PROFESSIONAL RESPONSIBILITY IN THE LIFE OF THE LAWYER

Second Edition

■ ■ ■

by

Carl A. Pierce

W. Allen Separk Distinguished Professor of Law Emeritus
University of Tennessee at Knoxville

Judy M. Cornett

College of Law Distinguished Professor of Law
University of Tennessee at Knoxville

Alex B. Long

Professor of Law
and
Associate Dean for Academic Affairs
University of Tennessee at Knoxville

Paula Schaefer

Associate Professor of Law
University of Tennessee at Knoxville

Cassandra Burke Robertson

Professor of Law
and
Director, Center for Professional Ethics
Case Western Reserve University

AMERICAN CASEBOOK SERIES®

WEST
ACADEMIC
PUBLISHING

American Casebook Series is a trademark registered in the U.S. Patent and Trademark Office.

© 2011 Thomson Reuters
© 2015 LEG, Inc. d/b/a West Academic
    444 Cedar Street, Suite 700
    St. Paul, MN 55101
    1-877-888-1330

West, West Academic Publishing, and West Academic are trademarks of West Publishing Corporation, used under license.

Printed in the United States of America

ISBN: 978-0-314-29090-8

To the many research assistants who helped with the development of these materials over the past fifteen years and the many more students who used, discussed, and constructively criticized the materials as they commenced their thinking about what conduct should be expected of lawyers engaged in the professionally responsible practice of law.

C.A.P.

To Rachel

J.M.C.

To Ann, Jeremy, and Abigail

A.B.L.

To Keith, Henry, and Ben and to my mentor Ann Covington

P.S.

To Joan Burke and Thom Robertson

C.B.R.

PREFACE

Although this book can usefully be read by anyone interested in learning about the regulation of the legal profession, the authors intend and expect that it will be read and discussed by students who are enrolled in an American law school and taking a required course that might variously be called Legal Ethics, Professional Responsibility, Legal Profession, or the Law Governing Lawyers. We also assume that most of our readers are attending law school because they aspire to embark on a career as a lawyer and are seeking the knowledge and skill necessary to secure admission to the bar, secure gainful employment as a lawyer, and thereafter enjoy a long and successful career practicing law. Thus, this book focuses on the rights and responsibilities of lawyers as such and, more particularly, their rights and responsibilities in connection with their practice of law.

A distinctive feature of this book is its organization. Basically, we present these materials as they relate to activities in which a lawyer is likely to engage at various times in the lawyer's career. Chronologically, we start with you in law school preparing to seek admission to the bar in one or more jurisdictions. Thereafter, we move to you seeking a job as a lawyer, then to you (or a law firm with which you have associated) seeking clients who you might represent, then to you relating to your clients and representing them in their dealings with third persons, and, then, at some point you or your law firm or a client terminating the client's representation. Every new lawyer will sooner or later be involved in each of these stages of what we call "the life cycle of the practice of law" as will recur throughout the lawyer's career. This book, then, introduces you to the law and professional responsibilities applicable to lawyers in each of the stages of this recurring life cycle in the order in which you are likely to confront them in the practice of law.

While most of this book is devoted to the study of the professional responsibilities of lawyers as they proceed through this recurring life cycle of the practice of law, we also have assumed that each of you is looking forward to a long life in the law, and that there are some professional opportunities and related issues that are likely to arise later in your career as a lawyer or at the end of your career. Thus, we examine the professional responsibilities associated with you eventually assuming supervisory or managerial responsibilities. Some of you will face these issues right out of law school, some will confront them sooner rather than later, and some will never face them other than as an observer of other lawyers who have become supervisors or managers. For organizational purposes, however, we treat these as "mid-career" opportunities and issues. Similarly, we treat becoming and being a judge as a mid-career opportunity giving rise to a distinctive set or mid-career issues facing those who would be judges, are judges, or return to law practice after having served as a judge.

We conclude by addressing some issues related to the end of your career as a lawyer—whenever or however that may occur. More reflectively, we also ask you to look forward to looking backward at what we hope will have been a rewarding life in the law.

In addition to organizing our book by reference to the life-cycle of a lawyer—both generally from beginning to end and more specifically from the beginning to the end of a lawyer's relationship with and representation of clients—we also organize the readings by reference to activities in which a lawyer engages, such as associating with law firms, seeking clients, establishing client-lawyer relationships, filing complaints, trying cases, terminating a representation, etc. In this regard, we proceed with an awareness that some lawyers limit their practices to the representation of clients in connection with prospective or pending litigation, and others limit their practices to the representation of clients in connection with the formation of business firms and business transaction. Still others limit their practices to mediation. Among litigators there are full and part-time prosecutors and there are lawyers who specialize in the representation of those accused of crime, both as public defenders and private practitioners. On the civil side, some lawyers represent plaintiffs only, and some lawyers represent defendants only. Some lawyers practice as full-time employees of government agencies. Some lawyers in private practice—commonly referred as in-house counsel—are full-time employees of a company and only represent it or its organizational affiliates. Government agencies and business firms are known as "organizational clients" and some lawyers who represent multiple clients only represent organizational clients and some only represent individuals. A lawyer's client may be sophisticated and experienced consumers of legal services. The client, on the other hand, might not be either sophisticated or experienced in the ways of the law, even to the extent of being what the ABA Model Rules refers to as "a client under a disability." Some clients will be paying the lawyer who represents them; some will not. One of the goals of this book, then, is to our readers' awareness of the variety of roles lawyers play, the variety of settings and circumstances in which those roles are played, and raise questions about how this variation may or should affect a lawyer's professional responsibilities.

With respect to subject matter coverage, this book addresses the issues typically covered in law school professional responsibility courses, but it also introduces our readers to some other topics as well. We focus on lawyers doing what lawyers do. In this regard, almost every Chapter addresses an activity in which a practicing lawyer will engage and begins with a problem that a lawyer has faced or may face in their practice of law. For the most part, the readings are rules, cases, and ethics opinions. The common core is that these primary legal materials involve lawyers speaking to lawyers. Although we also alert students to what law professors have to say on various issues, we primarily use the materials that the students are likely to use as they seek to comply with the law governing lawyers after they have entered practice. In the end, we think we have provided our readers with the information they will need to begin a career-long learning process that will enable them, first and foremost, to self-identify and self-resolve professional responsibility issues that inevitably will arise in a law practice. We also think of these materials as providing a solid foundation for a lawyer's participation in the processes through which the law governing lawyers is promulgated and enforced in America. We hope your reading and discussion of the materials in this book will inspire you to seek such an opportunity to improve the law governing lawyer and its enforcement.

To that end we have included many questions or problems throughout the book. In response to each of these questions or problems, our primary question to you will always be: "What do you think?" We think what you think is as important as what we or anyone think. We assume some, but not all, of these questions will be discussed in class. Actually, we know from our own experience that there is never enough time in a class for discussion of all the questions posed in a given chapter. We think, however, that each question is worthy of your attention and that you will be well served by at least taking a good faith stab at a tentative answer and explanation for the answer to each question We also think your questions are equally worthy of attention, and hope you will take the initiative to bring them to the attention of your professor and classmates.

With this second edition of the book, the original authors were fortunate enough to convince Professors Paula Schaefer and Cassandra Burke Robertson to come onboard as coauthors. Their contributions have greatly enhanced this new edition.

Finally, before you hustle off to examine the table of contents and start reading Chapter 1, please allow us to say thank you to a large group of students at the University of Tennessee College of Law. These students provided us with good questions and good answers. They offered constructive criticism. Among these students (with apologies to others whose contributions have been obscured from mind by the passage of time) are Anna Burck Williams, Craig Meredith, Travis Smuckler, James Inman, Sarah Swan, Jon Meagher Taylor Williams, Will Rogers, Anna Swift, Grayson Schleppegrell, Ashley Waddle, and Zachary Arnold. The virtues of this book are in large part due to the professionally responsible engagement of our students in their study of this very important, interesting, and challenging subject that provides the foundation for a rewarding career in a profession for which we have the greatest respect and to the further improvement of which we hope to contribute. So, let's turn to Part 1 and start thinking about the process through which you will become a lawyer and some of the core responsibilities you will assume when you are admitted to the bar. We trust this will whet your appetite for using this course and this book as an aid in the commencement of your life-long learning about what lawyers do and how they should behave.

> CARL A. PIERCE
> JUDY M. CORNETT
> ALEX B. LONG
> PAULA R.H. SCHAEFER
> CASSANDRA BURKE ROBERTSON

February 2015

ACKNOWLEDGMENTS

The authors gratefully acknowledge the following for permission to reprint material as follows:

Excerpt from *Suffering in Silence: The Tension Between Self-Disclosure and a Law School's Obligation to Report*, 18 AM. U.J. GENDER SOC. POL'Y & L. 121, 133 (2009) reprinted by permission of the American University Journal of Gender, Social Policy & the Law.

Excerpts from Formal Ethics Opinions 1995–12 and 2005–05 reprinted by permission of the Association of the Bar of the City of New York.

Celebrating 50 Years at SHB: John C. Dods reprinted by permission of Debbie Calton and Shook, Hardy & Bacon, L.L.P.

Excerpt from Margaret C. Benson, *Guardian ad Litem: The Grinch Need Not Apply*, CBA RECORD, Oct. 2008, at 38–40, reprinted by permission of the Chicago Bar Association and Margaret C. Benson.

Colorado Bar Association Formal Ethics Opinion 101 is reproduced by permission of the Colorado Bar Association and *The Colorado Lawyer*, where it was originally published. All rights reserved. Opinions are available online at http://www.cobar.org/index.cfm/ID/22347/CETH/Formal-Ethics-Opinions.

Oral History of the Honorable Ann K. Covington reprinted by permission of Ann K. Covington and Paula Schaefer.

Excerpt from Ted Schneyer, *"Professionalism" As Pathology: The ABA's Latest Policy Debate on Nonlawyer Ownership of Law Practice Entities*, 40 FORDHAM URB. L.J. 75, 110 n.126 (2012), reprinted by permission of Fordham Urban Law Journal. This article was originally published in the *Fordham Urban Law Journal* as Ted Schneyer, *"Professionalism" As Pathology: The ABA's Latest Policy Debate on Nonlawyer Ownership of Law Practice Entities*, 40 FORDHAM URB. L.J. 75 (2012).

Excerpt from Anthony E. Davis, *Legal Ethics and Risk Management: Complementary Visions of Lawyer Regulation*, 21 GEO. J. LEGAL ETHICS 95 (2008) reprinted with permission of the publisher, Georgetown Journal of Legal Ethics © 2008.

Steven Lubet, *A Life Well Lived*, 13 GEO. J. LEGAL ETHICS 575 (2000), reprinted with permission of the publisher, Georgetown Journal of Legal Ethics © 2000.

State Bar of Georgia, Formal Advisory Opinion 05–10, reprinted courtesy of the State Bar of Georgia.

Excerpt from Robert H. Jackson, *The Federal Prosecutor*, 24 J. AM. JUD. SOC'Y 18 (1940), reprinted by permission of the American Judicature Society.

Excerpt from David Hricik, *Dear Lawyer: If You Decide It's Not Economical to Represent Me, You Can Fire Me as Your Contingent Fee Client, but I Agree I Will Still Owe You a Fee*, 64 MERCER L. REV. 363 (2013), reprinted by permission of the Mercer Law Review.

Michigan Ethics Opinion Nos. RI-13 (1989), RI-223 (1995), and RI-310 (1998) reprinted by permission of The State Bar of Michigan.

Kansas City Legal 'Giant' John C. Dods III Dies, DAILY RECORD AND KANSAS CITY DAILY NEWS-PRESS, June 4, 2008, reprinted courtesy of Missouri Lawyers Media.

Excerpt from John F. Tobin, *The Boston Massacre Trials*, N.Y. ST. B.J. 12 (July/Aug. 2013) reprinted with permission from: New York State Bar Association *Journal*, July/August 2013, Vol. 85, No. 6, published by the New York State Bar Association, One Elk Street, Albany, New York 12207.

Oregon State Bar Association Formal Opinion Nos. 2005–159 and 2005–125 reprinted by permission of the Oregon State Bar.

Pennsylvania Bar Association Committee on Legal Ethics and Professional Responsibility Formal Opinion No. 94–35 reprinted by permission of the Pennsylvania Bar Association.

Carl A. Pierce, *Ethics 2000 and the Transactional Practitioner*, 3 TRANSACTIONS: TENN. J. BUS. L. Spring/Summer 2002, at 8, reprinted by permission of *Transactions* and Carl A. Pierce.

Restatement of the Law Third, The Law Governing Lawyers © 2000 by the American Law Institute. Reproduced with permission. All rights reserved.

Restatement, Second, Torts, copyright © 1977 by The American Law Institute. Reproduced with permission. All rights reserved.

Excerpt from Caprice L. Roberts, *The Fox Guarding the Henhouse?: Recusal and the Procedural Void in the Court of Last Resort*, 57 RUTGERS L. REV. 107, 109 (2004), reprinted by permission of the Rutgers Law Review.

Excerpt from Michael Pena, *Moses Lasky—Noted Trial Lawyer*, SAN FRANCISCO CHRONICLE, Apr. 18, 2002, http://www.sfgate.com/bayarea/article/Moses-Lasky-noted-trial-lawyer-2848793.php, republished with permission of Hearst Corporation; copyright 2002, permission conveyed through Copyright Clearance Center, Inc.

Excerpt from Judge Robert S. Lasnik and David Boerner, *The Legacy of Norm Maleng*, 84 WASH. L. REV. 3 (2009), reprinted by permission of the Washington Law Review.

Excerpt from Patricia Sullivan, *Federal Judge Robert R. Merhige Dies*, WASH. POST, Feb. 20, 2005, http://www.washingtonpost.com/politics/federal-judge-robert-r-merhige-dies/2012/05/31/gJQAdkJ4FV_story.html., republished with permission of Washington Post Co., copyright 2005; permission conveyed through Copyright Clearance Center, Inc.

Excerpt from Charles R. DiSalvo, *Attorney Gandhi's Questions*, W. VA. LAW., Jan.–Mar. 2014, at 36, reprinted by permission of the West Virginia Lawyer and Charles R. DiSalvo.

Excerpt from Fred C. Zacharias, *The Purposes of Lawyer Discipline*, 45 WM.& MARY L. REV. 675, 698 (2003), reprinted by permission of the William and Mary Law Review.

Excerpt from CHARLES W. WOLFRAM, MODERN LEGAL ETHICS © 1986 West Publishing Co., reprinted by permission of LEG, Inc. d/b/a West Academic.

SUMMARY OF CONTENTS

TABLE OF CONTENTS

TABLE OF CASES

The principal cases are in bold type.

TABLE OF RULES

PROFESSIONAL RESPONSIBILITY IN THE LIFE OF THE LAWYER

Second Edition

PART 1

ENTERING THE PROFESSION

■ ■ ■

As noted in the preface, this book is intended to be read and discussed by students who are enrolled in an American law school and taking a required course that might variously be called Legal Ethics, Professional Responsibility, Legal Profession, or Law Governing Lawyers. Most of our intended readers are attending law school because they aspire to embark on a career as a lawyer and are seeking the knowledge and skill necessary to secure admission to the bar, secure gainful employment as a lawyer, and thereafter enjoy a long and successful career practicing law. This book focuses on the rights and responsibilities of lawyers as such and, more particularly, their rights and responsibilities in connection with their practice of law.

The purpose of Part 1 is to provide a foundation for our subsequent study of a lawyer's professional rights and responsibilities. First, assuming that most of you aspire to be lawyers and that each of you has given some thought to what it will mean to be a lawyer, we begin in Chapter 1 with some information and thoughts about a lawyer's professional responsibilities. Chapter 2 addresses one's entry in the legal profession, including the rules governing the process of admission to the bar and how the rules of professional conduct that govern the behavior of the bar are promulgated. Chapter 3 addresses how those professional conduct rules are enforced, with a particular focus on the self-policing nature of the legal profession. Chapter 4 covers the process of how one becomes admitted to practice law in multiple jurisdictions and the law that protects the public (and lawyers, too) from the unauthorized practice of law by non-lawyers. Finally, Chapter 5 covers one of the special responsibilities one assumes upon entering the profession: the duty to provide access to justice through pro bono and other services.

* * *

CHAPTER 1

INTRODUCTION: A LAWYER'S PROFESSIONAL RESPONSIBILITIES

■ ■ ■

Chapter hypothetical. For more than a decade, you and your law firm have represented H.P. Simmons, a famous author known for her science fiction series *Immortal Beings*. After the final book in the series was published in 2012, H.P. announced that she was retiring from writing. *Immortal Beings* fans were devastated. Unbeknownst to these fans, H.P. recently released a new science fiction book, *The October Chronicles,* under the pen name Constance Fellows. You and two other lawyers at your law firm know about H.P.'s new book and pen name. You represented H.P. in negotiations with her new publisher, Little Blue Press.

A week ago, you were chatting with your spouse's best friend, Pat, at a dinner party. Pat always describes you as a "boring lawyer," so maybe you were showing off a little when you mentioned that your client H.P. Simmons just released a book under the pen name Constance Fellows. You immediately regretted the slip, and you swore Pat to secrecy. Pat assured you that your secret was safe as she pulled out her phone to order *The October Chronicles.*

This morning, you read a story in the *Sunday Times* reporting that H.P. Simmons has released a book under the pen name Constance Fellows. You feel certain that Pat is the source of the story and that the leak will soon be traced back to you.

* * *

This textbook prompts you to consider the issues you will face throughout your professional career from law school through your retirement. As a member of the legal profession, you will have numerous responsibilities and opportunities. You will represent clients who will trust you with some of the most important issues in their lives and businesses. You will also be a member of the bar, with the obligation to abide by professional conduct rules. Finally, you must decide what kind of person you will be in your personal and professional life. How will you treat others and contribute to your community? How will you balance the demands of being an attorney with obligations to your family, friends, and other interests?

Despite what you may have heard, the study of professional responsibility is not limited to the study of professional conduct rules. Professional responsibility is the study of every aspect of the lawyer's professional life: duties to clients, obligations to the bar, and the personal traits essential to being an excellent lawyer. This textbook provides a framework that will help you understand your various duties and opportunities to succeed as a professional.

* * *

A. FIDUCIARY DUTY TO CLIENTS

Please read Restatement (Third) of the Law Governing Lawyers §§ 16, 48–50 & 52–54.

* * *

Lawyers and clients are in a fiduciary relationship—a special relationship of trust and confidence. This means that when a lawyer agrees to represent a client in a matter, the lawyer must fulfill fiduciary duties of care and loyalty to the client. This is not something that the lawyer and client negotiate; the relationship is by definition fiduciary and comes with these responsibilities.

This text will often refer to the Restatement (Third) of the Law Governing Lawyers for a statement of the law of fiduciary duty. In practice, you would rely upon case law in the appropriate jurisdiction for a statement of the law.

The fiduciary duty of care requires a lawyer to act with the competence and diligence normally exercised by lawyers under similar circumstances. This is not a *reasonable person* standard but a *reasonable lawyer* standard. Clients can expect a level of knowledge and skill based on the lawyer's training and study. In order to perform competently, a lawyer must be mindful of the role that he or she is playing for the client. Advisor, negotiator, and courtroom advocate are just some of a lawyer's roles. The demands of each role are different and will be explored further throughout this book.

A lawyer's breach of the duty of care can give rise to liability for malpractice or professional negligence. You will see examples of such cases in various chapters in this textbook.

The lawyer's other duty to the client is the duty of loyalty. It requires the lawyer to protect client property and confidences, avoid prohibited conflicts of interests, and take no advantage arising from the attorney-client relationship. In many jurisdictions, the breach of the duty of loyalty gives rise to a cause of action for breach of fiduciary duty. You will also see cases involving these claims throughout the book.

As a lawyer, fiduciary duty to your client should be your touchstone. If you are in doubt about whether a course of conduct is right, you can often ask yourself if it is in your client's interest. Are you diligently working on your client's behalf? Are you providing the advice, advocacy, guidance, and representation your client deserves? Are you acting in your client's interest or in the interest of someone else or your own personal interest?

* * *

Problem 1.1. As you feared, the H.P. Simmons pen name leak was quickly traced to you. Your law firm released a statement publicly apologizing to H.P. Simmons and explaining that client confidentiality is of the utmost importance to the firm. *The October Chronicles* shot from number 4,709 to number 1 on the best-seller list within a week of the *Sunday Times* article. But that was no consolation to H.P. Simmons. In a subsequent article, H.P. was quoted as saying, "I certainly thought I could trust my lawyers with a secret. I am angry and devastated by this betrayal. I loved the freedom of releasing *The October Chronicles* without the pressure, hype, and expectation that always came with the release of an H.P. Simmons book. Now that has been taken from me."

Refer to the Restatement (Third) of the Law Governing Lawyers to determine the most appropriate cause of action for H.P. Simmons to assert in a lawsuit against you and your law firm. With citation to the pertinent section of the Restatement, explain what H.P would have to prove at trial to prevail on her claim.

* * *

B. PROFESSIONAL CONDUCT RULES

Another aspect of a lawyer's professional duty is the obligation to comply with professional conduct rules. These rules are adopted by the highest court of each state and by federal courts. In most jurisdictions, these rules are based to some extent upon the ABA's Model Rules of Professional Conduct. Most jurisdictions adapt the rules, which results in varying versions of the rules in each jurisdiction. This text will primarily refer you to the Model Rules, but it will sometimes reference variations on those rules adopted in various jurisdictions.

A lawyer may be disciplined for violating a professional conduct rule. Discipline can range from a private reprimand to suspension or even disbarment. You will read cases throughout this textbook in which an attorney faced possible discipline for violating a professional conduct rule.

Civil liability is not a consequence of violating a professional conduct rule. However, the same conduct that is the subject of discipline may be the subject of a client's lawsuit. For example, if a lawyer's lack of diligence results in the client's lawsuit being dismissed, the bar may discipline the attorney for violating Rule 1.3 (the rule requiring attorneys to be diligent) and the client may sue the attorney for violating the duty of care.

Professional conduct rules can be thought of as falling within one of three categories. These categories are not signaled within the professional conduct rules. As a result, students (and lawyers) sometimes perceive the rules as a mass of disconnected and meaningless obligations. Knowing the three categories can help you understand the purpose of a given rule so you can better understand what is necessary to comply with the rule's spirit—rather than merely following the technical letter of the rule. Understanding the categories can also help you see connections among the rules.

The first category contains rules that guide attorneys in fulfilling fiduciary obligations to their clients. Such rules address issues including competence, diligence, confidentiality, and avoiding conflicts of interest. As you know from reading Part A, attorneys owe fiduciary duties to their clients irrespective of the existence of these rules. But the professional conduct rules serve as an important reminder of these duties and a guide for fulfilling them. For example, it is an attorney's fiduciary duty to avoid conflicts of interest. Model Rule 1.7 generally prohibits a lawyer representing a client whose interests are adverse to another client.

Rules in the second category describe limits of what lawyers can do on a client's behalf. The rules in this category address situations when a lawyer *may* or *must* take action that is contrary to a client's stated interests. Some of these rules are adopted by the bar as an expression of its values—such as rules that protect the integrity of the legal process or the rights of third parties. Other professional conduct rules in this category recognize ethical dilemmas that attorneys may face in practice and give the attorney discretion to make a personal judgment within the rule's parameters—such as rules that allow the disclosure of client confidences to protect a third party in defined circumstances. Still other rules in this category mirror other sources of law—a lawyer is prohibited by law from participating in a client's crime.

Finally, rules in the third category are aimed at promoting and preserving the integrity of the profession. These rules cover topics such as attorney advertising, the duty to accept court appointments and provide pro bono service to those unable to pay, bar admission, disciplinary authority, and the obligation to report professional misconduct of a lawyer.

* * *

Problem 1.2. You receive a letter from the Disciplinary Counsel of the State Board of Attorney Conduct. The letter explains that H.P. Simmons and several lawyers (including lawyers from your firm) reported that you violated the confidentiality rule of professional conduct by revealing information learned in the representation of your client. The letter asks you to respond in writing within fourteen days and explains that your response will be considered as the Disciplinary Counsel determines whether to file a complaint for discipline.

Refer to the Model Rules of Professional Conduct to determine the specific provision you violated by disclosing your client's pen name. (The Table of Contents will be helpful as you search for the rule addressing confidentiality). Also, locate the professional conduct rule that requires a lawyer to report the professional misconduct of another lawyer. Must every rule violation be reported? Is the reporting obligation mandatory or permissive?

* * *

C. PERSONAL TRAITS ESSENTIAL TO BEING AN EXCELLENT LAWYER

Throughout this course, you should think about your personal values and the type of lawyer and person you want to be. What are your personal values and how will you reconcile those values with your other duties as a lawyer? What values do you hope to further develop in law school and as you begin practicing law?

A growing body of legal scholarship explores the qualities and traits of the best lawyers. Beyond complying with professional conduct rules and fulfilling obligations to clients, excellent lawyers share a number of key traits. They are effective in building relationships with others; they accept a special role in the legal system and society; they have a strong work ethic and work effectively with others; and they seek growth and fulfillment in their personal and professional lives. These traits and qualities are discussed in this part.

1. EFFECTIVE IN RELATIONSHIPS WITH AND TREATMENT OF OTHERS

The best lawyers are skilled at building and sustaining relationships with other people. They understand the importance of their relationships with all participants in the legal system—clients, colleagues, judges, opposing counsel, law office staff, and others. Adjectives used to describe these lawyers include: respectful, honest, trustworthy, civil, and courteous.

Notable research on how successful lawyers interact with others includes the following. The book *Best Practices for Legal Education* explains the need for lawyers to act with "honor, integrity, fair play, truthfulness, and candor" and to demonstrate "sensitivity and effectiveness with diverse clients and colleagues." Roy Stuckey et al., *Best Practices for Legal Education: A Vision and a Road Map*, 62 (2007), *available at* www.law.sc.edu/faculty/stuckey/best_practices/best_ practices-full.pdf [hereinafter "*Best Practices*"]. In her article *Lawyers as Leaders*, Professor Deborah L. Rhode describes a leader's values as including "integrity, honesty, trust, [and] an ethic of service." 2010 MICH. ST. L. REV. 413, 417 (2010). Professor Susan Brooks has researched and written about the importance of lawyers being "relationship-centered." She explains how lawyers should attend to client needs for "trust, respect, fair-mindedness, judgment, and perceptions around the opportunity to be heard." *Meeting the Professional Identity Challenge in Legal Education Through a Relationship-Centered Experiential Curriculum*, 41 U. BALT. L. REV. 395, 405–10 (2012). Finally, Professor Neil Hamilton's research into law firm evaluation systems reveals that firms consider integrity, honesty, and trustworthiness in evaluating attorneys. *Law Firm Competency Models and Student Professional Success: Building on a Foundation of Professional Formation/Professionalism*, 11 U. ST. THOMAS L.J. 6, 9 (2013).

2. ACCEPTS A SPECIAL ROLE IN THE LEGAL SYSTEM AND SOCIETY

Being a member of the legal profession means accepting the role of public servant—a person who provides access to the legal system and seeks individual and social justice. The best lawyers devote time to pro bono service, bar associations, and community. They show respect for the rule of law and courts and work to improve both.

Best Practices describes "respect for the rule of law" as one of five professional values deserving special attention in legal education. *Best Practices* authors explain, "As gatekeepers to the judicial system . . . lawyers have a special obligation to respect and foster respect for the rule of law, irrespective of their personal opinions about particular aspects of the law." *Best Practices*, at 64–65. The Carnegie Foundation's 2007 book on the future of legal education addresses the need for law students to be trained in providing both individual and social justice. William M. Sullivan et al., *Carnegie Foundation for the Advancement of Teaching, Educating Lawyers: Preparation for the Profession of Law* 14, 130–31 (2007) [hereinafter "*Carnegie Report*"]. The ABA's 1992 report on legal education describes two of the fundamental values of the legal profession as "striving to promote justice, fairness, and morality" and "contributing to the profession's fulfillment of its responsibility to enhance the capacity of law and legal institutions to do justice." American Bar Association, *Report of The Task Force on Law Schools and the Profession: Narrowing the Gap, Legal Education and Professional Development—An Educational Continuum* 140–41 (1992) [hereinafter "*MacCrate Report*"].

3. DEMONSTRATES A STRONG WORK ETHIC AND WORKS EFFECTIVELY WITH OTHERS

The profession's best lawyers demonstrate a strong work ethic and work effectively with others. They are responsive to clients and are hard-working, dependable, and self-motivated. Beyond that, outstanding lawyers have the ability to collaborate with and lead others.

In his article *Law Firm Competency Models*, Professor Neil Hamilton notes the following results from his survey of law firms concerning how they evaluate associates.

- Eight of the twenty-three competencies considered by eighteen large law firms in evaluating associates are directly related to an attorney's work habits and work ethic.

- Fifteen of eighteen law firms studied evaluate lawyers' initiative, ambition, drive, or strong work ethic, while sixteen of the firms evaluate lawyers' responsiveness to clients or dedication to client service.

- Seventeen of eighteen law firms in the study evaluate lawyers' "project management, including high quality, efficiency, and timeliness."

- All eighteen law firms studied evaluate lawyers' ability to initiate and maintain strong work and team relationships, while four of the subject firms specifically state that they evaluate the ability to work independently.

- Nine of eighteen studied firms evaluate an attorney's delegation, supervision, and mentoring, while two specifically evaluate "leadership."

Neil W. Hamilton, *Law Firm Competency Models and Student Professional Success: Building on a Foundation of Professional Formation/Professionalism*, 11 U. ST. THOMAS L.J. 6, 11 (2013).

4. CONTINUOUSLY STRIVES FOR PERSONAL GROWTH AND FULFILLMENT

Finally, the professional attorney continuously strives for personal and professional growth and fulfillment. The *MacCrate Report* notes that a fundamental value of the legal profession is "professional self-development" which includes seeking opportunities to increase knowledge and improve skills and selecting employment that will allow the lawyer to "develop as a professional and pursue his or her professional and personal goals." *MacCrate Report*, at 141. Professor Daisy Hurst Floyd explains that law students should "take the time to develop the inner life, to know who they are and what matters to them, to consider such questions as what their places are in the world, and how to practice law consistently with their values and morals." *We Can Do More*, 60 J. LEGAL EDUC. 129, 132 (2010). Professor Jerome Organ has researched lawyer satisfaction and happiness. He notes studies reflecting that lawyers disproportionately experience alcoholism, depression, and other mental health issues. Professor Organ urges further study of these issues and their relationship to lawyer satisfaction with the practice of law. *What Do We Know About the Satisfaction/Dissatisfaction of Lawyers? A Meta-Analysis of Research on Lawyer Satisfaction and Well-Being*, 8 U. ST. THOMAS L.J. 225, 268–70 (2011).

* * *

Problem 1.3. Why do you suppose our hypothetical lawyer revealed confidential information about client H.P. Simmons? Do you think most attorneys understand the confidentiality obligation? Why would a lawyer who understands the law and ethics of confidentiality nonetheless "slip up," and how can you avoid such mistakes in practice?

* * *

Profile of attorney professionalism. It would be easy for a professional responsibility text to focus only on the negative. After all, many cases worthy of inclusion in a professional responsibility textbook involve a lawyer's lapse of professional judgment. In an effort to highlight positive role models, each chapter of this text includes a "Profile of Attorney Professionalism." These short profiles feature attorneys who demonstrate exceptional professionalism in practice.

Before she became the first woman to serve on the Missouri Supreme Court, Ann Covington distinguished herself as a hard-working attorney who endeavored to provide exceptional service to her clients. She describes her early years in practice:

> I enjoyed [the practice of law] and it was extremely hard work. [I] have recognized . . . what a privilege it was to help people on a day-to-day basis, so to speak. Whereas, my practice later was more of a corporate representation, [when I first started practicing, the people who came to the office . . . placed] their business affairs or personal affairs in my hands. I felt terribly responsible for them. . . . One of the partners in [my firm], when I sometimes worried aloud about something, said: "Well, Ann, you didn't make these facts."

Well, of course I didn't make the facts, but when [a client] would come and say, "Here's my situation," I felt responsible. Certainly in divorces, when children were involved, in contested custody matters—those were difficult. But, dissolution of partnerships could be almost as deadly as dissolutions of marriage. So, those things were a strain. And beyond that, the cases in juvenile court. We were all expected to accept appointments as guardians ad litem for children or in some cases for persons who were parents who were unable to pay. Termination of parental rights case—those are heartbreaking. . . .

I was very involved with many, many, many of my clients. [It was] gratifying to be able to help them. . . . Sometimes I felt pleasure when an opposing party would come to me and say: "You're quite the barracuda; I would never have guessed." But [it was also gratifying when a client came in with flowers for me or] said, "I made these cookies for you and your family." Those kinds of things . . . were so rewarding, and I cherish that time.

Oral History of the Honorable Ann K. Covington, American Bar Association Women Trailblazers in the Law Project, *available at*: http://www.americanbar.org/directories/women_trailblazers_project_listing/the_honorable_ann_k_covington.html.

CHAPTER 2

ADMISSION TO THE BAR

■ ■ ■

Chapter hypothetical. Stephen Wood worked as a journalist for more than a decade before beginning law school. He was fired from his job at a national magazine after it was discovered that he had engaged in various forms of dishonesty, including plagiarizing passages from other authors' work and fabricating stories and quotes that were presented as fact. At one point, he reported a customer service representative for a major national company (which he named in the piece) had made derogatory and racist comments in interactions with customers. When Wood's fabrications came to light, he admitted that a number of stories had contained falsehoods. He admitted that the customer service story was one of the fabricated examples, and that to his knowledge, no such incident had ever happened. After being fired from his job, Wood obtained a J.D. degree and graduated with honors. He has worked for a year as a paralegal, and his boss reports that he has done a good job in the past year and supports his admission to the bar. You have been appointed to the local bar committee charged with evaluating Wood's application to the bar. What issues do you consider to determine whether Wood meets the character and fitness requirements? What questions would you ask at a panel hearing? If his prior record gives you concern, what kind of a record of rehabilitation would you want to see before approving his application?

* * *

This Chapter examines the requirements for bar admission, including the "good moral character" requirement. Additionally you will be introduced to the special responsibilities imposed upon you as an applicant for bar admission and upon lawyers who support your application.

* * *

A. JUDICIAL AUTHORITY TO REGULATE ADMISSION TO THE PRACTICE OF LAW

Each state has its own rules governing admission to the bar. Some states require attorneys to be members of a state bar association; these states are said to have a "unified" state bar. In other states, the state supreme court regulates admission to practice, and membership in a bar association is voluntary. In either case, the state supreme court generally retains power to set the requirements for admission to practice, as the judicial branch—rather than the legislative branch—generally exercises primary regulatory power over the practice of law. The following case deals with a constitutional challenge to a statute passed by the New Hampshire legislature, which would have required the bar to hold a referendum on de-unification.

IN RE PETITION OF NEW HAMPSHIRE BAR ASSOCIATION
855 A.2d 450 (2004)

NADEAU, J.

. . .

The Bar was first unified by this court in 1968 for a three-year trial period. Once unified, membership and the payment of dues to the Association were required of all lawyers as a condition to the practice of law in this State. In ordering unification, we acted to improve the administration of justice, to foster and maintain high standards of professional conduct, competence, and public service on the part of lawyers, and to ensure the existence of a continuing program of legal education for the legal profession. We did so on the basis that requiring compulsory enrollment of all members of the Bar of this State into one unit was "an integral part of the inherent power of this court to regulate the practice of law and to supervise" those who were engaged in it.

In 1972, this court again examined unification and concluded that the Association had benefited as an organization from its three-year experience, and had made substantial strides in internal organization, member participation, continuing legal education, professional competence, discipline, ethics, and finances. Consequently, we ordered the Bar unified on a permanent basis.

For thirty-one years thereafter, no legislation affecting the Association's unified status was enacted. However, during the 2003 legislative session, the New Hampshire General Court enacted RSA 311:7–g to:7–i. The Association argues that RSA 311:7–g and:7–h are unconstitutional. We agree that subsection:7–g is unconstitutional because the statute encroaches upon inherent judicial authority.

I. RSA 311:7–g

RSA 311:7–g is entitled "State Bar Association Membership; Vote Required" and provides:

I. The supreme court, pursuant to its power to regulate the practice of law under this chapter and its continuing supervisory authority over attorneys practicing before courts of this state, may assess fees for the purpose of regulating the practice of law and for maintaining a professional conduct committee.

II. The supreme court may require all persons engaged in the practice of law in this state to be members of the New Hampshire Bar Association; provided that the members of the Bar Association have approved the requirement pursuant to paragraph III.

III. The board of governors of the New Hampshire Bar Association shall place on the ballot with the election of officers of the association, the following question: "Shall membership in the New Hampshire Bar Association be required for all attorneys licensed to practice in this state?" An affirmative vote of a majority of those voting on the question, shall allow for the requirement by the supreme court under paragraph II. Approval by the membership under this paragraph shall be valid for a 5-year period beginning on the date of the affirmative vote.

RSA 311:7–g, I-III.

The Association contends, among other things, that this statute "infringes on the authority of the judicial branch to regulate the Bar in violation of the New Hampshire Constitution." (Emphasis omitted.) Specifically, the Association argues that "unification [is] the sole business of the Court," because the court retains "constitutionally-conferred authority to regulate the Bar." The Association further argues that the legislative enactment constitutes "an impermissible and affronting intrusion under the Separation of Powers Clause" and should be struck down as unconstitutional.

The State disagrees, contending that "the regulation of the . . . [A]ssociation and the practice of law in New Hampshire has historically been shared between the legislative and judicial branches of government." Because both branches have overlapping authority, the State argues that "either branch can act absent the initiative of the other." Moreover, the State argues that "assuming that regulation of the practice of law is, at least in part, an essential judicial function," nothing in RSA 311:7–g prevents the court from carrying out that function by, for example, prescribing ethical and educational standards for lawyers, as well as requiring them to make payments into public protection funds.

It is axiomatic that "the constitutionality of a legislative act is to be presumed." Petition of Governor and Executive Council, 151 N.H. 1, 4, 846 A.2d 1148, 1151 (2004) (quotation and brackets omitted). "However, if upon examination of [a] statute, there is a clear conflict with the Constitution [,] the court must declare the statute inoperative because the Constitution, and not the statute, is the paramount law." Hynes v. Hale, 146 N.H. 533, 535, 776 A.2d 722 (2001) (quotation omitted). Because we conclude that RSA 311:7–g is in clear conflict with Part I, Article 37 of the New Hampshire Constitution, we declare it to be unconstitutional.

Part I, Article 37 of the New Hampshire Constitution provides, in pertinent part: "In the government of this state, the three essential powers thereof, to wit, the legislative, executive, and judicial, ought to be kept as separate from, and independent of, each other, as the nature of a free government will admit." We have recognized, however, that the three branches of government, while distinct, often must "move in concert," whenever possible, as the practical and efficient operation of government is not served by the erection of "impenetrable barriers between the branches."

Ideally, then, there should exist "a cooperative accommodation among the three branches of government." McKay v. N.H. Compensation Appeals Bd., 143 N.H. 722, 726, 732 A.2d 1025 (1999) (quotation omitted). Indeed, a spirit of comity encourages cooperation between the branches in furtherance of mutual goals. But comity has limits. It does not constitutionally permit one branch to usurp the essential power of another. To do so would violate the separation of powers doctrine. When the actions of one branch of government defeat or materially impair the inherent functions of another branch, such actions are not constitutionally acceptable.

We conclude, consistent with our prior decisions, that the judicial branch of government retains ultimate authority to regulate the practice of law, and that in the exercise of that authority it is necessarily permitted to determine whether unification of the Bar is advantageous. The authority of the judicial branch is not the result of legislative inaction as suggested by the State, but is derived from its inherent authority to regulate the practice of law. Petition of N.H. Bar Ass'n, 110 N.H. 356, 357, 266 A.2d 853 (1970) ("The power and authority of the supreme court to supervise and regulate the practice of law has been recognized and acknowledged from an early date by custom, practice, judicial decision and statute."). In so holding, we conform to our precedent and share the view of other jurisdictions. Indeed, "[n]o court has held that the highest court of any state is without authority to unify its bar." Petition of Tennessee Bar Ass'n, 532 S.W.2d 224, 229 (Tenn.1975).

"Attorneys are officers of the court," Bryant's Case, 24 N.H. 149, 154 (1851), and ensuring their high caliber and competence through their admission into and exclusion from the Bar has long been recognized as an "exercise of judicial power," Ricker's Petition, 66 N.H. 207, 211, 29 A. 559 (1890) (quotation omitted). "In most, if not all, of the jurisdictions of this country, it is recognized that [t]he practice of law is so intimately connected with the exercise of judicial power in the administration of justice that the right to define and regulate the practice naturally and logically" belongs to the judiciary. Wallace v. Wallace, 225 Ga. 102, 166 S.E.2d 718, 723 (1969) (quotation omitted). Consequently, "[r]egulating the practice of law is a core function of the judicial branch." *Rosenkrantz*, 128 Cal.Rptr.2d 104, 59 P.3d at 211.

Indeed, for more than a century, this inherent authority has served as a fundamental tenet of our jurisprudence. Beginning with *Ricker's Petition* in 1890, Chief Justice Doe, writing for a unanimous court, noted that, "The constitution . . . vests in the courts all the judicial power of the state. The constitutional establishment of such courts appears to carry with it the power to establish a bar to practice in them." *Ricker's Petition*, 66 N.H. at 210, 29 A. 559 (quotation omitted). In 1968, Justice Lampron, in discussing Chief Justice Doe's analysis, wrote: "[T]his court held in *Ricker's Petition* that the authority to make reasonable rules for the admission and removal of members of the bar is necessarily inherent in every court, in order to enable it to discharge its duties, as much so as to preserve order." *In re Unification of the New Hampshire Bar*, 109 N.H. at 263, 248 A.2d 709 (citation and quotations omitted).

During the past three decades, this court has repeatedly recognized, without exception, that the authority to resolve the issue of unification lies within the judiciary's inherent power. When first confronted with the issue of unification in 1968, we stated:

> We hold that the determination of whether the administration of justice in New Hampshire will best be served by the compulsory enrollment of all the members of the Bar of this state into one unit to which the members must pay dues necessary to its efficient operation is an integral part of the inherent power of this court to regulate the practice of law and to supervise those engaged therein in New Hampshire. *Lawyers being thus uniquely related to, and subject to supervision and regulation by the judiciary, we hold that this court has jurisdiction to decide the issue of the unification of the Bar of this state. . . .*

Id. at 264, 248 A.2d 709 (emphasis added). In 1972, when the court ordered indefinite unification pursuant to "the court's continuing jurisdiction," *In re Unified New Hampshire Bar*, 112 N.H. at 207, 291 A.2d 600, it explicitly deemed the issue of unification to be "one of policy for the court," *id.* at 206, 291 A.2d 600.

. . .

Given the often overlapping actions of the branches, "[a]dmission to the practice of law and regulation of the conduct of attorneys in this State has been dealt with as an area of shared responsibility between the legislative and judicial branches." Rousseau v. Eshleman, 128 N.H. 564, 567, 519 A.2d 243 (1986). Although it is in the prerogative of the judicial branch "to regulate the practice of law, the legislature, under the police power, may act to protect the public interest, but in so doing, it acts in *aid* of the judiciary and *does not supersede or detract* from the power of the courts." *Wallace,* 166 S.E.2d at 723 (emphasis added). The regulation of the practice of law is a core judicial function. Because RSA 311:7–g has set in motion a vote on unification and may result in de-unification, contrary to our inherent authority and earlier order to regulate the practice of law through mandatory unification, we conclude that the statute is unconstitutional. The legislature, in effect, has created a mechanism by which a core function of the judiciary is usurped. Moreover, the statute allows those who participate in the referendum to annul our long-ago decision to unify the Bar. The legislature cannot, by empowering members of the Bar to negate a court order, do indirectly what it is prohibited from doing directly. For these reasons, we declare RSA 311:7–g to be unconstitutional.

The State argues that even if regulation of the legal profession is a core judicial function, RSA 311:7–g does not preclude the court from otherwise carrying out that function. We agree with the State that we might well be able to establish educational and ethical standards through different mechanisms. Indeed, we may even decide in the future to reexamine the question of unification. Because inherent constitutional authority allows the judicial branch to determine the most effective way to regulate the practice of law, however, we must remain free to structure the organized Bar as we deem necessary. The means by which the judicial branch chooses to organize the Bar, which it is charged with supervising, cannot be restricted by the other branches of government. *See* Sams v. Olah, 225 Ga. 497, 169 S.E.2d 790, 796 (1969) (noting that the judiciary cannot "be circumscribed or restricted in the performance of its duties related to its inherent power to regulate the practice of law"); *see also* 16A Am.Jur.2d *Constitutional Law* § 259 (1998) (courts cannot "be hampered or limited in the discharge of their functions by either of the other two branches"). Otherwise, inherent judicial power is compromised. Consequently, because we have elected to regulate the practice of law through unification, RSA 311:7–g, which permits de-unification without our involvement and contrary to our specific order, encroaches upon inherent judicial authority. . . .

III. Conclusion

Today, we neither redefine nor expand our inherent judicial power. Rather, we simply conform to our precedent. We reaffirm a well-established principle; that the inherent authority to regulate the practice of law lies with the judicial branch of government and includes the power to create a unified Bar.

* * *

B. UNITED STATES CITIZENSHIP

In its standard form application for preparations of a character report for submission to state bar admission official, the National Conference of Bar Examiners asks each applicant: "Of what country are you a citizen?" If the answer is any country other than the United States, the applicant must specify his or her immigration status.

* * *

Citizenship requirements. How far can a state go in denying bar admission to applicants who are not U.S. citizens? In In re Griffiths, 413 U.S. 717 (1973), a resident alien challenged, on Equal Protection grounds, Connecticut's refusal to allow her to sit for the bar exam. Noting that alienage is a suspect classification, the Court held that Connecticut had failed to "show that its purpose or interest is both constitutionally permissible and substantial, and that its use of the classification is necessary . . . to the accomplishment of its purpose or the safeguarding of its interest."

The Court rejected the state's proffered rationale that "the special role of the lawyer justifies excluding aliens from the practice of law" because "a resident alien lawyer might in the exercise of his functions ignore his responsibilities to the courts or even his clients in favor of the interest of a foreign power." Although the Court agreed that "[l]awyers do indeed occupy professional positions of responsibility and influence that impose on them duties correlative with their vital right of access to the courts" and that "lawyers have been leaders in government throughout the history of our country," the Court held that lawyers "are not officials of government by virtue of being lawyers. Nor does the status of holding a license to practice law place one so close to the core of the political process as to make him a formulator of government policy." Therefore, Connecticut's proffered rationale failed both because "the practice of law [does not offer] meaningful opportunities adversely to affect the interest of the United States" and because the plaintiff's willingness to take the oath required of lawyers indicated no risk that she would fail to protect the interest of clients.

A federal statute, 8 U.S.C. § 1621, establishes a default rule that undocumented immigrants are generally ineligible to apply for state professional licenses (including law licenses). However, the statute allows states to pass legislation to affirmatively provide for such eligibility. The California legislature passed such a law in January 2014, but the California Supreme Court still had to determine whether undocumented immigrants could satisfy the character and fitness standards. In the following case, the Court addressed two challenges to the licensure of undocumented immigrants.

IN RE GARCIA

315 P.3d 117 (Cal. 2014)

CANTIL-SAKAUYE, C.J.

I. Summary of Facts and State Bar Proceedings

The record before us indicates that applicant Garcia was born in Villa Jimenez, Mexico, on March 1, 1977. When he was 17 months old, his parents brought him to California, without inspection or documentation by immigration officials. He lived in California until 1986 (when he was nine years old) and then he and his parents moved back to Mexico. In 1994, when Garcia was 17 years old, he and his parents returned to California; again Garcia entered the country without documentation. At that time, Garcia's father had obtained lawful permanent resident status in the United States pursuant to federal immigration law, and on November 18, 1994, his father filed an immigration visa petition (form I-130 [petition for alien relative]) on Garcia's behalf. The petition was accepted by federal immigration officials on January 31, 1995. Under federal immigration law, the visa petition provides Garcia with a basis to apply for adjustment of his immigration status to that of a lawful permanent resident when an immigrant visa number becomes available. Under current provisions of federal immigration law, however, the number of available immigrant visas that may be issued each year is limited and is based upon an applicant's country of origin. Because the current backlog of persons of Mexican origin who are seeking immigrant visas is so large, as of the date of this opinion—more than 19 years after Garcia's visa petition was filed—a visa number still has not become available for Garcia.

Garcia has resided in California without interruption since 1994. During this period of time, he graduated from high school, attended Butte College, California State University at Chico, and Cal Northern School of Law. He received his law degree from Cal Northern School of Law in May 2009, and took and passed the July 2009 California bar examination.

[The Court first determined that California's statute complied with federal requirements to allow undocumented immigrants to become licensed attorneys. It then went on to consider additional arguments against admission raised by amicus curiae].

The objections relate to two circumstances: (1) the fact that, under federal law, undocumented immigrants are not lawfully authorized to be present in this country, and (2) the restrictions that federal law imposes upon the employment of undocumented immigrants in the United States. We discuss each of these subjects in turn.

1. Unlawful presence

Amicus curiae contends that because an undocumented immigrant is in violation of federal immigration law simply by being present in this country without authorization (8 U.S.C. §§ 1182, 1227), an undocumented immigrant cannot properly take the oath of office required of every attorney, which requires the individual to promise to " 'faithfully . . . discharge [the] duties of any attorney at law' " (quoting Bus. & Prof.Code, § 6067), including the duty " '[t]o support the Constitution and laws of the United States and of this state.' " (Quoting Bus. & Prof.Code, § 6068) Amicus curiae reasons that an undocumented immigrant cannot properly take the oath of office "since he will be in violation of federal law while he takes the oath and at all times later until he either becomes legal or leaves the United States."

Past California cases, however, do not support the proposition, implicit in amicus curiae's contention, that the fact that a bar applicant's past or present conduct may violate some law invariably renders the applicant unqualified to be admitted to the bar or to take the required oath of office. In Hallinan v. Committee of Bar Examiners (1966) 65 Cal.2d 447, 459, this court explained that "every intentional violation of the law is not, ipso facto, grounds for excluding an individual from membership in the legal profession. 'There is certain conduct involving fraud, perjury, theft, embezzlement, and bribery where there is no question that moral turpitude is involved. On the other hand, because the law does not always coincide exactly with principles of morality there are cases that are crimes that would not necessarily involve moral turpitude.' In such cases, investigation into the circumstances surrounding the commission of the act must reveal some independent act beyond the bare fact of a criminal conviction to show that the act demonstrates moral unfitness and justifies exclusion or other disciplinary action by the bar."

We conclude the fact that an undocumented immigrant is present in the United States without lawful authorization does not itself involve moral turpitude or demonstrate moral unfitness so as to justify exclusion from the State Bar, or prevent the individual from taking an oath promising faithfully to discharge the duty to support the Constitution and laws of the United States and California. Although an undocumented immigrant's presence in this country is unlawful and can result in a variety of civil sanctions under federal immigration law (such as removal from the country or denial of a desired adjustment in immigration status) (8 U.S.C. §§ 1227(a)(1)(B), 1255(i)), an undocumented immigrant's unauthorized presence does not constitute a criminal offense under federal law and thus is not subject to criminal sanctions. . . . Under these circumstances, we conclude that the fact that an undocumented immigrant's presence in this country violates federal statutes is not itself a sufficient or persuasive basis for denying undocumented immigrants, as a class, admission to the State Bar.

2. Employment restrictions

Amicus curiae further contends that it would be improper to grant a law license to an undocumented immigrant in light of the restrictions federal law places on the lawful employment of undocumented immigrants in the United States. . . .

All of the briefs agree that even if an undocumented immigrant is granted a license to practice law, federal law would prohibit an undocumented immigrant who lacks work authorization from practicing law as an "employee" of a law firm, corporation, or governmental entity. There is also general agreement that a licensed undocumented immigrant would not violate federal law if he or she provided legal services on a pro bono basis or outside the United States. The briefs disagree, however, regarding whether under current federal law a licensed undocumented immigrant without work authorization could lawfully practice law in this country as an "independent contractor," for example, as a sole practitioner. The briefs filed by the Committee and Garcia maintain that federal law would not bar a licensed undocumented immigrant from representing clients as a sole practitioner, but the amicus curiae brief filed by the United States Department of Justice states that federal law prohibits an undocumented immigrant who lacks work authorization from engaging in the practice of law for compensation in this country in any capacity, including as an independent contractor or sole practitioner. . . .

[T]his court's granting of a law license to undocumented immigrants would not override or otherwise affect the federal limitations upon the employment of undocumented immigrants. Nonetheless, for a number of reasons we conclude that existing federal limitations on the employment of undocumented immigrants do not justify excluding undocumented immigrants from admission to the State Bar.

First, as discussed above, the most directly applicable federal statute—section 1621—expressly authorizes a state, through a sufficiently explicit statute, to permit undocumented immigrants to obtain a professional license, notwithstanding the limitations on employment imposed by other federal statutes. No federal statute precludes a state from issuing a law license to an undocumented immigrant. Further, although the amicus curiae brief filed by the United States Department of Justice disagrees with the interpretation of federal immigration law relating to employment advanced by the Committee and Garcia, the brief at the same time emphasizes that "[t]he enforcement of the federal provisions governing employment by aliens is a responsibility of the federal government, and is not the proper subject of state-court proceedings, particularly in the context of state licensing" and urges this court not to "attempt to resolve any question about the types of legal services that Mr. Garcia may provide if granted a license."

Second, federal law restrictions on employment are subject to change, and under current federal immigration policy many undocumented immigrants are now eligible to obtain work authorization. Under the "deferred action for childhood arrivals" policy promulgated by the Secretary of the United States Department of Homeland Security (Secretary of Homeland Security) in June 2012, many undocumented immigrants who came to this country as children and were under the age of 30 when the new policy was adopted are eligible to obtain work authorization that is subject to renewal every two years.

Third, ... even with regard to an undocumented immigrant who lacks work authorization and faces significant federal law restrictions on his or her legal employment, we believe it would be inappropriate to deny a law license to such an individual on the basis of an assumption that he or she will not comply with the existing restrictions on employment imposed by federal law. Consistent with the provisions of Business and Professions Code section 6060.6,19 foreign law students who have passed the California bar examination and have been certified to this court by the Committee have been admitted to the State Bar, even though such individuals may lack authorization to work in the United States. Although it may be reasonable to assume that most foreign law students, when licensed, will return to their home countries to practice law, we rely upon these licensed attorneys to comply with their ethical obligations to act in accordance with all applicable legal constraints and do not condition or limit their law licenses. We conclude it is appropriate to treat qualified undocumented immigrants in the same manner. To the extent federal immigration law limitations on employment are ambiguous or in dispute, as in other contexts in which the governing legal constraints upon an attorney's conduct may be uncertain, we assume that a licensed undocumented immigrant will make all necessary inquiries and take appropriate steps to comply with applicable legal restrictions and will advise potential clients of any possible adverse or limiting effect the attorney's immigration status may pose.

For all of the foregoing reasons, we conclude there is no state law or state public policy that would justify precluding undocumented immigrants, as a class, from obtaining a law license in California.

* * *

C. RESIDENCY OR OTHER REQUISITE TIES TO THE STATE OF LICENSURE

In re Griffiths established that bar admission cannot be limited to U.S. citizens. But can states require bar applicants to have certain ties with the state of licensure? Do such requirements remain viable in an age of advanced technology that makes it easy to transact business without regard to state boundaries and in which many areas of law are increasingly federalized?

In Supreme Court of New Hampshire v. Piper, 470 U.S. 274 (1985), the Court held that New Hampshire's limitation of bar admission to state residents violated the Privileges and Immunities Clause. The plaintiff in *Piper* lived in Vermont, about 400 yards from the New Hampshire border, but because she was a nonresident, she was denied permission to take the New Hampshire bar. The state provided the following substantial reasons for its discrimination against nonresidents:

> "[N]onresident members would be less likely (i) to become, and remain, familiar with local rules and procedures; (ii) to behave ethically; (iii) to be available for court proceedings; and (iv) to do pro bono and other volunteer work in the State."

Holding that none of these reasons was "substantial," the Court expressed most concern about nonresidents' availability for court proceedings but noted that "the State can protect its interests through less restrictive means, [for example, by requiring] any lawyer who resides at a great distance to retain a local attorney who will be available for unscheduled meetings and hearings." Some states continue to require that all applicants for admission to its bar affirm their present intent to practice law in the state.

State residency requirements. Should a state be able to limit bar admission to state residents as a matter of state sovereignty? Justice Rehnquist, dissenting in *Piper*, thought so. Noting that the Privileges and Immunities Clause had been held applicable only to "nonresidents who seek to ply their trade interstate," he distinguished the practice of law as "one occupation that does not readily translate across state lines." Interestingly, Justice Rehnquist asserted that New Hampshire may well have "an interest in maximizing the number of resident lawyers so as to increase the quality of the pool from which its lawmakers can be drawn." Yet he disclaimed any reliance on the "notion that law is a superior profession." If Justice Rehnquist doesn't believe that law is a superior profession, then why would it be desirable to have attorneys available in the pool of potential lawmakers? What do you make of the fact that, according to the *Piper* majority, "[o]nly 8 of the 424 members of New Hampshire's bicameral legislature are lawyers?" Doesn't this fact undermine Justice Rehnquist's reasoning?

* * *

D. GRADUATING FROM LAW SCHOOL AND PASSING THE BAR EXAM

The American Bar Association, a private, voluntary association of approximately 400,000 lawyers as of 2008, serves as the accrediting agency for law schools nationwide. The ABA promulgates "Standards for Approval of Law Schools," and when a law school seeks ABA approval, it sends out teams composed of lawyers, judges, and law professors to inspect the law school and determine its compliance with the Standards. The ABA requires that the law school program prepare students for admission to the bar and for "effective and responsible participation in the legal profession." ABA Standards for Approval of Law Schools §. 3.01.

Most states recognize ABA accreditation of law schools by affording certain advantages to graduates of those schools. For example, Tennessee requires that any applicant for its bar be a graduate of an ABA-accredited law school or an in-state, non-ABA-accredited law school. The upshot of rules like Tennessee's is that a graduate of a non-ABA-accredited law school can practice law in only one state: the state where the non-accredited school is located. Other states' bars will be closed to her. Is this fair? Ask yourself whether it makes sense for a state to delegate its role as gatekeeper to the bar to a private organization.

The vast majority of American jurisdictions require that individuals who have not previously been admitted to the practice of law in another state (as well those who have been admitted elsewhere, but for less than five years) to pass a bar examination. One state—Wisconsin—recognizes a "diploma privilege" (exemption from taking the bar exam) for graduates of approved in-state law schools. There is no federal bar examination, the passage of which must be honored by all states. No state is required to honor one's passage of the bar examination in another state. Fourteen states have chosen to move toward greater standardization by adopting the Uniform Bar Examination, which is composed of standardized essay questions, multiple choice question, and two performance tests. All but three U.S. jurisdictions (Maryland, Wisconsin, and Puerto Rico), also require applicants to pass the Multistate Professional Responsibility Examination.

* * *

E. ESTABLISHING GOOD MORAL CHARACTER AND FITNESS TO PRACTICE LAW

All states require an applicant for a law license to show that he or she has good moral character. As you read the following material, ask yourself what good moral character means in the context of being licensed to practice law. Are states justified in imposing such a requirement?

* * *

Please read ABA Model Rules of Professional Conduct, Rule 8.1 and Comments.

* * *

1. GOOD MORAL CHARACTER

CORD V. GIBB

254 S.E.2d 71 (Va. 1979)

This is an appeal by Bonnie C. Cord from an order denying her the certificate of honest demeanor or good moral character required by Code § 54–60 as a prerequisite to her right to take the bar examination conducted by the Virginia Board of Bar Examiners. . . .

[Cord is a lawyer admitted to practice in the District of Columbia. When she applied for the Virginia bar, a three-person committee of practicing attorneys was appointed to investigate her "moral character and fitness." They discovered that she "had jointly purchased a home in a rural area of Warren County with Jeffery Blue, and that she and Blue jointly resided there." One committee member, "believing that Cord's living arrangement affected her character and fitness," recommended against admission. The trial court held a hearing at which Cord's neighbors testified to her " 'high character' and acceptance in the community." They testified that "her admission to the practice of law would not reflect adversely on the organized bar." Members of the D.C. bar also testified on her behalf. Nevertheless, the trial court refused to issue the certificate of good moral character " 'on the grounds that the living arrangement of Applicant would lower the public's opinion of the Bar as a whole.' "]

Whether a person meets the "honest demeanor, or good moral character" standard of Code § 54–60 is, of course, dependent upon the construction placed on those terms. The United States Supreme Court, recognizing that a state may require "high standards of qualification, such as good moral character or proficiency in its law, before it admits an applicant to the bar," has held that such qualifications, to pass constitutional muster, must have a "rational connection with the applicant's fitness or capacity to practice law." Schware v. Board of Bar Examiners, 353 U.S. 232, 239 (1957). . . .

Except for Cord's statement that she and a male to whom she was not married jointly owned and resided in the same dwelling, the record is devoid of any evidence which would otherwise reflect unfavorably on

Cord's professional competence, honest demeanor and good moral character. In fact, the evidence of a number of responsible citizens in the community where Cord resides establishes that she is of good character and honest demeanor. Likewise, the letters received from Cord's former employers vouch for her good moral character, as well as her professional competence.

While Cord's living arrangement may be unorthodox and unacceptable to some segments of society, this conduct bears no rational connection to her fitness to practice law. It cannot, therefore, serve to deny her the certificate required by Code § 54–60. . . .

Reversed and remanded.

* * *

Sexual activity in the character and fitness evaluation. As sexual mores have changed over time, courts have had to address what relevance, if any, sexual conduct might have in the character and fitness evaluation. The majority view is that "[p]rivate noncommercial sex acts between consenting adults are not relevant to prove fitness to practice law." Florida Bd. of Bar Examiners Re N.R.S., 403 So. 2d 1315, 1317 (Fla. 1981) (upholding admission of an applicant who had been excluded from the military based on his sexual orientation and had "refused to answer questions about his past sexual conduct" during the character and fitness process at a time when Florida criminalized same-sex sexual contact). However, sexual activity outside of the "consenting adults" framework is generally considered relevant to the fitness determination. *See, e.g.,* Vaughn v. Bd. of Bar Examiners for the Oklahoma Bar Ass'n, 759 P.2d 1026, 1027 (denying admission to an applicant who, while employed as a high-school teacher, had sexual relations with two of his fourteen-year-old students); In re Application of VanDenBossche, 724 N.E.2d 405, 407 (concluding that conduct involving a "lack of reliable judgment," including "physical contact with an intoxicated woman," was sufficiently serious to deny approval of licensure until more time had passed).

* * *

2.   FINANCIAL RESPONSIBILITY

IN RE STERN
943 A.2d. 1247 (Md. 2008)

BATTAGLIA, JUDGE

In this case we are asked to decide whether to grant the petition for admission to the Maryland Bar of Kevin Charles Stern, who has shown a pattern of financial irresponsibility, misrepresented his financial situation on his law school and Bar applications and exercised poor judgment with regard to a relationship with an underage female. Both the Character Committee and the State Board of Law Examiners recommended that Mr. Stern not be admitted, and we agree that Mr. Stern presently does not possess the requisite moral character and fitness for the practice of law required to be admitted to the Maryland Bar.

I. Background

On May 19, 2005, Kevin Charles Stern filed an application with the State Board of Law Examiners ("Board") for admission to the Maryland Bar. . . .

The Committee found that in 1993, Mr. Stern opened a credit account with Discover Card in order to meet his regular living expenses while attending Frostburg State University and to obtain cash advances to finance the startup of his business, Priority Plus, which provided various services to law firms including service of private process. As of May of 2001, the unpaid balance on the Discover Card account, the Committee found, was $11,190.00. Eventually, the Discover Card balance was sold to NCO Financial Systems, Inc., a debt collector. The Committee found that in 2006, after Mr. Stern had submitted his Bar application, he had negotiated a settlement with NCO. Just 33 days before the Committee hearing, on August 15, 2006, Mr. Stern's mother submitted a check to NCO for $6,000.00 in settlement of the debt. . . .

[The Court went through five more credit accounts opened by Stern between 1996 and 2002, between $700 and $10,000, all of which became delinquent and were sold to various collections agencies. Stern settled all of the accounts—usually for far less than face value, and after he had filed his bar application. Stern also had delinquent medical debts that were sold to a collections agency and settled for less than face value, as well as delinquent cell phone debt that was settled after Stern filed his bar application].

The Committee further found that, in 2007, Mr. Stern had a student loan payment of approximately $260.00 a month, that was in good standing; his only other outstanding debts were a Capital One credit card that had a balance of $479.00 and a PayPal account with a $50.00 balance. According to a Personal Financial Statement prepared with the help of a financial advisor, Mr. Stern also had savings of $21,500.00, two cars valued at $16,000.00, a bicycle worth $5,000.00, personal effects valued at $15,000.00, and $10,000.00 worth of artwork.

The Committee also determined that Mr. Stern had omitted various credit accounts and other problems either in his law school application or Bar application. In his law school application, dated January 15, 2002, in response to the question, "Do you have any charges or judgments pending against you?", Mr. Stern did not reveal the judgment entered against him, in 2000, for $4,476.91, the amount past due on the car loan purchased by

American General Finance. In his Bar application, dated May 1, 2005, in response to question 9(a), "During the last five years I have established or maintained credit with the following," Mr. Stern disclosed that he had established credit with Discover Financial Services and First USA Bank, but did not reveal the other accounts with which he had established credit, including American General Finance, Citibank Visa and Universal Card; in response to the following question on the Bar application, "9 (b) I presently owe money, some part of which has been delinquent for more than 90 days, to the following," Mr. Stern referred to two accounts, Discover Financial Services and Med 1 Yardmore Emergency Physician, but did not reveal the other credit accounts that had been delinquent for more than 90 days, including those with American General Finance, First USA Bank, Universal Card, Citibank Visa, as well as his unpaid bill with Cingular Wireless; in response to the question on the Bar application, "The following is a complete list of all suits in equity, actions at law, suits in bankruptcy or other statutory proceedings, matters in probate, lunacy, guardianship, and every other judicial or other administrative proceeding of every nature and kind, except divorce or criminal proceedings, to which I am or have been a party," Mr. Stern indicated that he had been a party in a tort action in the district court and that there was a pending case in the same court in which Discover Financial Services sought collection of an unpaid debt, but did not reveal the other accounts, which similarly, had resulted in judgments being entered, including the American General Finance, First USA Bank, Citibank Visa and Universal Card accounts. . . .

[B]efore the Committee, Mr. Stern proffered that he did not pay his outstanding debts because they became overwhelming, and he believed that making the required minimum payments would be pointless. He also claimed that he had recognized the error of his ways and had sought the assistance of a certified financial advisor. The Committee, although acknowledging the steps Mr. Stern had taken, found these contentions to be shallow. According to the Committee, before Mr. Stern had sought assistance of a financial advisor to correct his debt problems, he knew that his debts had to be paid and had assets to do so, but did not satisfy his obligations. Instead, he continued to increase his debt until no one would extend him further credit. Moreover, the Committee found, that Mr. Stern had not provided any documentation as to his actual income during the period when the debts were incurred, and that he had not explained why he had enough money in his budget in 2003 for a trip to Jamaica. The Committee also concluded that Mr. Stern paid off the majority of his debts with graduation gifts and a loan from his mother.

Mr. Stern also told the Committee that he did not reveal the American General Finance judgment because he was unaware of its existence until he gathered his information to complete his Bar application. The Committee determined, however, that this argument was unavailing, because . . . there was an affidavit from a private process company averring that Mr. Stern had been served with the summons on May 30, 2000 at 102 W. Pennsylvania Avenue, Suite 105, in Towson, Maryland, so that to believe Mr. Stern would require a lack of faith in the process server's certification.

Mr. Stern also testified before the Committee that he did not try to hide any of his financial information on his Bar application, that he did his best to disclose everything, that any mistakes he made were unintentional, and that all of his information was eventually disclosed. The Committee concluded, however, that Mr. Stern had not fully disclosed all of the institutions with which he had maintained credit, all of his unpaid debts, nor all of the legal actions pertaining to his delinquent accounts. . . .

The Character Committee issued a report dated March 28, 2007, in which the Committee found that Mr. Stern did not meet his burden of proof and then unanimously recommended that Mr. Stern be denied admission to the Maryland Bar based on the totality of the circumstances. . . .

[The Committee's report included the following findings:]

[T]he Committee believes that the Applicant has not shown a pattern of being fiscally responsible. For years, he allowed his debts to mount and made very few efforts to resolve the situation. He felt that paying nothing made sense back then and now feels his philosophy has been validated after discussing the matter with a financial advisor. Stern had a great revelation only recently that he should have at least communicated with his creditors in some fashion. Obviously, one form of communication would have been to pay something toward the bills. . . . Stern resented being labeled and harassed, presumably by creditors who were demanding payment.

Even now it is not difficult to conclude that the only reason for addressing the credit issues was the Bar application process. Had there been no application, Stern would likely still have unsatisfied judgments and unpaid bills. He does not appear to have altered his lifestyle or pared down his expenses as a means of generating funds to pay his outstanding accounts. He lists $68,500 worth of assets that include artwork, some of which he could have or can now use to pay his bills.

The fervent cleanup of his credit is belated and unconvincing. He used graduation gifts and a loan from his mother to pay his creditors. He now has a new major creditor, one whom he is in no hurry to repay. Stern's pattern of addressing his financial obligations does not bode well for someone who will be handling client funds and managing what is essentially a cash business. Stern has not demonstrated that he can be fiscally responsible with his own money and therefore, is unlikely to be so with the money of his clients. He commented that his mother is currently managing his money. However, her name will not be on the law license.

[The State Board of Law Examiners adopted the Committee's findings. Stern then appealed the Board's decision to the Maryland Supreme Court.]

II. Standard of Review

The issue before us is whether Mr. Stern has met his burden of proving that he possesses the present good moral character to practice law. Good moral character is denoted by "those qualities of truth-speaking, of a high sense of honor, of granite discretion, of the strictest observance of fiduciary responsibility." Thus, the "ultimate test of present moral character, applicable to original admissions to the Bar, is whether, viewing the applicant's character in the period subsequent to his misconduct, he has so convincingly rehabilitated himself that it is proper that he become a member of a profession which must stand free from all suspicion."

The Board's conclusions that an applicant does not possess the requisite moral character, and recommendation against admission to the Bar, are entitled to great weight. To properly exercise its responsibility, however, it is incumbent on this Court to make its own independent evaluation of the applicant's present moral character based upon testimony and evidence submitted before the Character Committee and the Board.

III. Discussion

Mr. Stern admits that he has been financially irresponsible, but argues that he has been rehabilitated, such that he now possesses good moral character and is fit to practice law. He contends that his rehabilitation is evidenced by the fact that he has paid many of his creditors and has developed a financial plan with the assistance of a financial advisor. He argues that he is motivated by his desire to become a member of the Bar in order to pursue a profession and gain financial stability. Mr. Stern also points out, that unlike many of our prior cases in which we have not admitted candidates to the Bar, his conduct was not criminal. With respect to his failure to disclose the American General Finance judgment on his law school application, Mr. Stern suggests that he was unaware, at that time, of the judgment; he also asserts that he did not intend to omit any financial information on his Bar application and that he fully disclosed the extent of his debt to the Committee. . . . . . He argues, in essence, that he has met his burden of proof and his admission should be granted. We disagree.

Our prior cases regarding Bar admissions are clear with respect to the impact of a failure to honor financial obligations. In *Application of Hyland*, we denied the admission to the Bar of a candidate who, prior to law school, pled guilty to fifteen counts of failure to remit sales taxes in violation of Pennsylvania state law and, in addition, failed to file federal employee withholding taxes, with regard to his operation of a restaurant. We noted that "[t]he conduct of an applicant in satisfying his or her financial obligations and exhibiting financial responsibility is an important factor in assessing good moral character," and that

> [g]iven the duties that attorneys are ordinarily required to perform, we think that the applicant's failure to carry out his significant legal obligation to satisfy his tax debt to the federal government and the Commonwealth of Pennsylvania is connected to his fitness to practice law. This conduct reflects adversely on the applicant's personal commitment to the proper administration of justice, as well as his honesty and truthfulness.

We noted that Hyland's inability to honor his financial obligations adversely reflected upon his ability to practice law:

> We shall consider those character traits that relate to the applicant's present fitness to practice law and to the State's legitimate interest in protecting prospective clients and the system of justice. We believe the record shows that the applicant does not appreciate the fiduciary responsibility incumbent upon an attorney when entrusted with the monies of another person. He does not appreciate the analogy between the tax obligations and the client trust account responsibilities. In addition to his lack of candor and contradictory testimony on critical issues, the applicant has displayed an inability to recognize his dereliction of a moral duty.

> We believe that the applicant's failure to honor his financial obligations evidences a disregard of a legal obligation and reflects adversely on his fitness to practice law.

. . . .

Mr. Stern has shown a pattern of financial irresponsibility. He allowed his debt to escalate and made very few efforts, if any, to resolve his financial obligations until he was faced with the possibility that his failure could hinder his admission to the Bar.

The Committee also found that Mr. Stern knew that his debts had to be paid and that he had assets to do so, but instead, he continued to increase his debt until no one would extend him further credit. He clearly did not take responsibility to generate funds sufficient to pay his debts by limiting his spending and selling assets. On his personal financial statement, requested by the Character Committee, Mr. Stern listed savings of $21,500.00, two vehicles valued at $16,000.00, a bicycle worth $5,000.00, personal effects valued at $15,000.00, and $10,000.00 worth of artwork, many of which could have been avoided or sold to meet his debt load. When assets are juxtaposed against the judgments, it becomes clear that Mr. Stern lived a lifestyle based on overdue credit and bad judgment.

Mr. Stern contends that unlike Application of Hyland, . . . and other cases in which we have denied admission, his conduct was not criminal. The fact that Mr. Stern was not the subject of criminal prosecution does not affect the fact that his financial misconduct does not bode well for someone who would be handling client funds as an attorney and in and of itself reflects adversely on his character and fitness to practice law. . . .

Additionally, Mr. Stern was not candid in regard to his disclosures on his law school and Bar applications. . . . We have emphasized the importance of candor in all of the Bar application process. Mr. Stern, in his law school application, did not reveal the judgment entered in connection with his unpaid car loan with American General Finance. In response to various questions on his Bar application, Mr. Stern did not reveal several suits filed against him related to delinquent credit accounts. . . .

Mr. Stern argues, nevertheless, that he had been rehabilitated because he has admitted his mistakes, has adopted a financial plan and has paid most of his creditors. While these actions are commendable, Mr. Stern fails to acknowledge the antecedent for his change; he satisfied his creditors only from the resources of others, specifically, a loan from his mother and gifts received after his graduation. Moreover, we agree that absent the exigency of the Bar admission process, Mr. Stern likely would have continued to ignore his financial obligations to repay his debt. Mr. Stern had allowed his debts to increase, and made very few efforts, if any, to resolve his financial obligations, even when it appears he had the means to do so. . . .

Conclusion

Therefore, after considering the totality of the circumstances surrounding Mr. Stern's conduct, and the fact that Mr. Stern bears the burden to prove his good moral character, our own independent review of the record leads us to conclude that Mr. Stern has failed to meet his burden, at this point in time, and his application for admission is denied

* * *

Good moral character. Clearly, this court believes that being a law-abiding citizen is not enough to establish "good moral character." What more is needed? Does the scrutiny of years-old financial delinquency make it more difficult for people from less privileged backgrounds to become lawyers? If you represented Mr. Stern, how would you advise him to demonstrate rehabilitation?

* * *

3. MENTAL HEALTH AND EMOTIONAL STABILITY

IN RE HENRY
841 N.W.2d 471 (S.D. 2013)

GILBERTSON, CHIEF JUSTICE.

Facts and Procedural History

Henry began attending the University of South Dakota School of Law in September 2007. Henry testified that during his second year of law school, he visited the University of South Dakota Student Counseling Center (the SCC) with his girlfriend to resolve some relationship issues. After his initial meeting, Henry had an individual counseling session at the SCC on March 17, 2009. He reported having auditory, visual, and tactile overstimulation, which affected his relationships, schoolwork, and employment. He also reported experiencing some anxiety and a period of five months in which he had experienced auditory hallucinations.

On March 24, 2009, Henry again visited the SCC. He reported that he had experienced racing thoughts followed by a great deal of energy and then a period of feeling down. Because of these reports, Henry took the Mini International Neuropsychiatric Interview (MINI). The interview indicated that he "met criteria for both Major Depressive Episode and Manic Episode, making a diagnosis of Bipolar Disorder most likely." Henry was diagnosed with Bipolar II Disorder on March 30, 2009.

On April 7, 2009, Henry visited the Sanford Vermillion Clinic to address his level of depression and anxiety. He was prescribed Symbyax, an antidepressant mood stabilizer. On April 14, Henry informed his counselor at the SCC that he was taking Symbyax. Two weeks later, however, Henry reported to his SCC counselor that he had stopped taking Symbyax "due to financial constraints." He also reported that he was depressed, and since he had stopped taking medication, his mood fluctuated frequently. However, at his hearing before the Board, Henry testified that it was actually the "horrific" side effects of the medication rather than "financial constraints" that caused him to discontinue taking the medication.

Henry completed his second year of law school in May 2009. That summer he had an internship in Sioux City but continued to live in Vermillion. For most of the summer, Henry discontinued counseling because he had not had "any episodes" and he was no longer affected "in any way and didn't really see the point in wasting the counselor's time."

Henry returned to the SCC on August 11, 2009. He testified that he informed the SCC that his prescribed medication "seemed to be 'stabilizing' as he had not been as fatigued." This was Henry's last counseling session of record while at the University of South Dakota. . . .

[Henry subsequently applied to take the Iowa bar, which asked him to undertake a psychological assessment.] The evaluation indicated that Henry exhibited low levels of anxiety. It also indicated that Henry "does not presently meet criteria for any psychological disorders." It stated that his "Bipolar II disorder is considered to be in full remission as it seems that he has not experienced either a depressed or hypomanic episode in approximately 1 year." The evaluation concluded, "There is no evidence to suggest any impairment in [Henry]'s ability to practice law in the state of Iowa due to problems in his psychological functioning." . . .

Following his admission to the Iowa bar, Henry sought admission to the South Dakota bar. . . . Shortly after taking the South Dakota bar exam, Henry went to the University of Iowa Hospitals and Clinic (the UIHC) in August 2012. Henry testified that he had just acquired health insurance through his employer and wanted to follow up on his bipolar disorder. At the time of the visit, Henry was experiencing some depression. Additionally, he indicated that he had one episode of low mood about once a year with each episode lasting about two weeks. Henry also thought he might have a milder form of mania exhibited by racing thoughts and excessive energy. The UIHC evaluation concluded that Henry had clear manic/hypomanic symptoms in his lifetime, but it was "less likely for him to have bipolar disorder." Dr. Thisayakron at the UIHC recommended that Henry try medication and counseling. He also prescribed Sertraline for anxiety and low mood. Henry was expected to follow up in five to six weeks; however, Henry did not follow up with the UIHC. Henry testified that he discontinued taking Sertraline due to "severe side-effects." He also indicated that he "clearly . . . did not have bipolar disorder or any disorder affecting [his] quality of life or [his] abilities." Thus, he "decided it was not worth the money to continue." . . .

[The Board of Law Examiners denied Henry's application to the South Dakota bar for several reasons, including a perceived lack of candor and the commission of two separate DUI offenses. In addition, the Board expressed concern regarding Henry's mental health.] The Board believed that Henry withheld some of his mental health records. It also expressed concern at Henry's decisions to discontinue recommended treatments without consulting the prescribing physician. The Board also noted periods of Henry's life that were affected by his mental health condition. Additionally, the Board believed that Henry showed disrespect to its members. . . .

Analysis and Decision

[Henry challenged the denial under the Americans with Disabilities Act, arguing] that the extent of the Board's inquiry into his mental health diagnosis along with the length of his character and fitness review violated the ADA. Henry contends that his prior diagnosis for bipolar disorder subjected him to a more thorough review process than other applicants. He asserts that this process violated the ADA.

The implementing regulations of the ADA state:

> A public entity shall not impose or apply eligibility criteria that screen out or tend to screen out an individual with a disability or any class of individuals with disabilities from fully and equally enjoying any service, program, or activity, unless such criteria can be shown to be necessary for the provision of the service, program, or activity being offered.

28 C.F.R. § 35.130(b)(8). Therefore, a general approach that denies all applicants who indicate a history of bipolar disorder on their bar application could violate the ADA. However, the Board did not conduct a generalized approach in this case. This is not a case of a blanket exclusion or inclusion. Instead, the Board conducted an individualized assessment to determine whether Henry met the "essential eligibility requirements" to practice law in the state. We conclude that the Board's individualized assessment of Henry's history of bipolar disorder did not violate the ADA. . . .

An individualized assessment of an applicant with a history of bipolar disorder is necessary to protect the public. Courts have routinely upheld bar application questions that ask whether an applicant has been treated for bipolar disorder, schizophrenia, paranoia, or any other psychotic disorder within a specific timeframe.

The rationale for these inquiries is that "bipolar disorder, schizophrenia, paranoia, and psychotic disorders are serious mental illnesses that may affect a person's ability to practice law." For instance, a Manic Episode, which can accompany bipolar disorder, may lead to the complete disregard of ethical concerns, even by those who are typically very conscientious. One can only imagine the risk this may pose to clients, who often entrust an attorney with their livelihood, freedom, or even life. Clients suffer as much from unintentional misconduct such as neglect as they would from the acts of an attorney caused by an intentional "evil motive." . . . Contrary to Henry's assertion, an individualized assessment of his diagnosis for bipolar disorder was necessary to evaluate whether his prior diagnosis may pose a threat to the public in the future.

Given that Henry indicated a prior diagnosis for bipolar disorder within five years of his application, it was necessary for the Board to obtain a complete picture of Henry's mental health history to determine whether potential symptoms of his bipolar disorder may affect his legal practice. It was also necessary that the Board receive Henry's records so that it could conduct an individual assessment of Henry's condition based on objective evidence from medical professionals. The Board's request was not unreasonable. . . .

The Board has a responsibility not just to the applicants, but also to the bar and citizens of its state to make sure that the attorneys it licenses are fit to practice. To maintain that public confidence, this Court must only license attorneys that are emotionally and mentally fit to practice law.

Conclusion

We conclude that Henry has not met his burden of proving good moral character by clear and convincing evidence. The cumulative effect of Henry's lack of candor, poor judgment, criminal record, and unreliability, paired with the unresolved issues regarding the status of Henry's mental health, justify the Board's decision. Thus, we agree with the Board's recommendation and note that Henry may reapply at a future date with the understanding that the Board is allowed to conduct an individual assessment into Henry's fitness to practice law, which includes a reasonable inquiry into Henry's mental health.

* * *

ADA challenges. In addition to the case above, a number of bar applicants have challenged the ability of bar examiners to ask about an applicant's mental impairments or history of substance abuse during the application process or to make application decisions on the basis of such characteristics. Dale v. Moore, 121 F.3d 624 (11th Cir. 1997) (bipolar disorder); Campbell v. Greisberger, 80 F.3d 703 (2d Cir. 1996) (schizophrenia); McCready v. Michigan State Bar, 881 F. Supp. 300 (W.D. Mich. 1995) (alcoholism and personality disorders); Johnson v. State of Kan., 888 F. Supp. 1073 (D. Kan. 1995) (bipolar disorder); Clark v. Virginia Bd. of Bar Examiners, 880 F. Supp. 430 (E.D. Va. 1995) (major depression). Applicants have had mixed success with these claims. In the past, it used to be common for states to ask about any history of mental health treatment. Now, most states have narrowed the inquiry to include only a specified set of particular diagnoses, such as those listed in the *Henry* decision: "bipolar disorder, schizophrenia, paranoia, or any other psychotic disorder."

DOJ investigation. In early 2014, the Department of Justice sent letters to officials in two states (Louisiana and Vermont) that used the standard admissions form promulgated by the National Conference of Bar Examiners. The DOJ alleged that three of the questions on the NCBE form impermissibly discriminated against individuals with disabilities and violated the ADA. The DOJ alleged that questions such as those discussed in the *Henry* opinion above are problematic because they "mak[e] discriminatory inquiries regarding bar applicants mental health and treatment," subject applicants "to burdensome supplemental investigations triggered by their mental health status or treatment," make "discriminatory admissions recommendations based on stereotypes of persons with disabilities," and fail "to provide adequate confidentiality protections." The DOJ also expressed concern that such burdensome review procedures would prevent law students and others from seeking help or treatment when warranted. As a result of the DOJ investigation, the NCBE agreed to change the standard character form, and will no longer ask whether the applicant has been diagnosed or treated for "bipolar disorder, schizophrenia, paranoia, or any other psychotic disorder." Instead, the standard application will ask whether, in the past five years, the applicant has "exhibited any conduct or behavior that could call into question [the applicant's] ability to practice law in a competent, ethical, and professional manner." *See* Anna Stolley Persky, *A Matter over Mind: State Bars May Probe Applicants' Behavior, but not Mental Health Status*, ABA JOURNAL (June 2014), at 20. States that do not use the standard NCBE form—or states that choose to supplement the standard form with additional questions—may or may not comply with the DOJ recommendations.

Challenging overbroad questions. Although many states are making narrower inquiries than they did in the past, there remains the possibility that some requests for information will not be "lawful" either because the information being sought is not rationally related to your fitness to practice law or because you have a privilege against disclosing the requested specified information that trumps the right of bar examiners to ask for it. Also, Comment [2] to Model Rule 8.1 states that the duty to be forthcoming is "subject to the provisions of the fifth amendment of the United States Constitution and corresponding provisions of state constitutions." The Comment, of course, is referring to the privilege against self-incrimination.

If you think that a request for information is unlawful or you think you have a legal privilege not to disclose the requested information, one option would be simply to refrain from disclosing the information. The course recommended by the ABA in Comment [2] to Model Rule 8.1 is for a person who is relying on a legal right not to answer a question to "do so openly and not use the right of nondisclosure as a justification for failure to comply with . . . this Rule." In other words, make your refusal explicit: do not answer falsely or merely leave the answer space blank. To do so would be seen as a misrepresentation rather than a refusal to answer.

One disability rights advocate has argued that applicants are justified in telling bar examiners that they will not respond to such questions:

> . . . I do think that given the fact that these inquiries are inappropriate, given that you all know that they discourage seeking help, and given, at least in some folks' view, that they're completely illegal because they target and burden people with disabilities in a process for which this inquiry is completely unnecessary for the public authority to do its work, I don't think you should answer.

Suffering in Silence: The Tension Between Self-Disclosure and a Law School's Obligation to Report, 18 AM. U. J. GENDER SOC. POL'Y & L. 121, 133 (2009) (statement of Ira Burnim).

Another approach would be to abdicate your rights or waive your privilege, reveal the information, and take your stand on the substantive irrelevance or inadequacy of the information as a ground for denial of your application for admission to the bar.

ABA Model Rule on Conditional Admission. The ABA has adopted a Model Rule on Conditional Admission that encourages jurisdictions to conditionally admit applicants who demonstrate rehabilitation from chemical dependency or successful mental health treatment when those conditions "caused conduct that would otherwise have rendered the applicant currently unfit to practice law." The rule is gaining traction in a number of states.

* * *

4. CANDOR IN THE BAR ADMISSION PROCESS

IN RE APPLICATION OF GOODSTEIN
1 N.E.3d 328 (Ohio 2013)

Daniel Robert Goodstein of Ada, Ohio, was expected to graduate from the Ohio Northern University Pettit College of Law in May 2013. He has applied as a candidate for admission but has not applied to take the bar exam.

Two members of the Hardin County Bar Association's admissions committee interviewed Goodstein. Although one of the interviewers noted that Goodstein had revealed a "situation" regarding the overpayment of unemployment benefits that he was working to repay, the committee recommended that his character, fitness, and moral qualifications be approved.

The Board of Commissioners on Character and Fitness exercised its authority to *sua sponte* investigate Goodstein's character. After conducting a hearing, a panel of the board issued a report expressing several concerns about Goodstein's character including (1) an administrative determination by the Ohio Department of Job and Family Services ("ODJFS") that the agency had overpaid him unemployment-compensation benefits and that the overpayment was due in part to fraud, (2) his failure to disclose his unemployment-compensation fraud on his original application, (3) his failure to disclose that he had been subject to discipline as an undergraduate at Xavier University for incidents involving alcohol, (4) his failure to disclose a speeding ticket, and (5) inaccuracies in the reporting of his employment history. . . .

The Underlying Improprieties

Unemployment—Benefits Fraud

The panel found that in February 2012, Goodstein sent the National Conference of Bar Examiners ("NCBE") an amendment to his application updating his response to one of the questions, but he did not submit the amendment to the Office of Bar Admissions. The amendment reflected that he had collected unemployment benefits after being "laid-off" from his employment as a sales representative for Total Quality Logistics[1] but that ODJFS had later determined that a portion of those benefits had been overpaid due to fraud. Goodstein reported in the amendment that ODJFS had determined that he became ineligible to receive unemployment benefits when he accepted a new job through an employment agency and then quit that job without providing notice to the employment agency. He explained that he had quit the new job because he could not afford the commute for the three weeks before he would have received his first paycheck.

Goodstein further stated in the amendment that by the time he learned that ODJFS expected him to repay a portion of the benefits that he had received, he had found work as a part-time janitor and that with the payments he received from unemployment and the work, he "was barely able to make [his] monthly rent and utilities payments." The panel initially believed that this statement indicated that Goodstein had been reporting his earnings to ODJFS and had been receiving a reduced unemployment benefit. At the hearing, however, Goodstein provided two ODJFS Determinations on Eligibility for Unemployment Benefits issued on April 28, 2010, and a later issued Director's Redetermination of

---

[1]   He did not initially disclose this employment on his application to register as a candidate for admission to the practice of law.

another determination that had been issued on that date, that proved otherwise.

One ODJFS determination disallowed Goodstein's claim for certain benefits on the finding that he had failed to report earnings from SMX Staffing (for the job that he had quit) for the period of September 6, 2009, through September 12, 2009, with the intent to obtain benefits to which he was not entitled. Goodstein appealed another determination regarding that job that had also gone against him, and the director of ODJFS issued a modified redetermination that was substantially similar to the appealed determination, characterizing the payment of benefits for the week that included Goodstein's voluntary termination of his employment as fraudulent because he had quit without just cause, while characterizing his claims for the ensuing period for the weeks of September 19, 2009, through December 26, 2009, as denied, but not fraudulent. Therefore, the director ordered Goodstein to repay 16 weeks of benefits at $198 per week, a total of $3,168.

A different ODJFS determination found that Goodstein had not reported his earnings from the Jewish Community Center for the period of January 03, 2010, through April 24, 2010, and that he had withheld that information with the intent of obtaining benefits to which he was not entitled. This determination declared that his collection of those benefits was fraudulent and ordered him to repay the $3,168 in benefits that he had received for that 16-week period.

While Goodstein sought to characterize his unemployment-benefits fraud solely as a misunderstanding about his eligibility following his voluntary termination of short-term employment, the panel expressed concern that he failed to acknowledge his "larger" fraud—falsely answering questions about his employment and income every week from at least January through May 2010 in order to collect unemployment benefits while he was gainfully employed—until he was cross-examined at the hearing. The panel was particularly troubled that Goldstein had disclosed the true nature of his "problem with ODJFS" to a law-school classmate, who testified at the hearing that Goodstein "had drawn unemployment while also having a job," yet had attempted to conceal it during the admissions process.

Goodstein paid $1,000 to ODJFS on July 14, 2010, and made two small payments totaling $43 on March 11, 2011. In September 2012, he told the admissions-committee interviewers that he was working hard to establish a repayment plan, but he made only two additional payments of $50 after that interview—one on November 30, 2012, and the other on January 4, 2013. At the time of that last payment, his outstanding balance, with accrued interest, was $6,705.04. Although Goodstein initially claimed that his ODJFS case manager had advised him that he could not make partial payments on his account because the overpayments had been fraudulently obtained, he conceded on cross-examination at the hearing that R.C. 4141.35 and an authoritative resource explaining repayment procedures appear to contemplate that repayment plans are acceptable, even in cases of fraud. And although Goodstein testified that he had an oral understanding with special counsel for the attorney general's office that he would make payments of $50 per month until he passed the bar exam and would increase his payments thereafter, he presented no documentary evidence to support this claim.

The panel noted that significant material inconsistencies became apparent when comparing Goodstein's application, his testimony, and the evidence presented at the hearing with regard to his employment history. While the amendment Goodstein submitted to the NCBE stated that his employment through the employment agency began on September 8, 2009, and ended on September 11, 2009, he testified at the hearing that he worked for only one day. The employment agency, however, reported that he worked for the company from September 9, 2009, through September 16, 2009. And while Goodstein testified that he obtained a job as a janitor at the Jewish Community Center in October or November 2009, the application submitted to this court states, and the employer confirmed, that he started working there as a "manager" in January 2010.

After the hearing, Goodstein filed a motion to correct his testimony to conform it to the documentary record, asserting that he had been confused about the date that he began working at the Jewish Community Center, and seeking to establish that the employment commenced in January 2010 as reported by the employer. The panel denied the motion, noting that the employer was asked only to confirm Goodstein's employment as a manager, not as a janitor—the position that he testified he accepted in November 2009—and that regardless of when the employment commenced, the record clearly established that he fraudulently collected unemployment benefits while employed until May 2010.

Underage Consumption of Alcohol at Xavier University

On his application, Goodstein answered "No" to Question 5A, which asked whether he had ever been subject to any disciplinary action at any educational institution. Xavier University reported to the NCBE that he had been disciplined for a November 2004 incident involving a keg party and that he had completed all sanctions imposed. At the hearing, Goodstein offered a letter from the Office of Residence Life at Xavier University detailing not one, but two separate incidents involving the underage consumption of alcohol. The sanction for the first offense, which occurred in September 2004, was five hours of community service, which he completed in October 2004. For his second offense, which occurred in November 2004, he wrote a paper about his experience consuming alcohol.

Goodstein testified that he had forgotten about these incidents until Xavier reported one of them to the NCBE and that he felt that they were residence-life issues separate from his academic record. The panel did not find his testimony to be credible in light of his brother-in-law's testimony that Goodstein first told him about the incidents in early 2012, which coincided with the timing of Goodstein's application to register as a candidate for admission to the practice of law.

Failure to Disclose Traffic Citation

The panel noted that Goodstein properly disclosed two traffic citations on his application but that he failed to disclose a third. While acknowledging that under ordinary circumstances such an omission would not be a cause for concern, the panel noted that in this case it was one of many misstatements and omissions, demonstrating, at a minimum, Goodstein's inattention to detail. . . .

Disposition

We adopt the findings of fact and conclusions of law of the board. Pursuant to [the Ohio rules governing bar admission], "[t]he applicant has the burden to prove by clear and convincing evidence that the applicant possesses the requisite character, fitness, and moral qualifications for admission to the practice of law. . . . A record manifesting a significant deficiency in the honesty, trustworthiness, diligence, or reliability of an applicant may constitute a basis for disapproval of the applicant."

In determining whether the record demonstrates such a deficiency, we consider a number of factors, including but not limited to an applicant's failure to provide complete and accurate information concerning the applicant's past; false statements, including omissions; and acts involving dishonesty, fraud, deceit, or misrepresentation.

The evidence demonstrates that in the year before he entered law school, Goodstein obtained unemployment benefits by making false representations about his employment status and earnings for a period of at least 17 weeks. Throughout these admissions proceedings, however, he attempted to characterize the overpayment of more than $6,000 in unemployment benefits as entirely the result of a misunderstanding about his eligibility for the benefits. In light of these acts, involving significant and repeated instances of dishonesty, fraud, deceit, or misrepresentation, and Goodstein's failure to fully disclose other unfavorable, but arguably less serious, information about his past, we agree that he has failed to demonstrate his character, fitness, and moral qualifications to practice law in Ohio.

Accordingly, we disapprove Goodstein's application to register as a candidate for admission to the practice of law. Provided that he first satisfies his full obligation to ODFJS of $6,705.04 plus interest accruing thereon, he may, however, reapply for admission to the practice of law by filing an entirely new application to register as a candidate and undergoing a new character and fitness evaluation, and he may apply to take the July 2015 bar exam.

* * *

Duty of disclosure. Note that Model Rule 8.1(b) requires more than truthful answers to questions posed by the bar admission officials. It requires the applicant to take the initiative to "disclose a material fact necessary to correct a misapprehension known by the person to have arisen in the matter," with Comment [1] explaining that this "requires correction of any prior misstatement in the matter that the applicant . . . may have made and the affirmative clarification of any misunderstanding on the part of the admissions . . . authority of which the person becomes aware."

The duty of candor for bar applicants. Is there some information about you that you would prefer not to share with the Board of Law Examiners? Might you be tempted to justify nondisclosure of adverse information by a narrow interpretation of the requests for information in the bar application? Be warned that doing so is risky business. As explained in Comment [1] to Model Rule 8.1, doing so may provide grounds for denial of the application for admission and also, if discovered subsequent to admission to the bar, would provide grounds for imposition of professional discipline, which could include disbarment. Non-compliance with the duty of candor in connection with a prior bar application could also serve as grounds for denial of a subsequent admission, such as when a lawyer licensed in one state seeks admission to the bar of another state. Even if the undisclosed information would not warrant denial of your application to the bar, failure to respond truthfully to all requests for information can justify the rejection of your application, and it would also warrant the imposition of professional discipline if your lie is discovered after your admission to the bar.

The duty of candor for lawyers providing references for others. The duty of candor imposed upon bar applicants by Model Rule 8.1 and numerous identical state rules apply with equal force to a lawyer serving as a reference for a bar applicant. The only difference is that a lawyer serving as a reference would not be able to invoke the applicant's privilege against self-incrimination as a justification for failure to truthfully respond to a question. It is important to distinguish the lawyer who is serving as a reference for a bar applicant and a lawyer who is representing or has represented a client in anticipation of or in connection with the client's application for admission to the bar. A lawyer representing a bar applicant is exempted from the affirmative disclosure requirements of Model Rule 8.1(b) if the information in question is protected by the lawyer's duty under Model Rule 1.6, and state counterparts, not to reveal information relating to the representation of client—a duty that will be examined in greater detail in later chapters.

* * *

Profile of attorney professionalism. In 1954, the Illinois Supreme Court denied George Anastaplo's application to practice law. Anastaplo's record was strong; he was described as an "unusually worthy applicant for admission," who had "joined the Air Force during the middle of World War II—flying as a navigator in every major theater of the military operations of that war," had received an honorable discharge, and had subsequently studied at the University of Chicago for both his undergraduate and law school education. In re Anastaplo, 366 U.S. 82, 98 (1961) (Black, J., dissenting). "His record throughout his life, both as a student and as a citizen, was unblemished." *Id.*

Nonetheless, Anastaplo was denied admission because he refused to answer a question about whether he had ever been a member of the Communist Party. When meeting with subcommittee members to discuss his application, Anastaplo also refused to answer questions about his political affiliation and religious beliefs. Anastaplo argued that the questions unconstitutionally infringed on his constitutional rights to free speech and association, and that they were not relevant to his ability to practice law. In his closing argument before the Illinois Committee on Character and Fitness, Anastaplo acknowledged that he had refused to answer a number of questions put before him, but argued that the committee should view this refusal as part of his dedication to the Constitution and laws of his country:

> You should be grateful that I have not made a complete submission to you, even though I have cooperated as fully as good conscience permits. . . . This is the problem of selecting the standards and methods the bar must employ if it is to help preserve and nourish that idealism, that vital interest in the problem of justice, that so often lies at the heart of the intelligent and sensitive law student's choice of career. This is an idealism which so many things about the bar, and even about bar admission practices, discourage and make unfashionable to defend or retain.

Id. at 104–05. The Illinois committee split on Anastaplo's case, with a majority voting against his admission. Not one of the committee members who had asked the challenged questions ultimately voted in his favor. Anastaplo sought review in the United States Supreme Court, but the Court ultimately denied relief by a vote of 5–4, deciding that the Illinois refusal would stand. The Court placed responsibility for Anastaplo's denial on the candidate himself: "We find nothing to suggest that he would not be admitted now if he decides to answer . . . In short, petitioner holds the key to admission in his own hands." In re Anastaplo, 366 U.S. 82, 96–97 (1961). Justice Black penned a vigorous dissent.

Although Anastaplo was never licensed to practice, he remained active in the scholarly side of law until his death in 2014. He taught in the University of Chicago's Basic Program of Liberal Education for Adults for nearly six decades, from 1957 to 2013, also taught at Loyola University School of Law in Chicago, and wrote numerous books and articles. He maintained a correspondence with Justice Black in the years following the decision. *See* George Anastaplo, *In Re Justice Hugo La Fayette Black (1886–1971): My More or Less "Personal" Experience of Him*, 44 LOY. U. CHI. L.J. 1271, 1279 (2013).

Justice Black asked for the final paragraph of his dissenting opinion to be read at his funeral in 1971, where Anastaplo and his young children were in attendance:

> Too many men are being driven to become government-fearing and time-serving because the Government is being permitted to strike out at those who are fearless enough to think as they please and say what they think. This trend must be halted if we are to keep faith with the Founders of our Nation and pass on to future generations of Americans the great heritage of freedom which they sacrificed so much to leave to us. The choice is clear to me. If we are to pass on that great heritage of freedom, we must return to the original language of the Bill of Rights. We must not be afraid to be free.

In re Anastaplo, 366 U.S. at 106 (Black, J., dissenting).

CHAPTER 3

REGULATION OF THE LEGAL PROFESSION: ENFORCING STANDARDS OF PROFESSIONAL CONDUCT

■ ■ ■

Chapter hypothetical. Rhett was a partner in the prestigious law firm Palsgraf & Pennoyer, LLP. The firm discovered that over a four-year period, Rhett had deposited in his personal bank account fourteen checks from the same client totaling $30,000 that, pursuant to the firm's partnership agreement, should have been deposited in the firm's account. Rhett explained that his family had been suffering some financial woes as a result of a family member's medical problems. He volunteered to repay the firm and offered to resign. The firm's management committee, consisting of several partners, refused Rhett's resignation offer and permitted him to stay on. The committee concluded that Rhett was under significant financial and emotional pressure when he deposited the checks, and that his actions were an aberration and were unlikely to be repeated. Therefore, they concluded Rhett's actions did not raise a serious question as to his fitness to practice law. The members of the committee did not inform all of the firm's other partners about Rhett's actions, fearing that Rhett was too emotionally fragile to handle the resulting attention.

An audit conducted by the firm a few months later revealed that Rhett's misappropriation of funds was more extensive than Rhett had admitted to. Again, concerned over Rhett's emotional state, the partners decided to "hold off for a while" in terms of taking action against Rhett. When Murray, another Palsgraf & Pennoyer partner who was not on the firm's management committee but who had worked with Rhett on the representation of the client at issue, learned about Rhett's actions and the committee's failure to inform the other partners, he was outraged. Murray quit the firm in protest, brought a civil action against the other partners for breach of the partnership agreement, and notified the New Dakota Board of Professional Responsibility about Rhett's actions. The Board subsequently brought disciplinary charges against Rhett, as well as charges against the partners on the management committee for their failure to inform the Board of Rhett's misconduct. Eventually, the story made the local news, and the client whose checks were misappropriated was furious with Murray about the resulting publicity and for disclosing information about the matter to the Board without first obtaining its consent. Rhett was never charged with a crime.

(A) Is Rhett subject to discipline under Rule 8.3?

(B) Are the members of the committee subject to discipline under Rule 8.3(a)?

(C) Was Murray obligated to obtain the client's consent before reporting to the Board?

(D) What disciplinary sanctions, if any, should be imposed upon Rhett?

* * *

In this Chapter we focus on the enforcement of the standards of professional conduct as have been promulgated in accord with the law and practice to which you were introduced in Chapter 2. The key enforcement mechanisms are (1) voluntary compliance, (2) enforcement by the imposition of professional discipline, such as a public reprimand or suspension of one's license to practice law, and (3) enforcement of the law governing lawyers through the imposition of civil and/or criminal liability. You should be familiar with the basic principles governing the imposition of criminal and civil liability, but need to be on the lookout for any departures from the basic principles because they are being applied to lawyers. After a moment's reflection on voluntary compliance, we will explore some general ideas about the misconduct that will warrant the imposition of professional discipline, the responsibilities of lawyers to actively participate in disciplinary process, and the various forms of discipline that might be imposed for professional misconduct. Then the chapter will look at the enforcement of the law governing lawyers through the imposition of civil or criminal liability and begin an ongoing exploration of the relationship between the standards governing the imposition of professional discipline and the standards governing the imposition of civil or criminal liability.

* * *

A. PROFESSIONAL DISCIPLINE

Please read ABA Model Rules of
Professional Conduct, Scope¶ [19].

Paragraph [10] of the Preamble to the ABA's Model Rules asserts that "[t]he legal profession is largely self-governing." In paragraph [11], the ABA explains that "self-regulation ... helps maintain the legal profession's independence from government domination." This is good because "[a]n independent legal profession is an important force in preserving government under law, for abuse of legal authority is more readily challenged by a profession whose members are not dependent on government for the right to practice." Given its relative autonomy, "[t]he profession has a responsibility to assure that its regulations are conceived in the public interest and not in furtherance of parochial or self-interested concerns of the bar."

Much of the energy of both the ABA and the state bar associations has been directed to the regulation of the legal profession. The ABA also undertook to regulate the conduct of lawyers when, in 1908, it adopted its Canons of Ethics and required its members to abide by them. In 1969, the ABA replaced the Canons with what became known as the Model Code of Professional Responsibility. Then, in 1983, the ABA replaced the Model Code of Professional Responsibility with its Model Rules of Professional Conduct and substantially amended the Model Rules in 2002.

As the ABA Rules are "model rules" without force of law, the ABA seeks to have its rules adopted by state supreme courts. To this end the ABA urges state bar associations to recommend the adoption of the ABA rules by their respective supreme courts. These rules form the basis of the professional disciplinary system in each state.

* * *

AMERICAN LAW INSTITUTE, RESTATEMENT OF THE LAW (THIRD), THE LAW GOVERNING LAWYERS

Title C. Professional Discipline

Introductory Note

From colonial times until late in the 19th century, lawyer discipline was almost entirely a function of courts and voluntary bar associations. A lawyer would be proceeded against in a show-cause proceeding before a court, at the suit either of an injured client, an adversary lawyer, or a voluntary bar association. A trial by the judge would ensue, with the most extreme sanction available being expulsion from the bar of the court. A lawyer admitted to several courts could, and often did, continue to practice before the other courts, unless and until successfully proceeded against there as well.

Disciplinary proceedings became increasingly formalized in the 20th century. Critical findings about the state of lawyer discipline were made by the 1979 ABA Special Committee on Evaluation of Disciplinary Enforcement, "Problems and Recommendations in Disciplinary Enforcement," chaired by Justice Tom Clark. In response, the ABA began work on what became, through a series of interim publications, the ABA Model Rules for Lawyer Disciplinary Enforcement (as amended 1996).

. . .

In most states and the District of Columbia, lawyer disciplinary proceedings are similar to and must comply with due-process standards applicable to administrative-enforcement proceedings. Many states have followed all or most of the recommended procedures and institutional arrangements specified in the ABA's Model Rules for Lawyer Disciplinary Enforcement, which were devised in light of applicable due process and similar constraints. Thereunder, a professional, independent disciplinary counsel is charged with responsibility to prosecute offenses, often following review by a screening body to determine whether probable cause exists warranting formal charges. Formal charges are heard by a neutral panel, composed primarily of lawyers but often having significant nonlawyer membership, appointed by the court and often without involvement of any bar association. Written charges make known to the lawyer the nature of the offense and its circumstances. Rules governing depositions in civil actions are applied; other discovery is conducted informally, subject to superintendence by the hearing panel. Beyond discovery, proceedings are governed by the rules of procedure and evidence applied in civil litigation. Some jurisdictions open the record of proceedings, including the hearing, once a determination of probable cause is made. The standard of proof in most jurisdictions is clear and convincing evidence, that is, evidence establishing the truth of the charged offense beyond a mere preponderance of the evidence but not necessarily beyond a reasonable doubt. Matters on which a responding lawyer bears the burden of persuasion must be proved by a preponderance of the evidence (on readmission, see below). Review is typically available in the highest court of the jurisdiction, which exercises independent judgment with respect to both findings of fact and conclusions of law on all issues, including the sanction imposed. . . .

* * *

One author has listed nine possible goals of professional discipline that have been advanced:

> (1) remedying an injured party's or the legal system's injury;
> (2) punishing a miscreant lawyer for past misconduct;
> (3) disabling the lawyer from committing future misconduct;
> (4) deterring future misconduct by the lawyer; (5) encouraging rehabilitation of the lawyer; (6) deterring future misconduct by other lawyers; (7) enhancing the image of the profession and the way the profession practices law; (8) protecting the integrity of the disciplinary process; and (9) balancing client protection and mercy to lawyers.

Fred C. Zacharias, *The Purposes of Lawyer Discipline*, 45 WM. & MARY L. REV. 675, 698 (2003). Of course, different people would rank these goals differently in terms of their relative importance. In addition, budgetary and other constraints might make it more difficult to achieve some of these goals than others. However, assuming that each of these are valid goals of professional discipline, consider how the disciplinary process should be structured in order to attain these goals. The ABA Model Rules of Lawyer Disciplinary Enforcement (http://www.americanbar.org/groups/professional_responsibility/resources/lawyer_ethics_regulation/model_rules_for_lawyer_disciplinary_enforcement.html) and ABA Standards for Imposing Lawyer Sanctions (http://www.americanbar.org/content/dam/aba/administrative/professional_responsibility/corrected_standards_sanctions_may2012_wfootnotes.authcheckdam.pdf) provide some suggestions for how states should structure their disciplinary systems.

What do you think? How does the disciplinary process compare with the adjudicative process in criminal cases? In civil cases?

1.   Who should be the adjudicators? Judges? Lawyers? Laypersons? An appropriate mix? Why? *See* ABA Model Rules of Lawyer Disciplinary Enforcement, Rules 2, 3, & 11.

2.   Who are or should be the prosecutors? Full-time disciplinary counsel? Lawyer volunteers? Law students participating in a disciplinary externships or clinics? Why? What are the responsibilities of disciplinary counsel? There are lawyers who specialize in prosecuting disciplinary cases against lawyers. *See* ABA Model Rules of Lawyer Disciplinary Enforcement, Rule 4. Many are career disciplinary counsel and are likely to be members of the National Organization of Bar Counsel (NOBC). Check out the NOBC website at http://www.nobc.org. Other lawyers are now specializing in the representation of lawyers who are respondents in disciplinary proceedings. They are likely to be members of the Association of Professional Responsibility Lawyers (APRL). Check out the APRL website at http://www.aprl.net.

3.   To what extent should disciplinary proceedings and impositions of discipline be confidential? Be a matter of public record? Be publicized by disciplinary counsel? *See* ABA Model Rules of Lawyer Disciplinary Enforcement, Rule 16.

4.   What should the statute of limitations be for disciplinary proceedings? *See* ABA Model Rules of Lawyer Disciplinary Enforcement, Rule 32.

5.   Who should have the burden of proof and what should that burden be?

* * *

Please read ABA Model Rules of Professional
Conduct, Rule 8.1 and Comments.

* * *

Self-incrimination. Comment [2] states that Model Rule 8.1 is subject to the right of the respondent to invoke his or her constitutional privilege against self-incrimination but goes on state that the respondent "should do so openly and not use the right of non-disclosure as a justification for a failure to comply with this Rule."

Voluntary compliance. Paragraph [16] of the Scope preceding the Model Rules provides that compliance with the rules of professional conduct "depends primarily upon understanding and voluntary compliance, secondarily upon reinforcement by peer and public opinion and finally, when necessary, upon enforcement through disciplinary proceedings." How likely is it that you will make a conscientious effort to understand the Rules of Professional Conduct and to voluntarily comply with the rules for no other reason than that is what is expected of you as a lawyer? How likely is it that you will do so even if there is no risk that a violation would be detected? How might peer or public opinion reinforce or undermine, as the case may be, either your personal commitment to abide by the rules or your disposition to "game" the rules? What role will the prospect of professional discipline and/or criminal or civil liability play in your decision-making about compliance with the Rules of Professional Conduct and other law governing lawyers? Please rethink each of these questions as applied to your classmates and then again as applied to America's lawyers. Finally, answer each of these questions about lawyers as a group as you think they would be answered in a public opinion survey of America's non-lawyers. Do you come up with the same answers?

* * *

B. MISCONDUCT

A necessary first step in the enforcement of standards of professional conduct is a determination that the lawyer has engaged in misconduct—misconduct that subjects the lawyer to professional discipline or criminal or civil liability. In some cases a lawyer's misconduct will subject the lawyer to professional discipline and both criminal and civil liability. In other cases conduct that does not subject the lawyer to civil or criminal liability will subject the lawyer to professional discipline. The following section explores some of the lawyer conduct that is branded as misconduct warranting the imposition of professional discipline.

* * *

Please read ABA Model Rules of Professional Conduct, Rule 8.4 and Comments.

* * *

The meaning of Rule 8.4(a). From reading Model Rule 8.4(a) you now know that it is misconduct to violate a Model Rule that requires you to do something or prohibits you from doing something. Note, however, the significant expansion of the reach of the rules by the inclusion within the specification of misconduct of an attempt to violate a rule, assisting or inducing another lawyer to violate a rule, and violating the rules through the act of another. Comment [1] sheds little light on the meaning of these terms. In terms of the prohibition on violating the rules through the acts of another, the typical fact pattern involves a lawyer using another (often a non-lawyer) to do something the lawyer is personally prohibited from doing. *See, e.g.*, State v. Grossberg, 705 A.2d 608 (Del. Super. Ct. 1997) (imposing discipline on lawyer who prepared his client to make statements in a television interview that the lawyer was prohibited by ethics rules from making).

The meaning of Rule 8.4(b) & (c). What criminal acts do *not* reflect adversely on a lawyer's honesty, trustworthiness, or fitness as a lawyer in other respects? For example, is driving under the influence a violation of Rule 8.4(b)? If the same lawyer is pulled over by a police officer on suspicion of driving under the influence and the lawyer lies to the officer about how much he has had to drink, is that "dishonesty, fraud, deceit, and misrepresentation" in violation of Rule 8.4(c)? Does it matter that the dishonesty occurs while the lawyer is not acting in his capacity as a lawyer?

* * *

Problem 3.1. Phillip, a lawyer, attends a deposition, during which he engages in abusive behavior toward opposing counsel and her client. Has he violated Rule 8.4(d)?

The meaning of Rule 8.4(d). Are you concerned about the breadth of the prohibition in Rule 8.4(d) against engaging in conduct that is prejudicial to the administration of justice? The rule has been applied in cases ranging from a lawyer who solicited sex from a minor, Attorney Grievance Commission v. Childress, 770 A.2d 685 (Md. 2001), to a lawyer who lied under oath, In re Mason, 736 A.2d 1019 (D.C. 1999). In Comment c to § 5 of the Restatement (Third) of the Law Governing Lawyers, we are told that this "catch-all" provision is "written broadly both to cover a wide array of offensive lawyer conduct and to prevent attempted technical manipulation of a rule stated more narrowly." However, "the breadth of such provisions creates the risk that a charge using only such language would fail to give fair warning of the nature of the charges to a lawyer respondent ... and that subjective and idiosyncratic considerations could influence a hearing panel or reviewing court in resolving a charge based only on it." Thus the Restatement cautions that "[t]ribunals ... should be circumspect in avoiding overbroad readings or resorting to standards other than those fairly encompassed within an applicable lawyer code."

What do you think? Rules 8.4(b) through (f) apply even though the lawyer is not engaged in the practice of law at the time of the misconduct. Do you think it is appropriate to subject lawyers to professional discipline for misconduct that is not related to their law practice? What is the rationale for doing so?

* * *

C. REPORTING PROFESSIONAL MISCONDUCT

In Chapter 1, Professor Hamilton identified as one of the five principles of professionalism that "each lawyer agrees ... to hold other lawyers accountable for meeting the minimum standards set forth in the Rules and to encourage them to realize core values and ideals of the profession." To what extent do the Rules of Professional Conduct require us to hold other lawyers accountable for professional misconduct?

* * *

Please read ABA Model Rules of Professional Conduct, Rule 8.3 and Comments.

* * *

The thresholds of Rule 8.3(a). According to ABA Formal Ethics Opinion 04–433 (2004), a lawyer's duty to report under Model Rule 8.3(a) arises if two thresholds are met: First, "the lawyer must 'know' of the violation; and the misconduct must raise a 'substantial question' as to the lawyer's honesty, trustworthiness or fitness as a lawyer."

The knowledge requirement. The Model Rules frequently refer to a lawyer's "knowledge." What constitutes "knowledge" for purposes of the rules? *See* Model Rule 1.0(f). What must the lawyer know before the reporting requirement of Rule 8.3(a) is triggered? With respect to the statement in Rule 1.0(f) that "knowledge may be inferred from circumstances," ABA Formal Ethics Opinion 04–433 states that "[m]ost cases and ethics opinions conclude that 'knowledge' is determined by an objective standard." Or, as the Mississippi Supreme Court put it,

> [the] standard must be an objective one, ... not tied to the subjective beliefs of the lawyer in question. The supporting evidence must be such that a reasonable lawyer under the

circumstances would have formed a firm opinion that the conduct in question had more likely than not occurred and that the conduct, if it did occur, raises a substantial question as to the purported offender's honesty, trustworthiness or fitness to practice law in other respects.

Attorney U v. Mississippi Bar, 678 So.2d 963, 972 (Miss. 1996). Is that a fair interpretation of Rule 1.0(f)? Should not knowledge be differentiated from reason to know, or even substantial reason to know?

Substantial questions. Presumably not all violations of the Rules of Professional Responsibility raise a substantial question about a lawyer's honesty, trustworthiness, and fitness as a lawyer in other respects. Which ones do? This is a question you will need to consider throughout your study of the Model Rules, but for the moment please consider what, if any, violations of Rule 8.4 or Rule 8.3 would raise such a substantial question. Comment [3] to Rule 8.3 suggests that the reporting requirement is limited to "those offenses that a self-regulating profession must vigorously endeavor to prevent." Does that explanation contribute to your understanding of the meaning of Rule 8.3(a)?

What do you think? If you know that a lawyer intentionally concealed the presence of water in the basement of his house when showing it to a prospective buyer, must you report this misconduct even though it did not occur in connection with the lawyer's practice?

The appropriate professional authority. Who is the appropriate professional authority to whom you must report another lawyer's misconduct? If the misconduct occurs in connection with litigation in which you have filed an appearance, is it sufficient to report the misconduct to the judge before whom the lawsuit is pending or must you also report it to the agency responsible for bar discipline? If you are an associate in a law firm, is it sufficient to inform the firm's managing partner of another lawyer's misconduct?

Timeliness. Rule 8.3(a) does not specify *when* a report of misconduct must be made. Opinions often say something along the lines of that a lawyer must report "within a reasonable time under the circumstances." United States v. Cantor, 897 F.Supp. 110 (S.D.N.Y. 1995). A comment to Massachusetts' version of Rule 8.3(a) provides that:

> [i]n most situations, a lawyer may defer making a report under this Rule until the matter has been concluded, but the report should be made as soon as practicable thereafter. An immediate report is ethically compelled, however, when a client or third person will likely be injured by a delay in reporting, such as where the lawyer has knowledge that another lawyer has embezzled client or fiduciary funds and delay may impair the ability to recover the funds.

Mass. Rules of Prof'l Conduct R. 8.3 cmt. 3A.

What do you think? Georgia's Rule 8.3 provides that a lawyer "should" inform the appropriate professional authority of another lawyer's violation of a rule of professional that raises a substantial question as to the lawyer's honesty, trustworthiness, or fitness as a lawyer in other respects. The Georgia rule also provides that there is no disciplinary penalty for a violation of Rule 8.3. Is this a good idea?

IN RE JAMES H. HIMMEL

533 N.E.2d 790 (Ill. 1988)

JUSTICE STAMOS delivered the opinion of the court:

This is a disciplinary proceeding against respondent, James H. Himmel. On January 22, 1986, the Administrator of the Attorney Registration and Disciplinary Commission (the Commission) filed a complaint with the Hearing Board, alleging that respondent violated Rule 1–103(a) of the Code of Professional Responsibility (the Code) (107 Ill.2d R. 1–103(a)) by failing to disclose to the Commission information concerning attorney misconduct. On October 15, 1986, the Hearing Board found that respondent had violated the rule and recommended that respondent be reprimanded ... We granted the Administrator's petition for leave to file exceptions to the Review Board's report and recommendation. . . .

We will briefly review the facts, which essentially involve three individuals: respondent, James H. Himmel, licensed to practice law in Illinois on November 6, 1975; his client, Tammy Forsberg, formerly known as Tammy McEathron; and her former attorney, John R. Casey.

The [disciplinary] complaint alleges that respondent had knowledge of John Casey's conversion of Forsberg's funds and respondent failed to inform the Commission of this misconduct. The facts are as follows.

In October 1978, Tammy Forsberg was injured in a motorcycle accident. In June 1980, she retained John R. Casey to represent her in any personal injury or property damage claim resulting from the accident. Sometime in 1981, Casey negotiated a settlement of $35,000 on Forsberg's behalf. Pursuant to an agreement between Forsberg and Casey, one-third of any monies received would be paid to Casey as his attorney fee.

In March 1981, Casey received the $35,000 settlement check, endorsed it, and deposited the check into his client trust fund account. Subsequently, Casey converted the funds.

Between 1981 and 1983, Forsberg unsuccessfully attempted to collect her $23,233.34 share of the settlement proceeds. In March 1983, Forsberg retained respondent to collect her money and agreed to pay him one-third of any funds recovered above $23,233.34.

Respondent investigated the matter and discovered that Casey had misappropriated the settlement funds. In April 1983, respondent drafted an agreement in which Casey would pay Forsberg $75,000 in settlement of any claim she might have against him for the misappropriated funds. By the terms of the agreement, Forsberg agreed not to initiate any criminal, civil, or attorney disciplinary action against Casey. This agreement was executed on April 11, 1983. Respondent stood to gain $17,000 or more if Casey honored the agreement. In February 1985, respondent filed suit against Casey for breaching the agreement, and a $100,000 judgment was entered against Casey. If Casey had satisfied the judgment, respondent's share would have been approximately $25,588.

The [disciplinary] complaint stated that at no time did respondent inform the Commission of Casey's misconduct. According to the Administrator, respondent's first contact with the Commission was in response to the Commission's inquiry regarding the lawsuit against Casey.

In April 1985, the Administrator filed a petition to have Casey suspended from practicing law because of his conversion of client funds and his conduct involving moral turpitude in matters unrelated to Forsberg's claim. Casey was subsequently disbarred on consent on November 5, 1985.

. . . Before retaining respondent, Forsberg collected $5,000 from Casey. After being retained, respondent made inquiries regarding Casey's conversion, contacting the insurance company that issued the settlement check, its attorney, Forsberg, her mother, her fiancé and Casey. Forsberg told respondent that she simply wanted her money back and specifically instructed respondent to take no other action. Because of respondent's efforts, Forsberg collected another $10,400 from Casey. Respondent received no fee in this case.

The Hearing Board found that respondent received unprivileged information that Casey converted Forsberg's funds, and that respondent failed to relate the information to the Commission in violation of Rule 1–103(a) of the Code. The Hearing Board noted, however, that respondent had been practicing law for 11 years, had no prior record of any complaints, obtained as good a result as could be expected in the case, and requested no fee for recovering the $23,233.34. Accordingly, the Hearing Board recommended a private reprimand.

Upon the Administrator's exceptions to the Hearing Board's recommendation, the Review Board reviewed the matter. The Review Board's report stated that the client had contacted the Commission prior to retaining respondent and, therefore, the Commission did have knowledge of the alleged misconduct. Further, the Review Board noted that respondent respected the client's wishes regarding not pursuing a claim with the Commission. Accordingly, the Review Board recommended that the complaint be dismissed.

The Administrator now raises three issues for review: (1) whether the Review Board erred in concluding that respondent's client had informed the Commission of misconduct by her former attorney; (2) whether the Review Board erred in concluding that respondent had not violated Rule 1–103(a); and (3) whether the proven misconduct warrants at least a censure.

As to the first issue, the Administrator contends that the Review Board erred in finding that Forsberg informed the Commission of Casey's misconduct prior to retaining respondent. In support of this contention, the Administrator cites to testimony in the record showing that while Forsberg contacted the Commission and received a complaint form, she did not fill out the form, return it, advise the Commission of the facts, or name whom she wished to complain about. The Administrator further contends that even if Forsberg had reported Casey's misconduct to the Commission, such an action would not have relieved respondent of his duty to report under Rule 1–103(a). Additionally, the Administrator argues that no evidence exists to prove that respondent failed to report because he assumed that Forsberg had already reported the matter.

Respondent argues that the record shows that Forsberg did contact the Commission and was forwarded a complaint form, and that the record is not clear that Forsberg failed to disclose Casey's name to the Commission. Respondent also argues that Forsberg directed respondent not to pursue the claim against Casey, a claim she had already begun to pursue.

We begin our analysis by examining whether a client's complaint of attorney misconduct to the Commission can be a defense to an attorney's failure to report the same misconduct. Respondent offers no authority for such a defense and our research has disclosed none. Common sense would dictate that if a lawyer has a duty under the Code, the actions of a client would not relieve the attorney of his own duty. Accordingly, while the parties dispute whether or not respondent's client informed the Commission, that question is irrelevant to our inquiry in this case. We have held that the canons of ethics in the Code constitute a safe guide for professional conduct, and attorneys may be disciplined for not observing them. The question is, then, whether or not respondent violated the Code, not whether Forsberg informed the Commission of Casey's misconduct.

As to respondent's argument that he did not report Casey's misconduct because his client directed him not to do so, we again note respondent's failure to suggest any legal support for such a defense. A lawyer, as an officer of the court, is duty-bound to uphold the rules in the Code. The title of Canon 1 (107 Ill.2d Canon 1) reflects this obligation: "A lawyer should assist in maintaining the integrity and competence of the legal profession." A lawyer may not choose to circumvent the rules by simply asserting that his client asked him to do so.

As to the second issue, the Administrator argues that the Review Board erred in concluding that respondent did not violate Rule 1–103(a). The Administrator urges acceptance of the Hearing Board's finding that respondent had unprivileged knowledge of Casey's conversion of client funds, and that respondent failed to disclose that information to the Commission. The Administrator states that respondent's knowledge of Casey's conversion of client funds was knowledge of illegal conduct involving moral turpitude. . . . Further, the Administrator argues that the information respondent received was not privileged. . . . Therefore, the Administrator concludes, respondent violated his ethical duty to report misconduct under Rule 1–103(a). According to the Administrator, failure to disclose the information deprived the Commission of evidence of serious misconduct, evidence that would have assisted in the Commission's investigation of Casey.

Respondent contends that the information was privileged information received from his client, Forsberg, and therefore he was under no obligation to disclose the matter to the Commission. Respondent argues that his failure to report Casey's misconduct was motivated by his respect for his client's wishes, not by his desire for financial gain. To support this assertion, respondent notes that his fee agreement with Forsberg was contingent upon her first receiving all the money Casey originally owed her. Further, respondent states that he has received no fee for his representation of Forsberg.

Our analysis of this issue begins with a reading of the applicable disciplinary rules. Rule 1–103(a) of the Code states: "(a) A lawyer possessing unprivileged knowledge of a violation of Rule 1–102(a)(3) or (4) shall report such knowledge to a tribunal or other authority empowered to investigate or act upon such violation." 107 Ill.2d R. 1–103(a).

[This rule] essentially track[s] the language of the American Bar Association Model Code of Professional Responsibility, upon which the Illinois Code was modeled. . . . Therefore, we find instructive the opinion of the American Bar Association's Committee on Ethics and Professional Responsibility that discusses the Model Code's Disciplinary Rule 1–103. . . . Informal Opinion 1210 states that under DR 1–103(a) it is the duty of a lawyer to report to the proper tribunal or authority any unprivileged knowledge of a lawyer's perpetration of any misconduct listed in Disciplinary Rule 1–102. . . . The opinion states that "the Code of Professional Responsibility through its Disciplinary Rules necessarily deals directly with reporting of lawyer misconduct or misconduct of others directly observed in the legal practice or the administration of justice." . . . This court has also emphasized the importance of a lawyer's duty to report misconduct. In the case *In re Anglin* (1988) because of the petitioner's refusal to answer questions regarding his knowledge of other persons' misconduct, we denied a petition for reinstatement to the roll of attorneys licensed to practice in Illinois. We stated, "Under Disciplinary Rule 1–103 a lawyer has the duty to report the misconduct of other lawyers. . . . Petitioner's belief in a code of silence indicates to us that he is not at present fully rehabilitated or fit to practice law." . . . Thus, if the present respondent's conduct did violate the rule on reporting misconduct, imposition of discipline for such a breach of duty is mandated.

The question whether the information that respondent possessed was protected by the attorney-client privilege, and thus exempt from the reporting rule, requires application of this court's definition of the privilege. We have stated that " '(1) [w]here legal advice of any kind is sought (2) from a professional legal adviser in his capacity as such, (3) the communications relating to that purpose, (4) made in confidence (5) by the client, (6) are at his instance permanently protected (7) from disclosure by himself or by the legal adviser, (8) except the protection be waived.' " We agree with the Administrator's argument that the communication regarding Casey's conduct does not meet this definition. The record does not suggest that this information was communicated by Forsberg to the respondent in confidence. We have held that information voluntarily disclosed by a client to an attorney, in the presence of third parties who are not agents of the client or attorney, is not privileged information. . . . In this case, Forsberg discussed the matter with respondent at various times while her mother and her fiancé were present. Consequently, unless the mother and fiancé were agents of respondent's client, the information communicated was not privileged. Moreover, we have also stated that matters intended by a client for disclosure by the client's attorney to third parties, who are not agents of either the client or the attorney, are not privileged. The record shows that respondent, with Forsberg's consent, discussed Casey's conversion of her funds with the insurance company involved, the insurance company's lawyer, and with Casey himself. Thus, . . . the information was not privileged.

Though respondent repeatedly asserts that his failure to report was motivated not by financial gain but by the request of his client, we do not deem such an argument relevant in this case. This court has stated that discipline may be appropriate even if no dishonest motive for the misconduct exists. . . . In addition, we have held that client approval of an attorney's action does not immunize an attorney from disciplinary action. . . . We have already dealt with, and dismissed, respondent's assertion that his conduct is acceptable because he was acting pursuant to his client's directions.

Respondent does not argue that Casey's conversion of Forsberg's funds was not illegal conduct involving moral turpitude under Rule 1–102(a)(3) or conduct involving dishonesty, fraud, deceit, or misrepresentation under Rule 1–102(a)(4). It is clear that conversion of client funds is, indeed, conduct involving moral turpitude. . . . We conclude, then, that respondent possessed unprivileged knowledge of Casey's conversion of client funds, which is illegal conduct involving moral turpitude, and that respondent failed in his duty to report such misconduct to the Commission. Because no defense exists, we agree with the Hearing Board's finding that respondent has violated Rule 1–103(a) and must be disciplined. . . .

* * *

Problem 3.2. *Himmel* was decided under the older Model Code standard as it existed in Illinois at the time. Assume that the case takes place today and Model Rule 8.3 applies. Assume further that Forsberg makes it clear to Himmel that she does not want Himmel to report Casey to the appropriate disciplinary authority and that Himmel complies with her instructions. Would Himmel be subject to discipline under Rule 8.3(c)? *See also* Model Rule 8.3, Comment [2].

What do you think? Assume that Ms. Forsberg had already reported Casey. Do you agree with the *Himmel* court that a lawyer is not excused from the reporting obligation if the misconduct has already been reported to the proper authority?

* * *

D. IMPOSING DISCIPLINARY SANCTIONS

IN RE JAMES H. HIMMEL
533 N.E.2d 790 (Ill. 1988)

[Authors' Note: See *supra* for the court's discussion of Mr. Himmel's misconduct.]

The third issue concerns the appropriate quantum of discipline to be imposed in this case. The Administrator contends that respondent's misconduct warrants at least a censure, although the Hearing Board recommended a private reprimand and the Review Board recommended dismissal of the matter entirely. In support of the request for a greater quantum of discipline, the Administrator cites to the purposes of attorney discipline, which include maintaining the integrity of the legal profession and safeguarding the administration of justice. The Administrator argues that these purposes will not be served unless respondent is publicly disciplined so that the profession will be on notice that a violation of Rule 1–103(a) will not be tolerated. The Administrator argues that a more severe sanction is necessary because respondent deprived the Commission of evidence of another attorney's conversion and thereby interfered with the Commission's investigative function. . . . [T]he Administrator notes that Casey converted many clients' funds after respondent's duty to report Casey arose. The Administrator also argues that both respondent and his client behaved in contravention of the Criminal Code's prohibition against compounding a crime by agreeing with Casey not to report him, in exchange for settlement funds.

In his defense, respondent reiterates his arguments that he was not motivated by desire for financial gain. He also states that Forsberg was pleased with his performance on her behalf. According to respondent, his failure to report was a "judgment call" which resulted positively in Forsberg's regaining some of her funds from Casey.

In evaluating the proper quantum of discipline to impose, we note that it is this court's responsibility to determine appropriate sanctions in attorney disciplinary cases. . . . We have stated that while recommendations of the Boards are to be considered, this court ultimately bears responsibility for deciding an appropriate sanction. . . . [w]hen determining the nature and extent of discipline to be imposed, the respondent's actions must be viewed in relationship "to the underlying purposes of our disciplinary process, which purposes are to maintain the integrity of the legal profession, to protect the administration of justice from reproach, and to safeguard the public. . . ."

Bearing these principles in mind, we agree with the Administrator that public discipline is necessary in this case to carry out the purposes of attorney discipline. While we have considered the Boards' recommendations in this matter, we cannot agree with the Review Board that respondent's conduct served to rectify a wrong and did not injure the bar, the public, or the administration of justice. Though we agree with the Hearing Board's assessment that respondent violated Rule 1–103 of the Code, we do not agree that the facts warrant only a private reprimand. As previously stated, the evidence proved that respondent possessed unprivileged knowledge of Casey's conversion of client funds, yet respondent did not report Casey's misconduct.

This failure to report resulted in interference with the Commission's investigation of Casey, and thus with the administration of justice. Perhaps some members of the public would have been spared from Casey's misconduct had respondent reported the information as soon as he knew of Casey's conversions of client funds. We are particularly disturbed by the fact that respondent chose to draft a settlement agreement with Casey rather than report his misconduct. As the Administrator has stated, by this conduct, both respondent and his client ran afoul of the Criminal Code's prohibition against compounding a crime, which states in section 32–1:

> "(a) A person compounds a crime when he receives or offers to another any consideration for a promise not to prosecute or aid in the prosecution of an offender.

> (b) Sentence. Compounding a crime is a petty offense." (Ill.Rev.Stat.1987, ch. 38, par. 32–1.)

Both respondent and his client stood to gain financially by agreeing not to prosecute or report Casey for conversion. According to the settlement agreement, respondent would have received $17,000 or more as his fee. If Casey had satisfied the judgment entered against him for failure to honor the settlement agreement, respondent would have collected approximately $25,588.

We have held ... that fairness dictates consideration of mitigating factors in disciplinary cases. Therefore, we do consider the fact that Forsberg recovered $10,400 through respondent's services, that respondent has practiced law for 11 years with no record of complaints, and that he requested no fee for minimum collection of Forsberg's funds. However, these considerations do not outweigh the serious nature of respondent's failure to report Casey, the resulting interference with the Commission's investigation of Casey, and respondent's ill-advised choice to settle with Casey rather than report his misconduct.

Accordingly, it is ordered that respondent be suspended from the practice of law for one year.

Respondent suspended.

* * *

Hierarchy of discipline. The ABA Standards for Imposing Lawyer Sanctions list a hierarchy of possible sanctions for misconduct. These include admonition (or non-public reprimand); reprimand (or public censure); interim suspension; suspension; disbarment; and the catch-all "other sanctions and remedies," which could include restitution or the requirement that the lawyer attend continuing legal education courses. Standards 2.2–2.8. In imposing sanctions, a court is directed to consider the duty violated, the lawyer's mental state, the potential or actual injury caused by the lawyer's misconduct, and any aggravating or mitigating circumstances. Standard 3.0. Certain duties (like the duty to maintain client confidences) are sufficiently weighty that when a lawyer intentionally violates the duty with the intent to benefit himself, disbarment or suspension is the presumptive punishment, at least when harm results to the client. *See* Standard 4.21. In contrast, when a lawyer *negligently* reveals information relating to representation of a client not otherwise lawfully permitted to be disclosed and this disclosure causes injury or potential injury to a client, the Standards suggest that reprimand should be the presumptive sanction. *See* Standard 4.23.

What do you think? What should be the appropriate discipline for Lawyer Casey? What should be the appropriate discipline for Lawyer Himmel?

Aggravating and mitigating factors. The ABA Standards for Imposing Lawyer Sanctions list several aggravating factors, the existence of which might justify a heightened sanction. These include prior disciplinary offenses, dishonest conduct, and a refusal to acknowledge wrongdoing. The Standards also list a number of mitigating factors, including absence of a prior disciplinary record, personal or emotional problems, and remorse. Should the fact that a lawyer was relatively inexperienced qualify as a mitigating factor in a disciplinary proceeding? Should the fact that a lawyer had a substance abuse problem at the relevant time qualify as an aggravating factor or a mitigating factor?

Disbarment. Standard 2.2 of the ABA Standards for Imposing Lawyer Sanctions provides that "[w]here disbarment is not permanent, procedures should be established for a lawyer who has been disbarred to apply for readmission ..." Are there circumstances under which disbarment should be permanent?

* * *

E. OTHER MEANS OF ENFORCEMENT

The possibility of criminal and/or civil liability may also play an important role in enforcing standards of professional conduct. For instance, the Foreword to the Restatement (Third) of the Law Governing Lawyers notes that "the remedy of malpractice liability . . . [is] practically of greater importance in most law practice than is the risk of disciplinary proceedings." Future chapters will examine how special rules of civil liability in the areas of agency, contract, and tort law have developed where lawyers are involved. Thus, the rules of civil liability may re-enforce and supplement the standards of professional conduct outlined in the rules of professional conduct. At the same time, there is a bit of tension between the disciplinary process and other areas of the law. Paragraph [20] in the Scope preceding the ABA's Model Rules provides that a violation of a rule of professional conduct "should not itself give rise to a cause of action against a lawyer nor should it create any presumption in such a case that a legal duty has been breached." Future chapters will explore this overlap between ethical duties and legal duties in more detail.

Criminal law may also help regulate the behavior of lawyers. In addition to the general body of criminal law, there are a few criminal statutes that specifically address lawyers. *See* N.Y. Jud. Law § 487 (making it a misdemeanor for a lawyer to engage in "any deceit or collusion, or consents to any deceit or collusion, with intent to deceive the court or any party"). Some have raised concerns about how the threat of criminal prosecution might deter lawyers from representing clients as diligently as they might otherwise. To this end, § 8 of the Restatement counsels that "[t]he traditional and appropriate activities of a lawyer in representing a client in accordance with the requirements of the applicable lawyer code are relevant factors for the tribunal in assessing the propriety of the lawyer's conduct under the criminal law."

* * *

Profile of attorney professionalism. The American legal profession has seen numerous codes of professional conduct. The current version of the ABA's Model Rules of Professional Conduct was adopted in 2002 (although it has been amended since then). Its origins can be traced much further back. As far back as colonial times, lawyers were sometimes required to take oaths of professional office that addressed misconduct. For example, a 1708 Connecticut statute contained an attorney oath prohibiting an attorney from doing any "falsehood" in court. Josiah Henry Benton, *The Lawyer's Official Oath and Office* 42 (1909).

In 1887, Alabama's state bar became the first to adopt an official code of professional ethics. Other state bar associations soon followed course. The Alabama bar's code was influenced heavily by George Sharswood's *Essay on Professional Ethics*. Sharswood was a law professor and dean at the University of Pennsylvania, who eventually became Chief Justice of Pennsylvania Supreme Court. As described by legal historian Carol Rice Andrews, "Sharswood structured his essay around three fundamental obligations: '[f]idelity to the court, fidelity to the client, [and] fidelity to the claims of truth and honor.'" Carol Rice Andrews, *Ethical Limits on Litigation Advocacy: A Historical Perspective*, 63 CASE WESTERN L. REV. 381, 409 (2012). "[A]lthough Sharswood believed that the lawyer should act with zeal on behalf of his client," he also believed that this obligation was tempered by the lawyer's obligations of fidelity to the court and to the truth. *Id.* at 411.

It would be a gross exaggeration to draw a straight line from Sharswood's *Essay on Professional Ethics* to the ABA's Model Rules of Professional Conduct. The ABA drew upon Alabama's code when it eventually adopted its 1908 Canons of Ethics, but there were significant differences between the documents. In 1969, the ABA put forth its Model Code of Professional Responsibility, which was later replaced by the 1983 Model Rules of Professional Conduct. The Model Rules were then amended substantially in 2002 as part of the ABA's Ethics 2000 initiative, and then again (although less substantially) in 2013 as part of the ABA's Ethics 20/20 initiative. Today, nearly every state uses the ABA's Model Rules as the model for their rules of professional conduct. The views of the legal profession have evolved over time as evidenced by the changing sets of ethics rules. But Judge Sharswood's *Essay* played an important role in the development of professional values and continues to influence the profession's thinking on those values.

CHAPTER 4

PRACTICING LAW

∎∎∎

Chapter hypothetical. Otis is a lawyer who lives and is licensed only in Old Dakota. Sharon is an old college friend who lives in New Dakota. Otis entered into an agreement with Sharon whereby Otis was to investigate and pursue claims of royalty payments due to Sharon under a mineral royalty lease with Volt, Inc., an Argentinian oil company that has an office in New Dakota. Under his agreement with Sharon, Otis was to "investigate, examine, copy, analyze, and interpret" documents relating to the mineral lease. Otis' compensation for his services under the agreement was based on a percentage share of the royalties recovered. Otis analyzed Sharon's lease with the oil company and gave her his opinion of its meaning. He also expressed opinions about legal theories for recovery of damages and discouraged pursuit of at least one theory. He drafted a demand letter to Volt in which he stated that the letter was a "single last effort to resolve issues short of litigation." Eventually, Sharon hired Isaac, a lawyer licensed in New Dakota, to file a court action against Volt. Isaac and Otis worked together, with Isaac eventually supporting Otis' motion for admission pro hac vice in a New Dakota state court.

Prior to trial, Isaac and Otis were able to obtain a substantial settlement on behalf of Sharon from the oil company. Isaac and Otis negotiated the settlement agreement with Cristina, an Argentinian lawyer (licensed only in Argentina) employed by Volt in its New Dakota office. Otis and Sharon had a falling out and Sharon refused to pay Otis his legal fees, claiming he was not entitled to them since he was not licensed to practice law in New Dakota. Otis has now filed suit, seeking to collect his fee under his agreement with Sharon.

Prior to the time he was admitted on a pro hac vice basis, all of Otis' conversations with Sharon, Isaac, and other individuals in New Dakota took place over the phone or by email from his office in Old Dakota.

(A) Assume that the New Dakota Board of Professional Responsibility brings a disciplinary charge against Otis for engaging in the unauthorized practice of law. Assume further that New Dakota has adopted ABA Model Rule 5.5. Is the Board likely to succeed? What if New Dakota has instead adopted the approach described in the *Birbrower* case (which is included in the chapter)?

(B) Assuming Otis is found to have engaged in the unauthorized practice of law in violation of New Dakota's Rules of Professional Conduct, should Otis be permitted to recover his fee?

(C) Has Cristina engaged in the unauthorized practice of law?

* * *

This chapter considers the unauthorized practice of law for both non-lawyers and lawyers. First, we consider the activities of a non-lawyer (including a law student) that may amount to the unauthorized practice of law. Second, we consider what a lawyer must do to avoid the unauthorized practice of law. This discussion considers both where an attorney should be licensed and the steps an attorney can take to practice on a temporary basis in a jurisdiction where he or she is unlicensed. Third, this chapter considers the issue of discipline for attorneys engaged in multi-jurisdictional practice. Two questions must be answered: (1) Which jurisdictions may discipline the attorney for misconduct?; and (2) Which jurisdiction's professional conduct rule applies when an attorney's conduct has a relationship to multiple jurisdictions? Finally, the chapter turns to licensing rules for foreign attorneys practicing in the U.S.

* * *

A. PREVENTING THE UNAUTHORIZED PRACTICE OF LAW BY NON-LAWYERS

Please read ABA Model Rules of Professional Conduct, Rule 5.5(a) and Comments [2] & [3].

You are currently a non-lawyer and therefore are prohibited from practicing law until you meet all the requirements for admission to the bar. Just what are you prohibited from doing at this pre-lawyer stage of your life and why? A related question is who gets to define what law-related activities non-lawyers may perform—the courts, the legislature, or some other governmental entity?

* * *

TENNESSEE CODE ANNOTATED
TITLE 23 ATTORNEYS-AT-LAW
UNAUTHORIZED PRACTICE AND IMPROPER CONDUCT

§ 23–3–101. Definitions.

As used in this chapter, unless the context otherwise requires:

(1) "Law business" means the advising or counseling for a valuable consideration of any person, firm, association, or corporation, as to any

secular law, or the drawing or the procuring of or assisting in the drawing for a valuable consideration of any paper, document or instrument affecting or relating to secular rights, or the doing of any act for a valuable consideration in a representative capacity, obtaining or tending to secure for any person, firm, association or corporation any property or property rights whatsoever, or the soliciting of clients directly or indirectly to provide such services; and

(2) "Practice of law" means the appearance as an advocate in a representative capacity or the drawing of papers, pleadings or documents or the performance of any act in such capacity in connection with proceedings pending or prospective before any court, commissioner, referee or any body, board, committee or commission constituted by law or having authority to settle controversies, or the soliciting of clients directly or indirectly to provide such services.

§ 23–3–103. Unlawful practice; crimes and offenses; fines and penalties.

(a) No person shall engage in the "practice of law" or do "law business," or both, as defined in § 23–3–101, unless such person has been duly licensed therefor, and while such person's license therefor is in full force and effect, nor shall any association or corporation engage in the "practice of the law" or do "law business," or both, as defined in § 23–3–101. . . .

(b) Any person, firm, association or corporation who violates the prohibition in subsection (a) commits a Class A misdemeanor and shall be subject to be sued for treble the amount which shall have been paid to such person, firm, association or corporation for any service rendered in violation hereof by the person, firm, association or corporation, . . .

(2) Any bar association bringing suit under this section is presumed to be acting in good faith and is granted a qualified immunity for the suit and the consequences of the suit. The presumption of good faith is rebuttable upon a showing by a preponderance of the evidence that the suit was brought for a malicious purpose.

* * *

PETITION OF BURSON
909 S.W.2d 768 (Tenn. 1995)

[The question in this case involved the constitutionality of a statutory provision that provided that taxpayers contesting the assessment of their real and personal property before boards of equalization may be represented by non-attorney agents. Specifically, the issue was whether the statute violated the separation of powers provisions of the Tennessee

Constitution by sanctioning the unauthorized practice of law and thereby infringing upon this Court's inherent authority to regulate the practice of law. The Tennessee Supreme Court stated that it possessed the inherent power to regulate the practice of law in Tennessee and included in this power was the right to prescribe and administer rules pertaining to the licensing and admission of attorneys. The Court acknowledged that the General Assembly had authority to enact legislation regarding the practice of law, but stated that "the exercise of such authority by the Legislature does not mean that this Court, in the exercise of its authority within the premises, may not require qualifications more extensive than those exacted by the Legislature."]

. . . [Ethical Consideration 3–5] appears in the Code of Professional Responsibility following Canon 3, which directs that "[a] lawyer should assist in preventing the unauthorized practice of law." The ethical consideration specifically provides as follows:

> It is neither necessary nor desirable to attempt the formulation of a single specific definition of what constitutes the practice of law. Functionally the practice of law relates to the rendition of services for others that call for the professional judgment of a lawyer. The essence of the professional judgment of the lawyer is his educated ability to relate the general body and philosophy of law to a specific legal problem of a client; and thus, the public interest will be better served if only lawyers are permitted to act in matters involving professional judgment. Where this professional judgment is not involved, non-lawyers, such as court clerks, police officers, abstracters, and many governmental employees, may engage in occupations that require a special knowledge of law in certain areas. But the services of a lawyer are essential in the public interest whenever the exercise of professional legal judgment is required.

Our decision to adopt the general standard contained within Ethical Consideration 3–5, is consistent with the rule observed in other jurisdictions. *See, e.g.*, [Conway-Bogue Realty Inv. Co. v. Denver Bar Ass'n, 135 Colo. 398, 312 P.2d 998, 1008 (1957)]. . . .

Applying the foregoing principles to the facts found by the Special Master, which are overwhelmingly supported by the record in this case, it is clear that no proof was introduced to show that the services performed for taxpayers or taxing authorities before the boards of equalization require the professional judgment of a lawyer.

* * *

Defining "the unauthorized practice of law." Read ABA Model Rule 5.5(a) and Comments [1] and [2]. Do they help explain what it means to "practice law" or engage in the unauthorized practice of law?

Preventing the unauthorized practice of law. One court has explained that the purpose of limiting the practice of law to those who have been duly licensed is "to protect the public from being advised and represented in legal matters by unqualified persons over whom the judicial department can exercise little, if any, control in the matter of infractions of the code of conduct which, in the public interest, lawyers are bound to observe." Others have offered somewhat more cynical explanations.

* * *

Problem 4.1. Marilyn is a nonlawyer. She has advertised in various local newspapers as "Marilyn's Secretarial Service" offering to perform typing services for "Do-It-Yourself" divorces, wills, resumes, and bankruptcies. Marilyn prepares, for a fee, all papers deemed by her to be needed for the pleading, filing, and securing of a dissolution of marriage, as well as detailed instructions as to how the suit should be filed, notice served, hearings set, trial conducted, and the final decree secured. She types up the documents for her customers after they have asked her to prepare a petition or an entire set of dissolution of marriage papers. Prior to typing up the papers, Marilyn asks her customers whether custody, child support, or alimony is involved. Marilyn has four sets of dissolution of marriage papers, and she chooses which set is appropriate for the particular customer. She then types out those papers, filling in the blank spaces with the appropriate information. She instructs her customers how the papers are to be signed, where they are to be filed, and how the customer should arrange for a final hearing. The New Dakota Board of Professional Responsibility recently filed a petition, charging that Marilyn has engaged in the unauthorized practice of law. You represent Marilyn. What arguments can you make in her defense? What arguments could you make if you represented the Board?

The Role of paraprofessionals. Paralegals and legal assistants play an ever-increasing role in the delivery of legal services. According to the Department of Labor Bureau of Labor Statistics, "[p]aralegals and legal assistants held about 263,800 jobs in 2008. Private law firms employed 71 percent; most of the remainder worked for corporate legal departments and various levels of government." There are currently approximately 260 ABA-approved paralegal training programs in the United States. With this increasing participation by paraprofessionals come questions about the appropriate scope of their role in the representation of clients. Note that Model Rule 5.5(a) not only prohibits a lawyer from engaging in the unauthorized practice of law but from assisting others in doing so.

* * *

The Ethical Responsibilities of Law Students and Those Who Employ Them

Through their work as law clerks in the summer, during the regular school year, or in legal clinics, law students frequently engage in activity that comes right up to the line of "practicing law." In some cases, law students may actually cross that line. In the case of students enrolled in a law school's legal clinic, this does not amount to the unauthorized practice of law. State statutes prohibiting the unauthorized practice of law frequently contain an exception for law school legal clinics. *See, e.g.,* N.C. Gen. Stat. § 84–8(1) (2005). In addition, some jurisdictions have established legal intern license programs, which permit law students to engage in the limited practice of law under the supervision of a licensed attorney. *See, e.g.,* Idaho Bar Commission Rule 221. Where neither type of provision is applicable, a lawyer employing a law student must supervise any work delegated to the student and retain responsibility for that work. *See* Model Rule 5.1, Comment [1]; *id.* Rule 5.3, Comment [1].

According to one source, "[t]he few courts that have considered the status of students admitted to practice under student practice rules have treated them as 'lawyers' for the purpose of analyzing lawyer and judicial ethics issues," even though they are not yet technically lawyers. Law students who do not practice under a special student practice rule but who nonetheless engage in conduct that would amount to a violation of the ethical rules governing lawyers may not be subject to discipline since those rules only apply to lawyers. *See* In re Wilkinson, 805 So.2d 142 (La. 2002) (involving dismissal of disciplinary complaint against individual who was a nonlawyer at the time of his negligent provision of legal services). However, as illustrated in Chapter 5, one's conduct prior to applying for admission to the bar is routinely taken into account during the bar application process. Moreover, it is well-established that non-lawyers who provide legal advice or render legal services for others assume a duty of care and may be held civilly liable for their negligence. Buscemi v. Intachai, 730 So.2d 329 (Fla. App. 1999).

Due to the nature of the cases undertaken by legal clinics, the potential for malpractice claims against such clinics is low. Peter A. Joy and Robert R. Kuehn, *Conflict of Interest and Competency Issues in Law Clinic Practice,* 9 CLINICAL L. REV. 493, n.45 (2002). According to one source, "there are no reported cases of professional liability claims against law students working in law school clinics." Andreas Bücker & William A. Woodruff, *The Bologna Process and German Legal Education: Developing Professional Competence Through Clinical Experiences,* 9 GERMAN L.J.

575, 602 (2008). However, there has been at least one malpractice claim filed against the director of a legal clinic. Juengain v. Johnson, 571 So.2d 167 (La. Ct. App. 1990). In addition, a licensed attorney who supervises a nonlawyer (such as a law student or law clerk) has an ethical obligation to properly supervise the nonlawyer and may face discipline or potential tort liability for the failure to do so. *See* In re Wilkinson, 805 So.2d 142 (La. 2002) (imposing discipline against attorney for his failure to properly supervise a law clerk in his office who provided incorrect legal advice to a client).

Another way a law student's involvement in a matter might be relevant is for purposes of assessing whether a conflict of interest exists. Future chapters will explore conflicts of interest. For now, it is enough to note the possibility that a lawyer and his or her firm may acquire a conflict of interest based upon the lawyer's involvement in a matter while still a law student. Thus, a law student who assists in the representation of a plaintiff while working for a law firm may find herself with a conflict of interest if, after becoming a lawyer, she goes to work for the law firm representing the defendant in the same matter. Moreover, the lawyer's conflict would be imputed to all of the other members of the law firm. Recognizing the potential hardships on a law student's employment prospects that such a rule creates, the Model Rules have, for a number of years, permitted law firms to employ "screening" devices in such situations that allow the firm to continue representing a client while screening the affected lawyer from any involvement in the matter. *See* Model Rule 1.10, Comment [4].

* * *

B. ATTORNEY LICENSURE IN ONE OR MORE JURISDICTIONS

Please read ABA Model Rules of Professional Conduct, Rule 5.5(a) & (b) and Comments [1]–[4].

* * *

Absent a professional conduct rule or law to the contrary, a lawyer who has an office or other "systematic or continuous presence" in a state must be licensed to practice there. Model Rule 5.5(b)(1). Further, even without an office in a state, a lawyer who wants to represent to the public that he or she is admitted to practice law in the jurisdiction must also be licensed there. Model Rule 5.5(b)(2). Failing to be licensed under these circumstances subjects an attorney to the same consequences as a non-attorney engaged in the unauthorized practice of law (as discussed in the previous section). For an attorney, he or she would also face discipline for violating Rule 5.5(a) by being engaged in the practice of law in a jurisdiction in violation of the legal profession's regulations.

Beyond being licensed in a state, a lawyer must also be admitted to practice in the federal courts where the lawyer wishes to appear on behalf of a client. Attorneys should be aware that federal courts also adopt professional conduct rules and may discipline attorneys for violating those rules.

In modern practice in the United States, many attorneys are licensed in multiple states. In some cases, it is because a lawyer has moved to a new state and needs to be licensed there so that the lawyer can practice there without being engaged in the unauthorized practice of law. In other cases, lawyers wish to be licensed in more than one state so that the lawyer can have a regular practice there, whether representing clients in litigation or non-litigation matters. Being licensed in two or more jurisdictions can be important for attorneys who live in an area where states border. It can also be important for attorneys who wish to develop a regular practice in a state even if the lawyer does not live near the state.

Lawyers who decide they need to be licensed in multiple jurisdictions have one major concern: what are the requirements for admission in the second (or third or fourth) state? In Supreme Court of Virginia v. Friedman, 487 U.S. 59 (1988), the Supreme Court considered the constitutionality of a Virginia court rule that required that any lawyer admitted in another jurisdiction who sought to be admitted "on motion" (i.e., without sitting for the Virginia bar exam) had to be a permanent resident of Virginia. The attorney in question lived in Maryland but earned her living working as an attorney in Virginia. The Court concluded that the rule violated the Privileges and Immunities Clause of the United States Constitution, Art. IV, § 2, cl. 1 because it was not closely related to the advancement of a substantial state interest. The Court acknowledged that the Commonwealth of Virginia had a substantial interest in assuring "that the admitted attorney has a stake in his or her professional licensure and a concomitant interest in the integrity and standards of the bar." However, the Court reasoned that there were other means of advancing that interest, such as requiring mandatory attendance at continuing legal education courses.

But of course, admission by motion is not an option in every state. Some states require every attorney to take the bar exam. Most states that allow admission by motion currently require an attorney to have practiced five of the past seven years in another jurisdiction. In 2012, the ABA amended its Model Rule on Admission by Motion. The Model Rule now permits admission on motion in a jurisdiction as long as the lawyer has practiced law in another jurisdiction for three of the immediately preceding five years. The attorney must also hold a degree from an ABA-accredited law school and demonstrates adequate character and fitness, including being in good standing—and not subject to any disciplinary proceeding—in all jurisdictions in which the lawyer is admitted. The Model Rule goes on to provide that if an applicant has failed a bar examination administered in the new jurisdiction within five years of the date of filing an application, the applicant is not eligible for admission on motion.

* * *

Problem 4.2. After graduation, you took the Virginia bar exam so that you could work in the Roanoke, Virginia office of the Palsgraf & Pennoyer law firm, which has offices in several states. Just after taking the exam, your firm's HR director tells you that the firm has an urgent need for new associates in its St. Louis, Missouri office. After agreeing to move there, you start to wonder if you will have to be licensed in Missouri. Assume that Missouri's Rule of Professional Conduct 5.5 is identical to Model Rule 5.5. Do you need to be licensed in Missouri even if you pass the Virginia bar exam?

* * *

C. SPECIAL RULES ALLOWING AN ATTORNEY TO ESTABLISH AN OFFICE IN A STATE WHERE THE ATTORNEY IS NOT LICENSED

Please read ABA Model Rules of Professional Conduct, Rule 5.5(d) and Comments [15]–[21].

The previous section noted that a person must be licensed in a state where she practices law, unless a professional conduct rule or law provides otherwise. States that follow the Model Rule 5.5(d) approach permits U.S. attorneys licensed in another state to establish an office in the state without being licensed there in two circumstances: (1) when the lawyer is in-house counsel, providing services to an employer located in the state; and (2) when the lawyer is providing services authorized by federal law or other law in the jurisdiction. Comment [17] provides that the attorney may be subject to registration in the state, even though the attorney is not required to be licensed there.

This rule also permits a foreign licensed attorney to provide legal services in a jurisdiction under similar circumstances. Those provisions are discussed in part F, below.

* * *

D. TEMPORARY PRACTICE OF LAW IN A STATE WHERE AN ATTORNEY IS UNLICENSED

Please read ABA Model Rules of Professional Conduct, Rule 5.5(c) and Comments [5]–[14].

An attorney licensed in a state may sometimes be asked to provide legal services that have a connection to another jurisdiction. The lawyer's client may ask the lawyer for advice about the law of another state. Or the lawyer's client may be sued in another state and ask the lawyer to represent the client there. A client that is a resident of another state may contact the lawyer seeking legal advice or preparation of a contract or legal document.

The lawyer in any of these circumstances is likely "practicing law," but is he or she practicing law in a state where he or she is unlicensed? If so, this conduct may amount to the unauthorized practice of law unless permitted by the law of the jurisdiction. This section considers California law and then the Model Rule 5.5(c) approach to this issue.

1. WHEN IS TEMPORARY PRACTICE THE UNAUTHORIZED PRACTICE OF LAW?

The next case, which sent shock waves through the bar when it was decided, addresses the situation in which an out-of-state attorney represents a client in a transaction related to a state in which the attorney is not licensed.

BIRBROWER, MONTALBANO, CONDON & FRANK, P.C. v. SUPERIOR COURT

949 P.2d 1 (Cal. 1998)

CHIN, JUSTICE.

Business and Professions Code section 6125 states: "No person shall practice law in California unless the person is an active member of the State Bar." We must decide whether an out-of-state law firm, not licensed to practice law in this state, violated section 6125 when it performed legal services in California for a California-based client under a fee agreement stipulating that California law would govern all matters in the representation.

I. BACKGROUND

The facts with respect to the unauthorized practice of law question are essentially undisputed. Birbrower is a professional law corporation incorporated in New York, with its principal place of business in New York. During 1992 and 1993, Birbrower attorneys, defendants Kevin F. Hobbs and Thomas A. Condon (Hobbs and Condon), performed substantial work in California relating to the law firm's representation of ESQ. Neither Hobbs nor Condon has ever been licensed to practice law in California. None of Birbrower's attorneys were [sic] licensed to practice law in California during Birbrower's ESQ representation.

ESQ is a California corporation with its principal place of business in Santa Clara County. In July 1992, the parties negotiated and executed the fee agreement in New York, providing that Birbrower would perform legal services for ESQ, including "All matters pertaining to the investigation of and prosecution of all claims and causes of action against TANDEM COMPUTERS INCORPORATED [Tandem]." [As part of the same agreement, ESQ-NY, a New York affiliate of ESQ, also retained Birbrower. Birbrower had provided legal services for ESQ-NY for several years prior to this agreement, including in connection with the agreement with Tandem at issue.] The "claims and causes of action" against Tandem, a Delaware corporation with its principal place of business in Santa Clara County, California, related to a software development and marketing contract between Tandem and ESQ dated March 16, 1990 (Tandem Agreement). The Tandem Agreement stated that "The internal laws of the State of California (irrespective of its choice of law principles) shall govern the validity of this Agreement, the construction of its terms, and the interpretation and enforcement of the rights and duties of the parties hereto." Birbrower asserts, and ESQ disputes, that ESQ knew Birbrower was not licensed to practice law in California.

While representing ESQ, Hobbs and Condon traveled to California on several occasions. In August 1992, they met in California with ESQ and its accountants. During these meetings, Hobbs and Condon discussed various matters related to ESQ's dispute with Tandem and strategy for resolving the dispute. They made recommendations and gave advice. During this California trip, Hobbs and Condon also met with Tandem representatives on four or five occasions during a two-day period. . . .

Around March or April 1993, Hobbs, Condon, and another Birbrower attorney visited California to interview potential arbitrators and to meet again with ESQ and its accountants. Birbrower had previously filed a demand for arbitration against Tandem with the San Francisco offices of the American Arbitration Association (AAA). In August 1993, Hobbs returned to California to assist ESQ in settling the Tandem matter. While in California, Hobbs met with ESQ and its accountants to discuss a proposed settlement agreement Tandem authored. Hobbs also met with Tandem representatives to discuss possible changes in the proposed agreement. Hobbs gave ESQ legal advice during this trip, including his opinion that ESQ should not settle with Tandem on the terms proposed.

ESQ eventually settled the Tandem dispute, and the matter never went to arbitration. . . .

In January 1994, ESQ sued Birbrower for legal malpractice and related claims. . . . Birbrower . . . filed a counterclaim, which included a claim for attorney fees for the work it performed in both California and New York. . . . ESQ moved for summary judgment and/or adjudication on the first through fourth causes of action of Birbrower's counterclaim . . . ESQ argued that by practicing law without a license in California and by failing to associate legal counsel while doing so, Birbrower violated section 6125, rendering the fee agreement unenforceable. . . . [The trial court and the Court of Appeal held that Birbrower violated section 6125 and that the fee agreement was therefore unenforceable.].

We granted review to determine whether Birbrower's actions and services performed while representing ESQ in California constituted the unauthorized practice of law under section 6125. . . .

II. DISCUSSION

A. The Unauthorized Practice of Law

The California Legislature enacted section 6125 in 1927 as part of the State Bar Act (the Act), a comprehensive scheme regulating the practice of law in the state. Since the Act's passage, the general rule has been that, although persons may represent themselves and their own interests regardless of State Bar membership, no one but an active member of the State Bar may practice law for another person in California. The prohibition against unauthorized law practice is within the state's police power and is designed to ensure that those performing legal services do so competently.

A violation of section 6125 is a misdemeanor. (§ 6126.) . . .

Although the Act did not define the term "practice law," case law explained it as " 'the doing and performing services in a court of justice in any matter depending therein throughout its various stages and in conformity with the adopted rules of procedure.' " People ex rel. Lawyers' Institute of San Diego v. Merchants' Protective Corp. (1922) 189 Cal. 531, 535, 209 P. 363 (*Merchants*). *Merchants* included in its definition legal advice and legal instrument and contract preparation, whether or not these subjects were rendered in the course of litigation. *Ibid.; see* People v. Ring (1937) 70 P.2d 281, 26 Cal. App. 2d. Supp. 768, 772–773 (*Ring*) (holding that single incident of practicing law in state without a license violates § 6125). . . .

In addition to not defining the term "practice law," the Act also did not define the meaning of "in California." In today's legal practice, questions often arise concerning whether the phrase refers to the nature of the legal services, or restricts the Act's application to those out-of-state attorneys who are physically present in the state.

Section 6125 has generated numerous opinions on the meaning of "practice law" but none on the meaning of "in California." In our view, the practice of law "in California" entails sufficient contact with the California client to render the nature of the legal service a clear legal representation. In addition to a quantitative analysis, we must consider the nature of the unlicensed lawyer's activities in the state. Mere fortuitous or attenuated contacts will not sustain a finding that the unlicensed lawyer practiced law "in California." The primary inquiry is whether the unlicensed lawyer engaged in sufficient activities in the state, or created a continuing relationship with the California client that included legal duties and obligations.

Our definition does not necessarily depend on or require the unlicensed lawyer's physical presence in the state. Physical presence here is one factor we may consider in deciding whether the unlicensed lawyer has violated section 6125, but it is by no means exclusive. For example, one may practice law in the state in violation of section 6125 although not physically present here by advising a California client on California law in connection with a California legal dispute by telephone, fax, computer, or other modern technological means. Conversely, although we decline to provide a comprehensive list of what activities constitute sufficient contact with the state, we do reject the notion that a person automatically practices law "in California" whenever that person practices California law anywhere, or "virtually" enters the state by telephone, fax, e-mail, or satellite. . . .

This interpretation acknowledges the tension that exists between interjurisdictional practice and the need to have a state-regulated bar. As stated in the American Bar Association Model Code of Professional Responsibility, Ethical Consideration EC 3–9, "Regulation of the practice of law is accomplished principally by the respective states. Authority to engage in the practice of law conferred in any jurisdiction is not per se a grant of the right to practice elsewhere, and it is improper for a lawyer to engage in practice where he is not permitted by law or by court order to do so. However, the demands of business and the mobility of our society pose distinct problems in the regulation of the practice of law by the states. In furtherance of the public interest, the legal profession should discourage regulation that unreasonably imposes territorial limitations upon the right of a lawyer to handle the legal affairs of his client or upon the opportunity of a client to obtain the services of a lawyer of his choice in all matters including the presentation of a contested matter in a tribunal before which the lawyer is not permanently admitted to practice." . . .

Exceptions to section 6125 do exist, but are generally limited to allowing out-of-state attorneys to make brief appearances before a state court or tribunal. They are narrowly drawn and strictly interpreted. For example, an out-of-state attorney not licensed to practice in California may be permitted, by consent of a trial judge, to appear in California in a particular pending action.

In addition, with the permission of the California court in which a particular cause is pending, out-of-state counsel may appear before a court as counsel pro hac vice. . . . The out-of-state attorney must also associate an active member of the California Bar as attorney of record and is subject to the Rules of Professional Conduct of the State Bar. . . .

The Act does not regulate practice before United States courts. . . .

B.   The Present Case

The undisputed facts here show that . . . our "sufficient contact" definition of "practice law in California" . . . would [not] excuse Birbrower's extensive practice in this state. Nor would any of the limited statutory exceptions to section 6125 apply to Birbrower's California practice. As the Court of Appeal observed, Birbrower engaged in unauthorized law practice in California on more than a limited basis, and no firm attorney engaged in that practice was an active member of the California State Bar. . . . [I]n 1992 and 1993, Birbrower attorneys traveled to California to discuss with ESQ and others various matters pertaining to the dispute between ESQ and Tandem. Hobbs and Condon discussed strategy for resolving the dispute and advised ESQ on this strategy. Furthermore, during California meetings with Tandem representatives in August 1992, Hobbs demanded Tandem pay $15 million, and Condon told Tandem he believed damages in the matter would exceed that amount if the parties proceeded to litigation. Also in California, Hobbs met with ESQ for the stated purpose of helping to reach a settlement agreement and to discuss the agreement that was eventually proposed. Birbrower attorneys also traveled to California to initiate arbitration proceedings before the matter was settled. As the Court of Appeal concluded, ". . . the Birbrower firm's in-state activities clearly constituted the [unauthorized] practice of law" in California.

Birbrower contends, however, that section 6125 is not meant to apply to any out-of-state attorneys. Instead, it argues that the statute is intended solely to prevent nonattorneys from practicing law. This contention is without merit because it contravenes the plain language of the statute. Section 6125 clearly states that no person shall practice law in California unless that person is a member of the State Bar. The statute does not differentiate between attorneys or nonattorneys, nor does it excuse a person who is a member of another state bar. . . .

Birbrower next argues that we do not further the statute's intent and purpose—to protect California citizens from incompetent attorneys—by enforcing it against out-of-state attorneys. Birbrower argues that because out-of-state attorneys have been licensed to practice in other jurisdictions, they have already demonstrated sufficient competence to protect California clients. But Birbrower's argument overlooks the obvious fact that other states' laws may differ substantially from California law. Competence in one jurisdiction does not necessarily guarantee competence in another. By applying section 6125 to out-of-state attorneys who engage in the extensive practice of law in California without becoming licensed in our state, we serve the statute's goal of assuring the competence of all attorneys practicing law in this state.

California is not alone in regulating who practices law in its jurisdiction. Many states have substantially similar statutes that serve to protect their citizens from unlicensed attorneys who engage in unauthorized legal practice. Like section 6125, these other state statutes protect local citizens "against the dangers of legal representation and advice given by persons not trained, examined and licensed for such work, whether they be laymen or lawyers from other jurisdictions." Spivak v. Sachs (1965) 16 N.Y.2d 163, 263 N.Y.S.2d 953, 956, 211 N.E.2d 329, 331. Whether an attorney is duly admitted in another state and is, in fact, competent to practice in California is irrelevant in the face of section 6125's language and purpose.... [A] decision to except out-of-state attorneys licensed in their own jurisdictions from section 6125 is more appropriately left to the California Legislature.

Assuming that section 6125 does apply to out-of-state attorneys not licensed here, Birbrower alternatively asks us to create an exception to section 6125 for work incidental to private arbitration or other alternative dispute resolution proceedings. Birbrower points to fundamental differences between private arbitration and legal proceedings, including procedural differences relating to discovery, rules of evidence, compulsory process, cross-examination of witnesses, and other areas. As Birbrower observes, in light of these differences, at least one court has decided that an out-of-state attorney could recover fees for services rendered in an arbitration proceeding. See Williamson v. John D. Quinn Const. Corp. (S.D.N.Y.1982) 537 F. Supp. 613, 616 (*Williamson*).

In *Williamson*, a New Jersey law firm was employed by a client's New York law firm to defend a construction contract arbitration in New York. It sought to recover fees solely related to the arbitration proceedings, even though the attorney who did the work was not licensed in New York, nor was the firm authorized to practice in the state. In allowing the New Jersey firm to recover its arbitration fees, the federal district court concluded that an arbitration tribunal is not a court of record, and its factfinding process is not similar to a court's process. The court relied on a local state bar report concluding that representing a client in an arbitration was not the unauthorized practice of law....

We decline Birbrower's invitation to craft an arbitration exception to section 6125's prohibition of the unlicensed practice of law in this state. Any exception for arbitration is best left to the Legislature, which has the authority to determine qualifications for admission to the State Bar and to decide what constitutes the practice of law. Even though the Legislature has spoken with respect to international arbitration and conciliation, it has not enacted a similar rule for private arbitration proceedings. . . .

Finally, Birbrower urges us to adopt an exception to section 6125 based on the unique circumstances of this case. Birbrower notes that "Multistate relationships are a common part of today's society and are to be dealt with in commonsense fashion." In many situations, strict adherence to rules prohibiting the unauthorized practice of law by out-of-state attorneys would be " 'grossly impractical and inefficient.' "

Although, as discussed . . . , we recognize the need to acknowledge and, in certain cases, accommodate the multistate nature of law practice, the facts here show that Birbrower's extensive activities within California amounted to considerably more than any of our state's recognized exceptions to section 6125 would allow. Accordingly, we reject Birbrower's suggestion that we except the firm from section 6125's rule under the circumstances here.

C. Compensation for Legal Services

Because Birbrower violated section 6125 when it engaged in the unlawful practice of law in California, the Court of Appeal found its fee agreement with ESQ unenforceable in its entirety. Without crediting Birbrower for some services performed in New York, for which fees were generated under the fee agreement, the court reasoned that the agreement was void and unenforceable because it included payment for services rendered to a California client in the state by an unlicensed out-of-state lawyer. . . . The Court of Appeal let stand, however, the trial court's decision to allow Birbrower to pursue its fifth cause of action in *quantum meruit*.

It is a general rule that an attorney is barred from recovering compensation for services rendered in another state where the attorney was not admitted to the bar.

. . . Because Birbrower practiced substantial law in this state in violation of section 6125, it cannot receive compensation under the fee agreement for any of the services it performed in California. Enforcing the fee agreement in its entirety would include payment for the unauthorized practice of law in California and would allow Birbrower to enforce an illegal contract.

Birbrower asserts that even if we agree with the Court of Appeal and find that none of the above exceptions allowing fees for unauthorized California services apply to the firm, it should be permitted to recover fees for those limited services it performed exclusively in New York under the agreement. . . .

We agree with Birbrower that it may be able to recover fees under the fee agreement for the limited legal services it performed for ESQ in New York to the extent they did not constitute practicing law in California, even though those services were performed for a California client. Because section 6125 applies to the practice of law in California, it does not, in general, regulate law practice in other states.

GEORGE, C.J., and MOSK, BAXTER, WERDEGAR and BROWN, JJ., concur.

ENNARD, JUSTICE, dissenting.

In California, it is a misdemeanor to practice law when one is not a member of the State Bar. In this case, New York lawyers who were not members of the California Bar traveled to this state on several occasions, attempting to resolve a contract dispute between their clients and another corporation through negotiation and private arbitration. Their clients included a New York corporation and a sister corporation incorporated in California; the lawyers had in previous years represented the principal owners of these corporations. The majority holds that the New York lawyers' activities in California constituted the unauthorized practice of law. I disagree.

The majority focuses its attention on the question of whether the New York lawyers had engaged in the practice of law in California, giving scant consideration to a decisive preliminary inquiry: whether, through their activities here, the New York lawyers had engaged in the practice of law at all. In my view, the record does not show that they did. In reaching a contrary conclusion, the majority relies on an overbroad definition of the term "practice of law." I would adhere to this court's decision in Baron v. City of Los Angeles (1970) 2 Cal. 3d 535, 86 Cal. Rptr. 673, 469 P.2d 353, more narrowly defining the practice of law as the representation of another in a judicial proceeding or an activity requiring the application of that degree of legal knowledge and technique possessed only by a trained legal mind. Under this definition, this case presents a triable issue of material fact as to whether the New York lawyers' California activities constituted the practice of law. . . .

. . . The *Baron* definition provides ample protection from incompetent legal practitioners without infringing upon the public's interest in obtaining advice and representation from other professionals, such as accountants and real estate brokers, whose skills in specialized areas may overlap with those of lawyers. This allows the public the freedom to choose professionals who may be able to provide the public with needed services at a more affordable cost. . . . As this court has recognized, there are proceedings in which nonattorneys "are competent" to represent others without undermining the protection of the public interest.

. . . The majority's overbroad definition would affect a host of common commercial activities. On point here are comments that Professor Deborah Rhode made in a 1981 article published in the *Stanford Law Review*: "For many individuals, most obviously accountants, bankers, real estate brokers, and insurance agents, it would be impossible to give intelligent counsel without reference to legal concerns that such statutes reserve as the exclusive province of attorneys. As one [American Bar Association] official active in unauthorized practice areas recently acknowledged, there is growing recognition that "all kinds of other professional people are practicing the law almost out of necessity.'" Moreover, since most legislation does not exempt gratuitous activity, much advice commonly imparted by friends, employers, political organizers, and newspaper commentators constitutes unauthorized practice. . . ." Rhode, *Policing the Professional Monopoly: A Constitutional and Empirical Analysis of Unauthorized Practice Prohibitions*, 34 STAN. L. REV. at p. 47, fns. omitted.

Unlike the majority, I would for the reasons given above adhere to the more narrowly drawn definition of the practice of law that this court articulated in *Baron* . . . : the representation of another in a judicial proceeding or an activity requiring the application of that degree of legal knowledge and technique possessed only by a trained legal mind. Applying that definition here, I conclude that the trial court should not have granted summary adjudication for plaintiffs based on the Birbrower lawyers' California activities. . . .

* * *

Partly in response to *Birbrower*, the ABA amended Model Rule 5.5 to explicitly permit the temporary practice of law in a jurisdiction in a broad set of circumstances enumerated in subsection (c). As you read it, map out the various means by which a lawyer can permissibly engage in the multi-jurisdictional practice of law.

Model Rule 5.5 serves both as a clarification and, some would say, a liberalization of the rules governing the unauthorized practice of law by a lawyer licensed in one jurisdiction but practicing law in another jurisdiction on a temporary basis. It may also serve as a starting point for yet further liberalization of restrictions on lawyers' freedom to engage in multi-jurisdictional practice at a time in which many aspects of America's legal life are transcending state borders. Do you think Rule 5.5 represents a step in the right direction?

Comment [4] to Model Rule 5.5, consistent with *Birbrower,* indicates that a lawyer can be engaged in the practice of law in a jurisdiction "even if the lawyer is not physically present" in a jurisdiction. Should Model Rule 5.5 include a definition of what it means to practice law "in a jurisdiction" for the limited purpose of regulating lawyers' multi-jurisdictional practice of law?

* * *

Problem 4.3. How would *Birbrower* have come out if California had adopted ABA Model Rule 5.5(c)?

* * *

2. PRO HAC VICE ADMISSION

Model Rule 5.5(c) explicitly notes pro hac vice admission is one means by which a lawyer may temporarily practice in a jurisdiction. Although such *pro hac vice* ("for this occasion") motions are routinely granted, there are some competing policy concerns. On the one hand, clients will often want to use lawyers with whom they have previously worked, and it might work a hardship on a client to be denied its lawyer of choice in a given matter. On the other hand, there is the concern regarding what form of oversight there will be with respect to these out-of-state lawyers.

Under the ABA's Model Rule on Pro Hac Vice Admission, the lawyer seeking admission must become familiar with the relevant local rules and procedures (including the rules of professional conduct). In addition, the party being represented by the lawyer practicing on a pro hac vice basis must also be represented by an in-state lawyer who serves as counsel of record and actively participates in the representation. As the report accompanying the Model Rule notes, "[t]hroughout the litigation, local counsel must remain responsible to the client and for the conduct of the proceeding. This includes advising the client of the lawyer's professional judgment when it differs from that of the out-of-state lawyer on contemplated actions." Some states require that both the in-state and out-of state lawyer sign all the pleadings, motions, briefs, and other papers and that the in-state lawyer personally appear for all court proceedings, unless excused by the court in which the case is pending.

As explained in one state's ethics opinion,

[T]ypical acts required of local counsel, such as moving of admission pro hac vice or the signing of pleadings, always carry with them affirmative ethical obligations. For example, in this, as in all circumstances, the signing of pleadings by an attorney constitutes a good faith representation regarding the pleadings and the conduct of the discovery procedure of which the pleadings are a part. There is nothing in the role of local counsel that changes this basic ethical responsibility. Local counsel, if he or she signs the pleadings, must be familiar with them and investigate them to the extent required by this good faith requirement.

State Bar of Georgia, Formal Advisory Op. 05–10 (2006). Local counsel may also be subject to discipline for the out-of-state lawyer's misconduct "when the local counsel knows of the abuse and ratifies it by his or her conduct." *Id.*

* * *

E. THE MULTI-STATE PRACTITIONER, DISCIPLINARY AUTHORITY, AND CHOICE OF LAW

What happens if a lawyer licensed in one state, but lawfully practicing in another state, commits an act that is unethical under one state's law but not the other's? Even if the act is unethical under the law of both states, which state has the power to discipline the lawyer?

* * *

Please read ABA Model Rules of Professional Conduct, Rule 8.5 and Comments [1]–[4].

* * *

Problem 4.4. Lawyer Juliana places an advertisement in the Massachusetts Yellow Pages for her firm in which she says her firm offers legal services to Connecticut and Massachusetts residents. Juliana is a member of the state bars of Connecticut and Pennsylvania but is not admitted in Massachusetts. However, her office is located close to the Massachusetts/Connecticut border, so she hopes to attract some clients from both states, but provide the services from her Connecticut office. Assume that the advertisement is determined to be false or misleading in violation of the ethical rules in place in Massachusetts, Connecticut, and Pennsylvania. In which jurisdiction(s) is Juliana subject to discipline? If the rules regarding lawyer advertising differ among the three states, which rule should a disciplinary authority in, say, Massachusetts apply?

Reciprocal discipline. If a lawyer is disciplined in a jurisdiction with authority to do so, should all jurisdictions in which the lawyer is licensed be required to impose the same discipline? Allowed to do so without a de novo proceeding? Rule 22, ¶ D of the ABA Model Rules for Lawyer Disciplinary Enforcement provides that all jurisdictions in which the offending lawyer is licensed should ordinarily treat a determination of misconduct by another jurisdiction as conclusive and should impose the identical discipline. Exceptions include where the proof of misconduct is especially weak or where the discipline imposed would be "offensive to the public policy of the jurisdiction." Should a jurisdiction ever be expected to impose reciprocal discipline where the lawyer's conduct—although violating the rules of the jurisdiction where the lawyer was disciplined—would not constitute a violation of its rules? When would it be offensive to public policy to do so?

* * *

F. INTERNATIONAL PERSPECTIVES

In light of globalization, United States jurisdictions are being faced with the question of the extent to which lawyers licensed in other countries should be allowed to practice law here in the states. Recognizing the practical effects of globalization, the ABA established a special commission, the Ethics 20/20 Commission, to consider how the rules of professional conduct could be adapted to adjust to the realities of globalization.

* * *

1. IN-HOUSE COUNSEL

**Please read ABA Model Rules of Professional Conduct,
Rule 5.5(d) & (e) and Comments [15]–[21].**

As noted by the Ethics 20/20 Commission in its Final Report, "many foreign-owned companies have substantial business and legal interests that involve numerous jurisdictions, including in the U.S." Not surprisingly, these companies might like the ability to employ a foreign lawyer as in-house counsel in an office within the United States. As a result, ABA Model Rule 5.5(d) was amended to give foreign lawyers greater authority to serve as in-house counsel in the United States. Under the rule, a foreign lawyer who is employed by a client may provide legal services to that client, provided the foreign lawyer is duly licensed in a foreign jurisdiction and is "subject to effective regulation and discipline by a duly constituted professional body or a public authority." However, where the services require advice on U.S. law, the advice must be based on the advice of a lawyer licensed to practice in the relevant jurisdiction.

2. TEMPORARY PRACTICE IN THE UNITED STATES BY FOREIGN LAWYERS

A lawyer licensed in a foreign jurisdiction may also need to provide legal services within the U.S. on a more temporary basis. In 2013, the ABA amended its Model Rule on Pro Hac Vice Admission to deal directly with the issue of lawyers licensed in a foreign jurisdiction who wish to provide legal services on a one-time basis. Under the new rule, a court may admit a foreign lawyer in a particular proceeding pending before the court to appear in a defined role as a lawyer, advisor, or consultant in that proceeding with an in-state lawyer. The in-state lawyer remains responsible to the client and responsible for the conduct of the proceeding, independently advising the client on the applicable substantive U.S. law, and advising the client whether the in-state lawyer's judgment differs from that of the foreign lawyer. In deciding whether to admit a foreign lawyer on a limited basis, a court may consider a variety of factors, including the experience of the foreign lawyer, the lawyer's familiarity with the relevant U.S. jurisdiction, and the lawyer's relationship with the client.

* * *

Profile of attorney professionalism. As the next chapter discusses in greater detail, access to justice is a pressing problem. The Washington Supreme Court recently summarized the problem:

> Our adversarial civil legal system is complex. It is unaffordable not only to low income people but . . . moderate income people as well (defined as families with incomes between 200% and 400% of the Federal Poverty Level). One example of the need for this rule is in the area of family relations which are governed by a myriad of statutes. Decisions relating to changes in family status (divorce, child residential placement, child support, etc.) fall within the exclusive province of our court system. Legal practice is required to conform to specific statewide and local procedures, and practitioners are required to use standard forms developed at both the statewide and local levels. Every day across this state, thousands of unrepresented (pro se) individuals seek to resolve important legal matters in our courts. Many of these are low income people who seek but cannot obtain help from an overtaxed, underfunded civil legal aid system. Many others are moderate income people for whom existing market rates for legal services are cost-prohibitive and who, unfortunately, must search for alternatives in the unregulated marketplace.

In the Matter of the Adoption of New APR 28—Limited Practice Rule for Limited License Legal Technicians (2012).

A task force of the New York Bar reached similar conclusions. It found that New Yorkers lacked legal assistance in:

- 99% of tenants in eviction cases in New York City and 98% of tenants in New York State;

- 97% of parents in child support proceedings in New York City and 95% of parents in New York State;

- 44% of homeowners in foreclosure cases in New York State.

Task Force to Expand Access to Civil Legal Services in New York (2010).

Some states have dealt with the access to justice problem by encouraging more *pro bono* work on the part of lawyers. Some state supreme courts have developed standardized legal forms (e.g., simple divorces) that are made available on court websites for litigants to use. Washington has dealt with the issue by recognizing the role of "limited license legal technicians," individuals "qualified by education, training and work experience who [are] authorized to engage in the limited practice of law in approved practice areas of law as specified by this rule and related regulations. The legal technician does not represent the client in court proceedings or negotiations, but provides limited legal assistance as set forth in this rule to a pro se client."

Under Washington's rule, a limited license legal technician could undertake the following actions:

(1) Obtain relevant facts, and explain the relevancy of such information to the client;

(2) Inform the client of applicable procedures, including deadlines, documents which must be filed, and the anticipated course of the legal proceeding;

(3) Inform the client of applicable procedures for proper service of process and filing of legal documents;

(4) Provide the client with self-help materials prepared by a Washington lawyer or approved by the Board, which contain information about relevant legal requirements, case law basis for the client's claim, and venue and jurisdiction requirements;

(5) Review documents or exhibits that the client has received from the opposing side, and explain them to the client;

(6) Select, complete, file, and effect service of forms that have been approved by the State of Washington, either through a governmental agency or by the Administrative Office of the Courts or the content of which is specified by statute; federal forms; forms prepared by a Washington lawyer; or forms approved by the Board; and advise the client of the significance of the selected forms to the client's case;

(7) Perform legal research and draft legal letters and documents beyond what is permitted in the previous paragraph, if the work is reviewed and approved by a Washington lawyer;

(8) Advise a client as to other documents that may be necessary to the client's case, and explain how such additional documents or pleadings may affect the client's case;

(9) Assist the client in obtaining necessary documents, such as birth, death, or marriage certificates.

Technicians would specifically be excluded from representing parties in an adjudicative proceeding or negotiating a party's legal rights and obligations.

Does this seem like a desirable approach?

* * *

Profile of attorney professionalism. Robert J. Kutak was the founder of the Kutak Rock law firm, one of the first truly national firms. According to his firm's biography, Kutak "was instrumental in developing the National Institute of Corrections (NIC) at the Department of Justice, and was a member of the blue-ribbon National Advisory Commission on Criminal Justice Standards and Goals." Kutak also served as an original member of the board of trustees of the national Legal Services Corporation. He was "a recognized expert in federal correctional reform and rehabilitation, serving the administrations of presidents of both parties in various capacities." He was also a delegate to two United Nations congresses on the prevention of crime and the treatment of prisoners. Kutak Rock LLP, http://www.kutakrock.com/robert-bob-kutak/.

Despite these achievements, Kutak's most lasting contribution was his service as Chairman of the American Bar Association's Special Commission on Evaluation of Professional Standards. This commission— which eventually became known as the Kutak Commission—was tasked in 1977 with revising the ABA's then-existing Model Code of Professional Responsibility. The Commission was established in the wake of the Watergate scandal when public confidence in the legal profession was low. The Kutak Commission proposed dramatic changes to the rules of professional conduct that were more specific in their scope. The work product of the Kutak Commission ultimately became the ABA's Model Rules of Professional Conduct, which still serve (in amended form) as the basis for most state rules of professional conduct. According to the noted legal ethics scholar Geoffrey Hazard, "few people have devoted so much public-spirited energy to improving the legal system." *Id.*

CHAPTER 5

PROVIDING ACCESS TO JUSTICE THROUGH PRO BONO AND OTHER SERVICE

■■■

Chapter hypothetical. Like many states, your state's supreme court recently created an Access to Justice Commission. The court is concerned that numerous citizens of the state need but are unable to pay for basic civil legal services. These individuals need legal advice and representation for matters related to child support, employment, housing, simple contract disputes, healthcare benefits, orders of protection, and other issues. Without a lawyer, these individuals often represent themselves, burdening the courts and compromising their legal rights. In other cases, those who cannot afford a lawyer simply forgo the court system.

A recent study by a non-profit group revealed that a staggering 1.5 million citizens of the state qualify financially for legal aid services. (The state has a population of 7 million). Despite the need, the state's legal service programs (legal aid organizations funded by the Legal Services Corporation and various other non-profit organizations) do not have the staff and volunteers to serve the state's citizens.

You have accepted the court's invitation to serve on the ten-person Access to Justice Commission. The Commission's charge is to improve access to justice for the state's citizens. The court has directed the committee to:

(1) Study the reasons that many law students and attorneys do not provide pro bono services to the poor.

(2) Develop a plan to encourage law students and attorneys to volunteer their time in (and provide financial support to) legal services programs in the state. This plan may include proposing court rules that promote pro bono service by law students, newly admitted attorneys, current attorneys, and retired members of the state bar.

* * *

For those who cannot afford to pay a lawyer, meaningful access to the courts is possible through the efforts of lawyers. Attorneys can volunteer their time at no charge, providing "pro bono" legal services to the economically disadvantaged. In an era of decreasing governmental financial support for legal aid organizations, lawyers' financial support to these organizations is another avenue to increase access to justice. Further, lawyers can accept cases—civil and criminal—in which they are appointed by a court to represent a party for little or no pay. Finally, attorneys can make a difference by their efforts to reform the law and in leadership roles in legal services organizations.

The Preamble to the Model Rules of Professional Conduct explains the attorney's obligation in this regard, describing lawyers as having "special responsibility for the quality of justice." Model Rules Preamble, ¶ 1. To improve access to justice, the Preamble urges lawyers to care for those who cannot afford legal assistance by devoting "professional time and resources and us[ing] civic influence to ensure equal access to our system of justice. . . ." Model Rules Preamble, ¶ 6.

The profession faces challenges putting these principles into practice. Legal educators and the bar must decide how best to inculcate a spirit of volunteerism in the next generation of lawyers. State courts and rule committees must endeavor to draft rules that encourage pro bono service and remove barriers to access to justice. Organizations that provide legal services to the poor must develop new programs that facilitate attorneys getting involved and making a difference. This chapter addresses these and other challenges faced by the profession as we work to provide access to justice.

* * *

A. LAW STUDENT PRO BONO SERVICE

1. PROMOTING LAW STUDENT PRO BONO SERVICE

In its accreditation standards, the American Bar Association requires that a law school's curriculum provide substantial opportunities for students to participate in pro bono legal services. ABA Standards for Approval of Law Schools, Standard 3.03(b)(2). In its interpretation of the rule, the ABA explains that schools are encouraged to promote pro bono consistent with Model Rule 6.1 priorities (primarily providing pro bono for persons of limited means and organizations that serve them). The interpretation further encourages law schools to provide students with opportunities to provide at least 50 hours of pro bono service while in law school. ABA Standards for Approval of Law Schools, Interpretation 303–3. Both the Standard and Interpretation acknowledge that pro bono opportunities in law school also may include the provision of law-related public services, such as (1) working to help groups protect and secure legal rights, (2) assisting charitable, religious and other groups that are unable to afford legal representation, and (3) participating in groups that educate the public about the law. ABA Standards for Approval of Law Schools, Standard 303(b)(2) and Interpretation 303–4.

U.S. law schools have adopted a variety of approaches to giving students opportunities to perform pro bono services. An Internet search reveals a good variety of programs instituted by schools around the country. Programs range from walk in clinics in which students answer legal questions from members of the community to programs that serve a specific group, like veterans or immigrant families. (You will have an opportunity to research these programs in Problem 5.1). Some law schools have hired full time staff to coordinate pro bono programs, while other schools' programs are run primarily through student organizations and faculty volunteers.

Law schools have reached different conclusions about whether pro bono service should be a graduation requirement or should be encouraged but not required. For example, Tulane University School of Law requires students to perform at least thirty hours of law-related, uncompensated pro bono service under an attorney's supervision. In another example, at The University of Tennessee College of Law, student pro bono service is not required, but students with exceptional pro bono service receive special recognition at commencement.

* * *

Problem 5.1. As a member of the Access to Justice Commission, you decide to search online for information about an interesting or innovative way that a law school (other than your own) promotes pro bono service. Be prepared to explain why you think law students would participate in the program or project you identify in your research.

Problem 5.2. Each member of the Access to Justice Commission agrees to survey three law students about the following issues. Take notes as you discuss these issues with three law students and be prepared to discuss the results in class:

(1) Should pro bono service be a graduation requirement at this law school? Why or why not?

(2) Has this law school taken appropriate steps to encourage pro bono service by students? What ideas do you have for improving the school's pro bono program?

(3) Have you participated in pro bono as a student? Why or why not?

2. PRO BONO BAR ADMISSION REQUIREMENT

In 2012, New York became the first state to adopt a rule that makes pro bono service a prerequisite to bar admission. Because the rule requires 50 hours of service prior to applying for bar admission, most applicants will perform this service during law school. Supporters of the proposal assert that the requirement will fill a need for legal services and provide real legal experience that prepares students for practice. Critics have concerns about forcing unwilling persons to perform legal services, both from the standpoint of the bar applicant (who has no choice in the matter) and of the client (who may be provided substandard legal services).

As this book goes to press, three other states (California, Montana, and New Jersey) are considering adopting a pro bono requirement for admission to the bar.

N.Y. Ct. Rules, § 520.16

Pro Bono Requirement for Bar Admission

(a) Fifty-hour pro bono requirement. Every applicant admitted to the New York State bar on or after January 1, 2015, other than applicants for admission without examination pursuant to section 520.10 of this Part, shall complete at least 50 hours of qualifying pro bono service prior to filing an application for admission with the appropriate Appellate Division department of the Supreme Court.

(b) Pro bono service defined. For purposes of this section, pro bono service is supervised pre-admission law-related work that:

(1) assists in the provision of legal services without charge for

(i) persons of limited means;

(ii) not-for-profit organizations; or

(iii) individuals, groups or organizations seeking to secure or promote access to justice, including, but not limited to, the protection of civil rights, civil liberties or public rights;

(2) assists in the provision of legal assistance in public service for a judicial, legislative, executive or other governmental entity; or

(3) provides legal services pursuant to subdivisions two and three of section 484 of the Judiciary Law, or pursuant to equivalent legal authority in the jurisdiction where the services are performed.

(c) Supervision required. All qualifying pre-admission pro bono work must be performed under the supervision of:

(1) a member of a law school faculty, including adjunct faculty, or an instructor employed by a law school;

(2) an attorney admitted to practice and in good standing in the jurisdiction where the work is performed; or

(3) in the case of a clerkship or externship in a court system, by a judge or attorney employed by the court system.

(d) Location of pro bono service. The 50 hours of pro bono service, or any portion thereof, may be completed in any state or territory of the United States, the District of Columbia, or any foreign country.

(e) Timing of pro bono service. The 50 hours of pro bono service may be performed at any time after the commencement of the applicant's legal studies and prior to filing an application for admission to the New York State bar.

(f) Proof required. Every applicant for admission shall file with the appropriate Appellate Division department an Affidavit of Compliance with the Pro Bono Requirement, describing the nature and dates of pro bono service and the number of hours completed. The Affidavit of Compliance shall include a certification by the supervising attorney or judge confirming the applicant's pro bono activities. For each position used to satisfy the 50-hour requirement, the applicant shall file a separate Affidavit of Compliance.

(g) Prohibition on political activities. An applicant may not satisfy any part of the 50-hour requirement by participating in partisan political activities.

* * *

Problem 5.3. Your state's Access to Justice Commission has voted in favor of proposing a bar admission pro bono requirement. You have agreed to take the lead drafting the proposed rule. Which aspects of the New York Rule will you incorporate into your rule? How will your proposal differ from the New York rule?

* * *

B. ATTORNEY PRO BONO SERVICE

Please read ABA Model Rules of Professional Conduct, Rule 6.1 and Comments.

Model Rule 6.1 provides that it is a lawyer's professional responsibility to provide legal representation to individuals unable to pay and that each lawyer should aspire to provide at least fifty hours of pro bono services each year. The rule creates a hierarchy of preferred services, stating that a "substantial majority" of the lawyer's pro bono services should be provided to individuals of limited means (or to organizations in order to meet the legal needs of individuals of limited means). Model Rule 6.1(a). Beyond that, subpart (b) guides lawyers in additional services that they may provide to fulfill their fifty-hour requirement, including providing substantially reduced fee representations to persons of limited means and participating in activities to improve the law. Model Rule 6.1(b). The comments provide some direction about who qualifies as a "person of limited means" under the rule. *See* Model Rule 6.1, Comment [3].

While many states do not set a goal for the number of pro bono hours an attorney should perform, twenty-nine states set a specific goal. Of these, most include a fifty-hour requirement like Model Rule 6.1. Some jurisdictions set a lower goal (20 hours in Mississippi and Florida), while others set a higher goal (80 hours in Oregon). Eight states suggest a specific financial contribution attorneys should make to support the provision of legal services to the poor.

A growing number of states encourage pro bono service by asking attorneys to report their pro bono hours (and sometimes also the amount of money donated to support legal aid organizations). Such reporting typically occurs when attorneys pay annual bar dues. Currently, eight states have adopted a mandatory reporting system. Even though pro bono is not mandatory in these states, attorneys are required to answer questions about how many hours of service they provided. Twelve states have adopted a permissive reporting scheme. Attorneys are asked for the information about pro bono hours, but are not required to provide it. The theory is that even though pro bono is not mandatory, knowing that they will be asked about their service may prompt attorneys to seek out pro bono opportunities.

Giving attorneys continuing legal education ("CLE") credit for time spent representing clients pro bono is another tool states use to encourage pro bono legal service. Currently, ten states have such rules. For example, in Arizona, attorneys can earn up to five of their fifteen required CLE credits through pro bono service each year. Under Arizona's rule, one credit hour of CLE is awarded for every five hours of pro bono service. In another example, Delaware allows attorneys to earn up to six hours of CLE credit every two years by performing pro bono work. Delaware allows attorneys to earn one hour of credit for every six hours of pro bono work.

Another avenue for increasing pro bono services is to increase the pool of attorneys able to provide those services. In thirty-eight jurisdictions, retired attorneys who are no longer active members of the bar are permitted to provide pro bono services under so called "emeritus attorney" professional conduct rules. Other rules allow in-house attorneys (practicing under a limited license because they did not take the bar exam in that state) to provide pro bono services in the state. *See, e.g.,* Tenn. Rules of Prof'l Conduct R. 5.5(e) (allowing in-house attorneys licensed in another jurisdiction to perform defined pro bono services in Tennessee); 22 N.Y.C.R.R. § 522.8 (permitting registered in-house attorneys licensed in another jurisdiction to perform defined pro bono services in New York).

Finally, states can make it easier for attorneys to perform pro bono service by relaxing the conflict of interest rules for "limited scope" pro bono representations. This issue is addressed more fully in Part C, below.

* * *

Problem 5.4. As a member of the Access to Justice Commission, which of the methods of encouraging pro bono service (discussed above) would you like to see incorporated into your state's professional conduct rules? Why do you think these are effective methods to encourage pro bono service?

Problem 5.5. Recall that the Access to Justice Commission was asked to study the reasons attorneys do not provide pro bono services and create a plan to address these issues. In your research, you find a recent report on pro bono prepared by an ABA standing committee. According to surveyed attorneys, the factors that most discouraged them from performing pro bono work in the previous year were:

(1) Lack of time.

(2) Commitment to family obligations.

(3) Lack of skills or experience in the practice area needed for the pro bono representation.

ABA Standing Committee on Pro Bono and Public Service, *Supporting Justice III: A Report on the Pro Bono Work of America's Lawyers,* p. 29–30 (March 2013).

What practical suggestions do you have about how the Access to Justice Commission, state bar, and legal services organizations can address these challenges?

Problem 5.6. For attorneys who would like to provide pro bono services but do not know how to get started, there are many online resources that can help. The American Bar Association's Directory of Pro Bono Programs provides an interactive map that allows a user to select a state and find a list of organizations in need of attorney volunteers. Look at the information provided for your state and decide which opportunity is of most interest to you.

C. CONFLICTS OF INTEREST AND A LAWYER'S PRO BONO LIMITED SCOPE REPRESENTATIONS AND OTHER VOLUNTEER ACTIVITIES

Please read ABA Model Rules of Professional Conduct, Rules 6.3–6.5 and Comments.

In Chapters 16 and 17, you will learn that a lawyer cannot represent a client when the lawyer or the lawyer's firm has a conflict of interest. Model Rules 6.3, 6.4, and 6.5 add a twist to the conflict of interest analysis for lawyers who are members of legal services organizations, engaged in law reform activities, or participants in limited legal services programs. Use these rules to answer the following questions.

* * *

Problem 5.7. You are asked to serve on the Board of Directors for the local Legal Aid organization. The partners in your firm are concerned that your membership on the board will create a conflict of interest for the firm. Legal Aid lawyers frequently represent tenants in eviction proceedings filed by the firm for an important client. Would your membership on the Board of Directors create a conflict of interest that would prevent the firm from representing the client in future cases adverse to Legal Aid clients?

Problem 5.8. Your local bar association hosts a Saturday morning walk-in legal clinic for low-income individuals. Attorneys meet the clients in person and provide legal advice during the clinic. Participants understand that there will not be a continuing attorney-client relationship, unless attorney and client agree otherwise. You would like to volunteer as an attorney for the walk-in clinic. Do you need to check for conflicts of interest between your law firm's clients and the individuals seeking advice at the clinic? If you recognize a conflict between an individual seeking advice at the clinic and a firm client, may you nonetheless provide advice to the individual on this one-time basis?

* * *

D. COURT APPOINTMENTS

Please read ABA Model Rules of Professional Conduct, Rule 6.2 and Comments.

Courts often appoint attorneys to represent individuals in criminal and sometimes even civil matters. Rule 6.2 provides that an attorney should generally accept such appointments absent good cause.

One good cause noted in Model Rule 6.2 is that the representation is likely to result in violation of professional conduct rules. Obviously, if the representation would create a conflict of interest, this is a proper basis to seek relief from the appointment. *See* Model Rules 1.7, 1.9, and 1.10. Attorneys also sometimes worry that their representation of an appointed client may violate the duty of competence. Courts generally dismiss these concerns, though, and expect attorneys to do the research and work necessary to perform competently. *See, e.g.,* Stern v. County Court, 773 P.2d 1074, 1080 (Colo. 1989) (agreeing with the trial court's determination that even if attorney was not competent to handle the criminal appointment, attorney was "very capable" of becoming competent).

An attorney may also want to avoid an appointment for a client that is unpopular or whose conduct or cause is troubling to the lawyer. For example, a lawyer may find it difficult to represent a person accused of abusing a child. Model Rule 6.2(c) provides that if the lawyer finds the client or cause is "so repugnant" that the lawyer's ability to represent the client is likely to be impaired, this is good cause to avoid the appointment. Nonetheless, comments to the rule reminds attorneys that it is our duty to accept a "fair share of unpopular matters or indigent or unpopular clients." Model Rule 6.2, Comment [1].

While attorneys are often paid for their work on court-appointed cases, sometimes they are asked to accept a representation pro bono. In other cases, appointed attorneys may receive pay that is substantially below market rates for paying clients. While most attorneys recognize the importance of pro bono service, they can face a financial strain when they are appointed to work on a significant case or several small cases for which they will receive little or no pay. Model Rule 6.2(b) provides that "unreasonable financial burden" is good cause to request relief from a court appointment. This issue was addressed in the following case.

HAGOPIAN V. JUSTICE ADMINISTRATIVE COMMISSION
18 So.3d 625 (Fla. Dist. Ct. App. 2009)

WALLACE, JUDGE.

I. THE FACTS

A. Introduction

In an effort to combat gang activity in Manatee County, the Statewide Prosecutor began charging persons alleged to be gang members with the offense of racketeering. Terry Green was one of the persons so charged. In 2008, an information was filed in the Manatee County Circuit Court charging Mr. Green and eleven codefendants with one count of racketeering and one count of conspiracy to commit racketeering. The circuit court appointed the public defender to represent one of Mr. Green's codefendants and appointed the five Manatee County attorneys whose names appeared on the registry list maintained by the clerk of the circuit court to represent five more of the codefendants. The circuit court could not appoint the Office of Criminal Conflict and Civil Regional Counsel to represent Mr. Green or any of his codefendants because of a conflict of interest. As a result of the shortage of available attorneys to represent the remaining defendants in Mr. Green's case and similar cases, the circuit court created an "Involuntary Appointment List" and began appointing attorneys whose names were placed on the Involuntary Appointment List to represent Mr. Green and other codefendants. The first two attorneys involuntarily appointed to represent Mr. Green were granted leave to withdraw because they lacked the requisite experience. The circuit court then appointed Mr. Hagopian, a sole practitioner, from the Involuntary Appointment List to represent Mr. Green. Mr. Hagopian moved to withdraw from Mr. Green's case, but the circuit court denied his motion. Mr. Hagopian now seeks review by certiorari of the order denying his motion to withdraw.

B. Chapter 2007–62

[The court describes the flat fee schedule for appointed counsel in the matter, explaining that it "obviously provides minimal compensation in cases that prove to be complicated or time-consuming for appointed counsel."]

G. The Order Appointing Mr. Hagopian and His Objection

On July 22, 2008, the circuit court entered an order in the *Brown* case appointing Mr. Hagopian to represent Mr. Green. . . . Mr. Hagopian promptly filed a motion to withdraw and requested a hearing. In his motion, Mr. Hagopian asserted four grounds for relief. First, the compensation available under section 27.5304 would be insufficient to compensate him for the work necessary to provide effective representation to Mr. Green. Second, the inadequacy of the compensation would inevitably give rise to a conflict of interest between Mr. Hagopian and the client and deprive Mr. Green of his right to conflict-free counsel. Third, the vast scope of the work necessary to handle the case would cause Mr. Hagopian to be unable to properly represent his existing clients, render him unable to accept new business, and ultimately lead to the ruin of his law practice. Fourth, the involuntary appointment would deprive Mr. Hagopian of his constitutional rights to due process of law, the right to contract, and the rights of association and free speech.

II. THE HEARING ON THE MOTION TO WITHDRAW

The circuit court promptly conducted an evidentiary hearing on Mr. Hagopian's motion to withdraw. In addition to Mr. Hagopian, three witnesses testified at the hearing: (1) Walt Smith, the trial court administrator of the Twelfth Judicial Circuit; (2) Mark Lipinski, an attorney board-certified in criminal law who practiced in Manatee

County; and (3) Joseph Campoli, an attorney appointed from the Involuntary Appointment List to represent one of the defendants in the *Agustin* case. [The court's discussion of the witnesses other than Mr. Hagopian is omitted].

[At the hearing, Mr. Hagopian testified that he] was admitted to the Florida Bar in 1993. The circuit court described Mr. Hagopian as "a former prosecutor who is now a prominent and successful solo practitioner. His Bradenton practice is about equally divided between civil and criminal cases[,] and his entire office staff consists of one secretary." Mr. Hagopian estimated his monthly overhead at $12,000.

Although Mr. Hagopian had not defended a RICO prosecution previously, he did not dispute his competency to handle such a case. Instead, as the circuit court noted, his objections to the appointment were "financial and ethical." Mr. Hagopian explained the vast scope of the State's case against Mr. Green with reference to a thirty-four-page discovery exhibit that he had received from the Statewide Prosecutor's Office:

> That is a listing . . . of 382 witnesses; 216 law enforcement witnesses, 178 from Manatee County Sheriff, 36 from the Bradenton Police Department, one from [the Florida Department of Law Enforcement], one from the Palmetto Police Department, 155 so-called civilian witnesses, 11 codefendants. If my addition is correct, that's 382 witnesses that are listed on the discovery exhibit. There are also 176 separate law enforcement police reports listed in that discovery exhibit. There are nine predicate acts listed for my client alone, Mr. Green, and there are a total of [11] codefendants.

Based on the complexity of the case, Mr. Hagopian estimated that it would take a minimum of 500 hours to investigate and prepare the case. This estimate did not include trial time. He expected that a trial could consume an additional two to six weeks. In addition to the demands that the case would place on his time, Mr. Hagopian anticipated that it would be necessary for him to hire an additional secretary to handle the administrative details of the case. However, under the JAC contract, attorneys may not be reimbursed for staff time devoted to a case.

Mr. Hagopian testified in detail about the impact that a case of this magnitude would have on his solo law practice. First, the demands of the case on his time would be so great that he believed he would be unable to effectively represent his existing clients. This would require him to seek to withdraw from matters he had already accepted and to return some retainers. Second, Mr. Hagopian also expected that the demands of the case would make it impossible for him to accept any new business for a substantial period of time. As a result, Mr. Hagopian explained, "If I were forced against my will to properly defend this individual, it could possibly shut my practice down."

Mr. Hagopian testified concerning his fee arrangements if he were to handle a similar matter for a private client: "I wouldn't even touch this case for anything less than $100,000 down, up-front, plus a trial fee of at least $50,000, plus depending on how much more I dig into it, another [$]50 to 100,000 for the work done." In response to a question from the circuit court, Mr. Hagopian testified that no attorney competent to defend the case would be willing to do the work for $75 per hour or even $110 per hour. After considering all of the circumstances-including the JAC's payment policies and practices-Mr. Hagopian concluded: "[T]here's just no way that I could possibly do this."

III. THE ORDER UNDER REVIEW

At the conclusion of the hearing on Mr. Hagopian's motion to withdraw, the circuit court entered a fourteen-page, single-spaced order [denying Mr. Hagopian's motion]. . . . Although we quash the circuit court's order, we praise the circuit court for its careful and thoughtful approach to this very difficult matter. The circuit court's conscientious handling of Mr. Hagopian's motion to withdraw has made this court's task much easier. [The court's detailed discussion of the order is omitted, as are a summary of the parties' arguments and a general discussion of the law].

VII. DISCUSSION

In considering the circuit court's denial of the motion to withdraw, we must put aside nostalgic conceptions of the practice of law in order to make a realistic assessment of what the involuntary appointment to Mr. Green's case actually meant for Mr. Hagopian and his solo law practice. For many people, lawyers and nonlawyers alike, the appointment of a lawyer from the private bar to represent an unpopular defendant accused of a serious crime brings to mind the image of Atticus Finch, the hero of Harper Lee's Pulitzer Prize-winning novel, *To Kill a Mockingbird*. Atticus Finch defended Tom Robinson, an indigent man charged with rape, "without mention of a fee, perpetuating in the eyes of readers everywhere the noble image of the lawyer dedicated to justice with no thought of . . . 'lucre.'" Arnold v. Kemp, 306 Ark. 294, 813 S.W.2d 770, 780 (1991) (Newbern, J., concurring). But the practice of law has changed drastically since the 1930s when the fictional Atticus Finch practiced law.

A number of factors have combined to increase the burden of involuntary appointments to criminal cases on members of the private bar in the modern era. First, the practice of criminal law has become increasingly complex and specialized. *See* Christopher D. Atwell, Comment, *Constitutional Challenges to Court Appointment: Increasing Recognition of an Unfair Burden*, 44 Sw. L.J. 1229, 1242–43 (1990).

Second, as the practice of law has changed, costs for personnel, libraries, equipment, and general overhead have increased significantly. *See id.* at 1243. Lawyers have also become expected to use computer-assisted legal research to ensure that their research is complete and up-to-date, but the costs of this service can be significant. *See* Michael Whiteman, *The Impact of the Internet and Other Electronic Sources on an Attorney's Duty of Competence under the Rules of Professional Conduct,* 11 Alb. L.J. Sci. & Tech. 89, 103 (2000) (concluding that computer-assisted legal research "has become recognized as a standard research technique among judges, lawyers[,] and law students, with price being perhaps the only thing holding back all attorneys from utilizing it in their research"). The lawyer's need to generate fees to pay these costs makes it more difficult to undertake appointed work for a reduced fee or for no fee at all. Third, competition among lawyers for business has become intense. *See Atwell,* 44 Sw. L.J. at 1243. Such competition makes it more difficult for a lawyer with a small office to undertake appointed work and continue to sustain his or her law practice.

These factors formed the backdrop for the testimony in the circuit court.... After a thorough consideration of the record in this extraordinary case, we conclude that Mr. Hagopian established two grounds under rule 4–6.2 supporting his withdrawal from further representation of Mr. Green. The three grounds described in the rule constitute a nonexclusive list of "circumstances that would justify 'good cause' to avoid court-ordered appointments." *In re Amendments,* 573 So.2d at 806. First, under rule 4–6.2(a), a lawyer may seek to avoid appointment by a court to represent a person when "representing the client is likely to result in violation of the Rules of Professional Conduct or of the law." ....

Here, the undisputed evidence established that the involuntary appointment to Mr. Green's case would make it impossible for Mr. Hagopian to handle the legal business of his existing clients and provide them with competent representation. Such derelictions by Mr. Hagopian would result in the violation of rules 4–1.1, 4–1.2(a), 4–1.3, and 4–1.4. Under these circumstances, Mr. Hagopian established good cause for moving to withdraw from Mr. Green's case. *See In re Amendments,* 573 So.2d at 806; ABA Formal Op. 06–441 at 4–5.

Second, under rule 4–6.2(b), a lawyer may seek to avoid an appointment by a court to represent a person when "representing the client is likely to result in an unreasonable financial burden on the lawyer." Here, the undisputed evidence established that the extraordinary time and effort that would be required to represent Mr. Green effectively-together with the minimal and uncertain compensation offered-threatened Mr. Hagopian with the ruin of his successful solo law practice. By any standard, the involuntary appointment to Mr. Green's defense was an unreasonable financial burden for Mr. Hagopian.

To be sure, under the circuit court's order, Mr. Hagopian was to be compensated at a higher rate for indigent defense than section 27.5304(12)(d) authorized-$110 per hour instead of $75 per hour. Still, the $110 hourly rate was substantially below the market rate for a successful lawyer such as Mr. Hagopian. Moreover, the $110 per-hour rate would not make up for losses resulting from time and resources devoted to the representation for which no compensation would be paid.

Furthermore, a focus on the enhanced hourly rate proposed by the circuit court overlooks the cost to Mr. Hagopian of the preclusion of other employment caused by the involuntary appointment. Generally speaking, payment at a below-market hourly rate for the defense of an indigent accused will be adequate in a routine felony prosecution. A criminal defense attorney can accept a routine case for a reduced fee and fit it into the balance of his or her practice. But the vast scope of Mr. Green's case threatened to overwhelm Mr. Hagopian's small office, requiring him to devote substantially all of his productive time to the case for an extended period. Under these circumstances, the hourly rate of $110 is inadequate because it does not replace income lost due to Mr. Hagopian's inability to handle the business of private clients who pay the market rate for his services.

When a lawyer is required to work exclusively on a single client's business for an extended period of time, work for existing clients must generally be postponed or referred to other attorneys. While the lawyer is working exclusively on one client's affairs, it is difficult-if not impossible-to accept new business. For such work on behalf of a single client performed on a "crash basis," the lawyer ought to receive a premium above his or her normal fee to compensate for the disruption to the lawyer's practice. [citations omitted]. The circumstances of the involuntary appointment of Mr. Hagopian to Mr. Green's case turn basic law office economics on its head by requiring Mr. Hagopian to work for one client on a "crash basis" at a rate substantially below the market rate for similar services.

For these reasons, Mr. Hagopian established grounds for withdrawal from further representation of Mr. Green under rule 4–6.2. The circuit court departed from the essential requirements of the law in denying Mr. Hagopian's motion to withdraw.

Before concluding, we address two matters pertinent to the limits of our decision. First, we emphasize the extraordinary nature of this case. Our decision to grant the petition and quash the circuit court's order is based on the undisputed evidence presented in the circuit court concerning the unusual complexity of the RICO prosecution against Mr.

Green and the ruinous effect the involuntary appointment will have on Mr. Hagopian's solo law practice. Our decision should not be read as granting lawyers a free pass to avoid unwanted appointments to represent indigent persons in more conventional prosecutions.

Second, we understand that our decision does not resolve the problem presented by this case. Mr. Green needs a lawyer, and he will not have the benefit of Mr. Hagopian's services. However, the only matter before us is whether the circuit court departed from the essential requirements of the law in denying Mr. Hagopian's motion to withdraw. We hold that it did, and we grant Mr. Hagopian's petition for writ of certiorari.

Unfortunately, no member of the criminal defense bar has volunteered to represent Mr. Green in the circuit court. At the conclusion of the hearing in the court below, the circuit judge remarked on the difficulties he had encountered in finding counsel for Mr. Green and expressed his hope that Mr. Green would soon have a lawyer. We appreciate the substantial efforts the circuit judge has made in this regard, and we share the concern he has expressed about finding counsel for Mr. Green.

VIII. CONCLUSION

For the reasons stated above, we grant the petition and quash the circuit court's order denying Mr. Hagopian's motion to withdraw.

* * *

Profile of attorney professionalism. Bill Colby was a young attorney when he accepted a pro bono case that would change the law, his clients' lives, and his own life.

It was 1987 when a partner in Bill Colby's law firm asked him to consider representing the Cruzan family in a dispute with the state of Missouri. In 1983, the Cruzans' daughter, Nancy, had been in a car accident that left her in a coma. Shortly after the accident and before anyone understood the extent of Nancy's injuries, the Cruzans agreed to a medical procedure to insert a feeding tube. Later, doctors determined that Nancy had no hope of recovery and diagnosed her condition as a "persistent vegetative state."

Once they understood that Nancy would never recover, the family asked for the feeding tube to be removed. The family agonized over the decision, but felt certain it would be Nancy's wish. The state-run hospital refused to remove Nancy's feeding tube without a court order. Unable to afford a lawyer, the Cruzans searched for an attorney willing to handle the case free of charge.

When he agreed to accept the case, Bill Colby expected he would be handling a one-day trial in probate court in southwestern Missouri.

Instead, for four years, he represented the Cruzan family in numerous courts, including the U.S. Supreme Court.

In his book *Long Goodbye: The Deaths of Nancy Cruzan*, Bill Colby tells the story of the Cruzan family's case. He describes the long hours he worked on the case, the weight of being at the center of politically charged litigation, and the professional and personal relationship he developed with the Cruzan family. Though he was not paid for his work, Bill Colby grew as a lawyer during the case, shaped the law concerning a patient's right to die in the United States, and zealously represented the Cruzan family.

William H. Colby, *Long Goodbye: The Deaths of Nancy Cruzan* (2002).

PART 2

ATTRACTING CLIENTS

■ ■ ■

Lawyers need clients. People who need legal services need lawyers. In the most general terms, the issue considered in this part is how prospective clients and lawyers get together. This process occurs in what may generally be called the market for legal services, or, more accurately, in a variety of markets through which lawyers and clients meet and eventually establish an attorney-client relationship. More particularly, however, the three chapters in this part will focus on the law governing the conduct of lawyers who are participating in these markets.

To provide a context for the material to follow, let us first try to picture what we will call the primary market for legal services. On the supply side will be America's lawyers, many of whom are associated with other lawyers in law firms. On the demand side will be those individuals who may need legal services for themselves or for organizations of which they are an owner or employee. Some, but by no means all, of these individuals will have the money or the access to the money needed to pay for the legal services.

Most of the law governing lawyers that regulates lawyer conduct in the market for legal services relates to lawyer conduct in the primary market for legal services in which lawyers, acting individually or in cooperation with other lawyers with whom they have associated in a law firm, seek to attract a sufficient number of fee-paying clients as will enable them to earn their livelihood as a practicing lawyer. We will examine this law in Chapter 7 (Advertising) and Chapter 8 (Solicitation).

Upon your graduation from law school and admission to the bar, some of you will have to or will choose to seek your clients in the primary market for legal services. This will be true if you hang out your own shingle as a sole practitioner or form a law firm with another new lawyer. Such new lawyers will need to let it be known that they are interested and capable of providing legal services to those in need and to encourage prospective clients to talk with them rather than some other lawyer. This, however, is the exception rather than the rule. Most new lawyers will gain access to their first clients by participating in what we will call the secondary market for lawyers—a market in which the demand side of the market to some extent consists of lawyers who have more clients than they can handle and want to hire lawyers to help them serve those clients and others they expect to be able to attract in the primary market for legal services. Because this is how most of you will get your first clients—by way of an assignment from a lawyer in a law firm which you have joined as a salaried employee—we treat associating with a law firm as one of the means lawyers use to gain access to clients. Thus, before we look at the law governing lawyers in the primary market for legal service, Chapter 6 takes a look at the law governing lawyers as relates to your quest for and employment as a lawyer in one of America's many law firms and your professional and legal status as an employee of a law firm.

CHAPTER 6

ASSOCIATING WITH LAW FIRMS

■ ■ ■

Chapter hypothetical. Associates in the law firm of Palsgraf & Pennoyer are typically eligible for partnership after eight years. The firm employs a two-tiered partnership track. An associate must spend at least one year as a non-equity partner before becoming eligible to become an equity partner. Non-equity partners are not required to bring in new clients, are not required to "buy in" as partners, and have limited voting rights with respect to firm decision making. Non-equity partners do not share in the firm profits and instead receive a salary with the potential for bonuses based on performance and the firm's profitability. The firm's publications do not draw any distinction between equity and non-equity partners and most clients do not know whether a lawyer is an equity or non-equity partner. Doreen has been a non-equity partner in Palsgraf & Pennoyer for nine months. Robert is an equity partner and the leader of the firm's litigation section. Ken is another equity partner in the litigation section. Phillip is an associate in the litigation section who is assigned most of his work by Ken.

* * *

Most of you, either prior to or shortly after graduation from law school, will make arrangements to become salaried lawyer-employees of a law firm, a corporate or governmental legal department, a legal services organization, or a district attorney's office. The Model Rules of Professional Conduct treat each of these organizations as "firms" for purposes of the Rules. Model Rule 1.0(c), Comment [3]. This is how you will gain access to your first clients—performing tasks for a client at the instruction and subject to the supervision of a more experienced lawyer. Thus, in this Chapter, we take a look at some of the law governing lawyer conduct in the job market for new lawyers. Also, because most of you will begin your career as a salaried employee, we want to alert you to some of the law governing lawyers of special importance to you as you begin your legal career. One of the most common complaints of newer lawyers is that they are not provided adequate training, supervision, or mentoring from their employers. Therefore, this Chapter focuses on the responsibilities of "subordinate lawyers" and those who supervise them. Finally, given the great increase in what the legal profession refers to as "lateral mobility" of lawyers between law firms, and the reality that many new lawyers will be asked to make such a move in the early years of their career, we also look at the law governing lawyers that applies when you decide to leave your law firm and hang out your own shingle or join another law firm.

* * *

A. HIRING AND ADVANCEMENT IN LAW FIRMS

Problem 6.1. Doreen is frustrated because Robert recently chose two male non-equity partners to assist him in a high-profile case. This has been a recurring problem for Doreen as she feels like most of the choice assignments are given to male colleagues. Doreen (who recently became engaged) recently expressed her frustration with Robert, but Robert has told her "not to worry your pretty little head over it since I figure you'll be quitting this firm soon enough to go be a full-time mother." You started work at the firm at the same time as Doreen, so she comes to you for advice.

* * *

New York Code of Professional Responsibility
DR 1–102 Misconduct

A. A lawyer or law firm shall not . . . (6) Unlawfully discriminate in the practice of law, including in hiring, promoting or otherwise determining conditions of employment, on the basis of age, race, creed, color, national origin, sex, disability, marital status, or sexual orientation. Where there is a tribunal with jurisdiction to hear a complaint, if timely brought, other than a Departmental Disciplinary Committee, a complaint based on unlawful discrimination shall be brought before such tribunal in the first instance. A certified copy of a determination by such a tribunal, which has become final and enforceable, and as to which the right to judicial or appellate review has been exhausted, finding that the lawyer has engaged in an unlawful discriminatory practice shall constitute *prima facie* evidence of professional misconduct in a disciplinary proceeding.

* * *

Vermont Rules of Professional Conduct
RULE 8.4 MISCONDUCT

It is professional misconduct for a lawyer to . . . (g) discriminate against any individual because of his or her race, color, religion, ancestry, national origin, sex, sexual orientation, place of birth or age, or against a qualified handicapped individual, in hiring, promoting or otherwise determining the conditions of employment of that individual; . . .

* * *

Please read ABA Model Rules of Professional Conduct, Rule 8.4(d) and Comment [3].

* * *

What do you think? Which of these three provisions do you prefer? If a lawyer engages in race or sex discrimination in hiring, has that lawyer engaged in "conduct that is prejudicial to the administration of justice" under Model Rule 8.4(d)?

* * *

HISHON V. KING & SPALDING
467 U.S. 69 (1984)

CHIEF JUSTICE BURGER delivered the opinion of the Court.

We granted certiorari to determine whether the District Court properly dismissed a Title VII complaint alleging that a law partnership discriminated against petitioner, a woman lawyer employed as an associate, when it failed to invite her to become a partner.

I

A

In 1972 petitioner Elizabeth Anderson Hishon accepted a position as an associate with respondent, a large Atlanta law firm established as a general partnership. When this suit was filed in 1980, the firm had more than 50 partners and employed approximately 50 attorneys as associates. Up to that time, no woman had ever served as a partner at the firm.

Petitioner alleges that the prospect of partnership was an important factor in her initial decision to accept employment with respondent. She alleges that respondent used the possibility of ultimate partnership as a recruiting device to induce petitioner and other young lawyers to become associates at the firm. According to the complaint, respondent represented that advancement to partnership after five or six years was "a matter of course" for associates "who receive[d] satisfactory evaluations" and that associates were promoted to partnership "on a fair and equal basis." Petitioner alleges that she relied on these representations when she accepted employment with respondent. The complaint further alleges that respondent's promise to consider her on a "fair and equal basis" created a binding employment contract.

In May 1978 the partnership considered and rejected Hishon for admission to the partnership; one year later, the partners again declined to invite her to become a partner. Once an associate is passed over for partnership at respondent's firm, the associate is notified to begin seeking employment elsewhere. Petitioner's employment as an associate terminated on December 31, 1979.

B

Hishon filed a charge with the Equal Employment Opportunity Commission on November 19, 1979, claiming that respondent had discriminated against her on the basis of her sex in violation of Title VII of the Civil Rights Act of 1964. . . . Ten days later the Commission issued a notice of right to sue, and on February 27, 1980, Hishon brought this action in the United States District Court for the Northern District of Georgia. She sought declaratory and injunctive relief, backpay, and compensatory damages "in lieu of reinstatement and promotion to partnership." This, of course, negates any claim for specific performance of the contract alleged.

The District Court dismissed the complaint on the ground that Title VII was inapplicable to the selection of partners by a partnership. A divided panel of the United States Court of Appeals for the Eleventh Circuit affirmed. We granted certiorari . . . and we reverse.

II

The issue before us is whether petitioner's allegations state a claim under Title VII, the relevant portion of which provides as follows:

"(a) It shall be an unlawful employment practice for an employer—

"(1) to fail or refuse to hire or to discharge any individual, or otherwise to discriminate against any individual with respect to his compensation, terms, conditions, or privileges of employment, because of such individual's race, color, religion, sex, or national origin." . . .

A

Petitioner alleges that respondent is an "employer" to whom Title VII is addressed. She then asserts that consideration for partnership was one of the "terms, conditions, or privileges of employment" as an associate with respondent.

Once a contractual relationship of employment is established, the provisions of Title VII attach and govern certain aspects of that relationship. In the context of Title VII, the contract of employment may be written or oral, formal or informal; an informal contract of employment may arise by the simple act of handing a job applicant a shovel and providing a workplace. The contractual relationship of employment triggers the provision of Title VII governing "terms, conditions, or privileges of employment." Title VII in turn forbids discrimination on the basis of "race, color, religion, sex, or national origin."

Because the underlying employment relationship is contractual, it follows that the "terms, conditions, or privileges of employment" clearly include benefits that are part of an employment contract. Here, petitioner in essence alleges that respondent made a contract to consider her for partnership. Indeed, this promise was allegedly a key contractual provision which induced her to accept employment. If the evidence at trial establishes that the parties contracted to have petitioner considered for partnership, that promise clearly was a term, condition, or privilege of her employment. Title VII would then bind respondent to consider petitioner for partnership as the statute provides, i.e., without regard to petitioner's sex. The contract she alleges would lead to the same result.

Petitioner's claim that a contract was made, however, is not the only allegation that would qualify respondent's consideration of petitioner for partnership as a term, condition, or privilege of employment. An employer may provide its employees with many benefits that it is under no obligation to furnish by any express or implied contract. Such a benefit, though not a contractual right of employment, may qualify as a "privileg[e]" of employment under Title VII. A benefit that is part and parcel of the employment relationship may not be doled out in a discriminatory fashion, even if the employer would be free under the employment contract simply not to provide the benefit at all. Those benefits that comprise the "incidents of employment," . . . or that form "an aspect of the relationship between the employer and employees," . . . may not be afforded in a manner contrary to Title VII.

Several allegations in petitioner's complaint would support the conclusion that the opportunity to become a partner was part and parcel of an associate's status as an employee at respondent's firm, independent of any allegation that such an opportunity was included in associates' employment contracts. Petitioner alleges that respondent's associates could regularly expect to be considered for partnership at the end of their "apprenticeships," and it appears that lawyers outside the firm were not routinely so considered. Thus, the benefit of partnership consideration was allegedly linked directly with an associate's status as an employee, and this linkage was far more than coincidental: petitioner alleges that respondent explicitly used the prospect of ultimate partnership to induce young lawyers to join the firm. Indeed, the importance of the partnership decision to a lawyer's status as an associate is underscored by the allegation that associates' employment is terminated if they are not elected to become partners. These allegations, if proved at trial, would suffice to show that partnership consideration was a term, condition, or privilege of an associate's employment at respondent's firm, and accordingly that partnership consideration must be without regard to sex.

III

We conclude that petitioner's complaint states a claim cognizable under Title VII. Petitioner therefore is entitled to her day in court to prove her allegations. The judgment of the Court of Appeals is reversed, and the case is remanded for further proceedings consistent with this opinion.

It is so ordered.

JUSTICE POWELL, concurring.

I write to make clear my understanding that the Court's opinion should not be read as extending Title VII to the management of a law firm by its partners. The reasoning of the Court's opinion does not require that the relationship among partners be characterized as an "employment" relationship to which Title VII would apply. The relationship among law partners differs markedly from that between employer and employee—including that between the partnership and its associates. The judgmental and sensitive decisions that must be made among the partners embrace a wide range of subjects. The essence of the law partnership is the common conduct of a shared enterprise. The relationship among law partners contemplates that decisions important to the partnership normally will be made by common agreement, . . . or consent among the partners. . . .

In admission decisions made by law firms, [however,] it is now widely recognized—as it should be—that in fact neither race nor sex is relevant. The qualities of mind, capacity to reason logically, ability to work under pressure, leadership, and the like are unrelated to race or sex. This is demonstrated by the success of women and minorities in law schools, in the practice of law, on the bench, and in positions of community, state, and national leadership. Law firms—and, of course, society—are the better for these changes.

* * *

Non-equity partners as "employees." In Clackamas Gastroenterology Assocs. v. Wells, 538 U.S. 440 (2003), the Supreme Court held that the fact that an individual is designated a partner or shareholder does not necessarily mean that the individual cannot be considered an "employee" for purposes of a statutory discrimination claim. Instead, the fundamental question is whether the individual is subject to the right of control by the employer. Many law firms rely on multi-tiered partnership structures in which non-equity partners sometimes lack management and decision-making authority. As a result, some law firm partners have argued (with varying degrees of success) that they were really employees for purposes of Title VII and related statutory discrimination laws. *See* EEOC v. Sidley Austin Brown & Wood,

315 F.3d 696 (7th Cir. 2002); Kirleis v. Dickie, McCamey & Chilcote, 2009 WL 3602008 (W.D. Pa., Oct. 28, 2009).

* * *

B. PRACTICING LAW AS A MEMBER OF A LAW FIRM

Problem 6.2. Ken, the partner at Palsgraf & Pennoyer, for whom Phillip does most of his work, has a problem with alcoholism. As a result, Ken has fallen behind on his caseload, so he has passed off some of his work to Phillip. Unfortunately, Phillip doesn't have any experience with the subject matter in question. He has been passing along his work product to Ken, but has never heard feedback from Ken other than the occasional two-word email stating "looks fine." Phillip is not so sure that his work product is fine. In fact, he's afraid his work is kind of shoddy. What advice do you have for Phillip?

* * *

Only a small portion of those newly admitted to the bar will begin their career as a partner in a law firm, a manager in a legal department, or as a lawyer with direct supervisory responsibilities over another lawyer. More will start as a sole practitioner, but only a portion of those will be able to hire a non-lawyer to assist them with their practice. Most new graduates will begin their professional career as what the ABA Model Rules call a "subordinate lawyer." Thus, this section focuses on the responsibilities of both supervising and subordinate lawyers. In a later chapter, we will examine more closely the special professional responsibilities imposed on lawyers who have the good fortune to become partners, managers, or supervisory lawyers.

1. PARTNERS, MANAGERS, AND SUPERVISORY LAWYERS

Please read ABA Model Rules of Professional Conduct, Rule 5.1 and Comments; and Rule 5.3 and Comments [1]–[3].

The lawyers who hire you as their employee or as an employee of the law firm with which they are associated may either be partners in the firm or possess comparable managerial authority in the firm or may have direct supervisory responsibility for your work on a matter. There may be more than one lawyer in the firm with managerial authority or supervisory responsibility for your work. Rule 5.1 of the ABA Model Rules of Professional Conduct is designed to ensure that these individuals take responsibility to promote a culture of ethical practice within the firm.

Model Rule 5.3 imposes comparable duties with respect to non-lawyers "employed or retained by or associated with a lawyer," the only difference being that Rule 5.3 refers to the non-lawyer's conduct being compatible with the professional obligations of the lawyer. This is because the Rules of Professional Conduct apply only to lawyers.

* * *

Problem 6.3. Assume that Alice is a partner at Pennoyer & Palsgraf, Bob is a senior associate at the firm, and Carol is a newer associate. Based on your reading of Rules 5.1 and 5.3 which of the following statements is most accurate?

(A) Bob has been assigned responsibility for supervising the work of Carol. Bob gave Carol instructions about how to proceed on a matter, but has not responded to any of her emails asking for clarification. Bob is not subject to discipline under Rule 5.1 since Bob is not a partner at the firm.

(B) Alice does not do any work with Carol, but knows that Carol's representation of a firm client fails to meet the level of competent representation. Alice does nothing in response, and the client suffers financial injury as a result of Carol's actions. Alice is not subject to discipline under Rule 5.1 because she did not have supervisory authority over Carol.

(C) Palsgraf & Pennoyer has no internal policies in place that would help ensure Carol is providing competent representation. The firm is subject to discipline under Rule 5.1.

(D) Alice knows that several legal assistants in the firm who work for other firm lawyers routinely engage in conduct that amounts to the unauthorized practice of law. Alice does nothing in response, since none of the legal assistants do work for Alice. Alice is subject to discipline under Rule 5.3.

* * *

2. "SUBORDINATE" LAWYERS

**Please read ABA Model Rules of Professional Conduct,
Rule 5.2 and Comments.**

* * *

DISCIPLINARY COUNSEL V. SMITH
918 N.E.2d 992 (Ohio 2009)

MOYER, C.J.

Respondent, Justin Martus Smith of Cleveland, Ohio ... was admitted to the practice of law in Ohio in 2000. The Board of

Commissioners on Grievances and Discipline recommends that we publicly reprimand respondent for his conduct in charging two clients excessive fees and representing them in legal matters for which he was not competent, while under the supervision of the owner of the law firm with which he was associated. We agree that respondent committed the misconduct found by the board and, accordingly, publicly reprimand respondent.

I. Procedural History

Relator, Disciplinary Counsel, filed a complaint against respondent, alleging violations of two Disciplinary Rules arising from respondent's conduct in helping two clients of his law firm to obtain compensation for injuries sustained in an auto accident. A panel of the board concluded that respondent had committed both violations of the Code of Professional Responsibility and recommended a public reprimand. The board adopted the panel's findings of fact, conclusions of law, and recommended sanction.

Respondent filed objections to the board's decision, arguing that the evidence did not support the findings that he had violated the Disciplinary Rules and thus that the complaint should be dismissed.

II. Misconduct

A. Factual Background

In May 2002, having been admitted to the practice of law in Ohio for two years and employed as an associate in the Chapman Law Firm, owned by Frank Chapman, respondent was assigned to the case of Louis and Florence Reiger. The Reigers were passengers in the vehicle of Marvin Seltzer and his wife when they were involved in an accident. Seltzer lost control of the car while driving on an Ohio expressway, causing it to flip into the median. Louis Reiger was seriously injured in the accident and required extensive medical treatment, hospitalization, and rehabilitation. Florence Reiger was also injured, although less seriously. She also required medical treatment and hospitalization.

After viewing the firm's advertisement in the yellow pages, the Reigers contacted the Chapman Law Firm, and respondent was assigned to the case. He visited Florence Reiger at the hospital and presented a contingent-fee agreement to her. The agreement provided for attorney fees of 33 1/3 percent of the gross amount if the case was settled without filing a lawsuit, 40 percent of the gross settlement or judgment if suit was filed, and 45 percent of the gross settlement or judgment following a trial or appeal. Respondent signed the agreement on behalf of the firm, and Florence signed on her own behalf and on behalf of her husband, Louis, as his attorney in fact. . . .

Seltzer was insured by a Geico automobile insurance policy with a $100,000-per-person limit for personal injury. He had no other assets that would allow for additional recovery. The Reigers, who were residents of New York, carried an insurance policy with State Farm Mutual Automobile Insurance Company ("State Farm") in New York. Their policy included personal-injury protection ("PIP") coverage of $175,000 per person. Under New York law, PIP coverage is no-fault insurance paid without a determination of liability. N.Y.Ins.Law 5101 et seq. PIP claims for medical and hospitalization expenses are paid directly to medical service providers. The providers may apply for the coverage themselves. Most importantly, New York law does not permit an attorney to collect a contingent fee from a client on PIP payments.

. . . Respondent testified that he possessed a general understanding of PIP coverage as no-fault insurance, but he did not research the permissibility of collecting legal fees. Respondent testified that he collected the fees because, after he questioned Chapman regarding fees on PIP recovery, Chapman instructed him to do so. Respondent stated that he did not feel that it was his responsibility to research whether fees could be collected from the PIP recovery, despite being the Reigers' attorney, because Chapman set fees for the firm.

. . . Even after one of the Reigers' children complained to respondent about the amount of the fees, Chapman told respondent that he was collecting 40 percent of the recovery. Respondent then sent a follow-up letter with greater detail to the Reigers.

A grievance was filed with the Office of Disciplinary Counsel regarding the attorney fees.

. . . The Reigers later sued respondent, Frank Chapman, and the Chapman Law Firm for legal malpractice and excessive fees. The case was settled when the Chapman Law Firm agreed to disgorge the attorney fees received on the PIP coverage of $83,261.17. The Reigers also received $18,738.83 under the malpractice insurance policy held by the firm.

B. Disciplinary Rule Violations

The board found that Respondent violated DR 2–106(A) ("A lawyer shall not enter into an agreement for, charge, or collect an illegal or clearly excessive fee"). We agree. Respondent has stipulated that the fees paid by the Reigers were excessive but argues that Chapman was responsible for charging those fees.

Although Chapman was the owner of the law firm, it was respondent who acted as the Reigers' attorney. Respondent signed the contingent-fee agreement, he filed suit on the Reigers' behalf, he submitted PIP claims on their behalf, he was the only attorney for the law firm that had any contact with them, and he prepared the disbursement sheets detailing their recovery and attorney fees.

It is undisputed that the fees charged in this case were excessive. New York state law controls the State Farm insurance policies held by the Reigers. New York law prohibits the collecting of a contingent fee from a client on PIP coverage. Respondent and the Chapman Law Firm were thus prevented by law from collecting fees based on the PIP recovery that their clients received. Despite this, . . . respondent collected 40 percent of the funds for his fees. He did so by reducing the disbursement that the Reigers should have received from the Geico liability coverage.

Respondent argues that he cannot be disciplined for his actions because Chapman had control of the fees and the firm's checkbook. Even though Chapman was his superior, respondent has a responsibility to his clients. Respondent's counsel stated at oral argument that respondent prepared the disbursement sheets as a scribe would, following the dictates of his superior. Actually, respondent is not a scribe but an attorney, responsible for zealously representing his clients' interests. We have stated previously that "new lawyers are just as accountable as more seasoned professionals for not complying with the Code of Professional Responsibility." Disciplinary Counsel v. Johnson, 106 Ohio St.3d 365, 2005-Ohio-5323, 835 N.E.2d 354, ¶ 39. The same general rule applies to lawyers who are directly supervised by their superiors within a law firm. A lawyer's obligations under the ethics rules are not diminished by the instructions of a supervising attorney.

Respondent claims that if only his conduct had occurred more recently, it would have fallen within the safe harbor of recently adopted Prof.Cond.R. 5.2. This assumption is incorrect. Prof.Cond.R. 5.2(a) states the general rule that "[a] lawyer is bound by the Ohio Rules of Professional Conduct notwithstanding that the lawyer acted at the direction of another person." The safe harbor appears in Prof.Cond.R. 5.2(b): "A subordinate lawyer does not violate the Ohio Rules of Professional Conduct if that lawyer acts in accordance with a supervisory lawyer's *reasonable* resolution of a question of professional duty." (Emphasis sic.)

Prof.Cond.R. 5.2(b) would not apply to the circumstances of this case regardless of its effective date. First, there was no ambiguity in the illegitimacy of the fees because New York law clearly prohibits the collection of a contingent fee from the client on PIP coverage. Second, respondent and Chapman were both insufficiently familiar with PIP coverage, and they did not properly research the question of attorney fees. Although respondent apparently posed the question to Chapman, and Chapman said he would look into it, it was unreasonable for respondent to rely on Chapman's directions under the circumstances. The nature of

PIP coverage as no-fault insurance that was to be paid directly to the Reigers' medical service providers should have alerted respondent to the issue of attorney fees. [Respondent should have sought] confirmation from Chapman that his research verified the permissibility of attorney fees, if not to research the question himself. There is no indication in the record that respondent ever followed up with Chapman after Chapman stated that he would contact another lawyer; nor did respondent verify the source of any information to which Chapman referred. Respondent even failed to take significant action after receiving complaints from the clients' family and Disciplinary Counsel. Under these circumstances, respondent was required to verify, at least minimally, the information he was given before he could reasonably rely on the instructions of his supervisor.

In addition to the unauthorized assessment of a fee against the Reigers on the PIP coverage, respondent should have recognized that the fees collected were excessive under the terms of the fee agreement. The agreement permitted a contingent fee of 40 percent only if it was necessary to file suit, while a lower fee of 33 1/3 percent was to be charged if no lawsuit was needed. Although respondent did file suit against Seltzer, and thereby recovered through Seltzer's Geico liability policy, no action was ever filed against State Farm. State Farm made payments under the Reigers' PIP coverage upon receipt of the proper forms. Even if legal fees could have been collected on the PIP recovery, the contingent-fee agreement permitted respondent to collect only 33 1/3 percent of the recovery, rather than the 40 percent he did collect. Since respondent signed the agreement on behalf of the law firm and prepared the disbursement sheets, there would be no reasonable basis for him to rely on Chapman for these purposes.

The board also found that respondent violated DR 6–101(A)(1) ("A lawyer shall not * * * [h]andle a legal matter which he knows or should know that he is not competent to handle, without associating with him a lawyer who is competent to handle it"). We agree. Respondent testified that he had a general understanding of PIP coverage but was unaware that he could not collect fees from the client. Respondent did not research the issue of attorney fees for helping a client obtain PIP benefits or associate with a lawyer who was familiar with PIP. He deferred to Chapman's statement that Chapman would speak to another lawyer, but at no time did respondent have any contact with outside counsel or even verify that Chapman had done so.

III. Sanction

The proper sanction for violations of the Disciplinary Rules is determined after consideration of "the duties violated, respondent's mental state, the injury caused, the existence of aggravating or mitigating circumstances, and applicable precedent." Disciplinary Counsel v. Evans (2000), 89 Ohio St.3d 497, 501, 733 N.E.2d 609.

[The court adopted the board's recommended sanction of a public reprimand.]

* * *

The interplay between Rules 5.1 and 5.2. Model Rules 5.1 and 5.2 envision a situation in which law firm partners and those with comparable authority will establish "ethical infrastructures" that will, among other things, help subordinate lawyers resolve any ethical dilemmas they may come across. Ted Schneyer, *Professional Discipline for Law Firms?*, 77 CORNELL L. REV. 1, 10 (1991) (stating that "a law firm's organization, policies, and operating procedures constitute an 'ethical infrastructure' "); Model Rule 5.1, Comment [3] ("Some firms, for example, have a procedure whereby junior lawyers can make confidential referrals of ethical problems directly to a designated senior partner or special committee."). At a minimum, Rule 5.2(b) contemplates that a subordinate lawyer facing an "arguable question of professional duty" may seek the guidance of a supervising lawyer for a "reasonable resolution" of the matter. Of course sometimes subordinate lawyers are left to sink or swim without much help from supervising lawyers. However, this does not excuse the subordinate's violation of the rules.

As Rule 5.2(a) makes clear, a subordinate may not follow clearly unethical orders. In theory, Rule 5.2(b) provides a limited defense for a subordinate lawyer who acts in accordance with a supervisor's reasonable resolution of an arguable question of professional duty. However, there are few reported decisions in which subordinate attorneys have successfully asserted Rule 5.2(b)'s "defense." *See, e.g.,* In re Kelley's Case, 627 A.2d 597, 600 (N.H. 1993) (rejecting associate's Rule 5.2(b) defense in conflict of interest case because "there could have been no 'reasonable' resolution of an 'arguable' question of duty"); *see also* Douglas R. Richmond, *Professional Responsibilities of Law Firm Associates* 199 (2007) (detailing cases).

Rule 5.2 and social psychology. Professor Andrew Perlman has suggested that Rule 5.2(b) is contrary to human nature. Using advanced social psychology, he argues that as a result of Rule 5.2(b), subordinate lawyers are in an opportune situation to ignore their own reasoned analysis and accept the instruction of a superior attorney. Factors such as hierarchal pressure and superior experience of a senior attorney, the threat of losing a job if instructions are not followed, and the mantra of "zealous representation" on behalf of clients all encourage (or at least justify) a subordinate lawyer to follow a questionable course of action while finding shelter under the veil of Rule 5.2(b).

Professor Perlman suggests that Rule 5.2(b) should be repealed and instead used only as a mitigating factor if a subordinate attorney has a disciplinary action brought against her. Furthermore, Perlman believes that the goals and purpose of Rule 5.2(b) would be better satisfied by granting whistleblower protection to attorneys and increasing the frequency and aggressiveness of actions against attorneys for failing to report another attorney as stated in Rule 8.3(a). Under this scheme, a subordinate attorney would be more likely to conduct her own research on "questionable" ethical issues, and the scheme would encourage that subordinate lawyer to report the senior attorney rather than mindlessly following instructions. Andrew M. Perlman, *Unethical Obedience by Subordinate Attorneys: Lessons from Social Psychology*, 36 HOFSTRA L. REV. 451 (2007).

* * *

C. LEAVING THE FIRM

1. WRONGFUL DISCHARGE OR EXPULSION

Problem 6.4. Phillip knows of several instances in which Ken's problems with alcohol have resulted in harm to a client. He is also aware of several instances of serious misconduct on the part of Ken, which Phillip believes raise a substantial question as to Ken's fitness to practice law. He is trying to decide what he should do. What advice do you have for him?

* * *

WIEDER V. SKALA
609 N.E.2d 105 (N.Y. 1992)

HANCOCK, JUDGE.

Plaintiff, a member of the Bar, has sued his former employer, a law firm. He claims he was wrongfully discharged as an associate because of his insistence that the firm comply with the governing disciplinary rules by reporting professional misconduct allegedly committed by another associate. The question presented is whether plaintiff has stated a claim for relief either for breach of contract or for the tort of wrongful discharge in violation of this State's public policy. The lower courts have dismissed both causes of action on motion as legally insufficient . . . on the strength of New York's employment-at-will doctrine. For reasons which follow, we modify the order and reinstate plaintiff's cause of action for breach of contract.

I.

In the complaint, which must be accepted as true on a dismissal motion . . . , plaintiff alleges that he was a commercial litigation attorney associated with defendant law firm from June 16, 1986 until March 18, 1988. In early 1987, plaintiff requested that the law firm represent him in the purchase of a condominium apartment. The firm agreed and assigned a fellow associate (L.L.) "to do 'everything that needs to be done' ". For several months, L.L. neglected plaintiff's real estate transaction and, to conceal his neglect, made several "false and fraudulent material misrepresentations". In September 1987, when plaintiff learned of L.L.'s neglect and false statements, he advised two of the firm's senior partners. They conceded that the firm was aware "that [L.L.] was a pathological liar and that [L.L.] had previously lied to [members of the firm] regarding the status of other pending legal matters". When plaintiff confronted L.L., he acknowledged that he had lied about the real estate transaction and later admitted in writing that he had committed "several acts of legal malpractice and fraud and deceit upon plaintiff and several other clients of the firm".

The complaint further alleges that, after plaintiff asked the firm partners to report L.L.'s misconduct to the Appellate Division Disciplinary Committee as required under DR 1–103(A) of the Code of Professional Responsibility, they declined to act. Later, in an effort to dissuade plaintiff from making the report himself, the partners told him that they would reimburse his losses. Plaintiff nonetheless met with the Committee "to discuss the entire matter". He withdrew his complaint, however, "because the [f]irm had indicated that it would fire plaintiff if he reported [L.L.'s] misconduct". Ultimately, in December 1987—as a result of plaintiff's insistence—the firm made a report concerning L.L.'s "numerous misrepresentations and [acts of] malpractice against clients of the [f]irm and acts of forgery of checks drawn on the [f]irm's account". Thereafter, two partners "continuously berated plaintiff for having caused them to report [the] misconduct". The firm nevertheless continued to employ plaintiff "because he was in charge of handling the most important litigation in the [f]irm". Plaintiff was fired in March 1988, a few days after he filed motion papers in that important case.

Plaintiff asserts that defendants wrongfully discharged him as a result of his insistence that L.L.'s misconduct be reported as required by DR 1–103(A). In his fourth cause of action, he alleges that the firm's termination constituted a breach of the employment relationship. In the fifth cause of action, he claims that his discharge was in violation of public policy and constituted a tort for which he seeks compensatory and punitive damages.

Defendants moved to dismiss the fourth and fifth causes of action as legally insufficient pursuant to CPLR 3211(a)(7). Supreme Court granted defendants' motion because his employment relationship was at will. . . .

The Appellate Division affirmed. . . . It also concluded that plaintiff failed to state a cause of action because, as an at-will employee, the firm could terminate him without cause. This Court granted leave to appeal.

II.

We discuss first whether, notwithstanding our firmly established employment-at-will doctrine, plaintiff has stated a legal claim for breach of contract in the fourth cause of action. The answer requires a review of the three cases in which that doctrine is fully explained.

The employment-at-will doctrine is a judicially created common-law rule "that where an employment is for an indefinite term it is presumed to be a hiring at will which may be freely terminated by either party at any time for any reason or even for no reason". . . . In *Murphy*, this Court dismissed the claim of an employee who alleged he had been discharged in bad faith in retaliation for his disclosure of accounting improprieties. In so doing, we expressly declined to follow other jurisdictions in adopting the tort-based abusive discharge cause of action for imposing "liability on employers where employees have been discharged for disclosing illegal activities on the part of their employers", being of the view 'that such a significant change in our law is best left to the Legislature". . . .

With respect to the contract cause of action asserted in *Murphy*, the Court held that plaintiff had not shown evidence of any express agreement limiting the employer's unfettered right to fire the employee. For this reason, the Court distinguished *Weiner v. McGraw-Hill, Inc* . . . where such an express limitation had been found in language in the employer's personnel handbook. Finally, in *Murphy*, the Court rejected the argument that plaintiff's discharge for disclosing improprieties violated a legally implied obligation in the employment contract requiring the employer to deal fairly and in good faith with the employee. . . .

Four years after *Murphy*, the Court decided Sabetay v. Sterling Drug, 506 N.E.2d 919 (N.Y. 1987). There, the Court dismissed the complaint of an employee who claimed he was fired for "blowing the whistle" and refusing to engage in improper and unethical activities. As in *Murphy*, the Court found no basis for an express limitation on the employer's right to discharge an at-will employee and, adhering to *Murphy* as a precedent, declined to base any such limitation on an implied-in-law obligation of dealing fairly and in good faith with its employee.

Not surprisingly, defendants' position here with respect to plaintiff's breach of contract cause of action is simple and direct, i.e., that: (1) as in

Murphy and *Sabetay,* plaintiff has shown no factual basis for an express limitation on the right to terminate of the type upheld in *Weiner;* and (2) *Murphy* and *Sabetay* rule out any basis for contractual relief under an obligation implied-in-law. We agree that plaintiff's complaint does not contain allegations that could come within the *Weiner* exception for express contractual limitations. . . . As to an implied-in-law duty, however, a different analysis and other considerations pertain. . . .

As plaintiff points out, his employment as a lawyer to render professional services as an associate with a law firm differs in several respects from the employments in *Murphy* and *Sabetay.* The plaintiffs in those cases were in the financial departments of their employers, both large companies. Although they performed accounting services, they did so in furtherance of their primary line responsibilities as part of corporate management. In contrast, plaintiff's performance of professional services for the firm's clients as a duly admitted member of the Bar was at the very core and, indeed, the only purpose of his association with defendants. Associates are, to be sure, employees of the firm but they remain independent officers of the court responsible in a broader public sense for their professional obligations. Practically speaking, plaintiff's duties and responsibilities as a lawyer and as an associate of the firm were so closely linked as to be incapable of separation. It is in this distinctive relationship between a law firm and a lawyer hired as an associate that plaintiff finds the implied-in-law obligation on which he founds his claim.

We agree with plaintiff that in any hiring of an attorney as an associate to practice law with a firm there is implied an understanding so fundamental to the relationship and essential to its purpose as to require no expression: that both the associate and the firm in conducting the practice will do so in accordance with the ethical standards of the profession. Erecting or countenancing disincentives to compliance with the applicable rules of professional conduct, plaintiff contends, would subvert the central professional purpose of his relationship with the firm—the lawful and ethical practice of law.

The particular rule of professional conduct implicated here (DR 1–103[A]), it must be noted, is critical to the unique function of self-regulation belonging to the legal profession. . . . To assure that the legal profession fulfills its responsibility of self-regulation, DR 1–103(A) places upon each lawyer and Judge the duty to report to the Disciplinary Committee of the Appellate Division any potential violations of the Disciplinary Rules that raise a "substantial question as to another lawyer's honesty, trustworthiness or fitness in other respects". Indeed, one commentator has noted that, "[t]he reporting requirement is nothing less than essential to the survival of the profession". . . .

Moreover, as plaintiff points out, failure to comply with the reporting requirement may result in suspension or disbarment. . . . Thus, by insisting that plaintiff disregard DR 1–103(A) defendants were not only making it impossible for plaintiff to fulfill his professional obligations but placing him in the position of having to choose between continued employment and his own potential suspension and disbarment. We agree with plaintiff that these unique characteristics of the legal profession in respect to this core Disciplinary Rule make the relationship of an associate to a law firm employer intrinsically different from that of the financial managers to the corporate employers in *Murphy* and *Sabetay*. The critical question is whether this distinction calls for a different rule regarding the implied obligation of good faith and fair dealing from that applied in *Murphy* and *Sabetay*. We believe that it does in this case, but we, by no means, suggest that each provision of the Code of Professional Responsibility should be deemed incorporated as an implied-in-law term in every contractual relationship between or among lawyers.

It is the law that in "every contract there is an implied undertaking on the part of each party that he will not intentionally and purposely do anything to prevent the other party from carrying out the agreement on his part". . . . The idea is simply that when A and B agree that B will do something it is understood that A will not prevent B from doing it. The concept is rooted in notions of common sense and fairness. . . .

Just such fundamental understanding, though unexpressed, was inherent in the relationship between plaintiff and defendant law firm. . . . Defendants, a firm of lawyers, hired plaintiff to practice law and this objective was the only basis for the employment relationship. Intrinsic to this relationship, of course, was the unstated but essential compact that in conducting the firm's legal practice both plaintiff and the firm would do so in compliance with the prevailing rules of conduct and ethical standards of the profession. Insisting that as an associate in their employ plaintiff must act unethically and in violation of one of the primary professional rules amounted to nothing less than a frustration of the only legitimate purpose of the employment relationship.

From the foregoing, it is evident that both *Murphy* and *Sabetay* are markedly different. The defendants in those cases were large manufacturing concerns—not law firms engaged with their employee in a common professional enterprise, as here. In neither *Murphy* nor *Sabetay* was the plaintiff required to act in a way that subverted the core purpose of the employment. . . . Thus, the case is distinguishable from *Murphy* and *Sabetay* where giving effect to the implied obligation would have been "inconsistent with" and "destructive of" an elemental term in the agreement. . . . We conclude, therefore, that plaintiff has stated a valid claim for breach of contract based on an implied-in-law obligation in his relationship with defendants.

III.

Plaintiff argues, moreover, . . . that the dictates of public policy in DR 1–103(A) have such force as to warrant our recognition of the tort of abusive discharge pleaded in the fifth cause of action. While the arguments are persuasive and the circumstances here compelling, we have consistently held that "significant alteration of employment relationships, such as the plaintiff urges, is best left to the Legislature". . . .

Accordingly, the judgment appealed from and the order of the Appellate Division brought up for review should be modified, with costs to plaintiff, by denying defendant's motion to dismiss the fourth cause of action and, as so modified, affirmed.

* * *

Wrongful discharge claims. *Wieder* refused to recognize the tort theory of wrongful or retaliatory discharge in violation of public policy. However, most courts have recognized some form of the tort. The theory is based on the notion that employer discretion must be limited to the extent that a firing threatens clear and substantial public policy. The tort "seeks to achieve a proper balance . . . among the employer's interest in operating a business efficiently and profitably, the employee's interest in earning a livelihood, and society's interest in seeing its public policies carried out." Balla v. Gambro, Inc., 584 N.E.2d 104 (Ill. 1991). Lawyers have sometimes brought such claims against their employers. Results have been mixed.

In Jacobson v. Knepper & Moga, P.C., 706 N.E.2d 491 (Ill. 1998), an associate brought a wrongful discharge claim, alleging he was fired in retaliation for reporting to a partner in the firm the fact that the firm was engaged in collection practices in violation of a statute. The Illinois Supreme Court held that the wrongful discharge theory, while available to other employees, is not available to lawyers. The court noted that the associate was already ethically obligated to report the misconduct to disciplinary authorities. "Therefore, the attorney's ethical obligations serve to adequately protect the public policy established by the collection statutes. Because sufficient safeguards exist in this situation, it is unnecessary to expand the limited and narrow tort of retaliatory discharge to the employee attorney." *Id.* at 493; *see also* Weiss v. Lonnquist, 293 P.3d 1264 (Wash. Ct. App. 2013) (concluding that the bar disciplinary process provides an adequate means of promoting the public policy in favor of candor to the tribunal and therefore dismissing attorney's wrongful discharge claim).

Other lawyers who claim to have been fired for reporting or threatening to report another lawyer's misconduct have enjoyed greater success with their wrongful discharge claims. *See* Crews v. Buckman Labs. Int'l, Inc., 78 S.W.3d 852 (Tenn. 2002) (permitting claim by in-house counsel); Matzkin v. Delaney, Zemetis, Donahue, Durham & Noonan, PC, No. CV044000288S, 2005 WL 2009277 (Conn. Super. Ct. July 19, 2005) (denying employer's motion to strike where lawyer was fired after insisting he was ethically obligated to report misconduct).

What do you think? Should a lawyer discharged under circumstances as in *Wieder* have a cause of action? If so, should it be recognized under a contract or tort theory? *See* Alex B. Long, *Retaliatory Discharge and the Ethical Rules Governing Attorneys*, 79 UNIVERSITY OF COLO. L. REV. 1045 (2008) (discussing benefits and drawbacks of both approaches).

Ethical constraints on firing whistleblowers. Currently, the Model Rules do not specifically address an employer's ability to fire an employee who raises concerns about possible professional misconduct. Is discharging a lawyer because of their good faith insistence on compliance with the rules of professional conduct "conduct prejudicial to the administration of justice" within the meaning of ABA Model Rule 8.4(d)? Should there be a rule of professional conduct that specifically prohibits such a wrongful discharge of a lawyer by a law firm? Should the profession go one step further and also prohibit lawyers from assisting a client who wrongfully discharges a lawyer-employee because the lawyer insisted on complying with the rules of professional conduct? *See e.g.,* Carl A. Pierce, *Client Misconduct in the 21st Century*, 35 U. MEM. L. REV. 731, 903–905 (2005) (calling more generally for a prohibition against a lawyer assisting a client in conduct the lawyer knows will "subject the client to civil liability for wrongful discharge of an employee in contravention of public policy as declared by statute, administrative regulation, or the state's highest court"); *see also* Alex B. Long, *Whistleblowing Attorneys and Ethical Infrastructures*, 68 MARYLAND L. REV. 786 (2009) (discussing this and other possible rules-based approaches to the problem).

Encouraging (or requiring) internal whistleblowing. Model Rule 8.3(a) imposes a duty to report serious misconduct to disciplinary authorities. Should there be a corresponding duty to first report serious misconduct to supervising attorneys *within* a law firm? According to a 2008 law review article, the law firm of Hinshaw & Culbertson required all lawyers in the firm to report misconduct to the firm's general counsel or the appropriate practice group or department head. Anthony E. Davis, *Legal Ethics and Risk Management: Complementary Visions of Lawyer Regulation*, 21 GEO. J. LEGAL ETHICS 95 (2008). The firm's employee handbook explained that all lawyers and non-lawyers in the firm are required to report (among other things) "any question or concern about the application of professional ethics rules to any client matter or to any other issue related to the operation of the Firm"; "any known or suspected violation of an applicable ethics rule"; "any verbal or written complaint of a client concerning fees or the handling of a matter not immediately resolved to the client's satisfaction accompanied by any express or implied threat that the client may file a disciplinary complaint or take legal action against the Firm or one or more of its attorneys"; "any known or suspected action or inaction which may lead to a claim of malpractice against the Firm or its attorneys"; and "any known or suspected instance of alcohol or other substance abuse." If you were a new associate in the firm and you knew of a firm partner who had engaged in one of these actions, would you report to the appropriate person? If you did so and were fired, would you have any kind of legal claim against the firm? Should you?

* * *

2. LATERAL MOVES

Please read Restatement (Third) of the Law Governing Lawyers § 9.

* * *

GRAUBARD MOLLEN DANNETT & HOROWITZ V. MOSKOVITZ
653 N.E.2d 1179 (N.Y. 1995)

KAYE, CHIEF JUDGE.

This appeal focuses on a modern-day law firm fixture: the revolving door. With charges of faithless deserting partners and countercharges of a vindictive abandoned firm, the key question becomes whether departing partners can "solicit" clients of the firm. Here we decide only that plaintiff law firm's allegations of breach of fiduciary duty, breach of contract and fraud are sufficient to withstand summary dismissal, which was the conclusion also reached by the trial court and Appellate Division.

The following factual account is drawn largely from the assertions of plaintiff law firm, the nonmovant, and denied in material part by defendants. As alleged in the amended complaint, defendant-appellant Irving Moskovitz, along with Seymour Graubard, in 1949 founded plaintiff law firm. Over the next 40 years, the firm grew to 35 lawyers, with four senior partners—Graubard, Moskovitz, Raymond Horowitz and Emmanuel Dannett. Defendant Peter Schiller joined the firm in 1949 and became a partner in 1956; defendant John Young arrived in 1964 and became a partner in 1971. Control of the firm, however, was centered in the four seniors (who initiated most of the business), especially Moskovitz, the firm's managing partner for 33 years, until 1982.

In 1959, Moskovitz brought into the firm as a client F. Hoffman LaRoche & Co., Ltd. and affiliates (Roche), a worldwide pharmaceutical group headquartered in Switzerland. Legal services for Roche were mainly in the area of international taxation, Moskovitz's specialty, although the firm also handled corporate and litigation matters for the client. In the late 1980s, billings to Roche exceeded $1 million per year.

Concerned with developing a plan both for transition of management to the junior partners and for retirement of the seniors, the firm in 1981 retained an outside consultant and in 1982 adopted a "Phasing Out and Retirement Program." . . .

At the time the agreement was presented, according to plaintiff, Moskovitz additionally assured the junior partners that the seniors would do all they could to secure the firm's future and to institutionalize clients, particularly key clients, by integrating them with other partners in the firm. Some time after the agreement was approved in April 1982, however, Moskovitz approached Graubard and suggested starting a new partnership with Horowitz, a proposal Graubard rejected. Soon thereafter, the firm signed a $1.5 million lease on new office space and moved into its new quarters.

At the end of the three-year phase-down, having received back his capital as well as compensation exceeding that provided in the retirement agreement, Moskovitz—then 73 years old—became "of counsel" to the firm. However, he soon became unhappy with the law firm and contacted legal search consultants (Alan Roberts & Associates) regarding a possible move, with his tax partners Schiller and Young, to another law firm. Moskovitz told Roberts that his client Roche would accompany him if it approved the new firm. On November 30, 1987 Roberts put Moskovitz in touch with LeBoeuf Lamb Leiby & MacCrae, a New York based firm, and a four-month negotiation ensued, culminating on April 29, 1988 in defendants' announced resignation from plaintiff law firm to join LeBoeuf.

According to plaintiff, LeBoeuf would not finalize any arrangement with defendants unless Roche approved the transfer of its business. Moskovitz likewise wanted to ensure that he would continue to represent Roche if he moved to LeBoeuf. In March 1988 Moskovitz asked Roche's tax director whether the company had any objection to representation by LeBoeuf if he were to move there. Defendants' meetings with Roche and with LeBoeuf became nearly contemporaneous: on March 4, defendants met with LeBoeuf partners at the Metropolitan Club and later that same week, Moskovitz met with Roche's domestic general counsel. On at least one occasion, in April 1988, Moskovitz arranged for the head of LeBoeuf's tax department to meet with Roche's general counsel. Furthermore, plaintiff firm was engaged in settlement negotiations of a tax audit matter for Roche from late 1987 and continuing into the first quarter 1988 with potentially serious financial consequences. Moskovitz asked for and received assurances from a Roche executive that he would continue to handle the matter if he joined LeBoeuf.

Defendants had planned to remain at the firm for two months beyond their announced resignation, continuing to draw their compensation, but one week later—on May 6—the firm locked them out of their offices and sued them for fraud, breach of fiduciary duty, breach of contract and unjust enrichment, seeking damages exceeding $10 million based upon lost revenues of the Roche account and $30 million in punitive damages. Defendants, consequently, began their association with LeBoeuf on May 9 and Roche immediately had its files transferred there.

In late 1989, defendants moved for summary judgment and plaintiff cross-moved for summary judgment on its breach of fiduciary duty claim. The court denied the motions. . . . On renewal in 1992 the trial court denied summary judgment finding that there were material questions of fact. The Appellate Division affirmed and granted leave to appeal to this Court on a certified question. Only Moskovitz appeals; plaintiff has not pursued a cross appeal from the denial of summary judgment on its breach of fiduciary duty claim.

Analysis

Breach of Fiduciary Duty

Both sides acknowledge the principle that law partners, no less than any other business or professional partners, are bound by a fiduciary duty requiring "the punctilio of an honor the most sensitive." Both sides acknowledge as well the principle that an attorney stands in a fiduciary relation to the client.

Translating principles into practice, however, presents a far greater problem.

Moskovitz insists that the venerable principle of fiduciary duty among law partners must in today's marketplace give way to the higher value of attorney responsibility to clients: keeping them informed of matters that affect them, allowing them counsel of their choice, and incident to that choice assuring unrestricted attorney mobility. He emphasizes that he had a direct, personal relationship with Roche, as its lawyer, for more than 30 years and therefore had not simply a right but actually an affirmative obligation to tell Roche, particularly in the midst of a serious tax matter he was handling for the client, that he was considering joining another law firm and ascertain whether it might have a conflict of interest there—and he did no more than that.

It is unquestionably difficult to draw hard lines defining lawyers' fiduciary duty to partners and their fiduciary duty to clients. That there may be overlap, tension, even conflict between the two spheres is underscored by the spate of literature concerning the current revolving door law firm culture. (*See generally*, Krane, *Ethical and Professional Issues Associated with Departing Attorneys*, printed in EMPLOYMENT LAW AND HUMAN RESOURCE ISSUES IN LAW FIRMS AND PROFESSIONAL PARTNERSHIPS, at 473 [1993]; Hillman, *Law Firms and their Partners: The Law and Ethics of Grabbing and Leaving*, 67 TEX L. REV. 1 [1988]; Johnson, *Solicitation of Law Firm Clients by Departing Partners and Associates: Tort, Fiduciary and Disciplinary Liability*, 50 U. PITT. L. REV. 1 [1988] . . .

One respected commentator opines that, while a departing partner's preresignation negotiations with firm clients in most businesses would probably constitute breach of the common-law obligation of loyalty to the firm, in the case of law practice, "the public policy favoring client freedom of choice in legal representation should override the firm's proprietary interest in holding its clientele" (Hazard, *Ethical Considerations in Withdrawal, Expulsion, and Retirement*, printed in WITHDRAWAL, RETIREMENT AND DISPUTES, op. cit., at 36).

We agree with the trial court and Appellate Division, however, that as a matter of principle, preresignation surreptitious "solicitation" of firm clients for a partner's personal gain—the issue posed to us—is actionable. Such conduct exceeds what is necessary to protect the important value of client freedom of choice in legal representation, and thoroughly undermines another important value—the loyalty owed partners (including law partners), which distinguishes partnerships (including law partnerships) from bazaars.

What, then, is the prohibited "solicitation"? As the trial court recognized, in classic understatement, the answer to that question is not "self-evident."

Given the procedural posture of the case before us, plainly this is not an occasion for drawing the hard lines. Factual variations can be crucial in determining whether an attorney's duties have been breached, and we cannot speculate as to what conclusions will follow from the facts yet to be found in the case before us. We can, however, set out certain broad parameters, as the trial court did.

At one end of the spectrum, where an attorney is dissatisfied with the existing association, taking steps to locate alternative space and affiliations would not violate a partner's fiduciary duties. That this may be a delicate venture, requiring confidentiality, is simple common sense and well illustrated by the eruption caused by defendants' announced resignation in the present case. As a matter of ethics, departing partners have been permitted to inform firm clients with whom they have a prior professional relationship about their impending withdrawal and new practice, and to remind the client of its freedom to retain counsel of its choice (New York County Lawyers Assn, Ethics Opn 679 [1991]; Assn of Bar of City of NY, Ethics Opn 80–65 [1982];. . . .

At the other end of the spectrum, secretly attempting to lure firm clients (even those the partner has brought into the firm and personally represented) to the new association, lying to clients about their rights with respect to the choice of counsel, lying to partners about plans to leave, and abandoning the firm on short notice (taking clients and files) would not be consistent with a partner's fiduciary duties.

Although the trial court harbored the belief that discovery would facilitate resolution of this dispute as a matter of law, and therefore invited renewal of plaintiff's cross motion for summary judgment, the volumes of depositions and affidavits have not in fact clarified the issues. With Moskovitz pointing to evidence that his preresignation conduct was nothing more than appropriate client informational service, and plaintiff law firm pointing to evidence that he was engaged in improper solicitation of Roche for his own benefit, no conclusion can be drawn at this juncture as to where on the spectrum this case falls. Plainly Moskovitz's summary judgment motion was correctly denied.

* * *

The ethics of "grabbing and leaving." ABA Model Rule 7.3, which is covered in a later chapter, addresses the solicitation of clients. Other rules of professional conduct might also apply. For example, according to ABA Formal Opinion 99–414, a departing lawyer who is responsible for the client's representation or who plays a principal role in the law firm's delivery of legal services in a current matter has an ethical duty to notify a client of the lawyer's impending departure. Although it will usually be a partner who is responsible for a client's representation, it is certainly possible that an associate could play "a principal role" in the firm's representation of the client. *See generally* Adler, Barish, Daniels, Levin & Creskoff v. Epstein, 393 A.2d 1175 (Pa. 1978) (involving associates who attempted to bring firm clients with them to new firm). According to the opinion, the duty to notify a client of the lawyer's impending departure is shared by the firm and the departing lawyer, and arises from the duty under Model Rule 1.4 to communicate with a client about matters that may affect the status of the client's matter. But there is no rule of professional conduct that speaks to the specific issue in *Graubard Mollen*. Instead, as the opinion suggests, the issue typically involves some combination of tort, fiduciary duty, and contract law principles.

The law of "grabbing and leaving." Both the ABA opinion and *Graubard Mollen* attempt to draw a line between notification of impending departure while still employed (permissible) and solicitation of clients while still employed (impermissible). Is there a clear difference between these actions?

Whose client? To whom does a client belong? The Restatement (Third) of the Law Governing Lawyers provides that with reference to a departing lawyer's duties to a firm, a client is the client of the firm. Restatement of the Law (Third), The Law Governing Lawyers § 9 cmt. i. Does the line the Restatement draws between pre-departure and post-departure solicitation of clients make sense from a liability standpoint?

* * *

3.   NON-COMPETITION AGREEMENTS

Please read ABA Model Rules of Professional Conduct, Rule 5.6(a) and Comments [1]–[3].

The use of non-competition agreements. In order to prevent a departing lawyer from "stealing" a firm's clients, it might be tempting for a law firm to enter into non-compete agreements with its lawyers that limit their ability to solicit or represent firm clients upon departure. These types of agreements are fairly common in other settings. However, Model Rule 5.6(a) prevents a firm from doing this on the theory that such agreements unfairly limit the ability of clients to choose their lawyers. As a result, courts in most jurisdictions have refused to enforce non-compete agreements between lawyers in violation of Rule 5.6(a) on the grounds that those agreements offend public policy.

In *Graubard Mollen*, the "Phasing Out and Retirement Program" referenced in the opinion contained the following language:

> "3. It is the spirit of the program that, during retirement, and even afterward, each of the retirees will not do anything to impair the firm's relationship with its existing clients and business.

> "4. The partners recognize that efforts towards institutionalization of the business of the firm is essential to the firm's continuing prosperity. In particular, the partners approaching phase-down and retirement will integrate, to the extent possible, relationships between the firm's clients and the other partners."

Does this agreement violate Rule 5.6(a)? Should it be enforceable under contract law?

* * *

Profile of attorney professionalism. Sandra Day received her law degree from Stanford in 1952, where she finished third in her class. She was a member of the *Stanford Law Review* and graduated Order of the Coif. Yet, she had difficulty finding a job after graduation. She called at least 40 law firms looking for a job but was unable to get a single interview.

> I was a woman, and they said, "We don't hire women," and that was a shock to me. . . . And it just came as a real shock because I had done well in law school, and it never entered my mind that I couldn't even get an interview." http://www.npr.org/2013/03/05/172982275/out-of-order-at-the-court-oconnor-on-being-the-first-female-justice.

At one point, Day was offered a job as a legal secretary.

Six months after law school, Day married her husband, John O'Connor, with whom she had three children. Over the course of her legal career, Sanda Day O'Connor served as a deputy county attorney, a solo practitioner, and assistant state attorney general. Later, she was appointed to the Arizona Supreme Court. In 1981, President Ronald Reagan appointed O'Connor as an Associate Justice of the Supreme Court. She retired from the Court in 2006.

CHAPTER 7

ADVERTISING

■ ■ ■

Chapter hypothetical. In response to concerns among the organized bar about the prevalence of lawyer advertisements in the state, the New Dakota Supreme Court recently amended its advertising rules for lawyers. Among other things, the new rules completely prohibit (1) ads that feature actors, celebrities, or similar spokespeople not affiliated with the law firm and (2) ads that rely on techniques to obtain attention that demonstrate a clear and intentional lack of relevance to the selection of counsel, including the portrayal of lawyers exhibiting characteristics clearly unrelated to legal competence. The rest of New Dakota's advertising rules track those found in the ABA's Model Rules of Professional Conduct.

The Law Office of Stephen A. Brill recently ran a television ad in which a local sports figure recommended Brill's services. The ad also featured Brill in a cape, flying over the city to visit a client. At the end of the ad, an animated dog named Sparky turns to the camera and says "Brill is the best!" One of Brill's competitors filed a complaint with the New Dakota Board of Professional Responsibility about the ad.

While the Board was investigating, it discovered that Brill runs a legal blog (called "BrillLaw"), in which he comments on recent legal cases involving personal injury and workers' compensation claims. (None of the parties were Brill's clients.) In all of the cases, the injured parties recovered substantial judgments. Readers are free to leave comments following Brill's posts. After discussing the cases, Brill typically ends the discussion with a sentence advising readers that if they are in a similar situation as the injured parties in the cases he discusses, they might want to consider contacting an attorney. The advertisements on the blog are all for the Law Office of Stephen A. Brill and contain a link to the firm's web page. On the firm's web page, there is a link entitled "Client Testimonials," in which clients discuss what an outstanding job Brill did in representing them. The Board has cited Brill for violations of the advertising rules described above for his television ads, his blog, and his website. You represent Brill.

(A) What arguments can you make on Brill's behalf in terms of the constitutionality of New Dakota's rule? (As you consider those arguments, also consider what arguments the Board might make.)

(B) Would Brill be subject to discipline if New Dakota instead had adopted the ABA's Model Rules?

* * *

One of the things new lawyers gain when they join a law firm is access to clients. The firm has more clients than they can serve, so it hires more lawyers. Young lawyers who "hang out their own shingle" will more immediately feel the need to figure out how to attract clients. In the end, however, all lawyers engaged in private practice must pay some attention to the task of attracting paying clients who want the lawyer or the lawyer's firm to provide them with needed legal services. Marketing a law practice is a multi-faceted activity. The following materials introduce you to some of the legal and professional responsibility issues lawyers face when trying to inform the public of their presence in the community and willingness to undertake the representation of clients and to "encourage" or "entice" potential clients to call their offices, rather than the office of another lawyer. This chapter examines lawyer advertising and the basic proposition that a lawyer's advertisements cannot be false or misleading. Chapter 8 examines "solicitation"—including in-person, live-telephone, real-time electronic, and targeted direct-mail communication.

* * *

A. THE CONSTITUTIONAL LANDSCAPE

Obviously, attempts to restrict what lawyers may include in their advertisements raise free speech concerns. The U.S. Supreme Court was first presented with a First Amendment challenge to restrictions on lawyer advertising in Bates v. State Bar of Arizona, 433 U.S. 350 (1977). *Bates* involved a blanket ban on lawyer advertisements. Arizona offered a host of justifications for the ban, including the arguments that lawyer advertisements damage the dignity of the legal profession, are inherently misleading, and tend to stir up litigation. The Court held that states cannot prohibit truthful, nondeceptive advertising of the availability of, and fees for, routine legal services. In the process, the Court rejected Arizona's proffered justifications for its blanket ban, finding that advertising by lawyers is not inevitably misleading and that "the postulated connection between advertising and the erosion of true professionalism to be severely strained." *Id.* at 368. Moreover, the Court cited some of the benefits of lawyer advertisements, including the fact that they may enable consumers to locate a suitable lawyer.

Less than a decade later, the Court decided Zauderer v. Office of Disciplinary Counsel, 471 U.S. 626 (1985). There, the Court was confronted with the question of whether a state may, consistent with the First Amendment, prohibit a lawyer from running newspaper advertisements containing nondeceptive illustrations. The Court concluded that the State of Ohio had failed to identify a substantial state interest that justified the restriction on speech. The Court rejected Ohio's argument that it had a substantial governmental interest in preserving the dignity of the profession that was advanced by the restriction on the inclusion of illustrations. In addition, the Court rejected the idea that a blanket ban on illustrations was justified simply because *some* illustrations might be deceptive or manipulative.

In *Zauderer*, the Court also considered whether it was permissible for the state to discipline a lawyer for failing to disclose certain information regarding fee arrangements in an advertisement. Specifically, the ad in question informed consumers that the law firm in question represented clients on a contingent fee basis, so "[i]f there is no recovery, no legal fees are owed by our clients." *Id.* at 631. However, the ad failed to inform consumers that there were some expenses they would be required to bear, regardless of whether they won or lost. The Court concluded that requiring attorneys to include this information in their ads was reasonably related to the goal of preventing deceptive advertising and was therefore constitutionally permissible.

The Court has also considered several cases involving lawyer solicitation of individual clients, a subject addressed in the next chapter. But *Bates* and *Zauderer* provide much of the constitutional backdrop concerning the ability of states to regulate lawyer advertisements. The ABA's Model Rules of Professional Conduct regarding advertising, which are covered in Part B in this chapter, take one approach to regulating such ads. Concerned over the proliferation of lawyer advertisements, several states have gone further in their attempts to regulate lawyer advertisements.

PUBLIC CITIZEN INC. v. LOUISIANA ATTORNEY DISCIPLINARY BOARD

632 F.3d 212 (5th Cir. 2011)

EDITH BROWN CLEMENT, CIRCUIT JUDGE:

Before the court is a First Amendment challenge to rules governing attorney advertising in Louisiana. Various Louisiana attorneys and law firms, as well as a national nonprofit organization with Louisiana members, filed suit against the Louisiana Attorney Discipline Board (LADB), a body tasked with investigating lawyer misconduct and making discipline recommendations to the Supreme Court of Louisiana, and two LADB officers. The plaintiffs argued that certain Louisiana Rules of Professional Conduct unconstitutionally infringe on the commercial speech of Louisiana lawyers.

FACTS AND PROCEEDINGS

In 2006, the Louisiana legislature adopted a resolution directing the Louisiana Supreme Court to study attorney advertising and to revise the related Rules of Professional Conduct. The Louisiana Supreme Court created a committee (LSCT Committee), the membership of which overlapped with that of the Louisiana State Bar Association's existing Rules of Professional Conduct Committee (LSBA Committee). The LSBA Committee was, at that time, already reviewing Louisiana's attorney advertising rules. At the request of the court, the LSBA Committee continued its work with the goal of submitting a set of proposed attorney advertising rules to the LSCT Committee for review.

It conducted a survey of Louisiana residents and a survey of members of the Louisiana Bar Association (Bar Members) regarding both groups' perceptions of attorney advertising within the state. The survey of Louisiana residents was conducted by telephone and yielded 600 responses from randomly-selected Louisianians from all regions of the state. It was approximately twelve minutes and thirty seconds long and consisted of thirty-two questions. A web survey sent by e-mail to nearly 18,000 Bar Members resulted in almost four thousand completed responses. It contained thirty-one questions. The LSBA Committee also held three focus group discussions, which involved a total of twenty-five respondents and were held in New Orleans, Lafayette, and Shreveport.

The LSBA Committee ultimately presented a report of its findings and conclusions to the Louisiana Supreme Court. The report endorsed the majority of the Louisiana Rules but recommended certain modifications making some rules more stringent and others less so. The Supreme Court adopted all of the proposed revisions and reissued the rules with a press release confirming their October 2009 effective date.

[The plaintiffs challenged the constitutionality of the rules.] [The district court] granted partial summary judgment to each group of plaintiffs and partial summary judgment to LADB and its officers. Of the three summary judgment rulings, only one was appealed. Public Citizen, Inc., Morris Bart, Morris Bart LLC, William N. Gee, III, and William N. Gee, III, Ltd. (collectively, the "Louisiana Plaintiffs"), maintain that six sub-parts of Rule 7.2(c) constitute unconstitutional restrictions on commercial speech. Rule 7.2(c) restricts the content of all advertisements and unsolicited written communications concerning a lawyer's services. The portions challenged on appeal are:

> *Rule 7.2(c)(1)(D)* prohibiting communications that "contain[ ] a reference or testimonial to past successes or results obtained . . . ;"

> *Rule   7.2(c)(1)(E)*   prohibiting   communications   that "promise[ ] results;"

Rule 7.2(c)(1)(I) prohibiting communications that "include a portrayal of a client by a non-client without disclaimer of such, as required by Rule 7.2(c)(10), or the depiction of any events or scenes or pictures that are not actual or authentic without disclaimer of such, as required by Rule 7.2(c)(10);"

Rule 7.2(c)(1)(J) prohibiting communications that "include[ ] the portrayal of a judge or a jury;"

Rule 7.2(c)(1)(L) prohibiting communications that "utilize[ ] a nickname, moniker, motto or trade name that states or implies an ability to obtain results in a matter;"

Rule 7.2(c)(10) requiring "[a]ny words or statements required by these Rules to appear in an advertisement or unsolicited written communication must be clearly legible if written or intelligible if spoken aloud. All disclosures and disclaimers required by these Rules shall be clear and conspicuous. Written disclosures and disclaimers shall use a print size at least as large as the largest print size used in the advertisement or unsolicited written communication, and, if televised or displayed electronically, shall be displayed for a sufficient time to enable the viewer to easily see and read the disclosure or disclaimer. Spoken disclosures and disclaimers shall be plainly audible and spoken at the same or slower rate of speed as the other spoken content of the advertisement. All disclosures and disclaimers used in advertisements that are televised or displayed electronically shall be both spoken aloud and written legibly."

The court will review the constitutionality of each of these rules seriatim.

DISCUSSION

The United States Supreme Court recognized that the First Amendment's protections apply to commercial speech in Virginia State Board of Pharmacy v. Virginia Citizens Consumer Council, Inc., 425 U.S. 748, 770 (1976). It later elaborated that this type of speech merits only "a limited measure of protection, commensurate with its subordinate position in the scale of First Amendment values, . . . allowing modes of regulation that might be impermissible in the realm of noncommercial expression." Ohralik v. Ohio State Bar Assoc., 436 U.S. 447, 456, 98 S.Ct. 1912, 56 L.Ed.2d 444 (1978). The Court specifically applied First Amendment protections to attorney advertising in Bates v. State Bar of Arizona, "holding that advertising by attorneys may not be subjected to blanket suppression . . . [but] not . . . that advertising by attorneys may not be regulated in any way." 433 U.S. 350, 383 (1977). It encouraged the bar to "assur[e] that advertising by attorneys flows both freely and cleanly." *Id.* at 384.

The Court later clarified that different types of commercial speech merit different levels of protection. Advertising that "is inherently likely to deceive or where the record indicates that a particular form or method . . . of advertising has in fact been deceptive" receives no protection and the State may prohibit it entirely. In re R.M.J., 455 U.S. 191, 202 (1982). Advertising that is potentially misleading—because it "may be presented in a way that is not deceptive"—may be regulated if it satisfies one of two standards. A regulation that restricts potentially misleading commercial speech will pass constitutional muster if "the regulation directly advances a substantial government interest" and "is not more extensive than is necessary to serve that interest." Cent. Hudson Gas & Elec. Corp. v. Pub. Serv. Comm'n, 447 U.S. 557, 566 (1980). A regulation that imposes a disclosure obligation on a potentially misleading form of advertising will survive First Amendment review if the required disclosure is "reasonably related to the State's interest in preventing deception of consumers." *Zauderer*, 471 U.S. at 651.

LADB, as "the party seeking to uphold a restriction on commercial speech[,] carries the burden of justifying it." Its burden is a "heavy" one, 44 Liquormart, Inc. v. Rhode Island, 517 U.S. 484, 516 (1996), that cannot be satisfied "by mere speculation or conjecture," Edenfield v. Fane, 507 U.S. 761, 770–71 (1993).

A.   Character of the Commercial Speech Targeted by the Louisiana Rules

. . . Rule 7.2(c)(1)(E) bars communications that "promise[ ] results." The district court found that "[t]he plain text of th[is] Rule prohibits only communications that are inherently misleading and untruthful." This court arrives at the same conclusion. A promise that a party will prevail in a future case is necessarily false and deceptive. No attorney can guarantee future results. Because these communications are necessarily misleading, LADB may freely regulate them and Rule 7.2(c)(1)(E) is not an unconstitutional restriction on commercial speech.

[Regarding] [t]he other five rules challenged by the Louisiana Plaintiffs . . . , [t]his court holds that the communications targeted by these rules may be presented in a non-deceptive manner and are not "inherently likely to deceive" the public. A depiction of a scene or picture can be presented in a non-deceptive way in an attorney advertisement. The portrayal of a judge in an advertisement may also be presented in a way that is not deceptive. Further, and as the district court determined, it is possible for an attorney to present past results in a manner that is not misleading. Finally, it is similarly obvious that a nickname or motto that might imply an ability to obtain results can be employed in a non-deceptive fashion.

Because these five challenged rules all target speech that is only potentially misleading, the First Amendment is implicated. The court must review these Louisiana Rules under *Central Hudson* or *Zauderer*. In accordance with these cases, we apply *Central Hudson* to the speech restrictions in Rules 7.2(c)(1)(D), (J), and (L) and *Zauderer* to the disclosure obligations set forth in Rules 7.2(c)(1)(I) and (c)(10).

B.   Applying Central Hudson to Advertising Restrictions

Under *Central Hudson*, a restriction on commercial speech survives First Amendment scrutiny if: (1) "the asserted governmental interest is substantial," (2) the regulation "directly advances" that interest, and (3) the regulation "is not more extensive than is necessary to serve that interest." This test is motivated by the principle that "people will perceive their own best interests if only they are well enough informed, and . . . the best means to that end is to open the channels of communication rather than to close them." *Va. Bd. of Pharmacy*, 425 U.S. at 770, 96 S.Ct. 1817.

1.   Substantial Government Interest

The first prong of *Central Hudson* requires LADB to offer a substantial government interest that is advanced by the challenged restrictions. [The LADB offered several purported interests advanced by the rules, including preventing lawyer advertising from becoming undignified and threatening the public's perception of the legal profession.]

The Supreme Court has recognized as substantial the government's interests in "ensuring the accuracy of commercial information in the marketplace" and "maintaining standards of ethical conduct in the licensed professions." *Edenfield*, 507 U.S. at 769–70. It has also characterized a State's interest "in regulating lawyers [a]s especially great since lawyers are essential to the primary governmental function of administering justice, and have historically been 'officers of the courts.' " Goldfarb v. Va. State Bar, 421 U.S. 773, 792 (1975) (citations omitted). By contrast, an interest in preserving attorneys' dignity in their communications with the public is not substantial. *Zauderer*, 471 U.S. at 647–48. "[T]he mere possibility that some members of the population might find advertising embarrassing or offensive cannot justify suppressing it. The same must hold true for advertising that some members of the bar might find beneath their dignity." *Id.* at 648.

In light of this precedent, the court holds that LADB has asserted at least two substantial government interests: protecting the public from unethical and potentially misleading lawyer advertising and preserving the ethical integrity of the legal profession.

2.   Narrowly Drawn to Materially Advance the Asserted Interests

The second and third prongs of the *Central Hudson* analysis require LADB to demonstrate that the challenged rules are narrowly drawn to materially advance the asserted substantial interests. To show that a regulation materially advances a substantial interest, LADB must "demonstrate[ ] that the harms it recites are real and that its restriction will in fact alleviate them to a material degree." *Edenfield,* 507 U.S. at 771 (invalidating regulations supported only by a "series of conclusory statements"). It may do so with empirical data, studies, and anecdotal evidence. The evidence on which it relies need not "exist pre-enactment." It may also "pertain[ ] to different locales altogether." *Went For It,* 515 U.S. at 628, 115 S.Ct. 2371. This requirement may also be satisfied with "history, consensus, and simple common sense." *Id.*

Finally, to show that a regulation is narrowly drawn, LADB must demonstrate that it is "not more extensive than is necessary to serve that interest." *W. States Med. Ctr.,* 535 U.S. at 367.

a.   Rule 7.2(c)(1)(D): Past Results

Rule 7.2(c)(1)(D) prohibits communications "containing a reference or testimonial to past successes or results obtained." The plain language of this rule imposes a blanket ban on all references or testimonials to past results in attorney advertisements.

Rule 7.2(c)(1)(D) prohibits statements "of opinion or quality and . . . [those] of objective facts that may support an inference of quality." [Peel v. Att'y Disciplinary Comm'n of Il., 496 U.S. 91, 101 (1990)]. A statement that a lawyer has tried 50 cases to a verdict, obtained a $1 million settlement, or procured a settlement for 90% of his clients, for example, are objective, verifiable facts regarding the attorney's past professional work. Conversely, statements such as "he helped me," "I received a large settlement," or "I'm glad I hired her" constitute subjective and unverifiable references.

It is well established that the inclusion of verifiable facts in attorney advertisements is protected by the First Amendment. *Zauderer,* 471 U.S. at 647–49, "[A] State [cannot] . . . prevent an attorney from making accurate statements of fact regarding the nature of his practice merely because it is possible that some readers will infer that he has some expertise in that area." *Zauderer,* 471 U.S. at 640 n. 9. Even if, as LADB argues, the prohibited speech has the potential for fostering unrealistic expectations in consumers, the First Amendment does not tolerate speech restrictions that are based only on a "fear that people would make bad decisions if given truthful information." *W. States Med. Ctr.,* 535 U.S. at 359. "It is precisely this kind of choice, between the dangers of suppressing information, and the dangers of its misuse if it is freely available, that the First Amendment makes for us." *Va. Bd. of Pharmacy,*

425 U.S. at 770. To the extent that Rule 7.2(c)(1)(D) prevents attorneys from presenting "truthful, non-deceptive information proposing a lawful commercial transaction," it violates the First Amendment. *Edenfield*, 507 U.S. at 765, 113 S.Ct. 1792.

"[A]dvertising claims as to the quality of services . . . [that] may be not susceptible of measurement or verification . . . may be so likely to be misleading as to warrant restriction." *Bates*, 433 U.S. at 383–84. LADB bears the burden to show that the unverifiable statements prohibited by Rule 7.2(c)(1)(D) are so likely to be misleading that it may prohibit them. To do so, LADB relies on selected responses from the two Louisiana surveys: (1) 83% of the interviewed public did not agree "client testimonials in lawyer advertisements are completely truthful"; (2) 26% agreed that lawyers endorsed by a testimonial have more influence on Louisiana courts; (3) 40% believe that lawyers are, generally, "dishonest"; and (4) 61% believe that Louisiana lawyer advertisements are "less truthful" than advertisements for other items or services.

These responses are either too general to provide sufficient support for the rule's prohibition or too specific to do so. The general responses indicate that the public has a poor perception of lawyers and lawyer advertisements. However, they fail to point to any specific harms or to how they will be alleviated by a ban on testimonials or references to past results. *Edenfield*, 507 U.S. at 771. The more specific survey responses provide information regarding client testimonials, but do not shed light on the rule's prohibition of only those testimonials specifically discussing the attorney's past results or of all mere "references" to past results in unsolicited advertisements. They might be read to show that a majority of the Louisiana public may be unswayed by testimonials—perhaps demonstrating that they are a poor advertising choice—but not that banning only those testimonials that relate to past results will "ensur[e] the accuracy of commercial information in the marketplace" or is required to uphold ethical standards in the profession. *Id.* Only a minority of survey respondents agreed that attorneys employing testimonials in their advertisements have greater influence on the courts, and the ambiguity of the question posed to them leaves open the possibility that they were expressing a belief that these attorneys could obtain better results, not a belief that they would do so improperly.

. . . The evidence is insufficient to show that unverifiable claims in the targeted speech are so likely to be misleading that a complete prohibition is appropriate. LADB has not met its burden under the second prong of *Central Hudson* to show that prohibiting all references or testimonials to past results in advertisements will materially advance the State's asserted interests in preventing consumer deception or setting standards for ethical conduct by Louisiana lawyers.

LADB also fails to satisfy the third prong of *Central Hudson*: establishing that the prohibition in Rule 7.2(c)(1)(D) is "no more extensive than reasonably necessary to further [its] substantial interests." The only evidence LADB submits on this point is the LSBA Committee's conclusory statement that a disclaimer could not alleviate its concerns regarding references or testimonials to past results. An unsupported assertion is insufficient to satisfy LADB's burden. *Edenfield*, 507 U.S. at 771 (invaliding rule because the record "contain[ed] nothing more than a series of conclusory statements"). The LSBA Committee also failed to explain how this speech differs from speech that it found could be appropriately and effectively addressed by a disclaimer. *See, e.g.*, Rule 7.2(1)(c)(I).

A disclaimer may be an acceptable way to alleviate the consumer deception that could result from this type of advertising. *See Bates*, 433 U.S. at 375; *see also Shapero*, 486 U.S. at 477–78 (indicating that States could enact less-restrictive measures to prevent deception, such as requiring an advertisement to be identified as such or to include instructions on how to report an inaccurate or misleading letter).

b. Rule 7.2(c)(1)(J): Portrayals of a Judge or Jury

Rule 7.2(c)(1)(J) prohibits attorney advertisements that "include [] the portrayal of a judge or a jury." LADB argues that this rule targets only speech that is inherently misleading because the inclusion of a judge or a jury in an attorney advertisement "impli[es] that a lawyer has undue influence with a judge or jury" and because an actual sitting judge or an impaneled jury could not participate in an advertisement. As discussed above, this court holds that a depiction of a judge or jury in a lawyer advertisement is not inherently misleading. LADB's argument to the contrary is based on an assumption that Louisianians are insufficiently sophisticated to avoid being misled by a courtroom not devoid of its normal occupants. The Supreme Court has explicitly instructed courts to reject such arguments when reviewing regulations of attorney advertising. *Bates*, 433 U.S. at 374–75 (rejecting attorney advertising restrictions based only on a belief that "the public is not sophisticated enough to realize the limitations of advertising").

Because the speech targeted by Rule 7.2(c)(1)(J) is only potentially misleading, the court undertakes a *Central Hudson* analysis of its restrictions. We conclude that the evidence submitted by LADB does not satisfy the second or third prongs of this test. First, LADB "has not demonstrated that the ban imposed by this rule advances its asserted interests in any direct and material way." There is no argument or evidence in the record connecting the "common sense observation" that "a communication that states or implies that the lawyer has the ability to influence improperly a court is likely to be false, deceptive, or misleading" to portrayals of a judge or jury in attorney advertisements generally. *Alexander*, 598 F.3d at 93 (internal quotation marks omitted). Second, the only evidence on the record to support narrow tailoring is the LSBA Committee's statement that "a disclaimer would not be able to cure or prevent the conduct from misleading and/or deceiving the public" and that Rule 7.2(c)(1)(D) is "narrowly-tailored to address the harm in question and to achieve the desired objective of protecting the public from false, misleading and/or deceptive advertising." The committee did not support these assertions with evidence or explanation and "[t]he record does not disclose any . . . evidence . . . that validates the[se] suppositions." *Edenfield*, 507 U.S. at 771. LADB has failed to demonstrate that its prohibition is "no more extensive than reasonably necessary"

c.   *Rule 7.2(c)(1)(L): Nicknames or Mottos that State or Imply an Ability to Obtain Results*

Rule 7.2(c)(1)(L) prohibits attorney advertising communications "utilizing a nickname, moniker, motto or trade name that states or implies an ability to obtain results in a matter." The district court analyzed this rule under *Central Hudson* and concluded that it "materially advances the State's interest in preventing deception of the public, and is narrowly tailored to meet those ends." This court undertakes the same analysis and arrives at the same conclusion.

To meet its burden to show that it has satisfied *Central Hudson*, LADB relies on the results of the two Louisiana surveys and three focus groups. Questions regarding the use of nicknames or mottos in attorney advertisements constituted approximately 50% of both surveys. In the telephone survey, members of the public were read nine specific mottos employed in Louisiana lawyer advertisements. The surveyors asked which of the nine mottos each participant recognized and then asked a series of questions about the effect of the advertisements containing mottos they recognized on their perceptions of Louisiana lawyers, Louisiana courts, and the advertising lawyer's ability to obtain results for clients. The internet survey of Bar Members used the same format and similar, but not identical, questions. The focus group participants were shown eight Louisiana attorney television advertisements and engaged in a group discussion of each advertisement.

The telephone survey showed that 59% of the public agreed that the advertisements implied that the featured attorneys can manipulate Louisiana courts and 32% agreed that these lawyers had greater influence over Louisiana courts. In addition, 61% of the public agreed that these advertisements promised that the lawyer would achieve a positive result and 78% of Bar Members agreed that they implied that the lawyers could obtain favorable results regardless of facts or law. Of the Bar Members surveyed, 66% agreed that these advertisements were implicitly misleading and 76% disagreed that the public was not misled by these advertisements. When various mottos were discussed within the focus groups, participants said that they viewed them negatively and found them to be misleading.

The court is satisfied that there is reliable and specific evidence on the record sufficient to support the restriction imposed by Rule 7.2(c)(1)(L). First, the survey and focus group responses consistently reveal that the advertisements containing these mottos misled the public, improperly promised results, and implied that the advertising lawyers could manipulate Louisiana courts. Second, they present the perceptions of a significant number of people from each of the two pools of respondents. One-half of each survey was directed at the use of mottos and nicknames in attorney advertisements. Participants were either shown existing attorney advertisements making use of mottos or asked whether they recognized specific mottos. Finally, the questions asked about the shown or recognized advertisements were not abstract or hypothetical. They targeted the specific elements of commercial speech implicated by this rule and sought and received the reactions of the public and Bar Members to that type of speech. The result is evidence that directly pertains to and supports the restriction set forth in Rule 7.2(c)(1)(L). The court holds that LADB has met its burden to show that this rule will advance its substantial interest in preventing consumer confusion.

C. Applying Rational Basis Review to Disclosure Requirements

The Supreme Court has held that " 'warning[s] or disclaimer[s] might be appropriately required ... in order to dissipate the possibility of consumer confusion or deception.' " *Zauderer*, 471 U.S. at 651, (quoting *In re R.M.J.*, 455 U.S. at 201 (alterations in original). Such disclosure requirements need only be "reasonably related to the State's interest in preventing deception of consumers." *Id.*

1. Rule 7.2(c)(1)(I): Portrayal of Clients, Scenes, or Pictures Without a Disclaimer

Rule 7.2(c)(1)(I) prohibits attorney advertisements that "include[ ] a portrayal of a client by a non-client without disclaimer ... or the depiction of any events or scenes or pictures that are not actual or authentic without disclaimer." To meet its burden to justify the disclosure requirements imposed by this rule, LADB relies on various responses from the Louisiana surveys. It argues that advertisements that employ reenactments, manufactured pictures, or actors to represent clients, without identifying the use of these devices can be deceptive and decrease public confidence in the Louisiana judicial system. It submits that disclaimers identifying these items will prevent their use from misleading the public or reflecting poorly on Louisiana attorneys and courts.

The survey responses highlighted by LADB indicate that 59% of the public and 63% of Bar Members could not always tell when a testimonial in a lawyer advertisement was provided by an actor rather than a real client. When asked about advertisements containing reenactments of accidents or accident victims, 29% of the public said that the featured attorneys have more influence on Louisiana courts; 54% of Bar Members believe that these advertisements imply that the attorney can obtain a positive result without regard to facts or law. In addition, 59% of the public said that these advertisements decrease their confidence in the integrity of Louisiana lawyers and 78% of Bar Members did not believe that these advertisements raised public opinion of the integrity of Louisiana lawyers. Focus group participants expressed negative opinions of the use of accident scenes and victims in attorney advertisements.

The evidence, combined with the court's "simple common sense," *Went For It*, 515 U.S. at 628, leads this court to conclude, as the district court did, that the disclaimers required by Rule 7.2(c)(1)(I) are reasonably related to the State's interests in preventing consumer deception. They are also sufficiently related to the substantial interest in promoting the ethical integrity of the legal profession. Rule 7.2(c)(1)(I)'s requirement that attorney advertisements explain when a "client" in an advertisement is portrayed by an actor, when a reenactment is a reenactment, or when a picture or drawing is a reproduction is a reasonable condition and one that is sufficiently related the substantial government interests at play.

2. Rule 7.2(c)(10): Format of Disclosures

The Louisiana Plaintiffs only challenge the portions of this rule that dictate the font size and speed of speech used in disclaimers and requiring that disclaimers be both spoken and written in televised or electronic advertisements. . . .

The Supreme Court has held that "[u]njustified or unduly burdensome disclosure requirements offend the First Amendment by chilling protected speech, but 'an advertiser's rights are adequately protected as long as disclosure requirements are reasonably related to the State's interest in preventing deception of consumers.'" *Milavetz*, 130 S.Ct. at 1339–40 (quoting *Zauderer*, 471 U.S. at 651).

[The court concluded that "[t]he record is devoid of evidence that Rule 7.2(c)(10)'s font size, speed of speech, and spoken/written provisions are 'reasonably related' to LADB's substantial interests in preventing consumer deception and preserving the ethical standards of the legal profession."]

In addition, a review of the record shows that the font size, speed of speech, and spoken/written requirements "effectively rule out" an attorney's ability to include one or more of the disclaimer-requiring elements in television, radio, and print advertisements of shorter length or smaller size. To comply with the Louisiana Rules, an attorney advertisement must include, both written in a large font and spoken slowly, at least all of the following information: (1) the lawyer's name and office location (Rule 7.2(a)); (2) a client's responsibility for costs (Rule 7.2(c)(6)); (3) all jurisdictions in which the lawyer is licensed (Rule 7.6(b)); (4) the use of simulated scenes or pictures or actors portraying clients (Rule 7.2(c)(1)(I)); and (5) the use of a spokesperson, whether the spokesperson is a lawyer, and whether the spokesperson is paid (Rule 7.5(b)(2)(c)).

In *Ibanez*, the Court struck down as "unduly burdensome" disclosure requirements that "effectively rule[d] out" an attorney's ability to include her specialty "on a business card or letterhead, or in a yellow pages listing." 512 U.S. at 146–47 (citing *Zauderer*, 471 U.S. at 651). The objected-to restrictions in Rule 7.2(c)(10) effectively rule out the ability of Louisiana lawyers to employ short advertisements of any kind. Accordingly, we hold that they are overly burdensome and violate the First Amendment.

CONCLUSION

For the reasons given above, the opinion of the district court is AFFIRMED with respect to Rules 7.2(c)(1)(E), 7.2(c)(1)(I), and 7.2(c)(1)(L). These rules do not regulate attorneys' commercial speech in a way that violates the First Amendment. With respect to Rules 7.2(c)(1)(D), 7.2(c)(1)(J), and 7.2(c)(10), the judgment of the district court is REVERSED.

* * *

Problem 7.1. In several opinions, judges in New Dakota have made positive statements about Stephen A. Brill's abilities as a lawyer. Therefore, Brill would like to run an advertisement that quotes from these opinions. Assume that a New Dakota advertising rule prohibits a lawyer from including a quotation from a judge about the lawyer's abilities unless the lawyer also includes a disclaimer to the effect that the judge's comments do not constitute an endorsement of the lawyer. Which of the constitutional tests described in *Public Citizen* would apply to such a regulation? Would such a regulation survive a constitutional challenge?

* * *

B. TRUTH IN ADVERTISING

Please read ABA Model Rules of Professional Conduct, Rule 7.1 and Comments; and Rule 7.2(a), (b)(1) & (c) and Comments [1]–[3].

* * *

Comparisons with other lawyers. What, if anything, will a lawyer have to be able to prove before he or she can advertise that "my fee rates are very reasonable"? What if the ad read "Low fees for uncontested divorces"? Should a lawyer be able to bill himself as "the toughest lawyer around"? Do you think the answer would be different if Model Rule 7.1, specified, as it did prior to its revision in 2002, that "[a] communication is false or misleading if it . . . compares the lawyer's services with other lawyers' services, unless the comparison can be factually substantiated"?

False or misleading communications. A lawyer has handled only one criminal case—a case in which she was appointed to defend an individual charged with criminal contempt of court for allegedly violating a protective order to stay away from his girlfriend. After the girlfriend failed to appear at two consecutive hearings, the case against the lawyer's client was dismissed with prejudice. Can the lawyer now advertise that she has never lost a criminal case?

What do you think? Can a lawyer present a staged jury argument in a TV advertisement? What if he displayed across the bottom of the screen the statement, "This is a dramatization"?

What do you think? May a lawyer advertise "No recovery/No fee" if the client will be expected to cover the costs associated with the representation? May a lawyer advertise "Free consultation" if the consultation is with a paralegal?

* * *

Problem 7.2. Over the past four years, Stephen A. Brill has represented three clients who recovered in excess of $1,000,000 in personal injury actions. Most of Brill's clients recovered significantly less during that timeframe. May Brill include in a TV ad the statement "Three $1,000,000 recoveries for clients in the past four years!"? What if he added the statement "Results obtained vary from case to case and no specific recovery can be guaranteed"?

* * *

C. THE NEW FRONTIER:
WEB-BASED COMMUNICATIONS

The advent of the Internet has given lawyers a new way to communicate with clients, potential clients, and the public. A web page is now standard for virtually every firm, whether large or small, and many sole practitioners also have web pages. Most web pages have stable content, containing information about the firm, links to profiles of the firm's lawyers, and perhaps some information about recent cases or practice specialties. Especially in the case of large firms, the web page might contain "newsletters" or other links to substantive legal information. Many lawyers also have their own blogs, a weblog on legal topics written by a lawyer.

Perhaps the most heated issue resulting from web sites and blogs is whether they should be regulated as attorney advertising. Most jurisdictions do regulate web sites as advertising, since they constitute unambiguous self-promotion. However, regulation of blogs has been much more controversial. Most bloggers argue that blogs embody primarily political speech, as opposed to commercial speech, and are therefore fully protected by the First Amendment. However, some scholars point out that most blogs contain self-promotional material that is subject to regulation as commercial speech.

In 2007 the New York Code of Professional Responsibility was amended to specifically include "weblogs" and "web sites" in its definition of "advertisement" if the website or blog has as its "primary purpose . . . the retention of the lawyer or law firm." The rules also provided that "[a]ny advertisement contained in a computer-accessed communication shall be retained for a period of not less than one year." The rules also prohibited solicitation by "real-time or interactive computer-accessed communication unless the recipient is a close friend, relative, former client or existing client." Although certain portions of the rules were attacked as violative of the First Amendment, the portions of the rules dealing specifically with web sites and blogs were not challenged. Therefore, to the extent that web sites or blogs have as their "primary purpose . . . the retention of the lawyer or law firm," they are subject to regulation in New York. It is still too early to detect a nationwide trend in the regulation of web sites and blogs as advertising. *See generally* Judy M. Cornett, *The Ethics of Blawging: A Genre Analysis*, 41 LOY. CHI. L.J. 221 (2009).

* * *

HUNTER V. VIRGINIA STATE BAR EX REL.
THIRD DISTRICT COMMITTEE

744 S.E.2d 611 (Va. 2013)

OPINION BY JUSTICE CLEO E. POWELL.

In this appeal of right by an attorney from a Virginia State Bar ("VSB") disciplinary proceeding before a three judge panel appointed pursuant to Code § 54.1–3935, we consider whether an attorney's blog posts are commercial speech ... and whether the panel ordered the attorney to post a disclaimer that is insufficient under Rule 7.2(a)(3) of the Virginia Rules of Professional Conduct.

I. FACTS AND PROCEEDINGS

Horace Frazier Hunter, an attorney with the law firm of Hunter & Lipton, PC, authors a trademarked blog titled "This Week in Richmond Criminal Defense," which is accessible from his law firm's website, www.hunterlipton.com/. This blog, which is not interactive, contains posts discussing a myriad of legal issues and cases, although the overwhelming majority are posts about cases in which Hunter obtained favorable results for his clients. Nowhere in these posts or on his website did Hunter include disclaimers.

On March 24, 2011, the VSB charged Hunter with violating [Virginia's advertising rules] by his posts on this blog. Specifically, the VSB argued that he violated rules 7.1 and 7.2 because his blog posts discussing his criminal cases were inherently misleading as they lacked disclaimers. . . .

In a hearing on October 18, 2011, the VSB presented evidence of Hunter's alleged violations. The VSB also entered all of the blog posts Hunter had posted on his blog to date. At that time, none of the posts entered contained disclaimers. Of these thirty unique posts, only five discussed legal, policy issues. The remaining twenty-five discussed cases. Hunter represented the defendant in twenty-two of these cases and identified that fact in the posts. In nineteen of these twenty-two posts, Hunter also specifically named his law firm. One of these posts described a case where a family hired Hunter to represent them in a wrongful death suit and the remaining twenty-one of these posts described criminal cases. In every criminal case described, Hunter's clients were either found not guilty, plea bargained to an agreed upon disposition, or had their charges reduced or dismissed.

At the hearing, Hunter testified that he has many reasons for writing his blog—including marketing, creation of a community presence for his firm, combatting any public perception that defendants charged with crimes are guilty until proven innocent, and showing commitment to criminal law. Hunter stated that he had offered to post a disclaimer on his blog, but the offered disclaimer was not satisfactory to the VSB. Hunter admitted that he only blogged about his cases that he won. . . .

Following the hearing, the VSB held that ... Hunter's website contained legal advertising was based on its factual finding that "[t]he postings of [Hunter's] case wins on his webpage advertise[d] cumulative case results." Moreover, the VSB found that at least one purpose of the website was commercial. The VSB further held that he violated Rule 7.2 by "disseminating case results in advertising without the required disclaimer" because the one that he proposed to the VSB was insufficient. The VSB imposed a public admonition with terms including a requirement that he remove case specific content for which he has not received consent and post a disclaimer that complies with Rule 7.2(a)(3) on all case-related posts.

Hunter appealed to a three judge panel of the circuit court and the court heard argument. . . . The court held VSB's interpretation of Rules 7.1 and 7.2 do not violate the First Amendment and that the record contained substantial evidence to support the VSB's determination that Hunter had violated those rules. The court imposed a public admonition and required Hunter to post the following disclaimer: "Case results depend upon a variety of factors unique to each case. Case results do not guarantee or predict a similar result in any future case." This appeal followed.

II. ANALYSIS

A. Whether "[t]he Ruling of the Circuit Court finding a violation of Rules 7.1(a)(4) and 7.2(a)(3) conflicts with the First Amendment to the Constitution of the United States."

Rule 7.1(a)(4), which is the specific portion of the Rule that the VSB argued that Hunter violated, states:

> (a) A lawyer shall not, on behalf of the lawyer or any other lawyer affiliated with the lawyer or the firm, use or participate in the use of any form of public communication if such communication contains a false, fraudulent, misleading, or deceptive statement or claim. For example, a communication violates this Rule if it:
>
> . . .
>
> (4) is likely to create an unjustified expectation about results the lawyer can achieve, or states or implies that the lawyer can achieve results by means that violate the Rules of Professional Conduct or other law.

The VSB also argues that Hunter violated the following subsection of Rule 7.2(a)(3):

(a) Subject to the requirements of Rules 7.1 and 7.3, a lawyer may advertise services through written, recorded, or electronic communications, including public media. In the determination of whether an advertisement violates this Rule, the advertisement shall be considered in its entirety, including any qualifying statements or disclaimers contained therein. Notwithstanding the requirements of Rule 7.1, an advertisement violates this Rule if it:

. . .

(3) advertises specific or cumulative case results, without a disclaimer that (i) puts the case results in a context that is not misleading; (ii) states that case results depend upon a variety of factors unique to each case; and (iii) further states that case results do not guarantee or predict a similar result in any future case undertaken by the lawyer. The disclaimer shall precede the communication of the case results. When the communication is in writing, the disclaimer shall be in bold type face and uppercase letters in a font size that is at least as large as the largest text used to advertise the specific or cumulative case results and in the same color and against the same colored background as the text used to advertise the specific or cumulative case results.

In response to these allegations, Hunter contends that speech concerning the judicial system is "quintessentially 'political speech'" which is within the marketplace of ideas. . . .

The VSB responds that Hunter's blog posts are inherently misleading commercial speech.

Turning to Hunter's argument that his blog posts are political, rather than commercial, speech, we note that "[t]he existence of 'commercial activity, in itself, is no justification for narrowing the protection of expression secured by the First Amendment.'" Bigelow v. Virginia, 421 U.S. 809, 818 (1975) (quoting Ginsburg v. United States, 383 U.S. 463, 474 (1966)). However, when speech that is both commercial and political is combined, the resulting speech is not automatically entitled to the level of protections afforded political speech. Board of Trustees of the State University of New York v. Fox, 492 U.S. 469, 474 (1989).

While it is settled that attorney advertising is commercial speech, Bates v. State Bar of Arizona, 433 U.S. 350, 363–64 (1977), *Bates* and its progeny were decided in the era of traditional media. In recent years, however, advertising has taken to new forms such as websites, blogs, and other social media forums, like Facebook and Twitter.

Thus, we must examine Hunter's speech to determine whether it is commercial speech, specifically, lawyer advertising.

> Advertising, like all public expression, may be subject to reasonable regulation that serves a legitimate public interest. To the extent that commercial activity is subject to regulation, the relationship of speech to that activity may be one factor, among others, to be considered in weighing the First Amendment interest against the governmental interest alleged. Advertising is not thereby stripped of all First Amendment protection. The relationship of speech to the marketplace of products or of services does not make it valueless in the marketplace of ideas.

Bigelow, 421 U.S. at 826 (internal citations omitted). Simply because the speech is an advertisement, references a specific product, or is economically motivated does not necessarily mean that it is commercial speech. Bolger v. Youngs Drug Products Corp., 463 U.S. 60, 67 (1983). "The combination of *all* these characteristics, however, provides strong support for the ... conclusion that [some blog posts] are properly characterized as commercial speech" even though they also discuss issues important to the public. *Id.* at 67–68 (emphasis in original).

Certainly, not all advertising is necessarily commercial, *e.g.*, public service announcements. However, all commercial speech is necessarily advertising. *See* Webster's Third New International Dictionary 31 (1993) (defining "advertisement" as "a calling attention to or making known [;]an informing or notifying[;] a calling to public attention[;] a statement calling attention to something[;] a public notice; esp[ecially] a paid notice or announcement published in some public print (as a newspaper, periodical, poster, or handbill) or broadcast over radio or television"). Indeed, the Supreme Court of the United States has said that "[t]he diverse motives, means, and messages of advertising may make speech 'commercial' in widely varying degrees." *Bigelow*, 421 U.S. at 826.

Here, Hunter's blog posts, while containing some political commentary, are commercial speech. Hunter has admitted that his motivation for the blog is at least in part economic. The posts are an advertisement in that they predominately describe cases where he has received a favorable result for his client. He unquestionably references a specific product, i.e., his lawyering skills as twenty-two of his twenty-five case related posts describe cases that he has successfully handled. Indeed, in nineteen of these posts, he specifically named his law firm in addition to naming himself as counsel.

Moreover, the blog is on his law firm's commercial website rather than an independent site dedicated to the blog. *See* Howard J. Bashman, How Appealing Blog (Feb. 11, 2013, 9:40 AM), http://howappealing.law. com (an independent blog by a Pennsylvania appellate attorney that is accessible through Law.com at http://legalblogwatch.typepad.com/). The website uses the same frame for the pages openly soliciting clients as it does for the blog, including the firm name, a photograph of Hunter and his law partner, and a "contact us" form. The homepage of the website on which Hunter posted his blog states only:

Do you need Richmond attorneys?

Hunter & Lipton, CP [sic] is a law practice in Richmond, Virginia specializing in litigation matters from administrative agency hearings to serious criminal cases. As experienced Richmond attorneys, we bring a genuine desire to help those who find themselves in difficult situations. Our partnership was founded on the idea that everyone, no matter what the circumstance, deserves a zealous advocate to fight on his or her behalf.

People make mistakes, and may even find themselves in situations not of their own making. And for these people, the system can be extraordinarily unforgiving and unjust-but you do not have to face this system alone.

If you find yourself in a difficult legal situation, the Richmond attorneys of Hunter & Lipton, LLP would consider it a privilege to represent you. Please contact our office with any questions or to schedule a consultation.

This non-interactive blog does not allow for discourse about the cases, as non-commercial commentary often would by allowing readers to post comments. *See, e.g.,* Law.com Legal Blog Watch, http://legalblogwatch. typepad.com/; Above the Law, http://abovethelaw.com/. *See also* JUNE LESTER & WALLACE C. KOEHLER, JR., FUNDAMENTALS OF INFORMATION STUDIES 102 (2d ed.2007) (observing that "[i]n contrast to the interaction possible in some other forms of web-published information, blog readers are most frequently permitted to leave comments and create threads of discussion"). Instead, in furtherance of his commercial pursuit, Hunter invites the reader to "contact us" the same way one seeking legal representation would contact the firm through the website.

Thus, the inclusion of five generalized, legal posts and three discussions about cases that he did not handle on his non-interactive blog, no more transform Hunter's otherwise self-promotional blog posts into political speech, "than opening sales presentations with a prayer or a Pledge of Allegiance would convert them into religious or political speech." *Fox*, 492 U.S. at 474–75. Indeed, unlike situations and topics where the subject matter is inherently, inextricably intertwined, Hunter chose to comingle sporadic political statements within his self-promoting blog posts in an attempt to camouflage the true commercial nature of his blog. "Advertisers should not be permitted to immunize false or misleading product information from government regulation simply by including references to public issues." *Bolger*, 463 U.S. at 68. When considered as a whole, the economically motivated blog overtly proposes a commercial transaction that is an advertisement of a specific product.

Having determined that Hunter's blog posts discussing his cases are commercial speech, we must determine whether the expression is protected by the First Amendment. [Applying the *Central Hudson* test, the court found that the blog posts had the potential to be misleading. The court then concluded that "the VSB has a substantial governmental interest in protecting the public from an attorney's self-promoting representations that could lead the public to mistakenly believe that they are guaranteed to obtain the same positive results if they were to hire Hunter" and the disclaimer requirement directly advanced that interest." Accordingly, as applied to Hunter's post, the restrictions were permissible.]

* * *

Social media as advertising. ABA Model Rule 7.2 generally permits lawyers to "advertise services through written, recorded or electronic communication." What qualifies as "advertising" for purposes of the rule? *See id.* Comment [1]. Under what circumstances would a lawyer's Facebook page or Twitter account be subject to the rules regarding advertising? Imagine, for example, a lawyer posts on her Facebook page, "Great day in court today. Won the slip and fall case!" Should this be treated as an advertisement for purposes of the rules? What other information would you need to know? *See generally* California Ethics Opinion No. 2012–186 (discussing application of ethics rule to lawyers' use of social media).

* * *

D. ADVERTISING LIMITED AND SPECIALIZED PRACTICES

In Peel v. Attorney Registration and Disciplinary Commission, 496 U.S. 91 (1990), the U.S. Supreme Court held that a state cannot prohibit attorneys from making truthful, nondeceptive statements regarding their specialization and qualifications. In that case, Peel's letterhead contained the following:

Gary E. Peel
Certified Civil Trial Specialist
By the National Board of Trial Advocacy
Licensed: Illinois, Missouri, Arizona.

Because each piece of information conveyed by the letterhead was true and verifiable, the Court held that it was protected by the First Amendment. However, the Court also left the door open for the states to require attorneys to provide consumers more information: "To the extent that potentially misleading statements of private certification or specialization could confuse consumers, a State might consider screening certifying organizations or requiring a disclaimer about the certifying organization or the standards of a specialty." *Id.* at 110.

* * *

Please read ABA Model Rules of Professional Conduct, Rule 7.4 and Comments.

* * *

Claiming "specialist" status. Comment [1] to Model Rule 7.4 permits a lawyer to call herself a specialist in an advertisement so long as the self-labeling is not misleading. But Rule 7.4(d) says a lawyer may not suggest that she is "*certified* as a specialist." (emphasis added). Is a prospective client likely to see any meaningful difference between these two claims? Unlike the ABA Model Rule, at least one jurisdiction prohibits a lawyer from calling herself a specialist unless she is certified as specialist in accordance with Supreme Court rules. Is this a good idea? Is such a prohibition constitutional?

* * *

E. LAW FIRM NAMES

Please read ABA Model Rules of Professional Conduct, Rule 7.5 and Comments.

* * *

Problem 7.3. Based on your reading of Model Rules 7.1 and 7.5, which of the following law firm names would be permissible?

(A) Sonya Goodman & Associates. [Assume that Sonya Goodman is the only lawyer in the firm, but has several paralegals working for her.]

(B) The Best Law Firm. [Assume no one in the firm has Best as a last name.]

(C) The Social Security Law Office. [Assume the firm handles
     social security cases.]

(D) None of the above.

Problem 7.4. Allen and Bailey practice together as partners. Their
firm is named Allen & Bailey. Conner desires to share office space and
office expenses with Allen and Bailey but does not desire to become a
partner in the firm. Further, Allen and Bailey will occasionally associate
Conner on certain cases, and Conner will occasionally associate Allen and
Bailey. Because they are practicing out of the same office, they want to
put a sign on the door that includes all three names. Can they do this
without violating Rule 7.5? Can they refer to themselves as "An
Association of Attorneys?"

Free speech and firm names. Based on your reading of *Public
Citizen*, *supra*, could a state constitutionally prohibit a law firm from
naming itself "The Ethics Rule Breaker Law Firm?" Why or why not?

* * *

F. CLIENT REFERRALS

Please read ABA Model Rules of Professional Conduct,
Rule 7.2(b) and Comments [5]–[8].

Model Rule 7.2 permits a lawyer to pay the costs associated with
advertising. However, it places limits on the ability of a lawyer to pay
others to recommend the lawyer's services. The rule also addresses other
forms of referral, including referral agreements and legal services plans.

1. REFERRALS IN GENERAL

Problem 7.5. Pat represented Shonna in a matter. Shonna was so
pleased with the job Pat did that she referred several of her friends to
Pat. In return, the next time Pat did legal work for Shonna, he reduced
his regular fee in appreciation. Is Pat subject to discipline? Could Pat give
a $10 gift certificate to a local restaurant in appreciation for her referrals?

2. LEGAL SERVICES PLANS AND
LAWYER REFERRAL SERVICES

A Michigan ethics opinion described the nature of legal services
plans:

> Most for-profit prepaid legal service plans are owned and
> operated by plan sponsors which, for a modest monthly charge,
> offer subscribers certain "covered" legal services for no additional
> cost and other specified services at reduced fees. The covered
> legal services are provided by participating lawyers and usually

include such services as unlimited telephone consultations and letter writing, and the preparation of simple wills. The reduced fee services usually cover court representation at a fixed hourly rate and contingency fee arrangements, both for less than fees customarily charged by lawyers for similar services. Certain matters are explicitly excluded, such as matters where the interests of two plan members are in direct conflict, suits against the plan's sponsor and complex matters.

State Bar of Michigan Standing Committee on Professional and Judicial Ethics Op. No. RI 223 (1995).

In contrast, a lawyer referral service is "an organization that holds itself out to the public as a lawyer referral service" and, presumably, provides "unbiased referrals to lawyers with appropriate experience" in the relevant subject area. Model Rule 7.2, Comment [6]. Model Rule 7.2 permits a lawyer to participate in a legal services plan or not-for-profit lawyer referral service or to pay the usual charges with such organizations. However, the lawyer must act reasonably to assure that the lawyer's activities are compatible with the lawyer's professional obligations, including the duty to maintain decisional independence, loyalty, and competence.

3. RECIPROCAL REFERRAL AGREEMENTS

Problem 7.6. Pat and Mike were old law school buddies who are each now solo practitioners. Pat practices criminal law and Mike practices family law. While reminiscing about old times, Pat said to Mike, "You're a heck of a lawyer. If I ever have a client who needs a divorce, I'm going to refer him to you. Will you do the same if one of your clients ever has a drunk driving case?" Mike said, "It's a deal, buddy." If Pat and Mike carry out this agreement, are they subject to discipline?

* * *

Profile of attorney professionalism. As mentioned in the introductory text to this chapter, one of the leading cases involving attorney advertising is Bates v. State Bar of Arizona, 433 U.S. 350 (1977). The attorneys at issue in that case were John Bates and Van O'Steen. Bates was named the most outstanding student in his class at Arizona State University College of Law in 1972, and O'Steen graduated cum laude. *Bates Participants Reflect on Landmark Case,* http://www.first amendmentcenter.org/bates-participants-reflect-on-landmark-case. After graduating, the young lawyers went to work for the Maricopa County Legal Aid Society before leaving to start their own firm. As Bates describes it, the lawyers wanted to focus on providing low-cost legal services to lower-income clients. "We wanted to change the existing system, which favored existing law firms, who did not seek clients among the unserved. In the provision of legal services, a huge number of people were being turned away because of lack of financial resources. We wanted to offer affordable legal services." *Id.*

To do this, they needed to advertise. Therefore, on February 22, 1976, they took out a newspaper ad. The scandalous ad read as follows: "Do you need a lawyer? Legal services at very reasonable fees." The ad then listed fees for various services. Less than two months later, Bates and O'Steen found themselves facing disciplinary charges for having violated Arizona's rule of professional conduct prohibiting a lawyer from advertising legal services "through newspaper or magazine advertisements, radio or television announcements, display advertisements in the city or telephone directories or other means of commercial publicity."

Bates and O'Steen challenged Arizona's prohibition on First Amendment grounds. After losing before the Arizona Supreme Court, they appealed to the United States Supreme Court. Arguing on behalf of the Arizona Bar was John Frank, the lawyer who successfully argued in favor of the "Miranda warning" at issue in *Miranda v. Arizona* before the Supreme Court. In a 5–4 decision, the Supreme Court held that Arizona's rule offended the First Amendment. The Arizona Bar defended its ban on several grounds, including the adverse effects that advertising might have on professionalism. Writing for the majority, Justice Blackmun rejected these arguments, finding "the postulated connection between advertising and the erosion of true professionalism to be severely strained." While recognizing potential dangers associated with lawyer advertising, Blackmun also noted the potential benefits in terms of improving access to justice:

> As the bar acknowledges, "the middle 70% of our population is not being reached or served adequately by the legal profession." ABA, *Revised Handbook on Prepaid Legal Services* 2 (1972). Among the reasons for this underutilization is fear of the cost, and an inability to locate a suitable lawyer. . . . The disciplinary rule at issue likely has served to burden access to legal services, particularly for the not-quite-poor and the unknowledgeable. A rule allowing restrained advertising would be in accord with the bar's obligation to "facilitate the process of intelligent selection of lawyers, and to assist in making legal services fully available."

Bates, 433 U.S. at 376–77.

Of course, lawyer advertisements remain controversial. John Frank, the lawyer defending Arizona's ban, said not long before his death, "My skin crawls and stomach screams when I see the ads for lawyers who promise to fight like tigers and at very low cost." For their part, Bates and O'Steen view the case as "victory for the public in general." *Bates*

Participants Reflect on Landmark Case, http://www.firstamendment center.org/bates-participants-reflect-on-landmark-case.

CHAPTER 8

SOLICITATION

■ ■ ■

Chapter hypothetical. The State of New Dakota recently enacted new rules of professional conduct regarding the solicitation of clients. According to the report of the state bar committee that drafted them, the rules were designed to protect consumers "against inappropriate solicitations or potentially misleading ads, as well as overly aggressive marketing," and to "benefit the bar by ensuring that the image of the legal profession is maintained at the highest possible level." The report cited several examples of what it viewed as overly aggressive advertising occurring in other states, but no evidence of similar marketing occurring in New Dakota. The new rules imposed a 30-day moratorium on the solicitation of clients with potential personal injury or wrongful death claims. The rule also prohibited lawyers who represented defendants or potential defendants in such instances from contacting injured parties or their representatives about the possibility of settlement for the same time period. The rule defined the term "solicitation" to mean "any advertisement initiated by or on behalf of a lawyer or law firm that is directed to, or targeted at, a specific recipient or group of recipients, or their family members or legal representatives, the primary purpose of which is the retention of the lawyer or law firm, and a significant motive for which is pecuniary gain. It does not include a proposal or other writing prepared and delivered in response to a specific request of a prospective client." The rest of New Dakota's advertising rules track those found in the ABA's Model Rules.

A few months ago, there was a terrible airplane crash in New Dakota. Over 100 passengers were killed. Hundreds of local residents also suffered property damage from falling debris from the crash. Sensing an opportunity, New Dakota lawyer Malcolm obtained the cell phone numbers of some of the families of the crash victims as well as the numbers for several of the property owners who suffered property damage as a result of the crash. Malcolm texted these individuals within a week of the crash and expressed his condolences while also offering his legal services in connection with the crash. That same week, Malcolm also placed advertisements on the Internet, offering to provide legal services in connection with the crash. Some of the family members of the crash victims and some of the property owners affected by the crash use ZMail, a free Web-mail service. ZMail uses web advertisements in an effort to pay for its system. ZMail uses a program that scans email messages for content and then uses an algorithm to place relevant, targeted advertisements in emails. When the family members and property owners exchanged emails with friends about the crash, they noticed that the replies they received from their friends contained Malcolm's advertisement on the side of the message. This is exactly what Malcolm had hoped would happen when he placed the advertisements.

When the New Dakota Board of Professional Responsibility found out about Malcolm's actions, it brought him up on disciplinary charges for violating the thirty-day moratorium. You represent Malcolm.

(A) What arguments can you make on his behalf in terms of the constitutionality of New Dakota's rule? (As you consider those arguments, also consider what arguments the Board might make.)

(B) Would Malcolm be subject to discipline if New Dakota instead had adopted the ABA's Model Rules?

* * *

Although advertising involves the active pursuit of clients—more active than many lawyers think is "professional"—it is typically regarded as a less aggressive and less threatening means of pursuing clients than the "solicitation" we will examine in this chapter. First we will consider solicitation by in-person contact—the "in-your-face pitch" and then turn our attention to two types of solicitation made possible by modern technology—solicitation of clients by live telephone and real-time electronic contact. Then, we look at a popular hybrid means of reaching prospective clients—using the mail to communicate directly with them either at home or at work. This Chapter will also provide us with the opportunity to reflect upon the future direction of the Supreme Court's constitutional oversight of the legal profession's regulation of the conduct of lawyers as they compete with other lawyers for the favor of those Americans who may be in need of legal services and be able to pay a lawyer to provide them.

* * *

A. IN-PERSON, LIVE TELEPHONE, AND REAL-TIME ELECTRONIC CONTACT

OHRALIK V. OHIO STATE BAR ASSOCIATION
436 U.S. 447 (1978)

MR. JUSTICE POWELL delivered the opinion of the Court.

In Bates v. State Bar of Arizona, 433 U.S. 350 (1977), this Court held that truthful advertising of "routine" legal services is protected by the First and Fourteenth Amendments against blanket prohibition by a State. The Court expressly reserved the question of the permissible scope of regulation of "in-person solicitation of clients. . . ." Today we . . . hold that the State—or the Bar acting with state authorization—constitutionally may discipline a lawyer for soliciting clients in person, for pecuniary gain, under circumstances likely to pose dangers that the State has a right to prevent.

I

Appellant, a member of the Ohio Bar, . . . learned . . . about an automobile accident . . . in which Carol McClintock, a young woman with whom appellant was casually acquainted, had been injured. Appellant made a telephone call to Ms. McClintock's parents, who informed him that their daughter was in the hospital. Appellant suggested that he might visit Carol in the hospital. Mrs. McClintock assented to the idea, but requested that appellant first stop by at her home.

During appellant's visit with the McClintocks, they explained that their daughter had been driving the family automobile on a local road when she was hit by an uninsured motorist. Both Carol and her passenger, Wanda Lou Holbert, were injured and hospitalized. In response to the McClintocks' expression of apprehension that they might be sued by Holbert, appellant explained that Ohio's guest statute would preclude such a suit. When appellant suggested to the McClintocks that they hire a lawyer, Mrs. McClintock retorted that such a decision would be up to Carol, who was 18 years old and would be the beneficiary of a successful claim.

Appellant proceeded to the hospital, where he found Carol lying in traction in her room. After a brief conversation about her condition, appellant told Carol he would represent her and asked her to sign an agreement. Carol said she would have to discuss the matter with her parents. She did not sign the agreement, but asked appellant to have her parents come to see her. Appellant also attempted to see Wanda Lou Holbert, but learned that she had just been released from the hospital. . . . He then departed for another visit with the McClintocks.

On his way appellant detoured to the scene of the accident, where he took a set of photographs. He also picked up a tape recorder, which he concealed under his raincoat before arriving at the McClintocks' residence. Once there, he re-examined their automobile insurance policy, discussed with them the law applicable to passengers, and explained the consequences of the fact that the driver who struck Carol's car was an uninsured motorist. Appellant discovered that the McClintocks' insurance policy would provide benefits of up to $12,500 each for Carol and Wanda Lou under an uninsured-motorist clause. Mrs. McClintock acknowledged that both Carol and Wanda Lou could sue for their injuries, but recounted to appellant that "Wanda swore up and down she would not do it." ... The McClintocks also told appellant that Carol had phoned to say that appellant could "go ahead" with her representation. Two days later appellant returned to Carol's hospital room to have her sign a contract, which provided that he would receive one-third of her recovery.

In the meantime, appellant obtained Wanda Lou's name and address from the McClintocks after telling them he wanted to ask her some questions about the accident. He then visited Wanda Lou at her home, without having been invited. He again concealed his tape recorder and recorded most of the conversation with Wanda Lou. After a brief, unproductive inquiry about the facts of the accident, appellant told Wanda Lou that he was representing Carol and that he had a "little tip" for Wanda Lou: the McClintocks' insurance policy contained an uninsured-motorist clause which might provide her with a recovery of up to $12,500. The young woman, who was 18 years of age and not a high school graduate at the time, replied to appellant's query about whether she was going to file a claim by stating that she really did not understand what was going on. Appellant offered to represent her, also, for a contingent fee of one-third of any recovery, and Wanda Lou stated "O.K."[4]

Wanda's mother attempted to repudiate her daughter's oral assent the following day, when appellant called on the telephone to speak to Wanda. Mrs. Holbert informed appellant that she and her daughter did not want to sue anyone or to have appellant represent them, and that if they decided to sue they would consult their own lawyer. Appellant insisted that Wanda had entered into a binding agreement. A month later Wanda confirmed in writing that she wanted neither to sue nor to be represented by appellant. She requested that appellant notify the insurance company that he was not her lawyer, as the company would not

---

[4]   Appellant told Wanda that she should indicate assent by stating "O.K.," which she did. Appellant later testified: "I would say that most of my clients have essentially that much of a communication. ... I think most of my clients, that's the way I practice law." ... In explaining the contingent-fee arrangement, appellant told Wanda Lou that his representation would not "cost [her] anything" because she would receive two-thirds of the recovery if appellant were successful in representing her but would not "have to pay [him] anything" otherwise.

release a check to her until he did so.[5] Carol also eventually discharged appellant. Although another lawyer represented her in concluding a settlement with the insurance company, she paid appellant one-third of her recovery[6] in settlement of his lawsuit against her for breach of contract.

Both Carol McClintock and Wanda Lou Holbert filed [disciplinary] complaints against appellant. . . . After a hearing, the Board found that appellant had violated Disciplinary Rules 2–103(A) and 2–104(A) of the Ohio Code of Professional Responsibility[9]. The Board rejected appellant's defense that his conduct was protected under the First and Fourteenth Amendments. The Supreme Court of Ohio adopted the findings of the Board, reiterated that appellant's conduct was not constitutionally protected, and increased the sanction of a public reprimand recommended by the Board to indefinite suspension.

. . . We now affirm the judgment of the Supreme Court of Ohio.

II

The solicitation of business by a lawyer through direct, in-person communication with the prospective client has long been viewed as inconsistent with the profession's ideal of the attorney-client relationship and as posing a significant potential for harm to the prospective client. It has been proscribed by the organized Bar for many years. Last Term the Court ruled that the justifications for prohibiting truthful, "restrained" advertising concerning "the availability and terms of routine legal services" are insufficient to override society's interest, safeguarded by the First and Fourteenth Amendments, in assuring the free flow of commercial information. *Bates*, 433 U.S., at 384. . . . The balance struck in *Bates* does not predetermine the outcome in this case. The entitlement of in-person solicitation of clients to the protection of the First Amendment differs from that of the kind of advertising approved in *Bates*, as does the strength of the State's countervailing interest in prohibition.

---

[5]   Before appellant would "disavow further interest and claim" in Wanda Lou's recovery, he insisted by letter that she first pay him the sum of $2,466.66, which represented one-third of his "conservative" estimate of the worth of her claim.

[6]   Carol recovered the full $12,500 and paid appellant $4,166.66. She testified that she paid the second lawyer $900 as compensation for his services.

[9]   DR 2–103(A) of the Ohio Code (1970) provides: "A lawyer shall not recommend employment, as a private practitioner, of himself, his partner, or associate to a non-lawyer who has not sought his advice regarding employment of a lawyer." DR 2–104(A) (1970) provides in relevant part: "A lawyer who has given unsolicited advice to a layman that he should obtain counsel or take legal action shall not accept employment resulting from that advice, except that: (1) A lawyer may accept employment by a close friend, relative, former client (if the advice is germane to the former employment), or one whom the lawyer reasonably believes to be a client."

A

Appellant contends that his solicitation of the two young women as clients is indistinguishable, for purposes of constitutional analysis, from the advertisement in *Bates*. Like that advertisement, his meetings with the prospective clients apprised them of their legal rights and of the availability of a lawyer to pursue their claims. According to appellant, such conduct is "presumptively an exercise of his free speech rights" which cannot be curtailed in the absence of proof that it actually caused a specific harm that the State has a compelling interest in preventing. But in-person solicitation of professional employment by a lawyer does not stand on a par with truthful advertising about the availability and terms of routine legal services. . . .

In-person solicitation by a lawyer of remunerative employment is a business transaction in which speech is an essential but subordinate component. While this does not remove the speech from the protection of the First Amendment, . . . it lowers the level of appropriate judicial scrutiny.

As applied in this case, the Disciplinary Rules are said to have limited the communication of two kinds of information. First, appellant's solicitation imparted to Carol McClintock and Wanda Lou Holbert certain information about his availability and the terms of his proposed legal services. In this respect, in-person solicitation serves much the same function as the advertisement at issue in *Bates*. But there are significant differences as well. Unlike a public advertisement, which simply provides information and leaves the recipient free to act upon it or not, in-person solicitation may exert pressure and often demands an immediate response, without providing an opportunity for comparison or reflection. The aim and effect of in-person solicitation may be to provide a one-sided presentation and to encourage speedy and perhaps uninformed decisionmaking; there is no opportunity for intervention or counter-education by agencies of the Bar, supervisory authorities, or persons close to the solicited individual. . . . In-person solicitation . . . actually may disserve the individual and societal interest, identified in *Bates*, in facilitating "informed and reliable decisionmaking." . . .

It also is argued that in-person solicitation may provide the solicited individual with information about his or her legal rights and remedies. In this case, appellant gave Wanda Lou a "tip" about the prospect of recovery based on the uninsured-motorist clause in the McClintocks' insurance policy, and he explained that clause and Ohio's guest statute to Carol McClintock's parents. But neither of the Disciplinary Rules here at issue prohibited appellant from communicating information to these young women about their legal rights and the prospects of obtaining a monetary recovery, or from recommending that they obtain counsel. DR 2–104(A) merely prohibited him from using the information as bait with which to obtain an agreement to represent them for a fee. The Rule does not prohibit a lawyer from giving unsolicited legal advice; it proscribes the acceptance of employment resulting from such advice.

. . . While entitled to some constitutional protection, appellant's conduct is subject to regulation in furtherance of important state interests.

B

The state interests implicated in this case are particularly strong. In addition to its general interest in protecting consumers and regulating commercial transactions, the State bears a special responsibility for maintaining standards among members of the licensed professions. "The interest of the States in regulating lawyers is especially great since lawyers are essential to the primary governmental function of administering justice, and have historically been 'officers of the courts.' " While lawyers act in part as "self-employed businessmen," they also act "as trusted agents of their clients, and as assistants to the court in search of a just solution to disputes."

. . . The substantive evils of solicitation have been stated over the years in sweeping terms: stirring up litigation, assertion of fraudulent claims, debasing the legal profession, and potential harm to the solicited client in the form of overreaching, overcharging, underrepresentation, and misrepresentation. The American Bar Association, as amicus curiae, defends the rule against solicitation primarily on three broad grounds: It is said that the prohibitions embodied in DR 2–103(A) and 2–104(A) serve to reduce the likelihood of overreaching and the exertion of undue influence on lay persons, to protect the privacy of individuals, and to avoid situations where the lawyer's exercise of judgment on behalf of the client will be clouded by his own pecuniary self-interest.

. . . [A]ppellant has conceded that the State has a legitimate and indeed "compelling" interest in preventing those aspects of solicitation that involve fraud, undue influence, intimidation, overreaching, and other forms of "vexatious conduct." We agree that protection of the public from these aspects of solicitation is a legitimate and important state interest.

III

Appellant's concession that strong state interests justify regulation to prevent the evils he enumerates would end this case but for his insistence that none of those evils was found to be present in his acts of solicitation. He challenges what he characterizes as the "indiscriminate application" of the Rules to him and thus attacks the validity of DR 2–103(A) and DR 2–104(A) not facially, but as applied to his acts of solicitation. And because no allegations or findings were made of the specific wrongs appellant concedes would justify disciplinary action, appellant . . . argues that we must decide whether a State may discipline him for solicitation per se without offending the First and Fourteenth Amendments.

. . . [A]ppellant errs in assuming that the constitutional validity of the judgment below depends on proof that his conduct constituted actual overreaching or inflicted some specific injury on Wanda Holbert or Carol McClintock. His assumption flows from the premise that nothing less than actual proved harm to the solicited individual would be a sufficiently important state interest to justify disciplining the attorney who solicits employment in person for pecuniary gain.

Appellant's argument misconceives the nature of the State's interest. The Rules prohibiting solicitation are prophylactic measures whose objective is the prevention of harm before it occurs. The Rules were applied in this case to discipline a lawyer for soliciting employment for pecuniary gain under circumstances likely to result in the adverse consequences the State seeks to avert. In such a situation, which is inherently conducive to overreaching and other forms of misconduct, the State has a strong interest in adopting and enforcing rules of conduct designed to protect the public from harmful solicitation by lawyers whom it has licensed.

The State's perception of the potential for harm in circumstances such as those presented in this case is well founded. The detrimental aspects of face-to-face selling even of ordinary consumer products have been recognized and addressed by the Federal Trade Commission, and it hardly need be said that the potential for overreaching is significantly greater when a lawyer, a professional trained in the art of persuasion, personally solicits an unsophisticated, injured, or distressed lay person[24]. Such an individual may place his trust in a lawyer, regardless of the latter's qualifications or the individual's actual need for legal representation, simply in response to persuasion under circumstances conducive to uninformed acquiescence. Although it is argued that personal solicitation is valuable because it may apprise a victim of misfortune of his legal rights, the very plight of that person not only makes him more vulnerable to influence but also may make advice all the more intrusive. Thus, under these adverse conditions the overtures of an uninvited lawyer may distress the solicited individual simply because of their obtrusiveness and the invasion of the individual's privacy, even when no other harm materializes. Under such circumstances, it is not

---

[24] Most lay persons are unfamiliar with the law, with how legal services normally are procured, and with typical arrangements between lawyer and client. To be sure, the same might be said about the lay person who seeks out a lawyer for the first time. But the critical distinction is that in the latter situation the prospective client has made an initial choice of a lawyer at least for purposes of a consultation; has chosen the time to seek legal advice; has had a prior opportunity to confer with family, friends, or a public or private referral agency; and has chosen whether to consult with the lawyer alone or accompanied.

unreasonable for the State to presume that in-person solicitation by lawyers more often than not will be injurious to the person solicited.

The efficacy of the State's effort to prevent such harm to prospective clients would be substantially diminished if, having proved a solicitation in circumstances like those of this case, the State were required in addition to prove actual injury. Unlike the advertising in *Bates*, in-person solicitation is not visible or otherwise open to public scrutiny. Often there is no witness other than the lawyer and the lay person whom he has solicited, rendering it difficult or impossible to obtain reliable proof of what actually took place. This would be especially true if the lay person were so distressed at the time of the solicitation that he could not recall specific details at a later date. If appellant's view were sustained, in-person solicitation would be virtually immune to effective oversight and regulation by the State or by the legal profession, in contravention of the State's strong interest in regulating members of the Bar in an effective, objective, and self-enforcing manner. It therefore is not unreasonable, or violative of the Constitution, for a State to respond with what in effect is a prophylactic rule.

On the basis of the undisputed facts of record, we conclude that the Disciplinary Rules constitutionally could be applied to appellant. He approached two young accident victims at a time when they were especially incapable of making informed judgments or of assessing and protecting their own interests. He solicited Carol McClintock in a hospital room where she lay in traction and sought out Wanda Lou Holbert on the day she came home from the hospital, knowing from his prior inquiries that she had just been released. Appellant urged his services upon the young women and used the information he had obtained from the McClintocks, and the fact of his agreement with Carol, to induce Wanda to say "O.K." in response to his solicitation. He employed a concealed tape recorder, seemingly to insure that he would have evidence of Wanda's oral assent to the representation. He emphasized that his fee would come out of the recovery, thereby tempting the young women with what sounded like a cost-free and therefore irresistible offer. He refused to withdraw when Mrs. Holbert requested him to do so only a day after the initial meeting between appellant and Wanda Lou and continued to represent himself to the insurance company as Wanda Holbert's lawyer.

The court below did not hold that these or other facts were proof of actual harm to Wanda Holbert or Carol McClintock but . . . the absence of explicit proof or findings of harm or injury is immaterial. The facts in this case present a striking example of the potential for overreaching that is inherent in a lawyer's in-person solicitation of professional employment. They also demonstrate the need for prophylactic regulation in furtherance of the State's interest in protecting the lay public. We hold that the

application of DR 2–103(A) and 2–104(A) to appellant does not offend the
Constitution.

   . . .

* * *

What do you think? Would the outcome in *Ohralik* have been
different if, instead of visiting Wanda Lou at the hospital, Ohralik had
called her on the telephone and offered to represent her? Why? What if
she had not been in the hospital, but was recuperating at home?

Runners and cappers. Imagine that instead of personally visiting
Wanda Lou, Ohralik hired a non-lawyer to approach Wanda Lou in the
hospital and make the same sales pitch that Ohralik made in the actual
case? (Such individuals are sometimes referred to as "runners" or
"cappers.") Would he still have been subject to discipline? *See* Model Rules
7.2(b) and 8.4(a).

* * *

IN RE PRIMUS
436 U.S. 412 (1978)

MR. JUSTICE POWELL delivered the opinion of the Court.

We consider on this appeal whether a State may punish a member of
its Bar who, seeking to further political and ideological goals through
associational activity, including litigation, advises a lay person of her
legal rights and discloses in a subsequent letter that free legal assistance
is available from a nonprofit organization with which the lawyer and her
associates are affiliated. . . .

I

Appellant, Edna Smith Primus, is a lawyer practicing in Columbia,
S. C. During the period in question, she was . . . an officer of and
cooperating lawyer with the Columbia branch of the American Civil
Liberties Union (ACLU). She received no compensation for her work on
behalf of the ACLU, but was paid a retainer as a legal consultant for the
South Carolina Council on Human Relations (Council), a nonprofit
organization with offices in Columbia.

During the summer of 1973, local and national newspapers reported
that pregnant mothers on public assistance in Aiken County, S.C. were
being sterilized or threatened with sterilization as a condition of the
continued receipt of medical assistance under the Medicaid program.
Concerned by this development, Gary Allen, an Aiken businessman and
officer of a local organization serving indigents, called the Council
requesting that one of its representatives come to Aiken to address some

of the women who had been sterilized. At the Council's behest, appellant, who had not known Allen previously, called him and arranged a meeting in his office in July 1973. Among those attending was Mary Etta Williams, who had been sterilized by Dr. Clovis H. Pierce after the birth of her third child. Williams and her grandmother attended the meeting because Allen, an old family friend, had invited them and because Williams wanted "[t]o see what it was all about. . . ." At the meeting, appellant advised those present, including Williams and the other women who had been sterilized by Dr. Pierce, of their legal rights and suggested the possibility of a lawsuit.

Early in August 1973 the ACLU informed appellant that it was willing to provide representation for Aiken mothers who had been sterilized. Appellant testified that after being advised by Allen that Williams wished to institute suit against Dr. Pierce, she decided to inform Williams of the ACLU's offer of free legal representation. Shortly after receiving appellant's letter[6]. . . Williams visited Dr. Pierce to discuss the progress of her third child, who was ill. At the doctor's office, she encountered his lawyer and at the latter's request signed a release of liability in the doctor's favor. Williams showed appellant's letter to the doctor and his lawyer, and they retained a copy. She then called appellant from the doctor's office and announced her intention not to sue. There was no further communication between appellant and Williams.

---

[6]   . . . [T]he letter stated:

August 30, 1973

Mrs. Marietta Williams
347 Sumter Street
Aiken, South Carolina 29801
Dear Mrs. Williams:

You will probably remember me from talking with you at Mr. Allen's office in July about the sterilization performed on you. The American Civil Liberties Union would like to file a lawsuit on your behalf for money against the doctor who performed the operation. We will be coming to Aiken in the near future and would like to explain what is involved so you can understand what is going on.

Now I have a question to ask of you. Would you object to talking to a women's magazine about the situation in Aiken? The magazine is doing a feature story on the whole sterilization problem and wants to talk to you and others in South Carolina. If you don't mind doing this, call me collect at 254–8151 on Friday before 5:00, if you receive this letter in time. Or call me on Tuesday morning (after Labor Day) collect.

I want to assure you that this interview is being done to show what is happening to women against their wishes, and is not being done to harm you in any way. But I want you to decide, so call me collect and let me know of your decision. This practice must stop.

About the lawsuit, if you are interested, let me know, and I'll let you know when we will come down to talk to you about it. We will be coming to talk to Mrs. Waters at the same time; she has already asked the American Civil Liberties Union to file a suit on her behalf.

Sincerely,
s/ Edna Smith
Edna Smith
Attorney-at-law

[In a disciplinary complaint, appellant was charged with engaging in] "solicitation in violation of the Canons of Ethics" by sending the August 30, 1973, letter to Williams. . . . Appellant . . . asserted, inter alia, that her conduct was protected by the First and Fourteenth Amendments . . .

. . . The panel filed a report recommending that appellant be found guilty of soliciting a client on behalf of the ACLU, in violation of Disciplinary Rules (DR) 2–103(D)(5)(a) and (c) and 2–104(A)(5) of the Supreme Court of South Carolina,[10] and that a private reprimand be issued. It noted that "[t]he evidence is inconclusive as to whether [appellant] solicited Mrs. Williams on her own behalf, but she did solicit Mrs. Williams on behalf of the ACLU, which would benefit financially in the event of successful prosecution of the suit for money damages." . . .

. . . [T]he Supreme Court of South Carolina entered an order which . . . increased the sanction, sua sponte, to a public reprimand.

. . . We now reverse.

II

This appeal concerns the tension between contending values of considerable moment to the legal profession and to society. Relying upon NAACP v. Button, 371 U.S. 415 (1963), and its progeny, appellant maintains that her activity involved constitutionally protected expression and association. In her view, South Carolina has not shown that the discipline meted out to her advances a subordinating state interest in a manner that avoids unnecessary abridgment of First Amendment freedoms. . . .

---

[10] [DR 2–103(D)(5)(a) and (c) provided as follows:]

(D) A lawyer shall not knowingly assist a person or organization that recommends, furnishes, or pays for legal services to promote the use of his services or those of his partners or associates. However, he may cooperate in a dignified manner with the legal service activities of any of the following, provided that his independent professional judgment is exercised in behalf of his client without interference or control by any organization or other person:

(5) Any other non-profit organization that recommends, furnishes, or pays for legal services to its members or beneficiaries, but only in those instances and to the extent that controlling constitutional interpretation at the time of the rendition of the services requires the allowance of such legal service activities, and only if the following conditions, unless prohibited by such interpretation, are met:

(a) The primary purposes of such organization do not include the rendition of legal services . . . [and]

(c) Such organization does not derive a financial benefit from the rendition of legal services by the lawyer.

[DR 2–104(A)(5) provided as follows:]

(A) A lawyer who has given unsolicited advice to a layman that he should obtain counsel or take legal action shall not accept employment resulting from that advice, except that:

(5) If success in asserting rights or defenses of his client in litigation in the nature of a class action is dependent upon the joinder of others, a lawyer may accept, but shall not seek, employment from those contacted for the purpose of obtaining their joinder.

[W]e decide today in Ohralik v. Ohio State Bar Assn., 436 U.S. 447, that the States may vindicate legitimate regulatory interests through proscription, in certain circumstances, of in-person solicitation by lawyers who seek to communicate purely commercial offers of legal assistance to lay persons.

Unlike the situation in *Ohralik*, however, appellant's act of solicitation took the form of a letter to a woman with whom appellant had discussed the possibility of seeking redress for an allegedly unconstitutional sterilization. This was not in-person solicitation for pecuniary gain. Appellant was communicating an offer of free assistance by attorneys associated with the ACLU, not an offer predicated on entitlement to a share of any monetary recovery. And her actions were undertaken to express personal political beliefs and to advance the civil-liberties objectives of the ACLU, rather than to derive financial gain. The question presented in this case is whether, in light of the values protected by the First and Fourteenth Amendments, these differences materially affect the scope of state regulation of the conduct of lawyers.

III

... [In *Button* this Court held] "that the activities of the NAACP, its affiliates and legal staff shown on this record are modes of expression and association protected by the First and Fourteenth Amendments which Virginia may not prohibit, under its power to regulate the legal profession, as improper solicitation of legal business violative of [state law] and the Canons of Professional Ethics." 371 U.S., at 428–429. The solicitation of prospective litigants, many of whom were not members of the NAACP or the Conference, for the purpose of furthering the civil-rights objectives of the organization and its members was held to come within the right " 'to engage in association for the advancement of beliefs and ideas.' " *Id.*, at 430. ...

Subsequent decisions have interpreted *Button* as establishing the principle that "collective activity undertaken to obtain meaningful access to the courts is a fundamental right within the protection of the First Amendment." United Transportation Union v. Michigan Bar, 401 U.S. 576, 585 (1971). ...

IV

We turn now to the question whether appellant's conduct implicates interests of free expression and association sufficient to justify the level of protection recognized in *Button* and subsequent cases. ...

... [T]he record does not support the state court's effort to draw a meaningful distinction between the ACLU and the NAACP. ... For the ACLU, as for the NAACP, "litigation is not a technique of resolving private differences"; it is "a form of political expression" and "political association." 371 U.S., at 429, 431.

... Appellant's letter of August 30, 1973, to Mrs. Williams thus comes within the generous zone of First Amendment protection reserved for associational freedoms. ...

V

South Carolina's action in punishing appellant for soliciting a prospective litigant by mail, on behalf of the ACLU, must withstand the "exacting scrutiny applicable to limitations on core First Amendment rights. ..." South Carolina must demonstrate "a subordinating interest which is compelling," and that the means employed in furtherance of that interest are "closely drawn to avoid unnecessary abridgment of associational freedoms."

Appellee contends that the disciplinary action taken in this case is part of a regulatory program aimed at the prevention of undue influence, overreaching, misrepresentation, invasion of privacy, conflict of interest, lay interference, and other evils that are thought to inhere generally in solicitation by lawyers of prospective clients, and to be present on the record before us. We do not dispute the importance of these interests. This Court's decision in *Button* makes clear, however, that "[b]road prophylactic rules in the area of free expression are suspect," and that "[p]recision of regulation must be the touchstone in an area so closely touching our most precious freedoms." 371 U.S., at 438. ...

A

The Disciplinary Rules in question sweep broadly. Under DR 2–103(D)(5), a lawyer employed by the ACLU or a similar organization may never give unsolicited advice to a lay person that he retain the organization's free services, and it would seem that one who merely assists or maintains a cooperative relationship with the organization also must suppress the giving of such advice if he or anyone associated with the organization will be involved in the ultimate litigation. ... Moreover, the Disciplinary Rules in question permit punishment for mere solicitation unaccompanied by proof of any of the substantive evils that appellee maintains were present in this case. In sum, the Rules in their present form have a distinct potential for dampening the kind of "cooperative activity that would make advocacy of litigation meaningful," as well as for permitting discretionary enforcement against unpopular causes.

B

... Where political expression or association is at issue, this Court has not tolerated the degree of imprecision that often characterizes government regulation of the conduct of commercial affairs. The approach we adopt today in *Ohralik*, 436 U.S. 447, that the State may proscribe in-person solicitation for pecuniary gain under circumstances likely to result in adverse consequences, cannot be applied to appellant's activity on behalf of the ACLU. Although a showing of potential danger may suffice in the former context, appellant may not be disciplined unless her activity in fact involved the type of misconduct at which South Carolina's broad prohibition is said to be directed.

The record does not support appellee's contention that undue influence, overreaching, misrepresentation, or invasion of privacy actually occurred in this case. Appellant's letter of August 30, 1973, followed up the earlier meeting—one concededly protected by the First and Fourteenth Amendments—by notifying Williams that the ACLU would be interested in supporting possible litigation. The letter imparted additional information material to making an informed decision about whether to authorize litigation, and permitted Williams an opportunity, which she exercised, for arriving at a deliberate decision. The letter was not facially misleading; indeed, it offered "to explain what is involved so you can understand what is going on." The transmittal of this letter—as contrasted with in-person solicitation—involved no appreciable invasion of privacy; nor did it afford any significant opportunity for overreaching or coercion. Moreover, the fact that there was a written communication lessens substantially the difficulty of policing solicitation practices that do offend valid rules of professional conduct. *See Ohralik*, 436 U.S., at 466–467. . . .

At bottom, the case against appellant rests on the proposition that a State may regulate in a prophylactic fashion all solicitation activities of lawyers because there may be some potential for overreaching, conflict of interest, or other substantive evils whenever a lawyer gives unsolicited advice and communicates an offer of representation to a layman. . . . In the context of political expression and association, however, a State must regulate with significantly greater precision.

VI

The State is free to fashion reasonable restrictions with respect to the time, place, and manner of solicitation by members of its Bar. . . . The State's special interest in regulating members whose profession it licenses, and who serve as officers of its courts, amply justifies the application of narrowly drawn rules to proscribe solicitation that in fact is misleading, overbearing, or involves other features of deception or improper influence. As we decide today in *Ohralik*, a State also may forbid in-person solicitation for pecuniary gain under circumstances likely to result in these evils. And a State may insist that lawyers not solicit on behalf of lay organizations that exert control over the actual conduct of any ensuing litigation. . . . Accordingly, nothing in this opinion should be read to foreclose carefully tailored regulation that does not abridge unnecessarily the associational freedom of nonprofit organizations, or their members, having characteristics like those of the NAACP or the ACLU.

    . . . The judgment of the Supreme Court of South Carolina is Reversed.

MR. JUSTICE BRENNAN took no part in the consideration or decision of this case.

* * *

Reconciling *Ohralik* and *Primus*. *Ohralik* involved in-person solicitation for pecuniary gain. *Primus* involved the solicitation of a prospective litigant by mail, on behalf of the ACLU. What then is the basis for distinguishing *Ohralik* and *Primus* and how do these cases affect the constitutional authority of the states to prohibit solicitation of clients by lawyers?

Dissenting and concurring opinions. Justice Rehnquist dissented in *Primus*. He questioned whether there was any principled distinction between the actions of the lawyers in *Primus* and *Ohralik* and suggested that even a lawyer who works for the ACLU or similar organization might be tempted to place the organization's political goals over those of the best interests of an individual client. For his part, Justice Marshall concurred in the outcomes in *Primus* and *Ohralik*, but wrote separately to emphasize his concern that unduly restrictive solicitation rules might deprive the consumers of legal services of important information. Did the Court draw the appropriate line in these cases in terms of a lawyer's pecuniary motive? Does Model Rule 7.3(a)?

* * *

Please read ABA Model Rules of Professional Conduct, Rule 7.3 and Comments.

* * *

Model Rule 7.3's exceptions. Obviously relying on the distinction drawn by the Court in *Primus*, Rule 7.3(a) limits its prohibition on marketing activities to those motivated by "the lawyer's pecuniary gain." Relying on *Ohralik*, Rule 7.3 draws a distinction between soliciting clients in real-time and soliciting clients in more indirect ways, such as through written communications. However, Rule 7.3(a) does allow lawyers to engage in real-time solicitation with respect to certain people, such as another lawyer or a family member. Why is real-time solicitation permitted in these cases?

The disciplinary rules post-*Ohralik* and *Primus*. In Edenfield v. Fane, 507 U.S. 761 (1993), Florida defended its ban on accountants' in-person solicitation of clients by analogy to *Ohralik*. However, the Court rejected this analogy because the solicitation at issue was directed at sophisticated business executives, not vulnerable accident victims, as in *Ohralik*. The Court emphasized that "the constitutionality of a ban on personal solicitation will depend upon the identity of the parties and the precise circumstances of the solicitation." *Id.* at 774. After *Edenfield* came down, the legal community expected a challenge to state bar regulations prohibiting solicitation of sophisticated business clients. But that challenge has not materialized, perhaps because lawyer solicitation of sophisticated clients already takes place via social channels. How are lawyers distinguishable from accountants?

Real-time electronic contact. The ABA takes the position that "real-time electronic contact" includes solicitation occurring in an Internet chat room. *Legislative History of the Model Rules of Professional Conduct* 254 (ABA 2005); *see also* Utah Rules of Prof'l Conduct R. 7.3 cmt. 1a (defining the term to mean "communication directed to a specific recipient and characterized by the immediacy and interactivity of response between individuals, such as that provided through . . . Internet 'chat rooms.' "). In contrast, the Philadelphia Bar Association concluded that the term did not apply to communications occurring in chat rooms. The Association reasoned that solicitation occurring in a chat room is different than in-person or telephone solicitation in that a participant "has the ability to simply leave the chat room at any time, solely within the participant's discretion." Philadelphia Bar Association Op. 2010–6.

The CAN-SPAM Act. In addition to the disciplinary rules governing solicitation of clients, there are state and federal laws that may apply. For instance, the federal CAN-SPAM Act, 15 U.S.C. § 7701 et seq., imposes specific requirements on those who send emails for the purpose of advertising or promoting a commercial product or service. These requirements include, among others, that the email not be deceptive or misleading, that it provide recipients with the ability to opt out of future mailings, and that the email is clearly and conspicuously identified as an advertisement or solicitation.

* * *

B. TARGETED DIRECT-MAIL SOLICITATION

In Shapero v. Kentucky Bar Association, 486 U.S. 466 (1988), the Court held that states cannot ban targeted direct mail solicitation of persons known to need legal services, as long as the letters are not false or deceptive. In *Shapero* a lawyer was disciplined for targeting persons facing foreclosure by mailing a letter offering a free consultation. In holding that Kentucky's blanket ban on targeted direct mail solicitation offended the First Amendment, the Court rejected the assertion that this case was simply "*Ohralik* in writing," *id.* at 475, and noted that solicitation letters are closer to the *Bates* pole than to the *Ohralik* pole on the marketing continuum: "A letter, like a printed advertisement (but unlike a lawyer), can readily be put in a drawer to be considered later, ignored, or discarded," *id.* at 467.

* * *

Please read ABA Model Rules of Professional Conduct, Rule 7.3(b) & (c) and Comments [5] and [7].

* * *

After almost two decades of invalidating state prohibitions on various forms of lawyer marketing, in 1995, the Court finally upheld a state regulation of targeted direct mail solicitation. As you read the following case, ask yourself whether it marks a revolution in the Court's view of lawyer marketing.

FLORIDA BAR v. WENT FOR IT, INC.
515 U.S. 618 (1995)

JUSTICE O'CONNOR delivered the opinion of the Court.

Rules of the Florida Bar prohibit personal injury lawyers from sending targeted direct-mail solicitations to victims and their relatives for 30 days following an accident or disaster. This case asks us to consider whether such rules violate the First and Fourteenth Amendments of the Constitution. We hold that in the circumstances presented here, they do not.

I

In 1989, the Florida Bar completed a 2-year study of the effects of lawyer advertising on public opinion. After conducting hearings, commissioning surveys, and reviewing extensive public commentary, the Bar determined that several changes to its advertising rules were in order. . . . Two of these amendments are at issue in this case. Rule 4–7.4(b)(1) provides that "[a] lawyer shall not send, or knowingly permit to be sent, . . . a written communication to a prospective client for the purpose of obtaining professional employment if: (A) the written communication concerns an action for personal injury or wrongful death or otherwise relates to an accident or disaster involving the person to whom the communication is addressed or a relative of that person, unless the accident or disaster occurred more than 30 days prior to the mailing of the communication." Rule 4–7.8(a) states that "[a] lawyer shall not accept referrals from a lawyer referral service unless the service: (1)

engages in no communication with the public and in no direct contact with prospective clients in a manner that would violate the Rules of Professional Conduct if the communication or contact were made by the lawyer." Together, these rules create a brief 30-day blackout period after an accident during which lawyers may not, directly or indirectly, single out accident victims or their relatives in order to solicit their business.

In March 1992, G. Stewart McHenry and his wholly owned lawyer referral service, Went For It, Inc., filed this action for declaratory and injunctive relief in the United States District Court for the Middle District of Florida challenging Rules 4.7–4(b)(1) and 4.7–8 as violative of the First and Fourteenth Amendments to the Constitution. McHenry alleged that he routinely sent targeted solicitations to accident victims or their survivors within 30 days after accidents and that he wished to continue doing so in the future. Went For It, Inc. represented that it wished to contact accident victims or their survivors within 30 days of accidents and to refer potential clients to participating Florida lawyers. In October 1992, McHenry was disbarred for reasons unrelated to this suit. . . .

The District Court . . . entered summary judgment for the plaintiffs, . . . relying on Bates v. State Bar of Arizona, 433 U.S. 350 (1977), and subsequent cases. The Eleventh Circuit affirmed on similar grounds. . . . We granted certiorari . . . and now reverse.

II

A

Constitutional protection for attorney advertising, and for commercial speech generally, is of recent vintage. . . .

In *Bates v. State Bar of Arizona*, supra, the Court struck a ban on price advertising for what it deemed "routine" legal services. . . . Expressing confidence that legal advertising would only be practicable for such simple, standardized services, the Court rejected the State's proffered justifications for regulation.

Nearly two decades of cases have built upon the foundation laid by *Bates*. It is now well established that lawyer advertising is commercial speech and, as such, is accorded a measure of First Amendment protection. Such First Amendment protection, of course, is not absolute. We have always been careful to distinguish commercial speech from speech at the First Amendment's core. . . . [W]e engage in "intermediate" scrutiny of restrictions on commercial speech, analyzing them under the framework set forth in Central Hudson Gas & Electric Corp. v. Public Service Comm'n of N.Y., 447 U.S. 557 (1980). Under *Central Hudson*, the government may freely regulate commercial speech that concerns unlawful activity or is misleading. . . . Commercial speech that falls into neither of those categories, like the advertising at issue here, may be regulated if the government satisfies a test consisting of three related prongs: first, the government must assert a substantial interest in support of its regulation; second, the government must demonstrate that the restriction on commercial speech directly and materially advances that interest; and third, the regulation must be " 'narrowly drawn,' ". . . .

B

"Unlike rational basis review, the *Central Hudson* standard does not permit us to supplant the precise interests put forward by the State with other suppositions,". . . . The Florida Bar asserts that it has a substantial interest in protecting the privacy and tranquility of personal injury victims and their loved ones against intrusive, unsolicited contact by lawyers. . . . This interest obviously factors into the Bar's paramount (and repeatedly professed) objective of curbing activities that "negatively affec[t] the administration of justice." . . . Because direct mail solicitations in the wake of accidents are perceived by the public as intrusive, the Bar argues, the reputation of the legal profession in the eyes of Floridians has suffered commensurately. . . . The regulation, then, is an effort to protect the flagging reputations of Florida lawyers by preventing them from engaging in conduct that, the Bar maintains, " 'is universally regarded as deplorable and beneath common decency because of its intrusion upon the special vulnerability and private grief of victims or their families.' "

. . . We have little trouble crediting the Bar's interest as substantial. On various occasions we have accepted the proposition that "States have a compelling interest in the practice of professions within their boundaries, and . . . as part of their power to protect the public health, safety, and other valid interests they have broad power to establish standards for licensing practitioners and regulating the practice of professions." Our precedents also leave no room for doubt that "the protection of potential clients' privacy is a substantial state interest."

. . . Under *Central Hudson*'s second prong, the State must demonstrate that the challenged regulation "advances the Government's interest 'in a direct and material way.' " That burden, we have explained, " 'is not satisfied by mere speculation and conjecture; rather, a governmental body seeking to sustain a restriction on commercial speech must demonstrate that the harms it recites are real and that its restriction will in fact alleviate them to a material degree.' " In *Edenfield*, the Court invalidated a Florida ban on in-person solicitation by certified public accountants (CPAs). We observed that the State Board of Accountancy had "present[ed] no studies that suggest personal solicitation of prospective business clients by CPAs creates the dangers of fraud, overreaching, or compromised independence that the Board claims to fear." Moreover, "[t]he record [did] not disclose any anecdotal evidence

... that validate[d] the Board's suppositions." ... In fact, we concluded that the only evidence in the record tended to "contradic[t] rather than strengthe[n] the Board's submissions."

... The direct-mail solicitation regulation before us does not suffer from such infirmities. The Florida Bar submitted a 106-page summary of its 2-year study of lawyer advertising and solicitation to the District Court. That summary contains data—both statistical and anecdotal—supporting the Bar's contentions that the Florida public views direct-mail solicitations in the immediate wake of accidents as an intrusion on privacy that reflects poorly upon the profession. As of June 1989, lawyers mailed 700,000 direct solicitations in Florida annually, 40% of which were aimed at accident victims or their survivors.... A survey of Florida adults commissioned by the Bar indicated that Floridians "have negative feelings about those attorneys who use direct mail advertising." ... Fifty-four percent of the general population surveyed said that contacting persons concerning accidents or similar events is a violation of privacy.... A random sampling of persons who received direct-mail advertising from lawyers in 1987 revealed that 45% believed that direct-mail solicitation is "designed to take advantage of gullible or unstable people"; 34% found such tactics "annoying or irritating"; 26% found it "an invasion of your privacy"; and 24% reported that it "made you angry." ... Significantly, 27% of direct-mail recipients reported that their regard for the legal profession and for the judicial process as a whole was "lower" as a result of receiving the direct mail....

The anecdotal record mustered by the Bar is noteworthy for its breadth and detail. With titles like "Scavenger Lawyers" (*The Miami Herald*, Sept. 29, 1987) and "Solicitors Out of Bounds" (*St. Petersburg Times*, Oct. 26, 1987), newspaper editorial pages in Florida have burgeoned with criticism of Florida lawyers who send targeted direct mail to victims shortly after accidents.... The study summary also includes page upon page of excerpts from complaints of direct-mail recipients. For example, a Florida citizen described how he was " 'appalled and angered by the brazen attempt' " of a law firm to solicit him by letter shortly after he was injured and his fiancée was killed in an auto accident.... Another found it " 'despicable and inexcusable' " that a Pensacola lawyer wrote to his mother three days after his father's funeral.... Another described how she was " 'astounded' " and then " 'very angry' " when she received a solicitation following a minor accident.... Still another described as " 'beyond comprehension' " a letter his nephew's family received the day of the nephew's funeral.... One citizen wrote, " 'I consider the unsolicited contact from you after my child's accident to be of the rankest form of ambulance chasing and in incredibly poor taste.... I cannot begin to express with my limited vocabulary the utter contempt in which I hold you and your kind.' " ...

In light of this showing—which respondents at no time refuted . . . —
we conclude that the Bar has satisfied the second prong of the *Central
Hudson* test. . . . After scouring the record, we are satisfied that the ban
on direct-mail solicitation in the immediate aftermath of accidents, unlike
the rule at issue in *Edenfield*, targets a concrete, nonspeculative harm.

In reaching a contrary conclusion, the Court of Appeals determined
that this case was governed squarely by Shapero v. Kentucky Bar Assn.,
486 U.S. 466 (1988). Making no mention of the Bar's study, the court
concluded that " 'a targeted letter [does not] invade the recipient's privacy
any more than does a substantively identical letter mailed at large. The
invasion, if any, occurs when the lawyer discovers the recipient's legal
affairs, not when he confronts the recipient with the discovery.' " . . .

While some of *Shapero*'s language might be read to support the Court
of Appeals' interpretation, *Shapero* differs in several fundamental
respects from the case before us. First and foremost, *Shapero*'s treatment
of privacy was casual. Contrary to the dissent's suggestions, . . . the State
in *Shapero* did not seek to justify its regulation as a measure undertaken
to prevent lawyers' invasions of privacy interests. . . . Rather, the State
focused exclusively on the special dangers of overreaching inhering in
targeted solicitations. . . . Second, in contrast to this case, *Shapero* dealt
with a broad ban on all direct-mail solicitations, whatever the time frame
and whoever the recipient. Finally, the State in *Shapero* assembled no
evidence attempting to demonstrate any actual harm caused by targeted
direct mail. The Court rejected the State's effort to justify a prophylactic
ban on the basis of blanket, untested assertions of undue influence and
overreaching. . . .

We find the Court's perfunctory treatment of privacy in *Shapero* to be
of little utility in assessing this ban on targeted solicitation of victims in
the immediate aftermath of accidents. While it is undoubtedly true that
many people find the image of lawyers sifting through accident and police
reports in pursuit of prospective clients unpalatable and invasive, this
case targets a different kind of intrusion. The Florida Bar has argued,
and the record reflects, that a principal purpose of the ban is "protecting
the personal privacy and tranquility of [Florida's] citizens from crass
commercial intrusion by attorneys upon their personal grief in times of
trauma." . . . The intrusion targeted by the Bar's regulation stems not
from the fact that a lawyer has learned about an accident or disaster (as
the Court of Appeals notes, in many instances a lawyer need only read
the newspaper to glean this information), but from the lawyer's
confrontation of victims or relatives with such information, while wounds
are still open, in order to solicit their business. In this respect, an
untargeted letter mailed to society at large is different in kind from a
targeted solicitation; the untargeted letter involves no willful or knowing
affront to or invasion of the tranquility of bereaved or injured individuals

and simply does not cause the same kind of reputational harm to the profession unearthed by the Florida Bar's study. . . .

The harm targeted by the Florida Bar cannot be eliminated by the targeted letter's brief journey to the trash can. The purpose of the 30-day targeted direct-mail ban is to forestall the outrage and irritation with the state-licensed legal profession that the practice of direct solicitation only days after accidents has engendered. The Bar is concerned not with citizens' "offense" in the abstract, . . . but with the demonstrable detrimental effects that such "offense" has on the profession it regulates[2]. Moreover, the harm posited by the Bar is as much a function of simple receipt of targeted solicitations within days of accidents as it is a function of the letters' contents. Throwing the letter away shortly after opening it may minimize the latter intrusion, but it does little to combat the former. . . .

Passing to *Central Hudson*'s third prong, we examine the relationship between the Florida Bar's interests and the means chosen to serve them. [With respect to this prong, the Court employs an intermediate test that is less stringent than the "least restrictive means" test but more stringent than rational basis review.]

Respondents levy a great deal of criticism, echoed in the dissent . . . at the scope of the Bar's restriction on targeted mail. "[B]y prohibiting written communications to all people, whatever their state of mind," respondents charge, the rule "keeps useful information from those accident victims who are ready, willing and able to utilize a lawyer's advice." This criticism may be parsed into two components. First, the rule does not distinguish between victims in terms of the severity of their injuries. According to respondents, the rule is unconstitutionally overinclusive insofar as it bans targeted mailings even to citizens whose injuries or grief are relatively minor. . . . Second, the rule may prevent citizens from learning about their legal options, particularly at a time when other actors—opposing counsel and insurance adjusters—may be clamoring for victims' attentions. Any benefit arising from the Bar's regulation, respondents implicitly contend, is outweighed by these costs.

We are not persuaded by respondents' allegations of constitutional infirmity. We find little deficiency in the ban's failure to distinguish among injured Floridians by the severity of their pain or the intensity of their grief. Indeed, it is hard to imagine the contours of a regulation that might satisfy respondents on this score. Rather than drawing difficult lines on the basis that some injuries are "severe" and some situations

---

[2] Missing this nuance altogether, the dissent asserts apocalyptically that we are "unsettl[ing] leading First Amendment precedents". . . . We do no such thing. There is an obvious difference between situations in which the Government acts in its own interests, or on behalf of entities it regulates, and situations in which the Government is motivated primarily by paternalism. . . .

appropriate (and others, presumably, inappropriate) for grief, anger, or emotion, the Florida Bar has crafted a ban applicable to all postaccident or disaster solicitations for a brief 30-day period. . . . The Bar's rule is reasonably well-tailored to its stated objective of eliminating targeted mailings whose type and timing are a source of distress to Floridians, distress that has caused many of them to lose respect for the legal profession.

Respondents' second point would have force if the Bar's rule were not limited to a brief period and if there were not many other ways for injured Floridians to learn about the availability of legal representation during that time. Our lawyer advertising cases have afforded lawyers a great deal of leeway to devise innovative ways to attract new business. Florida permits lawyers to advertise on prime-time television and radio as well as in newspapers and other media. They may rent space on billboards. They may send untargeted letters to the general population, or to discrete segments thereof. There are, of course, pages upon pages devoted to lawyers in the Yellow Pages of Florida telephone directories. These listings are organized alphabetically and by area of specialty. . . . These ample alternative channels for receipt of information about the availability of legal representation during the 30-day period following accidents may explain why, despite the ample evidence, testimony, and commentary submitted by those favoring (as well as opposing) unrestricted direct-mail solicitation, respondents have not pointed to— and we have not independently found—a single example of an individual case in which immediate solicitation helped to avoid, or failure to solicit within 30 days brought about, the harms that concern the dissent. . . . In fact, the record contains considerable empirical survey information suggesting that Floridians have little difficulty finding lawyers when they need one. . . . Finding no basis to question the commonsense conclusion that the many alternative channels for communicating necessary information about attorneys are sufficient, we see no defect in Florida's regulation.

III

Speech by professionals obviously has many dimensions. There are circumstances in which we will accord speech by attorneys on public issues and matters of legal representation the strongest protection our Constitution has to offer. *See, e.g.,* Gentile v. State Bar of Nevada, 501 U.S. 1030 (1991). This case, however, concerns pure commercial advertising, for which we have always reserved a lesser degree of protection under the First Amendment. Particularly because the standards and conduct of state-licensed lawyers have traditionally been subject to extensive regulation by the States, it is all the more appropriate that we limit our scrutiny of state regulations to a level commensurate with the " 'subordinate position' " of commercial speech in the scale of First Amendment values.

We believe that the Florida Bar's 30-day restriction on targeted direct-mail solicitation of accident victims and their relatives withstands scrutiny under the three-part *Central Hudson* test that we have devised for this context. The Bar has substantial interest both in protecting injured Floridians from invasive conduct by lawyers and in preventing the erosion of confidence in the profession that such repeated invasions have engendered. The Bar's proffered study, unrebutted by respondents below, provides evidence indicating that the harms it targets are far from illusory. The palliative devised by the Bar to address these harms is narrow both in scope and in duration. The Constitution, in our view, requires nothing more.

The judgment of the Court of Appeals, accordingly, is reversed.

JUSTICE KENNEDY, with whom JUSTICE STEVENS, JUSTICE SOUTER, and JUSTICE GINSBURG join, dissenting.

. . .

Although I agree with the Court that the case can be resolved by following the three-part inquiry we have identified to assess restrictions on commercial speech, . . . [i]t would oversimplify to say that what we consider here is commercial speech and nothing more, for in many instances the banned communications may be vital to the recipients' right to petition the courts for redress of grievances. . . .

As the Court notes, the first of the *Central Hudson* factors to be considered is whether the interest the State pursues in enacting the speech restriction is a substantial one. . . . The State says two different interests meet this standard. The first is the interest "in protecting the personal privacy and tranquility" of the victim and his or her family. As the Court notes, that interest has recognition in our decisions as a general matter; but it does not follow that the privacy interest in the cases the majority cites is applicable here. The problem the Court confronts, and cannot overcome, is our recent decision in Shapero v. Kentucky Bar Assn., 486 U.S. 466 (1988). In assessing the importance of the interest in that solicitation case, we made an explicit distinction between direct in-person solicitations and direct mail solicitations. *Shapero*, like this case, involved a direct mail solicitation, and there the State recited its fears of "overreaching and undue influence." . . . We found, however, no such dangers presented by direct mail advertising. We reasoned that "[a] letter, like a printed advertisement (but unlike a lawyer), can readily be put in a drawer to be considered later, ignored, or discarded." . . . .

To avoid the controlling effect of *Shapero* in the case before us, the Court seeks to declare that a different privacy interest is implicated. As it sees the matter, the substantial concern is that victims or their families will be offended by receiving a solicitation during their grief and trauma. But we do not allow restrictions on speech to be justified on the ground that the expression might offend the listener. . . .

   . . .

In the face of these difficulties of logic and precedent, the State and the opinion of the Court turn to a second interest: protecting the reputation and dignity of the legal profession. The argument is, it seems fair to say, that all are demeaned by the crass behavior of a few. The argument takes a further step in the amicus brief filed by the Association of Trial Lawyers of America. There it is said that disrespect for the profession from this sort of solicitation (but presumably from no other sort of solicitation) results in lower jury verdicts. In a sense, of course, these arguments are circular. While disrespect will arise from an unethical or improper practice, the majority begs a most critical question by assuming that direct mail solicitations constitute such a practice. The fact is, however, that direct solicitation may serve vital purposes and promote the administration of justice, and to the extent the bar seeks to protect lawyers' reputations by preventing them from engaging in speech some deem offensive, the State is doing nothing more (as amicus the Association of Trial Lawyers of America is at least candid enough to admit) than manipulating the public's opinion by suppressing speech that informs us how the legal system works. The disrespect argument thus proceeds from the very assumption it tries to prove, which is to say that solicitations within 30 days serve no legitimate purpose. This, of course, is censorship pure and simple; and censorship is antithetical to the first principles of free expression.

II

Even were the interests asserted substantial, the regulation here fails the second part of the *Central Hudson* test, which requires that the dangers the State seeks to eliminate be real and that a speech restriction or ban advance that asserted State interest in a direct and material way. . . . Here, what the State has offered falls well short of demonstrating that the harms it is trying to redress are real, let alone that the regulation directly and materially advances the State's interests. The parties and the Court have [relied upon] a document prepared by the Florida Bar, one of the adverse parties, and submitted to the District Court in this case. . . . This document includes no actual surveys, few indications of sample size or selection procedures, no explanations of methodology, and no discussion of excluded results. There is no description of the statistical universe or scientific framework that permits any productive use of the information ... The most generous reading of this document permits identification of 34 pages on which direct mail solicitation is arguably discussed. Of these, only two are even a synopsis of a study of the attitudes of Floridians towards such solicitations. The bulk of the remaining pages include comments by lawyers about direct mail (some of them favorable), excerpts from citizen complaints about such solicitation, and a few excerpts from newspaper articles on the topic. Our cases require something more than a few pages of self-serving and unsupported statements by the State to demonstrate that a regulation directly and materially advances the elimination of a real harm when the State seeks to suppress truthful and nondeceptive speech. . . .

III

. . . Were it appropriate to reach the third part of the *Central Hudson* test, it would be clear that the relationship between the Bar's interests and the means chosen to serve them is not a reasonable fit. The Bar's rule creates a flat ban that prohibits far more speech than necessary to serve the purported state interest. Even assuming that interest were legitimate, there is a wild disproportion between the harm supposed and the speech ban enforced. . . .

. . . The only seeming justification for the State's restriction is the one the Court itself offers, which is that attorneys can and do resort to other ways of communicating important legal information to potential clients. Quite aside from the latent protectionism for the established bar that the argument discloses, it fails for the more fundamental reason that it concedes the necessity for the very representation the attorneys solicit and the State seeks to ban. The accident victims who are prejudiced to vindicate the State's purported desire for more dignity in the legal profession will be the very persons who most need legal advice, for they are the victims who, because they lack education, linguistic ability, or familiarity with the legal system, are unable to seek out legal services. . . .

. . . The State's restriction deprives accident victims of information which may be critical to their right to make a claim for compensation for injuries. The telephone book and general advertisements may serve this purpose in part; but the direct solicitation ban will fall on those who most need legal representation: for those with minor injuries, the victims too ill-informed to know an attorney may be interested in their cases; for those with serious injuries, the victims too ill-informed to know that time is of the essence if counsel is to assemble evidence and warn them not to enter into settlement negotiations or evidentiary discussions with investigators for opposing parties. . . . A solicitation letter is not a contract. Nothing in the record shows that these communications do not at the least serve the purpose of informing the prospective client that he or she has a number of different attorneys from whom to choose, so that the decision to select counsel, after an interview with one or more interested attorneys, can be deliberate and informed. . . .

IV

It is most ironic that, for the first time since *Bates v. State Bar of Arizona*, the Court now orders a major retreat from the constitutional guarantees for commercial speech in order to shield its own profession from public criticism. . . . There is no authority for the proposition that the Constitution permits the State to promote the public image of the legal profession by suppressing information about the profession's business aspects. If public respect for the profession erodes because solicitation distorts the idea of the law as most lawyers see it, it must be remembered that real progress begins with more rational speech, not less. . . .

. . . By validating Florida's rule, today's majority is complicit in the Bar's censorship. For these reasons, I dissent from the opinion of the Court and from its judgment.

* * *

Post-*Went For It*. Following *Went For It*, a number of jurisdictions adopted similar cooling off periods. Conn. Rules of Prof'l Conduct R. 7.3(b)(5) (imposing a forty-day moratorium on "written or electronic communication concern[ing] an action for personal injury or wrongful death"); Ga. Rules of Prof'l Conduct R. 7.3(a)(3) (imposing a thirty-day moratorium on "written communication concern[ing] an action for personal injury or wrongful death"); Tenn. Rules of Prof'l Conduct R. 7.3(b)(3) (imposing a thirty-day moratorium of potential clients by written, recorded, or electronic communication or by in-person, telephone, or real-time electronic contact" if "the communication concerns an action for personal injury, worker's compensation, wrongful death, or otherwise relates to an accident or disaster involving the person to whom the communication is addressed").

What do you think? Is *Went-For-It* merely a logical extension of the invasion of privacy and known vulnerability prongs of *Ohralik* or has the majority laid a completely new foundation for the evaluation of restraints on lawyers' commercial speech that will permit the Court to uphold restrictions on lawyer advertising and solicitation if the bar can "document" that the activity in question causes a significant number of people to think poorly of the legal profession?

* * *

Profile of attorney professionalism. Edna Smith Primus was the lawyer whose actions were at issue in the *Primus* case included in this chapter. Primus, "the daughter of a sharecropper," was the "first black woman to graduate from the law school of the University of South Carolina" in 1972 and was only the third black woman to be admitted to the South Carolina Bar. *Supreme Court Clears Black Woman Attorney*, JET, Sept. 14, 1978, at 6. Roughly a year after receiving her law degree, Primus became involved in the events that led to the Supreme Court decision that bears her name. Primus, a frequent advocate for the underrepresented, was an attorney with the South Carolina Council on Human Relations (SCCHR), a group that "played a key role in fostering better living and social conditions for African-Americans and promoting racial harmony within South Carolina and the South generally." *Records of the South Carolina Council on Human Relations,* South Caroliniana Library, The University of South Carolina *available at* http://library.sc. edu/socar/mnscrpts/scchr.html (last visited Jan. 14, 2015). Primus also served as a legal services attorney in the city of Columbia and served in the role of managing attorney of that office for many years.

Edna Primus sought to advance the rights of women and minorities throughout her long legal career. Her professional life serves as an example of principled and persistent advocacy that highlights the important role of lawyers as active members in their communities.

PART 3

THE CLIENT-LAWYER RELATIONSHIP

■ ■ ■

Now that you have attracted a prospective client, you are ready to form an attorney-client relationship and then commence your representation of the client. In Part 3, we examine the attorney-client relationship as it will be established by express or implied agreement between the lawyer and client and also as it continues, is terminated, and to some extent persists after its termination. Although all the various issues that can arise in an ongoing attorney-client relationship can be addressed by agreement between the lawyer and client when the relationship is first formed, we have chosen to subdivide our examination of the various facets of the attorney-client relationship and to differentiate between those facets that are necessarily addressed when the attorney and client agree to establish their relationship—such as the scope of the representation and the fee to be paid by the client for the lawyer's services—and the facets of the relationship that more typically play out during the performance, termination, and afterlife of the relationship. Thus, Section 1 focuses on the formation of the attorney-client relationship, with chapters focusing on the agreement between the lawyer and client about the scope of the representation to be provided by the lawyer, the fee to be paid by the client, and the related duty of safekeeping client funds and property. In this section we will also introduce the lawyer's duties to prospective clients whom the lawyer chooses not to represent. Subsequent sections then focus on selected aspects of an ongoing attorney-client relationship—communication and decision-making in Section 2; competence and diligence in Section 3; confidentiality and privileges in Section 4; and loyalty in Section 5. Finally in Section 6, we examine the termination of the attorney-client relationship and the duties lawyers owe to their former clients. In all these chapters, the focus is on the legal and professional relationship between the lawyer and the client rather than on the lawyer's relationships with third persons with whom the lawyer may interact while representing the client.

SECTION 1

ESTABLISHING THE CLIENT-LAWYER RELATIONSHIP

■ ■ ■

This section includes three chapters that focus on the formation of the attorney-client relationship, with particular focus on the negotiation of the agreement between the lawyer and the client by which the lawyer undertakes to provide specified services to the client, and the client either agrees to pay the lawyer for the services rendered or the lawyer agrees to provide the services for free. In Chapter 9, we first focus on the dealings between a lawyer and a prospective client that may, or may not, result in an attorney-client relationship between them. Included in Chapter 9 will be our consideration of a lawyer's duties to prospective clients whom the lawyer chooses not to represent and a focus on the lawyer's ability to limit the scope of representation. Chapter 10 focuses on the client's promise to pay the lawyer a fee and to reimburse the lawyer for costs incurred by the lawyer on the client's behalf. Chapter 11 then examines the responsibilities of lawyers after they receive payment or are otherwise entrusted to keep safe client funds and property.

CHAPTER 9

ESTABLISHING A CLIENT-LAWYER RELATIONSHIP

■ ■ ■

Chapter hypothetical. Elizabeth had been toying with the idea of bringing a personal injury suit against another individual but had never quite gotten around to it. One day, she visited Palsgraf & Pennoyer LLP's website and noticed that Darren, a lawyer in the firm, did personal injury work. The firm's site has a link entitled "Contact Us." When a visitor clicks on this link, a screen comes up that asks, "Think you might need a lawyer?" There is a box in the screen in which the visitor is invited to briefly describe the nature of the visitor's legal issue and to leave a name, phone number, and email. Elizabeth filled out the form, describing in detail the incident that led to her injury. A paralegal retrieved Elizabeth's information and passed it along to Darren, who, unfortunately, misplaced the information. Elizabeth never received a response, so she figured she must not have had a good claim. Two weeks after Elizabeth filled out the form on the website, the statute of limitations on her claim ran out. Elizabeth has since spoken to another lawyer who informed her that she had a strong claim, but that she could no longer pursue it due to the statute of limitations.

Darren agreed to represent another client, Agnes, about the possibility of representing her. Agnes explained that she and her husband had already gone through mediation and agreed upon a settlement and distribution of the marital assets. Agnes explained that she did not want to renegotiate the agreement; she simply wanted to make sure that the agreement was clear enough so that there would not be any interpretation issues that might result in future litigation. "I'm sick of the whole thing and I just want to be done with it," an obviously distraught Agnes told Darren. Darren documented his agreement with Agnes in a letter:

Dear Agnes:

This letter will confirm that you have retained my law firm for the purpose of reviewing a Property Settlement Agreement that was the product of divorce mediation.

This letter will further confirm that I have not conducted any discovery in this matter on your behalf. I have not reviewed income tax returns or other financial documentation to confirm or verify your husband's income for the past several years. I have no information concerning the gross and net values of the property you and your husband own.

Based upon the fact that I have not had an opportunity to conduct full and complete discovery in this matter, including but not limited to appraisals of real estate and business interests, depositions and interrogatories, I am not in a position to advise you as to whether or not the Agreement is fair and equitable and whether or not you should execute the Agreement as prepared. In sum, I am not in a position to make a recommendation or determination that the Property Settlement Agreement as prepared represents a fair and reasonable compromise of the issues concerning equitable distribution or whether the amount of alimony and/or child support that you will receive under the terms of the Agreement is an amount that would be awarded to you if, in fact, this matter proceeded to trial.

After reviewing the Agreement with you, I am satisfied that you understand the terms and conditions of the Agreement; that you feel that you are receiving a fair and equitable amount of the assets that were acquired during the marriage; and that the amount of support that is provided in the Agreement will, in fact, provide you with an income that will allow you to maintain a respectable lifestyle.

I will use my best efforts to review the Agreement for clarity and precision in an attempt to reduce the potential for future litigation. [The rest of the agreement discussed the firm's fee and other billing matters.]

Agnes entered into the Property Settlement Agreement. Several months later, she learned that her husband had hidden substantial assets from her during the mediation. A simple review of the couple's tax returns and other financial records by a reasonably competent attorney would have revealed these assets. As a result, she sought to have the Agreement set aside. In addition, she sued Darren and Palsgraf & Pennoyer LLP for malpractice for failing to protect her interests and also filed a disciplinary complaint against them in connection with Darren's representation of her in the matter.

(A) Is Darren subject to discipline and/or liability for malpractice based on his handling of Elizabeth's matter?

(B) Is Darren subject to discipline and/or liability for malpractice based on his handling of Agnes' matter?

(C) Imagine that you work with Darren at Palsgraf & Pennoyer and saw a draft of his letter to Agnes before he mailed it. What suggestions do you have in terms of revising the letter so that it more clearly complies with Model Rule 1.2(c) and limits the firm's potential liability?

* * *

Assuming a lawyer's advertising or solicitation efforts have been successful in attracting a prospective client, there remains the final step of entering into a client-attorney relationship. As discussed in Chapter 1, a lawyer assumes various common law and ethical duties by entering into a client-attorney relationship. This includes a duty to competently and diligently pursue the client's interests. Therefore, it is essential that the parties understand the scope of the lawyer's anticipated representation.

* * *

A. BECOMING A PERSON'S LAWYER

The ABA Model Rules of Professional Conduct do not contain a definition of a "client" or a specification of circumstances in which a lawyer will be held to have created an attorney-client relationship. Rather, paragraph [17] of the Preamble and Scope simply refers a reader to substantive state or federal law to determine whether a client-lawyer relationship exists. This is an important omission because "[m]ost of the duties flowing from the client-lawyer relationship attach only after the client has requested the lawyer to render legal services and the lawyer has agreed to do so."

* * *

1. AGREEING OR UNDERTAKING TO REPRESENT ANOTHER

Please read Restatement (Third) of the Law Governing Lawyers § 14.

* * *

Problem 9.1. Lawyer Belinda routinely advertises her services as a personal injury lawyer. Miles telephones Belinda's office and tells Belinda's secretary that Miles was hurt when he fell in a store about a year ago and would like Belinda to represent Miles in a personal injury action. Belinda's secretary tells Miles to bring in any medical bills or other relevant information he might have. She also arranged a medical examination for Miles with the store's insurance company. However, Belinda's secretary does not tell Miles that Belinda would then decide whether to take the case. Miles delivers the information to Belinda's office the next day. Due to an oversight, Belinda does not communicate with Miles for 30 days, and then eventually tells Miles that she does not wish to take the case. By then, the statute of limitations had run on Miles' claims. Could a jury applying the test from the *Restatement* find that an attorney-client relationship existed between Belinda and Miles prior to Belinda's communication declining representation? *See* DeVaux v. American Home Assurance Co., 444 N.E.2d 355 (Mass. 1983).

* * *

2. DUTIES TO PROSPECTIVE CLIENTS

Please read ABA Model Rules of Professional Conduct, Rule 1.18 and Comments [1]–[3] & [9].

Please read Restatement (Third) of the Law Governing Lawyers § 15.

* * *

TOGSTAD V. VESELY, OTTO, MILLER & KEEFE

291 N.W.2d 686 (Minn. 1980) (en banc)

PER CURIAM.

[As a result of medical malpractice by a hospital and a physician, Mr. Togstad was left paralyzed on the right side and unable to speak.]

About 14 months after her husband's hospitalization began, plaintiff Joan Togstad met with attorney Jerre Miller regarding her husband's condition. Neither she nor her husband was personally acquainted with Miller or his law firm prior to that time. John Togstad's former work supervisor, Ted Bucholz, made the appointment and accompanied Mrs. Togstad to Miller's office. Bucholz was present when Mrs. Togstad and Miller discussed the case.

Mrs. Togstad testified that she told Miller "everything that happened at the hospital,". . . . She stated that she "believed" she had told Miller "about the procedure and what was undertaken, what was done, and what happened." She brought no records with her. Miller took notes and asked questions during the meeting, which lasted 45 minutes to an hour. At its conclusion, according to Mrs. Togstad, Miller said that "he did not think we had a legal case, however, he was going to discuss this with his partner." She understood that if Miller changed his mind after talking to his partner, he would call her. Mrs. Togstad "gave it" a few days and, since she did not hear from Miller, decided "that they had come to the conclusion that there wasn't a case." No fee arrangements were discussed, no medical authorizations were requested, nor was Mrs. Togstad billed for the interview.

Mrs. Togstad denied that Miller had told her his firm did not have expertise in the medical malpractice field, urged her to see another attorney, or related to her that the statute of limitations for medical malpractice actions was two years. She did not consult another attorney until one year after she talked to Miller. Mrs. Togstad indicated that she did not confer with another attorney earlier because of her reliance on Miller's "legal advice" that they "did not have a case."

On cross-examination, Mrs. Togstad was asked whether she went to Miller's office "to see if he would take the case of [her] husband * * *." She replied, "Well, I guess it was to go for legal advice, what to do, where shall we go from here? That is what we went for." Again in response to defense counsel's questions, Mrs. Togstad testified as follows:

Q. And it was clear to you, was it not, that what was taking place was a preliminary discussion between a prospective client and lawyer as to whether or not they wanted to enter into an attorney-client relationship?

A. I am not sure how to answer that. It was for legal advice as to what to do.

Q. And Mr. Miller was discussing with you your problem and indicating whether he, as a lawyer, wished to take the case, isn't that true?

A. Yes.

On re-direct examination, Mrs. Togstad acknowledged that when she left Miller's office she understood that she had been given a "qualified, quality legal opinion that [she and her husband] did not have a malpractice case."

Miller's testimony was different in some respects from that of Mrs. Togstad. Like Mrs. Togstad, Miller testified that Mr. Bucholz arranged and was present at the meeting, which lasted about 45 minutes. According to Miller, Mrs. Togstad described the hospital incident, including the conduct of the nurses. He asked her questions, to which she responded. Miller testified that "[t]he only thing I told her [Mrs. Togstad] after we had pretty much finished the conversation was that there was nothing related in her factual circumstances that told me that she had a case that our firm would be interested in undertaking."

Miller also claimed he related to Mrs. Togstad "that because of the grievous nature of the injuries sustained by her husband, that this was only my opinion and she was encouraged to ask another attorney if she wished for another opinion" and "she ought to do so promptly." He testified that he informed Mrs. Togstad that his firm "was not engaged as experts" in the area of medical malpractice, and that they associated with the Charles Hvass firm in cases of that nature. Miller stated that at the end of the conference he told Mrs. Togstad that he would consult with

Charles Hvass and if Hvass's opinion differed from his, Miller would so inform her. Miller recollected that he called Hvass a "couple days" later and discussed the case with him. It was Miller's impression that Hvass thought there was no liability for malpractice in the case. Consequently, Miller did not communicate with Mrs. Togstad further.

On cross-examination, Miller testified as follows:

Q. Now, so there is no misunderstanding, and I am reading from your deposition, you understood that she was consulting with you as a lawyer, isn't that correct?

A. That's correct.

Q. That she was seeking legal advice from a professional attorney licensed to practice in this state and in this community?

A. I think you and I did have another interpretation or use of the term "Advice". She was there to see whether or not she had a case and whether the firm would accept it.

Q. We have two aspects; number one, your legal opinion concerning liability of a case for malpractice; number two, whether there was or wasn't liability, whether you would accept it, your firm, two separate elements, right?

A. I would say so. . . . Certainly, she was seeking my opinion as an attorney in the sense of whether or not there was a case that the firm would be interested in undertaking.

Kenneth Green, a Minneapolis attorney, was called as an expert by plaintiffs. He stated that in rendering legal advice regarding a claim of medical malpractice, the "minimum" an attorney should do would be to request medical authorizations from the client, review the hospital records, and consult with an expert in the field. John McNulty, a Minneapolis attorney, and Charles Hvass testified as experts on behalf of the defendants. McNulty stated that when an attorney is consulted as to whether he will take a case, the lawyer's only responsibility in refusing it is to so inform the party. He testified, however, that when a lawyer is asked his legal opinion on the merits of a medical malpractice claim, community standards require that the attorney check hospital records and consult with an expert before rendering his opinion.

Hvass stated that he had no recollection of Miller's calling him in October 1972 relative to the Togstad matter. He testified that:

A. * * * when a person comes in to me about a medical malpractice action, based upon what the individual has told me, I have to make a decision as to whether or not there probably is or probably is not, based upon that information, medical malpractice. And if, in my judgment, based upon what the client has told me, there is not medical malpractice, I will so inform the client.

Hvass stated, however, that he would never render a "categorical" opinion. In addition, Hvass acknowledged that if he were consulted for a "legal opinion" regarding medical malpractice and 14 months had expired since the incident in question, "ordinary care and diligence" would require him to inform the party of the two-year statute of limitations applicable to that type of action.

This case was submitted to the jury by way of a special verdict form. The jury found that Dr. Blake and the hospital were negligent and that Dr. Blake's negligence (but not the hospital's) was a direct cause of the injuries sustained by John Togstad; that there was an attorney-client contractual relationship between Mrs. Togstad and Miller; that Miller was negligent in rendering advice regarding the possible claims of Mr. and Mrs. Togstad; that, but for Miller's negligence, plaintiffs would have been successful in the prosecution of a legal action against Dr. Blake; and that neither Mr. nor Mrs. Togstad was negligent in pursuing their claims against Dr. Blake. The jury awarded damages to Mr. Togstad of $610,500 and to Mrs. Togstad of $39,000. . . .

. . . In a legal malpractice action of the type involved here, four elements must be shown: (1) that an attorney-client relationship existed; (2) that defendant acted negligently or in breach of contract; (3) that such acts were the proximate cause of the plaintiffs' damages; (4) that but for defendant's conduct the plaintiffs would have been successful in the prosecution of their medical malpractice claim.

. . . The thrust of Mrs. Togstad's testimony is that she went to Miller for legal advice, was told there wasn't a case, and relied upon this advice in failing to pursue the claim for medical malpractice. In addition, according to Mrs. Togstad, Miller did not qualify his legal opinion by urging her to seek advice from another attorney, nor did Miller inform her that he lacked expertise in the medical malpractice area. Assuming this testimony is true, . . . we believe a jury could properly find that Mrs. Togstad sought and received legal advice from Miller under circumstances which made it reasonably foreseeable to Miller that Mrs. Togstad would be injured if the advice were negligently given. Thus, under either a tort or contract analysis, there is sufficient evidence in the record to support the existence of an attorney-client relationship.

. . . [D]efendants [also] assert that a new trial should be awarded on the ground that the trial court erred by refusing to instruct the jury that Miller's failure to inform Mrs. Togstad of the two-year statute of limitations for medical malpractice could not constitute negligence. . . .

. . . [T]here is adequate evidence supporting the claim that Miller was also negligent in failing to advise Mrs. Togstad of the two-year medical malpractice limitations period and thus the trial court acted properly in refusing to instruct the jury in the manner urged by defendants. One of defendants' expert witnesses, Charles Hvass, testified:

> Q. Now, Mr. Hvass, where you are consulted for a legal opinion and advice concerning malpractice and 14 months have elapsed (since the incident in question), wouldn't you hold yourself out as competent to give a legal opinion and advice to these people concerning their rights, wouldn't ordinary care and diligence require that you inform them that there is a two-year statute of limitations within which they have to act or lose their rights?

> A. Yes. I believe I would have advised someone of the two-year period of limitation, yes.

Consequently, based on the testimony of Mrs. Togstad, i.e., that she requested and received legal advice from Miller concerning the malpractice claim, and the above testimony of Hvass, we must reject the defendants' contention, as it was reasonable for a jury to determine that Miller acted negligently in failing to inform Mrs. Togstad of the applicable limitations period.

. . . Based on the foregoing, we hold that the jury's findings are adequately supported by the record. Accordingly we uphold the trial court's denial of defendants' motion for judgment notwithstanding the jury verdict. . . .

* * *

Togstad **and Rule 1.18.** *Togstad* involved a legal malpractice claim, not the disciplinary process, and was decided before the adoption of Model Rule 1.18. Regardless, would Mrs. Togstad qualify as a prospective client under Rule 1.18 today? Why or why not?

Law firm websites and prospective clients. ABA Formal Opinion No. 10–457 (2010) notes the possibility that a law firm website that invites inquiries may create a prospective client-lawyer relationship under Rule 1.18. "Lawyers who respond to website-initiated inquiries about legal services should consider the possibility that Rule 1.18 may apply."

* * *

B. THE CONSTITUTIONAL RIGHT TO COUNSEL OF CHOICE

The law governing lawyers places a high value on respecting a client's decision regarding the choice of an attorney and preserving a client-attorney relationship once it has been formed. Numerous rules of professional conduct further this value. So does constitutional law.

In United States v. Gonzalez-Lopez, 548 U.S. 140 (2006), a criminal defendant hired an out-of-state lawyer to represent him. The trial court erroneously denied the attorney's petition for admission pro hac vice. As a result, the defendant was forced to hire another attorney and was convicted. The Eighth Circuit held that the district court had erred in denying the petition pro hac vice, and that the error was not subject to harmless error analysis, thus warranting automatic reversal. On appeal, the Supreme Court held that the trial court erroneously deprived the defendant of his constitutional right to counsel of choice. The Sixth Amendment provides that "[i]n all criminal prosecutions, the accused shall enjoy the right . . . to have the Assistance of Counsel for his defense." The Court concluded that a defendant who does not require appointed counsel and is erroneously denied counsel of choice is not required to demonstrate that the substitute counsel rendered ineffective assistance.

> Different attorneys will pursue different strategies with regard to investigation and discovery, development of the theory of defense, selection of the jury, presentation of the witnesses, and style of witness examination and jury argument. And the choice of attorney will affect whether and on what terms the defendant cooperates with the prosecution, plea bargains, or decides instead to go to trial. In light of these myriad aspects of representation, the erroneous denial of counsel bears directly on the "framework within which the trial proceeds,"—or indeed on whether it proceeds at all. It is impossible to know what different choices the rejected counsel would have made, and then to quantify the impact of those different choices on the outcome of the proceedings. Many counseled decisions, including those involving plea bargains and cooperation with the government, do not even concern the conduct of the trial at all. Harmless-error analysis in such a context would be a speculative inquiry into what might have occurred in an alternate universe.

Id. at 150. Ultimately, "the Sixth Amendment right to counsel of choice . . . commands, not that a trial be fair, but that a particular guarantee of fairness be provided—to wit, that the accused be defended by the counsel he believes to be best." *Id.* at 146.

* * *

C. CLARIFYING THE SCOPE OF REPRESENTATION

Please read ABA Model Rules of Professional Conduct, Rule 1.5(b) and Comments [2] & [5].

* * *

Problem 9.2. Lawyer Darren has regularly represented Hannah in Hannah's real estate investments. Darren has always been paid on the same hourly basis. Hannah has now asked Darren to help Hannah set up a new corporation. Darren agrees to do so and sends a confirmation letter to Hannah several days later and after Darren has started work on the matter. The letter confirms that Darren will use his best efforts to help Hannah set up a new corporation. The letter says nothing about Darren's fee (which Hannah assumes will involve the same hourly rate Darren has charged in real estate matters). Is Darren subject to discipline?

(A) Yes, because Darren failed to communicate the basis or rate of the fee.

(B) Yes, because Darren did not send the confirmation letter until after he had already commenced representation.

(C) No, because Darren has represented Hannah on a regular basis.

(D) Yes, because Hannah did not sign the agreement.

* * *

A writing requirement? Model Rule 1.5(b) requires that a lawyer communicate the scope of representation to the client, but does not require that the lawyer do so in writing. Why not?

* * *

D. AGREEING TO LIMIT THE SCOPE OF REPRESENTATION

Please read ABA Model Rules of Professional Conduct, Rule 1.2(c) and Comments [6]–[8].

1. IN GENERAL

NICHOLS V. KELLER
19 Cal.Rptr.2d 601 (Ct. App. 1993)

MARTIN, ACTING PRESIDING JUSTICE.

Plaintiff appeals from summary judgments in a legal malpractice action arising from an industrial accident.

In December 1987, Zurn Industries employed the 46-year-old plaintiff at a cogeneration plant construction project in Crow's Landing, Stanislaus County. Zurn was a subcontractor and Kiewit Industrial was the general contractor on the project. Plaintiff had been a union boilermaker for over 24 years. On December 7, plaintiff commenced work on the exterior of a large boiler [when he was injured on the job].

On February 24, 1988, plaintiff and his wife met with defendant E. Paul Fulfer, an attorney with the defendant firm of Fulfer & Fulfer, to discuss plaintiff's accident and legal rights and remedies. At the conclusion of the meeting, defendant Fulfer had plaintiff sign a workers' compensation application for adjudication of claim. Fulfer executed the form as "applicant's attorney" and filed the application on plaintiff's behalf with the Stockton office of the Division of Industrial Accidents/California Department of Industrial Relations. . . . Defendant Fulfer then associated defendant Edward Keller, an attorney with defendant firm of LaCoste, Keller, Mello & Land, to prosecute the workers' compensation claim. Fulfer signed a formal pleading bearing the caption "association of attorneys" on January 20, 1989.

Defendant Keller met with plaintiff on March 28, 1988, and said he would represent plaintiff in his pending workers' compensation matter against Zurn Industries and Aetna Casualty and Surety Company. Defendant Keller continued to represent plaintiff in the workers' compensation proceeding until July 1989.

Sometime in 1989, plaintiff and his wife traveled from their home in Nevada to a workers' compensation medical appointment in the San Francisco area. On their return trip, they visited the Boilermakers Union Hall in Pittsburg, California. Plaintiff and his wife spoke with union employees Jim Wilson and Greg Bingham regarding plaintiff's accident at the cogeneration plant. They suggested plaintiff meet with another attorney and scheduled an appointment with James Butler of the law offices of William L. Veen in San Francisco.

On July 7, 1989, plaintiff and his wife met with attorney Butler. According to plaintiff, "At this meeting I learned for the first time that a third-party claim could and very likely should have been brought in regards to my industrial injury in December 1987, and that my wife and I may have a legal claim against Edward C. Keller and Elbert Paul Fulfer, attorneys, who had failed to advise or inform us of these facts."

On March 21, 1990, plaintiff filed a complaint for damages in Stanislaus County Superior Court. Plaintiff named attorneys Keller, Fulfer, and their respective law firms as defendants. He alleged causes of action for legal malpractice. . . .

On December 17, 1990, defendant Fulfer and his law firm filed a motion for summary judgment. Defendants alleged . . . the attorney-client relationship, if any, which existed between defendant Fulfer and plaintiff was limited solely to the subject matter of plaintiff's workers' compensation claim. . . .

On January 31, 1991, the court filed a minute order granting defendants' motions for summary judgment. . . . "Defendant KELLER's motion for summary judgment is granted. . . . [I]t is undisputed that the representation was undertaken for the limited purpose of the workman's compensation claim. Furthermore, an attorney's obligation does not include a duty to advise on all possible alternatives no matter how remote or tenuous. . . ."

On April 4, 1991, plaintiff filed a notice of appeal.

DISCUSSION

I.   DID DEFENDANTS OWE PLAINTIFF A DUTY TO ADVISE HIM OF THE POSSIBILITY OF A THIRD-PARTY CIVIL LAWSUIT AND THE APPLICABLE STATUTE OF LIMITATIONS?

Plaintiff contends: "[A]n attorney does have a duty to provide sound advice in furtherance of the client's best interests. Mr. Nichols, a man of limited education ... went to respondents seeking legal advice and representation from members of the Bar of California regarding any and all legal remedies he might be eligible for arising from his work injury. Respondents' failure to advise appellant that he may have a third party claim; respondents' failure to advise appellant regarding the applicable statute of limitations; and respondents' failure to refer appellant to an attorney experienced in third party actions was a breach of that duty. . . ."

Actionable legal malpractice is compounded of the same basic elements as other kinds of actionable negligence: duty, breach of duty, causation, and damage. The elements of a cause of action for professional negligence are (1) the duty of the professional to use such skill, prudence and diligence as other members of the profession commonly possess and exercise; (2) breach of that duty; (3) a causal connection between the negligent conduct and the resulting injury; and (4) actual loss or damage resulting from the professional negligence. . . . An attorney, by accepting employment to give legal advice or render legal services, impliedly agrees to use ordinary judgment, care, skill, and diligence in the performance of the tasks he or she undertakes.

The question of the existence of a legal duty of care in a given factual situation presents a question of law which is to be determined by the courts alone. . . . Absent the existence of a duty by the professional to the claimant, there can be no breach and no negligence.

One legal scholar has noted:

"An attorney advising or representing an injured employee concerning workers' compensation benefits must consider whether the employee should also pursue a lawsuit for civil damages against (1) a third party ... or (2) the employee's employer or coworker, or the employer's workers' compensation insurer. . . . For comparable injuries, damages recoveries often greatly exceed workers' compensation recoveries.

"The compensation attorney should either personally conduct a skilled and careful inquiry into the prospects for obtaining damages for the client that would exceed recoverable workers' compensation benefits or refer the client to an attorney who is competent to determine the prospects for such a recovery. . . .

"A workers' compensation attorney's failure to file and pursue a timely lawsuit for civil damages, or to refer the client to another lawyer for that purpose, can be the basis for a legal malpractice action. . . .

"Often, it is prudent to initiate both a compensation claim and a civil action, and to pursue both until it is determined that one of them will provide a full recovery. . . ." (Peyrat, *Cal. Workers' Damages Practice* (Cont. Ed. Bar 1985) § 1.4, pp. 4–5.)

A significant area of exposure for the workers' compensation attorney concerns that attorney's responsibility for counseling regarding a potential third-party action. One of an attorney's basic functions is to advise. Liability can exist because the attorney failed to provide advice. Not only should an attorney furnish advice when requested, but he or she should also volunteer opinions when necessary to further the client's objectives. The attorney need not advise and caution of every possible alternative, but only of those that may result in adverse consequences if not considered. Generally speaking, a workers' compensation attorney should be able to limit the retention to the compensation claim if the client is cautioned (1) there may be other remedies which the attorney will not investigate and (2) other counsel should be consulted on such matters. However, even when a retention is expressly limited, the attorney may still have a duty to alert the client to legal problems which are reasonably apparent, even though they fall outside the scope of the retention. The rationale is that, as between the lay client and the attorney, the latter is more qualified to recognize and analyze the client's legal needs. The attorney need not represent the client on such matters. Nevertheless, the attorney should inform the client of the limitations of the attorney's representation and of the possible need for other counsel. (2 Mallen & Smith, *Legal Malpractice* (3d ed. 1989) §§ 19.5, 19.5, 19.28, pp. 159–162, 229–233 . . .).

In their motions for summary judgment, defendant attorneys maintained they agreed to undertake only a limited employment. Attorney Fulfer asserted he agreed to represent plaintiff in the workers' compensation matter only and, even then, for two specific purposes: (1) to file a workers' compensation application on plaintiff's behalf and (2) to refer plaintiff to defendant Keller, so the latter could actually prosecute the workers' compensation claim on plaintiff's behalf. Attorney Keller argued the attorney-client relationship between the plaintiff and himself was solely for the purpose of representation in the workers' compensation claim. Keller claimed he owed only a duty to prosecute that claim and not to prosecute any possible third-party claim or to advise plaintiff as to the prosecution of such a claim. Defendants reiterate these positions on appeal.

In his opposition to the motions for summary judgment, plaintiff attached the declaration of attorney Yale Jones, a certified specialist in workers' compensation law. Jones declared attorney Fulfer acted below the standard of care of an attorney in the Stockton area by failing to (1) advise plaintiff of the different remedies available through the Workers' Compensation Appeal Board and through a civil action; (2) advise plaintiff of the statute of limitations applicable to plaintiff's third-party action; (3) advise plaintiff to consult another attorney concerning any available rights and remedies plaintiff might have against third parties; and (4) provide plaintiff with written advice regarding which rights defendant Fulfer would protect or which needed to be reviewed by other competent attorneys and what would happen in the event plaintiff did not protect those rights. Attorney Jones also declared defendant Keller acted below the standard of care for the same reasons.

. . . The lower court's minute order concluded: "[I]t is undisputed that the representation was undertaken for the limited purpose of the workman's compensation claim. Furthermore, an attorney's obligation does not include a duty to advise on all possible alternatives no matter how remote or tenuous. . . ."

A determination that defendants owe plaintiff no duty of care would negate an essential element of plaintiff's cause of action for negligence and would constitute a complete defense. . . .

Foreseeability of harm, though not determinative, has become the chief factor in duty analysis. . . . The question of foreseeability in a "duty" context is a limited one for the court and is readily contrasted with the fact-specific foreseeability questions bearing on negligence (breach of duty) and causation posed to the jury or trier of fact. . . .

It seems to us the foreseeability factor compels a finding of duty in cases of this type. A trained attorney is more qualified to recognize and analyze legal needs than a lay client, and, at least in part, this is the reason a party seeks out and retains an attorney to represent and advise him or her in legal matters. (2 Mallen & Smith, *Legal Malpractice, supra,* §§ 19.5, 19.28, pp. 159–162, 229–233.). . . .

. . . In the context of personal injury consultations between lawyer and layperson, it is reasonably foreseeable the latter will offer a selective or incomplete recitation of the facts underlying the claim; request legal assistance by employing such everyday terms as "workers' compensation," "disability," and "unemployment"; and rely upon the consulting lawyer to describe the array of legal remedies available, alert the layperson to any apparent legal problems, and, if appropriate, indicate limitations on the retention of counsel and the need for other counsel. In the event the lawyer fails to so advise the layperson, it is also reasonably foreseeable the layperson will fail to ask relevant questions regarding the existence of other remedies and be deprived of relief through a combination of ignorance and lack or failure of understanding. And, if counsel elects to limit or prescribe his representation of the client, i.e., to a workers' compensation claim only without reference or regard to any third party or collateral claims which the client might pursue if adequately advised, then counsel must make such limitations in representation very clear to his client. Thus, a lawyer who signs an application for adjudication of a workers' compensation claim and a lawyer who accepts a referral to prosecute the claim owe the claimant a duty of care to advise on available remedies, including third-party actions. . . .

. . . The lower court erroneously granted summary judgment on the duty element of legal negligence and reversal is required. . . .

* * *

Informed consent. Model Rule 1.2(c) provides that a lawyer may limit the scope of the representation if the limitation is reasonable under the circumstances and the client gives informed consent. Imagine that you are Keller, the second defendant in *Nichols.* What would you need to say to the plaintiff in order to be deemed to have complied with this rule? *See* Model Rule 1.0(e). How does a lawyer's ethical duty in this situation relate to the lawyer's duty under tort law?

* * *

Problem 9.3. A corporation wishes to hire Palsgraf & Pennoyer LLP to litigate a substantial suit. During negotiations, the corporation proposes a litigation budget. The law firm explains to the corporation's inside legal counsel that it can litigate the case within that budget but only by conducting limited discovery, which could materially lessen the likelihood of success. Is this a reasonable limitation on the scope of representation as contemplated by Rule 1.2(c)?

* * *

2. ENHANCING ACCESS TO JUSTICE BY PROVIDING LIMITED SCOPE REPRESENTATION

The idea that a lawyer and client should be allowed to limit the scope of the representation to be provided by the lawyer in order to reduce the cost of representation to an amount a low or moderate-income client could afford is an idea whose time has only recently come. This has been in part because the idea of limiting the representation in order to render the services affordable seemed inconsistent with the lawyers' often proclaimed declaration that all Americans are entitled to equal access to justice without regard to income or wealth and that equal access to justice means equal access to a full-service lawyer. Less than full-service violated the bar's commitment to equal access. With respect to legal services, every client was deemed to need and be entitled to a Cadillac, and rather than permit the sale of a Chevy, or a used Chevy, the profession encouraged lawyers to provide full-service pro bono representation to persons unable to afford a lawyer and to support funding of legal services programs that would provide full-service representation to those who met the program's income guidelines. This ideal then ran head-on into cuts in funding for legal service programs and the reality that the pro bono efforts of the bar fell far short of the demand for legal services from persons unable to pay the fees typically charged for a full-service representation. One manifestation of the problem was the increased presence of low and moderate-income pro se litigants in America's state trial courts, particularly those whose jurisdiction embraced domestic relations, landlord-tenant, and small claims. This led some lawyers to rethink the idea that lawyers should provide only full-service representation and to embrace the idea that from the perspective of low- and moderate-income clients, as well as the courts, limited scope representation would be better than no representation.

In approving the use of limited-scope fee agreements, an ethics opinion from Colorado explicitly links limited-scope representation to improving access to justice:

> A lawyer who provides a client with some, but not all, of the work normally involved in litigation is said to be providing "unbundled" legal services. By this unbundling, a person who cannot afford full representation can receive at least some legal assistance. In certain circumstances, it may be preferable for a lay person to have limited legal services rather than no services at all.

Ethics Op. of the Colorado Bar Ass'n, Formal Op. 101 (1998). The opinion goes on, however, to note some of the special ethical concerns raised when a lawyer limits the scope of a client's representation.

* * *

Model Rule 6.5. As part of the effort to expand access to justice for those unable to afford full legal representation, legal service organizations, other non-profit organizations, and some courts have established programs—variously called legal-advice hotlines, advice-only clinics, or pro se counseling programs—through which volunteer lawyers undertake to provide limited short-term legal services to clients as permitted by Model Rule 1.2(c). In addition to questions about the reasonableness of the limited scope of the representation being provided, lawyers have also been concerned about how the conflict of interest rules apply to the representation of clients in these short-term limited service programs. These concerns are addressed in ABA Model Rule 6.5, which was added to the Model Rules in 2002 in response to a recommendation from the Ethics 2000 Commission.

* * *

E. DECLINING TO TAKE A CASE

**Please read ABA Model Rules of Professional Conduct,
Rule 1.16(a) and Comments; and Rule 6.2 and Comments.**

* * *

The client-lawyer relationship is contractual in nature. Therefore, both sides are generally free to enter into a relationship or decline to do so. There may be some instances in which a lawyer is required to decline representation. For example, ABA Model Rule 1.16(a) prohibits a lawyer from representing a client where the representation would result in a violation of the rules of professional conduct or other law or where "the lawyer's physical or mental condition materially impairs the lawyer's ability to represent the client. . . ." Obvious examples would include where the lawyer lacks the competence to represent a client or is under a conflict of interest.

In other instances, a lawyer may choose to decline a client for various reasons. Sometimes a client or his cause might be repugnant to a lawyer. Model Rule 1.2(b) tries to alleviate concerns over the representation of repugnant clients or causes by noting that a lawyer's representation of a client "does not constitute an endorsement of the client's political, economic, social or moral views or activities." Model Rule 1.2 At the same time, one leading legal ethicist has argued that "[i]t is proper . . . to publicly challenge lawyers to justify their representation of particular clients." Monroe H. Freedman, *Response, The Lawyer's Moral Obligation of Justification*, 74 TEX. L. REV. 111, 112 (1995).

Some states have placed other limitations on a lawyer's ability to decline representation. In California, for example, a lawyer may not unlawfully discriminate "on the basis of race, national origin, sex, sexual orientation, religion, age or disability in . . . accepting or termination of representation of any client." Cal. R.P.C 2–400; *see also* Stropnicky v. Nathanson, 19 M.D.L.R. 39 (M.C.A.D. 1997) (concluding lawyer, who specialized in handling divorce cases for women, violated state anti-discrimination law by refusing to take on a male client).

With court appointments, lawyers have considerably less discretion in terms of who they represent. ABA Model Rule 6.2 places limits on a lawyer's freedom to accept and decline representation. Courts possess the authority to compel an attorney to accept an appointment. States vary as to their level of compensation for court-appointed lawyers, but given the overall low rate of pay, some attorneys might be tempted to avoid a court appointment.

* * *

Problem 9.4. Lawyer Darren is appointed to represent a minor seeking a judge's permission to obtain an abortion against her parents' wishes. Darren inquires of the state bar's ethics committee whether he is ethically permitted to avoid the appointment. Darren states that "he is a devout Catholic and cannot, under any circumstances, advocate a point of view ultimately resulting in what he considers to be the loss of human life. The religious beliefs are so compelling that counsel fears his own personal interests will subject him to conflicting interests and impair his independent professional judgment." Should Darren be excused under Rule 6.2? If so, under which part? *See generally* Tennessee Formal Ethics Opinion 96–F–140 (1996) (involving this scenario); Ernest F. Lidge, III, *The Lawyer's Moral Autonomy and Formal Opinion 140*, 33 TENN. B.J. 12 (Jan./Feb. 1997) (discussing the case).

* * *

Constitutional limitations on court's power of appointment. In Family Division Trial Lawyers v. Moultrie, 725 F.2d 695 (D.C. Cir. 1984), D.C. lawyers challenged the constitutionality of a requirement that lawyers who requested court appointments in juvenile delinquency cases—for which they would be reasonably compensated by the District—to accept appointments to represent indigent parents in child neglect proceedings without compensation. They challenged the appointment practice as involuntary servitude, a taking of their property, and as a denial of equal protection.

The district court dismissed the Thirteenth Amendment and "taking" claims stating, first, that compelled public service is not, in and of itself, involuntary servitude, even when imposed on a limited segment of the population. Specifically, requiring attorneys to take pro bono cases is neither involuntary servitude nor a per se "taking." The district court acknowledged, however, that if a system of compulsory assignments without pay sufficiently burdened individual attorneys so that their ability to earn a livelihood was endangered, it could constitute a prohibitive "taking" of property, but nonetheless dismissed the claim because the appellants did not refute the defendant's averment that "neglect cases do not usually require substantial . . . efforts," and "the burden placed on an attorney by neglect appointments does not impair the attorney's ability to engage in remunerative practice."

The district court also accepted the defendant's claim that the lawyers did not state a claim for violation of the equal protection clause because "it is entirely rational to select lawyers who have expressed an interest in Family Division appointments to take on neglect cases; lawyers who request appointment to Family Division actions may be presumed to be more experienced in family legal issues and therefore may be presumed capable of providing more skilled counsel." . . .

The D.C. Court of Appeals upheld the dismissal of the Thirteenth Amendment involuntary servitude claim and, relying on United States v. Dillon, 346 F.2d 633 (9th Cir. 1965), cert. denied, 382 U.S. 978, also rejected the plaintiffs' claim that uncompensated appointments were not a per se violation of the takings clause of the Fifth Amendment. Noting, however, that an unreasonable amount of required uncompensated service might qualify as a taking if it denies the plaintiff-lawyers the opportunity to maintain a remunerative practice as family lawyers before the Family Division, the court denied the motion for summary judgment on the takings claim, primarily because:

> The stakes in this case are too great not only for the lawyers and court personnel but also for the parents and children involved in neglect cases to let stand a judgment mistakenly entered without any judicial inquiry upon "facts"—that representation of parents in neglect cases entails minimum time and effort and need exact no substantial premium in time or talent from legal advocates— which are widely perceived in the local bar and in the community at large, not to be true, and which have been the core of a decade-old controversy.

With respect to the equal protection challenge, the court held that "the appellants' right to earn a living as lawyers is not so fundamental that it triggers strict judicial scrutiny of the challenged system; if the system reflects a rational choice aimed at furthering legitimate state interests, a court must uphold it." With this said, however, the court found the factual record insufficient to support a holding that the appointment system was rational, reasoning that the District Court acted rationally in presuming that lawyers who regularly practice before the Family Division are best able to represent parents in neglect proceedings, and in requiring more from recipients of the public fisc than from other attorneys.

> At some point, even initially rationally motivated restrictions on the pool of attorneys assigned pro bono cases may result in such enormous demands on the time and energy of these appointed attorneys that they cease to be rational either in the results they engender of ineffective representation for indigent parents, or the burdens they impose on the chosen attorneys: For example, to require the one most experienced neglect lawyer in the local bar to take on all pro bono assignments would surely not survive even a rational means test. It is by no means clear from the sparse record before us whether this point has been reached or even approached. Since the constitutional claim at issue is the discriminatory application of the system, not just its design, further fact finding is required.

* * *

What do you think? EC 2–27 of the Model Code declares rather grandly that "[h]istory is replete with instances of distinguished and sacrificial services by lawyers who have represented unpopular clients and causes." Perhaps the best-known literary example of an exemplary lawyer is Atticus Finch in *To Kill a Mockingbird*. What sort of client or cause would you find repugnant enough to cause you to decline representation?

* * *

Profile of attorney professionalism. Perhaps the most famous real-life example of a lawyer representing an unpopular client or cause is John Adams' representation of the British soldiers accused of murder in the Boston Massacre in 1770. Boston radicals used the incident to whip up public anger toward the British Crown. At the time, Adams was a 34-year-old lawyer who was asked to represent the soldiers when no one else would. "Although he realized he would be vilified by the town's inhabitants and the press, thus jeopardizing his thriving legal practice, Adams . . . immediately agreed to do so, firm in his belief that all persons accused of a crime were entitled to an effective legal defense." John F. Tobin, *The Boston Massacre Trials*, N.Y. STATE BAR JOURNAL 12 (July/August 2013). Adams was indeed vilified: "Within days of agreeing to defend Preston and the soldiers, rocks were thrown through the windows of Adams's home and he was jeered by passersby on the streets." *Id.* Adams was accused of having been bribed to take the case. David McCullough, *John Adams* 68 (2001). Ultimately, the commanding officer and six of the soldiers involved were acquitted. Two other soldiers were convicted of manslaughter.

The local paper criticized Adams for representing the soldiers, and Adams claimed to have lost more than half of his practice as a result of his representation. *Id.* at 68. However, Adams' career, of course, survived. Over time, his public standing actually improved as a result of his actions. Looking back on his life's accomplishments, Adams remarked:

> The part I took in defense of Captain Preston and the soldiers procured me anxiety and obloquy enough. It was, however, . . . one of the best pieces of service I ever rendered my country. Judgment of death against those soldiers would have been as foul a stain upon this country as the executions of the Quakers or witches anciently. As the evidence was, the verdict of the jury was exactly right.

Tobin, supra at 17.

CHAPTER 10

BILLING THE CLIENT

■ ■ ■

Chapter hypothetical. Katherine hired Lynn, a lawyer, to represent her in a probate matter in New Dakota. Katherine's husband, Robert, died intestate. The couple had several children and Robert had several other living relatives. Under the law of New Dakota, Katherine was entitled to one-third of Robert's estate. Katherine was unsure as to the value of the estate, but provided Lynn with a list of the contents of a safe in which Robert kept many of his records as well as some other valuables. The list described stock that Robert owned in ten different large corporations. Unfortunately, one of Robert's relatives had taken some of the valuables from the safe after Robert's passing and removed them across state lines to Old Dakota. Eventually, Lynn was able to compel the relative to return the valuables and determined the value of Robert's estate to be $1.8 million. Most of the value of the estate was derived from the stock Robert had owned. Lynn spent approximately 50 hours on the matter. After the matter was resolved and Katherine had received her $600,000 from the estate, Lynn sent Katherine a bill for $200,000. This represented the one-third contingent fee she said Katherine had orally agreed to. Katherine claimed to have agreed to no such thing and told Lynn that she had spoken to other lawyers around town who said they charged, on average, around $200 an hour on probate matters. Angered, Katherine filed a disciplinary complaint against Lynn.

(A) Is Lynn subject to discipline?

(B) Can Lynn enforce the fee agreement if she sues Katherine to recover her fee?

* * *

In addition to the scope and objectives of the representation, another issue that the lawyer and client should discuss at the outset of the relationship is fees. Although most lawyers are sincerely committed to the public service goals of their profession, they also practice law in the hope of making at least a decent living. The materials in this and the following chapter address some of the issues that arise with respect to the determination of what, if anything, a client will owe his or her lawyers for services rendered and costs incurred.

* * *

A. REASONABLENESS OF FEES AND OTHER CHARGES

Please read ABA Model Rules of Professional Conduct, Rule 1.5(a) & (b) and Comments [1], [2] & [4].

* * *

BROBECK, PHLEGER & HARRISON V. TELEX CORPORATION

602 F.2d 866 (9th Cir. 1979)

PER CURIAM:

This is a diversity action in which the plaintiff, the San Francisco law firm of Brobeck, Phleger & Harrison ("Brobeck"), sued the Telex Corporation and Telex Computer Products, Inc. ("Telex") to recover $1,000,000 in attorney's fees. . . . Brobeck sent Telex a bill for $1,000,000, that it claimed Telex owed it under their written contingency fee agreement. When Telex refused to pay, Brobeck brought this action. Both parties filed motions for summary judgment. The district court granted Brobeck's motion, awarding Brobeck $1,000,000 plus interest. Telex now appeals.

Telex was the plaintiff in antitrust litigation against IBM in the United States District Court for the Northern District of Oklahoma. On November 9, 1973 the District Court found that IBM had violated § 2 of the Sherman Act . . . and entered judgment for Telex in the amount of $259.5 million, plus costs and attorney's fees of $1.2 million. The court also entered judgment in the sum of $21.9 million for IBM on its counterclaims against Telex for misappropriation of trade secrets and copyright infringement.

On appeal, the Tenth Circuit reversed the entire judgment that Telex had won in the district court. . . . It also reduced the judgment against Telex on IBM's counterclaim to $18.5 million and affirmed the district court's judgment as modified.

Having had reversed one of the largest antitrust judgments in history, Telex officials decided to press the Tenth Circuit's decision to the United States Supreme Court. To maximize Telex's chances for having its petition for certiorari granted, they decided to search for the best available lawyer. They compiled a list of the preeminent antitrust and Supreme Court lawyers in the country, and Roger Wheeler, Telex's Chairman of the Board, settled on Moses Lasky of the Brobeck firm as the best possibility.

Wheeler and his assistant made preliminary phone calls to Lasky on February 3, 4, and 13, 1975 to determine whether Lasky was willing to prepare the petition for certiorari. Lasky stated he would be interested if he was able to rearrange his workload. When asked about a fee, Lasky stated that, although he would want a retainer, it was the policy of the Brobeck firm to determine fees after the services were performed. Wheeler, however, wanted an agreement fixing fees in advance. . . .

[Lasky agreed to represent Telex. The parties entered into a complicated fee agreement under which Brobeck would be entitled to a minimum fee of $1 million. Telex's President submitted a check for $25,000 as the agreed retainer.]

. . . Lasky, as agreed, prepared the petition for certiorari and filed it in July 1975. He also obtained a stay of mandate from the Tenth Circuit pending final disposition of the action by the Supreme Court. In the meantime Telex began to consider seriously the possibility of settlement with IBM by having Telex withdraw its petition in exchange for a discharge of the counterclaim judgment.

. . . Lasky, at Telex's request, prepared a reply brief to IBM's opposition to the petition for certiorari, and sent it to the Supreme Court on September 17th for filing. . . .

On October 2 IBM officials became aware that the Supreme Court's decision on the petition was imminent. They contacted Telex and the parties agreed that IBM would release its counterclaim judgment against Telex in exchange for Telex's dismissal of its petition for certiorari. On October 3, at the request of [Telex], Lasky had the petition for certiorari withdrawn. Thereafter, he sent a bill to Telex for $1,000,000. When Telex refused to pay, Brobeck filed its complaint. On the basis of depositions and exhibits, the district court granted Brobeck's motion for summary judgment.

. . . Telex argues that it, not Brobeck, is entitled to summary judgment, or alternatively, to go to trial to determine the meaning of the contract. Telex raises three contentions:

[The first two contentions are omitted];

3) the fee awarded under the contract was so excessive as to render it unconscionable. . . .

There is no dispute about the facts leading to Telex's engagement of the Brobeck firm. Telex was an enterprise threatened with bankruptcy. It had won one of the largest money judgments in history, but that judgment had been reversed in its entirety by the Tenth Circuit. In order to maximize its chances of gaining review by the United States Supreme Court, it sought to hire the most experienced and capable lawyer it could possibly find. After compiling a list of highly qualified lawyers, it settled on Lasky as the most able. Lasky was interested but wanted to bill Telex on hourly basis. After Telex insisted on a contingent fee arrangement,

Lasky made it clear that he would consent to such an arrangement only if he would receive a sizable contingent fee in the event of success.

In these circumstances, the contract between Telex and Brobeck was not so unconscionable that "no man in his senses and not under a delusion would make on the one hand, and as no honest and fair man would accept on the other." This is not a case where one party took advantage of another's ignorance, exerted superior bargaining power, or disguised unfair terms in small print. Rather, Telex, a multi-million dollar corporation, represented by able counsel, sought to secure the best attorney it could find to prepare its petition for certiorari, insisting on a contingent fee contract. Brobeck fulfilled its obligation to gain a stay of judgment and to prepare and file the petition for certiorari. Although the minimum fee was clearly high, Telex received substantial value from Brobeck's services. For, as Telex acknowledged, Brobeck's petition provided Telex with the leverage to secure a discharge of its counterclaim judgment, thereby saving it from possible bankruptcy in the event the Supreme Court denied its petition for certiorari. We conclude that such a contract was not unconscionable.

The judgment of the district court is affirmed.

* * *

BUSHMAN v. STATE BAR OF CALIFORNIA
11 Cal.3d 558 (1974) (en banc)

BY THE COURT.

This is a proceeding to review a recommendation of the State Bar of California that Ted Bushman be suspended from the practice of law for one year. Bushman was found by the State Bar Disciplinary Board to have charged and attempted to collect an exorbitant and unconscionable fee from clients. . . .

. . . Bushman was retained by Barbara Cox, aged 16, her mother and father (Mr. and Mrs. Stroud), and Ralph Hughes (hereinafter referred to as the defendants) in connection with an action filed by Barbara's husband, Neal W. Cox, for divorce and custody of a minor child of the marriage. The only substantial issue in Cox's action was custody. Barbara's parents were named as defendants because it was alleged they might have had physical custody of the child, and Hughes was involved because he allegedly was having sexual relations with Barbara and there was a possibility that he would be charged with statutory rape.

Cox was represented by attorney Gertrude Chern. At Bushman's request, the defendants signed a promissory note for $5,000, payable $300 forthwith and the balance at $50 a month. They also signed a retainer agreement providing for an hourly fee of not less than $60. Barbara was a minor, her parents were on welfare, and there was no community property of the Cox marriage. Bushman advised the defendants it was the policy of his office that, whenever attorney Chern was the opposing counsel in a custody matter, a minimum retainer of $5,000 was required without regard to the time spent by Bushman on the case or to other factors, because Mrs. Chern would generate a "paper war." Subsequently, when Cox visited Bushman's office in connection with a possible reconciliation with Barbara, Bushman unsuccessfully sought to induce him to add his signature to the promissory note.

All the pleadings and negotiations on behalf of Cox were handled by an associate of Mrs. Chern. The action did not involve any juvenile court or criminal matters, and the custody issue was resolved by a stipulation of the parties in favor of Barbara, following the usual custody investigation and report of the county probation department. The fee charged Cox by his attorney was $300, plus costs, representing five and one-half hours of work.

The court ordered that the husband pay Bushman a fee of $300, and $60 in costs; Bushman did not advise the court of the $5,000 note signed by the wife and others or of the sums paid thereon. There was nothing unusual or novel in pleadings or research in the Cox case. Bushman filed on Barbara's behalf a demurrer, cross-complaint, petition for appointment of a guardian-ad-litem, and stipulation to a probation report, as well as an answer to the complaint, and a declaration of points and authorities. He attended two hearings on orders to show cause, and subpoenaed and interviewed a doctor.

Bushman claimed that he spent over 100 hours on the case, which at $60 an hour would call for a fee of $6,000. However, he billed the defendants for only $2,800 plus $60 in costs which, at the $60 an hour rate, would amount to far less than 100 hours of time spent. The reasonable value of Bushman's services in the action was the amount awarded by the court, i.e., $300 and $60 in costs.

. . . It is settled that gross overcharge of a fee by an attorney may warrant discipline. The test is whether the fee is "so exorbitant and wholly disproportionate to the services performed as to shock the conscience." Herrscher v. State Bar, 4 Cal. 2d 399, 401–402 (1935). In *Herrscher* this court stated that most cases warranting discipline on this ground involved an element of fraud or overreaching by the attorney, so that the fee charged, under the circumstances, constituted a practical appropriation of the client's funds. . . .

[U]nder all the circumstances, the fee charged by Bushman was so exorbitant and wholly disproportionate to the services rendered to the defendants as to shock the conscience. An examination of the file in the

Cox matter reveals that only a simple, almost routine series of documents was filed by Bushman on Barbara's behalf. Although he asserts that the case was "quite involved," he is unable to articulate any complex issues which required extensive research or specialized skills. The only documentation in the file indicating any research whatever is a one-page "Points and Authorities" filed in support of an order to show cause, which cites the text of five statutes and one case, without any argument. Aside from interviews with the defendants and a doctor, the only additional services performed by Bushman were two appearances in court for hearings on orders to show cause. He failed to substantiate his claim of 100 hours spent on the Cox case.... It is of some significance in this connection that Cox's attorney spent slightly more than five hours on the case.

... In view of the fact that Bushman was dealing with persons in clearly impecunious circumstances, including a minor on welfare, that the marriage was of short duration and there was no community property, that he failed to reveal to the court in the face of a court-awarded fee of $300 to be paid by the husband, that he held a $5,000 promissory note from the wife and her parents, and that the amount of the note and the $2,800 bill he sent the defendants were grossly disproportionate to the value of the services he had rendered, his course of conduct with regard to the fee in the Cox matter contained an element of fraud or overreaching warranting disciplinary action.

Bushman attacks the finding of the board that the only substantial issue in the Cox case was custody. He contends that the board made this determination on the basis of hindsight and that at the time the promissory note was signed there was the possibility of an action in the juvenile court against Barbara, and the possibility of a statutory rape charge against Hughes, as well as contempt proceedings against the Strouds. The only evidence of any substance in the record that Bushman might be called upon to defend such charges was a random threat by Cox's attorney to cause a charge of statutory rape to be filed against Hughes. Clearly, the board's conclusion that the only substantial issue related to child custody is supported by the record.

Petitioner maintains that the board failed to consider the fact that his efforts on Barbara's behalf were successful in that she was ultimately awarded custody of the child, and that there was no element of concealment in his conduct since he revealed to the defendants why the fee would be so high, and they were free to consult another attorney. We do not deem these matters to be of sufficient significance to outweigh the clear showing set out above that Bushman was guilty of overreaching and unconscionable conduct....

It is ordered that petitioner be suspended from the practice of law for a period of one year.

* * *

Model Rule 1.5(a) and reasonable fees. *Bushman* was decided under a different standard from the reasonableness standard articulated by Model Rule 1.5(a). Would the application of the factors for determining the reasonableness of a fee have yielded a different result in *Bushman*?

The importance of reasonable fees. As *Brobeck* illustrates, there is at least the potential that a lawyer who charges an unreasonable or clearly excessive fee may wind up recovering nothing under the fee agreement. As a matter of contract law, an unconscionable fee agreement might be unenforceable. But the Model Rules impose a higher standard on lawyers, subjecting a lawyer to discipline for charging an "unreasonable" fee. What justifies this higher standard? As stated by one court,

> [t]he court is an instrument of society for the administration of justice. Justice should be administered economically, efficiently, and expeditiously. The attorney's fee is, therefore, a very important factor in the administration of justice, and if it is not determined with proper relation to that fact it results in a species of social malpractice that undermines the confidence of the public in the bench and bar. It does more than that; it brings the court into disrepute and destroys its power to perform adequately the function of its creation.

Baruch v. Giblin, 164 So. 831, 833 (Fla. 1935).

* * *

Problem 10.1. When may an attorney bill two or more clients for work done simultaneously? Imagine that an attorney has three clients, each of whom has a motion set on the same day. The attorney attends the motion hearing, and argues each client's motion in turn. She spends a total of three hours in court. May she bill each client for the full three hours? Must she apportion the time equally among the clients (one hour per client)? What if she would have spent the entire three hours in court for one client anyway, due to the waiting time for the motion to be heard?

Or imagine that an associate is flying to a deposition on behalf of Client A. While on the plane, he works on a drafting project for Client B. May he bill both Client A and Client B for the time spent on the drafting project (when he would have been in the air for Client A anyway)? Or must he deduct the time he spends on Client B's project from the flying time he bills to Client A? Imagine that the associate has an annual billing requirement of 1800 hours.

See ABA Formal Ethics Opinion 93–379 (1993).

What do you think? It is not uncommon for a lawyer and client to remember things differently when it comes to the amount of the agreed-upon fee. Similarly, it is not uncommon for a client to object to what it views as an unreasonable charge for expenses. In light of the potential for honest misunderstandings and disagreements, should Model Rule 1.5(b) be amended to require that all fee agreements be in writing?

* * *

B. NON-REFUNDABLE RETAINERS

IN THE MATTER OF COOPERMAN
83 N.Y.2d 465, 611 N.Y.S.2d 465 (1994)

BELLACOSA, JUSTICE.

In 1990, the petitioner, Grievance Committee [charged] attorney Cooperman with 15 specifications of professional misconduct [relating] to his use of . . . special nonrefundable retainer fee agreements.

[One such agreement was] in connection with a probate proceeding. It states in pertinent part: "For the MINIMAL FEE and NON-REFUNDABLE amount of Five Thousand ($5,000.00) Dollars, I will act as your counsel." The agreement further provided: "This is the minimum fee no matter how much or how little work I do in this investigatory stage * * * and will remain the minimum fee and not refundable even if you decide prior to my completion of the investigation that you wish to discontinue the use of my services for any reason whatsoever." The client discharged Cooperman, who refused to provide the client with an itemized bill of services rendered or refund any portion of the fee, citing the unconditional nonrefundable fee agreement.

. . . We agree with the Appellate Division in this disciplinary matter that special nonrefundable retainer fee agreements clash with public policy and transgress provisions of the Code of Professional Responsibility, essentially because these fee agreements compromise the client's absolute right to terminate the unique fiduciary attorney-client relationship.

The particular analysis begins with a reflection on the nature of the attorney-client relationship. Sir Francis Bacon observed, "[t]he greatest trust between [people] is the trust of giving counsel." This unique fiduciary reliance, stemming from people hiring attorneys to exercise professional judgment on a client's behalf—"giving counsel"—is imbued with ultimate trust and confidence. The attorney's obligations, therefore, transcend those prevailing in the commercial market place. The duty to deal fairly, honestly and with undivided loyalty superimposes onto the attorney-client relationship a set of special and unique duties, including maintaining confidentiality, avoiding conflicts of interest, operating competently, safeguarding client property and honoring the clients' interests over the lawyer's. To the public and clients, few features could be more paramount than the fee—the costs of legal services.

The Code of Professional Responsibility reflects this central ingredient by specifically mandating, without exception, that an attorney "shall not enter into an agreement for, charge, or collect an illegal or excessive fee" (DR 2–106[A]). . . . Accordingly, attorney-client fee agreements are a matter of special concern to the courts and are enforceable and affected by lofty principles different from those applicable to commonplace commercial contracts. . . .

The unqualified right to terminate the attorney-client relationship at any time has been assiduously protected by the courts. An attorney, however, is not left without recourse for unfair terminations lacking cause. If a client exercises the right to discharge an attorney after some services are performed but prior to the completion of the services for which the fee was agreed upon, the discharged attorney is entitled to recover compensation from the client measured by the fair and reasonable value of the completed services. We have recognized that permitting a discharged attorney "to recover the reasonable value of services rendered in quantum meruit, a principle inherently designed to prevent unjust enrichment, strikes the delicate balance between the need to deter clients from taking undue advantage of attorneys, on the one hand, and the public policy favoring the right of a client to terminate the attorney-client relationship without inhibition on the other."

Correspondingly and by cogent logic and extension of the governing precepts, we hold that the use of a special nonrefundable retainer fee agreement clashes with public policy because it inappropriately compromises the right to sever the fiduciary services relationship with the lawyer. Special nonrefundable retainer fee agreements diminish the core of the fiduciary relationship by substantially altering and economically chilling the client's unbridled prerogative to walk away from the lawyer. To answer that the client can technically still terminate misses the reality of the economic coercion that pervades such matters. If special nonrefundable retainers are allowed to flourish, clients would be relegated to hostage status in an unwanted fiduciary relationship—an utter anomaly. Such circumstance would impose a penalty on a client for daring to invoke a hollow right to discharge. . . . Instead of becoming responsible for fair value of actual services rendered, the firing client would lose the entire "nonrefundable" fee, no matter what legal services, if any, were rendered. This would be a shameful, not honorable, professional denouement. . . .

Our holding today makes the conduct of trading in special nonrefundable retainer fee agreements subject to appropriate professional discipline. Moreover, we intend no effect or disturbance with respect to other types of appropriate and ethical fee agreements.... Minimum fee arrangements and general retainers that provide for fees, not laden with the nonrefundability impediment irrespective of any services, will continue to be valid and not subject in and of themselves to professional discipline....

Accordingly, the order of the Appellate Division should be affirmed, with costs.

* * *

General retainers vs. special nonrefundable fee agreements. *Cooperman* draws a distinction between general retainers and special nonrefundable fee agreements. The former is an arrangement by which the client pays to reserve the services of a lawyer in the future. This fee is "nonrefundable" in the sense that the fee is earned upon payment. In contrast, special nonrefundable fee agreements involve fees paid in advance by a client for a specific legal service. They ostensibly become "nonrefundable" when, as in *Cooperman*, the fee agreement designates them as such. While most court and ethics opinions side with *Cooperman*, *see* Or. Eth. Op. 2005–151 (concluding that doing so would amount to charging an excessive fee and designating such a fee as nonrefundable may be false or misleading in violation of the rules of professional conduct), some permit these types of arrangements. *See* Grievance Administrator, Attorney Grievance Commission v. Cooper, 757 N.W.2d 867 (Mich. 2008).

* * *

Problem 10.2. Lawyer agrees to represent Client in a probate matter. The parties agree that Lawyer's fee will be $5,000, payable in advance, and that the fee is nonrefundable. The day after entering into the agreement and before Lawyer has done any work on the matter or incurred any other detriment, Client changes her mind, fires Lawyer, and hires a new lawyer. Lawyer, citing the fee agreement, refuses to refund Client's money. Is Lawyer subject to discipline under Model Rule 1.5? If so, on what grounds?

* * *

C. CONTINGENT FEES

1. IN GENERAL

Lawyer's fees and the costs associated with the provision of legal services can be quite high and in many cases will be beyond the means of the person needing the legal services. There is also an element of risk associated with hiring a lawyer because even the best lawyer cannot guarantee a favorable outcome. Among those with the financial means to hire a lawyer there are some who will not be willing to bear the risk of investing considerable sums of money to hire a lawyer when they cannot be sure the outcome will be favorable. Such individuals will hire a lawyer only if the lawyer will agree not only to provide the needed legal services, but also to "finance" the representation by agreeing to provide the needed services with payment of fees and/or reimbursement of costs due only if there is a favorable outcome. Such "contingent fee" arrangements are most often associated with the representation of plaintiffs in tort cases who cannot afford to pay a fixed fee, but they are also used in numerous other situations in which the lawyer and client agree that the lawyer will bear the risk that a considerable investment of time and money necessary for legal representation will not yield a favorable outcome. The contingent fee, then, represents the method employed to compensate the lawyer for the reasonable value of services rendered and costs incurred and for assuming the risk of not being paid or reimbursed if the representation does not result in a favorable outcome.

Contingent fees are fees contingent upon the outcome of the matter, usually litigation. In a contingent fee arrangement, the lawyer agrees to represent the client for an agreed-upon percentage of any recovery. Contingent fees have been justified on the ground that they improve access to justice for those who would not be financially able to pay an hourly fee; the lawyer bears the risk of the representation. If the representation produces a monetary *res*, the lawyer is paid; if not, the lawyer gets no fee.

Contingent fees have been criticized on a number of grounds. First, it is said that contingent fees can result in a windfall to the lawyer, if the liability of the defendant is clear, and a large recovery is obtained with little effort on the lawyer's part. Second, it has been asserted that contingent fees stir up litigation by encouraging lawyers to bring nonmeritorious lawsuits in order to extract nuisance-value settlements from which the lawyer's fee can be paid. Finally, contingent fees potentially create a conflict of interest between attorney and client. The lawyer's interest may be in a sure, quick recovery, while the client's interest may be in a more prolonged, more risky representation that may result in a larger recovery.

In 1994 the American Bar Association Standing Committee on Ethics and Professional Responsibility was presented with a number of inquiries regarding the propriety of contingent fees in a number of situations. The Committee opined that the charging of a contingent fee in most instances does not violate ethical standards "as long as the fee is appropriate in the circumstances and reasonable in amount, and as long as the client has been fully advised on the availability of alternative fee arrangements." ABA Formal Ethics Opinion 94–389 (1994).

However, there are other constraints on contingent fees, some of them statutory. For example, federal law limits the fee for claimants' attorneys in Social Security cases to 25% of any back pay award. 42 U.S.C. § 406(a)(2)(A). Some states, likewise, impose statutory limits on attorney fees. *See, e.g.*, Tenn. Code Ann. § 29–26–120 (placing cap on attorney fee in medical malpractice cases of 33 1/3% of total recovery). There are also other ethical limits on the charging of contingent fees.

* * *

2.   ENTERING INTO A CONTINGENT-FEE AGREEMENT

Please read ABA Model Rules of Professional Conduct, Rule 1.5(a) & (c) and Comment [3].

Procedural requirements. Model Rule 1.5 singles out contingent fee agreements for special treatment and imposes additional requirements on lawyers who draft them. Why? What concerns justify this special treatment?

* * *

3.   PROHIBITED CONTINGENT FEES

a.   Domestic Relations Cases

Please read ABA Model Rules of Professional Conduct, Rule 1.5(d)(1) and Comment [6].

* * *

Fee agreements in violation of public policy. In addition to the contract defense of unconscionability, a contract that offends public policy may be also unenforceable as a matter of contract law. RESTATEMENT (SECOND) OF CONTRACTS § 178 (1979). While there is some dispute as to whether a fee agreement that violates a rule of professional conduct for lawyers offends public policy for purposes of this contract defense, *see* Benjamin P. Cooper, *Taking Rules Seriously: The Rise of Lawyer Rules as Substantive Law and the Public Policy Exception in Contract Law*, 35 CARDOZO L. REV. 267 (2013), courts often find fee agreements that violate some portion of Rule 1.5 to offend public policy. *See, e.g.,* Maxwell Schuman & Co. v. Edwards, 663 S.E.2d 329, 333 (N.C. Ct. App. 2008). The public policy underlying the ban on charging contingent fees in the situations mentioned in Model Rule 1.5(d)(1) is one of encouraging reconciliation "by removing any incentive to the attorney to press forward with the divorce." Guenard v. Burke, 443 N.E.2d 892, 895 (Mass. 1982). Courts typically declare fee agreements that violate Rule 1.5(d)(1) to be unenforceable as against public policy, but permit a lawyer to recover the reasonable value of services rendered. *See, e.g., Maxwell Schuman & Co.,* 663 S.E.2d at 333. Should such recovery in *quantum meruit* be the norm in these cases?

* * *

Problem 10.3. Client retains Lawyer's services because Client's ex-husband has failed to make court-ordered child support payments over the past six months. Client and Lawyer enter into a contingent fee agreement, under which Lawyer's fee will be 10% of whatever portion of the balance owed by the ex-husband that Lawyer is able to collect on Client's behalf. Is Lawyer subject to discipline?

* * *

b. Criminal Cases

Please read ABA Model Rules of Professional Conduct, Rule 1.5(d)(2).

* * *

Justifications for the prohibition on contingent fees. Assume that a criminal defendant is charged with murder. He enters into a fee agreement with a lawyer, under which the defendant agrees to pay the lawyer $50,000 to represent him and an additional $50,000 if the client is found not guilty for any reason. Why should the lawyer be subject to discipline for entering into such an agreement? One justification has been that, unlike representation of a plaintiff in a civil matter, "legal services in criminal cases do not produce a res with which to pay the fee." Model Code of Prof'l Resp. EC 2–20. That may be true, but is that a good reason for banning the use of contingent fees in criminal cases? What justifies Model Rule 1.5(d)(2)'s prohibition?

* * *

c.   **Alternative Fee Agreements**

NEW YORK COUNTY LAWYERS' ASSOCIATION
COMMITTEE ON PROFESSIONAL ETHICS
FORMAL OPINION NUMBER 736
September 21, 2006

QUESTION:

In a retainer agreement with a client in a personal injury matter in which the lawyer represents the plaintiff, may a lawyer ethically include a provision that permits the attorney to unilaterally change from a contingency to hourly fee basis if the client refuses a settlement offer that the lawyer considers fair and reasonable?

OPINION:

The question posed to the Committee is whether, in a personal injury matter, a lawyer may ethically propose or enter into a fee agreement with the plaintiff-client that *begins* as contingent but *may become* hourly if the client declines a settlement offer deemed fair and reasonable by the lawyer.

We conclude that such conduct is ethically prohibited.

The contingency fee is not unique to the personal injury field, and is utilized in a variety of areas of practice. Here, our primary concern is with the most typical use of the contingency fee: on behalf of an injured personal injury plaintiff. A contingency fee makes representation possible for personal injury clients, many of whom cannot afford an hourly fee. If after a period of ongoing litigation representation, a lawyer were permitted to invoke the proposed arrangement and require the client to begin paying by the hour, we believe that the resulting financial pressure to settle would violate the client's right to make that settlement decision.

This conclusion is supported by authorities from jurisdictions outside New York. For example, ABA 94–389 states that:

> All contingent fee agreements carry certain risks: the risk that the case will require substantially more work than the lawyer anticipated; the risk that there will be no judgment, or only an unenforceable one; the risk of changes in the law ... *and the risk that the client will require the lawyer to reject what the lawyer considers a good settlement or otherwise to continue the proceedings much further than in the lawyer's judgment they should be pursued.*

Thus, the uncertainty that accompanies a contingency fee case cuts both ways, and can result in a quick windfall (to the lawyer's benefit) or unanticipated months of extra work for the lawyer. This is a risk that the lawyer accepts by entering into the contingency fee arrangement and may not eliminate by including the proposed provision

In New York, DR 7–101(A) provides that a lawyer shall not intentionally "fail to seek the lawful objectives of the client. . . ." EC 7–7 provides that, generally speaking, "the authority to make decisions is exclusively that of the client and, if made within the framework of the law, such decisions are binding on the lawyer," and that "it is for the client to decide whether to accept a settlement offer. . . ."[1] We find, therefore, that the proposed provision would violate the client's right to decide whether to settle because the lawyer, as fiduciary for the client, is best positioned to evaluate the implications of the provision at the outset. For example, the New York Court of Appeals has written that the attorney client relationship:

> is imbued with ultimate trust and confidence. The attorney's obligations, therefore, transcend those prevailing in the commercial market place. . . . To the public and clients, few features could be more paramount that the fee—the costs of legal services. Accordingly, attorney-client fee agreements are a matter of special concern to the courts and are enforceable and affected by lofty principles different from those applicable to commonplace commercial contracts.

Conclusion

In a retainer agreement with a client in a personal injury case, a lawyer may *not* ethically include a provision that permits the attorney to unilaterally change from a contingency to hourly fee basis, prospectively, if the client refuses a settlement offer that the lawyer considers fair and reasonable.[2]

* * *

Reverse contingent fees. Another variation on the contingent fee is the "reverse contingent fee," which is "a fee based on the amount of money saved a client rather than the amount of money recovered for a client." ABA Formal Ethics Opinion 93–373 (1993). The opinion found no ethical prohibition on such fees "so long as the reasonableness and informed consent requirements of Rule 1.5 are satisfied." At least one court has disagreed. In Wunschel Law Firm, P.C. v. Clabaugh, 291 N.W.2d 331 (Iowa 1980), a defendant's attorney sued the defendant for

---

[1] The ABA Model Rules of Professional Conduct, while not binding in New York, are consistent. ABA Model Rule 1.2(a) provides that, "A lawyer shall abide by a client's decision whether to settle a matter."

[2] Our conclusion is limited to the personal injury context. We leave to another day the issue of whether or not a lawyer may in other contexts, such as commercial litigation involving "sophisticated" clients, include the provision in the fee agreement and, for example, agree in advance as to what will constitute a "reasonable" settlement offer.

unpaid attorney's fees under an agreement whereby the defendant was to pay the lawyer one-third of any amount saved. The defendant had been sued for defamation; the complaint sought $17,500 in damages. The jury awarded only 10% of that—$1750—a savings of $15,750. Thus, the defendant's lawyer sought an award of $5250. The Iowa Supreme Court held that the lawyer's contract with the client was void as against public policy; the reverse contingent fee was unreasonable because it was based only on speculation.

* * *

D. SHARING FEES WITH OTHER LAWYERS

Please read ABA Model Rules of Professional Conduct, Rule 1.5(e) and Comments [7] & [8].

* * *

Problem 10.4. Jack, an attorney, was retained by James and Lisa to represent their minor child in connection with a lawsuit alleging injuries sustained during the child's birth. Jack agreed to represent the couple. However, Jack had little experience with medical malpractice cases. So, a few months later and before Jack had done much work on the case, Jack referred the case to Geoffrey, a medical malpractice attorney. Jack had previously referred several cases to Geoffrey in exchange for a percentage of the attorney's fees paid to Geoffrey's law firm in connection with the referred cases.

All of the above parties met in Geoffrey's office to discuss the representation. They all agree that James and Lisa agreed that Geoffrey would be their new lawyer. However, beyond that, they all have different recollections as to what transpired. Jack contends that all parties understood that Jack would receive 1/3 of the attorney's fees paid to Geoffrey in exchange for Jack's referral. Geoffrey maintains the referral fee was 1/5 of the fees paid to Geoffrey, while James and Lisa don't recall agreeing to any kind of referral fee. Geoffrey entered into a written contingency fee agreement with James and Lisa whereby they agreed that Geoffrey would receive 1/3 of the amount recovered from their suit as payment for legal services. All parties agree that there was no reference in the written contingency fee agreement to any separate fee-sharing agreement between Jack and Geoffrey.

Prior to trial, the defendant in the malpractice case offered to settle for $1.2 million. James and Lisa were pleased with the offer and wanted to accept it. However, Geoffrey persuaded them to hold out for more. Eventually, the defendant upped his settlement offer to $1.5 million. James and Lisa accepted. After receiving the money from the defendant, Geoffrey sent a check to Jack in the amount of $100,000 which represented 1/5 of the 1/3 fee ($500,000) Geoffrey collected. Jack demanded that Geoffrey pay him $166,666, which would represent 1/3 of the 1/3 fee Geoffrey received. Geoffrey refused and now Jack has filed suit, seeking to recover the fee to which he believes he is entitled.

(A) Assuming Jack is able to establish that an agreement did exist in accordance with his version of events, did the agreement between Jack and Geoffrey comply with Model Rule 1.5(e)?

(B) Assuming Jack is able to establish that an agreement did exist in accordance with his version of events, is the agreement enforceable? Should Jack at least be allowed to recover on a quantum meruit basis?

* * *

Fee-splitting arrangements. Model Rule 1.5(e) addresses two different kinds of situations: (1) true co-counsel relationships and (2) referral situations in which one lawyer refers a client to another lawyer and seeks a fee for the referral. The latter arrangement is permissible only if (in addition to the other requirements of Rule 1.5(e)) "each lawyer assumes joint responsibility for the representation." Model Rule 1.5(e)(1). Comment [7] explains that "[j]oint responsibility for the representation entails financial and ethical responsibility for the representation." What is the point of this requirement? What is the concern more generally with fee-splitting arrangements between lawyers in different firms?

Fee-splitting arrangements in violation of public policy. Section 47, comment i of the Restatement (Third) of the Law Governing Lawyers takes the position that a fee agreement that fails to comply with Rule 1.5(e) is unenforceable against a client. Should it be enforceable as between two lawyers? *See id.*; Kaplan v. Pavalon & Gifford, 12 F.3d 87 (7th Cir. 1993).

* * *

E. EXPENSES

Please read ABA Model Rules of Professional Conduct, Rule 1.5 and Comment [1]; and Rule 1.8(e) and Comment [10].

* * *

Reasonable fees for expenses. Comment [1] to Model Rule 1.5 addresses the cost of services performed in-house or other out-of-pocket expenses incurred in the course of representation. With regard to things like copying costs or long-distance charges, a firm may charge "a reasonable amount to which the client has agreed in advance or by charging an amount that reasonably reflects the cost incurred" by the firm. The "cost incurred" may also include things like (in the case of copying costs), costs to help offset the salary of the photocopier operator. *See* ABA Formal Ethics Opinion 93–379 (1993). At the same time, ABA Formal Ethics Opinion 93–379 warns that a lawyer should not use other firm resources as an additional source of profit for the law firm: "The lawyer's stock in trade is the sale of legal services, not photocopy paper, tuna fish sandwiches, computer time or messenger services."

* * *

Problem 10.5. Edwin is a lawyer who represents an indigent client, Ralph, in a personal injury action. While his suit was pending, Ralph's car broke down. Ralph could not afford to repair the car and was in danger of losing his job as a result of the lack of reliable transportation, so Edwin paid the $500 repair bill for him. Ralph also suffered some medical problems (which were unrelated to his personal injury action) that required hospitalization. Edwin loaned money (interest-free) to Ralph to cover the hospital bills. As part of his fee agreement, Edwin also agreed to pay all of Ralph's court costs and litigation expenses. Is Edwin subject to discipline?

* * *

Alternative approaches. Some jurisdictions have considered what role an attorney can or should play in a client's search for a third party lender for a loan to tide the client over during the litigation process. In Florida, it is "discouraged" for an attorney to assist a client in obtaining a litigation loan. Even so, the state bar has outlined the strict guidelines under which an attorney could in fact do so. First, an attorney must conduct a conference with the client in which the attorney "discusses with the client whether the costs of the transaction outweigh the benefits of receiving the funds immediately and the other potential problems that can arise." However, the attorney can only give the client names of such lenders; lawyers are not allowed to contact the lender on behalf of the client. Furthermore, the lending institution is not to have any influence over the course of the litigation even though the lender can obtain a security interest in a portion of the recovery of a case. Finally, the attorney cannot have any ownership interest in the lending institution or receive any profits from the referral. Fla. Ethics Op. 00–03 (2002).

In New York, an attorney is also allowed to give a client the names of several litigation lenders. As in Florida, the attorney cannot own any interest in the lending institution or receive any compensation for the referral. Additionally, the lender cannot have any control over the litigation. Finally, the state bar reminds lawyers that the lender will desire information about the facts and merits of the case, but the attorney must be extremely careful to not violate the confidentiality provisions of Rule 1.6(a). N.Y. State Ethics Op. 769 (2003).

Should other states adopt such rules? Is there a danger in an attorney giving a client a list of litigation lenders? Will such loans encourage plaintiffs to see a case through trial rather than settling? How do the potential dangers in this relationship differ from those that exist when an attorney lends money directly to a client?

Litigation funding. Historically, third parties were prohibited from encouraging or funding litigation through champerty and maintenance laws. Given the increased costs of legal representation, some have argued for a relaxation of the traditional rules prohibiting third-party funding of litigation. Thus, it has been argued, third-party litigation funding by commercial entities may be a means of increasing access to justice. Jasminka Kalajdzic, Peter Cashman, & Alana Longmoore, *Justice for Profit: A Comparative Analysis of Australian, Canadian, and U.S. Third Party Litigation Funding*, 61 AM. J. COMP. L. 93, 100 (2013). What are the concerns with allowing more third-party litigation funding? Would the benefits of this approach outweigh the costs?

* * *

Profile of attorney professionalism. Recall that in *Brobeck*, Telex hired a lawyer, Moses Lasky, to represent the company on appeal before the Supreme Court because the company wanted to increase its chances for having its petition for certiorari granted. According to his obituary, Lasky "had a national reputation as a brilliant trial and appellate lawyer." During his career, he represented several high-profile clients, including Howard Hughes, the Union Oil Co., and the Oakland Raiders.

> A native of Denver, Mr. Lasky enrolled in the University of Colorado at the age of 14. He graduated with a bachelor's and law degree at age 20. Too young to be admitted to the bar, he instead enrolled in Harvard Law School, where he earned a master's degree.

> The son of Polish immigrants, Mr. Lasky financed much of his education by selling veterinary manuals door to door.

Michael Pena, *Moses Lasky—Noted Trial Lawyer*, SAN FRANCISCO CHRONICLE, Apr. 18, 2002, http://www.sfgate.com/bayarea/article/Moses-Lasky-noted-trial-lawyer-2848793.php

According to one local judge, Lasky "was the best lawyer I will ever see in my lifetime." *Id.* At the age of 72, Lasky left the Brobeck firm and founded the firm of Lasky, Haas, Cohler & Munter. He ended up practicing law well into his 80s.

CHAPTER 11

SAFEKEEPING CLIENT FUNDS AND PROPERTY

■ ■ ■

Chapter hypothetical. Lawyer Joan has represented Lita in a number of matters. One of these was a personal injury case against Brett. This case eventually settled, and Brett gave Joan a settlement check, which Joan deposited in her general business account before disbursing the proceeds to Lita two weeks later. At the same time this matter was pending, Joan was representing Lita in her divorce from Vince. Unfortunately, Joan and Lita had never signed a formal fee agreement and their recollections differed as to the agreed-upon fee. Eventually, Vince agreed to pay Lita $50,000 in settlement of the divorce. In July, Joan informed Lita that she had received the check from Vince and that she would be keeping $10,000 as payment of her fee "as we agreed." Lita objected, arguing that they had agreed on a lesser figure and that, in any event, $10,000 was unreasonable. Joan believed in good faith both that she and Lita had agreed to the $10,000 amount and that this amount was reasonable. Therefore, she placed the $10,000 in her general business account and disbursed the rest of the settlement proceeds to Lita. Lita then fired Joan, sued to collect the $10,000, and, in January of the following year, filed a request for production of documents seeking Joan's business records relating to the representation. Joan was unable to comply with the request for production because, in keeping with her bookkeeping practices, she had destroyed all financial records relating to the representation six months after the termination of representation. Is Joan subject to discipline?

* * *

A. TRUST ACCOUNTS AND THE OBLIGATION TO SAFEGUARD CLIENT PROPERTY

Please read ABA Model Rules of Professional Conduct, Rule 1.15(a)–(d) and Comments.

* * *

There are three common situations in which a lawyer will hold funds on behalf of a client. First, the client may be asked to provide an advance

241

on fees and expenses (often called a retainer) before the lawyer performs work on behalf of the client. Once the lawyer has earned the fees and the client has approved the bill, then the funds become the lawyer's property and should be moved out of the client trust account.

A second common situation occurs when the lawyer negotiates a settlement on the client's behalf. Typically, the opposing party will write a check to the lawyer, who then deposits it in the client trust account. Again, some portion of the settlement may accrue to the attorney (for example, if the attorney and client had agreed on a contingency fee) or to a third party (as payment of litigation expenses or court costs). The lawyer will typically provide the client with an accounting and will transfer funds out of the trust account once the settlement check has cleared.

Finally, in the third situation, the lawyer may hold funds as the administrator of a client's estate or as part of an escrow arrangement for a business or real estate transaction. In all of these situations, a lawyer who holds client funds or property acts as a fiduciary with regard to those funds and must comply with the state rules on safekeeping client property.

States often impose specific requirements in terms of the client trust accounts mentioned in Rule 1.15. For example, in Idaho,

> (A) All trust accounts maintained by members of the Idaho State Bar shall be clearly identified as such
>
>> (i) Lawyers who practice in Idaho shall deposit all funds held in trust in this jurisdiction in accordance with Rule 1.15(a) of the Idaho Rules of Professional Conduct in accounts clearly identified as "trust" or "escrow" accounts, referred to herein as "trust accounts," and shall take all steps necessary to inform the depository institution of the purpose and identity of such accounts.
>>
>> (ii) Funds held in trust include funds held in any fiduciary capacity, whether as trustee, agent, guardian, executor or otherwise. Attorney trust accounts shall be maintained only in financial institutions approved by the Idaho Supreme Court or the Idaho State Bar.

Idaho Bar Commission Rule 302. In addition, a financial institution acting as a depository for client trust accounts is required to file "with the Idaho State Bar an agreement, in a form provided by the Bar, to report to Bar Counsel in the event any properly payable instrument is presented against an attorney trust account containing funds insufficient to honor the instrument in full." *Id.* Rule 302(C).

Model Rule on Financial Recordkeeping. Comment [1] to Model Rule 1.15 requires that a lawyer hold property of others "with the care required of a professional fiduciary." The ABA's Model Rule on Financial Recordkeeping "is intended to give further definition to the requirements of Rule 1.15." The Model Rule on Financial Recordkeeping requires the lawyer to maintain detailed financial records, including "receipt and disbursement journals," "ledger records for all trust accounts," "copies of retainer and compensation agreements with clients," "copies of bills . . . to clients," and "checkbook registers." With respect to trust accounts required by Rule 1.15, the Model Rule on Financial Recordkeeping requires signatories to the account to be admitted to practice in the jurisdiction.

Failure to properly safeguard funds and property. Failing to properly account for a client's funds or other property is one of the most common bases of attorney discipline. Because the duty to keep accurate records falls upon the attorney, violations are generally easy to prove. The more difficult question in cases involving violations of Model Rule 1.15 is the proper sanction. As you read the following cases, consider the mitigating or aggravating factors that led the courts to choose the particular disciplinary sanctions they imposed.

* * *

SKOUTERIS V. BOARD OF PROFESSIONAL RESPONSIBILITY

2014 WL 686690 (Tenn. 2014) (not for publication)

LEE, JUSTICE.

This is a direct appeal of an attorney disciplinary proceeding involving six complaints of professional misconduct. The trial court affirmed the hearing panel's decision that the attorney had violated multiple Rules of Professional Conduct and should be disbarred from the practice of law. After review of the evidence presented and the applicable law, we affirm the judgment of the trial court. . . .

We begin our review with a summary of the evidence presented to the Panel and reviewed by the Trial Court.

A. Pruett Case

In October 2005, Tiffany Pruett was seriously injured in an automobile accident. Mr. Skouteris visited Ms. Pruett in the hospital. After Ms. Pruett was released from the hospital, she agreed for Mr. Skouteris, who had previously handled some minor legal matters for her, to represent her in her claim for damages. According to Ms. Pruett, Mr. Skouteris agreed to represent her at no charge because he was concerned for her and her son. Mr. Skouteris, however, testified that Ms. Pruett orally agreed to pay him a one-third contingency fee. Mr. Skouteris admitted that there was no written contingency fee agreement.

In March 2007, Mr. Skouteris settled Ms. Pruett's claim for $197,480. On April 16, 2007, Mr. Skouteris deposited Ms. Pruett's settlement check in his trust account. According to Ms. Pruett, Mr. Skouteris did not tell her about the settlement until several months later and did not provide her with any settlement documents. When Mr. Skouteris advised her of the settlement, he told her he would pay her medical bills and send her the remaining settlement funds. In June 2007, instead of disbursing the remaining balance of the settlement to Ms. Pruett, Mr. Skouteris began depositing payments in small amounts—such as $1000 or $2500—into Ms. Pruett's bank account on an irregular basis. Mr. Skouteris testified that Ms. Pruett requested this method of distribution. Ms. Pruett, however, testified that she never agreed to accept periodic disbursements, was strapped for money, and repeatedly requested that the entire balance be sent to her.

Mr. Skouteris did not maintain Ms. Pruett's funds in his trust account. The ending balance in Mr. Skouteris's trust account for the time period spanning April 13, 2007, through May 14, 2007, was $204,662.28, which included Ms. Pruett's $197,480 settlement deposit. The ending balance of Mr. Skouteris's trust account on June 14, 2007, was less than $197,480, even though Mr. Skouteris had not disbursed any of Ms. Pruett's settlement proceeds. In the following months, the balance in Mr. Skouteris's trust account declined even further below the total amount of Ms. Pruett's settlement proceeds. Mr. Skouteris admitted that as of June 13, 2008, he did not have sufficient funds in his trust account to cover his obligations to Ms. Pruett. Two of the payments that Mr. Skouteris made to Ms. Pruett were drawn on Mr. Skouteris's personal checking account, rather than his trust account. Mr. Skouteris continued disbursing Ms. Pruett's settlement proceeds to her in small increments from July 2007 to August 2008.

As of June 2008, no disbursements had been made from Ms. Pruett's settlement proceeds other than the payment of one of her medical bills in November 2007 and the periodic deposits into her bank account. Mr. Skouteris testified that he was holding approximately $80,000 in his trust account in order to ensure payment for a hospital lien, yet the balance in his trust account was not sufficient to pay the hospital lien. Ms. Pruett testified that Mr. Skouteris told her on several occasions that all of her other medical bills had been paid. Ms. Pruett discovered that her medical bills had not been paid when she applied for a student loan and learned that her credit rating had been adversely affected by Mr. Skouteris's failure to pay her medical providers.

Ms. Pruett testified that she had repeatedly asked Mr. Skouteris to send her proof of the payments that he had allegedly made to her medical providers, but he did not do so. In July 2008, Ms. Pruett became frustrated with Mr. Skouteris's lack of communication regarding the status of her settlement. She sent him an e-mail in which she requested a face-to-face meeting with him, and also demanded that he produce documentation of her settlement balance and disbursements to her medical providers, as well as an explanation regarding the hospital lien. Ms. Pruett met with Mr. Skouteris on July 30, 2008, but he did not provide her with any of the requested information.

As of August 2008—approximately sixteen months after Mr. Skouteris received and deposited Ms. Pruett's $197,480 settlement—Mr. Skouteris had paid Ms. Pruett $96,518.05 and her medical providers $7,944.29. There should have been a balance of at least $93,017.66 in Mr. Skouteris's trust account to cover his remaining obligations to Ms. Pruett, her medical providers, and any attorney fees he was owed. Mr. Skouteris's trust account, however, contained a balance of only $1,361.51.

This same month, Ms. Pruett hired attorney Mark Vorder-Bruegge to assist her in recovering her full settlement proceeds from Mr. Skouteris. Mr. Vorder-Bruegge corresponded several times with Mr. Skouteris about Ms. Pruett's claim, and on November 21, 2008, he made a formal written demand to Mr. Skouteris that he immediately disburse the entire remaining balance of Ms. Pruett's settlement funds. Mr. Skouteris did not comply with this demand. On September 15, 2009, Ms. Pruett sued Mr. Skouteris. Mr. Skouteris did not respond to the lawsuit, and on September 27, 2010, a default judgment was entered, finding that Mr. Skouteris had committed the intentional tort of conversion of Ms. Pruett's property and money, and that Mr. Skouteris had lied to Ms. Pruett regarding the payments due to her medical providers by assuring her that the bills were paid when they were not. The default judgment ordered Mr. Skouteris to pay $93,017.66 in compensatory damages and $300,000 in punitive damages. Mr. Skouteris moved to set aside the default judgment, but the motion was denied and no appeal was taken. As of the date of his hearing before the Panel, Ms. Pruett's judgment against him remained unsatisfied.

On July 3, 2009, Mr. Skouteris sent Mr. Vorder-Bruegge a check for $32,018.05, which Mr. Skouteris deemed to be the approximate amount due Ms. Pruett. He arrived at this amount by taking the amount of her settlement ($197,480), deducting the periodic disbursements that he had made to her ($96,518.05), deducting the payments that he had made to her medical providers ($7,944.29), and deducting a one-third contingency attorney fee after subtracting Ms. Pruett's medical expenses from her settlement ($56,781.57). According to Mr. Vorder-Bruegge and Ms. Pruett, this was the first time that Mr. Skouteris had claimed that he would be charging Ms. Pruett an attorney fee. Mr. Skouteris's trust account did not have a sufficient balance to cover the $32,018.05 check, but the bank honored the check.

When asked to provide an explanation for his failure to maintain Ms. Pruett's settlement funds in his trust account, Mr. Skouteris testified:

> Well, I mean, I had been going through a tough time, personal-wise. So I think it affected my—I mean I think I'm still a good lawyer, not such a great accountant and at that point in time I had lost both of my parents and went through a divorce. And I think I just didn't take care of my business well. I wasn't as precise in taking care of [t]his stuff the way I should have.

> In late 2007, early 2008, I tore my Achilles tendon and had to have surgery on that. So I was out for about a month. Then I was on [crutches] and such for about three months.

B. Cox Case

Mr. Skouteris represented Valerie Cox in a claim for damages arising out of an August 25, 2008 automobile accident. Mr. Skouteris settled the claim for $12,000. On May 19, 2009, he deposited Ms. Cox's settlement check into his operating account, rather than his trust account. Mr. Skouteris admitted this was a mistake on his part.

Before receiving Ms. Cox's settlement check, Mr. Skouteris learned that the State of Florida asserted a lien for unpaid child support against Ms. Cox's funds in an amount in excess of $14,000. In light of the outstanding Florida lien for child support, Mr. Skouteris testified that he sought the advice of twenty attorneys and the Board concerning how to deal with Ms. Cox's settlement proceeds. After seeking this advice, Mr. Skouteris did not disburse the balance of Ms. Cox's settlement to Ms. Cox or the State of Florida. Nor did he file an interpleader action to allow a court to determine how the funds should be disbursed.

As of the time of the Panel hearing, Mr. Skouteris had not disbursed the settlement proceeds. Mr. Skouteris testified that he had kept the money because Ms. Cox wanted to avoid having to satisfy the State of Florida's child support lien. Mr. Skouteris acknowledged, however, that he only offered to relinquish Ms. Cox's funds after Ms. Cox filed a complaint against him with the Board.

C. Crawford Case

Mr. Skouteris represented Gary Crawford on a contingency fee basis in a claim for damages arising out of an automobile accident. Mr. Skouteris admitted that there was no written contingency fee agreement signed by Mr. Crawford. Mr. Skouteris settled Mr. Crawford's claim for $6,500 and deposited the settlement check in his trust account on June

11, 2008. The ending balance of Mr. Skouteris's trust account as of August 15, 2008, was $1,361.51, but Mr. Skouteris had not distributed any funds to Mr. Crawford. Mr. Crawford's settlement proceeds were disbursed on June 27, 2009. According to Mr. Skouteris, he delayed distributing Mr. Crawford's settlement proceeds for more than a year because Mr. Crawford disputed payment of some of his medical bills. Mr. Skouteris admitted that he failed to respond to the Board's request for information in a timely manner.

D. Baker Case

Mr. Skouteris represented Jacqueline Baker, a minor, in a personal injury action resulting from an automobile accident that occurred in November 2007. Ms. Baker's case was settled for $100,000, and on September 18, 2008, the settlement check was deposited in Mr. Skouteris's trust account. The court order approving the settlement provided that the proceeds would be distributed as follows: $30,000 to Mr. Skouteris for his attorney fee; $18,423 to Blue-Cross Blue-Shield; $10,900 to Ms. Baker's father for her dental care; and the balance of $40,677 to Ms. Baker's father for her use and benefit. Mr. Skouteris made all of these disbursements except for the balance of $40,677, which he retained at the request of Mr. Baker. Before Mr. Skouteris had finished disbursing all of Ms. Baker's settlement proceeds, in July 2009, the balance of Mr. Skouteris's trust account fell to −$3,360.69.

Mr. Skouteris issued payments on Ms. Baker's behalf for educational expenses totaling $1,049, and when Ms. Baker turned eighteen years old in August 2009, Mr. Skouteris also made payments to her in August and September 2009 of $3,500 and $1,000, respectively. Thus, in October, 2009, Mr. Skouteris still owed Ms. Baker $35,128. As of October 15, 2009, the balance of Mr. Skouteris's trust account was $1,603.89.

In January 2010, the balance of Mr. Skouteris's trust account fell even further to $982.38. On February 4, 2010, Mr. Skouteris wrote a check to Ms. Baker in the amount of $17,564, reflecting one-half of the outstanding $35,128 balance that he owed her. Mr. Skouteris was charged a fee for insufficient funds on that check, but the bank honored it. As of February 12, 2010, Mr. Skouteris held only $131.38 in his trust account, but still owed $17,564 to Ms. Baker. On February 26, 2010, Mr. Skouteris wrote another check to Ms. Baker for the remaining $17,564. The only deposits made to Mr. Skouteris's trust account during the period from January until March 2010 were settlement proceeds from other clients; thus, the February 26, 2010 check to Ms. Baker cleared due to deposits belonging to other clients. Ms. Baker eventually received her full settlement from Mr. Skouteris. Mr. Skouteris admitted that he failed to respond to the Board's request for information in a timely manner.

E. Davis Case

Mr. Skouteris represented Danzel Davis, a minor, in a premises liability matter. Mr. Skouteris settled the case and received two settlement checks totaling $9,000, which he deposited into his trust account on June 23, 2009, and June 30, 2009. The balance in his trust account throughout the month of June was a negative balance. The account statement for July 14, 2009, reflects an ending balance of $3,360.69.

Mr. Skouteris paid Mr. Davis $1,000 on August 19, 2009. On October 30, 2009, because Mr. Davis had reached the age of majority, an Order of Dismissal was entered in Mr. Davis's case providing that he was entitled to receive the remainder of his funds without judicial oversight. Mr. Skouteris did not disburse any additional proceeds to Mr. Davis until August 19, 2010, when Mr. Skouteris wrote Mr. Davis a check for $4,250. In addition to the negative balance in Mr. Skouteris's account on July 14, 2009, the account statements for January 2010, February 2010, and April 2010 all reflect a total balance of less than $4,250. Mr. Skouteris testified that he doubted that he had a written contingency fee agreement with Mr. Davis, and none was produced. Mr. Skouteris admitted that he failed to respond to the Board's request for information in a timely manner.

F. Levick Case

Mr. Skouteris represented Justin Levick in a personal injury claim arising out of an automobile accident in August 2010. Mr. Skouteris did not provide Mr. Levick with a written contingency fee agreement. Mr. Skouteris settled Mr. Levick's case for $3,000 and deposited Mr. Levick's settlement check in his trust account on November 12, 2010. At one point during the October 15 to November 15, 2010 statement period—during which time Mr. Skouteris held Mr. Levick's funds, but before any disbursements had been made—the balance in Mr. Skouteris's trust account was—$1,443.50. On August 15, 2011, the day that Mr. Levick filed a disciplinary complaint with the Board, Mr. Skouteris disbursed $1,970 in settlement proceeds to Mr. Levick.

IV.A.

Based on these facts, the Panel found that Mr. Skouteris violated Rules of Professional Conduct 1.1, 1.3, 1.4(a), 1.4(b), 1.5(c), 1.15(a), 1.15(c), 1.16(d), 8.1(b), 8.4(a), 8.4(b), 8.4(c), and 8.4(d).

In determining that disbarment was the appropriate sanction, the Panel analyzed the relevant aggravating and mitigating factors applicable to Mr. Skouteris's case, and consulted the ABA Standards for Imposing Lawyer Sanctions ("ABA Standards"). . . . the Hearing Panel found that each of the following aggravating factors justified a further increase in Mr. Skouteris's disciplinary sanction:

a. His action evidenced a dishonest and selfish motive;

b. His conduct evidenced a pattern of misconduct;

c. He engaged in multiple offenses;

d. He refused to acknowledge the wrongful nature of his conduct;

e. His victims were particularly vulnerable in that they were his clients and relied on him to represent and care for their interest;

f. He had substantial experience in the practice of law; and

g. He evidenced an indifference to making restitution.

Further, the Panel found that Mr. Skouteris had previously been disciplined twice for failing to disburse settlement proceeds and that no mitigating factors applied.

B.

In this appeal, Mr. Skouteris raises four issues: (1) the Board was allowed to twice amend its Petition for Discipline to present "a cumulative effect of relative [sic] insignificant charges"; (2) that the cumulative effect of allowing the amendments to the Petition for Discipline unfairly prejudiced Mr. Skouteris; (3) that the Trial Court failed to consider the proof submitted by Mr. Skouteris; and (4) that the Trial Court misinterpreted the proof relative to Mr. Skouteris's prior disciplinary offenses. We have thoroughly considered all of Mr. Skouteris's arguments and find that each lacks merit.

In issues (1) and (2), Mr. Skouteris argues that the consolidation of six complaints of misconduct, which were filed in three separate Petitions for Discipline, was unfairly prejudicial to him. According to Mr. Skouteris, these complaints, considered separately, would not have been significant enough to warrant the attention of the Board, and added together, they had the cumulative effect of being unduly prejudicial. . . .

The consolidated complaints against Mr. Skouteris contained similar issues that occurred in the same time frame and involved the same bank statements. Mr. Skouteris had sufficient notice of the allegations to prepare his defense. The alleged misconduct in the three petitions was not insignificant and merited the attention of the Board. Mr. Skouteris's argument that he was unfairly prejudiced by the Panel's decisions to grant the Board's motions to amend its Petition for Discipline lacks merit. . . .

The Board presented uncontroverted evidence that, after accepting and depositing their settlement checks, Mr. Skouteris failed to maintain sufficient funds in his trust account to cover his obligations to Ms. Pruett, Ms. Cox, Mr. Crawford, Ms. Baker, Mr. Davis, and Mr. Levick. Mr. Skouteris did not provide competent representation to his clients and failed to act with reasonable diligence and promptness in disbursing their settlement proceeds. He failed to keep his clients informed about their cases and to respond to their requests for information. Mr. Skouteris failed to have written attorney fee agreements signed by Ms. Pruett, Mr. Levick, Mr. Crawford, and Mr. Davis. Mr. Skouteris failed to provide a written statement showing the disbursement of his clients' funds. He did not keep Ms. Cox's funds separate from his operating funds. In Ms. Pruett's case, he failed to cooperate with her new lawyer by providing information, documents and work product. Mr. Skouteris failed to respond to the Board after complaints were filed in Mr. Crawford's, Ms. Baker's, and Mr. Davis's cases. Mr. Skouteris violated multiple Rules of Professional Conduct, engaged in conduct involving dishonesty, deceit and misrepresentation, and engaged in conduct that was prejudicial to the administration of justice.

Mr. Skouteris argues that the Panel and Trial Court overlooked four factual matters. First, he notes that Mr. Crawford, Ms. Baker, Mr. Davis, and Mr. Levick ultimately "received every cent" of their settlements. The record, however, indicates that the Panel and Trial Court considered this fact, but concluded that Mr. Skouteris had caused actual injury to Ms. Pruett and Ms. Cox because they were deprived of their settlement funds, and that Ms. Baker, Mr. Crawford, Mr. Levick, and Mr. Davis were subjected to potentially serious injury by Mr. Skouteris's mishandling of their funds. These findings, as well as the Panel's subsequent Order noting that restitution was still owed to Ms. Pruett and Ms. Cox, make clear that the Panel considered the fact that Mr. Crawford, Ms. Baker, Mr. Davis, and Mr. Levick ultimately received their full settlements.

Second, Mr. Skouteris argues that the Panel and Trial Court failed to note that Ms. Cox, Mr. Crawford, and Ms. Baker did not testify before the Panel. However, it was not necessary for them to testify. There was sufficient evidence introduced to prove that Mr. Skouteris had mishandled the settlement proceeds of Ms. Cox, Mr. Crawford, and Ms. Baker without the benefit of their testimony.

Third, Mr. Skouteris argues that the Panel and Trial Court only looked to the balance of Mr. Skouteris's trust account, rather than considering Mr. Skouteris's testimony that Mr. Crawford was responsible for delaying Mr. Skouteris's ability to disburse his settlement proceeds. Mr. Skouteris failed to maintain Mr. Crawford's settlement proceeds in his trust account. It makes no difference that Mr. Crawford may have delayed the distribution of his settlement proceeds.

Fourth, Mr. Skouteris argues that the Panel and Trial Court failed to recognize that he owed no legal duty to Jill Alston, the complainant in Ms. Baker's case. This is irrelevant. The complainant's identity would have no bearing on the findings of the Panel and the Trial Court that Mr.

Skouteris failed to maintain Ms. Baker's settlement funds in his trust account.

In his next issue, Mr. Skouteris argues that the Trial Court mistakenly concluded that he had previously been suspended for professional misconduct on two occasions—rather than admonished twice and publicly reprimanded once. Mr. Skouteris is correct that this statement of the Trial Court was inaccurate, but this error was of no consequence due to the extent and severity of Mr. Skouteris's misconduct and the appropriate punishment for each violation.

Although not listed as an issue in his brief, Mr. Skouteris argues that disbarment was an inappropriate sanction for his misconduct, and suggests that a more appropriate sanction is the imposition of a five-year suspension with the last three years served on a probationary status. Mr. Skouteris's continued insistence that his misconduct was limited to trivial accounting errors is troubling. In finding that Mr. Skouteris's misconduct amounted to conversion for personal gain, the Panel correctly noted: "It is obvious that Mr. Skouteris converted funds in his trust account for personal use in that he utilized any funds available to keep his practice afloat and to make payments to others and to make withdrawals for himself." Even if Mr. Skouteris intended to pay his clients all that they were owed in due time, converting their property for his own use for any period of time was a serious ethical violation and a breach of his fiduciary duty. By continuing to describe his trust account violations as insignificant, Mr. Skouteris shows a lack of understanding that his conduct is wrong. Mr. Skouteris also argues that his punishment should be reduced in light of his twenty-four-year law career. Under the ABA Standards, however, substantial experience in the practice of law is an aggravating factor, not a mitigating factor.

CONCLUSION

For the foregoing reasons, the judgment of the Trial Court is affirmed, and Mr. Skouteris is disbarred from the practice of law. Costs of this appeal are assessed to George E. Skouteris, Jr. and his surety, for which execution may issue if necessary.

* * *

DISCIPLINARY BOARD V. BECKER
504 N.W.2d 303 (N.D.1993)

MESCHKE, JUSTICE.

The Disciplinary Board recommends a public reprimand of Donald R. Becker for negligently handling a client's property. Because there was little or no actual injury after prompt restitution, we direct a private reprimand of Becker.

Becker became a member of the North Dakota Bar in 1983. Beginning October 1988, he represented Dennis Mees on several criminal charges. Mees paid Becker a $2,000 initial retainer, another $1,000 later, and $500 was due after sentencing. Around October 18, 1989, postal officials returned to Becker five pieces of Mees's gold jewelry, three rings and two bracelets, seized at the time of Mees's arrest. Mees asked Becker to deliver the jewelry to Mees's fiancée in Texas. Becker agreed to do so.

Around November 28, 1989, Becker told Mees that the jewelry had been stolen from the console inside Becker's car during the Thanksgiving holiday. Because it was doubtful that the jewelry could be recovered and, with the concurrence of Mees, to avoid further publicity before Mees's impending sentencing on criminal charges, Becker made no police report.

Because the loss was not covered by Becker's insurance, Becker agreed with Mees to forgo further payment for his work and to perform other legal services to offset the value of the jewelry. After considerable work, Becker discussed the continuing representation in July 1990 with Mees, then in prison. According to Becker, it was understood that the additional work had exceeded the worth of the jewelry, and that the arrangement would end with the completion of a pending name-change petition. In August 1990, Becker sent Mees a statement that itemized $6,421.78 in services, transfers, and expenses for Mees.

Mees wrote back, accusing Becker of stealing the jewelry. Mees later made a disciplinary complaint that Becker stole the jewelry.

In February 1991, formal disciplinary proceedings were begun against Becker for violating NDRPC 1.15 by failing to safekeep the property of a client. From a stipulation, disciplinary counsel summarized the evidence to a hearing panel. The panel concluded that, because "the jewelry was missing and therefore could not be valued by an independent third party, ... the lawyer's negligence ... caused injury or potential injury to a client." The panel recommended that Becker be publicly reprimanded and assessed costs of $350. The Disciplinary Board unanimously adopted the panel's findings and submitted that recommendation to this court for disciplinary action.

Becker admits the violation and does not contest the costs, but he argues that, "because the value of services, money and goods provided Mees was in excess of the value of the jewelry," Mees suffered no "loss or potential loss." Therefore, Becker argues, a private reprimand is the correct sanction.

The relevant part of NDRPC 1.15 says:

(a) A lawyer shall hold property of clients or third persons that is in a lawyer's possession in connection with a representation separate from the lawyer's own property. Funds shall be deposited in one or more identifiable interest bearing trust accounts. . . . Other property shall be identified as such and appropriately safeguarded.

Becker negligently failed to appropriately safeguard property that his client entrusted to him. That fact is undisputed, and the only question is what sanction applies.

This court adopted the North Dakota Standards for Imposing Lawyer Sanctions (NDSILS) in 1988 based on the American Bar Association's Standards of Imposing Lawyer Sanctions (February 1986). See NDCC Court Rules Annotated 1009 (1992–93). The purposes of the standards are "to promote: (1) consideration of all factors relevant to imposing the appropriate level of sanction in an individual case; (2) consideration of the appropriate weight of such fact[or]s in light of the stated goals of lawyer discipline; (3) consistency in the imposition of disciplinary sanctions for the same or similar offenses. . . ." NDSILS 1.3. Those purposes aid us in selecting the appropriate sanction.

Either of two related standards could apply here. NDSILS 4.13 says:

Reprimand is generally appropriate when a lawyer is negligent in dealing with client property and causes injury or potential injury to a client.

NDSILS 4.14 reads:

Admonition is generally appropriate when a lawyer is negligent in dealing with client property and causes little or no actual or potential injury to a client.

In the standards, "reprimand" means "public reprimand," while "admonition" denotes "private reprimand." NDSILS 2.4 and 2.5. The question here is the extent of the injury for selection of the correct sanction.

Ironically, this dispute about the correct sanction results in publicizing the sanction, even if we apply a private reprimand. See Disciplinary Board v. Amundson, 297 N.W.2d 433, 444 (N.D.1980) ("Private reprimands are issued by the Disciplinary Board, not this court, although we may review the decision of the Disciplinary Board to issue a private reprimand."). Still, the public airing has the wholesome aspect of informing other lawyers, thereby discouraging similar carelessness. The differential in our decision lies largely in the severity of the offense on this lawyer's record.

For sanction selection, an "injury" is

harm to a client, the public, the legal system, or the profession which results from a lawyer's misconduct. The level of injury can range from "serious" injury to "little or no" injury; a reference to "injury" alone indicates any level of injury greater than "little or no" injury.

. . . .

"Potential injury" is the harm to a client, the public, the legal system or the profession that is reasonably foreseeable at the time of the lawyer's misconduct, and which, but for some intervening factor or event, would probably have resulted from the lawyer's misconduct.

NDSILS Definitions at NDCC Court Rules Annotated 1010. Mees was clearly injured by Becker's carelessness in carrying a client's valuable property around in his car. In the end, however, little or no actual injury resulted to Mees after Becker's restitution via legal services.

Recognizing the lack of actual injury, disciplinary counsel urges that the controlling factor is the "potential injury" to the profession. Disciplinary counsel argues it this way: "Had Becker not left the jewelry in the console, there would not be the dispute over its value or the nagging question, reflecting so poorly on the profession, of whether it really was stolen."

Becker and Mees placed divergent values on the lost jewelry: $5,500 by Becker, and $8,840 by Mees. Becker testified that he impulsively obtained an appraisal by a local Fargo jeweler before the loss, speculating that he might be asked to accept the jewelry in lieu of fees. This appraisal "indicated that the retail value of the jewelry would be approximately $5,500.00 and a fair market value would be approximately ½ that amount." On the other hand, Mees's estimate came from a jeweler who sometimes appraised items sight unseen, and who had otherwise given Mees and his fiancée blank letterhead stationery "so that they could type up their own lists of jewelry and appraisals." With Mees's criminal record, disciplinary counsel concedes that Mees's appraisal has "little credibility." The clearest and most convincing evidence, the appraisal by a local jeweler for Becker, is practically an independent appraisal. See NDPRLDD 3.5(C) (standard of proof is clear and convincing evidence). This local appraisal placed the value of the jewelry at under $5,500.

If a sentimental value existed, Mees might yet have an unreimbursed injury, even after restitution. It was stipulated, however, that "Mees at one time observed that he would just as soon have his cash as a nest egg and have fees paid by the lost jewelry." If the jewelry had more than a monetary value to Mees, he would not have been so agreeable to offsetting its loss for services and to delaying his complaint to the channels of discipline. No sentimental value affects our analysis.

Disciplinary counsel examined Becker's files to appraise the work done for Mees. The work included defending federal criminal proceedings, where Mees was convicted and sentenced for mail fraud, aiding and abetting, possession of firearms by a convicted felon, false oath, and failure to disclose; defending later state criminal charges, where Mees was convicted and sentenced for theft of property and bail jumping; resisting revocation of Mees's insurance license in Texas; resisting enforcement of a lien against the property of Mee's fiancée; and performing various other miscellaneous services, including resisting collection claims against Mees and his wife, assisting his wife and stepdaughter on some claims, presenting a name-change petition for Mees, and paying some shipping charges, as well as making some cash payments to, and purchases for, Mees in the amount of $523; all totaling $6,421.78.

Disciplinary counsel concedes that "the additional work done far exceeded what one might expect as incidental to representation in criminal proceedings for a flat fee, . . ." and that the amounts charged by Becker were reasonable. Thus, Becker's legal work adequately compensated for the lost jewelry.

Uncharacteristically, the hearing panel and Disciplinary Board did not address aggravating and mitigating circumstances, as NDPRLDD 3.1(F) requires: "Mitigating or aggravating circumstances which affect the nature or degree of discipline to be imposed in a matter shall be fully set forth in its report." Disciplinary counsel urges that "it is plain" that Becker's earlier disbarment in 1977 by the Supreme Court of Arizona "is entitled to weight in aggravation" under NDSILS 9.22(a). We disagree.

Arizona disbarred Becker for a completely unrelated type of offense. Disciplinary counsel concedes that her investigation confirms Becker's full disclosure and the extensive investigation that was made when he applied for admission in North Dakota. He was admitted to practice in this state, and has not been disciplined here. In fact, another gold watch and some tools were later returned by postal officials to Becker, safeguarded by him, and delivered for Mees. No pattern of misconduct is present. Becker's remote conduct does not aggravate this unintentional violation.

"The least culpable mental state is negligence, when a lawyer fails to be aware of a substantial risk that circumstances exist or that a result will follow, which failure is a deviation from the standard of care that a reasonable lawyer would exercise in the situation." Prefatory material to the current Model Standards For Imposing Lawyer Sanctions, ABA/BNA Lawyers' Manual on Professional Conduct at 01:805–806 (Published by the American Bar Association and the Bureau of National Affairs; 6–17–92). Under NDSILS 9.32(d), mitigating factors include "timely good faith effort to make restitution or to rectify consequences of misconduct." While services, rather than money, are not ordinarily an acceptable form of restitution, it was agreed upon in this case. Here, coming after completion of agreed restitution, the lateness of the complaint lessens its impact.

Becker readily made restitution before Mees complained to disciplinary authorities.

> Lawyers who make restitution voluntarily and on their own initiative demonstrate both a recognition of their ethical violation and their responsibility to the injured client. . . . Such conduct should be considered as mitigation. . . .

Model Standards For Imposing Lawyer Sanctions 9.4, Commentary, ABA/BNA Lawyers' Manual on Professional Conduct at 01:841. See also Matter of Walton, 251 N.W.2d 762 (N.D.1977) (prompt restitution is an important mitigating factor). By promptly acknowledging his carelessness, readily making restitution, and fully cooperating in the disciplinary process, Becker has rectified his negligence and compensated for the injury.

Accordingly, we conclude that Mees suffered little or no actual injury, and that there is no practical injury to the profession. We order that Donald R. Becker be privately reprimanded, and that he pay costs of $350.

* * *

B. HANDLING DISPUTED FUNDS

Please read ABA Model Rules of Professional Conduct, Rule 1.15(e) and Comment [4].

Disputes about the disposition of funds held in trust can arise between an attorney and client (as when the client objects to the amount of attorney's fees claimed by the attorney) or between the client and a third party (as when a creditor of the client asserts a claim to the funds). When disputes about the proper disposition of funds arise, Model Rule 1.15 directs attorneys to release any undisputed funds and retain in trust only those whose ownership is disputed. The court in the *Skouteris* mentioned one way that such disputes can properly be resolved: the attorney can file an interpleader action with a court to determine priority of ownership. In other cases, such as the garnishment action in the following case, a third party may file a court action seeking to enforce a property interest in the funds. As you read the following case, ask yourself what the law firm could have done to protect its interest in payment.

Interest on Lawyers' Trust Accounts ("IOLTA"). In the following case, you will also see client trust accounts referred to as "IOLTA" accounts. IOLTA programs, which have been established in all fifty states, use the interest paid on lawyers' trust accounts to provide funding for legal aid to low-income state residents in civil matters. If each client's funds were held in a separate account, any interest earned would normally be less that the administrative fees associated with the account. However, by allowing clients' funds to be pooled together, the interest earned in the aggregate can be significant. IOLTA accounts survived a constitutional "takings" challenge in in Brown v. Legal Found. of Washington, 538 U.S. 216 (2003). The Supreme Court concluded that using the money for public purposes would indeed be an unconstitutional taking, but held that no damages would be due when clients suffered no loss of funds. That is, as long as administrative expenses would outweigh the interest payable to any individual client, the client had suffered no compensable loss and the state need not disgorge the interest payments. Although IOLTA accounts survived the constitutional challenge, they faced a greater practical test after 2008, when sustained low interest rates significantly reduced the amount of funds available for legal aid. The ABA estimated in 2013 that nationwide IOLTA funding had dropped from $371 million a year in 2007 to $93.2 million in 2011. As a result, states have had to look for other sources to fund civil legal aid, and many legal aid agencies have been forced to lay off employees and reduce the number of clients they can serve.

* * *

HADASSAH V. SCHWARTZ

966 N.E.2d 298 (Ohio Ct. App. 2011)

FISCHER, JUSTICE.

[Hadassah, The Women's Zionist Organization of America, Inc. ("Hadassah") prevailed in a lawsuit against Robert L. Schwartz, obtaining a judgment for $2.2 million dollars. Hadassah's attorneys knew that Schwartz had deposited $150,000 with his law firm, Bieser, Greer & Landis, L.L.P. ("BG&L"). Hadassah then filed a garnishment action to obtain the funds held by the law firm. The trial court ruled that Hadassah had a right to garnish the funds. Schwartz appealed, arguing that the funds had been designated as an advance payment of legal fees and should not be subject to garnishment.]

For the reasons stated below, we determine that Schwartz's appeal is without merit, and we affirm the judgment of the trial court. . . . A debtor's funds generally are not exempt from garnishment merely because the funds are placed with an attorney.

Ohio law authorizes Hadassah to enforce its judgment against Schwartz by collecting Schwartz's property in the possession of BG&L. BG&L asserted in its answer that the money Schwartz had paid to BG&L had been deposited in an IOLTA account and that the funds served as a retainer for legal services. Neither BG&L nor Schwartz produced the alleged retainer agreement, and nothing in the record indicates that BG&L acquired an ownership interest in the retainer or that the retainer was nonrefundable.

The Ohio Rules of Professional Conduct mandate that property belonging to a client or third party be kept in a client's trust account and that property belonging to an attorney be kept separate from a client's property. Prof.Cond.R. 1.15. BG&L kept Schwartz's $150,000 retainer in an IOLTA account, which indicates that, at that specific point in time, Schwartz, and not BG&L, retained the ownership rights over the $150,000 retainer. Therefore, the retainer was property subject to garnishment. . . .

Schwartz argues that "[p]arties should * * * be able to prepare for protracted litigation by adequately funding their legal defense and trusting that the funds will be secured as anticipated." Schwartz contends that garnishment of BG&L's IOLTA account deprived him of representation and that this deprivation was unfair in the absence of evidence that Schwartz had engaged in collusion or concealment to avoid garnishment. Schwartz also argues that public policy forbids the "gamesmanship" employed by Hadassah where, as Schwartz alleges, Hadassah had demanded that Schwartz place $150,000 in BG&L's custody during settlement negotiations, with the intent that settlement would not take place.

Schwartz's equitable arguments fail. Schwartz's accusation that Hadassah engaged in bad-faith settlement tactics is without support in the record. As to the other equitable arguments, garnishment is a purely statutory procedure, and we are not in the position to create exemptions to the garnishment statute.

Although we sympathize with Schwartz's argument that garnishment of an IOLTA account might deprive a client of legal representation, a client in Schwartz's position could avoid this result by reaching a representation agreement with the attorney that gives the attorney an ownership interest in some or all of the legal fee upon receipt, so long as the agreement was not used as a tool to evade garnishment and did not place the attorney in the position of receiving an excessive fee. See Prof. Cond. R. 1.5. And if the legislature wishes to add attorney-retainer fees to the list of exemptions, it can do so.

Schwartz also relies on several provisions of Ohio's Uniform Commercial Code governing secured transactions to argue that BG&L

had a superior interest to that of the creditor Hadassah in the $150,000 retainer held in the IOLTA account. Secured-transactions principles do not apply in this case, because neither BG&L nor Schwartz produced the representation agreement, and so there is no evidence of a written document creating a security interest in the funds. Thus, the record does not show that BG&L and Schwartz created a security interest

In conclusion, we determine that the trial court did not err in ordering garnishment of Schwartz's funds in BG&L's IOLTA account. We overrule the assignment of error, and we affirm the judgment of the trial court.

* * *

C. SUPPORTING LAWYERS' FUNDS FOR CLIENT PROTECTION

Please read ABA Model Rules of Professional Conduct, Rule 1.15 and Comment [6].

Funds for Client Protection. As an example of the kind of fund for client protection mentioned in Comment [6], New York's Lawyers' Fund for Client Protection provides a remedy up to a maximum of $300,000 for law clients of lawyers injured as a result of dishonest conduct by a lawyer admitted to practice in New York. The remedy is available to those clients "who cannot get reimbursement from the lawyer who caused the loss, or from insurance or other sources." The fund is financed through a mandatory registration fee. http://www.nylawfund.org/faq.html.

* * *

Profile of attorney professionalism. Attorney Christopher Marinello, often described as the "Sherlock Holmes of art crime," has made a career out of returning property to its rightful owners. *See* Sarah Cascone, *Chris Marinello is the Sherlock Holmes of Art Crime*, ArtNet News *at* http://news.artnet.com/in-brief/chris-marinello-is-the-sherlock-holmes-of-art-crime-166601 (November 16, 2014).

Over the last twenty years, Marinello has overseen the return of more than $300 million in stolen artwork. In 2013, he founded the firm Art Recovery International. In 2012, he represented the family of Paul Rosenberg seeking the return of an Henri Matisse painting, *Woman in Blue in Front of a Fireplace*, that was allegedly looted by Nazi operatives in 1941 and had ended up in a Norwegian museum. Art Recovery International reported on its website that "it was the strength of the moral claim that persuaded [the museum] to restitute this painting unconditionally to the Rosenberg heirs" in 2014. Marinello has also worked closely with law enforcement. In one case, he notified U.S.

Homeland Security officials that a painting at a Long Island gallery was believed to be another Nazi-looted painting, this one a portrait of a young Jewish girl with her pet rabbit. The painting was one of several that had been looted from the family home in Brussels when the family fled the Nazi Occupation in 1944. After an investigation, the gallery owner agreed to turn over the painting and Marinello was able to return the painting to the girl, who had survived the war by hiding with her family in the Belgian countryside and was now an elderly woman living in Belgium. ArtDaily.org, *A Child's Portrait, Looted During the War, is Returned to Its Owner*, at http://artdaily.com/news/34691/A-Child-s-Portrait--Looted-During-the-War-is-Returned-to-Its-Owner#.VMWiZP54rYg[/url].

Marinello is a graduate of the University of Miami School of Law. For several years, he has taught a class on Law and Ethics in the Art Market at New York University School of Law. On the Art Recovery website, Marinello credits his legal experience for developing his "proficiency for negotiating complex title disputes between collectors, dealers, museums and insurance companies."

SECTION 2

COMMUNICATION AND DECISION-MAKING

■ ■ ■

Communication between a lawyer and a prospective client is an essential aspect of the process through which they eventually enter into an attorney-client relationship. It is not uncommon for lawyers and prospective clients to commence their attorney-client relationship without discussion or resolution of many of the issues concerning these subjects that might arise during the lawyer's representation of the client. This does not mean, of course, that the issues will not arise and need to resolved at some later point in time. For that to occur there will need to be communication between lawyer and client and a decision or decisions will need to be made concerning the lawyer's representation of the client. As an overriding issue, then, this Section addresses communication and decision-making within an attorney-client relationship.

We will start with a few simple observations. First, clients may be more interested in communication with the lawyer than the lawyer is interested in communicating with the client. Similarly, clients may want more of a role in decision-making than the lawyer would prefer. Some clients may want more of each than other clients. The success or failure of the representation will affect both lawyer and client, but differently, and this may affect their attitudes about communication and the allocation of decision-making authority between them. On the other hand, the lawyer is presumed to have special expertise and the client is presumed to be in need of the lawyer's assistance. In this regard, however, some clients may need, or think they need, less assistance than others. Such clients may want more information and say in their representation. Lawyers may think a client needs more assistance than the client thinks is needed, and this may affect the lawyer's inclination to communicate and actively involve the client in decision-making concerning the representation.

In Chapter 12, we consider communication and decision-making within an attorney-client relationship between a lawyer and a client thought to be capable of making decisions concerning his or her representation. This chapter also explores these issues in circumstances when the client is thought to be "impaired."

CHAPTER 12

COMMUNICATION AND DECISION-MAKING

■ ■ ■

Chapter hypothetical. Bob is a lawyer with Palsgraf & Pennoyer who represents Lucille's Cupcakes, a one-person business. Lucille's is being sued on various theories by Neil, a former distributor. Lucille, the owner, comes to you and tells you that she is unhappy with Bob's representation and would like your advice. Apparently, Bob wants to implead Ronnie's Motors, a business that was involved in the transaction with Neil that led to the lawsuits. But Lucille does not wish to implead Ronnie's Motors because she has a longstanding business relationship with Ronnie that she does not want to jeopardize. Lucille says that Bob told her that she was paying him to make those kinds of decisions and he wasn't about to be micromanaged. Lucille also just found out that Bob agreed with Neil's lawyer to waive a potentially valid statute of limitations defense Lucille had in exchange for Neil's agreement to drop another of his claims against Lucille's. Lucille is not at all happy to have learned about Bob's decision and wants to assert the statute of limitations defense regardless of Bob's agreement.

What advice do you have for Lucille?

* * *

In the course of any representation, many decisions must be made. The lawyer is the client's agent and representative, but does that mean the lawyer can make all decisions on the client's behalf? Does it mean that the lawyer does not have to tell the client what is going on? The following materials will introduce you to the ethical and legal dimensions of the need for communication between lawyer and client and the allocation of decision-making authority between lawyer and client. Who's in charge? Who should be in charge?

* * *

A. IN GENERAL

* * *

1. COMMUNICATION

**Please read ABA Model Rules of Professional Conduct,
Rule 1.4 and Comments.**

Problem 12.1. Lawyer is representing a client in a divorce. The client calls the lawyer several times a day wanting to discuss his case. These conversations have lasted as long as an hour. The lawyer eventually stopped returning the client's calls unless she has some specific information for the client. Is the lawyer violating Rule 1.4 by not returning all of the client's phone calls? What would you recommend that the lawyer do to address this problem?

* * *

2. ALLOCATION OF DECISION-MAKING AUTHORITY

**Please read ABA Model Rules of Professional Conduct,
Rule 1.2(a) and Comments [1]–[4] & [13];
and Rule 1.4(a)(2).**

OLFE V. GORDON

93 Wis.2d 173, 286 N.W.2d 573 (1980)

CALLOW, JUSTICE.

Early in 1971 Olfe, a widow about sixty-two years of age, was approached by Elmer J. Demman (Demman) who proposed buying Olfe's three-family house and the land upon which it was situated for the purpose of constructing an office building. A verbal agreement was reached between Olfe and Demman in which Demman was to purchase the property for $87,000. Olfe, after meeting with Demman and his attorney, decided she needed an attorney. Olfe consulted Gordon, telling him that she wanted a first mortgage. Olfe testified that when she left the office Gordon "was going to go ahead with getting the documents ready to sign for a first mortgage." On two subsequent occasions, Olfe testified she had contact with Gordon during which she was told that work was proceeding on obtaining a first mortgage for her.

On September 15, 1971, Olfe, Gordon, Demman, and Attorney C. J. Schloemer met with Demman's attorney at his office. Gordon told Olfe he brought Schloemer, his law partner, to the meeting because Schloemer "was well versed" in real estate matters. The first offer Demman's attorney presented to Schloemer was unacceptable, and a second offer to purchase was prepared and presented to Schloemer who reviewed the document and handed it to Gordon. Gordon looked at the document and asked Olfe to sign it. Prior to signing the offer to purchase, Olfe asked: " 'This isn't a second mortgage, is it?' " Gordon gave no answer and Schloemer said: "It is second only to cost of construction." Olfe signed the offer to purchase. She testified she understood Schloemer's remark to mean "that a second mortgage was only on the new building that was going to go up and that the land and the home on it was still under first mortgage." Olfe testified she did not read the document because "I'm not very good at legal terms and that is the reason I hired an attorney to represent me to read it and to see that I was signing for a first mortgage."

Olfe received about $22,500 of the purchase price on November 4, 1971, the date of the closing. The balance of about $64,500 was to be paid in two equal installments during the two succeeding years. No subsequent payments were ever made to Olfe prior to a foreclosure proceeding which was commenced by Continental Savings and Loan, the holder of the first mortgage. It was at this time that Olfe discovered she had only a second mortgage on the entire property. A judgment of foreclosure was entered. Schloemer later negotiated on Olfe's behalf a sale of her second mortgage interest to Continental Savings and Loan for $37,500.

Olfe commenced this action against Gordon and his professional liability insurer to recover the difference between the unpaid principal balance on the mortgage note and the amount which she had received from Continental Savings and Loan. Her complaint alleged she hired Gordon to protect and represent her interest and that "she wanted a first mortgage on said premises if the said purchaser was unable to pay the entire sum of the sale price at the closing." . . .

Olfe's appeal presents two issues: (1) Is expert testimony required to establish the standard of care on the part of an attorney in a malpractice action; and if so, is such testimony required to establish negligence on the part of Gordon? (2) Does the record contain sufficient credible evidence, when taken in the light most favorable to Olfe, to warrant sending the case to the jury?

. . . .

. . . Olfe's first two allegations, that Gordon failed to provide in the offer to purchase that Olfe's security interest would be a first mortgage and that he failed to draft or cause to be drafted a mortgage that would be senior to any other Demman would obtain on the premises of sale, are contentions that Gordon is liable for damages caused by his negligent disregard of Olfe's instructions. The legal theory on which these allegations are premised is well established:

> "It has generally been recognized that an attorney may be liable for all losses caused by his failure to follow with reasonable

promptness and care the explicit instructions of his client. Moreover, an attorney's honest belief that the instructions were not in the best interests of his client provides no defense to a suit for malpractice."

The attorney-client relationship in such contexts is one of agent to principal, and as an agent the attorney "must act in conformity with his authority and instructions and is responsible to his principal if he violates this duty." While actions for disregard of instructions can be based upon fiduciary and contractual principles, the principal's cause of action for an agent's breach of duty may also lie in tort. "[I]f a paid agent does something wrongful, either knowing it to be wrong, or acting negligently, the principal may have either an action of tort or an action of contract." . . . Expert testimony is not required to show that the agent (attorney) has violated his duty.

Olfe does not allege that she was harmed by a lack of legal expertise on the part of Gordon. She does not assert that Gordon failed to comply with statutes prescribing the necessary formalities concerning the documents' validity. Rather, she seeks to hold Gordon liable for his failure to effectuate her intent, even though the documents he prepared were not legally invalid. While preparation of an offer to purchase and preparation of a mortgage involve "special knowledge or skill or experience on subjects which are not within the realm of the ordinary experience of mankind, and which require special learning, study, or experience," proof of negligence in failing to follow specific instructions concerning the nature and purpose of the documents desired does not require expert testimony. This case is controlled by the law of agency, and the attorney-client relationship does not alter Gordon's alleged relationship to Olfe as an agent to his principal. As such, duties of care owed Olfe by Gordon are established not by the legal profession's standards but by the law of agency. A jury is competent to understand and apply the standards of care to which agents are held. This case falls within the exception to the rule that expert testimony is necessary to establish the negligence of attorneys. Here Olfe concedes that the documents drafted by Gordon were valid instruments but argues they failed to effectuate her intent and were inconsistent with her specific instructions. We conclude that expert testimony was not required to establish the applicable standard of care and Gordon's alleged departure from that standard in order to have a jury determine the merits of Olfe's allegations that Gordon was negligent in that he failed to properly draft documents consistent with Olfe's instructions.

. . . .

To establish a prima facie case subjecting an agent to liability in tort, the principal must show a duty of care owed by the agent to the principal, a breach of that duty, and injury to the principal as a proximate result of the breach. In contending that Olfe's proof does not establish a prima facie case, Gordon asserts that his alleged breach of the duty to obey the instructions of his principal was not the cause of Olfe's injury. Gordon relies on the following statement from Lien v. Pitts, 46 Wis.2d 35, 46, 174 N.W.2d 462, 468 (1970): " 'It is a rule of long-standing that the signing of an instrument raises a strong presumption that its contents are understood by the signer, and such presumption is not overcome by his statements that he did not understand the nature of the instrument which he signed.' "

. . . .

Olfe, however, seeks recovery from her agent, employed to protect her interests, and in so doing she does not rely solely on her statement that she did not understand the contents of the instruments. She testified she asked, " 'This isn't a second mortgage, is it?' " Gordon gave no answer, and Schloemer said, "It is second only to cost of construction." In our view, Gordon's silence and Schloemer's answer could reasonably be viewed by one or more jurors as misinforming Olfe or insufficiently informing her, as she alleges. These responses could be viewed as having the effect of reinforcing Olfe's perception of the standing of the mortgage.

Moreover, Gordon's argument overlooks Olfe's contention that the reason she employed Gordon was that she desired her security interest in the property sold to Demman to be legally protected. Had Olfe desired to make the sale in an informal manner and take as security Demman's assertion that he would pay her, there would have been no need to employ Gordon to prepare an offer to purchase and a mortgage. Olfe cannot be barred from recovery merely because she concluded Gordon had properly performed the services for which he was employed.

. . . .

* * *

Breach of duty? What was the failure of Gordon (and Schloemer) in this case: a failure to carry out Olfe's objectives, a failure to communicate, or both?

Allocation of decision-making authority. Section 21(1) of the Restatement (Third) of the Law Governing Lawyers provides that, subject to the limitations mentioned below, a client and lawyer "may agree which of them will make specified decisions." However, there are some decisions that are reserved for either the client or the lawyer to make. Model Rule 1.2(a) lists several decisions that are ultimately for the client to make. Section 22(2) of the Restatement contains a similar list but also includes a decision "whether to appeal in a civil proceeding or criminal prosecution." Similarly, § 23 of the Restatement lists two areas in which a lawyer retains the ultimate decision-making authority "that may not be overridden by an agreement with or an instruction from the client." These are, first, the lawyer's right "to refuse to perform, counsel, or assist future or ongoing acts in the representation that the lawyer reasonably believes to be unlawful," and second, the lawyer's right "to make decisions or take actions in the representation that the lawyer reasonably believes to be required by law or an order of a tribunal."

* * *

Problem 12.2. Attorney Art tells client Clarence that Art does not think they should file a motion for summary judgment in Clarence's case. Art explains it will be costly, they will have a very slim chance of winning, and they may even annoy the judge by filing the motion. Clarence responds, "I'll leave it up to you." Do you think Art had an obligation to discuss whether to file a motion for summary judgment with the client or would it have been appropriate for Art to make this decision without input from Clarence?

Just days before the summary judgment motion deadline, Clarence tells Art, "I've changed my mind. I think we need to file a motion for summary judgment." Art continues to believe it is a bad idea for the reasons he has explained to Clarence when they originally discussed the issue. What should Art do? *See* Restatement (Third) of the Law Governing Lawyers 21, cmt. d.

Means vs. objectives. Aside from the limitations on decision-making discussed above, the Restatement provides that "[a] client may give instructions to a lawyer during the representation ... just as any other principal may instruct an agent." *Id.* § 21 cmt. d. Model Rule 1.2(a) and Comment [2] to the rule are more equivocal in nature. When it comes to the means used to carry out a client's objectives, a lawyer must reasonably consult with the client about the means to be used to accomplish the client's objectives. Comment [2] suggests that clients "normally defer" to a lawyer's decisions as to "technical, legal, and tactical matters." What happens, however, if the client does not defer? Must the lawyer abide by the client's decision as to what is traditionally a matter of lawyer discretion?

* * *

JONES V. BARNES
463 U.S. 745 (1983)

CHIEF JUSTICE BURGER delivered the opinion of the Court.

We granted certiorari to consider whether defense counsel assigned to prosecute an appeal from a criminal conviction has a constitutional duty to raise every nonfrivolous issue requested by the defendant.

In 1976, Richard Butts was robbed at knifepoint by four men in the lobby of an apartment building; he was badly beaten and his watch and money were taken. Butts informed a Housing Authority Detective that he recognized one of his assailants as a person known to him as "Froggy," and gave a physical description of the person to the detective. The following day the detective arrested respondent David Barnes, who is known as "Froggy."

[Respondent was convicted of first and second degree robbery and second degree assault.]

[Attorney Michael Melinger was appointed by the Appellate Division of the Supreme Court of New York, Second Department to represent respondent on appeal.] Respondent sent Melinger a letter listing several claims that he felt should be raised. Included were claims that Butts' identification testimony should have been suppressed, that the trial judge improperly excluded psychiatric evidence, and that respondent's trial counsel was ineffective. Respondent also enclosed a copy of a *pro se* brief he had written.

In a return letter, Melinger accepted some but rejected most of the suggested claims, stating that they would not aid respondent in obtaining a new trial and that they could not be raised on appeal because they were not based on evidence in the record. Melinger then listed seven potential claims of error that he was considering including in his brief, and invited respondent's "reflections and suggestions" with regard to those seven issues. The record does not reveal any response to this letter.

Melinger's brief to the Appellate Division concentrated on three of the seven points he had raised in his letter to respondent: improper exclusion of psychiatric evidence, failure to suppress Butts' identification testimony, and improper cross-examination of respondent by the trial judge. In addition, Melinger submitted respondent's own *pro se* brief. Thereafter, respondent filed two more *pro se* briefs, raising three more of the seven issues Melinger had identified.

At oral argument, Melinger argued the three points presented in his own brief, but not the arguments raised in the *pro se* briefs. On May 22, 1978, the Appellate Division affirmed by summary order. The New York Court of Appeals denied leave to appeal.

[In an omitted portion of the opinion the Court describes a series of unsuccessful *pro se* attempts by Butts to have his conviction overturned on the ground of ineffective assistance of counsel.]

Respondent then returned to United States District Court for the second time, with a petition for habeas corpus based on the claim of ineffective assistance by appellate counsel. The District Court ... dismissed the petition, holding that the record gave no support to the claim of ineffective assistance of appellate counsel on "any ... standard which could reasonably be applied." The District Court concluded: "It is not required that an attorney argue every conceivable issue on appeal, especially when some may be without merit. Indeed, it is his professional duty to choose among potential issues, according to his judgment as to their merit and his tactical approach."

A divided panel of the Court of Appeals reversed, 665 F.2d 427 (CA2 1981). Laying down a new standard, the majority held that when "the appellant requests that [his attorney] raise additional colorable points [on appeal], counsel must argue the additional points to the full extent of his professional ability." *Id.*, at 433. In the view of the majority, this conclusion followed from Anders v. California, 386 U.S. 738, 87 S. Ct. 1396, 18 L. Ed. 2d 493 (1967). In *Anders*, this Court held that an appointed attorney must advocate his client's cause vigorously and may not withdraw from a nonfrivolous appeal. The Court of Appeals majority held that, since *Anders* bars counsel from abandoning a nonfrivolous appeal, it also bars counsel from abandoning a nonfrivolous issue on appeal. ...

The court concluded that Melinger had not met the above standard in that he had failed to press at least two nonfrivolous claims: the trial judge's failure to instruct on accessory liability and ineffective assistance of trial counsel. The fact that these issues had been raised in respondent's own *pro se* briefs did not cure the error, since "[a] pro se brief is no substitute for the advocacy of experienced counsel." *Ibid.* The court reversed and remanded, with instructions to grant the writ of habeas corpus unless the State assigned new counsel and granted a new appeal.

We granted certiorari, and we reverse.

II

In announcing a new *per se* rule that appellate counsel must raise every nonfrivolous issue requested by the client, the Court of Appeals relied primarily upon *Anders v. California, supra*. There is, of course, no constitutional right to an appeal, but in Griffin v. Illinois, 351 U.S. 12, 18, 76 S. Ct. 585, 590, 100 L. Ed. 891 (1955), and Douglas v. California, 372 U.S. 353, 83 S. Ct. 814, 9 L. Ed. 2d 811 (1963), the Court held that if an appeal is open to those who can pay for it, an appeal must be provided for an indigent. It is also recognized that the accused has the ultimate authority to make certain fundamental decisions regarding the case, as to whether to plead guilty, waive a jury, testify in his or her own behalf, or take an appeal, *see* Wainwright v. Sykes, 433 U.S. 72, 93 n. 1, 97 S. Ct. 2497, 2509 n. 1, 53 L. Ed. 2d 594 (1977) (BURGER, C.J., concurring); ABA Standards for Criminal Justice 4–5.2, 21–2.2 (2d ed. 1980). In addition, we have held that, with some limitations, a defendant may elect to act as his or her own advocate, Faretta v. California, 422 U.S. 806, 95 S. Ct. 2525, 45 L. Ed. 2d 562 (1975). Neither *Anders* nor any other decision of this Court suggests, however, that the indigent defendant has a constitutional right to compel appointed counsel to press nonfrivolous points requested by the client, if counsel, as a matter of professional judgment, decides not to present those points.

This Court, in holding that a State must provide counsel for an indigent appellant on his first appeal as of right, recognized the superior ability of trained counsel in the "examination into the record, research of the law, and marshalling of arguments on [the appellant's] behalf," Douglas v. California, 372 U.S., at 358, 83 S. Ct., at 817. Yet by promulgating a *per se* rule that the client, not the professional advocate, must be allowed to decide what issues are to be pressed, the Court of Appeals seriously undermines the ability of counsel to present the client's case in accord with counsel's professional evaluation.

Experienced advocates since time beyond memory have emphasized the importance of winnowing out weaker arguments on appeal and focusing on one central issue if possible, or at most on a few key issues. Justice Jackson, after observing appellate advocates for many years, stated:

> "One of the first tests of a discriminating advocate is to select the question, or questions, that he will present orally. Legal contentions, like the currency, depreciate through over-issue. The mind of an appellate judge is habitually receptive to the suggestion that a lower court committed an error. But receptiveness declines as the number of assigned errors increases. Multiplicity hints at lack of confidence in any one.... [E]xperience on the bench convinces me that multiplying assignments of error will dilute and weaken a good case and will not save a bad one." Jackson, *Advocacy Before the Supreme Court*, 25 Temple L.Q. 115, 119 (1951).

Justice Jackson's observation echoes the advice of countless advocates before him and since. An authoritative work on appellate practice observes:

> "Most cases present only one, two, or three significant questions.... Usually, ... if you cannot win on a few major points, the others are not likely to help, and to attempt to deal

with a great many in the limited number of pages allowed for briefs will mean that none may receive adequate attention. The effect of adding weak arguments will be to dilute the force of the stronger ones." R. Stern, *Appellate Practice in the United States* 266 (1981).

There can hardly be any question about the importance of having the appellate advocate examine the record with a view to selecting the most promising issues for review. This has assumed a greater importance in an era when oral argument is strictly limited in most courts—often to as little as 15 minutes—and when page limits on briefs are widely imposed. *See, e.g.,* Fed. Rules App. Proc. 28(g); McKinney's 1982 New York Rules of Court §§ 670.17(g)(2), 670.22. Even in a court that imposes no time or page limits, however, the new *per se* rule laid down by the Court of Appeals is contrary to all experience and logic. A brief that raises every colorable issue runs the risk of burying good arguments—those that, in the words of the great advocate John W. Davis, "go for the jugular," Davis, *The Argument of an Appeal*, 26 A.B.A.J. 895, 897 (1940)—in a verbal mound made up of strong and weak contentions. *See generally, e.g.,* Godbold, *Twenty Pages and Twenty Minutes—Effective Advocacy on Appeal*, 30 SW.L.J. 801 (1976).[6]

This Court's decision in *Anders*, far from giving support to the new *per se* rule announced by the Court of Appeals, is to the contrary. *Anders* recognized that the role of the advocate "requires that he support his client's appeal to the best of his ability." 386 U.S., at 744, 87 S. Ct., at 1400. Here the appointed counsel did just that. For judges to second-guess reasonable professional judgments and impose on appointed counsel a duty to raise every "colorable" claim suggested by a client would disserve the very goal of vigorous and effective advocacy that underlies *Anders*. Nothing in the Constitution or our interpretation of that document requires such a standard. The judgment of the Court of Appeals is accordingly

---

[6]   The ABA Model Rules of Professional Conduct provide: "A lawyer shall abide by a client's decisions concerning the objectives of representation . . . and shall consult with the client as to the means by which they are to be pursued. . . . In a criminal case, the lawyer shall abide by the client's decision, . . . as to a plea to be entered, whether to waive jury trial and whether the client will testify." Model Rules of Professional Conduct, Proposed Rule 1.2(a) (Final Draft 1982). With the exception of these specified fundamental decisions, an attorney's duty is to take professional responsibility for the conduct of the case, after consulting with his client. Respondent points to the ABA Standards for Criminal Appeals, which appear to indicate that counsel should accede to a client's insistence on pressing a particular contention on appeal, *see* ABA Standards for Criminal Justice 21–3.2, at 21–42 (2d ed. 1980). The ABA Defense Function Standards provide, however, that, with the exceptions specified above, strategic and tactical decisions are the exclusive province of the defense counsel, after consultation with the client. *See* ABA Standards for Criminal Justice 4–5.2 (2d ed. 1980). *See also* ABA Project on Standards for Criminal Justice, The Prosecution Function and The Defense Function § 5.2 (Tent. Draft 1970). In any event, the fact that the ABA may have chosen to recognize a given practice as desirable or appropriate does not mean that that practice is required by the Constitution.

Reversed.

* * *

Justice Brennan's dissent. In a dissenting opinion, Justice Brennan argued that the right to assistance of counsel carries with it a right on the part of a defendant to insist upon the assertion of any nonfrivolous argument the defendant wishes to assert. Brennan believed that the ruling "denigrates the values of individual autonomy and dignity central to many constitutional rights, especially those Fifth and Sixth Amendment rights that come into play in the criminal process." For example, a criminal defendant might wish to plead innocence even though other strategies are more likely to succeed. He might wish to advance an argument for political reasons or to protect third parties. These decisions might be unwise and a competent lawyer would try to talk the defendant out of advancing them. But given the stakes involved, Brennan argued, the defendant has the constitutional right to advance them, provided they are not frivolous. Is Brennan right?

* * *

B. A LAWYER'S POWER TO OBLIGATE THE CLIENT IN DEALINGS WITH OTHERS

When will a client be bound by the actions of a lawyer, such as agreeing to a settlement or a continuance of a lawsuit, receiving notice from a third party, or making an admission on behalf of the client? Does the client have a cause of action against the lawyer if the lawyer took action not authorized by the client? The law of agency answers these questions.

A client will be bound by a lawyer's actions if the lawyer has either actual authority or apparent authority to bind the client. Both are discussed below. These concepts are also important for determining a lawyer's liability to a client. If the lawyer took action on behalf of the client even though the lawyer did not have the express or implied authority to do so, then the lawyer will face liability to the client for exceeding actual authority.

Actual authority. Section 26 of the Restatement (Third) of the Law Governing Lawyers explains that a lawyer has *actual authority* on behalf of a client in proceedings before a tribunal or in dealings with third parties when the client has expressly or impliedly authorized the act or ratifies the act after learning what the lawyer has done, or if the lawyer has irrevocable authority conferred by law to do or refrain from doing the act in question. Model Rule 1.2 also addresses issues of actual authority. The rule directs lawyers to abide by the client's decisions about the objectives of the representation. Stated another way, the lawyer has express authority to achieve the client's stated objectives, such as "I want a first mortgage" or "I want you to help me get a divorce." Model Rule 1.2 also explains a lawyer's implied authority: "A lawyer may take such actions on behalf of the client as is impliedly authorized to carry out the representation."

If the lawyer has actual authority to act on behalf of the client, the lawyer has both the power and the right to obligate the client. The client is obligated by the lawyer's action, and assuming the lawyer was not negligent, the client has no claim against the lawyer for adverse consequences resulting from the lawyer's actions.

Actual authority can be revoked by the client. Section 31(2) of the Restatement (Third) of the Law Governing Lawyers identifies five events that will terminate, or revoke, the lawyer's actual authority to act on behalf of the client. They are (1) discharge of the lawyer by the client, (2) withdrawal of the lawyer from the representation, (3) death of the client or in the case of a corporation or similar organization, loss of its legal capacity to function as such, (4) death, incapacity, disbarment, or suspension of the lawyer, or a court order requiring the lawyer to terminate the client's representation, or (5) completion of the representation. This list should also include a communication from the client to the lawyer revoking the client's prior grant of authority to the lawyer. A client can terminate a lawyer's actual authority to take action on behalf of the client without discharging the lawyer. All it takes is a message delivered to the lawyer.

Apparent authority. Even in the absence of actual authority, a lawyer may have *apparent authority.* Section 27 of the Restatement (Third) of the Law Governing Lawyers specifies that a lawyer's act is considered to be that of the client "if the tribunal or third person reasonably assumes that the lawyer is authorized to do the act on the basis of the client's (and not the lawyer's) manifestations of such authorization." A lawyer's apparent authority ends only when the third party or court knows or has reason to know that the lawyer no longer has actual authority. *See* Restatement (Third) of the Law Governing Lawyers § 31(3). If the lawyer acts within the scope of the apparent but not actual authority, the client will be obligated but probably will not be happy. The client will be able to hold the lawyer liable for the adverse consequences because the lawyer exceeded actual authority.

* * *

Problem 12.3. At a pretrial conference in a medical malpractice case, lawyer Daryl for the defendant Ricardo General Hospital agrees with opposing counsel that neither party will call more than one expert witness at the trial. Opposing counsel is not aware that Daryl's corporate client (which has many similar cases) instructs its lawyers to present expert testimony from at least two witnesses in every medical malpractice case involving more than a certain amount in claimed damages. Judge knows of the client's practice but does not inform opposing counsel. Will the client be bound by the agreement? *See* Restatement (Third) of the Law Governing Lawyers § 27 cmt. c, ill. 2.

Problem 12.4. Lawyer Jordan represents Sadee in a civil action in which the court orders counsel either to appear at a pretrial conference with authority to settle the case or to arrange for the presence of a person so authorized. Sadee has not been informed of the order and has not authorized Jordan to approve a settlement. Jordan, without disclosing that lack of authority, attends the conference and agrees to a settlement he thinks will be acceptable to Sadee. What are the possible adverse consequences that may flow from this conduct? *See id.* cmt. d, ill. 3.

* * *

C. IDENTIFYING THE DULY AUTHORIZED CONSTITUENTS OF YOUR ORGANIZATIONAL CLIENTS

ABA Model Rule 1.13 addresses the representation of organizational clients. Rule 1.13(a) provides that "a lawyer employed or retained by an organization represents the organization acting through its duly authorized constituents." Comment [1] explains that an organizational client is a legal entity, but that it can only act through its officers, directors, employees, shareholders, and other constituents. The entity is your client. Absent a separate agreement, the constituents are not clients. Comment [1] further explains that Rule 1.13 is applicable to unincorporated associations, such as partnerships, and that the catchall reference to "other constituents" was meant to embrace persons whose status in an unincorporated organization was equivalent to that of an officer, the directors, employees, or shareholder of a corporation.

What is conspicuously absent from the comment is any discussion of who among the various constituents of an organizational client is a "duly authorized" constituent through whom the organization can act. This is an important issue for lawyers who represent organizations. First, only a duly empowered or authorized constituent of the organization can enter into a legally binding client-lawyer relationship. Second, only a duly authorized constituent can make the decisions concerning the organization's representation that must or may be made by the client. Third, the lawyer must direct such communication concerning the organization's representation as is required by Rule 1.4 to a duly authorized constituent and must not reveal information relating to the organization's representation to a person who is not a duly authorized constituent. Finally, as will be explored in greater depth in a later chapter, there are situations in which a lawyer for an organization will be required by Rule 1.13 to consult with the constituent(s) who possess "the highest authority" to act on behalf of the organization.

* * *

D. REPRESENTING CLIENTS WITH DISABILITIES OR DIMINISHED CAPACITY

* * *

1. IN GENERAL

Please read ABA Model Rules of Professional Conduct, Rule 1.14 and Comments.

* * *

Problem 12.5. Melissa is eighteen years old. She has Down syndrome. When she was a child, her parents divorced, and her mother, Helen, was granted custody. As Melissa approached age eighteen, she expressed a desire to live with her father. Because Helen wanted Melissa to continue to live with her, she instituted an action seeking guardianship of Melissa once she became an adult. Her father is contesting Helen's action and wants to be appointed guardian. Pursuant to a New Dakota court rule, the trial court appointed Paul to act as Melissa's attorney in the matter. Paul spoke with several experts who had dealt with Melissa, and they offered conflicting opinions as to whether Melissa was competent to make a decision as to who she wanted to live with. Melissa has made it clear to Paul that she wishes to live with her father, but Paul has serious doubts as to whether Melissa fully understands what is at stake and whether living with her father is truly in Melissa's best interests. He is conflicted about what he should do at the scheduled hearing, so he comes to you for advice as to his ethical obligations. What advice do you have for him?

* * *

As noted above, there is much room for disagreement about the extent of the capacity of some clients to make adequately considered decisions in connection with the client's representation and how that affects the responsibilities of the lawyer to communicate with the client and to involve the client in decisions affecting the client's interest. The legal profession, however, has also recognized that some clients' capacity to make adequately considered decisions concerning their representation can be diminished due to legal incompetency, mental problems, or other reasons. How does such impairment affect the lawyer's responsibilities concerning communication with the client and the respective roles of lawyer, client, and others in decision-making concerning the impaired client's representation?

* * *

The uncertain contours of Model Rule 1.14. Numerous commentators have expressed concern over the failure of Model Rule 1.14 to create clear standards for attorneys to follow. For example, Rule 1.14(a) requires that the "lawyer shall, as far as reasonably possible, maintain a normal client-lawyer relationship with the client" even when the client has diminished capacity "to make adequately considered decisions in connection with a representation." What specifically should the lawyer do to comply with this rule? Comment [2] counsels that the lawyer should "treat the client with attention and respect" and states that "[e]ven if the person has a legal representative, the lawyer should as far as possible accord the represented person the status of client, particularly in maintaining communication." However, Comment [4] suggests that "[i]f a legal representative has already been appointed for the client, the lawyer should ordinarily look to the representative for decisions on behalf of the client." Are these two comments reconcilable? Section 24(2) of the Restatement fleshes out the lawyer's responsibility toward a client with diminished capacity by stating, "A lawyer . . . must . . . pursue the lawyer's reasonable view of the client's objectives or interests as the client would define them if able to make adequately considered decisions on the matter, even if the client . . . gives contrary instructions." Is this directive more satisfactory than the requirements of Model Rule 1.14? If a lawyer acted contrary to her client's instructions on the ground that the client had diminished capacity, would the client have a cause of action for legal malpractice, or a basis for a disciplinary complaint, against the lawyer?

Determining "diminished capacity." How can a lawyer determine that a client has diminished capacity? Comment [6] advises that "[i]n appropriate circumstances, the lawyer may seek guidance from an appropriate diagnostician." But Rule 1.14(c) cautions that "[i]nformation relating to the representation of a client with diminished capacity is protected by Rule 1.6." How then would the lawyer seek guidance from an appropriate diagnostician? And what would constitute "appropriate circumstances" for seeking such guidance? Comment [6] lists a number of factors the lawyer may consider in deciding to seek such guidance. Do these factors provide a sufficient foundation upon which to make a decision to seek diagnostic guidance?

* * *

Please read Restatement (Third) of the Law Governing Lawyers § 24 and Comments.

* * *

What do you think? Section 24(3) spells out two circumstances in which the lawyer is not required to respect the decisions of the client's legal representative. Should the Model Rules be amended to add such a provision?

* * *

Guardian ad litem vs. Appointed counsel. In some instances, a court will appoint a guardian ad litem (GAL) for a child or other person lacking the capacity to make decisions. In others, the child or other person may be represented by counsel, appointed or otherwise. One court has explained the difference between the two roles:

> A court-appointed counsel's services are to the child. Counsel acts as an independent legal advocate for the best interests of the child and takes an active part in the hearing, ranging from subpoenaing and cross-examining witnesses to appealing the decision, if warranted. If the purpose of the appointment is for legal advocacy, then counsel would be appointed. A court-appointed guardian ad litem's services are to the court on behalf of the child. The GAL acts as an independent fact finder, investigator and evaluator as to what furthers the best interests of the child. The GAL submits a written report to the court and is available to testify. If the purpose of the appointment is for independent investigation and fact finding, then a GAL would be appointed. The GAL can be an attorney, a social worker, a mental health professional or other appropriate person. These rules are not intended to expand the circumstances when such appointments are to be made; neither are these appointments to be made routinely.

In the Matter of M.R., 638 A.2d 1274 (N.J. 1994).

* * *

OREGON STATE BAR ASSOCIATON BOARD OF GOVERENORS,
COMPETENCE AND DILIGENCE:
REQUESTING A GUARDIAN AD LITEM IN A
JUVENILE DEPENDENCY CASE
FORMAL OPINION NUMBER 2005-159

Facts:

The Juvenile Court appoints guardians ad litem (GALs), who are often lawyers, for mentally ill parents in some dependency cases and termination-of-parental-rights cases.

Questions:

1.   May a lawyer for a parent ethically request a GAL for the client?

2.   When a lawyer acts as a GAL, does the lawyer have the same ethical duties, obligations, and powers as in a regular lawyer-client relationship?

3.   After the appointment of the GAL for the mentally ill parent, is the lawyer obligated to take direction from the GAL?

. . . .

Discussion:

It is generally accepted that it is error for a court to proceed without appointment of a GAL for a party when facts strongly suggest a lack of mental competency. United States v. 30.64 Acres, 795 F2d 796, 806 (9th Cir 1986). Similarly, it is a violation of due process to fail to appoint a GAL for a mentally incompetent parent in a termination-of parental-rights proceeding. State ex rel. Juv. Dept. v. Evjen, 107 Or App 659, 813 P2d 1092 (1991).

1.   Seeking Appointment of a GAL.

Although a marginally competent client can be difficult to represent, a lawyer must maintain as regular a lawyer-client relationship as possible and adjust representation to accommodate a client's limited capacity before resorting to a request for a GAL. This is reflected, *inter alia*, in Oregon RPC 1.14 . . . . Consequently, and as a general proposition, lawyers for parents should not invade a typical client's rights beyond the extent to which it reasonably appears necessary for the lawyer to do so. In other words, lawyers should request GALs for their clients only when a client consistently demonstrates a lack of capacity to act in his or her own interests and it is unlikely that the client will be able to attain the requisite mental capacity to assist in the proceedings in a reasonable time.[1]

---

[1]   It has been suggested that the parent's lawyer should seek a GAL only if "serious harm is imminent, intervention is necessary, no other ameliorative development is foreseeable, and non-lawyers would be justified in seeking guardianship." Paul R. Tremblay, *On Persuasion and*

. . . .

In determining whether the client can adequately act in his or her own interests, the lawyer needs to examine whether the client can give direction on the decisions that the lawyer must ethically defer to the client. Short of a client's being totally noncommunicative or unavailable due to his or her condition, a lawyer can most often explain the decisions that the client faces in simple terms and elicit a sufficient response to allow the lawyer to proceed with the representation. Standards for representation in juvenile dependency cases and termination-of-parental-rights cases recognize that the lawyer should always seek the lawful objectives of the client and should not substitute the lawyer's judgment for the client's in decisions that are the responsibility of the client. However, the lawyer may make other necessary decisions consistent with the client's direction on these essential issues.

2.   Distinguishing the Role of GAL and Lawyer.

There is no requirement that a GAL be a lawyer, and non-lawyers frequently serve as GALs. Thus, when a lawyer acts as a GAL, the lawyer is performing a non-lawyer function and does not have the same ethical duties, obligations, and powers in the guardian-ward relationship as in a lawyer-client relationship, although both a lawyer and a GAL have a fiduciary relationship with the client or ward.

Oregon courts have indicated that a GAL has authority to settle claims on behalf of an incapacitated person and, with prior court approval, a GAL may confess judgment on behalf of the incapacitated person. The GAL's authority essentially substitutes for the incapacitated person's authority to make these decisions in the proceeding. "In the law of adult incompetents, the role of the GAL has sometimes been held to incorporate the concept of substituted judgment, whereby the GAL attempts to make decisions for the ward based on what the GAL thinks the particular ward would have wanted had the ward not been incompetent." Ann M. Haralambie, The Child's Lawyer: A Guide to Representing Children in Custody, Adoption and Protection Cases (ABA 1993).

3.   Taking Direction from Client's GAL.

Because the rationale for the appointment of a GAL is to have someone who can make decisions for the incompetent client, after the appointment of the GAL the lawyer for the parent generally must take direction from the GAL and can make stipulations and agreements and do other acts at the GAL's direction that the parent could do if the parent were competent. It is improper for the parent's lawyer to act contrary to

Paternalism: Lawyer Decisionmaking and the Questionably Competent Client, 1997 UTAH L REV 515, 566.

the direction of a GAL who is adequately asserting the client's interests. *See, e.g.,* Brode v. Brode, 298 S.E.2d 443 (SC 1982) (improper and beyond scope of lawyer's authority for lawyer to appeal from decision authorizing sterilization of profoundly retarded handicapped minor, when GAL did not choose to appeal); Developmental Disabilities Advocacy Ctr. Inc. v. Melton, 521 F. Supp 365 (DNH 1981), vacated and remanded on other grounds, 689 F.2d 281 (1st Cir 1982) (lawyers in agency established by statute to advocate for rights of disabled persons may not act independently of incompetent client's GAL).

When a GAL is appointed for an incompetent client, "appointment of a parent or other adult does not absolve the lawyer of the duty to make an independent determination of the client's interests." Martha Matthews, *Ten Thousand Tiny Clients: The Ethical Duty of Representation in Children's Class Action Cases,* 64 FORDHAM L REV 1435, 1446 (1996). Parents' lawyers should serve as a monitor to assure that the GAL adequately asserts the incapacitated client's interests. Furthermore, the lawyer has a responsibility to inquire periodically whether the client's competence has changed and, if appropriate, request removal of the GAL. Such inquiries should occur at every critical stage in the proceeding.

* * *

2.   COMMUNICATION

COMMITTEE ON PROFESSIONAL ETHICS OF THE
NEW YORK CITY BAR ASSOCIATION
Formal Opinion Number 1995–12 (Excerpt)

. . . .

QUESTION

Must a lawyer, who cannot communicate directly with a client in a mutually understood language, consider the need for the services of an interpreter and take steps to secure the services of a qualified interpreter to insure competent and zealous representation, to preserve client confidences, and to avoid unlawful discrimination?

OPINION

Lawyers are increasingly being called upon to advise and represent persons with whom they cannot communicate directly because the lawyer and the client do not share a common language. Often, the only effective method of communication is through a language (foreign or sign) interpreter.

. . . .

Since communication with a non-English-speaking client or a deaf client may only be effective or even possible if conducted with an interpreter, it is questionable whether a lawyer can competently represent his or her client without considering the need for, and, in some instances, securing the services of, an interpreter.

It is axiomatic that adequate communication between lawyer and client, is necessary to render competent legal services. *Cf.* ABA Model Rules of Professional Conduct, Rule 1.4. In addition to being the means by which a client is provided with the advice and information needed to make informed decisions, *see* EC 7–8, adequate communication is the means by which the lawyer obtains the information necessary to prepare for the handling of the client's legal matter.

. . . .

. . . When the need for an interpreter is apparent or it is reasonable to conclude that an interpreter is required for effective communication, failure to take steps with the client to secure an interpreter may be a breach of the duty to represent the client competently.

Moreover, the lawyer may not passively leave the decision as to the need for or the securing of an interpreter entirely to the client's discretion. Once it is evident that, without an interpreter, effective lawyer-client communications are questionable or not possible, failure of a lawyer to take steps to help the client understand the significance of the interpreter for adequate communication and to take, when necessary, steps to secure interpreter services may violate the lawyer's duty to represent the client zealously.

. . . .

In sum, when a language barrier impedes the ability for the lawyer and the client to communicate effectively, the lawyer must be sensitive to the needs for interpreter services and take steps to secure interpreter services, when needed, to avoid unlawful discrimination or prejudice.

CONCLUSION

A lawyer who represents a client with whom direct communications cannot be maintained in a mutually understood language, must evaluate the need for qualified interpreter service and take steps to secure the services of an interpreter, when needed for effective lawyer-client communications, to provide competent and zealous representation, preserve client confidences and avoid unlawful discrimination or prejudice in the practice of law.

* * *

Legal obligations. Law offices are covered as places of public accommodation under Title III of the Americans with Disabilities Act

(ADA). The ADA requires such entities "to take such steps as may be necessary to ensure that no individual with a disability is ... denied services ... because of the absence of auxiliary aids and services," such as qualified interpreters. 42 U.S.C. § 12182(b)(2)(A)(ii).

* * *

Profile of attorney professionalism.

Georgia, a 94-year-old nursing home resident, is a widow with two senior-citizen-aged children. She worked for years as a hotel maid, laboring hard for the monthly social security benefits that are her only income. She owns no home, no pension, no bank accounts. Suffering from Alzheimers and a host of physical problems, she spends her days sitting in a wheelchair looking at the television.

Georgia was born in the same year that the income tax, stainless steel and assembly line were introduced in America. No longer able to feed or care for herself, she needed someone to make decisions for her and to ensure that she has the best quality of life possible, so her son Alfred filed a petition to be appointed guardian.

But Probate Judge Mary Ellen Coghlan needed to know if Alfred's appointment would be in his mother's best interests. Could he take care of her? Would he? Because neither Georgia nor her family could afford to pay an attorney, Judge Coghlan appointed Chicago Volunteer Legal Services as guardian ad litem (GAL). Volunteer Eve Epstein agreed to take the case.

. . . .

Eve traveled to Georgia's south side nursing home and visited with her in her room. After noting that Georgia was neat and clean and that her room looked tidy, she tried to engage her in conversation, without much luck. Eve spoke with the nursing home staff who confirmed that Alfred was a frequent and kind visitor. Eve also spoke with Georgia's daughter who resides in an assisted living program due to her own medical problems. She wanted her brother to be guardian of their mother. After a thorough investigation, Eve recommended that Alfred be appointed guardian and Judge Coghlan made the appointment.

A few days later, Alfred sent Eve a letter. "Miss Epstein, I would like to thank you for all the help I received from you. I know I could never pay you for your time, so I just wanted to thank you with all my heart. Maybe you could get a cup of coffee to go with your lunch." He'd enclosed a $10 bill with the letter.

. . . .

Kim Halvorsen, an associate at Clifford Law Offices, is GAL for 55-year old Michael, who has dementia and lives in a nursing home. His wife and his mother both wanted to be his guardian and both wanted the other woman out of his life. When the wife was given limited guardianship, the mother was given visitation rights. Unfortunately, the women frequently tried to visit at the same time and got into fights. When one altercation turned physical and the police had to escort them from the home, staff threatened to ban them both. Kim went to court and got a specific visitation schedule to keep the two women apart. They still fight and both call Kim regularly complaining about the other. Kim has her work cut out for her as she tries to do what is best for Michael.

Kim got the case because Clifford Law Offices adopted the Adult GAL Program as its firm-wide pro bono program, and committed to handle two cases per attorney per year. Managing partner, Thomas K. Prindable, who took the firm's first case himself, admires the work of the Probate Court and the work that GALs perform. "When you go in these Probate courtrooms it makes your heart just open up. There are wonderful people working very hard to ensure that the weakest members of our society are protected. It's an honor to be part of that."

Margaret C. Benson, *Guardian Ad Litem: The Grinch Need Not Apply*, CBA RECORD, Oct. 2008, at 38–40.

SECTION 3

COMPETENCE AND DILIGENCE

■ ■ ■

In Torts you learned the duty of care each of us owes to all with whom we come into contact. In this section, we focus on the duty of care owed by a particular subset of all persons—lawyers—to a particular subset of persons—clients—by virtue of their agreement to establish an attorney-client relationship. This duty is typically discussed in terms of the lawyer's duty to competently and diligently represent the client. Chapter 13 addresses this duty as well as the extent to which a lawyer's failure to perform duties to her client may subject the lawyer to discipline or civil liability.

CHAPTER 13

COMPETENT AND DILIGENT REPRESENTATION OF A CLIENT

■ ■ ■

Chapter hypothetical. Miranda is a solo practitioner who has been in practice for three years. As a solo practitioner, Miranda has a heavy caseload. Most of her work involves personal injury cases, but she recently agreed to take a criminal case involving Jill, an employee at a prison hospital accused of altering a public document. Prior to her representation of Jill, Miranda had never had a criminal case. Miranda's only prior knowledge of criminal law came from having taken Criminal Law in her first semester of law school. (She made a C+ in the class.)

Jill was accused of altering the medical records of a prisoner who had undergone medical treatment in an attempt to cover up medical malpractice. Eventually, Jill was placed on leave while the prison conducted an internal investigation. Prison officials requested that Jill participate in the investigation and informed her that none of her statements could be used against her in a subsequent criminal proceeding. They further advised that if she did not participate in the internal investigation, Jill could be disciplined. They told her they wished to interview her within twenty-four hours. Miranda researched the law and concluded that any statements Jill made as part of the investigation would not be deemed to be compelled by the state and would therefore not be protected under her Fifth Amendment privilege against self-incrimination. Therefore, she reasoned, the statements could then be used against Jill in any subsequent criminal proceedings. As a result, Miranda advised Jill not to participate in the internal investigation. Jill took Miranda's advice and was fired from her job. She was eventually reinstated but lost several months' pay in the meantime. The criminal charges were eventually dropped. She has now sued Miranda for legal malpractice.

At the time Miranda advised Jill, the well-established constitutional rule was that when a public employee is faced with the choice between forfeiting her job and incriminating herself, any subsequent statements made are compelled and, under the Fifth Amendment, cannot be used in a criminal proceeding. Garrity v. New Jersey, 385 U.S. 493 (1967). Miranda based her opinion on this decision but did not read any of the decisions from lower courts applying the *Garrity* rule to specific instances of allegedly coercive conduct. The lower court decisions from within the controlling federal circuit hold that where an employer's statement is ambiguous as to whether an employee will be fired for refusing to incriminate herself, the test is whether a reasonable employee would believe that the statements constituted a threat of termination. If so, any statements would be treated as being compelled.

* * *

Lawyers cannot guarantee that the work they will perform on behalf of clients will produce the outcome the client wants. All the lawyer can do is work competently with the law and facts to make it as likely as reasonably possible that the client's objectives for the representation will be accomplished. These materials introduce you to some of the legal and professional responsibility issues which arise when clients are dissatisfied with their lawyer's performance, including the possibility of a legal malpractice action.

* * *

A. DISCIPLINARY RULES

1. COMPETENCE

Please read ABA Model Rules of Professional Conduct, Rule 1.1 and Comments.

* * *

Model Rule 1.1 lists four components of competence. The first two—legal knowledge and skill—can be acquired through legal education and experience. Comment [1] to Rule 1.1 states that representation in some matters may require only the "proficiency . . . of a general practitioner," while in others, "[e]xpertise in a particular field of law may be required." How will you know the required level of expertise that is necessary in a given case? Does criminal defense require expertise? Criminal defense in a capital case? Comment [2] notes that competence in a given matter may be achieved either through "necessary study" or through "association of a lawyer of established competence." Do these two means of acquiring competence correspond to the situations in which generalized knowledge vs. specialized knowledge is required? Note also that Rule 1.1 imposes an ongoing duty upon all lawyers to keep up to date with changes in the law and its practice "including the benefits and risks associated with relevant technology." *Id.* Comment [8].

The third and fourth components of competence—thoroughness and preparation—would seem to depend on simple hard work at least as much as study and experience. Note that Comment [5] explains that thoroughness and preparation includes adequate investigation into both the factual and legal elements of a problem. *See, e.g.*, Goebel v. Lauderdale, 214 Cal. App.3d 1502 (1989) (involving lawyers who provided advice to a client that would have violated a state penal code); Lawrence Duncan MacLachlan, *Gandy Dancers on the Web: How the Internet Has Raised the Bar on Lawyers' Professional Responsibility to Research and Know the Law*, 13 GEO. J. LEGAL ETHICS 607 (2000).

* * *

Problem 13.1. Refer back to the Chapter Hypothetical. Putting aside for now the question of whether Miranda competently represented Jill, was Miranda competent to take on the representation in the first place? *See* Model Rule 1.1., Comments [1]–[4].

* * *

2. DILIGENCE

Please read ABA Model Rules of Professional Conduct, Rule 1.3 and Comments.

Comment [1] to Model Rule 1.3 provides that a lawyer must act with "commitment and dedication to the interests of the client and with zeal in advocacy upon the client's behalf. However, the comment also warns that this duty "does not require the use of offensive tactics or preclude the treating of all persons involved in the legal process with courtesy and respect." Is the balance between "zeal" and "courtesy and respect" a difficult one to maintain? Comment [3] warns against procrastination, noting that the "client's interests can often be adversely affected by the passage of time" and that "delay can cause a client needless anxiety and undermine confidence in the lawyer's trustworthiness." The comment identifies as heavy caseloads as one possible cause of such delay.

* * *

B. CIVIL LIABILITY FOR MALPRACTICE

Please read Restatement (Third) of the Law Governing Lawyers §§ 48, 50 & 52–54.

* * *

A legal malpractice claim is a claim of professional negligence. As such, a plaintiff must establish all of the elements of the standard tort action for negligence: duty, breach, causation (both causation in fact and proximate cause), and damages. In terms of the duty requirement, a lawyer typically only owes a duty to a client. (The issue of when a client-attorney client relationship exists was covered in Chapter 9.) Possible exceptions to that general rule include where the client has invited a third party to rely upon the lawyer's services and where a third party is the intended beneficiary of the representation (such as in the case of a will). The issues of breach, causation, and damages pose their own set of problems. In addition, some special rules that apply only in the case of professional negligence (or at least in the case of a lawyer's negligence) have also developed.

Establishing the standard of care. Compare § 52(1) of the Restatement with Model Rules 1.1 and 1.3, both of which articulate standards of care. Which standard is clearer? Is it helpful that the Restatement standard is limited to the legal malpractice context?

Violation of disciplinary rules as evidence of malpractice. Paragraph [20] of the Scope preceding the Model Rules advises that the "[v]iolation of a Rule should not itself give rise to a cause of action against a lawyer," because, in part, the rules "are designed . . . to provide a structure for regulating conduct through disciplinary agencies." *See also* Restatement (Third) of the Law Governing Lawyers § 52(2)(a). The violation of a disciplinary rule is not negligence *per se*, as that term is used in tort law. Paragraph [20] also goes on to provide that violation of a rule should not "create any presumption in such a case that a legal duty has been breached." Why shouldn't it? If, for example, a lawyer has violated her duty of communication under Model Rule 1.4, why should that not be sufficient to at least establish a presumption that the lawyer breached her duty to the client for purposes of a tort action? What evidentiary role should the disciplinary rules play in a malpractice action?

* * *

1.   MALPRACTICE IN NON-LITIGATION SETTINGS

DAVIS V. DAMRELL
119 Cal.App.3d 883 (1981)

RACANELLI, ACTING PRESIDING JUSTICE.

Appellant challenges the summary judgment entered on her complaint for legal malpractice, contending that the issue of negligence concerning the implications of an unsettled proposition of law presented triable questions of fact. However, in light of the record and governing precedents, the contention is proven meritless. Accordingly, we affirm the judgment for the reasons which follow.

The record reveals the following salient facts and circumstances: In 1970 appellant retained respondent Frank C. Damrell Sr., a former California Superior Court Judge, to represent her in a dissolution proceeding. Appellant's husband, David K. McMillin, a career Army officer, then possessed a vested right to a federal pension upon retirement from active duty. In response to appellant's inquiry whether a community interest attached to her husband's federal military "retirement pay," respondent advised her that such federal military pension did not constitute divisible community property. A property settlement agreement subsequently executed by the parties contained no provision for the allocation or distribution of community property interests in the military pension. In 1973 Mr. McMillin retired from active duty and apparently has been receiving regular military pension payments ever since.

In 1974 the California Supreme Court determined that vested retirement benefits, including federal military pensions, constituted community property subject to equal division between the spouses in the event of dissolution. (In re Marriage of Fithian (1974) 10 Cal.3d 592, 596, 111 Cal.Rptr. 369, 517 P.2d 449, cert. den. 419 U.S. 825, 95 S.Ct. 41, 42 L.Ed.2d 48.)

Respondent, who was admitted to the bar in 1935, had recently resumed the practice of law following his retirement after 15 years of judicial service. During that time, he had maintained a close familiarity with the developing law in the field of pension rights and benefits. His personal interest in this particular area, which predated his judicial service, led to his closely monitoring the leading decision of Wissner v. Wissner (1950) 338 U.S. 655, 70 S.Ct. 398, 94 L.Ed. 424 (establishing the supremacy of a federal statute governing disposition of the proceeds of a military service life insurance policy).[2]

Following the Supreme Court's clarification of the "error-in-judgment" rule to require the exercise of an informed judgment in order to avoid a charge of professional negligence (see Smith v. Lewis (1975) 13 Cal.3d 349, 118 Cal.Rptr. 621, 530 P.2d 589), appellant instituted suit claiming, *inter alia*, that respondent's failure to advise her of the unsettled state of the relevant law deprived her of the opportunity to actively litigate and pursue such unsettled points of law and thus amounted to professional negligence. Appellant submitted the counter declaration of Lawrence W. Thorpe, an attorney experienced in domestic relations litigation, which stated in essence that respondent had failed to meet the minimum standards of professional practice by inaccurately

---

[2] In a supporting declaration respondent traced his familiarity with a line of cases following the earlier *French* rule (French v. French (1941) 17 Cal.2d 775, 112 P.2d 235 (holding that a nonvested military pension was a mere expectancy not subject to division as community property), overruled in In re Marriage of Brown (1976) 15 Cal.3d 838, 126 Cal.Rptr. 633, 544 P.2d 561). His special interest in the Wissner litigation (due in part to his long acquaintanceship with the Wissner family) motivated him to follow the progress of that litigation from its inception in the same court in which he was to eventually serve, including frequent discussions of a professional nature with the respective attorneys involved in the litigation.

advising appellant that the community property character of military retirement benefits was fully settled.

I

It is well established that an attorney is liable for damages sustained by a client as a result of the negligent performance of his professional duties. When the challenged conduct or omission relates to matters not within the common knowledge of a layman, the question of professional negligence will generally require expert testimony for appropriate factual resolution. But it is equally settled that no liability will attach "for lack of knowledge as to the true state of the law where a doubtful or debatable point is involved." (Sprague v. Morgan (1960) 185 Cal.App.2d 519, 523, 8 Cal.Rptr. 347; accord Smith v. Lewis, supra, 13 Cal.3d 349, 358–359, 118 Cal.Rptr. 621, 530 P.2d 589; see generally 1 Witkin, op. cit., ss. 150–152, pp. 161–164; Annot. (1977) 78 A.L.R.3d 255.) In reaffirming the long-established principle immunizing the legal practitioner from liability resulting from an honest error in judgment concerning a doubtful or debatable point of law, the California Supreme Court imposed the added condition that reasonable legal research be first undertaken "in an effort to ascertain relevant legal principles and to make an informed decision as to a course of conduct based upon an intelligent assessment of the problem." (Smith v. Lewis, supra, 13 Cal.3d 349, 359, 118 Cal.Rptr. 621, 530 P.2d 589.) Thus, the controlling test invokes a two-pronged inquiry: (1) whether the state of the law was unsettled at the time the professional advice was rendered; (2) and whether that advice was based upon the exercise of an informed judgment. We believe both inquiries must be answered affirmatively herein.

At the time of the challenged conduct substantial uncertainty existed relating to the community character of federal pension benefits, provoking considerable debate concerning the nature and vesting of federal retirement benefits as well as questions of federal supremacy. (See Smith v. Lewis, supra, 13 Cal.3d at p. 357, 118 Cal.Rptr. 621, 530 P.2d 589, and authorities there cited.) It was not until the 1974 Fithian decision that vested military retirement benefits were authoritatively determined to be subject to California community property law. Indeed, no sooner had the jurisprudential dust settled than the court forthrightly repudiated its earlier language excluding nonvested pension rights from community property treatment. (In re Marriage of Brown, supra, 15 Cal.3d 838, 851, fn. 14, 126 Cal.Rptr. 633, 544 P.2d 561 disapproving contrary statements in a number of decisions including In re Marriage of Jones (1975) 13 Cal.3d 457, 119 Cal.Rptr. 108, 531 P.2d 420; Smith v. Lewis, supra, 13 Cal.3d 349, 118 Cal.Rptr. 621, 520 P.2d 589; In re Marriage of Fithian, supra, 10 Cal.3d 592, 111 Cal.Rptr. 369, 517 P.2d 449.) Of course, those subsequent decisions are temporally irrelevant to the question to be decided herein relating to the state of the relevant law in 1970 which as previously noted postured clearly arguable issues "upon which reasonable lawyers could differ." (Smith v. Lewis, supra, at p. 357, 118 Cal.Rptr. 621, 520 P.2d 589; accord Henn v. Henn (1980) 26 Cal.3d 323, 328, 161 Cal.Rptr. 502, 605 P.2d 10.) Thus, we conclude as a matter of law, the subject of the community character of vested military retirement benefits inherently involved an unsettled point of law; accordingly, respondent's failure to anticipate its future resolution characterized in a recent decision as a "180 degree shift in the law" (Ruchti v. Goldfein (1980) 113 Cal.App.3d 928, 934, 170 Cal.Rptr. 375) cannot serve as the basis for professional negligence by reason of an erroneous but otherwise informed judgment.

Unlike the factual record disclosed in *Smith* supporting a theory of actionable negligence, the record indisputably demonstrates respondent's continuing legal research and knowledgeable familiarity with the state of existing law pertinent to the community property aspect of federal retirement benefits. In sharp contrast with Mrs. Smith's counsel, respondent was fully aware of the then controlling precedents and relevant literature, supplemented by a wealth of judicial experience in numerous domestic relations matters involving a variety of retirement benefits issues. Based upon the sum of that legal knowledge and practical experience, respondent rendered his now questioned opinion that a federal military pension was not subject to division under community property law. While in hindsight that professional advice ultimately proved erroneous, nonetheless it represented a reasoned exercise of an informed judgment grounded upon a professional evaluation of applicable legal principles. Under such uncontroverted circumstances, respondent's error in judgment on a question of law is immune from a claim of professional negligence.

II

We reject appellant's further contention that given the unsettled state of the law at the time the advice was rendered, respondent was under a duty to so advise his client in order to permit an informed choice whether to litigate the claim at trial and on appeal. While we recognize that an attorney owes a basic obligation to provide sound advice in furtherance of a client's best interests (see ABA Code of Prof. Responsibility, Canon 7, Ethical Considerations, 7–7, 7–8), such obligation does not include a duty to advise on all possible alternatives no matter how remote or tenuous. To impose such an extraordinary duty would effectively undermine the attorney-client relationship and vitiate the salutary purpose of the error-in-judgment rule. As a matter of policy, an attorney should not be required to compromise or attenuate an otherwise sound exercise of informed judgment with added advice concerning the unsettled nature of relevant legal principles. Under the venerable error-in-judgment rule, if an attorney acting in good faith exercises an honest and informed discretion in providing professional advice, the failure to anticipate correctly the resolution of an unsettled legal principle does not constitute culpable conduct. To require the attorney to further advise a client of the uncertainty in the law would render the exercise of such professional judgment meaningless. "The fact that greater prudence might have caused him to initiate what he believed to be a futile (appeal) . . . cannot, in lieu of a showing that he should have known it to be otherwise, now cause him to be subjected to a judgment of malpractice." (Sprague v. Morgan, *supra*, 185 Cal.App.2d 519, 523, 8 Cal.Rptr. 347.) In short, the exercise of sound professional judgment rests upon considerations of legal perception and not prescience.

In conclusion, we find no error in the judgment below.

* * *

WOOD V. MCGRATH, NORTH, MULLIN & KRATZ, P.C.
589 N.W.2d 103 (Neb. 1999)

CONNOLLY, J.

We granted the appellant, Beverly J. Wood's petition for further review of the Nebraska Court of Appeals' decision. The Court of Appeals concluded that as a matter of law, Timothy J. Pugh, an attorney with the appellee, the law firm of McGrath, North, Mullin & Kratz, P.C. (McGrath), did not breach the standard of care or commit legal malpractice by failing to inform Wood that the law relating to two issues relevant to a divorce settlement was unsettled and that the settlement resolved those issues against her. We reverse the Court of Appeals' decision and conclude that the doctrine of judgmental immunity does not apply to an attorney's failure to inform a client of unsettled legal issues relevant to a settlement agreement.

BACKGROUND

Wood brought a legal malpractice action against McGrath, alleging that Pugh had negligently represented her in a dissolution action. The underlying dissolution action was concluded by settlement and decree. In her petition against McGrath, Wood alleged that Pugh allowed her to accept less than her share of the marital estate and was negligent by, inter alia, failing to inform her that (1) the settlement reflected a distribution which excluded all rights to then unvested stock options which her husband held through his employment at Werner Enterprises, Inc.; (2) the state of the law indicated that a trial court could likely include all such stock options within the marital estate; (3) the settlement reflected a distribution which excluded approximately $210,489 from the marital estate to account for potential capital gains tax on the stock that the couple owned; and (4) the state of the law indicated that a trial court could likely value the Werner stock without deducting any potential capital gains tax.

At trial, Wood testified that Pugh told her the settlement awarded her 40 percent of the marital estate and that when she asked if that was appropriate, she said Pugh told her a judge would award her anywhere from 35 to 50 percent-that she could do better or worse than the settlement by going to trial. However, Wood testified that Pugh never discussed the different terms of the settlement, never mentioned any alternatives to settling, never provided any reasons to reject the settlement, and never discussed the potential outcome of a trial. She stated that she would not have signed the agreement if Pugh had told her that a trial court might include the unvested stock options as part of the marital estate and that a trial court might prohibit the deduction of potential capital gains tax when valuing the stock, contrary to what the settlement proposed.

Two attorneys testified as expert witnesses for Wood. David Domina stated that when a property settlement raises the issue of unvested stock options, the decision is the client's whether to pursue the issue to trial or to nonetheless settle the issue and that a lawyer breaches the applicable standard of care by failing to inform the client of the existence of the issue and the related law. Domina testified that when a settlement agreement deducts potential capital gains taxes from the value of a marital estate, a lawyer breaches the applicable standard of care by failing to inform a client of the effect of the deduction and the related law. Paul Galter testified that given the terms of the settlement agreement presented to Wood, Pugh breached the standard of care because Pugh did not give Wood sufficient information on the unvested stock options and capital gains tax issues. Galter stated that Pugh had a duty to tell Wood that the agreement raised the issues; to explain their effects to Wood; and to explain what the relevant law on the issues was, including what courts in other jurisdictions had held, before permitting her to sign the agreement.

At the close of Wood's evidence, McGrath moved for a directed verdict, which the court sustained on the issues of the stock valuation and the exclusion of unvested stock options.

On appeal, Wood asserted, inter alia, that the trial court erred in granting McGrath's directed verdict, arguing that Pugh breached the standard of care by failing to properly advise her in regard to the settlement agreement.

The Court of Appeals noted that the law on both the inclusion of unvested stock options in the marital estate and the consideration of potential capital gains taxes in valuing the estate were unsettled in Nebraska at the time the parties entered into the agreement. Wood v. McGrath, North, 7 Neb.App. 262, 581 N.W.2d 107 (1998). Accordingly, the court held that the judgmental immunity rule applied and concluded that Pugh's acts and omissions relating to the issues were not negligent as a matter of law. The court then stated that "Pugh, upon exercise of informed judgment, was not obligated to give additional advice regarding the unsettled nature of relevant legal principles." Id. at 282, 581 N.W.2d at 121.

ASSIGNMENT OF ERROR

In her petition for further review, Wood asserts that the Court of Appeals erred in affirming the trial court's judgment.

ANALYSIS

Wood argues that the doctrine of judgmental immunity does not apply to Pugh's failure to inform her of the law relating to the unvested stock options and capital gains tax deduction issues; that the settlement resolved those issues against her; and that given the body of law on the issues at the time, a trial judge might have resolved those issues in her favor. McGrath notes that the law regarding those issues was unsettled in Nebraska when Pugh represented Wood and argues that the doctrine of judgmental immunity applies to an attorney's decision regarding unsettled law, citing Baker v. Fabian, Thielen & Thielen, 254 Neb. 697, 578 N.W.2d 446 (1998). McGrath thus contends that when presenting a client with a settlement, an attorney has no duty to inform a client of possible options when the law relating to a relevant issue is unsettled.

In *Baker, supra,* this court held that an attorney is not liable for an error in judgment on a point of law which has not been settled by this court and on which reasonable doubt may be entertained by well-informed lawyers. Thus, an attorney's judgment or recommendation on an unsettled point of law is immune from suit, and the attorney has no duty to accurately predict the future course of unsettled law. This immunity rule encourages practicing attorneys in this state to predict, in a professional manner, the outcome of legal issues relevant to their clients' cases. See Canon 7, EC 7–3 and 7–5, of the Code of Professional Responsibility. However, Pugh's recommendations (or lack thereof) on the unvested stock options and capital gains tax issues are not before us. Rather, the issue is whether the doctrine of judgmental immunity applies to Pugh's failure to inform Wood that the law relating to unvested stock options and potential capital gains tax issues, while unsettled in Nebraska, were settled in other jurisdictions in a manner which would have been favorable to Wood. The question of whether an attorney owes a duty to inform a client of the unsettled nature of relevant law was not addressed in *Baker*. Thus, we must determine whether to extend the *Baker* judgmental immunity rule to an attorney's failure to inform a client of unsettled legal issues relevant to a settlement agreement.

"[W]e insist that lawyers ... advise clients with respect to settlements with the same skill, knowledge, and diligence with which they pursue all other legal tasks." Bruning v. Law Offices of Ronald J. Palagi, 250 Neb. 677, 689, 551 N.W.2d 266, 272 (1996) (citing Grayson v. Wofsey, Rosen, Kweskin & Kuriansky, 231 Conn. 168, 646 A.2d 195 (1994)). See, also, McWhirt v. Heavey, 250 Neb. 536, 550 N.W.2d 327 (1996). We declined in McWhirt v. Heavey, 250 Neb. at 547, 550 N.W.2d at 335, "'to adopt a rule that insulates attorneys from exposure to malpractice claims arising from their negligence in settled cases if the attorney's conduct has damaged the client.'" We decline to adopt such a rule now.

The decision to settle a controversy is the client's. See Canon 7, EC 7–7. If a client is to meaningfully make that decision, he or she needs to have the information necessary to assess the risks and benefits of either settling or proceeding to trial. "A lawyer should exert his or her best efforts to ensure that decisions of a client are made only after the client has been informed of relevant considerations." Canon 7, EC 7–8. The desire is that a client's decision to settle is an informed one.

The attorney's research efforts may not resolve doubts or may lead to the conclusion that only hindsight or future judicial decisions will provide accurate answers. The attorney's responsibilities to the client may not be satisfied concerning a material issue simply by determining that a proposition is doubtful or by unilaterally deciding the issue. Where there are reasonable alternatives, the attorney should inform the client that the issue is uncertain, unsettled or debatable and allow the client to make the decision. 2 Ronald E. Mallen & Jeffrey M. Smith, Legal Malpractice § 17.15 at 531–32 (4th ed.1996).

Additionally, an allegation that an attorney is negligent by failing to inform a client of an unsettled legal issue relevant to a settlement does not demand that an attorney accurately predict the future course of unsettled law. Thus, an allegation that an attorney did not properly inform a client of relevant unsettled legal issues does not provide the same need for immunity from suit as does an attorney's judgment or recommendation in an area of unsettled law.

Ultimately, we cannot support what would be the clear result of extending the judgmental immunity rule in the instant case. If we conclude that the judgmental immunity rule applies to an attorney's failure to inform a client of unsettled legal issues relevant to a settlement, an attorney could forgo conducting research or providing a client with information on a relevant legal issue once he or she determined that the legal issue at hand was unsettled in this state. We fail to see how this result promotes the settlement of disputes in a client's best interests.

We conclude that the doctrine of judgmental immunity does not apply to an attorney's failure to inform a client of unsettled legal issues relevant to a settlement. Our conclusion makes no judgment as to whether Pugh was negligent. It imposes no additional duty as a matter of law to research or inform a client on unsettled legal matters. Rather, it simply directs that consistent with Bruning v. Law Offices of Ronald J. Palagi, 250 Neb. 677, 551 N.W.2d 266 (1996); McWhirt v. Heavey, 250 Neb. 536, 550 N.W.2d 327 (1996); and McVaney v. Baird, Holm, McEachen, 237 Neb. 451, 466 N.W.2d 499 (1991), whether an attorney is negligent for such a failure is determined by whether the attorney exercised the same skill, knowledge, and diligence as attorneys of ordinary skill and capacity commonly possess and exercise in the performance of all other legal tasks. At the same time, an attorney's ultimate recommendation in an area of unsettled law is immune from suit. Baker v. Fabian, Thielen & Thielen, supra. Such a result gives the client the benefit of both professional advice and the information necessary to make an informed decision whether to settle a dispute.

CONCLUSION

The Court of Appeals erred in concluding that Pugh was not negligent as a matter of law in failing to inform Wood of the unsettled nature of the law regarding whether unvested stock options were part of the marital estate and whether the marital estate's unvested stock options should have been valued without deducting potential capital gains tax. Accordingly, we reverse the Court of Appeals' decision and remand the cause to the Court of Appeals with directions to remand the cause to the district court for a new trial.

* * *

The scope of the "informed judgment" or "error-in-judgment" rule. Assume that there is a split of authority at the time a lawyer decides to file an action. The lawyer proceeds on the assumption that the law is in her client's favor but is unaware of the contrary decisional law. Eventually, the court rules against the lawyer's position. Do the rules from *Damrell* and *Wood* protect the lawyer from a malpractice claim? In your opinion, which opinion gets the issue right?

* * *

Problem 13.2. Refer back to the Chapter Hypothetical. You represent Jill in her malpractice suit against Miranda. Is she likely to be successful? How can you establish Miranda's failure to meet the requisite standard of care?

* * *

2. MALPRACTICE IN THE LITIGATION SETTING

SIMKO V. BLAKE

532 N.W.2d 842 (Mich. 1994)

MALLETT, JUSTICE

. . . .

I

Plaintiffs Arthur Louis Simko, Margaret Simko, and Tara Marie Simko filed suit against defendant Marvin Blake, an attorney, alleging that the defendant committed professional malpractice in failing to adequately represent Arthur Simko in a prosecution of possessing over 650 grams of cocaine, M.C.L. § 333.7401(2)(a)(i); M.S.A. § 14.15(7401)(2)(a)(i), and possession of a firearm in the commission or attempt to commit a felony, M.C.L. § 750.227b; M.S.A. § 28.424(2). Although the defendant was convicted and the conviction eventually was reversed by the Court of Appeals, Mr. Simko spent more than two years in prison.

In the underlying criminal case, on the night of March 6, 1987, a state police officer observed a speeding car traveling with its lights flashing in an apparent effort to attract the officer's attention. The car exited the highway and stopped to wait for the police car. The driver of the vehicle alighted from his car and told the police that the passenger, Arthur Simko, needed medical attention.

Plaintiff appeared flushed, was perspiring, and his breathing was labored. The officer summoned an ambulance. While waiting for the ambulance to arrive, the officer discovered what appeared to be drug paraphernalia on the floor of the car. A further search of the car revealed a cup containing cocaine residue, a bullet in plaintiff's pocket, a pistol in the glove compartment, a pistol in the trunk, several rounds of ammunition, and 988 grams of a substance containing cocaine.

Arthur Simko was represented by Marvin Blake. At the close of the prosecution's case, and again at the close of defendant's case, Mr. Blake moved for a directed verdict on the ground that the evidence was insufficient to convict plaintiff. The trial judge denied both motions. Mr. Simko was ultimately found guilty by the jury and sentenced to mandatory sentences of life without parole plus two years.

Arthur Simko then retained another attorney and appealed his conviction. The Court of Appeals reversed; however, by that time, he had already served two years of his prison sentence.

At the time plaintiff filed his appeal, he also filed a legal malpractice action against defendant. Arthur Simko alleged that the defendant failed to properly investigate his case and failed to properly prepare to defend him. Specifically, Mr. Simko alleged that Mr. Blake did not produce any witnesses in his defense besides Mr. Simko himself, failed to produce plaintiff's personal physician who had been treating him for a pinched nerve and who prescribed medication that would have offered an explanation of his medical condition at the time of arrest, and failed to provide Mr. Simko with the name and location of the hotel where Mr. Simko had spent the day before he was arrested that may have protected him from impeachment.*

The malpractice action was dismissed by the trial court when it granted defendant's motion for summary disposition. The trial court stated:

> The proximate cause of his conviction was the trial court's error in denying the motion for directed verdict in favor of the defendant in the underlying case.

> The Court of Appeals, in holding that a directed verdict should have been granted indirectly not only stated that the trial court here erred but that the jury erred as well.

> By holding that the standard was satisfied for the granting of a motion for directed verdict, in effect, the Court of Appeals held that a reasonable well-instructed jury could not convict based upon the evidence presented during the course of the trial.

> The jury in the underlying case by virtue of the Court of Appeals decision acted unreasonably in light of evidence presented for the jury to consider.

> As a result, the defendant Blake cannot possibly be held responsible for the acts of an unreasonable jury.

The Court of Appeals affirmed, stating that

[b]y challenging the sufficiency of the evidence against Simko, Blake raised a complete and ultimately successful defense to both charges. . . . Blake was not Simko's insurer against all possible misfortune. . . . His duty was to raise an adequate defense to the criminal charges, not to protect Simko from judge and jury. [201 Mich.App. 191, 195, 506 N.W.2d 258 (1993).]

We affirm the decision of the Court of Appeals and hold that Marvin Blake fulfilled his duty to Arthur Simko.

---

* Editor's note: The police were in possession of the name and address of a hotel in Florida at which Simko had spent the previous day. At trial, Simko's testimony was impeached because he could not remember the name of the hotel.

II

We hold that defendant's motion for summary disposition was properly granted by the trial court because the plaintiffs failed to state a claim upon which relief can be granted. Plaintiffs' complaint and pleadings failed to state a breach of duty.

Pursuant to MCR 2.116(C)(8), a motion for summary disposition is granted if the claim is so clearly unenforceable as a matter of law that no factual development could possibly justify recovery. A motion of summary disposition is tested on the pleadings alone, and all factual allegations contained in the complaint must be accepted as true.

III

In order to state an action for legal malpractice, the plaintiff has the burden of adequately alleging the following elements:

(1) the existence of an attorney-client relationship;

(2) negligence in the legal representation of the plaintiff;

(3) that the negligence was a proximate cause of an injury; and

(4) the fact and extent of the injury alleged.

[The parties admitted that an attorney-client relationship existed.] Thus, the issue is not whether a duty existed, but rather the extent of that duty once invoked.

It is well established that "[a]n attorney is obligated to use reasonable skill, care, discretion and judgment in representing a client." Lipton v. Boesky, 110 Mich.App. 589, 594, 313 N.W.2d 163 (1981). Further, according to SJI2d 30.01, all attorneys have a duty to behave as would an attorney "of ordinary learning, judgment or skill . . . under the same or similar circumstances . . . ."

An attorney has the duty to fashion such a strategy so that it is consistent with prevailing Michigan law. However, an attorney does not have a duty to insure or guarantee the most favorable outcome possible. An attorney is never bound to exercise extraordinary diligence, or act beyond the knowledge, skill, and ability ordinarily possessed by members of the legal profession.

To require attorneys, or other professionals, to act over and beyond average skill, learning, and ability, would be an unreasonable burden on the profession and the legal system. As the Court of Appeals stated:

There is no motion that can be filed, no amount of research in preparation, no level of skill, nor degree of perfection that could anticipate every error or completely shield a client from the occasional aberrant ruling of a fallible judge or an intransigent jury. To impose a duty on attorneys to do more than that which is legally adequate to fully vindicate a client's rights would require our legal system, already overburdened, to digest unnecessarily inordinate quantities of additional motions and evidence that, in most cases, will prove to be superfluous. And, *because no amount of work can guarantee a favorable result, attorneys would never know when the work they do is sufficiently more than adequate to be enough to protect not only their clients from error, but themselves from liability.* [201 Mich.App. at 194, 506 N.W.2d 258 (emphasis added).]

Lastly, mere errors in judgment by a lawyer are generally not grounds for a malpractice action where the attorney acts in good faith and exercises reasonable care, skill, and diligence. Baker v. Beal, 225 N.W.2d 106, 112 (Iowa 1975). Where an attorney acts in good faith and in honest belief that his acts and omissions are well founded in law and are in the best interest of his client, he is not answerable for mere errors in judgment. Rorrer v. Cooke, 313 N.C. 338, 340–342, 329 S.E.2d 355 (1985). . . . 1 Mallen & Smith, Legal Malpractice (3d ed.), §§ 14.12 to 14.17, pp. 836–853:

> [T]here can be no liability for acts and omissions by an attorney in the conduct of litigation which are based on an honest exercise of professional judgment. This is a sound rule. Otherwise every losing litigant would be able to sue his attorney if he could find another attorney who was willing to second guess the decisions of the first attorney with the advantage of hindsight . . . . To hold that an attorney may not be held liable for the choice of trial tactics and the conduct of a case based on professional judgment is not to say, however, that an attorney may not be held liable for any of his actions in relation to a trial. He is still bound to exercise a reasonable degree of skill and care in all his professional undertakings. [Woodruff v. Tomlin, 616 F.2d 924, 930 (C.A.6 1980) (citations omitted).]

IV

We find that the defendant acted as would an attorney of ordinary learning, judgment, or skill under the same or similar circumstances, and his alleged acts and omissions were a matter of trial tactics based on reasonable professional judgment.

From October 12 through October 15, 1987, Mr. Simko's trial was held in the Recorder's Court for the City of Detroit, before the Honorable Craig S. Strong. Mr. Simko was the only witness to testify. Dr. Karbal and Mrs. Simko were not called as witnesses because Mr. Blake did not feel that they would be beneficial to the defense's case. Following the prosecution's presentation of the case, and again after the defense rested, Mr. Blake moved for a directed verdict of acquittal. Both motions were denied by Judge Strong. On October 15, 1987, Mr. Simko was convicted by the jury as charged.

We find, as a matter of law, that the plaintiffs' allegations could not support a breach of duty because they are based on mere errors of professional judgment and not breaches of reasonable care. Plaintiffs' allegations of breach of duty are contained in ¶¶ 10(a)–(k) of plaintiffs' complaint. The only specific allegations that could have altered the outcome of Mr. Simko's trial are contained in ¶¶ 10(d)–(i).5 Plaintiffs alleged that defendant should have called other witnesses besides Mr. Simko, including Mr. Simko's physician, Dr. Michael Karbal, and Mr. Simko's wife, Margaret Simko. In addition, ¶ 10(i) alleges that Mr. Blake failed to ascertain the name and location of the hotel where Mr. Simko had allegedly spent the day before he was arrested.

First, it is a tactical decision whether to call particular witnesses, as long as the attorney acts with full knowledge of the law and in good faith. *Woodruff, supra* at 933. *Woodruff* held that a charge of malpractice on the basis of an attorney's decision to not cross-examine an expert witness did not constitute malpractice. Similarly, in Frank v. Bloom, 634 F.2d 1245, 1256–1257 (C.A. 10 1980), the court stated that it will afford latitude to the attorney when making tactical strategies:

> [I]t is the duty of the attorney who is a professional to determine trial strategy. If the client had the last word on this, the client could be his or her own lawyer.

Here, plaintiffs are alleging that defendant was negligent in not calling Dr. Karbal and Mrs. Simko. This, however, is a tactical decision that this Court may not question. Perhaps defendant made an error of judgment in deciding not to call particular witnesses, and perhaps another attorney would have made a different decision; however, tactical decisions do not constitute grounds for a legal malpractice action. *Woodruff, supra.* Plaintiffs' claim that certain witnesses should have been called is nothing but an assertion that another lawyer might have conducted the trial differently, a matter of professional opinion that does not allege violation of the duty to perform as a reasonably competent criminal defense lawyer.

Second, the failure to ascertain the name and location of the hotel where a client was located at a particular time does not constitute negligence. There is no duty to infallibly protect a client from impeachment. This would be an impossible standard for defense counsel to meet and would violate and extend beyond the well-established reasonable care standard.

V

We conclude that there was no legal basis for holding that Mr. Blake's actions constituted negligence, or otherwise constitute malpractice. When an attorney fashions a trial strategy consistent with the governing principles of law and reasonable professional judgment, the attorney's conduct is legally adequate. Accordingly, we affirm the decision of the Court of Appeals and hold that the defendant fulfilled his duty to his client.

LEVIN, Justice (dissenting).

. . . .

I

The majority states:

[A]ttorneys must only act as would an attorney of ordinary learning, judgment, or skill under the same or similar circumstances.

A

I agree that a lawyer need "only act" as would a lawyer of ordinary learning, judgment, diligence, or skill under the same or similar circumstances. But he must *so act*. If the majority were to allow this case to come to trial, the evidence were to show, and a trier of fact were to find, that a lawyer of ordinary learning, judgment, diligence, or skill, under the same or similar circumstances, would have avoided errors that Blake allegedly committed, then Blake is, or should be, subject to liability for damage found to have resulted from conviction of an offense subjecting Simko to a sentence of life in prison and actual incarceration for over two years.

. . . .

B

The majority also states that "mere errors in judgment by a lawyer are *generally* not grounds for a malpractice action where the attorney acts in good faith and exercises reasonable care, skill, and diligence." (Emphasis added.) It is implicit in the formulation adopted by the majority, requiring a lawyer to act as would a lawyer of "ordinary learning, *judgment*, or skill," that errors of judgment may constitute negligence. Whether an error of judgment, or a "mere" error of judgment, constitutes negligence depends on whether a lawyer of ordinary learning, judgment, diligence, or skill would have avoided the error or "mere" error of judgment. That "generally" is a question of fact for the trier of fact to decide.

. . . .

III

Blake's motion for summary disposition was filed on the basis that the Simkos "failed to state a claim on which relief can be granted." In finding facts on this second appellate review, the majority ignores that only the pleadings may be considered by the circuit court and the appellate courts in ruling on such a motion.

The majority finds, as a matter of fact or law, that the "alleged acts and omissions were trial tactics based on good faith and reasonable professional judgment." The complaint particularized concerning the errors claimed by Simko. In response to the motion for summary disposition, the Simkos filed an affidavit of a lawyer stating that in his opinion Blake had erred. Blake did not file an affidavit in support of the motion for summary disposition, probably because no such support is required or permitted. Nevertheless the majority finds, as a matter of fact or law, that Blake acted in good faith and exercised reasonable professional judgment.

The majority finds, as a matter of fact or law, that certain witnesses were not called because Blake "did not feel that they would be beneficial to the defense's case."

Because Blake did not file an affidavit in support of his motion for summary disposition, and, even if he had, it could not properly have been considered in deciding the motion, there is no record support for fact finding by the majority.

Because there is no factual record, the majority does not have a basis for asserting that the witnesses were not called because Blake "did not feel that they would be beneficial to defense's case." Since there is no record, we do not know whether either or both witnesses were interviewed by Blake, and what might have occurred during any such interview. The silent record no more justifies a finding that Blake had a reason for not calling the witnesses, than it would a finding that he simply neglected or overlooked calling them. A silent record supports no finding of fact at all.

. . . .

* * *

Trial tactics and the "error in judgment" rule. Relying on a Sixth Circuit opinion (*Woodruff*), *Simko* held that if the failure to call a witness was error, it was a "mere error in judgment" and such errors "are generally not grounds for a malpractice action where the attorney acts in good faith and exercises reasonable care, skill, and diligence." Are *Simko* and *Woodruff* "merely" applications of the "error in judgment" rule from *Damrell* to trial tactics or are the courts applying a different standard altogether? Is there a good reason to give lawyers more leeway in the case of trial tactics than other kinds of decisions?

* * *

Problem 13.3. Assume that the trial court in *Simko* denied Blake's motion for summary disposition and that the malpractice case proceeded to trial. In which of the following situations would the rule that the Michigan Supreme Court ultimately applied bar recovery for Simko at trial?

(A) Simko's expert witness testified that any reasonable attorney would have called Simko's doctor as a witness.

(B) The evidence presented established that the reason why Blake failed to introduce the doctor's testimony was because he failed to interview the doctor after being told about him by Simko.

Establishing causation in legal malpractice actions. As is the case with most negligence claims, a plaintiff alleging legal malpractice must establish that the defendant's negligence resulted in damages. The trial court in *Simko* appears to have dismissed the malpractice action on causation grounds. How is a legal malpractice plaintiff supposed to prove that the lawyer's negligence was a cause in fact of the plaintiff's damages? A proximate cause? Where the allegation of malpractice involves conduct related to civil litigation, there generally must be a "trial within a trial"— a trial within the broader legal malpractice trial in which the plaintiff's underlying case is tried as it should have been, absent the alleged negligence. If this trial establishes that the plaintiff would not have obtained a better result even in the absence of the lawyer's negligence, the malpractice case is over. What if the alleged malpractice occurs in the transactional setting? For example, how could a plaintiff establish that a lawyer's negligence in negotiating a contract resulted in unfavorable terms for the plaintiff without asking a jury to engage in guesswork?

Problem 13.4. Assume in the Chapter Hypothetical that Miranda provided deficient advice in connection with Jill's criminal matter and, as a result, Jill was convicted of forgery and other crimes. If a plaintiff alleging malpractice in a prior civil matter must establish that the lawyer's negligence resulted in the plaintiff obtaining a worse result, what should it take for a criminal defendant to establish a malpractice claim against his lawyer? *See* Restatement (Third) of the Law Governing Lawyers § 53 cmt. d.

Public defender immunity. Lawyers who are employed by the Federal Public Defenders Office enjoy statutory immunity from malpractice liability. 18 U.S.C. § 3006A(g)(2)(A). Should lawyers who are *appointed* by a court to represent indigent criminal defendants enjoy immunity from malpractice liability? The majority of courts to consider the issue have said no. *See* Mooney v. Frazier, 693 S.E.2d 333 (W. Va. 2010) (rejecting majority rule).

* * *

C. AGREEMENTS PROSPECTIVELY LIMITING A LAWYER'S LIABILITY

Please read ABA Model Rules of Professional Conduct, Rule 1.8(h)(1) & (k) and Comment [14].

* * *

Rationale for Rule 1.8(h)(1). Comment [14] explains that agreements prospectively limiting the lawyer's liability are prohibited because such agreements "are likely to undermine competent and diligent representation." Is this rationale persuasive?

* * *

D. SETTLING MALPRACTICE CLAIMS

Please read ABA Model Rules of Professional Conduct, Rule 1.8(h)(2) & (k) and Comment [15].

* * *

Rationale for Rule 1.8(h)(2). Model Rule 1.8(h)(2) requires a lawyer who wishes to settle a malpractice claim with an unrepresented client to advise the client "in writing of the desirability of seeking" counsel and to give the client "a reasonable opportunity to seek the advice of independent legal counsel." Comment [15] explains that this requirement results from "the danger that a lawyer will take unfair advantage of an unrepresented client." Does this rule represent a jaded view of attorneys or is it a realistic assessment of human nature?

* * *

E. MALPRACTICE INSURANCE

Law students probably don't give much thought to malpractice insurance, but for lawyers it is a very important topic. As you read the following materials, ask yourself whether malpractice insurance coverage should be voluntary or mandatory.

1. MANDATORY PROFESSIONAL LIABILITY INSURANCE

One issue related to malpractice insurance is whether a lawyer should be required to carry such insurance and, if not, whether the lawyer must disclose this fact to a client. There are several possible approaches to this issue. Oregon is the only state that makes legal malpractice insurance mandatory. Roughly half of the states require lawyers to disclose the fact that they do not carry professional liability insurance. Benjamin P. Cooper, *Attorney Self-Disclosure*, 79 U. CIN. L. REV. 697, 712 (2010). A few states require lawyers to inform their clients directly of the fact that they do not maintain malpractice insurance above a certain level. *See, e.g.*, Ohio Code of Professional Responsibility DR 1–104. In keeping with the ABA Model Court Rule on Insurance Disclosure, a greater number require only that a lawyer disclose on their annual registration statements to the state bar whether they maintain liability insurance. A number of states have rejected proposals that would have required disclosure in some form. Susan Saab Fortney, *Law as Profession: Examining the Role of Accountability*, 40 FORDHAM URB. L.J. 177, 195–96 (2012).

Recall from Chapter 12 that a lawyer has a duty under Model Rule 1.4(b) to "explain a matter to the extent reasonably necessary to permit the client to make informed decisions regarding the representation." Does this rule impose upon a lawyer a duty to inform a client about the lawyer's failure to carry liability insurance?

* * *

2. FILING CLAIMS AND NOTIFYING CLIENTS

The American Bar Association Standing Committee on Lawyers' Professional Liability notes, "All insurance policies include language requiring the insured to give prompt notice to the insurance company of a malpractice claim or suit. This requirement enables the insurer to defend the claim or, when possible, to mitigate or avoid a loss." American Bar Association Standing Committee on Lawyers' Professional Liability, *Selecting Legal Malpractice Insurance* 9 (2003). But must a lawyer inform the client about her malpractice? According to the ABA committee, the lawyer must, as a matter of professional responsibility, "inform[ ] the client of any errors committed by the attorney that may result in harm to the client's interest." The committee based its opinion on the lawyer's duty of communication under Model Rule 1.4. What decisions might a client have to make as a result of the lawyer's malpractice in his case?

A lawyer's failure to notify a client about a possible mistake may also make the client that much madder if and when the client learns of the mistake. The failure to inform a client of the lawyer's possible malpractice might also toll the statute of limitations. Thus, the committee concludes, "The bottom line is that it is in the attorney's and the client's best interest to disclose any errors to the client as soon as possible."

* * *

Profile of attorney professionalism. Memphis attorney Lucian Pera, a self-described "legal ethics geek," represents lawyers and law firms in matters ranging from malpractice to professional discipline. He also regularly advises law firms on issues of loss prevention. Lucian explains, "Basically, any time a lawyer or law firm has any kind of ethics problem, or claim, or similar issue, I can get called in to help."

Why does a lawyer need a legal ethics expert? Lucian notes the growing complexity and sophistication of the law governing the practice of law and its importance to lawyers. He explains, "[T]hose of us who practice in the ethics area, either just for our own law firms, or for other clients, tend to be the holders of lots of specialized, 'geeky' knowledge – knowledge most other lawyers are very comfortable not knowing and relying on us for." Lucian regularly writes articles and gives seminars on ethics and loss prevention issues. He says this is useful to "sensitize lawyers to the fact that there is actually specialized knowledge about ethics and loss prevention that can be very useful when a lawyer is in a pinch."

It is not always easy for lawyers to decide to hire another lawyer. Lucian says that lawyers can be slow to ask for help, but they are happy when they make the call. "I enjoy this work because I can do for lawyers, using my ethics 'geek' knowledge and experience, just what we lawyers do for clients – I help solve lawyers' problems so that can get back to representing their own clients. You would be amazed how happy lawyers can be after they realize they can get this kind of help."

For five years, Lucian was a member of the ABA Ethics 2000 Commission that studied and revised the Model Rules of Professional Conduct. Lucian notes that most states adopted the Ethics 2000 rule amendments within five years and explains that this brought much greater uniformity to the law of attorney ethics. "That's an incredibly good development, because the practice of law, even in the smallest states and the most isolated towns, involves lawyers working across jurisdictional lines more than ever before. For example, the conflict of interest rules are today more uniform, across more American jurisdictions, than ever before in history. Ethics 2000 is responsible for that, and it was great to be a part of that."

Lucian stays in touch with clients and friends by sending a card every January to celebrate Elvis Presley's birthday. Each card features a photo of The King provided by *The Commercial Appeal*, the daily newspaper in Memphis. Lucian has represented the newspaper for years. Lucian says that sending the card "combines my long-time work with *The Commercial Appeal*, a native Memphian's love of Elvis, and a mission to share with folks outside Memphis a little bit of history from The Cultural Center of The Universe."

SECTION 4

CONFIDENTIALITY

■ ■ ■

This Section begins your introduction to the law and rules of professional responsibility which relate to the protection of information a lawyer may acquire or produce in connection with the lawyer's representation of a client. Chapter 14 alerts you to the lawyer's affirmative professional responsibilities to refrain from disclosing or misusing information relating to the client's representation as well as the exceptions to this rule that permit or sometimes require disclosure of such information. Chapter 15 addresses two legal tools a lawyer may use to protect information the client wants to keep confidential—the attorney-client privilege—a rule of evidence—and the work-product doctrine—a rule of civil procedure—each of which can be used to prevent the use of legal process to compel the disclosure of certain information relating to a lawyer's representation of her client. The goal is to provide an informational starting point for further thought about how you might conduct your practice so as to be a professionally responsible steward of the information you acquire or produce in connection with your representation of your clients.

CHAPTER 14

DUTY OF CONFIDENTIALITY

■ ■ ■

Chapter hypothetical. Cynthia Burns is a long-time friend who knows you handle family law issues in your law practice. One night, she calls you at home and says she wants you to be her lawyer because she wants a divorce. She says her husband has been unfaithful, and she cannot tolerate being married to him anymore. You agree to represent her and within the week, you file a petition for divorce in the appropriate court. You are worried about your client's mental and physical health. She says she is not sleeping or eating well because she is so stressed about the end of her marriage.

* * *

A. PROTECTING CONFIDENTIAL INFORMATION

Please read ABA Model Rules of Professional Conduct, Rule 1.6(a) & (c) and Comments [1]–[5].

Please read Restatement (Third) of the Law Governing Lawyers §§ 16(3) & 49.

* * *

As a fiduciary, lawyers owe their clients a duty of confidentiality. Unauthorized disclosure of client confidences is a breach of that duty and can result in liability for the lawyer. Such a disclosure is the subject of the case *Perez v. Kirk and Carrigan,* excerpted below. *See also* Restatement (Third) of the Law Governing Lawyers § 49 (2000).

Beyond civil liability, a lawyer can be disciplined for disclosing client confidences. This is the subject of Model Rule 1.6(a). The rule provides that an attorney must not reveal "information relating to the representation of the client" unless the client consents, the disclosure is impliedly authorized to carry out the representation, or an exception applies. Though the confidentiality exceptions vary from state to state, most jurisdictions have adopted a general rule governing confidentiality substantially similar to that found in Model Rule 1.6(a). This rule provides broad protection. The information that must be kept confidential can come from the client or from some other source. Not only is "embarrassing" information covered by the rule, but all information no matter how seemingly mundane. Even if the client revealed the same information to a third party, the lawyer cannot reveal that information absent the client's consent or an exception.

While some believe this rule is broader than necessary to protect clients, the rule has the advantage of simplicity. Except to the extent an exception applies or auhorized to carry out the representation, a lawyer should not tell anyone about the lawyer's clients, their problems, or the work the lawyer is doing on their behalf.

It is worth noting the distinction between the attorney-client privilege and the attorney's ethical and fiduciary duty of confidentiality. The attorney-client privilege allows attorney and client to refuse to testify regarding (or produce a document reflecting) a communication made in confidence between attorney and client for the purpose of obtaining or providing legal advice. Restatement (Third) of the Law Governing Lawyers § 68 (2000). Some attorneys incorrectly believe that only privileged information must be kept confidential. But this is incorrect; whether privileged or not privileged, if information is learned through the lawyer's representation of the client, the lawyer may not reveal it absent authorization or exception. The attorney-client privilege and work product doctrine will be discussed in detail in Chapter 15.

A relatively recent addition to Model Rule 1.6 is subpart (c). This part of the rule addresses an attorney's obligation to competently protect confidential client information. Because this duty also touches upon special issues related to protecting privilege and work product, it will be discussed in Chapter 15.

* * *

Problem 14.1. While you are representing your friend Cynthia Burns in her divorce, you run into a mutual friend Ross Conner. Ross asks if you sense that Cynthia has been worried about something lately. He says he saw her the other day and she seemed depressed. Separately consider each of the following possible responses to Ross's question. Analyze whether one or more of these responses would violate your obligation under Rule 1.6(a).

(1) "Cynthia hired me to file a petition for divorce on her behalf. I can't really say anything else about the situation."

(2) "Cynthia learned recently that her husband cheated on her. I think that is probably why she seems depressed."

(3) "I'm really worried about her, too! She told me that she has not been sleeping or eating. What can we do to cheer her up?"

Problem 14.2. Suppose for purposes of this question only that you turned down the opportunity to represent Cynthia in her divorce, but only after she mentioned her husband's infidelity. If you are not (and never were) Cynthia's lawyer, do you have an obligation to keep the information about her cheating husband confidential? Refer to Model Rule 1.18 in your analysis.

Problem 14.3. As you represent Cynthia in the divorce proceedings, which categories of information do you believe you are impliedly authorized to reveal to your opposing counsel? Can you reveal information about Cynthia's case to a partner or associate in your law firm consistent with your obligation under Rule 1.6(a)? Consider Comment [5] to Rule 1.6 as you answer both questions in this problem.

Problem 14.4. If you reveal confidential information to mutual friend Ross Conner concerning Cynthia, does Cynthia have a valid cause of action against you for breach of fiduciary duty? Consider the following case.

* * *

PEREZ V. KIRK & CARRIGAN

822 S.W.2d 261 (Tex. Ct. App. 1991)

DORSEY, JUSTICE.

Ruben Perez appeals a summary judgment rendered against him on his causes of action against the law firm of Kirk & Carrigan, and against Dana Kirk and Steve Carrigan individually (henceforth all three will be collectively referred to as "Kirk & Carrigan"). We reverse the summary judgment and remand this case for trial.

The present suit arises from a school bus accident on September 21, 1989, in Alton, Texas. Ruben Perez was employed by Valley Coca-Cola Bottling Company as a truck driver. On the morning of the accident, Perez attempted to stop his truck at a stop sign along his route, but the truck's brakes failed to stop the truck, which collided with the school bus. The loaded bus was knocked into a pond and 21 children died. Perez suffered injuries from the collision and was taken to a local hospital to be treated.

The day after the accident, Kirk & Carrigan, lawyers who had been hired to represent Valley Coca-Cola Bottling Company, visited Perez in the hospital for the purpose of taking his statement. Perez claims that the lawyers told him that they were his lawyers too and that anything he told them would be kept confidential. With this understanding, Perez gave them a sworn statement concerning the accident[2]. However, after taking

---

[2] Among other things, Perez generally stated that he had a previous accident while driving a Coke truck in 1987 for which he was given a citation, that he had a speeding violation in 1988, that he had not filled out a daily checklist to show that he had checked the brakes on the morning of the accident, that he had never before experienced problems with the brakes on his

Perez' statement, Kirk & Carrigan had no further contact with him. Instead, Kirk & Carrigan made arrangements for criminal defense attorney Joseph Connors to represent Perez. Connors was paid by National Union Fire Insurance Company which covered both Valley Coca-Cola and Perez for liability in connection with the accident.

Some time after Connors began representing Perez, Kirk & Carrigan, without telling either Perez or Connors, turned Perez' statement over to the Hidalgo County District Attorney's Office. Kirk & Carrigan contend that Perez' statement was provided in a good faith attempt to fully comply with a request of the district attorney's office and under threat of subpoena if they did not voluntarily comply. Partly on the basis of this statement, the district attorney was able to obtain a grand jury indictment of Perez for involuntary manslaughter for his actions in connection with the accident.[3]

Ruben Perez filed the present suit . . . assert[ing] numerous causes of action against Kirk & Carrigan for breach of fiduciary duty, negligent and intentional infliction of emotional distress, violation of the Texas Deceptive Trade Practices—Consumer Protection Act [the "DTPA"] and conspiracy to violate . . . the Texas Insurance Code. . . . Perez complained generally by his petition that Kirk & Carrigan had caused him to suffer public humiliation and emotional distress by turning over his supposedly confidential statement to the district attorney. In addition to the turnover of this statement, Perez alleged generally that Kirk & Carrigan, Valley Coca-Cola, and National Union engaged in an overall plan to shift the blame for the accident away from them and onto Perez, by concealing information tending to show that Valley Coca-Cola's faulty maintenance of the brakes on the truck was the real cause of the accident.

Kirk & Carrigan moved for summary judgment on all of the claims made against them by Perez, on the grounds that no attorney-client or other fiduciary relationship existed, that even if a fiduciary relationship did exist no damages resulted from the asserted breach, that all of Perez' claims basically allege groundless prosecution and therefore constitute an invalid claim for malicious prosecution, that Perez was not a consumer

---

truck and that they were working just before the accident, that he tried to apply the brakes to stop the truck, but that the brakes for the trailer were not working at all to stop the truck (the truck had two sets of brakes: the ones for the cab worked; the ones for the trailer did not and the greater weight of the trailer had the effect of pushing the entire truck, even though the cab brakes were working), that Perez did not have enough time to apply the emergency brakes, and that there was nothing the managers or supervisors at Valley Coca-Cola could have done to prevent the accident.

[3] By his summary judgment affidavit offered in support of Perez, Joseph Connors stated that, in his professional opinion as a board certified criminal law specialist, if he had known that the statement had been provided and had been able to have Perez explain his lack of training or knowledge about the brake system to the grand jury, Perez would not have been indicted for manslaughter. . . .

under the DTPA, and that Perez failed to state a cause of action for conspiracy to violate the Texas Insurance Code. . . .

By his sole point of error, Perez complains simply that the trial court erred in granting Kirk & Carrigan's motion for summary judgment. The movant for summary judgment has the burden of showing that there is no genuine issue of material fact and that he is entitled to judgment as a matter of law. In deciding whether there is a disputed material fact issue precluding a summary judgment, evidence favorable to the non-movant will be taken as true, every reasonable inference must be indulged in the non-movant's favor, and any doubts must be resolved in his favor. . . .

Breach of Fiduciary Duty

With regard to Perez' cause of action for breach of the fiduciary duty of good faith and fair dealing, Kirk and Carrigan contend that no attorney-client relationship existed and no fiduciary duty arose, because Perez never sought legal advice from them.

An agreement to form an attorney-client relationship may be implied from the conduct of the parties. Moreover, the relationship does not depend upon the payment of a fee, but may exist as a result of rendering services gratuitously.[4]

In the present case, viewing the summary judgment evidence in the light most favorable to Perez, Kirk & Carrigan told him that, in addition to representing Valley Coca Cola, they were also Perez' lawyers and that they were going to help him. Perez did not challenge this assertion, and he cooperated with the lawyers in giving his statement to them, even though he did not offer, nor was he asked, to pay the lawyers' fees. We hold that this was sufficient to imply the creation of an attorney-client relationship at the time Perez gave his statement to Kirk & Carrigan.

The existence of this relationship encouraged Perez to trust Kirk & Carrigan, and gave rise to a corresponding duty on the part of the attorneys not to violate this position of trust. Accordingly, the relation between attorney and client is highly fiduciary in nature, and their dealings with each other are subject to the same scrutiny as a transaction between trustee and beneficiary. Specifically, the relationship between attorney and client has been described as one of uberrima fides, which means, "most abundant good faith," requiring absolute and perfect candor, openness and honesty, and the absence of any concealment or deception. In addition, because of the openness and candor within this relationship, certain communications between attorney and client are privileged from disclosure in either civil or criminal proceedings under

---

[4] An attorney's fiduciary responsibilities may arise even during preliminary consultations regarding the attorney's possible retention if the attorney enters into discussion of the client's legal problems with a view toward undertaking representation.

the provisions of Tex. R. Civ. Evid. 503 and Tex. R. Crim. Evid. 503, respectively. . . .

Kirk & Carrigan seek to avoid this claim of breach, on the ground that the attorney-client privilege did not apply to the present statement, because unnecessary third parties were present at the time it was given. . . . However, whether or not the Rule 503 attorney-client privilege extended to Perez' statement, Kirk & Carrigan initially obtained the statement from Perez on the understanding that it would be kept confidential. Thus, regardless of whether from an evidentiary standpoint the privilege attached, Kirk & Carrigan breached their fiduciary duty to Perez either by wrongfully disclosing a privileged statement or by wrongfully representing that an unprivileged statement would be kept confidential. Either characterization shows a clear lack of honesty toward, and a deception of, Perez by his own attorneys regarding the degree of confidentiality with which they intended to treat the statement.

This type of deceitful and fraudulent conduct within the attorney-client relationship has been treated as a tortious breach of duty in other contexts. *See* Burgin v. Godwin, 167 S.W.2d 614 (Tex.Civ.App.—Amarillo 1942, writ ref'd w.o.m.). . . .

In *Burgin*, for instance, the attorneys had a written agreement with their client for compensation, which the parties subsequently modified by an oral agreement. The attorneys later attempted to avoid the oral modification by asserting the statute of frauds. In holding that the attorneys were not entitled to the protections of the statute of frauds, the Amarillo Court of Appeals reasoned that the attorneys were under a duty to act with the most scrupulous fidelity and reveal to their client the exact status brought about by the contractual relationship and the need to reduce the oral modification to writing. . . .

Similarly, in the present case, the attorneys were at least under a fiduciary duty not to misrepresent to Perez that his conversations with them were confidential. Kirk & Carrigan should not now be able to assert the lack of attorney-client privilege (as the attorneys in *Burgin* were not allowed to assert the statute of frauds) to excuse the harm caused by their own misrepresentation to Perez. We hold that it was error for the trial court to grant summary judgment on the ground that Kirk & Carrigan did not owe or breach a fiduciary duty to Perez.

In addition, however, even assuming a breach of fiduciary duty, Kirk & Carrigan also contend that summary judgment may be sustained on the ground that Perez could show no damages resulting from the breach. Kirk & Carrigan contend that their dissemination of Perez' statement could not have caused him any damages in the way of emotional distress, because the statement merely revealed Perez' own version of what happened. We do not agree. Mental anguish consists of the emotional response of the plaintiff caused by the tortfeasor's conduct. It includes, among other things, the mental sensation of pain resulting from public humiliation.

Regardless of the fact that Perez himself made the present statement, he did not necessarily intend it to be a public response as Kirk & Carrigan contend, but only a private and confidential discussion with his attorneys. Perez alleged that the publicity caused by his indictment, resulting from the revelation of the statement to the district attorney in breach of that confidentiality, caused him to suffer emotional distress and mental anguish. We hold that Perez has made a valid claim for such damages. . . .

In conclusion, for the reasons stated above, we sustain Perez' point of error. We REVERSE the summary judgment rendered against Perez and REMAND this case for trial.

* * *

B. EXCEPTIONS TO THE LAWYER'S DUTY OF CONFIDENTIALITY

Please read ABA Model Rules of Professional Conduct, Rule 1.6(b) and Comments [6]–[17].

* * *

The confidentiality exceptions found in Model Rule 1.6(b) reflect situations in which the bar has determined a lawyer may disclose confidential information even though the client would prefer otherwise. Because these exceptions are contrary to the client's stated interests, the Model Rules refer to these exceptions as "Disclosure Adverse to Client." *See* Heading to Model Rule 1.6, Comments [6]–[17]. The exceptions reflect a policy decision that the defined interests of a third party or the lawyer's own interests outweigh the client's interest in confidentiality. The confidentiality exceptions have evolved over time. For example, in 2002, Model Rule 1.6(b) contained only four exceptions; in 2015, it contains seven.

Lawyers should be aware that confidentiality exceptions vary widely from jurisdiction to jurisdiction. Some examples of the differences are highlighted throughout this chapter. In practice, it is important to consult the jurisdiction's rule to determine whether a lawyer is prohibited, permitted, or required to disclose client confidences in a given situation.

This chapter focuses on the confidentiality exceptions contained in Model Rule 1.6(b). Other professional conduct rules (addressed throughout this textbook) cross-reference Rule 1.6(b), permitting disclosure of client confidences in a given situation if permitted by Rule

1.6(b). *See* Model Rule 1.6(b), Comment [17], citing Rules 1.2(d), 4.1(b), 8.1 and 8.3. Other rules permit the disclosure of confidences under the circumstances defined by the rule and without reference to Rule 1.6(b). *See* Model Rule 3.3 (concerning disclosure of a client's criminal or fraudulent conduct in a legal proceeding to the tribunal) and Model Rule 1.13(c) (concerning disclosure of organizational client's agent's misconduct to protect the organization from substantial injury).

1. DISCLOSURE REASONABLY NECESSARY TO PREVENT DEATH OR SUBSTANTIAL BODILY HARM

Please read ABA Model Rules of Professional Conduct, Rule 1.6(b)(1) and Comments [6], [16] & [17].

* * *

Model Rule 1.6(b)(1) permits, but does not require, the lawyer to disclose client confidences to the extent the lawyer reasonably believes necessary to prevent "reasonably certain death or substantial bodily harm." There are a number of possible alternative approaches with respect to the exception contained in Rule 1.6(b)(1). In some jurisdictions, the exception is stated in mandatory, rather than permissive, terms. Thus, a lawyer *must* disclose information to the extent reasonably necessary to prevent reasonably certain death or substantial bodily harm. *See, e.g.*, Ill. Rules of Prof'l Conduct R. 1.6(b). Prior to its amendment in 2002, the ABA Model Rule permitted a lawyer to disclose information relating to the representation to the extent the lawyer reasonably believes necessary to prevent the client from committing a criminal act the lawyer believes is likely to result in *imminent* death or substantial bodily harm.

* * *

Problem 14.5. While you are still representing Cynthia Burns in her divorce, she comes to your office and shows you a gun. She tells you she purchased it so she can "kill her cheating husband." What steps, if any, should you take prior to disclosing Cynthia's plan? If you determine that Cynthia is serious, would you disclose her plan to someone? If yes, to whom would you make your disclosure? Do Comments [6], [16], and [17] help you answer these questions?

* * *

2. DISCLOSURE REASONABLY NECESSARY TO PREVENT OR RECTIFY THE CONSEQUENCES OF CLIENT CRIME OR FRAUD

Please read ABA Model Rules of Professional Conduct, Rule 1.6(b)(2) & (3) and Comments [7], [8], [16] & [17].

* * *

The focus of subparts 2 and 3 of Model Rule 1.6(b) is preventing or mitigating the financial consequences of client crime or fraud. The rule requires that the client used the lawyer's services in furtherance of the crime or fraud. A crime is conduct for which there is a criminal penalty. In its simplest terms, fraud is lying to someone to obtain money. Fraud can be the basis of civil or criminal liability.

An attorney who believes his or her services are being used to perpetrate a crime or fraud should be concerned about the prospect of liability—not only for the client but also for the lawyer. Generally, a lawyer is not insulated from civil or criminal liability simply because she was acting on a client's behalf. Restatement (Third) of the Law Governing Lawyers §§ 8, 56 (2000). Thus, it is in the client's interest and the lawyer's that the client ceases the misconduct. The lawyer's ability to disclose client fraud may be significant in this circumstance. A client inclined to ignore the lawyer's advice to stop engaging in misconduct may be persuaded if the client understands the lawyer has the power to reveal the misconduct.

As is the case with the exception permitting disclosure to prevent death or substantial bodily harm, jurisdictions have taken different approaches with respect to the exception contained in Model Rule 1.6(b)(2) and (3). Below is a representative sample:

- Indiana Rule of Professional Conduct, Rule 1.6(b)(2): "may" reveal "to the extent the lawyer reasonably believes necessary . . . to prevent the client from committing a crime . . . ."

- Texas Rules of Professional Conduct, Rule 1.05(c)(7): "may" reveal "when the lawyer has reason to believe it is necessary to do so in order to prevent the client from committing a criminal or fraudulent act."

- Alaska Rules of Professional Conduct, Rule 1.6(b)(2): "may" reveal "to the extent the lawyer reasonably believes necessary to prevent a client from committing a crime or fraud that is reasonably certain to result in substantial injury to the financial interests or property of another. . . ."

- Wisconsin Rules of Professional Conduct, Rule 1.6(b): "shall reveal . . . to the extent the lawyer reasonably believes necessary to prevent the client from committing a criminal or fraudulent act that the lawyer reasonably believes is likely to result in death or substantial bodily harm or in substantial injury to the financial interest or property of another."

- New Jersey Rules of Professional Conduct, Rule 1.6(b)(1): "shall reveal . . . to the proper authorities, as soon as, and to the extent the lawyer reasonably believes necessary, to prevent the client or another person from committing a criminal, illegal or fraudulent act that the lawyer reasonably believes is likely to result in . . . substantial injury to the financial interests or property of another."

- Florida Rules of Professional Conduct, Rule 1.6(b)(1): "must reveal . . . to the extent the lawyer reasonably believes necessary to prevent a client from committing a crime."

* * *

Problem 14.6. You are working with Cynthia Burns to complete a draft of answers to interrogatories. As she talks to you about edits to the draft interrogatories, she mentions that she has found a clever way to hide assets from her soon-to-be ex-husband. She has invested about $10,000 in Bitcoins over the past year. You believe that failing to disclose the Bitcoin investment will amount to falsely answering one of the interrogatories and will ultimately defraud Burns' husband out of marital assets.

Outline a script for what you will say to Cynthia to dissuade her from lying about the $10,000 in assets. In addition to Rule 1.6(b)(2), do any other professional conduct rules apply in this situation?

Problem 14.7. During the course of your representation of Cynthia Burns in her divorce, she casually mentions an unrelated real estate venture. Cynthia admits that she has put in place a scheme to defraud investors of substantial sums of money. You counsel Cynthia that her conduct will harm the investors, and you explain the civil and criminal consequences of her conduct. You urge her to take corrective action, but Cynthia laughs and says, "I'll take my chances." Under Model Rule 1.6(b)(2) or (3), may you disclose confidential information to protect the investors from financial harm?

* * *

3. DISCLOSURE REASONABLY NECESSARY TO SECURE LEGAL ADVICE

Please read ABA Model Rules of Professional Conduct, Rule 1.6(b)(4) and Comments [9], [16] & [17].

* * *

Model Rule 1.6(b)(4) allows a lawyer to disclose confidential client information in order to obtain legal advice about the lawyer's compliance with professional conduct rules. This rule encourages attorneys to seek help in determining how to fulfill their professional conduct obligations.

* * *

Problem 14.8. You have completed some research and believe you may be participating in Cynthia Burns' fraud if you do not reveal the $10,000 in Bitcoins in answers to interrogatories (referenced in Problem 14.6). You want to get a second opinion about how you should handle the situation. Who might you consult in order to determine your professional conduct obligations and what can you reveal to him or her?

* * *

4. DISCLOSURE REASONABLY NECESSARY TO ESTABLISH A CLAIM OR DEFENSE BY THE LAWYER

Please read ABA Model Rules of Professional Conduct, Rule 1.6(b)(5) and Comments [10], [11], [16] & [17].

* * *

Model Rule 1.6(b)(5) allows a lawyer to disclose confidences to the extent necessary: (1) for the lawyer to state a claim or defense in a "controversy" with the client; (2) for the lawyer to defend against a "criminal charge or civil claim" based upon conduct in which client was involved; or (3) for the lawyer "to respond to allegations in any proceeding" related to the lawyer's representation of the client. The first category covers disclosure in a lawyer's lawsuit against a client for an unpaid fee, as well as disclosure to defend against a client's malpractice claim. The second category encompasses the lawyer's ability to defend against a civil lawsuit filed by a third party claiming, for example, that lawyer and client defrauded the third party. This second category also allows the lawyer to disclose confidences to the extent necessary to defend against a criminal charge arising out of the lawyer's representation of the client. Finally, the third category allows a lawyer to disclose client confidences to respond to a proceeding such as an ethics complaint against the lawyer.

In this age of online customer reviews, can a lawyer defend against a negative client review on a website like Yelp or AVVO? Review Rule 1.6(b)(5) and Comments [10], [11], [16], and [17] as you consider this issue in the context of Problem 14.9.

* * *

Problem 14.9. After the conclusion of Cynthia Burns' divorce, your secretary alerts you to a negative, anonymous review on Yelp. You read the review and immediately realize it was posted by Cynthia Burns. Cynthia's post reads:

> *This attorney cost me a fortune in my divorce! The ironic thing is that we were friends when I hired her, but we aren't friends anymore. If you want to have two coins to rub together at the end of your divorce, I highly recommend getting a different lawyer!*

You immediately respond with the following post:

> *I want my clients to be happy with my representation, but I refuse to lie and cheat for them. The client who wrote this review wanted to hide $10,000 in Bitcoins from her husband. I won't be a party to fraud! I convinced her that she had to tell the truth when we answered interrogatories about her assets. Sorry that this client doesn't have her 10,000 Bitcoins to rub together, but I refuse to lie for any client.*

Have you violated Rule 1.6 or was your disclosure consistent with Rule 1.6(b)(5)? Do Comments [10], [11], [16], and [17] help or hurt an argument that your disclosure is appropriate?

* * *

5. DISCLOSURE REASONABLY NECESSARY TO COMPLY WITH OTHER LAW OR A COURT ORDER

Please read ABA Model Rules of Professional Conduct, Rule 1.6(b)(6) and Comments [12] & [15]–[17].

* * *

Model Rule 1.6(b)(6) permits an attorney to disclose confidential client information to the extent necessary to comply with "other law" or "a court order." The "court order" exception may arise in litigation (in discovery or at trial) when an attorney asserts that certain information is protected by the attorney-client privilege, but the court nonetheless orders the disclosure of the information. Comment [15] explains that a lawyer "should assert on behalf of the client all nonfrivolous claims" that the disclosure is not authorized by law. The comment concludes that if ultimately compelled to disclose information, the lawyer should consult with the client about a possible appeal and if review is not sought, the lawyer may reveal the information consistent with the court's order.

The "other law" exception is addressed in Comment [12]. It provides that the question of whether other law trumps the confidentiality rule is "a question of law beyond the scope of these Rules." Thus, if an attorney learns information in the representation of a client (such as information about child abuse) and the attorney's research reveals a legal obligation to reveal that information (such as a statute requiring persons to report child abuse to a state agency), the attorney must conduct additional research to determine which obligation prevails. The answer can vary from jurisdiction to jurisdiction. The following case from Onondaga County, New York, resolves the question of whether New York public health laws supersede a New York attorney's duty of confidentiality to his client.

* * *

PEOPLE V. BELGE

372 N.Y.S.2d 798 (Onondaga Co. Ct. 1975)

ORMAND N. GALE, JUDGE.

In the summer of 1973 Robert F. Garrow, Jr. stood charged in Hamilton County with the crime of murder. The Defendant was assigned two attorneys, Frank H. Armani and Francis R. Belge. A defense of insanity had been interposed by counsel for Mr. Garrow. During the course of the discussions between Garrow and his two counsel, three other murders were admitted by Garrow, one being in Onondaga County. On or about September of 1973 Mr. Belge conducted his own investigation based upon what his client had told him and with the assistance of a friend the location of the body of Alicia Hauck was found in Oakwood Cemetery in Syracuse. Mr. Belge personally inspected the body and was satisfied, presumably, that this was the Alicia Hauck that his client had told him that he murdered.

This discovery was not disclosed to the authorities, but became public during the trial of Mr. Garrow in June of 1974, when to affirmatively establish the defense of insanity, these three other murders were brought before the jury by the defense in the Hamilton County trial. Public indignation reached the fever pitch; statements were made by the District Attorney of Onondaga County relative to the situation and he caused the Grand Jury of Onondaga County, then sitting, to conduct a thorough investigation. As a result of this investigation Frank Armani was No Billed by the Grand Jury but Indictment No. 75–55 was returned as against Francis R. Belge, Esq., accusing him of having violated § 4200(1) of the Public Health Law, which, in essence, requires that a decent burial be accorded the dead, and § 4143 of the Public Health Law, which, in essence, requires anyone knowing of the death of a person without medical attendance, to report the same to the proper authorities. Defense counsel moves for a dismissal of the Indictment on the grounds that a confidential, privileged communication existed between him and Mr. Garrow, which should excuse the attorney from making full disclosure to the authorities.

The National Association of Criminal Defense Lawyers, as Amicus Curiae . . . succinctly state the issue in the following language:

> If this indictment stands, "The attorney-client privilege will be effectively destroyed. No defendant will be able to freely discuss the facts of his case with his attorney. No attorney will be able to listen to those facts without being faced with the Hobson's choice of violating the law or violating his professional code of Ethics."

. . . .

In the most recent issue of the New York State Bar Journal (June 1975) there is an article by Jack B. Weinstein, entitled "Educating Ethical Lawyers." In a sub-caption to this article is the following language which is pertinent: "The most difficult ethical dilemmas result from the frequent conflicts between the obligation to one's client and those to the legal system and to society. It is in this area that legal education has its greatest responsibility, and can have its greatest effects." In the course of his article Mr. Weinstein states that there are three major types of pressure facing a practicing lawyer. He uses the following language to describe these:

> First, there are those that originate in the attorney's search for his own well-being. Second, pressures arise from the attorney's obligation to his client. Third, the lawyer has certain obligations to the courts, the legal system, and society in general.

Our system of criminal justice is an adversary system and the interests of the state are not absolute, or even paramount. "The dignity of the individual is respected to the point that even when the citizen is known by the state to have committed a heinous offense, the individual is nevertheless accorded such rights as counsel, trial by jury, due process, and the privilege against self incrimination."[3]

A trial is in part a search for truth, but it is only partly a search for truth. The mantle of innocence is flung over the defendant to such an extent that he is safeguarded by rules of evidence which frequently keep out absolute truth, much to the chagrin of juries. Nevertheless, this has been a part of our system since our laws were taken from the laws of

---

[3]   Criminal Law Bulletin (Dec. 1974). Article by Monroe H. Freedman.

England and over these many years has been found to best protect a balance between the rights of the individual and the rights of society.

The concept of the right to counsel has again been with us for a long time, but since the decision of Gideon v. Wainwright, 372 U.S. 335, it has been extended more and more so that at the present time a defendant is entitled to have counsel at a parole hearing or a probation violation hearing.

The effectiveness of counsel is only as great as the confidentiality of its client-attorney relationship. If the lawyer cannot get all the facts about the case, he can only give his client half of a defense. This, of necessity, involves the client telling his attorney everything remotely connected with the crime.

Apparently, in the instant case, after analyzing all the evidence, and after hearing of the bizarre episodes in the life of their client, they decided that the only possibility of salvation was in a defense of insanity. For the client to disclose not only everything about this particular crime but also everything about other crimes which might have a bearing upon his defense, requires the strictest confidence in, and on the part of, the attorney.

When the facts of the other homicides became public, as a result of the defendant's testimony to substantiate his claim of insanity, "Members of the public were shocked at the apparent callousness of these lawyers, whose conduct was seen as typifying the unhealthy lack of concern of most lawyers with the public interest and with simple decency." A hue and cry went up from the press and other news media suggesting that the attorneys should be found guilty of such crimes as obstruction of justice or becoming an accomplice after the fact. From a layman's standpoint, this certainly was a logical conclusion. However, the constitution of the United States of America attempts to preserve the dignity of the individual and to do that guarantees him the services of an attorney who will bring to the bar and to the bench every conceivable protection from the inroads of the state against such rights as are vested in the constitution for one accused of crime. Among those substantial constitutional rights is that a defendant does not have to incriminate himself. His attorneys were bound to uphold that concept and maintain what has been called a sacred trust of confidentiality.

The following language from the brief of the Amicus Curiae further points up the statements just made:

> The client's Fifth Amendment rights cannot be violated by his attorney. There is no viable distinction between the personal papers and criminal evidence in the hands or mind of the client. Because the discovery of the body of Alicia Hauck would have presented "a significant link in a chain of evidence tending to

establish his guilt" (Leary v. United States, 395 U.S. 6 (1969)), Garrow was constitutionally exempt from any statutory requirement to disclose the location of the body. And Attorney Belge, as Garrow's attorney, was not only equally exempt, but under a positive stricture precluding such disclosure. Garrow, although constitutionally privileged against a requirement of compulsory disclosure, was free to make such a revelation if he chose to do so. Attorney Belge was affirmatively required to withhold disclosure. The criminal defendant's self-incrimination rights become completely nugatory if compulsory disclosure can be exacted through his attorney.

In the case at bar we must weigh the importance of the general privilege of confidentiality in the performance of the defendant's duties as an attorney, against the inroads of such a privilege, on the fair administration of criminal justice as well as the heart tearing that went on in the victim's family by reason of their uncertainty as to the whereabouts of Alicia Hauck. In this type situation the Court must balance the rights of the individual against the rights of society as a whole. There is no question but Attorney Belge's failure to bring to the attention of the authorities the whereabouts of Alicia Hauck when he first verified it, prevented bringing Garrow to the immediate bar of justice for this particular murder. This was in a sense, obstruction of justice. This duty, I am sure, loomed large in the mind of Attorney Belge. However, against this was the Fifth Amendment right of his client, Garrow, not to incriminate himself. If the Grand Jury had returned an indictment charging Mr. Belge with obstruction of justice under a proper statute, the work of this Court would have been much more difficult than it is.

There must always be a conflict between the obstruction of the administration of criminal justice and the preservation of the right against self-incrimination which permeates the mind of the attorney as the alter ego of his client. But that is not the situation before this Court. We have the Fifth Amendment right, derived from the constitution, on the one hand, as against the trivia of a pseudo-criminal statute on the other, which has seldom been brought into play. Clearly the latter is completely out of focus when placed alongside the client-attorney privilege. An examination of the Grand Jury testimony sheds little light on their reasoning. The testimony of Mr. Armani added nothing new to the facts as already presented to the Grand Jury. He and Mr. Belge were co-counsel. Both were answerable to the Canons of professional ethics. The Grand Jury chose to indict one and not the other. It appears as if that body were grasping at straws.

It is the decision of this Court that Francis R. Belge conducted himself as an officer of the Court with all the zeal at his command to protect the constitutional rights of his client. Both on the grounds of a privileged communication and in the interests of justice the Indictment is dismissed.

* * *

6. DISCLOSURE REASONABLY NECESSARY TO DETECT CONFLICTS OF INTEREST

Please read ABA Model Rules of Professional Conduct, Rule 1.6(b)(7) and Comments [13], [14], [16] & [17].

* * *

When a lawyer considers moving to a new firm and when groups of lawyers consider merging two firms, it is necessary to know whether the change will create a conflict of interest. For example, assume that lawyer Sue has practiced law for many years at a small law firm. Sue would like to join a new law firm, but Sue and the new firm want to be sure that such a move would not create a conflict of interest. A conflict of interest would exist if Sue represents ABC Lighting in a pending matter and her proposed new firm currently has a case adverse to ABC Lighting.

Model Rule 1.6(b)(7) allows lawyers in Sue's situation to reveal information necessary to detect and resolve conflicts of interest. The rule prohibits revealing information that would compromise the attorney-client privilege or otherwise prejudice a client. Conflicts of interest will be addressed further in Chapters 16, 17, and 19.

* * *

Profile of attorney professionalism. Jamie Kunz and Dale Coventry knew that their client Andrew Wilson killed a security guard in a Chicago McDonald's in 1982. But Wilson was never charged with the crime. Instead, an innocent man, Alton Logan, was convicted and sentenced to life in prison.

Attorneys Kunz and Coventry knew that prosecutors had the wrong man in 1982. They describe Wilson as "kind of gleeful" when he told them that he was the one who killed the McDonald's security guard but that Logan had been charged with the crime. Kunz and Coventry even watched parts of the Logan trial. They did not want to see an innocent man go to jail, but they knew they had a legal and ethical obligation not to disclose their client's confession to the crime.

In a 2008 interview, Coventry acknowledged public sentiment that the lawyers should have disclosed that the wrong man was in prison. Coventry said that while the issue is not "morally clear" the requirement that lawyers maintain client confidentiality is essential to our legal system. Coventry and Kunz explained that they researched the issue and sought legal advice on the issue, and determined that they could not disclose their client's information. They concluded that even if they did disclose the information, it would likely be inadmissible in court because their disclosure would have violated the attorney-client privilege.

When asked if they were silent to avoid disbarment, Coventry answered, "I don't think I considered [disbarment] as much as I considered my responsibility to my client. I was very concerned to protect him."

Coventry and Kunz recognized they could reveal Wilson's confession if they had his permission. They asked Wilson if he would agree that they could disclose his identity as the shooter after Wilson's death. He agreed. So when Wilson died in 2007, Coventry and Kunz disclosed that Wilson had committed the murder. Their disclosure eventually lead to Alton Logan's release from prison in 2008. He had served twenty-six years behind bars for a crime he did not commit.

60 Minutes, *26-Year Secret Kept Innocent Man in Prison*, http://www.cbs news.com/news/26-year-secret-kept-innocent-man-in-prison/1/.

While many people criticized Coventry and Kunz for their silence, they acted consistent with their legal and professional obligations under Illinois law. Some states have concluded that a different professional conduct rule is appropriate in this situation. Both Massachusetts and Alaska have adopted rules permitting attorneys to disclose confidential client information to the extent necessary to prevent the wrongful execution or incarceration of another.

CHAPTER 15

ATTORNEY-CLIENT PRIVILEGE, WORK PRODUCT, AND COMPETENTLY PROTECTING CLIENT INFORMATION

■ ■ ■

Chapter Hypothetical. You represent Convinsio Corporation in litigation with its competitor Kinsera Inc. Both companies are in the business of providing web-based marketing services for nonprofit corporations. In January 2015, Kinsera filed a complaint in federal court alleging claims against Convinsio for copyright infringement. Kinsera alleges that in April and May 2014, Convinsio improperly accessed Kinsera's password-protected website and copied Kinsera's proprietary and copyrighted computer program codes which it then improperly used to develop its own website. Convinsio denies these allegations. The case has now entered the discovery phase.

* * *

A. THE ATTORNEY-CLIENT PRIVILEGE

Please read ABA Model Rules of Professional Conduct, Rule 1.6 and Comment [3].

Please read Restatement (Third) of the Law Governing Lawyers §§ 68–72 & 86.

In litigation, lawyer and client cannot be compelled to testify or otherwise provide information regarding their communications made in confidence for the purpose of obtaining or providing legal assistance. This is the attorney-client privilege. The purpose of the attorney-client privilege is to encourage open, unguarded communication between attorney and client, so that the client is more likely to receive appropriate legal advice. *See* Hunt v. Blackburn, 128 U.S. 464, 470, 9 S.Ct. 125, 127 (1888) (explaining that attorney-client privilege "is founded upon the necessity, in the interest and administration of justice, of the aid of persons having knowledge of the law and skilled in its practice, which assistance can only be safely and readily availed of when free from the consequences or the apprehension of disclosure.").

It may be helpful to consider an example. Suppose a client emails his attorney with a question about whether the client has a cause of action for employment discrimination. The email is protected by the attorney-client privilege because it reflects a confidential communication between attorney and client for the purpose of seeking legal advice. The attorney's confidential response to the client—analyzing the client's chance of prevailing in an employment discrimination suit—is also privileged.

In order to invoke the attorney-client privilege, the attorney must object when the information is requested in litigation, such as in a written discovery request, in a deposition, or at trial. For example, suppose that opposing counsel makes a request for production of documents that seeks: "All email communications between Plaintiff and Plaintiff's attorney from June 1, 2014 to the present." The law of attorney-client privilege provides the basis for counsel to refuse the request. The attorney would object in writing ("Plaintiff objects to producing the requested information because it is protected by the attorney-client privilege."), refuse to produce the information, and describe the withheld documents on a "privilege log" (required by Federal Rule of Civil Procedure 26(b)(5)(A) and state court rules of civil procedure).

The privilege protects from disclosure the attorney-client communication, but that does not mean facts can be hidden from an opponent by communicating them to an attorney. For example, suppose a client's confidential email to her attorney states, "I ran the red light, but I still think the accident happened because the defendant was speeding. Do you think I can win anyway?" While the email between attorney and client is privileged, the client's belief that she ran the red light is not. Because of privilege, the defendant cannot obtain the email in discovery or ask the client "What did you tell your attorney about the accident?" However, the defendant is entitled to ask the plaintiff (in an interrogatory, request for admissions, or in a deposition), "Did you run the red light?" There is no basis to object that the information is privileged simply because it was communicated to an attorney.

At first blush, the attorney's duty of confidentiality and the attorney-client privilege may appear to be similar, but they are different in several important ways. First, the source of law for each is distinct. An attorney has a legal duty of confidentiality because of the fiduciary relationship between attorney and client. This duty is also a professional conduct obligation embodied in Model Rule 1.6. The attorney-client privilege is an evidentiary privilege that is embodied in rules of evidence, statutes and/or case law depending on the jurisdiction. In federal court, Federal Rule of Evidence 501 provides that privilege is "governed by the principles of the common law as they may be interpreted by courts of the United States in light of reason and experience." This evidentiary rule also provides that if the state law applies in the case, then state privilege law applies. As a result, federal courts look to state privilege law to resolve privilege issues in cases filed in the court based on diversity jurisdiction.

Second, more information is encompassed within the confidentiality obligation than within attorney-client privilege. Under Rule 1.6, a lawyer must keep in confidence *all information* learned in the representation of a client. This includes privileged information (such as a client's email to her lawyer seeking legal advice about an issue) and non-privileged information (such as the client's name, the type of lawsuit the lawyer filed on the client's behalf, information the client's friend told the lawyer, and information the client told the lawyer in the presence of a third party). As a result, an attorney can violate the duty of confidentiality by disclosing even non-privileged information. Recall the hypotheticals about client Cynthia Burns' divorce in the previous chapter. Suppose that Cynthia's attorney discloses to a friend, "Cynthia's divorce is getting messy. Her husband claims in a court filing that she is a heroin addict." The attorney has not disclosed privileged information, but the attorney has violated the confidentiality obligation.

Third, the contexts in which the issues of confidentiality and privilege arise are different. The confidentiality duty obligates a lawyer to not discuss with third parties any information learned while representing clients, absent client consent or an exception. In contrast, the attorney-client privilege is invoked in litigation. It is the basis for an attorney to object to any question seeking information about confidential communications between client and attorney for the purpose of giving or receiving legal advice.

Finally, consequences of disclosure are distinct. If an attorney violates the confidentiality obligation, the attorney may be disciplined by the bar and may be sued by the client for violating fiduciary duty. When privileged information is disclosed to a third party by an attorney or client, a court may be asked to determine whether the disclosure waived the privilege. If the court finds privilege was waived, the information may be offered as evidence at trial. The issue of privilege waiver will be discussed further later in this chapter.

* * *

The attorney-client privilege extends to organizational clients, such as corporations. Federal courts disagreed about which employees' communications with counsel were covered by the privilege until the U.S. Supreme Court addressed the issue in the following case.

[handwritten: foreign subsidiary & illegal bribes. IRs demanded docs.]

UPJOHN COMPANY V. UNITED STATES

[handwritten: ACP applies to corp. ✓]

449 U.S. 383 (1981)

JUSTICE REHNQUIST delivered the opinion of the Court.

We granted certiorari in this case to address important questions concerning the scope of the attorney-client privilege in the corporate context and the applicability of the work-product doctrine in proceedings to enforce tax summonses.... With respect to the privilege question the parties and various amici have described our task as one of choosing between two "tests" which have gained adherents in the courts of appeals. We are acutely aware, however, that we sit to decide concrete cases and not abstract propositions of law. We decline to lay down a broad rule or series of rules to govern all conceivable future questions in this area, even were we able to do so. We can and do, however, conclude that the attorney-client privilege protects the communications involved in this case from compelled disclosure and that the work-product doctrine does apply in tax summons enforcement proceedings.

I

Petitioner Upjohn Co. manufactures and sells pharmaceuticals here and abroad. In January 1976 independent accountants conducting an audit of one of Upjohn's foreign subsidiaries discovered that the subsidiary made payments to or for the benefit of foreign government officials in order to secure government business. The accountants, so informed petitioner, Mr. Gerard Thomas, Upjohn's Vice President, Secretary, and General Counsel. Thomas is a member of the Michigan and New York Bars, and has been Upjohn's General Counsel for 20 years. He consulted with outside counsel and R.T. Parfet, Jr., Upjohn's Chairman of the Board. It was decided that the company would conduct an internal investigation of what were termed "questionable payments." As part of this investigation the attorneys prepared a letter containing a questionnaire which was sent to "All Foreign General and Area Managers" over the Chairman's signature. The letter began by noting recent disclosures that several American companies made "possibly illegal" payments to foreign government officials and emphasized that the management needed full information concerning any such payments made by Upjohn. The letter indicated that the Chairman had asked Thomas, identified as "the company's General Counsel," "to conduct an investigation for the purpose of determining the nature and magnitude of any payments made by the Upjohn Company or any of its subsidiaries to any employee or official of a foreign government." The questionnaire sought detailed information concerning such payments. Managers were instructed to treat the investigation as "highly confidential" and not to discuss it with anyone other than Upjohn employees who might be helpful in providing the requested information. Responses were to be sent directly to Thomas. Thomas and outside counsel also interviewed the recipients of the questionnaire and some 33 other Upjohn officers or employees as part of the investigation.

On March 26, 1976, the company voluntarily submitted a preliminary report to the Securities and Exchange Commission on Form 8–K disclosing certain questionable payments. A copy of the report was simultaneously submitted to the Internal Revenue Service, which immediately began an investigation to determine the tax consequences of the payments. Special agents conducting the investigation were given lists by Upjohn of all those interviewed and all who had responded to the questionnaire. On November 23, 1976, the Service issued a summons pursuant to 26 U.S.C. § 7602 demanding production of:

> All files relative to the investigation conducted under the supervision of Gerard Thomas to identify payments to employees of foreign governments and any political contributions made by the Upjohn Company or any of its affiliates since January 1, 1971 and to determine whether any funds of the Upjohn Company had been improperly accounted for on the corporate books during the same period.

> The records should include but not be limited to written questionnaires sent to managers of the Upjohn Company's foreign affiliates, and memorandums or notes of the interviews conducted in the United States and abroad with officers and employees of the Upjohn Company and its subsidiaries.

... The company declined to produce the documents specified in the second paragraph on the grounds that they were protected from disclosure by the attorney-client privilege and constituted the work product of attorneys prepared in anticipation of litigation. On August 31, 1977, the United States filed a petition seeking enforcement of the summons ... in the United States District Court for the Western District of Michigan. That court ... concluded that the summons should be enforced. Petitioners appealed to the Court of Appeals for the Sixth Circuit which ... agreed that the privilege did not apply "[t]o the extent that the communications were made by officers and agents not responsible for directing Upjohn's actions in response to legal advice ... for the simple reason that the communications were not the 'client's.'" ... Noting that Upjohn's counsel had interviewed officials such as the Chairman and President, the Court of Appeals remanded to the District Court so that a determination of who was within the "control group" could be made. In a concluding footnote the court stated that the work-product doctrine "is not applicable to administrative summonses issued under 26 U.S.C. § 7602." ...

II

Federal Rule of Evidence 501 provides that "the privilege of a witness . . . shall be governed by the principles of the common law as they may be interpreted by the courts of the United States in light of reason and experience." The attorney-client privilege is the oldest of the privileges for confidential communications known to the common law. 8 J. Wigmore, Evidence § 2290 (McNaughton rev. 1961). Its purpose is to encourage full and frank communication between attorneys and their clients and thereby promote broader public interests in the observance of law and administration of justice. The privilege recognizes that sound legal advice or advocacy serves public ends and that such advice or advocacy depends upon the lawyer's being fully informed by the client. . . . Admittedly complications in the application of the privilege arise when the client is a corporation, which in theory is an artificial creature of the law, and not an individual; but this Court has assumed that the privilege applies when the client is a corporation . . . , and the Government does not contest the general proposition.

The Court of Appeals, however, considered the application of the privilege in the corporate context to present a "different problem," since the client was an inanimate entity and "only the senior management, guiding and integrating the several operations, . . . can be said to possess an identity analogous to the corporation as a whole." . . . The first case to articulate the so-called "control group test" adopted by the court below, Philadelphia v. Westinghouse Electric Corp., 210 F. Supp. 483, 485 (E.D. Pa.), *petition for mandamus and prohibition denied sub nom.* General Electric Co. v. Kirkpatrick, 312 F.2d 742 (CA3 1962), *cert. denied*, 372 U.S. 943 (1963), reflected a similar conceptual approach:

> Keeping in mind that the question is, Is it the corporation which is seeking the lawyer's advice when the asserted privileged communication is made?, the most satisfactory solution, I think, is that if the employee making the communication, of whatever rank he may be, is in a position to control or even to take a substantial part in a decision about any action which the corporation may take upon the advice of the attorney, . . . then, in effect, *he is (or personifies) the corporation* when he makes his disclosure to the lawyer and the privilege would apply. (Emphasis supplied.)

Such a view, we think, overlooks the fact that the privilege exists to protect not only the giving of professional advice to those who can act on it but also the giving of information to the lawyer to enable him to give sound and informed advice. . . .

In the case of the individual client the provider of information and the person who acts on the lawyer's advice are one and the same. In the corporate context, however, it will frequently be employees beyond the control group as defined by the court below—"officers and agents ... responsible for directing [the company's] actions in response to legal advice"—who will possess the information needed by the corporation's lawyers. Middle-level—and indeed lower-level—employees can, by actions within the scope of their employment, embroil the corporation in serious legal difficulties, and it is only natural that these employees would have the relevant information needed by corporate counsel if he is adequately to advise the client with respect to such actual or potential difficulties. This fact was noted in Diversified Industries, Inc. v. Meredith, 572 F.2d 596, 608–09 (CA8 1978) (en banc):

> In a corporation, it may be necessary to glean information relevant to a legal problem from middle management or non-management personnel as well as from top executives. The attorney dealing with a complex legal problem "is thus faced with a 'Hobson's choice.' If he interviews employees not having 'the very highest authority,' their communications to him will not be privileged. If, on the other hand, he interviews only those employees with the 'very highest authority,' he may find it extremely difficult, if not impossible, to determine what happened."

. . .

The control group test adopted by the court below thus frustrates the very purpose of the privilege by discouraging the communication of relevant information by employees of the client to attorneys seeking to render legal advice to the client corporation. The attorney's advice will also frequently be more significant to noncontrol group members than to those who officially sanction the advice, and the control group test makes it more difficult to convey full and frank legal advice to the employees who will put into effect the client corporation's policy.

The narrow scope given the attorney-client privilege by the court below not only makes it difficult for corporate attorneys to formulate sound advice when their client is faced with a specific legal problem but also threatens to limit the valuable efforts of corporate counsel to ensure their client's compliance with the law. In light of the vast and complicated array of regulatory legislation confronting the modern corporation, corporations, unlike most individuals, "constantly go to lawyers to find out how to obey the law," . . . particularly since compliance with the law in this area is hardly an instinctive matter . . . [2]. The test adopted by the

---

[2]   The Government argues that the risk of civil or criminal liability suffices to ensure that corporations will seek legal advice in the absence of the protection of the privilege. This response ignores the fact that the depth and quality of any investigations, to ensure compliance with the law would suffer, even were they undertaken. The response also proves too much, since it applies to all communications covered by the privilege: an individual trying to comply with the law or

court below is difficult to apply in practice, though no abstractly formulated and unvarying "test" will necessarily enable courts to decide questions such as this with mathematical precision. But if the purpose of the attorney-client privilege is to be served, the attorney and client must be able to predict with some degree of certainty whether particular discussions will be protected. An uncertain privilege, or one which purports to be certain but results in widely varying applications by the courts, is little better than no privilege at all. The very terms of the test adopted by the court below suggest the unpredictability of its application. The test restricts the availability of the privilege to those officers who play a "substantial role" in deciding and directing a corporation's legal response. Disparate decisions in cases applying this test illustrate its unpredictability.

The communications at issue were made by Upjohn employees[3] to counsel for Upjohn acting as such, at the direction of corporate superiors in order to secure legal advice from counsel. . . . Information, not available from upper-echelon management, was needed to supply a basis for legal advice concerning compliance with securities and tax laws, foreign laws, currency regulations, duties to shareholders, and potential litigation in each of these areas. The communications concerned matters within the scope of the employees' corporate duties, and the employees themselves were sufficiently aware that they were being questioned in order that the corporation could obtain legal advice. The questionnaire identified Thomas as "the company's General Counsel" and referred in its opening sentence to the possible illegality of payments such as the ones on which information was sought. . . . A statement of policy accompanying the questionnaire clearly indicated the legal implications of the investigation. . . . This statement was issued to Upjohn employees worldwide, so that even those interviewees not receiving a questionnaire were aware of the legal implications of the interviews. Pursuant to explicit instructions from the Chairman of the Board, the communications were considered "highly confidential" when made . . . and have been kept confidential by the company. Consistent with the underlying purposes of the attorney-client privilege, these communications must be protected against compelled disclosure.

The Court of Appeals declined to extend the attorney-client privilege beyond the limits of the control group test for fear that doing so would

---

faced with a legal problem also has strong incentive to disclose information to his lawyer, yet the common law has recognized the value of the privilege in further facilitating communications.

   [3] Seven of the eighty-six employees interviewed by counsel had terminated their employment with Upjohn at the time of the interview. . . . Petitioners argue that the privilege should nonetheless apply to communications by these former employees concerning activities during their period of employment. Neither the District Court nor the Court of Appeals had occasion to address this issue, and we decline to decide it without the benefit of treatment below.

entail severe burdens on discovery and create a broad "zone of silence" over corporate affairs. Application of the attorney-client privilege to communications such as those involved here, however, puts the adversary in no worse position than if the communications had never taken place. The privilege only protects disclosure of communications; it does not protect disclosure of the underlying facts by those who communicated with the attorney:

> [T]he protection of the privilege extends only to *communications* and not to facts. A fact is one thing and a communication concerning that fact is an entirely different thing. The client cannot be compelled to answer the question, "What did you say or write to the attorney?" but may not refuse to disclose any relevant fact within his knowledge merely because he incorporated a statement of such fact into his communication to his attorney.

Philadelphia v. Westinghouse Electric Corp., 205 F. Supp. 830, 831. . . . Here the Government was free to question the employees who communicated with Thomas and outside counsel. Upjohn has provided the IRS with a list of such employees, and the IRS has already interviewed some 25 of them. While it would probably be more convenient for the Government to secure the results of petitioner's internal investigation by simply subpoenaing the questionnaires and notes taken by petitioner's attorneys, such considerations of convenience do not overcome the policies served by the attorney-client privilege. As Justice Jackson noted in his concurring opinion in Hickman v. Taylor, [329 U.S. 495, 516 (1947)]: "Discovery was hardly intended to enable a learned profession to perform its functions . . . on wits borrowed from the adversary."

[W]e conclude that the narrow "control group test" sanctioned by the Court of Appeals, in this case cannot, consistent with "the principles of the common law as . . . interpreted . . . in the light of reason and experience," Fed. Rule Evid. 501, govern the development of the law in this area. . . . Accordingly, the judgment of the Court of Appeals is reversed, and the case remanded for further proceedings.

[Concurring in part and concurring in the judgment, CHIEF JUSTICE BURGER joined in Part I of the Court's opinion but objected to the Court's refusal to "articulate a standard that will govern similar cases and afford guidance to corporations, counsel advising them, and federal courts."]

* * *

When state law (rather than federal law) is applicable, the contours of the organizational client's attorney-client privilege may be defined differently. For example, Illinois courts apply the control group test.

Consolidation Coal Co. v. Bucyrus-Erie Co., 432 N.E.2d 250, 257–58 (Ill. 1982) (holding that the control group test is applicable in the corporate client context and elaborating on which individuals should be considered members of the control group). In Arizona, the communications encompassed within the organizational client's attorney-client privilege are described in the following excerpt.

All communications initiated by the employee and made in confidence to counsel, in which the communicating employee is directly seeking legal advice [on behalf of the corporation] are privileged. In contrast, where an investigation is initiated by the corporation, factual communications from the corporate employees to corporate counsel are within the corporation's privilege only if they concern the employee's own conduct within the scope of his or her employment and are made to assist counsel in assessing or responding to the legal consequences of that conduct for the corporate client.

Samaritan Foundation v. Goodfarb, 862 P.2d 870 (Ariz. 1993) (en banc).

Additional issues related to organizational clients and privilege are considered in Chapter 25.

* * *

Problem 15.1. Kinsera's First Request for Production of Documents to Convinsio contains the following request: "Produce all communications sent from Convinsio employees or received by Convinsio employees that refer or relate to the Kinsera website during the time period of April 1, 2014 to May 31, 2014." During your review of Convinsio's documents, you found a number of documents that you know you must produce in response to this request. You also found the following documents that you think may be protected by the attorney-client privilege. Analyze whether each document is or is not protected by the attorney-client privilege.

(A) In a May 5, 2014 email, Convinsio's marketing director, Rhonda Harvey, tells attorney Henry Lee that Convinsio is creating a new website that contains similar elements to that found on Kinsera's website. Rhonda wants Henry to provide advice about whether Convinsio is doing anything that violates copyright law or any other law.

(B) In another May 5, 2014 email, Henry Lee responds to Rhonda Harvey's email and tells her he'll need additional information to answer her question. He asks her some questions about the new website that Convinsio is developing and how it is similar to Kinsera's website.

(C) Rhonda Harvey's handwritten notes (dated May 5, 2014), outline a telephone conversation between Rhonda Harvey and Henry Lee concerning steps Convinsio should take to avoid infringing Kinsera's copyright as Convinsio develops its new website.

Problem 15.2. What steps should you take to assert the attorney-client privilege when you respond to Kinsera's First Request for Production of Documents to Convinsio?

* * *

B. WORK PRODUCT DOCTRINE

Please read Restatement (Third) of the Law Governing Lawyers §§ 87–90.

Please read Federal Rules of Civil Procedure, Rule 26(b)(3) & (4).

Work product doctrine (also known as "work product protection") is a body of law that protects information prepared for trial or in anticipation of litigation by a party or a party's agent. The purpose of the doctrine is to allow parties to prepare for litigation without fear that an opponent will gain access to that work. Even though many attorneys would say they *always* anticipate litigation, work product doctrine only applies to work product that was prepared for pending or threatened litigation. There must be a nexus between the litigation (or the imminent litigation) and the preparation of work product. An example of work product is an attorney's notes from interviews with witnesses who may have knowledge about the facts of a lawsuit the attorney is planning to file.

The law of work product allows a party to refuse to produce that information to an opponent in discovery or at trial. In federal court, the authority for work product protection is found in Federal Rule of Civil Procedure 26(b)(3) and (4) and case law, including the still-important case Hickman v. Taylor, 329 U.S. 495 (1947). In that case, the U.S. Supreme Court first articulated the work product doctrine.

In a case pending in federal court, federal work product doctrine applies even if state law applies to the underlying claim. (Recall that this is different from the law of attorney-client privilege). For cases pending in state court, state law defines work product protection.

Like attorney-client privilege, an attorney must object to producing work product if it is requested in discovery or of a witness at trial. Unlike privileged information, though, there are some circumstances in which a party may be allowed access to an opponent's work product. Under Federal Rule of Civil Procedure 26(b)(3)(A), a party may obtain an opponent's work product if it is otherwise within the scope of discovery and the party "has substantial need for the materials to prepare its case and cannot, without undue hardship, obtain their substantial equivalent by other means." The law provides greater protection for work product that includes an attorney's opinions and mental impressions. Under Federal Rule of Civil Procedure 26(b)(3)(B), a court that allows discovery of work product must protect against disclosure "the mental impressions, conclusions, opinions, or legal theories of a party's attorney or other representative concerning the litigation."

* * *

Problem 15.3. The litigation between Kinsera and Convinsio has received a bit of media attention. In an apparent effort to persuade clients that Convinsio is the "bad guy" in the dispute, Kinsera posted the following information on the home page of its website. (The post is in an area available to the public and not password-protected).

Copyright Infringement Litigation

We know our clients have heard reports about our copyright infringement lawsuit against Convinsio. We want to assure you that we will prevail in this litigation.

In November 2014, a former Convinsio employee alerted Kinsera of Convinsio's illegal conduct. He told us that in spring 2014, Convinsio executives directed employees to improperly access Kinsera's website with a password that was improperly and illegally obtained. With access to this password-protected area, Convinsio was able to use Kinsera's copyright protected computer code to create a new Convinsio website. When this Convinsio employee complained to his superiors about their illegal conduct, he was fired. Then he bravely contacted Kinsera and agreed to sign an affidavit under penalty of perjury detailing Convinsio's illegal conduct. With this and other information uncovered in our investigation, we know we will win our lawsuit against Convinsio.

After you saw this information on Kinsera's website, you served Kinsera with Convinsio's Second Request for Production of Documents seeking a copy of the affidavit. Kinsera refused to provide the affidavit, objecting that it is protected by the work product doctrine. The issue of work product waiver will be addressed in the following Part C. But as a threshold matter (without reference to the issue of waiver), analyze whether the affidavit appears to constitute work product protected from disclosure in litigation.

* * *

C. PRIVILEGE AND WORK PRODUCT EXCEPTIONS AND WAIVER

* * *

1. EXCEPTIONS AND WAIVER THROUGH INTENTIONAL CONDUCT

Please read Restatement (Third) of the Law Governing Lawyers §§ 78–85 & 91–93.

The law recognizes a number of exceptions to the attorney-client privilege. The attorney-client privilege cannot be invoked to prohibit a lawyer from disclosing information necessary to resolve a fee dispute with the client or to defend the lawyer against a charge of misconduct in representing the client. The law also recognizes exceptions to the privilege in defined circumstances when an attorney-client communication is relevant to: (1) a dispute concerning the client-decedent's disposition of property; (2) a claimed breach of a client-fiduciary's duties to beneficiaries of a trust; (3) a claimed breach of an organizational client's manager's fiduciary duties. In all three of these situations, it is in the interest of the ultimate beneficiary of the attorney-client relationship for the otherwise privileged communications to be disclosed.

There is a "crime-fraud" exception to both the attorney-client privilege and work product protection. If the client consulted the lawyer for assistance in committing a crime or fraud that was ultimately accomplished, the privilege or work product protection does not apply.

Attorney-client privilege and work product protection can be waived by the client's (or the client's authorized agent's) intentional conduct. Waiver can occur when the client agrees to waive privilege or work-product protection. Privilege and work product can also be waived by putting the content of privileged or work product protected communications at issue in litigation. This arises when a client asserts that she relied upon the advice of counsel as a defense in a criminal or civil case. Such "at issue" waiver can also occur when the client claims the lawyer's assistance was ineffective or negligent. Privilege and work product can also be waived by allowing a witness to employ the material while testifying or in preparing to testify. A client's attorney's failure to object when privileged or work product protected information is requested in litigation is also a means by which the privilege can be waived.

Finally, intentional disclosure of privileged information (to a third party) or of work product (if the disclosure increases the likelihood of access by an adverse party) can result in a court finding a waiver. In the age of electronic communication, it is easier than ever for clients to voluntarily disclose privileged information to third parties. Disclosure can be as simple as forwarding an attorney's email to a friend or posting an attorney's legal advice or work product on Facebook or a blog. If opposing counsel learns about such a disclosure (by reading it on Facebook, for example) he or she will likely request that the court find the privilege waived. In the case of intentional disclosures, the court may find that the privilege is waived for all related communications on the same subject matter. These issues are addressed in the following case.

* * *

LENZ V. UNIVERSAL MUSIC CORP.

No. C 07–03783 JF (PVT), Docket No. 297 (Oct. 22, 2010)

ORDER GRANTING IN PART AND DENYING IN PART DEFENDANTS' MOTION TO COMPEL PRODUCTION OF PRIVILEGED DOCUMENTS AND TESTIMONY

PATRICIA V. TRUMBULL, UNITED STATES MAGISTRATE JUDGE.

INTRODUCTION

Defendant Universal Music Corporation, Universal Music Publishing, Inc. and Universal Music Publishing Group (collectively "defendants") move to compel production of documents and testimony withheld on the basis of waived claim of attorney-client privilege. Plaintiff Stephanie Lenz opposes the motion. Having reviewed the papers and considered the arguments of counsel, defendants' motion to compel is granted in part and denied in part.

BACKGROUND

Plaintiff Lenz alleges that defendant Universal improperly notified the video-sharing website, YouTube, that the 29 second video of her young toddler dancing to Prince's musical composition "Let's Go Crazy" was an unauthorized use. Universal administers the copyrights for a number of Prince's musical compositions, including "Let's Go Crazy." As a result of the June 4, 2007 notice from Universal, YouTube removed the video from its website until Lenz later sent two counter-notices demanding that her video be restored. YouTube restored her video to its website a few weeks afterwards.

Plaintiff Lenz alleges that defendant Universal knew or should have known that it was a self-evident non-infringing fair use under 17 U.S.C. § 107. Plaintiff Lenz also alleges that she has incurred substantial and irreparable injury, including "harm to her free speech rights under the First Amendment," and to her "sense of freedom to express herself."

During the pendency of this action, defendant Universal notes that Lenz has made repeated disclosures to third parties regarding her confidential communications with legal counsel and has referenced "multiple subjects related to this litigation and [her] allegations before the court." Specifically, it notes that the multiple disclosures by plaintiff Lenz have related to the actual motive for pursuing the action, discussions regarding certain legal strategies, "core allegations" in the action, and have occurred in emails, electronic chats with online friends, and on her personal blog located at www.piggyhawk.wordpress.com. For example, plaintiff has stated that the action provides a forum for her lawyers at Electronic Frontier Foundation to "get [ ] their teeth into UMG [Universal Music Group]" for sending takedown notices.

In light of the above, defendant Universal moves [to] compel plaintiff (1) to produce all responsive documents withheld on the basis of a claim of attorney-client privilege, where plaintiff has waived the privilege as to the subject matter of the communications by breaching the confidentiality of communications with her counsel; and (2) to compel plaintiff to testify further at deposition regarding such matters.

LEGAL STANDARD

"Parties may obtain discovery regarding any nonprivileged matter that is relevant to any party's claim or defense. . . ." Fed.R.Civ.P. 26(b). "For good cause, the court may order discovery of any matter relevant to the subject matter involved in the action." *Id.* "Relevant information need not be admissible at the trial if the discovery appears reasonably calculated to lead to the discovery of admissible evidence." *Id.*

"The scope of discovery permissible under Rule 26 should be liberally construed; the rule contemplates discovery into any matter that bears on or that reasonably could lead to other matter that could bear on any issue that is or may be raised in a case." Phoenix Solutions, Inc. v. Wells Fargo Bank, N.A., et al., 254 F.R.D. 568, 575 (N.D.Cal.2008). Permissible discovery, however, may be limited by relevant privileges, including the attorney-client privilege. *Id.* "As a general matter, '[a] party is not entitled to discovery of information protected by the attorney-client privilege.'" *Id.* "Because the attorney-client privilege is in derogation of the search for truth, it is 'narrowly and strictly construed.'" Verizon California, Inc. v. Ronald A. Katz Technology Licensing, 266 F.Supp.2d 1144, 1147 (C.D.Cal.2003) (internal citations omitted).

The party asserting the attorney-client privilege bears the burden of proving that it applies. Pauline Weil, et al. v. Investment/Indicators, Research and Management, Inc., et al., 647 F.2d 18, 25 (9th Cir.1981) (internal citations omitted). "One of the elements that the asserting party must prove is that it has not waived the privilege." *Id.*

"The disclosure of confidential information resulting in the waiver of the attorney-client privilege constitutes waiver of privilege as to communications relating to the subject matter that has been put at issue." *Phoenix Solutions, Inc. v. Wells Fargo Bank, N.A., et al.,* 254 F.R.D. at 575. "The privilege which protects attorney-client communications may not be used both as a sword and a shield." Akamai Technologies, Inc. v. Digital Island, Inc., 2002 WL 1285126 *8 (N.D.Cal.2002).

"The doctrine of waiver of attorney-client privilege is rooted in notions of fundamental fairness." Michael E. Tennenbaum, et al. v. Deloitte & Touche, 77 F.3d 337, 340 (9th Cir.1996). "Its principal purpose is to protect against the unfairness that would result from a privilege holder selectively disclosing privileged communications to an adversary, revealing those that support the cause while claiming the shelter of the privilege to avoid disclosing those that are less favorable." *Id.* at 340–341.

"[I]t has been widely held that voluntary disclosure of the content of a privileged attorney communication constitutes waiver of the privilege as to all other such communications on the same subject." *Pauline Weil, et al. v. Investment/Indicators, Research and Management, Inc., et al, supra,* 647 F.2d at 24.

DISCUSSION

I.   Communications By Plaintiff

The following three categories of communications are at issue: (1) communications regarding plaintiff's motivation for pursuing the action; (2) communications regarding specific legal strategies; and (3) communications regarding the substance of plaintiff's factual allegations.

At plaintiff Lenz's deposition, her counsel stated at the outset, that with respect to communications plaintiff had had with the Electronic Frontier Foundation, she would only be allowed to authenticate what she had previously written, to verify the date, time, place, and person she communicated with, and to clarify her understanding of her own words. Plaintiff's counsel instructed her not to answer any questions outside these parameters.

A.   Communications Regarding Plaintiff's Motivation for Pursuing the Action

Plaintiff Lenz asserts that she is pursuing the action to vindicate her First Amendment right of free expression. However, defendant Universal contends that plaintiff's communications with third parties suggest alternative motives for pursuing the action.

On June 14, 2007, plaintiff sent the following email:

They [EFF] are very, very interested in the case. I imagine so. I've never heard of anything like it. She [EFF lawyer Marcia Hoffman] said that Universal Music Group is creating a trend of just going all over the web claiming copyright infringement left and right & that they're breaking laws & such to do it. So EFF is pretty well salivating over getting their teeth into UMG yet again.

In another email to her mother on that same day, plaintiff stated that she couldn't "say much," but that EFF was planning a "publicity blitz and/or a lawsuit against Universal." She further stated that EFF would be funding this endeavor and that "[a]ny lawyer fees would come out of the settlement."

In her blog, plaintiff posted the following:

> Today, I got an e-mail from someone at EFF. He asked some questions, asked to see the correspondence from YouTube, asked to see the video, etc. I forwarded everything to him and explained that I'm sensitive to copyright issues and have some knowledge on the topic . . . The letter [from EFF] seemed to have the tone of "this sounds familiar and is something we're interested in talking about."

Plaintiff Lenz contends that the waiver doctrine is rooted in principles of fairness, and that the court should scrutinize the basis for defendant Universal's waiver argument and whether any prejudice results from the lack of any further discovery. *See, e.g.,* Opp. at 6–7. (Comments 1–3).

Here, plaintiff has voluntarily waived the privilege as to communications with her attorney regarding the possible motives for bringing the action. Plaintiff's communications with third parties relate to the actual substance of her conversations with her attorney. Therefore, in the interests of fundamental fairness, defendant Universal shall obtain further discovery regarding communications involving this subject matter. Accordingly, defendant Universal's motion to compel further discovery regarding plaintiff's communications with her attorneys as to her motives for bringing the action is granted.

B. Communications Regarding Legal Strategies

Plaintiff also made disclosures to third parties regarding specific legal strategies.

In a Gmail Chat, plaintiff disclosed to her friend her communications with EFF regarding re-pleading the complaint:

> we're going back to the same judge with more facts, more case law and strengthening the federal aspect. We're dropping the state charge, which was that they violated the contract w/YouTube . . . this way their threat of [h]itting me with a SLAPP suit ('pay our lawyers') is dust . . . b/c the SLAPP statute is a state thing, not a federal. If I make no state claim, they can't

respond with the SLAPP allegation . . . thing is, they're fighting YouTube over the federal thing right now too . . . so in my case it's like "pick a federal law you're accusing me of breaking" it's lose-lose for them on [DMCA] front but they can't admit publicly that they're filing DMCA notices b/c that would obliterate the YouTube fight they're having . . . I told [EFF counsel] Corynne [McSherry] that since pursuing the federal portion of the case achieves the ends I have in mind, that's fine to drop the state portion (that they filed a false DMCA notice, tha[t] they're accusing me of copyright infringement and that a ruling in our case could clarify a cloudy decision known as "Rossi")

Plaintiff relayed the same conversation in another Gmail Chat with another friend that same day.

Plaintiff also revealed EFF's legal strategy relating to the timing of filing the lawsuit. As noted above, on June 14, 2007, she revealed to her mother that she and EFF were communicating about a "publicity blitz" for her case. Apparently, additional correspondence reveals efforts by plaintiff and EFF to coordinate the filing of the complaint and the re-posting of the video on YouTube.

On June 21, 2007, plaintiff informed her chat friend that EFF was ready to file her complaint at that time. She stated "they [the lawyers] said I can blog it [the case] discretely but I've decided it's less hassle just to point on Monday and what [sic.] the hit counter on my video go ding ding ding. It should be reinstated by YouTube and then what=watch."

On July 18, 2007, plaintiff had another chat with a friend:

me [plaintiff]: hey, EFF may file my suit today

Erin [plaintiff's friend]: oh? That's good, yes?

Me [plaintiff]: yeah[,] it was held up b/c were waiting for YouTube to restore the video, which they never did.

See, e.g., Opp. at 7–8. (Comments 4–6).

As discussed above, plaintiff has voluntarily waived privilege here. Contrary to plaintiff's assertion that her communications were analogous to her having merely disclosed that she had spoken to an attorney and that EFF was taking the case, plaintiff disclosed the actual substance of her communications with her attorney. Nonetheless, her communications regarding certain specific legal strategies, including whether to drop the state law claim for interference, whether she had potential exposure to a SLAPP suit, and her discussions regarding the timing of the filing of the lawsuit are not relevant. Plaintiff's communications with her attorney regarding the "clarification about the *Rossi* decision," however, are relevant. Accordingly, defendant Universal's motion to compel further discovery regarding plaintiff's communications with her attorney as to the specific legal strategies identified above is granted in part and denied in part.

C. Communications Regarding Plaintiff's Factual Allegations

In conversations with third parties, plaintiff further disclosed communications she had with her attorneys regarding certain factual allegations.

On April 16, 2008, plaintiff stated in a Gmail Chat with her friend the following:

> you'll love the brief my lawyer wrote up, once it's a finished public document ... She's really going after UMPG & now Prince is the villain as well. Our lawsuit was filed before we knew he had a hand in it. Now she's kind of hinting that they're doing this b/c Prince bullied them into it and that there's been ample public proof that he wants everyone targeted, no matter whether they're actually guilty of anything. It's delicious.

Several months later, plaintiff stated that:

> I asked [EFF counsel Corynne McSherry] if she though they [Universal] were holding out to the last minute to settle & she thinks that b/c it's Prince, they have to fight ... [Plaintiff's Friend:] You think Prince is forcing them to fight it out instead of trying to settle? [Plaintiff:] I think that's what Corynne thinks.

In another communication, plaintiff stated:

> [Reporter from "Zerogossip.com"]: You contacted the Electronic Frontier Foundation. What are you hoping for?

> [Plaintiff]: When I contacted EFF, I did so at the suggestion of a friend of mine who's a lawyer in Canada. I wanted to know my rights, how to protect myself in case UPMG sued me and in what way (if any) I had infringed copyright. In discussing the situation with one of the EFF lawyers, we came to the conclusion that I did not infringe the copyright and eventually we decided to file this lawsuit.

On June 12, 2007, plaintiff responded on her blog to a reader, who asked about a fair use defense. Plaintiff wrote: "You're right Richard. Mine's not a 'fair use' case at all. Nor is it a parody. It's something different. I've never heard of anything like it, which is why I contacted EFF." At plaintiff's deposition, she stated that "[a]t the time it may have been my opinion. It may have been I was misunderstanding what I'd been told by counsel."

As before, the court finds that plaintiff has voluntarily waived the privilege here. In the interests of fundamental fairness, defendant

Universal shall obtain further discovery regarding plaintiff's communications with her attorney on this subject matter as well. Accordingly, defendant Universal's motion to compel further discovery regarding plaintiff's communications with her attorney as to the specific factual allegations set forth above is granted.

CONCLUSION

For the foregoing reasons, defendants' motion to compel is granted in part and denied in part. Plaintiff Lenz shall produce further responsive documents no later than November 8, 2010. Defendant Universal may depose plaintiff on the subject matters set forth above for no more than 2 hours and the deposition shall be held no later than December 1, 2010.

IT IS SO ORDERED.

* * *

Problem 15.4. Refer to the facts in Problem 15.3. Assume that the affidavit is otherwise protected by the work product doctrine. Analyze whether Kinsera waived work product protection by disclosing information about the affidavit on its website.

* * *

2.   INADVERTENT DISCLOSURE AND WAIVER

**Please read ABA Model Rules of Professional Conduct,
Rule 4.4(b) and Comments [2]–[3].**

**Please read Federal Rules of Evidence,
Rule 502(a), (b) & (f).**

**Please read Federal Rules of Civil Procedure,
Rule 26(b)(5)(B).**

In the age of electronic communication, inadvertent disclosure of privileged and work product protected information is a common occurrence. The most common inadvertent disclosure scenario occurs in litigation during discovery. One party requests that the other produce documents relevant to the case. The responding party objects to producing privileged and work product protected documents, but accidentally includes one or more privileged or work product protected documents in its document production. This is a common mistake given of the volume of documents that attorneys must review in a document production. It is impossible to detect and correctly code all of the privileged documents with 100% accuracy. Inadvertent disclosure can also happen outside of discovery, such as when a lawyer mistakenly sends an email intended for a client to opposing counsel.

Privilege is not necessarily waived by an inadvertent disclosure. Federal courts follow Federal Rule of Evidence 502(b) to determine if such a disclosure results in waiver. The rule provides that the disclosure of a privileged or work product protected document does not result in waiver if: (1) the disclosure was "inadvertent"; (2) the privilege holder took "reasonable steps" to prevent disclosure; and (3) the privilege holder "promptly took reasonable steps to rectify the error," including following Federal Rule of Civil Procedure 26(b)(5)(B). In state court, the issue of privilege waiver may be resolved by reference to case law or a rule of evidence, typically containing a test similar to Federal Rule of Evidence 502(b).

Professional conduct authorities in most jurisdictions require recipients of an inadvertent disclosure to at least notify the sending attorney. Professional conduct rules in approximately thirty states follow Model Rule 4.4(b), which provides that if a receiving attorney knows (or reasonably should know) that a document was inadvertently sent, then the receiving attorney shall promptly notify the sender. Some states have adopted professional conduct rules that require even more of the recipient than notice, such as retrieving the document if it was already disseminated, returning it to the sending attorney, and using the document only if a waiver ruling is obtained from the court. *See, e.g.,* Tenn. Rules of Prof'l Conduct R. 4.4(b). In other states, case law or ethics opinions address the receiving attorney's obligation upon receipt of an inadvertent disclosure.

Despite such authority in most jurisdictions, sending attorneys often learn of their own inadvertent disclosures at a deposition when opposing counsel hands a privileged document to the witness. Perhaps receiving attorneys rationalize that notice was not necessary because (in their opinion) the disclosure was not "inadvertent."

When sending attorneys learn that they inadvertently disclosed a privileged document, they may be able to use a rule of civil procedure to protect the content of the document from further use and disclosure pending a ruling on waiver. In federal court, Federal Rule of Civil Procedure 26(b)(5)(B) provides that a party may assert a claim of privilege or work product for documents it has already produced in discovery. Once the receiving party has been alerted to this claim it (1) must promptly return, sequester, or destroy the information; (2) must not use or disclose the information until the claim is resolved; (3) must take steps to retrieve the information (if it had already disclosed prior to receiving notice); and (4) may present the information to the court for a determination of the issue. Similar rules of procedure have been adopted in some state courts.

The bottom line is that inadvertent disclosure and waiver is a complicated issue today. Because the issue of waiver turns on the facts of each case, parties often file opposing briefs arguing about the Rule 502(b) factors: whether the disclosure was inadvertent, whether the sending party took reasonable steps to prevent the disclosure, and whether the sending party took reasonable steps to rectify the error. It is difficult to predict whether a court will find privilege waived under the facts of any given case given the subjective standard embodied in Rule 502(b). These disputes can jeopardize the attorney-client privilege and increase the costs of litigation. As a result, parties are increasingly employing "clawback" agreements and court orders to address the issue of inadvertent disclosure and privilege waiver. Such agreements are considered in the following section.

* * *

Problem 15.5. When you responded to Kinsera's discovery requests in Problem 15.1, you objected on Convinsio's behalf to producing Rhonda Harvey's handwritten notes on the grounds that they are protected by the attorney-client privilege. You even listed the document on the privilege log that you provided to opposing counsel. Nonetheless, your paralegal has just alerted you that a copy of the notes was apparently produced to Kinsera two months ago. You and your paralegal have no idea how this happened.

Do you think Kinsera's attorney had an obligation under Rule 4.4(b) to inform you of the disclosure? What are the possible consequences of counsel's failure to do so?

What steps should you take in order to seek the return of the notes and to prevent their use in the pending litigation? Analyze whether the court will find that you waived the attorney-client privilege given the circumstances of your disclosure. (For purposes of this latter question, assume that the parties do not have a clawback agreement or order in the case. Clawback provisions will be discussed in the following part).

* * *

D. COMPETENTLY PROTECTING CONFIDENTIAL CLIENT INFORMATION AND REDUCING THE RISK OF PRIVILEGE WAIVER

Please read ABA Model Rules of Professional Conduct, Rule 1.1 and Comment [8]; and Rule 1.6(c) and Comments [18] & [19].

Please read Federal Rules of Evidence, Rule 502(d) & (e).

Please read Federal Rules of Civil Procedure, Rule 16(b)(3); and Rule 26(f)(3)(D).

Protecting confidential client information is more difficult today than ever before. To provide some perspective, consider an attorney's practice forty years ago. Lawyers and clients communicated primarily in person, by phone, and by letter. Lawyers dictated pleadings, contracts, and correspondence to secretaries who prepared the documents on typewriters. The client's file was kept in a manila folder, housed in a file cabinet in the lawyer's office. In the present-day law practice, lawyers and clients use technology to communicate, creating a trail of electronic communications every day. Lawyers draft and edit correspondence and documents for clients, using various computers, tablets, and phones. Client information is not only found in a physical file cabinet, but on numerous devices, programs, platforms, and in the cloud. A client's confidences can be accessed by a hacker, compromised through a computer virus, accidentally forwarded via email to an adversary, and lost when a cell phone is left in a taxi.

In short, today's client's confidential information is easily created, copied, accessed, and disseminated. This helps lawyers be productive and facilitates lawyer-client communication. But it also creates a risk that unauthorized persons will be able to access the client's information and that attorneys will inadvertently forward confidential information to third parties.

In the information age, competently protecting confidential client information requires an understanding of technology and the risks associated with using it. According to Comment [8] to Model Rule 1.1, in order to maintain competence, lawyers must stay up-to-date about the benefits and risks of technology. Model Rule 1.6(c) provides that a lawyer shall make "reasonable efforts" to prevent inadvertent or unauthorized disclosure of or access to confidential client information. Comments [18] and [19] address "reasonable efforts" attorneys should take to protect confidentiality. The guidance is general, rather than specific. In short, the ABA explains that what is reasonable depends on the sensitivity of the client's information, the risk of disclosure absent additional security, and the financial and practical costs of implementing additional safeguards.

Comment [19] addresses an attorney's duties when transmitting communications. The comment explains that the lawyer's duty does not require the lawyer to use special security measures if the method of communication "affords a reasonable expectation of privacy."

Because technology is constantly changing, the risks and preventative measures are a moving target. Further, risk tolerance differs from client to client, even among the clients of a single firm. Some clients may need (or insist upon) additional measures to ensure their information is protected.

As a result, lawyers must be vigilant in assuring themselves that they understand their clients' needs and that they are taking appropriate steps to protect confidentiality. Simply handing the issue over to the firm's information technology person (or staff) is not enough. Attorneys must work with the technology experts to understand the vulnerabilities of client information, the range of actions possible to protect against unauthorized access and inadvertent disclosure, and the risks that remain despite such efforts. Cyber security experts encourage attorneys to develop data protection systems that include encryption, strong passwords, multi-factor authentication for remote access, anti-virus and anti-spyware software, and firewalls. Additional security for phones, tablets, and laptops can include limiting certain functionality (like printing) and adding the ability to wipe devices remotely if stolen. Firms can also protect client information by limiting who within the firm can access it and how it can be disseminated (such as by prohibiting flash drives and emails to and from non-firm email accounts). Whichever methods are adopted, attorney and law firm staff training, periodic audits, and constant vigilance are essential.

Resources are available to lawyers struggling with the intersection between technology and confidentiality. For example, the International Legal Technology Association ("ILTA") provides its members with information about using technology in law practice. According to ILTA's website, its LegalSEC® initiative "seeks to provide the legal community with guidelines for risk-based information security programs that are achievable, measurable and mature." The ABA has plans to create a website that will contain frequently updated information and resources to help attorneys protect confidentiality in light of modern technology. The Sedona Conference's Working Group 11 is preparing primers on data security and data privacy, as well as a document that will provide an overview of reasonable and unreasonable security measures.

Beyond protecting confidentiality generally, there are additional steps attorneys should take to protect against privilege and work product waiver (referred to collectively here as privilege waiver). This chapter has already highlighted the events that typically precipitate an attorney requesting a finding of privilege waiver: (1) intentional disclosure of privileged information by a party that comes to the attention of opposing counsel; and (2) inadvertent disclosure of privileged information by an attorney to opposing counsel.

Attorneys can lessen the risk of privilege waiver by attacking these issues. The first step is addressing party/client disclosures of privileged information. Today's clients live their lives online. They use email, blogs, and social media to communicate with family, friends, customers, and acquaintances. This is not just individuals, but also clients that are business entities and governmental agencies. When clients share privileged or work product protected information in those forums, it is possible that an opposing party or attorney will learn about the disclosure and seek a waiver ruling. This is what happened in the *Lenz v. Universal Music Corporation* case. To address this issue, attorneys must educate their clients about privilege and how it is waived. Clients need to understand that their own disclosures are a major risk to the attorney-client privilege. To make the lesson memorable, attorneys should share concrete examples with their clients, perhaps telling them what happened in a case like *Lenz*.

The next step in reducing the privilege waiver risk is addressing inadvertent disclosure. Attorneys, not clients, are the primary cause of inadvertent disclosure and privilege waiver in litigation. Inadvertent disclosure should be attacked on two fronts: pre-production privilege review and clawback agreements and orders. In an ideal world, an attorney would detect and withhold every privileged document from a document production. But in litigation today, that is not always possible or practical. There are often so many documents (electronic, paper, or both) and such a tight discovery schedule and budget that it is not feasible for even careful attorneys to detect and withhold every privileged document.

Clawback agreements and orders can provide a client with protection in the event that privileged or work product documents slip through a document review and are disclosed to opposing counsel. A clawback agreement (which is ideally incorporated into a court order) describes the circumstances in which a privileged or work product protected document can be "clawed back" without waiving privilege or work product protection. Both Federal Rule of Civil Procedure 26 and Federal Rule of Evidence 502 contemplate clawback agreements (though the term "clawback" is only found in the comments and not in the text of these federal rules) as a way to protect against privilege waiver.

It is not enough simply to have a clawback agreement or order. The clawback must provide predictable protection against privilege waiver. For example, a clawback might provide that if a privileged document is disclosed the receiving attorney "must return it, must not disseminate it, and will not seek a waiver ruling based on the disclosure." More subjective clawback provisions often result in motion practice, with the receiving party asserting privilege is waived because the disclosure was not "inadvertent," that the sending attorney did not "promptly" request the document's return, or arguing that some other provision of the clawback was not satisfied. *See, e.g.,* Mt. Hawley Insurance Company v. Felman Production, Inc., 271 F.R.D. 125, 133–36 (SD. W.Va. 2010) (as required by parties' clawback, the court analyzed whether producing party took "reasonable precautions" to avoid disclosure of privileged email and ultimately determined the precautions were not reasonable and the privilege was waived).

Because avoiding cost and uncertainty is the goal, attorneys should strive to draft clawback provisions that provide predictable protection against waiver. For suggestions on drafting better clawback provisions and other tips for avoiding privilege waiver, see Paula Schaefer, *Technology's Triple Threat to the Attorney-Client Privilege,* 2013 J. PROF. LAW. 171, 191–93 (2013). In every case, an attorney should explain to the client the efforts that will be made to detect privileged documents pre-production, the protection the clawback will provide if documents are inadvertently produced, and the risks that will remain despite having a clawback in place. Because it is the client's privileged information that is at stake, the client should have the final word on how much risk is acceptable.

* * *

Profile of attorney professionalism. Loyalty to clients demands that attorneys protect the attorney-client privilege. This can be particularly difficult when a court orders the disclosure of information the attorney believes is privileged. This was the situation for attorney John Lawrence. Attorney Lawrence's former client, Jeffrey McDermott, was indicted for the murder of Elwood McKown. Prosecutors wanted to call Lawrence as a witness to testify about information McDermott told him when they were in an attorney-client relationship. The prosecution asserted this was proper because McDermott had waived the attorney-client privilege by telling a third party about the content of a discussion between McDermott and Lawrence. In a hearing on a motion to compel the attorney's testimony, the prosecution presented a witness (who happened to be John Lawrence's brother, Warren Lawrence) who testified that McDermott told him of a conversation with John Lawrence in which McDermott told John Lawrence he had killed Elwood McKown.

The court was not convinced that the privilege had been waived, noting that the prosecution had only presented the uncorroborated testimony of a single witness. Nonetheless, the court ordered attorney

Lawrence to answer leading questions about the content of the conversation with McDermott. If attorney Lawrence admitted the content, then the court would find a waiver and expect Lawrence to testify further about the otherwise privileged information.

John Lawrence appeared with counsel and refused to answer any question about conversations he had with his client. The court found attorney Lawrence in criminal contempt of court, and sentenced him to a thirty-day jail term and imposed a $250 fine.

John Lawrence then appealed, arguing that without a prior finding that the privilege had been waived, an attorney cannot be compelled to disclose a privileged conversation with his client. The appellate court agreed, finding the trial court abused its discretion. An attorney cannot be required to disclose privileged information so that a court can decide whether the client waived the privilege; the waiver decision must precede an order that the attorney testify. State v. McDermott, 598 N.E.2d 147, 148–50 (Ohio App. 1991).

SECTION 5

LOYALTY

■ ■ ■

One of the fiduciary duties lawyers owe to their clients is loyalty. While the duty of loyalty encompasses numerous responsibilities, it also means that the lawyer must serve as the partisan of her client, or alternatively stated, as an advocate of the client. As the client's partisan and/or advocate, the lawyer must, to the fullest lawful extent, elevate the client's interests over everyone else's interests, including the lawyer's own interest. With an awareness that there are many situations in which a lawyer might be tempted to be disloyal to a client, the legal profession has developed a set of rules that either require the lawyer to decline or withdraw from a representation affected by a conflict of interest or, at least, to disclose the temptation to the client or prospective client and allow the client to decide whether the client wants to take the risk that the lawyer might be less of a partisan advocate than otherwise would be the case. Model Rule 1.7 is the centerpiece of these rules, with additional rules found in Rule 1.8.

Chapter 16 addresses conflicts of interest that arise because the lawyer is representing more than one client at the same time. Chapter 16 focuses on conflicts of interests that arise because the lawyer is representing a client whose interests are directly adverse to the interests of one of the lawyer's other clients. In addition, the chapter focuses on situations in which there is a substantial risk that the lawyer's representation of one client will be materially limited by the lawyer's obligations to another client or perhaps by the lawyer's own interests. Chapter 17 focuses on situations in which a lawyer's interests may conflict with those of a client.

CHAPTER 16

REPRESENTING MULTIPLE CLIENTS: CONCURRENT CONFLICTS OF INTEREST

■ ■ ■

Chapter hypothetical. Lawyer Jacobs of the Lessner Law Firm had handled the firm's representation of Twible in a couple of recent matters and is currently representing Twible in a collection matter against Houghton. At the same time, Lawyer Sullivan of the firm agreed to represent O'Brien in a claim against Twible. Sullivan fully disclosed to O'Brien that the firm had represented Twible in the other matters and was currently representing him in the collection matter. O'Brien's complaint charged Twible with assault and battery and sought punitive and exemplary damages, charging that the assault and battery by Twible was willful, wanton, malicious, premeditated, and vindictive. The complaint sought damages of $20,000 from Twible. In addition, the firm attached his home. Is there a concurrent conflict of interest under Rule 1.7(a)(1)? Why is there any concern at all in this case?

* * *

A. GENERAL PRINCIPLES

One of the core duties lawyers owe to their clients is loyalty. This means that the lawyer must serve as the partisan of her client, or alternatively stated, as an advocate of the client. As the client's partisan and/or advocate, the lawyer must, to the fullest lawful extent, elevate the client's interests over everyone else's interests, including the lawyer's own interest. With an awareness that there are many situations in which a lawyer might be tempted to be disloyal to a client, the legal profession has developed a set of rules that either require the lawyer to decline or withdraw from a representation affected by a conflict of interest or, at least, to disclose the temptation to the client or prospective client and allow the client to decide whether they want to take the risk that the lawyer might be less of a partisan advocate than otherwise would be the case. Model Rule 1.7 is the centerpiece of these rules, with additional rules found in Model Rule 1.8.

1. IDENTIFYING CONFLICTS OF INTEREST

Please read ABA Model Rules of Professional Conduct, Rule 1.7(a) and Comments [1]–[4], [6] & [8].

* * *

The first step to avoid or resolve conflicts of interest relating to your representation of a client is to identify that you might have a conflict of interest. Also given that there may be different rules applicable to different kinds of conflicts of interest, you will need to identify what kind of conflict you might have. The conflicts of interest that we will examine in this section are those that will either preclude a lawyer from undertaking or continuing the representation of a client or will need to be resolved through a process in which the affected person or persons gives informed consent to the representation. We emphasize at this point that we are talking about a sensitivity to the possibility that your representation is affected by a conflict of interest that will need to be avoided or resolved. What you suspect or fear might be such a conflict of interest may turn out not to be so, leaving you free to continue your representation without jumping through any extra hoops. On the other hand, further examination may reveal that your initial suspicion or fear was well-founded. The problem, of course, is that if you are insensitive to or clueless about possible conflicts, you will not do the investigation, research and thinking that will enable you to determine whether you have a conflict of interest, and, if so, what you are required to do in order to resolve it. This section introduces you to the primary types of conflicts of interest of which you must be aware in order to avoid discipline, involuntary disqualification, or liability for representing a client in violation of rules prohibiting you from doing so or doing so without the informed consent of the person to whom you must remain loyal.

Comment [3] states that a lawyer should adopt reasonable procedures to determine whether a conflict of interest exists and warns that "ignorance caused by a failure to institute such procedures will not excuse a lawyer's violation of this rule." Why is Model Rule 1.7 a "strict responsibility" rule? Failing to properly identify and handle conflicts of interest to can lead to attorney discipline. More often, however, litigation conflicts are addressed in litigation through a motion seeking to disqualify the attorney or law firm from representing one or more clients.

2. CONFLICTS OF INTEREST PRECLUDING THE REPRESENTATION OF A CLIENT

Please read ABA Model Rules of Professional Conduct, Rule 1.7(b) and Comments [14]–[22]; and Rule 1.0(e) and Comments [6] & [7].

* * *

Having determined that a proposed or ongoing representation of a client involves a conflict of interest, now we have to decide what to do. One possibility is to decline the proposed representation (or terminate an ongoing representation). Comment [2] describes this as the question of "whether the conflict is consentable." Some conflicts are consentable and some are not. Which ones are and which ones are not? This is a question that has to be asked and answered by a lawyer every time a proposed or ongoing representation involves a conflict of interest as defined by Model Rule 1.7(a).

Determining consentability. Note that the lawyer is the gatekeeper who must determine whether she is allowed to ask a client to consent to a directly adverse representation. The lawyer herself must first "believe" (a subjective standard)—"reasonably" (an objective standard)—that she can "provide competent and diligent representation to each affected client." Is it realistic to expect a lawyer to play this role? After all, we are asking a lawyer to turn down a prospective client who may have a very lucrative matter unrelated to the matter in which the lawyer is already representing an adverse client. Should more procedural safeguards be required, such as requiring the lawyer to secure the written approval of a disinterested and independent lawyer? Or less drastically, should the lawyer at least be required to advise the client in writing of the desirability of seeking the advice of independent legal counsel and to give the client a reasonable opportunity to do so? As you will see in Chapter 17 when we look at conflicts between the lawyer's interests and those of the client, such advice is required by Model Rule 1.8(a) when a lawyer engages in a business transaction with a client and by Model Rule 1.8(h) when a lawyer settles a claim for legal malpractice with a client or former client not represented by another lawyer in the matter.

Client consent to representation involving a conflict of interest. If you are not prohibited from undertaking or continuing the representation of a client by Model Rule 1.7(b)(1), (2), or (3), you still have more work to do before you can proceed with a representation involving a concurrent conflict of interest. You must comply with and document your compliance with a special set of procedures designed to protect prospective clients and clients as they decide whether they want you—conflict of interest notwithstanding—to commence or continue their representation.

Memorializing consent. Comment [7] to Model Rule 1.0 indicates that informed consent "usually" requires an affirmative response, but then notes that consent may be inferred from the conduct of a client with adequate information. The client's consent, however, must be confirmed in writing—a requirement that can be satisfied by the lawyer sending a memo to the client confirming the client's prior oral consent—a memo that client may never read. Should the client's informed consent be in a writing signed by the client either before or within a reasonable time after commencing the representation?

What do you think? A reading of Model Rule 1.7(b) should suggest that consent to a conflict is the exception, not the norm. Should that be the case? What is the justification for eliminating the freedom of consenting adult lawyers and clients to agree to a representation of the client by the lawyer that involves a conflict of interest?

* * *

3.   IMPUTED OR VICARIOUS CONFLICTS OF INTEREST

Please read ABA Model Rules of Professional Conduct, Rule 1.10(a) & (c) and Comments [1]–[4] & [6]; and Rule 1.0(c) and Comments [2]–[4].

* * *

Determining association. How do you tell whether two lawyers are associated with each other in a law firm? If there clearly is a law firm in which two or more lawyers are associated, how do you determine whether yet another lawyer, or another law firm is "associated with" the law firm for the purpose of imputing conflicts of interest?

Imputation. Why are all conflicts other than personal interest conflicts automatically imputed from the personally disqualified lawyer to all lawyers associated in a firm with the personally disqualified lawyer rather than limiting the vicarious disqualification to cases in which the presence of the personally disqualified lawyer in the firm presents a significant risk of materially limiting the representation of the client by other lawyers in the firm?

* * *

B. DIRECT ADVERSITY

**Please read ABA Model Rules of Professional Conduct,
Rule 1.7(a)(1) & (b) and Comment [6]; and Rule 1.10(a) and
Comments [1] & [2].**

* * *

COMMITTEE ON LEGAL ETHICS v. FRAME

433 S.E.2d 579 (W. Va. 1993)

PER CURIAM:

I.

On August 10, 1988, Wesley Metheney, a member of the law firm of Wilson, Frame & Metheney in Morgantown, West Virginia, filed a civil action entitled Baamonde, et al. v. Markwoods, Inc., dba J & J Home Sales (hereinafter "Markwoods"). Mr. Baamonde alleged that he had injured his knee while walking up steps to inspect a mobile home on J & J Home Sales' lot. Mr. Baamonde sought $500,000 in damages and $100,000 loss of consortium damages for his wife. The summons and complaint were served on . . . Ms. Vickie Lynn McMillen, vice president and manager of the family-owned mobile home company, Markwoods. Ms. McMillen . . . provided them to her local insurance agent that same day. Ms. McMillen had been employed by J & J Homes Sales since 1978, having become a majority stockholder in 1984 holding fifty-two percent of the outstanding shares.

Markwoods' insurer, Erie Insurance, retained Russell Clawges, Jr., to defend the action. Mr. Clawges contacted Ms. McMillen on August 24, 1988, and informed her of his representation. . . . Subsequent to [a conversation with Erie on May 30, 1989], Ms. McMillen had no further contact with either Erie or Mr. Clawges and assumed that the lawsuit had been resolved.

In early 1989, Ms. McMillen contacted Mr. Frame regarding representation in a divorce action. During their initial consultation on March 7, 1989, Ms. McMillen discussed her interest in Markwoods and her concern that her husband not receive any portion of the company through the divorce. Although the evidence is unclear, there was apparently was some reference during that meeting to the Baamonde suit. Ms. McMillen testified that Mr. Frame asked her if his firm was suing the corporation. Ms. McMillen also testified that she had been under the impression that the matter had been settled and that she did not understand the significance of the discussion.

Mr. Frame assumed representation of Ms. McMillen and filed a divorce complaint on her behalf. . . . [but because Mr. Frame had a scheduling conflict, Mr. Michael Benninger, an associate in the Frame firm, assumed responsibility for the representation of Ms. McMillen and attended the final hearing as Ms. Ms. McMillen's counsel.]

Upon receipt of a motion for summary judgment on behalf of Markwoods, Mr. Metheney requested that Mr. Benninger research the legal issues raised in the motion. When Mr. Benninger noticed Ms. McMillen's affidavit, included within that motion for summary judgment, he realized that his firm was representing Ms. McMillen in her divorce while suing her corporation in a separate action. He also understood that she was going to appear as an adverse witness at the trial of the Baamonde action. Mr. Benninger researched the potential conflict question and conferred with Mr. Metheney and Mr. Frame. They concluded that there was no conflict of interest because their firm had sued the corporate entity rather than Ms. McMillen personally. They also concluded that they need not discuss the issue with either Ms. McMillen or the Baamondes since they perceived no conflict of interest.

On June 27, 1989, for reasons not now apparent to Ms. McMillen, she first realized that the firm representing her in the divorce action also represented a plaintiff suing her corporation. Ms. McMillen contacted Mr. Clawges on or about June 30, 1989, and complained of what she perceived to be a conflict of interest. On the day of the scheduled Baamonde trial, July 10, 1989, Mr. Clawges orally moved to disqualify the law firm of Wilson, Frame & Metheney based upon the alleged conflict of interest. The lower court denied the motion, ruling that no confidential information had been disclosed and that the motion was untimely. The trial proceeded, and the case settled within policy limits. Upon the conclusion of the proceedings, Ms. McMillen expressed her anger and sense of betrayal to Mr. Benninger and traveled to Kingwood to hire attorney Virginia Hopkins to substitute as counsel in the divorce action.

On September 15, 1989, Ms. McMillen filed an ethics complaint with the West Virginia State Bar. . . .

II.

Rule 1.7(a) of the West Virginia Rules of Professional Conduct provides as follows: "(a) A lawyer shall not represent a client if the representation of that client will be directly adverse to another client, unless: (1) the lawyer reasonably believes the representation will not adversely affect the relationship with the other client; and (2) each client consents after consultation." The Respondents maintain that they had no duty to refrain from representation or obtain consent because no direct adversity existed between the two clients, Ms. McMillen and Mr. Baamonde. By definition, no violation of Rule 1.7(a) can occur if representation of one client will not be directly adverse to another client.

With regard to the interpretation of the phrase "directly adverse," the comment to Rule 1.7(a) provides the following guidance:

> Thus, a lawyer ordinarily may not act as advocate against a person the lawyer represents in some other matter, even if it is wholly unrelated. On the other hand, simultaneous representation in unrelated matters of clients whose interests are only generally adverse, such as competing economic enterprises, does not require consent of the respective clients. Paragraph (a) applies only when the representation of one client would be directly adverse to the other.

The Committee maintains that the Respondents' representation of Mr. Baamonde in his personal injury lawsuit was directly adverse to Ms. McMillen in her capacity as a majority shareholder, corporate officer, and manager of Markwoods. The Respondents contend that although Ms. McMillen and Mr. Baamonde were on opposing sides of the personal injury action, the Respondents were not representing Ms. McMillen in that personal injury action. They simply represented Ms. McMillen in a divorce action while representing Mr. Baamonde in an unrelated personal injury action. Ms. McMillen acknowledges that no information was disclosed or sought by the Respondents concerning the Baamonde case, and Ms. McMillen was also unable to identify any prejudice or misfortune resulting from the simultaneous misrepresentation. Ms. McMillen did, however, appear as a witness in the Baamonde case regarding the general business of Markwoods and was cross-examined by Mr. Metheney of the Respondents' law firm.

The conclusive question is whether representation of one client was directly adverse to the other. . . .

We . . . addressed the "directly adverse" requirement in State ex rel. Morgan Stanley & Co., Inc. v. MacQueen, 187 W. Va. 97, 416 S.E.2d 55 (1992). In that case, we recognized that being named as a party to a lawsuit is not a prerequisite to creating the direct adversity element needed to establish a conflict of interest. . . . Morgan Stanley involved an attempt to disqualify a law firm based, in part, upon the provisions of Rule 1.7(a). The firm represented both the State and certain state employees in the State's action to recover investment fund losses. In finding that a conflict of interest existed, we also explained that "[t]he critical issue is the existence or potentiality of conflicts of interest and not the inclusion of all adverse parties in a lawsuit." Id. at 102, 416 S.E.2d at 60. Similarly, while Ms. McMillen was not personally named as a defendant in the Baamonde suit, her status as a majority shareholder of the named defendant corporation created a potential, if not actual, conflict of interest.

We agree with the Committee's findings that the Respondents' representation of Mr. Baamonde "was directly adverse to Ms. McMillen in her capacity as a majority shareholder, corporate officer, and manager of Markwoods, Inc." While the Respondents did not directly represent Ms. McMillen in the personal injury suit, they did represent Ms. McMillen in an unrelated divorce action; she was still their client, and Rule 1.7(a) still applies. The Respondents also appear to place great emphasis on the fact that no deleterious impact was actually created by the simultaneous representation. That begs the question. To establish an ethical violation under Rule 1.7(a), one does not have to prove prejudicial impact, negative result, or an exchange of confidential information. The only prerequisites for the establishment of an ethical violation are those clearly set forth in the rule itself; namely, representation of one client that is "directly adverse" to another client without the consent of each client. The "directly adverse" language does not imply that a bad result must occur before representation is impermissible. It is the interests of the clients with which the rule is concerned, not the result obtained.[1]

In the present case, representation of Mr. Baamonde entailed cross-examination of Ms. McMillen. The Committee contends that direct adversity automatically exists when a lawyer's representation of one client entails cross-examination of an adverse witness who is also the lawyer's client. In formal opinion 92–367, issued by the American Bar Association Committee on Ethics and Professional Responsibility, the Committee explained: "A lawyer who in the course of representing a client examines another client as an adverse witness in a matter unrelated to the lawyer's representation of the other client, ... will likely face a conflict that is disqualifying in the absence of appropriate client consent." ... The Committee concluded that a "lawyer's examining the lawyer's client as an adverse witness, or conducting third[-]party discovery of a client, will ordinarily present a conflict of interest...." The Committee opined that such examination or discovery is likely to create the following problems:

> (1) to pit the duty of loyalty to each client against the duty of loyalty to the other; (2) to risk breaching the duty of confidentiality to the client-witness; and (3) to present a tension between the lawyer's own pecuniary interest in continued employment by the client-witness and the lawyer's ability to effectively represent the litigation client.

... The American Bar Association opinion further notes that cross-examination of a lawyer's own client could potentially jeopardize client

---

[1] While the results of simultaneous representation are not dispositive of the determination as to whether an ethical violation has occurred, the fact that no negative consequences were suffered certainly merits consideration in our determination of the appropriate discipline for such violation.

confidences. "First, to the extent a lawyer's general familiarity with how a client's mind works is relevant and useful information, it may also be disqualifying information within the contemplation of Rule 1.8(b). . . ." Second, the opinion explains that if the lawyer had acquired confidential information relevant to the cross-examination, the lawyer may overcompensate and fail to cross-examine fully and fail to adequately represent the litigation client.

We conclude that the simultaneous representation of Mr. Baamonde and Ms. McMillen, while fortunately resulting in no actual harm, presented such dangers as contemplated above and constitutes a violation of Rule 1.7(a). . . .

For their own protection from charges of ethical violations and in consideration of their clients' interests, attorneys should remain mindful of actual or potential conflicts of interest resulting from simultaneous representation. Any doubt regarding whether a conflict exists should be resolved in favor of informing the client(s) of the concerns and allowing the client(s) an opportunity to consent to continued representation or to seek new counsel.

The Committee found that the Respondents in the present case exercised poor judgment.[4] To the extent that the Respondents could have averted this disciplinary proceeding by assuring that Ms. McMillen and Mr. Baamonde understood and approved of the relationship between the Baamonde's suit and the Respondents' law firm, we agree. We adopt the findings and recommendation of the Committee and hereby order a public reprimand against Mr. Frame and further order that the costs of this proceeding be assessed against him.

Public reprimand ordered.

NEELY, JUSTICE, dissenting:

The majority accurately sets out the standard for determining whether representation of one client is directly adverse to another: the duration and intimacy of the lawyer's relationship with the clients involved; the functions performed by the lawyer; the likelihood of actual conflict; and the likelihood of prejudice. If Ms. McMillen were a named party in the Baamonde action, the case against Mr. Frame would be unassailable.

Ms. McMillen is in fact two steps removed from the arena of the Baamonde case: the real party in interest in that case was not Ms. McMillen and was not the corporation in which Ms. McMillen owns a

---

[4] We emphasize that neither this Court nor the Committee assigns any unethical intent to Mr. Frame in this matter. As the Committee pointed out, the incident is an example of poor judgment rather than malicious or deceptive intent. We therefore attribute no improper motive to Mr. Frame or any member of his law firm.

controlling interest, but rather the corporation's insurer. Under the unity of interest doctrine, there is no representation of a client "directly adverse" to another client where, as here, the suit is against a corporation's insurer and not against the individual or the corporation the individual owns in terms of whose ox will actually be gored.

When Ms. McMillen retained Clark Frame as her divorce lawyer, Mr. Frame informed her of his representation in the Baamonde matter. Ms. McMillen expressed no concern. Ms. McMillen obviously retained Mr. Frame because he is among the foremost lawyers in West Virginia and has a reputation for representing clients aggressively and successfully. Had Mr. Frame failed to disclose to Ms. McMillen the posture of the cases while actually aware of the possible conflict, his actions would deserve sanction. Had Ms. McMillen (who was soon if not immediately armed with full knowledge of the nature of both actions), registered an objection during months of continued contact with Mr. Frame, her case would be more plausible. Instead, Ms. McMillen gets this ridiculous opportunity to act out because, obviously, she did not get what from her perspective would have been a perfect result in her divorce action. Meanwhile the escutcheon of a highly-regarded lawyer in this state is needlessly besmirched.

* * *

Subordinate responsibility. No discipline was imposed against Mr. Benninger, the associate who identified the conflict and brought it to the attention of Mr. Frame. The Disciplinary Committee explained that this was due to his "genuine attempts to alert his senior partners of the conflict." Is this sound reasoning? What would be a better explanation?

Subjective perceptions. Note that in *Frame*, the lawyers explicitly addressed whether they had a conflict of interest and decided they did not. The disciplinary authority and reviewing court disagreed with the lawyers' judgments. What's going on here? Were these particular lawyers just ethically uninformed? Were there special circumstances in the two cases that made the conflicts hard to spot? Does it worry you that the judgment of these lawyers was later second-guessed?

Conflicts in class actions. Comment [25] provides that neither the lawyer for the class nor the lawyer for the opponent in a class action needs to get client consent before undertaking representation directly adverse to an unnamed class member. Is this rule consistent with the other prohibitions and exceptions in Model Rule 1.7 and its comments? What are the public policy considerations underlying this rule?

* * *

C. MATERIAL LIMITATION CONFLICTS

There are many instances in which lawyers may find themselves representing clients who are not on opposing sides of a matter but whose interests may be sufficiently divergent that the lawyer's effective representation of one client will interfere with the lawyer's representation of the other client. Such interference might be insignificant, significant, or substantial. This section introduces you to the law and rules of professional conduct that govern the lawyer's conduct in situations in which the lawyer is not representing interests directly adverse to a client but the lawyer's representation of the client may nonetheless be limited by the lawyer's performance of her duty owed to another client.

* * *

Please read ABA Model Rules of Professional Conduct, Rule 1.7(a)(2) & (b) and Comments [8], [13], [17], [20] & [23]; and Rule 1.10(a).

* * *

Risk of conflict. Model Rule 1.7(a)(2) prohibits concurrent representation if there is a "significant risk" that the representation of one client will be "materially limited" by the lawyer's representation of another client. How are these crucial terms defined? Comment [8] gives some guidance: "a conflict of interest exists if there is a significant risk that a lawyer's ability to consider, recommend or carry out an appropriate course of action for the client will be materially limited as a result of the lawyer's other responsibilities or interests." Keep this definition in mind as you read the rest of the material in this chapter.

* * *

IN RE CLAUSEN'S CASE
53 A.3d 621 (N.H. 2012)

LYNN, J.:

The respondent, K. William Clauson, appeals an order of the Supreme Court Professional Conduct Committee (PCC) suspending him from the practice of law for six months based upon its finding that he violated New Hampshire Rules of Professional Conduct (Rules) 1.1, 1.7, 1.9(a), and 8.4(a). Because we find that the respondent violated only Rules 1.7 and 8.4(a), we affirm in part, reverse in part, vacate in part, and remand.

I

The record supports the following facts. On June 20, 2009, Todd Gray was arrested for assault arising out of an incident that occurred early in the morning of June 14, 2009, at the home he shared with his wife Brenda and their children. In the supporting affidavit for the arrest warrant, State Trooper Nathan Hamilton stated that he learned the following in the course of investigating the incident. Mr. and Mrs. Gray attended a graduation party in Vermont on the night of June 13 and became intoxicated. Mrs. Gray told Hamilton that, after returning home with their daughter Amber, a dispute arose during which Mr. Gray broke a bathroom mirror, threw furniture over, and slapped Mrs. Gray in the face. Mr. Gray later told Hamilton that he had punched the mirror in response to his wife's "bickering," and that she had scratched him on the side of the neck. Some time after speaking with Mrs. Gray, Hamilton located Amber and asked her what happened. She said that after hearing the sound of the mirror breaking, she approached the bathroom and had "some words" with her father, and in response he backed her into a wall and slapped her in the face. After that, according to Amber, Mrs. Gray approached Mr. Gray and slapped him on the back of the head; Mr. Gray then threw Mrs. Gray into a refrigerator, table, and chair, slapped her, and, after Amber called the police, left the house. Trooper Hamilton returned to obtain a written statement from Mrs. Gray later on June 14, but she declined to provide one and said she did not want the investigation to proceed.

After his arrest on June 20, Mr. Gray appeared before a bail commissioner, who released him on $500 personal recognizance and ordered him not to contact Mrs. Gray or Amber or go within 100 yards of them. On June 22, Mrs. Gray sought the respondent's assistance in lifting the no-contact condition of the bail order so that Mr. Gray could return home. The respondent, an attorney licensed to practice in New Hampshire since 1971, agreed to represent her in the matter. After speaking with Mr. Gray by telephone to obtain his consent to appear in the district court on his behalf, the respondent filed a motion entitled "Brenda Gray and Todd Gray's Emergency Motion for Immediate Hearing on Bail Conditions." The respondent appeared with Mrs. Gray for a hearing on the motion on June 23 in the Lebanon District Court (Cirone, J.). He told the court that Mrs. Gray did not consider herself a victim in the case and wanted the no-contact condition lifted. The court, however, declined to rule on the matter because Mr. Gray was not present.

On June 30, the respondent again appeared on behalf of the Grays to request the no-contact condition be lifted. Mr. Gray was also arraigned at that hearing and entered a not guilty plea through the respondent, who had by that time agreed to represent him in the criminal case. At some point, the court expressed its concern that the respondent's joint representation of the Grays presented a possible conflict of interest. Mrs. Gray then testified that she was not afraid of her husband and wanted him to return home, and engaged in a discussion with the court about the matter. Mr. Gray did not speak during that hearing. The court issued an order the next day lifting the no-contact condition of the bail order.

The respondent represented Mr. Gray in his criminal case. After the court scheduled a trial to take place in November, the State agreed to place the charges on file for one year without a finding, conditioned on Mr. Gray's good behavior and completion of an anger management course.

The Attorney Discipline Office issued a notice of charges against the respondent in August 2010 alleging violations of Rules 1.7(a), 1.9(a), 1.1, and 8.4(a). A hearing panel found that the respondent violated each Rule as charged and recommended: (1) a sanction of three months suspension; (2) a requirement to take the Multistate Professional Responsibility Exam (MPRE) and earn a 90% passing score; (3) attendance at twelve hours of continuing education seminars; and (4) payment of all expenses incurred in the investigation and prosecution of the matter. After hearing oral argument, the PCC found violations of each of the Rules, as charged, issued a six-month suspension, and required the respondent to complete an MPRE course and pass the examination. The respondent appealed.

II

We first consider whether the respondent violated the Rules. The PCC's finding of a violation must be supported by clear and convincing evidence.

A. Concurrent Conflict of Interest

The PCC first concluded that the respondent violated Rule 1.7(a), which provides:

(a) Except as provided in paragraph (b), a lawyer shall not represent a client if the representation involves a concurrent conflict of interest. A concurrent conflict of interest exists if:

. . .

(2) there is a significant risk that the representation of one or more clients will be materially limited by the lawyer's responsibilities to another client, a former client or a third person or by a personal interest of the lawyer.

(b) Notwithstanding the existence of a concurrent conflict of interest under paragraph (a), a lawyer may represent a client if:

(1) the lawyer reasonably believes that the lawyer will be able to provide competent and diligent representation to each affected client;

(2) the representation is not prohibited by law;

(3) the representation does not involve the assertion of a claim by one client against another client represented by the lawyer in the same litigation or other proceeding before a tribunal; and

(4) each affected client gives informed consent, confirmed in writing.

Comment 8 to the ABA Model Rules explains further:

Even where there is no direct adverseness, a conflict of interest exists if there is a significant risk that a lawyer's ability to consider, recommend or carry out an appropriate course of action for the client will be materially limited as a result of the lawyer's other responsibilities or interests .... The conflict in effect forecloses alternatives that would otherwise be available to the client. The mere possibility of subsequent harm does not itself require disclosure and consent. The critical questions are the likelihood that a difference in interests will eventuate and, if it does, whether it will materially interfere with the lawyer's independent professional judgment in considering alternatives or foreclose courses of action that reasonably should be pursued on behalf of the client.

N.H. R. Prof. Conduct 1.7, ABA Model Code Comment 8.

Because the respondent does not contend that he obtained informed, written consent, our analysis is limited to whether his representation of Mr. and Mrs. Gray presented a significant risk that his representation of one would be materially limited by his responsibilities to the other.

The respondent advances several arguments as to why his representation of the Grays did not violate Rule 1.7: (1) that their respective interests were aligned insofar as each wanted the no-contact order lifted; (2) that his representation of Mr. Gray in the underlying criminal case was contingent upon his review of the police file; and (3) that because both Mr. and Mrs. Gray denied that the alleged assault even occurred, his representation of each would never be materially limited by his responsibilities to the other.

The first argument is unpersuasive because it pertains to the actual alignment of the Grays' interests—not the risk that the respondent's responsibilities to one would materially limit his representation of the other. See Wyatt's Case, 159 N.H. 285, 298, 982 A.2d 396 (2009) (Rule 1.7(b) (the former version of Rule 1.7(a)(2)) "is broad, and focuses not upon direct adversity at the outset, but the risk that it or other material limitations may arise in the course of the dual representation" (citation omitted)); see also R. Flamm, Lawyer Disqualification § 4.1, at 61 (2003) ("In a situation where a lawyer concurrently represents two or more parties with respect to the same subject matter there is usually a chance that their interests will, at some point, diverge.").

The second argument is also unpersuasive because the PCC found that the respondent represented Mr. Gray in the general criminal case before the June 30 hearing. The record supports that finding, particularly given that the respondent entered a not guilty plea on Mr. Gray's behalf at the June 30 hearing. Moreover, the finding of a concurrent conflict may be predicated solely upon the respondent's representation of the Grays in the two hearings convened for the purpose of lifting the no-contact condition of the bail order. Whether or not we accept that the respondent's representation of Mr. Gray on the criminal assault charge was contingent upon receiving and reviewing the police file, it is undisputed that the respondent represented both Mr. and Mrs. Gray at the bail hearings. Because there is no evidence in the record that the respondent provided Mrs. Gray with any additional legal services after the June 30 hearing, we limit our analysis of Rule 1.7 to the two hearings on the bail conditions.

We conclude that the joint representation presented several significant risks that the respondent's responsibilities to Mrs. Gray would materially limit his representation of Mr. Gray. First, the respondent's responsibilities to Mrs. Gray included an obligation to offer candid and independent advice which, if given, could have conflicted with Mr. Gray's interest in removing the no-contact provision and defending against the underlying assault charge. For example, the respondent knew that Mrs. Gray had an obligation to tell the truth in the bail hearing. A disinterested lawyer might have examined the facts, explained to Mrs. Gray the risks of telling the court that the assault never happened notwithstanding substantial evidence to the contrary, and, accordingly, advised her to refrain from denying the assault took place. Similarly, a disinterested lawyer might have foreseen a possibility that Mrs. Gray would change her mind and opt later to proceed as a willing witness for the prosecution. In that event, prudence might also dictate advising her to refrain from supporting removal of the no-contact order lest she later face exposure to cross-examination based upon her prior statements to the court (a possibility made even more pronounced in light of her having told Trooper Hamilton on the night of the incident that Mr. Gray had, in fact, assaulted her). But providing such advice obviously would have been detrimental to Mr. Gray's interest in lifting the no-contact condition and defending against the criminal case. This situation presented the primary risk arising from a concurrent conflict of interest under Rule 1.7(a)(2): divided loyalties that might inhibit the lawyer's range of options in advising a client.

The respondent's responsibilities to Mrs. Gray could also materially limit his representation of Mr. Gray were the case against him to proceed to trial. At trial, the respondent's obligation to Mr. Gray would be to cross-examine witnesses against him as vigorously as possible. Yet his ability to cross-examine Mrs. Gray—an inevitable witness for the prosecution—would be limited by Rule 1.9(c)(2), which prohibits a lawyer who has "formerly represented a client in a matter" from revealing information "relating to the representation." Rule 1.7(a)(2) expressly applies to such a situation by virtue of its reference to a lawyer's "responsibilities to . . . a former client." Although Rule 1.6 would allow the respondent to reveal such information if he obtained Mrs. Gray's informed consent, the fact that she supported lifting the no-contact order on June 30 did not make her continued support of her husband a foregone conclusion. In the event that Mrs. Gray withheld her consent to allow the respondent to use information "relating to the representation"— information he presumably obtained when he initially interviewed her about the matter—the respondent could not effectively advocate on behalf of Mr. Gray and would likely be forced to withdraw.

The foregoing discussion makes clear that the respondent's third argument—that because the Grays denied the assault took place meant "there could be no occasion when . . . [the respondent's] representation would be 'materially limited' by his responsibilities to each"—also lacks merit. Whether or not the respondent was in fact satisfied that there was no assault, his loyalties to Mr. Gray in seeking to lift the no-contact order and defend him against the charged crime could have compromised his ability to provide independent and disinterested advice to Mrs. Gray. *See* In re O'Brien, 26 A.3d 203, 209 (Del.2011) ("Rule 1.7(a) is an objective standard and does not rely upon the lawyer's subjective belief about his ability to remain impartial."). The risk that the respondent's loyalties would be divided was made even more palpable by the evidence the police had collected against Mr. Gray, including that Mrs. Gray told Trooper Hamilton that Mr. Gray had hit her and that Amber told Hamilton that Mr. Gray had not only hit Mrs. Gray, but also pushed her into a table and a refrigerator. The respondent's ability to counsel Mrs. Gray either to stay silent at the bail hearing or to reconsider her support for her husband given that the State was pursuing the charges against him was impaired by his obligation to advocate effectively for Mr. Gray. See N.H. R. Prof. Conduct 1.7, ABA Model Code Comment 8. Thus, we agree with the PCC that clear and convincing evidence supports a finding that the respondent violated Rule 1.7(a)(2) when he represented both Mr. and Mrs. Gray.

The PCC also determined, without elaboration, that this conflict was unwaivable because the respondent could not have "reasonably believed" that he could provide effective and diligent representation notwithstanding the conflict. See N.H. R. Prof. Conduct 1.7(b)(1). This conclusion was unnecessary to the disposition of the matter because it is undisputed that the respondent did not obtain informed consent under Rule 1.7(b)(4). Thus, we need not address it.

Because the respondent violated Rule 1.7(a), he also violated Rule 8.4(a), which provides: "It is professional misconduct for a lawyer to . . . violate . . . the Rules of Professional Conduct . . . ." *See Wyatt's Case*, 159 N.H. at 306, 982 A.2d 396. [The court went on to decide that although the lawyer had violated Rule 1.7 and 8.4, he had not violated Rule 1.1 or 1.9, and the court therefore remanded the case for reconsideration of the appropriate sanction].

* * *

Problem 16.1. Lawyer Smith represents Lettley, a criminal defendant charged with first-degree murder. Lawyer Smith also happens to represent another criminal defendant in an unrelated matter. The other client confesses to Smith (in confidence) that he actually committed the murder of which Lettley is accused. Is there a conflict under Rule 1.7(a)(2) and, if so, why? *See* Lettley v. State, 746 A.2d 392 (Md. 2000).

Consequences of conflicts in the criminal defense setting. Assume in the above problem that Smith seeks permission from the court to withdraw as counsel, that the court refuses to allow her to withdraw, and that Lettley is convicted. Should Lettley's conviction be overturned on the grounds of ineffective assistance of counsel in violation of the Sixth Amendment to the United States Constitution? Lettley was lucky that his lawyer recognized the conflict and sought permission to withdraw, as the Supreme Court has denied relief to defendants who failed to object to common representation at trial. In Cuyler v. Sullivan, 446 U.S. 335 (1980), the Supreme Court held that "[in] order to establish a violation of the Sixth Amendment, a defendant who raised no objection at trial must demonstrate that an actual conflict of interest adversely affected his lawyer's performance." Thus, the mere "possibility of conflict is insufficient to impugn a criminal conviction. In order to demonstrate a violation of his Sixth Amendment rights, a defendant must establish that an actual conflict of interest adversely affected his lawyer's performance." This standard applies regardless of whether the defense attorney is appointed or privately retained. But what if the criminal defendant, through counsel, does advise the court about the possibility of a conflict? Courts have held under these circumstances that if the trial court fails to take "adequate steps to ascertain whether the risk was too remote to warrant separate counsel," Holloway v. Arkansas, 435 U.S. 475, 484 (1978), or improperly requires joint or dual representation, then reversal is automatic, without a showing of prejudice, or adverse effect upon the representation. *Lettley*, 746 A.2d 392.

Representation of co-defendants. Husband and Wife both face drug trafficking charges. Lawyer represents both spouses. Both spouses have signed an agreement waiving any potential conflicts that may arise. Prior to trial, Prosecutor offers the following plea deal (which no defense attorney would have reasonably foreseen): (1) Both spouses accept responsibility for half of the drugs and serve 8 years each or (2) One spouse accepts full responsibility for the drugs and serve the full 25-year minimum term while the other spouse would go free. Both clients have confessed the crime to Lawyer. Does Lawyer have a conflict of interest under Rule 1.7(a)(2)? If so, why? Could the waiver still be effective? *See* Thomas v. State, 551 S.E.2d 254 (S.C. 2001).

What do you think? Note that neither Model Rule 1.7 itself nor Comment [23] establishes an absolute prohibition on joint representation of criminal co-defendants. Should it? What are the benefits—to the clients, to counsel, to the justice system—of joint representation of criminal co-defendants? What are the ethical risks?

Joint representation in civil litigation. Lawyer wants to jointly represent Biological Mother and Adoptive Parents in an adoption. Is there a possible conflict under Model Rule 1.7(a)(2)? If so, could the parties validly consent to the representation and waive the conflict in advance?

What do you think? Model Rule 1.8(g) and Comment [13] single out two situations—aggregate acceptance of a settlement in a civil case and aggregate acceptance of a guilty or nolo contendere plea in a criminal case—as so risky that a lawyer representing multiple clients must get the informed consent of each in writing to the settlement or plea. Why is this situation so risky? Notice that this requirement applies only to aggregate settlements or pleas, not to individual ones. Why?

Positional conflicts. Comment [24] describes a particular type of material limitation conflict, the "positional conflict." Note that in a positional conflict, the two (or more) clients who are represented by the same lawyer are not themselves adversaries. Rather, it is only the "legal position" taken on behalf of one client that may result in an adverse effect on another client. The conflict is disqualifying "if there is a significant risk that a lawyer's actions on behalf of one client will materially limit the lawyer's effectiveness in representing another client in a different case."

* * *

Problem 16.2. You are a lawyer who also happens to be a defendant in a legal malpractice action brought by a former prospective client. Your lawyer is arguing on your behalf before the Eastern Division Court of Appeals in the state in which you are practicing that a lawyer owes no duty of care to prospective clients. You have recently been asked by a prospective client in another matter to represent her in a malpractice suit she wants to bring against a lawyer for his alleged failure to alert her to the imminent running of the statute of limitations in a case in which the lawyer had declined to represent her. That suit would be filed in a trial court within a different appellate division of the same state. What should you do?

* * *

D. CONSENT TO CONFLICTS

Please read ABA Model Rules of Professional Conduct, Rule 1.7 and Comments [18]–[22].

* * *

AN UNNAMED ATTORNEY V. KENTUCKY BAR ASSOCIATION
186 S.W.3d 741 (Ky. 2006)

LAMBERT, C. J.

Movant, An Unnamed Attorney, moves this Court to impose the sanction of a Private Reprimand in the above referenced disciplinary proceeding.

In early 2003, Movant was employed as an attorney by John and Jane Doe, husband and wife, to perform an investigation of the circumstances surrounding the fatal shooting of Mrs. Doe's former husband. Neither Mr. nor Mrs. Doe had been charged with any crime in connection with that occurrence; however, they were concerned that one or both of them might be charged with a crime as the official investigation proceeded. The Does advised Movant that neither of them had played any role in the shooting and that they had a common alibi. They sought to employ Movant to investigate the shooting on their behalf, in the hope that the investigation would produce evidence supporting their claim that they were innocent of any involvement.

Movant advised the Does that a conflict of interest could arise in the course of his work on their behalf. He also advised them that if a conflict of interest did arise he might be required to withdraw from the joint employment. However, he did not advise them that any and all information obtained during the joint representation or obtained in any communication to him by them would be available to each client and exchanged freely between the clients in the absence of a conflict of interest. Movant asserts that he did not anticipate the possibility that the interests of the Does would become so materially divergent that there would be a conflict of interest in providing the results of the investigation to each of them. He acknowledges that he did not explain the potential ramifications of joint representation in that regard.

After discussing the aforementioned aspects of the employment, Movant agreed to undertake the investigation for a flat fee of $7,500. The Does made an initial payment of $2,500, and Movant commenced work on their behalf. They paid him an additional $3,000 after he began work, leaving a balance of $2,000 still unpaid.

The investigation produced information that indicated that one of the Does was directly involved in the shooting, contrary to what Movant had been told. Upon discovery of this information, and following communications with the KBA Ethics Hotline, Movant determined that he should withdraw from the joint employment. Furthermore, Movant concluded that he should not disclose certain results of his investigation to either Mr. or Mrs. Doe without the consent of each of them, which they declined to give. Movant encouraged each of them to obtain new counsel, and they followed this advice.

After receiving a bar complaint from the Does, the Inquiry Commission authorized a Charge against Movant pursuant to SCR 3.190. The Charge contains two counts, both of which are based on the allegation that Movant did not adequately explain the potential for a conflict of interest and the potential consequences of such a conflict. Count I alleges that Movant violated SCR 3.130–1.4(b), which states: "a lawyer should explain a matter to the extent reasonably necessary to permit the client to make informed decisions regarding the representation." Count II alleges that Movant violated SCR 3.130–1.7(2)(b) which states:

> A lawyer shall not represent a client if the representation of that client may be materially limited by the lawyer's responsibilities to another client or to a third person, or by the lawyer's own interests, unless:
>
> (1) The lawyer reasonably believes the representation will not be adversely affected; and
>
> (2) The client consents after consultation. When representation of multiple clients in a single matter is undertaken, the consultation shall include explanation of the implications of the common representation and the advantages and risks involved.

This rule does not absolutely prohibit common representation. As neither of the Does had been charged at the time the representation commenced, the rule only required that Movant reasonably believe the representation of each client would not be adversely affected by the dual representation, and that each of the clients consent after consultation. In the context of common representation, consent must be informed, and this requires that each client be made aware of the full consequences of such representation. This includes the meaning of confidentiality, and the reasonably foreseeable means that conflicts could adversely affect the interests of each client. Such communication must "include explanation of the implications of the common representation."

In this case there was a lack of required communication by Movant. Specifically, Movant failed to explain that there would be no confidentiality as between the two clients and the lawyer, that all information discovered would be furnished to both, and that each client was owed the same duty. When the investigation uncovered information that was favorable to one client but harmful to the other, Movant refused to release the information he had gathered without the acquiescence of both clients, which was not given. This resulted from his failure to initially explain the implications of common representation to both clients. When the investigation revealed that one of the clients was involved in the homicide, Movant had a duty with respect to that client to keep that fact confidential. On the other hand, he had a duty to the other client to provide exculpatory information which necessarily included information he was obligated to keep confidential.

It should be noted that the advice given in the Ethics Hotline opinion does not shield Movant from this Charge, as the Charge arises from the commencement of the representation and before the events that led him to request an Ethics Hotline opinion. This case well illustrates the potential peril lawyers face when undertaking joint representation. SCR 3.130–1.7(2)(b) is mandatory and the consent element must be informed consent, including a full explanation of all foreseeable ramifications.

The KBA has expressed its agreement with the motion made by Movant, and we feel that the punishment is appropriate, especially in light of the unique factors of this case. We hereby grant the motion and, it is ORDERED that:

1.   Movant, An Unnamed Attorney, is hereby privately reprimanded for violations of SCR 3.130–1.4(b) and SCR 3.130–1.7(2)(b).

2.   In accordance with SCR 3.450, Movant is directed to pay costs in the amount of $49.60, for which execution may issue from this Court upon finality of this Opinion and Order.

* * *

GLADERMA LABS., L.P. v, ACTAVIS MID ATLANTIC, LLC
927 F.Supp.2d 390 (N.D. Tex. 2013)

KINKEADE, J.

Before the Court is Plaintiffs Galderma Laboratories, L.P., Galderma S.A., and Galderma Research & Development, S.N.C.'s (collectively "Galderma") Motion to Disqualify Vinson & Elkins, LLP. The Court conducted a hearing on this motion on October 28, 2012. . . . The Court

DENIES Galderma's Motion (Doc. No. 18) because Galderma gave informed consent to Vinson & Elkins's ("V & E") representation of clients directly adverse to Galderma in matters that are not substantially related to V & E's representation of Galderma.

I. Factual Background

Galderma is a worldwide leader in the research, development, and manufacturing of branded dermatological products. Galderma is headquartered in Fort Worth where it employs approximately 240 people. Galderma and its affiliates have operations around the world, employing thousands of people and reporting worldwide sales of 1.4 billion euros for the year 2011 alone.

As a complex, global company, Galderma routinely encounters legal issues and the legal system. Galderma has its own legal department to address these issues. The legal department is headed by its Vice President and General Counsel, Quinton Cassady. Mr. Cassady is a lawyer who has practiced law for over 20 years and has been general counsel for Galderma for over 10 of those years. In addition to an inhouse legal department, Galderma, through Mr. Cassady, frequently engages outside counsel to assist with a wide range of issues. Over the past 10 years, Galderma has been represented by large law firms including DLA Piper, Paul Hastings, and Vinson & Elkins, LLP ("V & E"). Galderma also engages smaller law firms as needed.

In 2003, Galderma and V & E began its attorney-client relationship. V & E sent Galderma an engagement letter. As part of the engagement letter, V & E sought Galderma's consent to broadly waive future conflicts of interest, subject to specific limitations identified in the engagement letter. The waiver contained in the engagement letter is as follows:

> We understand and agree that this is not an exclusive agreement, and you are free to retain any other counsel of your choosing. We recognize that we shall be disqualified from representing any other client with interest materially and directly adverse to yours (i) in any matter which is substantially related to our representation of you and (ii) with respect to any matter where there is a reasonable probability that confidential information you furnished to us could be used to your disadvantage. You understand and agree that, with those exceptions, we are free to represent other clients, including clients whose interests may conflict with [y]ours in litigation, business transactions, or other legal matters. You agree that our representing you in this matter will not prevent or disqualify us from representing clients adverse to you in other matters and that you consent in advance to our undertaking such adverse representations.

On behalf of Galderma, Mr. Cassady signed that he understood and, on behalf of Galderma, agreed to the terms and conditions of engaging V & E, including the waiver of future conflicts of interest.

Beginning in 2003, Galderma engaged V & E for legal advice relating to employee benefit plans, Galderma's 401(k) plan, health care benefit programs, employment issues, and other issues relating to the administration of such programs. V & E continued to advise Galderma on employment and benefits issues into July of 2012.

In June 2012, while V & E was advising Galderma on employment issues, Galderma, represented by DLA Piper and Munck Wilson Mandala, filed this intellectual property lawsuit against Actavis Mid Atlantic, LLC ("Actavis"). At that time, V & E had already represented various Actavis entities in intellectual property matters for six years. Without any additional communication to Galderma, V & E began working on this matter for Actavis, and in July 2012, V & E filed Actavis's answer and counterclaims.

In July 2012, Galderma received a copy of Actavis's answer and counterclaims, and became aware that V & E was representing Actavis. After brief discussions in late July between Mr. Cassady and V & E, Galderma asked V & E to withdraw from representing Actavis. On August 6, 2012, V & E chose to terminate its attorney-client relationship with Galderma rather than Actavis. On that same day, V & E stated that it would not withdraw from representing Actavis, because Galderma had consented to V & E representing adverse parties in litigation when it signed the waiver of future conflicts in the 2003 engagement letter. Galderma then brought this motion to disqualify.

II. Galderma's Motion to Disqualify

Galderma now moves to disqualify V & E from representing Actavis in the underlying patent litigation. The briefing of the parties has been wide-ranging, but at oral arguments, counsel acknowledged that the crux of the issue is this: whether or not Galderma, a sophisticated client, represented by in-house counsel gave informed consent when it agreed to a general, open-ended waiver of future conflicts of interest in V & E's 2003 engagement letter. Galderma argues that its consent was not "informed consent" when its own, in-house lawyer signed the agreement on its behalf because V & E did not advise Galderma of any specifics with regards to what future conflicts Galderma may be waiving. V & E argues that in this case, because Galderma is a highly sophisticated client who is a regular user of legal services and was represented by its own counsel, the waiver language is reasonably adequate to advise Galderma of the material risks of waiving future conflicts, despite being general and open-ended.

A. Legal Framework for Resolving Ethics Questions

. . . The Court must give careful consideration to motions to disqualify because of the potential for abuse. Disqualification motions may be used as "procedural weapons" to advance purely tactical purposes. A disqualification inquiry, particularly when instigated by an opponent, presents a palpable risk of unfairly denying a party the counsel of his choosing. When the Model Rules are invoked as procedural weapons, the party subverts the purpose of the ethical rules. MODEL RULES OF PROF'L CONDUCT, Scope, cmt. 20 (2010).

When a client hires multiple firms, that creates inadvertent problems for the ethical system in at least two ways. One is when the client hires every large and small firm possible to prevent any local firm from being on the other side. The second problem happens in cases such as this, where a client hires a firm for work that is important, but small in size compared to some unrelated large matters. The ABA recognized this problem may occur:

> When corporate clients with multiple operating divisions hire tens if not hundreds of law firms, the idea that, for example, a corporation in Miami retaining the Florida office of a national law firm to negotiate a lease should preclude that firm's New York office from taking an adverse position in a totally unrelated commercial dispute against another division of the same corporation strikes some as placing unreasonable limitations on the opportunities of both clients and lawyers.

Sophisticated clients can retain their adversary's counsel of choice in unrelated matters while attempting to invalidate prospective waivers of future conflicts when that counsel later becomes adverse to them. Large firms would never be able to take on small, specialized matters for a client unless the firms could reasonably protect against this potential abuse by preserving their ability to practice in other areas where the client has chosen to retain different counsel.

B. Ethical Standards for Waiver of Future Conflicts

With the ABA canons of ethics as a guide, informed by state and local rules, the Court considers the ethical standards relevant to this specific case.

As a general rule, a lawyer is not allowed to sue his own client, which he concurrently represents in other matters. This holding mirrors the position of the ABA Model Rules of Professional Conduct ("Model rules"), which provide that, "[e]xcept as provided in paragraph (b) a lawyer shall not represent a client if the representation involves a concurrent conflict of interest." MODEL RULES OF PROF'L CONDUCT R. 1.7 (2010). Rule 1.7(b) creates an exception.

Notwithstanding the existence of a concurrent conflict of interest under paragraph (a), a lawyer may represent a client if:

(1) the lawyer reasonably believes that the lawyer will be able to provide competent and diligent representation to each affected client;

(2) the representation is not prohibited by law;

(3) the representation does not involve the assertion of a claim by one client against another client represented by the lawyer in the same litigation or other proceeding before a tribunal; and

(4) each affected client gives informed consent, confirmed in writing. Id. R. 1.7(b).

"Informed consent" denotes the agreement by a person to a proposed course of conduct after the lawyer has communicated adequate information and explanation about the material risks of and reasonably available alternatives to the proposed course of conduct. Id. R. 1.0(e). . . .

Under the Model Rules, a client's waiver of future conflicts is valid when the client gives informed consent. MODEL RULES OF PROF'L CONDUCT R. 1.7(b) (2010). Clearly, all clients, even the most sophisticated, must give informed consent. What disclosure from an attorney is reasonably adequate to allow for informed consent for a particular client is not clear. The Model Rules, the Comments to the Model Rules, and the Formal Opinions of the ABA's Committee on Ethics and Professional Responsibility outline a number of factors for courts to consider in determining whether a client has given informed consent to waive future conflicts of interest.

1. ABA Model Rules and Applicable Comments

One source for determining how to apply the Model Rules is the comments to the Model Rules. The comments do not add obligations to the Model Rules but provide guidance for practicing in compliance with the Rules. Id. Preamble, cmt. 14. The text of each Rule is authoritative, but the Comments are intended as guides to interpretation. Id. Preamble, cmt. 21.

The Comments to Rule 1.7, governing current client conflicts, recognize that a lawyer may properly request a client to waive future conflicts, subject to the test in Rule 1.7(b). Id. 1.7, cmt. 22. The effectiveness of the waiver is generally determined by the extent to which the client reasonably understands the material risk that the waiver entails.

When dealing with a waiver of future conflicts, a specific waiver of a particular type of conflict has the greatest likelihood of being effective. A general and open-ended waiver will ordinarily be ineffective, because the client will likely not have understood the material risks involved. Consent using a general or open-ended waiver is not per se ineffective, but considering the entire spectrum of clients, a general and open-ended waiver is likely to be ineffective because the vast majority of clients are not in a position to understand the material risks from the open-ended language of the waiver itself.

The same comment highlights that consent to a general, open-ended waiver is more likely to be effective when dealing with a narrow set of circumstances. If the client is an experienced user of the legal services involved and is reasonably informed regarding the risk that a conflict may arise, that consent is more likely to be effective. The consent is particularly likely to be effective when the client is independently represented by other counsel in giving consent and the consent is limited to future conflicts unrelated to the subject of the representation.

The comments to Rule 1.0, which defines "informed consent," mirror the comments to Rule 1.7. For consent to be "informed," the lawyer must take reasonable steps to ensure that the client or other person possesses information reasonably adequate to make an informed decision. Id. R. 1.0, cmt. 6. Ordinarily, this requires communication that includes a disclosure of the facts and circumstances giving rise to the situation, any explanation reasonably necessary to inform the client or other person of the material advantages and disadvantages of the proposed course of conduct and a discussion of the client's or other person's options and alternatives. The more experienced the client is in legal matters generally and in making decisions of the type involved, the less information and explanation is needed for a client's consent to be informed. Id. When dealing with a client who is independently represented by other counsel in giving the consent, generally the client should be assumed to have given informed consent. Just like Rule 1.7, Rule 1.0 shows there is a vast difference in what type of disclosure is necessary to ensure that a client has reasonably adequate information to make an informed decision, depending on the sophistication of the client and, importantly, whether or not the client is represented by an independent lawyer. . . .

D. Whether or Not Galderma Gave Informed Consent to the Waiver of Future Conflicts

To meet its burden of showing informed consent, V & E must show that it provided reasonably adequate information for Galderma to understand the material risks of waiving future conflicts of interest. MODEL RULES OF PROF'L CONDUCT R. 1.0, cmt. 6 (2010). Two related questions in this test form the analysis. The first question is whether the information disclosed is reasonably adequate for a client to form informed consent. If the waiver does, the second question is, whether or not the disclosure is reasonably adequate for the particular client involved in this case. The focus of the first question is on what information is being disclosed, and the focus of the second question is on circumstances pertaining to the client.

1. Whether V & E's Disclosure Is Reasonably Adequate for a Client to Form Informed Consent

Rule 1.0 provides three basic factors to help determine whether a disclosure is reasonably adequate to allow for informed consent. See id., 1.0(e). Rule 1.0(e) identifies that informed consent is characterized by: 1) agreement to a proposed course of conduct, 2) after the lawyer has communicated adequate information and explanation about the material risks, and 3) the lawyer has proposed reasonably available alternatives to the proposed course of conduct. The language of the agreement is a primary source for determining whether or not a particular client's consent is informed.

The waiver language at issue in this case is found in V & E's 2003 engagement letter. First, the 2003 engagement letter identifies a course of conduct with regard to concurrent conflicts of interest. Second, the engagement letter includes an explanation of the material risk in waiving future conflicts of interest. Third, the letter explains an alternative course of conduct for Galderma. All of these favor a finding that Galderma's agreement manifested informed consent.

First, the Court examines the language for whether or not the parties agreed to a course of conduct with regard to conflicts of interest. The letter, in relevant part, states:

> We recognize that we shall be disqualified from representing any other client with interests materially and directly adverse to yours (i) in any matter which is substantially related to our representation of you and (ii) with respect to any matter where there is a reasonable probability that confidential information you furnished to us could be used to your disadvantage. You understand and agree that, with those exceptions, we are free to represent other clients, including clients whose interests may conflict with yours in litigation, business transactions, or other legal matters.

These sentences, the bulk of the waiver language, identify a course of conduct for the parties. The course of conduct identified is that V & E is given wide ranging freedom to represent other clients, including those whose interests conflict with Galderma. The outer boundaries of the parties agreed course of conduct is defined in the previous sentence. Despite V & E's freedom to represent other clients with conflicting interests, V & E would not be able to represent a client in a material and directly adverse manner where the adverse representation is substantially related to the representation of Galderma, or there is a reasonable probability that confidential information Galderma furnished could be used to its disadvantage. The course of conduct identified in the waiver language provides for broad freedom for V & E to represent clients with whom it would otherwise have a conflict of interest, limited by specifically identified situations.

Galderma argues the waiver is open-ended and vague, which makes it unenforceable. First, an open-ended waiver is not per se unenforceable. See MODEL RULES OF PROF'L CONDUCT R. 1.7, cmt. 22 (2010) (allowing for the validity of open-ended waivers). Second, simply because a waiver is general, does not mean it is vague. The waiver language in the contract signed by Galderma provides a framework for determining in the future, when a conflict arises, whether or not V & E will be disqualified.

Galderma maintains that the provisions of the waiver must be more specific so that a person who reads the waiver can know whether the parties anticipated a particular party or a particular type of legal matter. . . . While specifying a particular party or type of legal matter does make it more likely that the waiver will be effective for a wider range of clients, using a general framework for determining a course of conduct does not render the waiver unenforceable. The waiver language supports a finding of informed consent because it provides a course of conduct by which the parties can manage future conflicts relating to the attorney-client relationship.

Second, the Court looks to see whether or not the waiver language includes any explanation of the material risk of waiving future conflicts of interest. Waiver language that informs the client of the material risk of waiving future conflicts supports a finding of informed consent. See MODEL RULES OF PROF'L CONDUCT R. 1.0(e) (2010); V & E waiver language in this case informs Galderma that if they agree, Vinson and Elkins representation of Galderma, "will not prevent or disqualify us from representing clients adverse to you in other matters." The previous language explains that V & E is not necessarily disqualified when representing another client with interests "materially and directly adverse to [Galderma]." The waiver explains that agreeing to the waiver risks V & E advocating for another client directly against Galderma. This is exactly the risk of which Galderma now claims they were not informed. This language explains the material risk in waiving future conflicts, and so this language also supports a finding of informed consent.

Third, the Court looks to see whether the waiver language contains any explanation of reasonably available alternatives to the proposed course of conduct. When the waiver language includes explanation of alternatives to the course of conduct, this also supports a finding that the client gave informed consent. See MODEL RULES OF PROF'L CONDUCT R. 1.0(e) (2010). In this case, the alternative course of conduct is for Galderma to hire other counsel. The waiver language tells Galderma, "You are free to retain any other counsel of your choosing." Elsewhere, the engagement letter tells Galderma that V & E's representation of Galderma is based on the parties' mutual consent. The language in the waiver and the agreement as a whole identifies at least one alternative; Galderma need not engage V & E on this matter if they do not wish to consent to the proposed terms and conditions. This language, although the least clear of the three factors, also supports a finding of informed consent. . . .

The Court concludes that the waiver in the 2003 engagement letter is reasonably adequate to allow clients in some circumstances to understand the material risk of waiving future conflicts of interest. The language discloses a course of conduct for determining when V & E will be disqualified, explains the material risk that V & E may be directly adverse to the client, and explains an alternative, that the client need not hire V & E if it does not wish to consent. The Court must next examine Galderma's sophistication and whether Galderma was independently represented in the waiver to determine whether or not the disclosure provided was reasonably adequate to allow Galderma to understand the material risks of waiving future conflicts. Id. R. 1.0, cmt. 6 & R. 1.7, cmt. 22.

2. Whether V & E's Disclosure Is Reasonably Adequate for Galderma to Form Informed Consent

For the general, open-ended waiver to be valid in this case, V & E must still establish that the disclosure was reasonably adequate to allow Galderma to understand the material risks involved. The communication necessary to obtain informed consent varies with the situation involved. Id. R. 1.0, cmt. 6. The principal considerations at this point in the analysis are the sophistication of the parties and whether the client was represented by counsel independent of the law firm seeking the waiver. See RESTATEMENT (THIRD) LAW GOVERNING LAWYERS § 122, cmt. c(i) (2000). . . .

Cassady claims now that he did not intend to consent to V & E representing a generic drug manufacturer when he signed the 2003 engagement letter. The language in the Model Rules is clear; informed consent turns on an objective standard of reasonable disclosure and reasonable understanding. See MODEL RULES OF PROF'L CONDUCT R. 1.0 & 1.7 (2010). Mr. Cassady's current declaration that he did not actually intend for Galderma to consent does [not] make a general waiver invalid because when a sophisticated party is represented by independent counsel a general, open-ended waiver is still likely to be reasonably adequate disclosure. . . .

3. Whether Galderma Gave Informed Consent to the Waiver of Future Conflicts of Interest

V & E's disclosure is general and open-ended. In many cases, and for many clients, the disclosure in this case would likely not be reasonably adequate to allow a client to make an informed decision. [However,] Galderma is a sophisticated client who has experience engaging multiple large law firms and has twice signed similar waiver provisions with at least one other law firm it has hired. Finally, having the benefit of its own independent counsel to advise Galderma on what the language meant, Galderma, through its own counsel, chose to sign the engagement letter which included the waiver of future conflicts.

Given the 2002 amendment to the Model Rules on informed consent and waivers of future conflicts, the authority related to those changes, and the evidence in this case, the Court concludes that Galderma gave informed consent to V & E's representation of clients directly adverse to Galderma in substantially unrelated litigation. Because V & E's representation of Actavis falls within the scope of that informed consent, V & E is not disqualified from representing Actavis.

* * *

Revocation of Consent: Problem 16.3. Clients A and B validly consent to Lawyer representing them jointly as co-defendants in a breach of contract action. On the eve of trial and after months of pretrial discovery on the part of all the parties, Client A withdraws consent to the joint representation for reasons not justified by the conduct of Lawyer or Client B and insists that Lawyer cease representing Client B. At this point, it would be difficult and expensive for Client B to find separate representation for the impending trial. Should Client A's revocation of consent prevent the lawyer from representing either client? *See* Comment [21] and Restatement (Third) of the Law Governing Lawyers § 122, cmt. f, illustration 6.

Aggregate settlements. In recent years, courts have grown stricter with the requirements for certification of a class action. As a result, it has become more common for plaintiffs' attorneys to represent a group of litigants pursuing similar claims and for defendants to agree to a "global" settlement that resolves all claims at once. Model Rule 1.8(g) allows such agreements only if "each client gives informed consent, in a writing signed by the client," and requires that "[t]he lawyer's disclosure shall include the existence and nature of all the claims or pleas involved and of the participation of each person in the settlement." These requirements can make it difficult to make large-scale settlement agreements that involve many plaintiffs. The American Law Institute (ALI) has proposed amending the aggregate settlement rule to allow plaintiffs in some cases to agree *ex ante* that they will accept an aggregate settlement offer approved by a supermajority of similarly situated claimants, but so far courts have generally struck down settlement contracts based on such prospective agreements. For an excellent discussion of the ethical issues involved in nonclass aggregate litigation, *see* Nancy J. Moore, *Ethical Issues in Mass Tort Plaintiffs' Representation: Beyond the Aggregate Settlement Rule*, 81 FORDHAM L. REV. 3233 (2013).

* * *

E. CONFLICTS IN TRANSACTIONAL REPRESENTATION

Please read ABA Model Rules of Professional Conduct, Rule 1.7 and Comments [7] & [26]–[35].

* * *

Note that Comments [7] and [26]–[35] to Model Rule 1.7 address conflicts that may arise in transactional (non-litigation) matters. These issues will be addressed in the Transactional Practice chapter.

* * *

Profile of attorney professionalism. In 2011, Richel Rivers and Mary Evelyn McNamara formed the law firm of Rivers ♦ McNamara PLLC in Austin, Texas, where they primarily practice family law. Family law can be challenging; as the firm's website points out, "Family Law cases present some of the most complicated and emotional problems people face." The legal system can appear overwhelming to Family Law clients who are already facing personal difficulties, but McNamara and Rivers are committed to helping their clients navigate through the legal system and are known for offering legal guidance with compassion and understanding of their clients' experience. A particularly sensitive challenge in the family law practice area involves the lawyer's ability to manage the conduct of the case in compliance with legal rules of professional conduct and litigation practice that the client may find bewildering. The conflicts-of-interest rules of professional conduct present an early challenge to an attorney's decision to accept a family law client.

Prior to forming their new firm, Rivers and McNamara had been partners in a large, full-service law firm with several practice groups. In that setting, the broad scope of Family Law issues presented many potential conflicts of interest with former and current clients of attorneys in other practice areas. McNamara noted that if the Estate Planning section prepared wills for both a husband and wife, then the Family Law section could not represent either former client against the other in a subsequent divorce matter because substantially related issues of the character and extent of their estate were the subject of both the prior representation and the later divorce matter. Similarly, if the Business section prepared business formation documents for a married couple, the Family Law section could not represent either spouse in a subsequent divorce if the representation in reasonable probability would involve use of confidential information to the disadvantage of one of the former clients, or if issues presented in the prior business formation representation were substantially related to the divorce matter.

Conflicts arising from a firm's disparate practice areas became less common once Rivers and McNamara moved to their own firm, which is smaller and more specialized. Other types of conflicts, however, arise in large and small firms alike. One of the common issues involves consultations with prospective clients. Many initial consultations do not result in the prospective client hiring the firm, but the consultation itself still creates a conflict that is likely to prevent the firm from representing the consulting party's spouse in a related matter. This creates opportunities for troubling manipulation: a client aware of the conflicts rules could consult with several attorneys with the intent of creating a conflict that would preclude those attorneys from representing the other spouse. The Model Rules discourage this conduct by specifying that "a person who communicates with a lawyer for the purpose of disqualifying the lawyer is not a 'prospective client,'" and is therefore not entitled to the protections that prospective clients would ordinarily be afforded. *See* Model Rule 1.18, comment [2]. Some state-specific rules, such as in Texas, do not provide this explicit exception to the initial consultation conflict scenario. Furthermore, as McNamara explained, "it can be difficult to discern whether the multiple consultations are for the legitimate purposes of obtaining second opinions and gauging the capabilities of various lawyers or for the ethically suspect purpose of unfairly conflicting competent counsel from representing the opposing party." Attorneys therefore must treat every consultation carefully.

Robust intake procedures help ensure that potential conflicts are identified and managed from the beginning. Rivers explained that a conflicts-checking routine is undertaken when a prospective client first contacts the firm: "Our intake procedures require that the legal assistant identify the inquiring party immediately and perform a conflicts check against our listings of both prior clients and prior prospective client consultations." Only after the conflict check has been performed will an initial consultation be scheduled for the prospective client to meet with an attorney at the firm.

CHAPTER 17

RESOLVING CONFLICTS OF INTEREST BETWEEN LAWYER AND CLIENT

■ ■ ■

Chapter hypothetical. You are a partner in a five-member law firm. You own 1,000 shares of stock in a mid-sized corporation which are worth $50 per share. There are 10,000 shares of issued and outstanding stock. A prospective client has asked you to represent her in an employment discrimination suit against the corporation in which she is seeking $500,000. She suggests a 30% contingent fee, which you may assume is reasonable under the circumstances.

(A) May you accept the case, and if so, what requirements will you need to meet?

(B) You are concerned that the prospective client seems to have a litigious nature, as she has filed several lawsuits against various entities in the past three years. Can you accept the representation contingent upon the client agreeing to waive any potential claim against you?

* * *

A. FAMILY OR OTHER CLOSE PERSONAL RELATIONSHIPS AS A MATERIAL LIMITATION ON A CLIENT'S REPRESENTATION

1. REPRESENTING INTERESTS ADVERSE TO A "RELATED" PERSON

Problem 17.1. You are a practicing lawyer, but you also co-own a car dealership with a long-time friend. You each have a 50% interest in the dealership. A partner in your law firm has been asked to bring a slip and fall lawsuit against a motel corporation in which your friend/business partner has a 75% interest. What should you do?

Problem 17.2. You are a second-year associate in a large law firm. You have an uncle who has always been like a father to you. Indeed, ever since your father divorced your mother, this uncle has been your surrogate father. Your uncle has recently been discharged by his employer as part of a downsizing and has filed a lawsuit against his employer alleging age discrimination. Knowing how important this lawsuit is to your uncle, you are distressed to learn that the partner in your law firm to whom you report is representing your uncle's employer. Although you have not been asked to help at this point, you fear that you will be asked to do so. You know that you could not do anything that would hurt your uncle. What should you do?

* * *

2. REPRESENTING INTERESTS ADVERSE TO A PERSON REPRESENTED BY A "RELATED" LAWYER

Please read ABA Model Rules of Professional Conduct, Rule 1.7 and Comment [11].

* * *

Prior to the revision of the ABA Model Rules in 2002, Rule 1.8(i) addressed the issue now discussed in Comment [11] to Rule 1.7. Rule 1.8(i) specified that

> [a] lawyer related to another lawyer as parent, child, sibling or spouse shall not represent a client in a representation directly adverse to a person whom the lawyer knows is represented by the other lawyer except upon consent by the client after consultation regarding the relationship.

Comment [6] explained that paragraph (i) applies to related lawyers who are in different firms: "The disqualification stated in paragraph (i) is personal and is not imputed to members of firms with whom the lawyers are associated." The vicarious disqualification in Rule 1.10(a) did not apply to a disqualification required by Rule 1.8(i).

* * *

As women began entering law school in larger numbers in the 1970s, the issue of spouses' representing adverse parties began to arise with greater frequency. With increased gender diversity in the profession, more lawyers married lawyers. The ABA addressed this issue in Formal Ethics Opinion 340 (1975). The ABA concluded that there is no per se prohibition on spouses' representing adverse parties; however, the ABA cautioned that "[m]arriage partners who are lawyers must guard carefully at all times against inadvertent violations of their professional responsibilities arising by reason of the marital relationship." An example of an inadvertent violation would be a telephone message left by one spouse's client on the answering machine in the marital home, and inadvertently heard by the other spouse.

[handwritten margin notes: charged / appointed counsel / convicted / finds out dating (8 mos.) / moved for new trial → ineffective assistance due to COI / duty of loyalty/breach conf. / they didn't tell him → can choose his own counsel / Reversed]

Comment [11] to current Rule 1.7 makes it clear that lawyers related to one another and representing adverse parties must obtain informed consent to the representation.

* * *

PEOPLE V. JACKSON

167 Cal.App.3d 829, 213 Cal.Rptr. 521 (1985).

PUGLIA, PRESIDING JUSTICE.

A jury convicted defendant of assault with intent to commit rape (Pen.Code, § 220), finding contemporaneous use of a deadly weapon (Pen.Code, § 12022, subd. (b)). Before sentencing, defendant discharged court-appointed trial counsel. Through retained counsel he moved for a new trial on grounds of ineffective assistance of counsel and prosecutorial misconduct. The crux of defendant's complaint was the existence of an ongoing "dating" relationship between trial counsel and the prosecutor. According to defendant's declaration in support of his motion for new trial, this relationship had not been disclosed to him. The record does not reveal when or in what manner the relationship ultimately became known to defendant. It is inferable, however, that defendant had no knowledge of it until after the conclusion of the trial.

Following an evidentiary hearing, the court denied the new trial motion. Imposition of sentence followed. On appeal, defendant renews his claims of ineffective assistance of counsel and prosecutorial misconduct. We shall reverse on the first ground.

I

The evidence at the new trial hearing establishes that defense counsel and the prosecutor began "dating" about eight months before defendant was charged. They continued to meet on "a regular basis" for movie and dinner dates, etc. throughout the duration of the criminal proceedings against defendant. During that time they appeared as counsel in directly adverse roles representing defendant and the People respectively at the preliminary examination, at pretrial settlement conferences, and at trial. They were never married nor engaged to each other nor did they ever live together.

Defense counsel and the prosecutor did not inform defendant or the court of their relationship. Defense counsel never divulged any confidential defense information to the prosecution. He testified he believed the situation created no possibility of conflict of interest and therefore did not require disclosure.

II

"It is settled that an indigent charged with committing a criminal offense is entitled to legal assistance unimpaired by the influence of conflicting interests." As guaranteed by section 15 of article I of the California Constitution, the right to effective assistance of counsel ". . . means more than mere competence. Lawyering may be deficient when conflict of interest deprives the client of undivided loyalty and effort." Under the California standard, appellate courts may not "indulge in nice calculations as to the amount of [resulting] prejudice" when a conviction is attacked on the ground that an appointed lawyer was influenced by conflict of interest. "[E]ven a potential conflict may require reversal if the record supports 'an informed speculation' that appellant's right to effective representation was prejudicially affected." "Proof of an 'actual conflict' is not required."

. . . "It is essential that the public have absolute confidence in the integrity and impartiality of our system of criminal justice. This requires that public officials not only in fact properly discharge their responsibilities but also that such officials avoid, as much as is possible, the appearance of impropriety." . . . As distinct from parties to casual social contacts, those who are involved in a sustained dating relationship over a period of months are normally perceived, if not in fact, as sharing a strong emotional or romantic bond. (Cf. Comment, Ethical Concerns of Lawyers Who Are Related by Kinship or Marriage (1981) 60 Oregon L. Rev. 399, 400.) Such an apparently close relationship between counsel directly opposing each other in a criminal prosecution naturally and reasonably gives rise to speculation that the professional judgment of counsel as well as the zealous representation to which an accused is entitled has been compromised. No matter how well intentioned defense counsel is in carrying out his responsibilities to the accused, he may be subject to subtle influences manifested, for example, in a reluctance to engage in abrasive confrontation with opposing counsel during settlement negotiations and trial advocacy.

A criminal defendant's "right to decide for himself who best can conduct the case must be respected wherever feasible." Accordingly, counsel involved in a potential conflict situation such as that disclosed by this record may not proceed with the defense without first explaining fully to the accused the nature of his relationship with opposing counsel and affording the accused the opportunity, if he so desires, to secure counsel unencumbered by potential divided loyalties.

Given the nature of the relationship shown here, the absence of disclosure inevitably fuels informed speculation as to the existence of a disabling conflict. Defendant is then left with no recourse but to impugn the loyalty and adequacy of his appointed counsel. Since the situation created by counsel's lack of disclosure defies its quantification, actual prejudice need not be shown by defendant as a condition to relief. A potential if not an actual conflict has been demonstrated and thus the appearance, at least, of impropriety. In these circumstances, we are foreclosed from "indulg[ing] in nice calculations as to the amount of [resulting] prejudice."

The judgment is reversed.

* * *

Other relationships. Does a conflict of interest exist when opposing parties are represented by a full-time county prosecutor and a criminal defense attorney who are siblings? The Supreme Court of Ohio Board of Commissioners on Grievances and Discipline considered this question and concluded that the situation "creates a conflict because the sibling relationship is a personal interest which could affect the lawyers' exercise of professional judgment on behalf of the clients." Supreme Court of Ohio Board of Commissioners on Grievances and Discipline Opinion Number 91–22 (1991). The opinion noted that state ethics opinion were somewhat split on this and similar issues, see, e.g., Alabama State Bar General Counsel and Disciplinary Comm'n, Op. 85–74 (1985) (concluding that a lawyer or his law partner may represent a criminal defendant even though the lawyer's brother is assistant district attorney and may prosecute the same case), but concluded that, given the special role that prosecutors play and the need for the public to be confident that there is no conflict, the situation created an unwaivable conflict of interest. Do you agree with the approach taken by the Ohio ethics opinion?

* * *

Please read ABA Model Rules of Professional Conduct, Rule 1.8 and Comments; and Rule 1.10(a) and Comment [3].

* * *

B. CLIENT INTERESTS ADVERSE TO A THIRD PARTY WHO IS PAYING THE LAWYER'S FEES OR SALARY

Model Rule 1.8 offers guidance on specific types of conflicts of interest. One of the most common situations involves a third party who pays the lawyer to represent another person. This often happens in the context of insurance defense, where the insurance company pays an attorney to defend the insured. It may also happen in the context of criminal representation, where family members or others may pay for an attorney to represent the defendant.

* * *

1. CONSENT TO THIRD-PARTY PAYMENT

Please read ABA Model Rules of Professional Conduct, Rule 1.7 and Comment [13]; and Rule 1.8(f) and Comments [11] & [12].

* * *

IN RE DISCIPLINE OF REENER
325 P.3d 104 (Utah 2014)

DURHAM, J.

Attorney Jere Reneer appeals the decision of the Utah Supreme Court's Ethics and Discipline Committee (discipline committee) to privately admonish him for violating rules 1.8(f) and 8.4(a) of the Utah Rules of Professional Conduct. We hold that the Office of Professional Conduct (OPC) did not produce substantial evidence that Mr. Reneer violated rule 1.8(f) by failing to obtain the informed consent of his client to receive compensation from a third party. Moreover, rule 8.4(a) may not be used as an independent ground for attorney discipline. We therefore reverse the discipline committee's order admonishing Mr. Reneer.

BACKGROUND

After the police arrested Thomas Broude for criminal trespass and aggravated assault, Joe Scheeler at the Utah Legal Group (ULG) contacted Mr. Broude through the mail about legal representation. Mr. Scheeler is not an attorney, and ULG is not a law firm, but rather a marketing company that recruits paying clients for Utah attorneys. Mr. Broude spoke with Mr. Scheeler and then requested that his mother, Judy Carey, also speak with Mr. Scheeler because she would be paying for the legal representation. Ms. Carey met with Mr. Scheeler and signed a contract with ULG. The contract specified that in exchange for Ms. Carey's agreement to pay $6,000, ULG would find and retain an attorney for Mr. Broude. The contract stated ULG would pay all attorney's fees, monitor Mr. Broude's cases, and resolve disputes between the attorney and the client.

Ms. Carey incorrectly believed that ULG was a law firm that would represent her son. Ms. Carey alleged that ULG's ads represented that it would "kick ass" and could "get things accomplished that no other firm could." Ms. Carey claimed that Mr. Scheeler told her that without ULG's help, her son would face extensive jail time, probation, and fines, but that if she retained ULG, Mr. Broude would avoid jail. Ms. Carey also alleged that when she expressed her concern about ULG's high fee and mentioned the possibility of a public defender, Mr. Scheeler told her that if she did not want to see her son go to jail, she should think twice about getting a public defender.

After Ms. Carey signed the contract, ULG contacted Mr. Reneer, and he agreed to represent Mr. Broude for a flat fee of $2,500. Mr. Reneer was not aware of the amount Ms. Carey agreed to pay ULG. Neither Ms. Carey nor Mr. Broude ever signed a separate fee agreement with Mr. Reneer. Mr. Reneer and an associate at his firm, Reneer & Associates, met with Mr. Broude to discuss his two cases, requested discovery from the prosecutors, and represented Mr. Broude at several pretrial hearings. Despite Mr. Broude's prior criminal history, Reneer & Associates negotiated a plea in abeyance for the criminal trespass charge and a plea agreement on the aggravated assault charge, lowering the charge from a third-degree felony to a class A misdemeanor. The court sentenced Mr. Broude to 365 days in jail on the reduced charge, but suspended all but 120 days of the sentence. Mr. Broude's jail sentence was 60 days less than the 180 days recommended by Adult Probation and Parole in the presentence report.

Due to Mr. Scheeler's alleged promise that Mr. Broude would not receive a jail sentence, Ms. Carey was unhappy with this result. Ms. Carey wrote a letter to Mr. Scheeler expressing her discontent and stating her intention to stop making payments toward the remaining debt she still owed to ULG. Ms. Carey then submitted a complaint against Mr. Reneer to the Utah State Bar Consumer Assistance Program. The complaint incorrectly referred to Mr. Reneer as an attorney working for the law firm "Utah Legal Group." In her complaint, Ms. Carey sought a waiver of the $1,600 she still owed ULG, as well as a $1,000 refund from the money she had already paid to ULG.

The OPC investigated Ms. Carey's complaint and concluded that Mr. Reneer may have violated (1) rule 1.5(b) of the Utah Rules of Professional Conduct, which requires that a lawyer communicate the scope of representation and the basis and rate of fees to the client; (2) rule 1.8(f), which prohibits a lawyer from accepting compensation from one other than the client without the client's informed consent to do so; (3) rule 5.4(a), which prohibits a lawyer from sharing legal fees with a nonlawyer; and (4) rule 8.4(a), which defines professional misconduct for a lawyer. The OPC then referred the matter to a screening panel of the discipline committee for further investigation.

The screening panel held a hearing to investigate the potential violations identified by the OPC. Ms. Carey, Mr. Reneer, and an associate at Mr. Reneer's firm all testified, but Mr. Broude did not attend the hearing. The screening panel found that Mr. Reneer violated rules 1.8(f) and 8.4(a) because he failed to obtain informed consent from Mr. Broude to receive compensation from Ms. Carey or ULG. The panel determined that Mr. Reneer's conduct caused little or no injury and recommended that he be privately admonished for the violations.

Mr. Reneer filed an exception to the screening panel's recommendation with the discipline committee. Because Mr. Reneer did not request a new hearing, the discipline committee made its determination based on the record before the screening panel. The discipline committee concluded that Mr. Reneer provided competent representation to his client and that the outcome was reasonable, but determined that substantial evidence supported the screening panel's findings that Mr. Reneer violated rules 1.8(f) and 8.4(a). The discipline committee issued an order privately admonishing Mr. Reneer for the violations. Mr. Reneer appealed the discipline committee's ruling. . . .

ANALYSIS

I. RULE 1.8(f)

Rule 1.8(f) of the Utah Rules of Professional Conduct states that "[a] lawyer shall not accept compensation for representing a client from one other than the client unless . . . the client gives informed consent." The rules define informed consent as "the agreement by a person to a proposed course of conduct after the lawyer has communicated adequate information and explanation about the material risks of and reasonably available alternatives to the proposed course of conduct." UTAH R. PROF'L CONDUCT R. 1.0(f). Informed consent is required when a third party pays a lawyer's fee "[b]ecause third-party payers frequently have interests that differ from those of the client, including interests in minimizing the amount spent on the representation and in learning how the representation is progressing." Id. R. 1.8 cmt. 11. "Sometimes, it will be sufficient for the lawyer to obtain the client's informed consent regarding the fact of the payment and the identity of the third-party payer." Id. R. 1.8 cmt. 12. Nevertheless, for consent to be fully informed, an attorney must "explain the nature and implications of the conflict in enough detail so that the parties can understand" the conflict being waived.

In this case we review the screening panel's factual finding that Mr. Reneer did not obtain his client's informed consent to receive compensation from his client's mother by way of ULG. We agree that substantial evidence would support a finding that Mr. Reneer failed to secure his client's written consent. Mr. Reneer testified that it was his practice to send a letter to all new clients, informing them of the importance of attending hearings and providing all documentation relevant to their case. But the form letter makes no mention of third-party payments, and Mr. Reneer admitted that it was possible that he never sent the letter to Mr. Broude. Mr. Reneer testified that the letter was the only written communication he exchanged with a new client referred to him by ULG.

Written consent, however, is not required to comply with rule 1.8(f). The rule only requires the client's "informed consent"; it does not state that consent must be in writing. The structure of rule 1.8 confirms that a writing is not required. Two of the conflicts described in rule 1.8 explicitly require a client's written informed consent to waive the conflict. UTAH R. PROF'L CONDUCT R. 1.8(a) (business transactions with a client); id. R. 1.8(g) (aggregate settlement of the claims of two or more clients). Thus the omission of a written consent requirement in rule 1.8(f) must be seen as purposeful, allowing for a client's oral manifestation of consent.

The screening panel received no evidence—much less substantial evidence—of the absence of Mr. Broude's oral informed consent. Testimony about the presence or absence of informed consent could have been obtained most readily from two sources: Mr. Broude or Mr. Reneer. But Mr. Broude did not provide any testimony to the screening panel, and the panel never asked Mr. Reneer if he obtained Mr. Broude's informed consent to receive compensation from a third party. Mr. Reneer testified that he did not remember telling his client how much ULG promised to pay him for the representation, but rule 1.8 does not require an attorney to disclose the amount of compensation paid to the attorney by a third party. The comments to rule 1.8 suggest that if a third-party fee arrangement does not create a rule 1.7 conflict of interest, "informed consent regarding the fact of the payment and the identity of the third-party payer" may be sufficient. Id. R. 1.8 cmt. 12.

The OPC suggests that because Mr. Reneer did not provide evidence that he obtained his client's informed consent, the screening panel's finding that Mr. Reneer failed to do so should be upheld. Mr. Reneer, however, did not bear the burden of proving compliance with the rules of professional conduct. Rather, the OPC bore the burden of producing evidence showing that Mr. Reneer did not comply. SUP.CT. R. PROF'L PRACTICE 14–517(c) ("The burden of proof in proceedings seeking discipline . . . is on the OPC"). In the absence of testimony or other evidence on this issue, the screening panel may not presume noncompliance. Therefore the panel's finding of fact that Mr. Reneer failed to obtain his client's informed consent, as required by rule 1.8(f), is not supported by substantial evidence.

II. RULE 8.4(a)

Mr. Reneer's alleged violation of rule 8.4(a) of the Utah Rules of Professional Conduct likewise does not support the order of admonishment. Rule 8.4(a) provides that "[i]t is professional misconduct for a lawyer to . . . violate . . . the Rules of Professional Conduct." The comments to this rule clarify that "[a] violation of paragraph (a) based solely on the lawyer's violation of another Rule of Professional Conduct shall not be charged as a separate violation." UTAH R. PROF'L CONDUCT R. 8.4 cmt. 1a. Because Mr. Reneer's alleged violation of 8.4(a) was based upon the charge that he violated rule 1.8(f), it may not stand as an independent ground for discipline.

CONCLUSION

Substantial evidence does not support a violation of rule 1.8(f). And rule 8.4(a) is not a basis for discipline in this case. We therefore reverse the order admonishing Mr. Reneer.

* * *

2. INSURANCE CONFLICTS

Third-party payment of legal fees can get especially complicated in the insurance context. Most insurance liability contracts state that the insurance company will pay to defend the insured against certain lawsuits and will pay to indemnify the insured against judgments arising out of such suits. They also allow the insurance company to choose and hire defense counsel. Usually, the interests of the insurer and insured will be aligned: both have an interest in asserting that the insured was not at fault in the incident, and both have an interest in minimizing the potential liability if the insured is found to be at fault. As you can imagine, however, conflicts often arise. Sometimes, there may be an allegation that the insured was engaging in activity not covered by the insurance policy. For example, some policies cover only the insured's negligent conduct, and will not cover the insured's intentional conduct. Thus, if there is evidence that the insured acted intentionally, the insurance company would benefit from information—it wouldn't be liable to pay the ultimate judgment. The insured, however, would be disadvantaged by that information. In other cases, there might be particular categories of damages (commonly including punitive damages, for example) that would not be covered by insurance. Finally, another common conflict arises when potential liability under the policy could exceed the policy limit.

States take different approaches in how they handle the conflicts that can arise. One of the key questions, of course, is determining who the client is. Some states provide that defense counsel represents both the insured and the insurer as co-clients. Other states provide that counsel represents only the insured. In either case, however, separate counsel may be necessary when conflicts arise between the interests of the insured and the insurance company. In the following case, the court had to decide whether an insurance company policy that required the company's "prior approval" of defense counsel services violated the Rules of Professional Conduct.

* * *

IN THE MATTER OF THE RULES OF PROFESSIONAL CONDUCT AND INSURER IMPOSED BILLING RULES AND PROCEDURES

2 P.3d 806 (Mont. 2000)

LEAPHART, J.

In an original application for declaratory judgment, Petitioners assert that insurer-imposed billing rules and procedures violate the Rules of Professional Conduct.

We address the following issues:

1. May an attorney licensed to practice law in Montana, or admitted pro hac vice, agree to abide by an insurer's billing and practice rules which impose conditions limiting or directing the scope and extent of the representation of his or her client, the insured?

2. May an attorney licensed to practice law in Montana, or admitted pro hac vice, be required to submit detailed descriptions of professional services to outside persons or entities without first obtaining the informed consent of his or her client and do so without violating client confidentiality? . . .

Discussion

. . . 1.   May an attorney licensed to practice law in Montana, or admitted pro hac vice, agree to abide by an insurer's billing and practice rules which impose conditions limiting or directing the scope and extent of the representation of his or her client, the insured? [The court stated there were several Rules of Professional Conduct that were relevant, including Rule 1.1 (Competence), Rule 2.1 (Advice), and Rule 1.8(f) (accepting compensation from one other than the client).]

In the present case, the parties do not dispute that insurers' billing and practice rules typically "impose conditions [upon an attorney appointed by an insurer to represent an insured] limiting or directing the scope and extent of the representation of his or her client." The Petitioners have focused on the requirement of prior approval in insurers' billing and practice rules. We therefore address that condition of representation while recognizing that other conditions limiting or directing the scope and extent of representation of a client may also implicate the Rules of Professional Conduct.

As a representative set of litigation guidelines, we briefly consider the guidelines submitted by the St. Paul Companies (hereafter, St. Paul). The declared policy of St. Paul's Litigation Management Plan (hereafter, the Plan) is to "[p]rovide a systematic and appropriate defense for St. Paul and its insureds, and to vigorously defend nonmeritorious claims and claims where the demands are excessive."...

[T]he Plan states that "[m]otion practice, discovery and research are items that have historically caused us some concern and which we plan to monitor closely. While we foresee very few differences of opinion, we require that defense counsel secure the consent of the claim professional prior to scheduling depositions, undertaking research, employing experts or preparing motions"....

Thus, the Plan expressly requires prior approval before a defense attorney may undertake to schedule depositions, conduct research, employ experts, or prepare motions. The Plan concludes that "[w]e understand that any conflicts between the St. Paul Litigation Management Plan and the exercise of your independent judgment to protect the interests of the insured must be resolved in favor of the insured. We expect, however, to be given an opportunity to resolve any such conflicts with you before you take any action that is in substantial contravention of the Plan."

A. Whether Montana has recognized the dual representation doctrine under the Montana Rules of Professional Conduct.

Petitioners assert that the insured is the sole client of a defense attorney appointed by an insurer to represent an insured pursuant to an insurance policy (hereafter, defense counsel) and that a requirement of prior approval in insurance billing and practice rules impermissibly interferes with a defense counsel's exercise of his independent judgment and his duty of undivided loyalty to his client. Petitioners argue that because the relationship of insurer and insured is permeated with potential conflicts, they cannot be co-clients of defense counsel.

Respondents argue that under Montana law, the rule is that in the absence of a real conflict, the insurer and insured are dual clients of defense counsel. From this fundamental premise, Respondents argue that as a co-client of defense counsel, the insurer may require pre-approval of attorney activities to assure adequate consultation. Respondents argue further that defense counsel must abide by a client's decisions about the objectives of representation and that defense counsel are obliged to consult with a client about the means for the objectives of representation. Respondents also argue that under Montana law, an insurer is vicariously liable for the conduct of defense counsel and that an insurer's control of litigation justifies holding an insurer vicariously liable for the conduct of defense counsel.

We conclude that Respondents have misconstrued our past decisions. This Court has not held that under the Rules of Professional Conduct, an insurer and an insured are co-clients of defense counsel....

None of these decisions addressed whether insurers and insureds are co-clients under the Rules of Professional Conduct, and none of them addressed whether defense counsels' compliance with insurance contracts that repose "absolute" control of litigation in insurers violated the Rules of Professional Conduct.

We note that Respondents argue that insurance contracts effectively place absolute control of litigation with insurers. However, Respondents' claim of absolute control of litigation cannot be reconciled with their insistence that whenever a conflict may arise between their litigation guidelines and an attorney's ethical obligations, the attorney is to follow the ethical course of action. Respondents' assertion that defense counsel are not only free to but must follow their independent judgment is inconsistent with their claim that insurers have absolute control of litigation.

B.   Whether insurers and insureds are co-clients under Montana's Rules of Professional Conduct.

We turn to the question whether an insurer is a client of defense counsel under the Rules of Professional Conduct. We note that some other courts have concluded that the insurer is not a client of defense counsel. In Atlanta Int. Ins. Co. v. Bell (1991), 438 Mich. 512, 475 N.W.2d 294, the court addressed whether defense counsel retained by an insurer to defend its insured may be sued by the insurer for professional malpractice. Recognizing the general rule that an attorney will only be held liable for negligence to his client, the court determined that "the relationship between the insurer and the retained defense counsel [is] less than a client-attorney relationship." *Bell*, 475 N.W.2d at 297. The court further determined, however, that although the insurer is not a client of defense counsel, the defense counsel nevertheless "occupies a fiduciary relationship to the insured, as well as to the insurance company." *Bell*, 475 N.W.2d at 297. Recognizing further that "the tripartite relationship between insured, insurer, and defense counsel contains rife possibility [sic] of conflict," *Bell*, 475 N.W.2d at 297, the court reasoned that "[t]o hold that an attorney-client relationship exists between insurer and defense counsel could indeed work mischief, yet to hold that a mere commercial relationship exists would work obfuscation and injustice." *Bell*, 475 N.W.2d at 297.

Nor is Michigan unique in concluding that the insured is the sole client of defense counsel. . . .

Respondents argue vigorously that the interests of an insurer and an insured usually coincide and that most litigation is settled within an insured's coverage limits. These arguments gloss over the stark reality that the relationship between an insurer and insured is permeated with potential conflicts. Compare Thomas D. Morgan, *What Insurance*

Scholars Should Know About Professional Responsibility, 4 Conn.Ins.L.J. 1, 7–8, 1997 (concluding that designating insurer "a second client . . . would routinely create the potential for conflicts of interest"); Kent D. Syverud, *What Professional Responsibility Scholars Should Know About Insurance*, 4 CONN. INS. L.J. 17, 23–24, 1997 (recognizing "[b]oth insurance companies and insureds have important and meaningful stakes in the outcome [of] a lawsuit against the insureds, stakes that include not just the money that the insurance company must pay in defense and settlement, but also the uninsured liabilities of the insured, which include not just any judgment in excess of liability limits, but also the insured's reputation and other non-economic stakes. The history of liability insurance suggests that unbridled control of the defense of litigation by either the insurance company or the insured creates incentives for the party exercising that control to take advantage of the other"). Compare also Restatement (Third) of the Law Governing Lawyers § 215, Comment f(5) (Proposed Final Draft No. 2, 1998) . . . (recognizing "[m]aterial divergence[s] of interest might exist between a liability insurer and an insured. . . . Such occasions for conflict may exist at the outset of the representation or may be created by events that occur thereafter"). In cases where an insured's exposure exceeds his insurance coverage, where the insurer provides a defense subject to a reservation of rights, and where an insurer's obligation to indemnify its insured may be excused because of a policy defense, there are potential conflicts of interest.

We reject Respondents' implicit premise that the Rules of Professional Conduct need not apply when the interests of insurers and insureds coincide. The Rules of Professional Conduct have application in all cases involving attorneys and clients. Moreover, whether the interests of insurers and insureds coincide can best be determined with the perfect clarity of hindsight. Before the final resolution of any claim against an insured, there clearly exists the potential for conflicts of interest to arise. Further, we reject the suggestion that the contractual relationship between insurer and insured supersedes or waives defense counsels' obligations under the Rules of Professional Conduct. We decline to recognize a vast exception to the Rules of Professional Conduct that would sanction relationships colored with the appearance of impropriety in order to accommodate the asserted economic exigencies of the insurance market. . . . We hold that under the Rules of Professional Conduct, the insured is the sole client of defense counsel.

We caution, however, that this holding should not be construed to mean that defense counsel have a "blank check" to escalate litigation costs nor that defense counsel need not ever consult with insurers. Under Rule 1.5, M.R.Prof.Conduct, for example, an attorney must charge reasonable fees. See Rule 1.5, M.R.Prof.Conduct (providing in part that "[a] lawyer's fees shall be reasonable"). Nor, finally, should our holding be taken to signal that defense counsel cannot be held accountable for their work.

Respondents argue further, however, that even if an insurer is not a co-client of defense counsel, an insurer's control of litigation is necessary and appropriate. Respondents argue that the insurer must control the litigation in order to meet its duties to the insured to indemnify and to provide a defense. Further, Respondents argue that the insured has a good faith duty to cooperate with the insurer in defense of a claim that warrants an insurer's control of litigation, and that in any event insureds agree to insurers' control of litigation. Respondents also argue that insureds typically contract for a limited defense that does not protect their reputational interests and that they are not entitled to unlimited expenditures on their behalf. Further, Respondents assert that insurers and insureds have "aligned" interests in minimizing litigation costs and settlements.

None of these arguments is persuasive. Animating them is the deeply flawed premise that by contract insurers and insureds may dispense with the Rules of Professional Conduct. . . .

We conclude that whether the requirement of prior approval seldom results in denials of authorization for defense counsel to perform legal services begs the question whether the requirement of prior approval violates the Rules of Professional Conduct. Without reaching the issue here, moreover, we caution further that a mere requirement of consultation may be indistinguishable, in its interference with a defense counsel's exercise of independent judgment and ability to provide competent representation, from a requirement of prior approval. Further, the entitlement of insurers not to pay for overpriced or unnecessary services, which Petitioners do not dispute, also begs the question whether the requirement of prior approval violates the Rules of Professional Conduct.

Finally, Respondents argue that their billing and practice rules do not interfere with defense counsels' freedom of action. As previously discussed, they suggest that when an insurer denies approval for particular actions that defense counsel propose, nothing prevents defense counsel from exercising their independent judgment and doing the very thing for which the insurer has denied approval. We reject Respondents' underlying dubious premise that the threat of withholding payment does not interfere with the independent judgment of defense counsel. The very action taken by Petitioners in seeking declaratory relief in the present case is a blunt repudiation of that speculative premise. Further, if the threat of withholding payment were quite as toothless as Respondents suggest, we doubt that they would make such a threat, let alone that they would expressly incorporate it in their billing and practice rules.

C. Whether the requirement of prior approval violates the Rules of Professional Conduct.

Having concluded that the insured is the sole client of defense counsel, we turn to the fundamental issue whether the requirement of prior approval in billing and practice rules conflicts with defense counsels' duties under the Rules of Professional Conduct. The parties appear to agree that defense counsel may not abide by agreements limiting the scope of representation that interfere with their duties under the Rules of Professional Conduct. Compare Annotated Model Rules of Professional Conduct (Fourth ed. Center for Professional Responsibility American Bar Association) Rule 1.2, p. 12, Comment [4] (concluding "[t]he objectives or scope of services provided by a lawyer may be limited by agreement with the client or by the terms under which the lawyer's services are made available to the client. . . . [5] An agreement concerning the scope of representation must accord with the Rules of Professional Conduct and other law. Thus, the client may not be asked to agree to representation so limited in scope as to violate Rule 1.1").

We conclude that the requirement of prior approval fundamentally interferes with defense counsels' exercise of their independent judgment, as required by Rule 1.8(f), M.R.Prof.Conduct. Further, prior approval creates a substantial appearance of impropriety in its suggestion that it is insurers rather than defense counsel who control the day to day details of a defense.

Montana is not alone in rejecting arrangements that fetter lawyers' undivided duty of loyalty to their clients and their independence of professional judgment in representing their clients. In Petition of Youngblood (Tenn.1995), 895 S.W.2d 322, the court determined that for inhouse attorney employees of an insurance company to represent insureds was not a per se ethical violation. However, the *Youngblood* court emphasized the loyalty that an attorney owes an insured and concluded that

> Some of the usual characteristics incident to [the employer-employee] relationship cannot exist between the insurer and the attorney representing an insured. The employer cannot control the details of the attorney's performance, dictate the strategy or tactics employed, or limit the attorney's professional discretion with regard to the representation. Any policy, arrangement or device which effectively limits, by design or operation, the attorney's professional judgment on behalf of or loyalty to the client is prohibited by the Code, and, undoubtedly, would not be consistent with public policy.

Youngblood, 895 S.W.2d at 328. The court went to conclude that "[t]he same loyalty is owed the client whether the attorney is employed and paid by the client, is a salaried employee of the insurer, or is an independent contractor engaged by the insurer." *Youngblood*, 895 S.W.2d at 328. . . .

We hold that defense counsel in Montana who submit to the requirement of prior approval violate their duties under the Rules of Professional Conduct to exercise their independent judgment and to give their undivided loyalty to insureds. Compare Rule 1.7(b) (providing "[a] lawyer shall not represent a client if the representation of that client may be materially limited by the lawyer's responsibility to another client or to a third person"); Annotated Model Rules of Professional Conduct, Comment [4] to Rule 1.7 (concluding "[t]he critical questions are the likelihood that a conflict will eventuate and, if it does, whether it will materially interfere with the lawyer's independent professional judgment in considering alternatives or foreclose courses of action that reasonably should be pursued on behalf of the client"); State v. Jones (1996), 278 Mont. 121, 125, 923 P.2d 560, 563 (concluding "[t]he duty of loyalty is 'perhaps the most basic of counsel's duties' "). [The court's discussion of the second issue is omitted.]

* * *

The tripartite relationship. Other courts have concluded that defense counsel in these kinds of situations represent both the insurer and the insured. *See, e.g.*, Nevada Yellow Cab Corp. v. Eighth Judicial Dist. Court, 152 P.3d 737 (Nev. 2007).

* * *

C. BUSINESS TRANSACTIONS WITH CLIENTS

Please read ABA Model Rule of Professional Conduct,
Rule 1.8(a), (c), (d) & (k) and
Comments [1]–[3], [9] & [20].

Lawyers must proceed with caution when entering business transactions with clients. Some of the more common transactions include an attorney's attempt to seek a loan from a client, an attorney's attempt to obtain an investment from a client in the lawyer's side business, or an attorney's desire to invest in a client's business. If the client later determines he or she is unhappy with the transaction, the client may sue the lawyer for breach of fiduciary duty, undue influence, or a similar cause of action. (Alternatively, if the lawyer sues the client over the transaction, the attorney can expect the client to raise the lawyer's breach of fiduciary duty or undue influence as a defense). Lawyers must remember that these are not arm's length transactions. Courts will presume the transaction is the product of attorney abuse of client trust and the attorney can only overcome that presumption by showing that attorney went to great lengths to protect the client. The first case that follows addresses this issue.

In an effort to guide attorneys in fulfilling their fiduciary duty, professional conduct rules provide detailed direction regarding the steps attorneys should take prior to entering a transaction with a client. Under Model Rule 1.8(a), an attorney entering a business transaction with a client must: (1) ensure that the transaction's terms are fair and reasonable and fully disclosed to the client in writing; (2) provide the client advice in writing that it is desirable for the attorney to obtain independent counsel; and (3) obtain informed, written consent of the client to the terms of the transaction including the lawyer's role in the transaction. The discipline consequences of failing to comply with such a professional conduct rule are addressed in the second case.

* * *

SECURITY FEDERAL SAVINGS & LOAN ASSOCIATION OF NASHVILLE V. RIVIERA, LTD.

856 S.W.2d 709 (Tenn. 1992)

CANTRELL, J.

[This case arose out of a failed business transaction between Tom Robinson, a business professional and engineer, and Mickey Ridings, who is an accountant and former IRS auditor as well as a licensed attorney. Ridings specialized in financial planning. He advised Robinson's companies on pensions and benefits, and he also provided personal financial advice to Robinson. Ridings also partnered with Jack Redditt the partnership Riviera, Ltd. The Riviera partnership sold an apartment building to Robinson. After the transaction was completed, Robinson learned that the building was worth less than anticipated. In addition, Robinson found that he could not take advantage of favorable tax benefit that attorney Ridings had told him would be available.]

. . .

II.

We will address the fraud claim first. Mr. Robinson says that he was induced to enter into the transaction because of Mr. Ridings' fraudulent misrepresentations concerning the value of the property and the ability to take advantage of Riviera's 1987 losses. We think all the parties would concede that the representations concerning the tax benefits turned out to be false. Although the appellees assert that Mr. Robinson failed to prove the value of the property as of the date of the sale, the proof does fairly establish that the property was worth far less than the $2,500,000 to $2,700,000 represented by Mr. Ridings.

False representations alone, however, will not affect the validity of a transaction. The purchaser must have relied on the misrepresentations, and the reliance must have been reasonable under the circumstances.

If this were an arm's length transaction, we do not think Mr. Robinson could claim that his reliance on the representations about the property's value and the tax consequences was reasonable. He is a well-informed and sophisticated businessman accustomed to regarding such hyperbole with a jaundiced eye. Concerning the tax consequences of the sale, Mr. Robinson was actually warned . . . to obtain independent advice before signing the agreement. Moreover, the representations about the property's value had so little substantive underpinning that one much less astute than Mr. Robinson should have been suspicious.

Under these circumstances we do not think Mr. Robinson has made out a case on the basis of Mr. Ridings' fraudulent representations.

III.

A.

It is another matter, however, if the transaction was not at arm's length. As Justice Cardozo said in his famous quote in Meinhard v. Salmon, 249 N.Y. 458, 164 N.E. 545 (1928):

> "Many forms of conduct permissible in a workaday world for those acting at arm's length, are forbidden to those bound by fiduciary ties. A trustee is held to something stricter than the morals of the market place. Not honesty alone, but the punctilio of an honor the most sensitive, is then the standard of behavior."

Id. at 464, 164 N.E. at 546.

It would be difficult to find a legal principle that enjoys a wider application. In Turner v. Leathers, 191 Tenn. 292, 232 S.W.2d 269 (1950), the Supreme Court of Tennessee quoted Pomeroy's *Equity Jurisprudence*, 5th Ed., Vol. 3, § 956, p. 792:

> Whenever two persons stand in such a relation that, while it continues, confidence is necessarily reposed by one, and the influence which naturally grows out of that confidence is possessed by the other, and this confidence is abused, or the influence is exerted to obtain an advantage at the expense of the confiding party, the person so availing himself of his position will not be permitted to retain the advantage, *although the transaction could not have been impeached if no confidential relation had existed.*

Id. at 298, 232 S.W.2d at 271 (emphasis in original).

This same principle applies to the whole reach of confidential and fiduciary relationships: trustee and beneficiary, attorney and client, confidential friend and adviser.

In Bayliss v. Williams, 46 Tenn. (Cold.) 440 (1869), the Supreme Court applied the same rule to a relationship founded on trust and confidence alone without any contractual obligations. The court said:

> Though Williams was not, by employment for compensation, their attorney or agent, he put himself in that relation by reason of friendship and gratuitous service proferred by him, and accepted by them, and of confidence upon and by them in him;
>
> . . . .

Id. at 442.

B.

We think it is inescapable that Mr. Ridings was in a position of trust and confidence with respect to Mr. Robinson. Even the most astute business people are not experts on every aspect of their trade. They rely on the advice of skilled professionals—especially in the maze of regulations presided over by the IRS. Although Mr. Ridings seeks to avoid a finding of a fiduciary relationship by showing that he was not acting as Mr. Robinson's attorney at the time of the Riviera transaction, it is not necessary to show employment to perform services connected with the transaction. Nor is it necessary to show employment of any sort at the precise time of the transaction. Not many attorney-client relationships involve continuous day-to-day legal obligations, but the relationship of trust and confidence reaches across the gaps in actual employment and endures until it is clearly terminated.

In addition, Mr. Ridings overlooks the fact that the same principles of fiduciary duty apply to other relationships such as that of confidential friend and adviser. The proof clearly shows that as to his personal taxes, Mr. Robinson relied upon the advice of Mr. Ridings.

Considering all the evidence in this case we are of the opinion that the evidence preponderates against the chancellor's finding that no fiduciary relationship existed between Mr. Ridings and Mr. Robinson.

C.

Transactions between persons in a confidential relationship are not automatically invalid. The relationship of trust and confidence between persons in a fiduciary relationship, however, commands the close attention of the courts to the fairness of any transaction between them. The law raises a presumption that the transaction is invalid and the evidence required to overcome the presumption is determined by the circumstances of each case. The factors which are important in determining whether a transaction is fair include: (1) whether the fiduciary made a full and frank disclosure of all relevant information within his possession; (2) whether the consideration was adequate; and (3) whether the principal had independent advice before completing the transaction.

We are of the opinion that Mr. Ridings has failed to show that the transaction was fair. In fact, the proof demonstrates that the agreement was decidedly unfair to Mr. Robinson. Although Mr. Ridings maintains that he did not profit from the transaction, and the chancellor so found, we think the evidence clearly preponderates against that finding. Mr. Ridings got out from under the liability for the partnership debt, which in itself was a substantial benefit. By the terms of the agreement, he was also to receive $125,000 for his limited partnership interest which cost him nothing. The property was worth substantially less than the value represented to Mr. Robinson, and, when the plan to reap a tax benefit failed, most of the consideration for the transaction vanished.

* * *

IOWA SUPREME COURT ATTORNEY DISCIPLINARY BD. v. WINTROUB

745 N.W.2d 469 (Iowa 2008)

APPEL, J.

In this case, we consider the sanctions recommended by the Iowa Supreme Court Grievance Commission (Commission) against a previously suspended Iowa lawyer who allegedly engaged in improper business transactions with a client, neglected a client matter, and improperly retained an unearned fee. For the reasons expressed below, we reprimand the lawyer for his misconduct, but impose no further sanction in addition to his previously imposed two-year suspension. . . .

Bergman Matters

The undisputed facts reveal that Wintroub and Bergman were close personal friends for many years before the two entered into an attorney-client relationship. Over time, Bergman retained Wintroub to represent him on legal matters, usually involving litigation. Bergman frequently employed more than one attorney on the same matter, however, and Wintroub was not Bergman's attorney for business, corporate, or personal financial matters. The parties stipulated that Bergman believed that Wintroub was acting in his best interest at all times relevant to this disciplinary proceeding and that Bergman trusted Wintroub to do what was right.

In January 1994, Wintroub formed a Nebraska corporation called Takara Enterprises, Inc. for the purpose of buying, promoting, and selling artwork created by Seikichi Takara. In January 1999, at a time when Wintroub was representing Bergman in at least two lawsuits, Wintroub sold Bergman 22.5 shares of stock in Takara, Inc. for the sum of $150,000. Wintroub did not advise Bergman, a sophisticated investor, to seek independent counsel in connection with the transaction.

Shortly thereafter, Wintroub also procured a personal loan from Bergman. By May 25, 1999, loans totaling $275,000 from Bergman to Wintroub were memorialized in a promissory note drafted by Wintroub. The loan was unsecured and bore a rate of zero percent interest.

Prior to formalizing the loan, Wintroub made several disclosures to Bergman. He told Bergman that (1) he had monies owed to him from his principal client; (2) he had expanded his business in reliance on this client; (3) he had invested his personal financial resources to pay the expenses of his law practice; (4) he had exhausted his credit; (5) he had no other source of funds to keep his law practice in operation; (6) without the loan he might have to cut back his law practice, but would continue to represent Bergman; and (7) he had no idea when he would be able to repay the loan, but that it would certainly be a while. Wintroub did not advise Bergman to seek independent counsel to review the loan documents or transaction.

In 2000 and 2001, Bergman asked Wintroub to start paying on the promissory note, but Wintroub was unable to do so. In December 2000, Wintroub released John Sens, an associate, from his law firm. Sens had previously been assigned several of the Bergman matters. On February 21, 2001, Bergman terminated Wintroub's representation in a litigation matter adverse to James Moyer. Bergman then retained Sens as counsel. Sens sent Wintroub letters dated February 27, March 28, April 4, and June 13 asking Wintroub to deliver the Moyer file to him. Wintroub had conversations with Sens and Bergman in an attempt to persuade them to allow him to continue the representation. Among other things, Wintroub claimed that he intended the attorney's fees earned in the Moyer matter to be a source of repayment of the Bergman loan. Bergman, however, refused and, on September 12, 2001, filed a declaratory judgment action against Wintroub that, among other things, sought the return of the Moyer file. At this point, Wintroub returned the file. He also declared bankruptcy, thereby frustrating efforts by Bergman to collect on the loan.

Discussion.

A. Business Relations with Client.

Wintroub engaged in two business transactions with a client in which he and his client admittedly had conflicting interests. While there is no blanket prohibition on such transactions, our ethical rules in this area are very demanding. We have long held that when an attorney engages in business transactions with a client involving conflicting interests, the burden is on the attorney to show that he acted in good faith and made full disclosures. As a result of this burden, a record that fails to show affirmatively that a client was fully advised about the facts of a transaction or its legal consequences leads to an ethical violation.

We have further found that full disclosure means more than simply disclosing the material terms of a transaction. Full disclosure means the use of active diligence on the part of the attorney to "fully disclose every relevant fact and circumstance which the client should know to make an intelligent decision concerning the wisdom of entering the agreement." Further, the attorney must give the same kind of legal advice that the client would have received if the transaction involved a stranger and not the attorney. More recently, we emphasized that lawyers engaged in business transactions with clients involving conflicting interests " 'have a duty to explain carefully, clearly and cogently why independent legal advice is required.' "

Wintroub made significant material disclosures in connection with both of the Bergman transactions. In connection with the sale of stock in Takara, Inc., however, the stipulation upon which this case was tried did not show that Wintroub disclosed the financial performance of the company through financial statements, annual reports, or oral summaries for the period beginning in January 1994, when Wintroub formed Takara, until the time of Bergman's investment in January 1999. As a result, Wintroub has failed to meet his burden of showing full disclosure of every relevant fact and circumstance as required by our cases involving business relations with clients. Further, there is no record that Wintroub advised Bergman regarding the lack of liquidity ordinarily associated with minority interests in closely held corporations or the lack of control minority interests have over management. Finally, Wintroub admits that he did not advise Bergman of the need to obtain independent counsel in connection with the transaction. Because of Wintroub's failure to demonstrate full factual disclosure and his failure to urge Bergman to seek independent counsel, we conclude Wintroub violated DR 5–104(A) (a lawyer shall not enter into a business transaction with a client if they have differing interests therein and the client expects the lawyer to exercise professional judgment therein for the protection of the client unless the client has consented after full disclosure).

In connection with the personal loan, Wintroub made a robust disclosure of his own dire financial circumstances. Nevertheless, Wintroub committed an ethical violation when he failed to urge Bergman to seek independent counsel prior to entering into this substantial transaction and to explain why independent counsel was important. In connection with the loan transaction, competent independent counsel would have engaged in an interactive process that would have questioned the unsecured nature of the loan, the lack of interest or timetable for repayment, and possible contingencies that could arise, likely demonstrating why the unstructured nature of the loan was not in Bergman's best interests. While Wintroub may have fairly disclosed his financial circumstances, competent counsel would have explored Bergman's own financial needs and the potential for the unstructured loan transaction serving as a point of contention in the future. The record is devoid of evidence that Wintroub made any of these disclosures. We conclude that Wintroub violated DR 5–104(A) in connection with the loan transaction.

We reiterate, again, our statement that perhaps the safest and best course for an attorney is to decline to personally participate in business transactions where the attorney and the client have differing interests. The high standard of disclosure expected in these situations is difficult to meet. By insisting that the client obtain independent legal advice, the attorney may avoid any perception that his communications with his client have been colored or less than candid on the transaction in question, but even so, full disclosure of all relevant facts and circumstances is required.

* * *

D. ADDITIONAL TYPES OF CONFLICTS

Use of information related to the representation of a client. Lawyers may not use information learned from their clients in a way that disadvantages the client. For example, the hypothetical in Comment [2] notes that lawyers may learn that their client plans to develop a new shopping center, which is likely to raise surrounding property values. Lawyers may not use that information to invest in surrounding property (or to recommend such an investment to others) if there is a chance that the client may want to purchase the property and extend the development; in such a case, the lawyer would be competing with the client. Comment [2] states that "[t]he Rule does not prohibit uses that do not disadvantage the client," which suggests that the lawyer's investment in surrounding property would not violate the rule as long as the client had no interest in purchasing it—thus requiring, at least implicitly, client consent to the investment, as the lawyer cannot be sure of the client's plans without asking. However, it is important to remember that other sources of law may prohibit lawyer action even where Model Rule 1.8 is silent. So, for example, a lawyer may learn confidential information about a publicly-traded company that is likely to affect the stock price. Even if the client would not suffer any disadvantage, the lawyer cannot trade on that information without running afoul of federal insider-trading regulation.

Receipt of gifts. Although Model Rule 1.8(c) does not prohibit a lawyer from accepting a gift from a client, as Comment [6] notes, a gift may be voidable under the doctrine of undue influence. If a confidential or fiduciary relationship exists between a donee and a donor, the burden of proof is typically placed on the donee to show by clear and convincing evidence that the donor made the gift voluntarily and with a full understanding of the facts. *See, e.g.*, Matter of Herm's Estate, 284 N.W.2d 191, 200 (Iowa 1979). The fact that a gift is substantial or disproportionate may make it less likely for a fiduciary to satisfy this standard. Roberts-Douglas v. Meares, 624 A.2d 405, 422 (D.C. 1992).

Acquiring literary or media rights relating to a client's representation. What is the point of the prohibition in 1.8(d)? D.C. Ethics Opinion 334 (2004) dealt with an inquiry involving the situation in which a lawyer would receive compensation from media representatives for the lawyer's cooperation and the rights to the lawyer's story concerning the lawyer's representation of a client. The opinion concluded that there was no violation of D.C.'s version of Model Rule 1.8(d) because the rule only prohibits a lawyer from acquiring literary or media rights, not selling his own rights. However, the opinion noted that the proposed arrangement raised "serious concerns" under the more general standard of Model Rule 1.7(a)(2) regarding conflicts of interest arising from the lawyer's personal interests and the interests of the client.

Making loans or gifts to clients to assist with living expenses. If a client loans money to his or her attorney, that transaction is governed by 1.8(a), as discussed in the cases above. When lawyers loan money to clients, however, that is governed by 1.8(e) and comment [10], which prohibits lawyers from "making or guaranteeing loans to their clients for living expenses, because to do so would encourage clients to pursue lawsuits that might not otherwise be brought and because such assistance gives lawyers too great a financial stake in the litigation." Some have argued that this rule exacerbates a disparity in bargaining power, especially in cases where the defendant is significantly wealthier than the plaintiff. Looking back at the introductory chapter hypothetical, imagine that the plaintiff suing for employment discrimination is currently unemployed and facing possible foreclosure. If the defendant offers a settlement significantly lower than what the plaintiff could reasonably expect to win at trial, might the plaintiff nevertheless feel economically pressured to accept a quick settlement? Third party lending was historically prohibited as "maintenance and champerty" that impermissibly encouraged litigation. Now, however, that perception is diminishing, and in a growing number of states, third-party lenders may offer loans to the client to be repaid out of a later judgment or settlement.

Limitations on malpractice remedies. Model Rule 1.8(h) contains strict requirements for lawyers who seek to limit their potential malpractice liability. Prospective waivers of malpractice remedies are enforceable only if the client was separately represented in making the agreement. Retrospective settlement agreements for particular claims require that the client be "advised in writing of the desirability of seeking and . . . given a reasonable opportunity to seek the advice of independent legal counsel in connection therewith."

Sex with clients. Does there really need to be a disciplinary rule for this? Rule 1.7(a)(2) already prohibits a lawyer from representing a client where the lawyer's independent professional judgment is materially limited. What, if anything, does Rule 1.8(j) add to Rule 1.7(a)(2)? Some have argued that the specific rule is redundant. Others believe that a specific rule simplifies disciplinary proceedings in cases where other types of misconduct may co-exist, especially in cases involving an imbalance of power or coercive conduct. The following excerpt discusses how the rule is applied in a transactional setting:

CARL A. PIERCE, *ETHICS 2000 AND THE TRANSACTIONAL PRACTITIONER*

3 Transactions: TENN. J. BUS. L. 7 (Spring/Summer 2002)

IX. Sexual Relations with Constituents of Organizational Clients: A new Rule 1.8(j) prohibits a lawyer from having sexual relations with a client unless a consensual sexual relationship existed between them before the client-lawyer relationship was formed. The related Comments do not offer a definition of sexual relations, but Comment [19] explains how the prohibition applies to lawyers who represent organizational clients. Without differentiation between in-house counsel or outside counsel, a lawyer for an organizational client may not have sexual relations with an organizational constituent who supervises, directs, or regularly consults with the lawyer concerning the organization's legal matters.[1] A new Rule 1.8(k) and Comment [20] clarify that this prohibition does not apply to other lawyers associated with the sexually active lawyer in a firm. In short, the lawyer working with an organizational constituent may not be a lover as well as a lawyer, but would be allowed to be a matchmaker on behalf of other lawyers in the firm.

The new comments do not explain the relationship between Rule 1.8(j) and Rule 1.7, the general conflict of interest rule, beyond noting in a new Comment [18] that sexual relationships that predate the client-lawyer relationship might materially limit the lawyer's representation of the client and thereby require compliance with Rule 1.7. What this

---

[1] In ABA Formal Ethics Opinion 92–364 (1992), the ABA Standing Committee on Ethics and Professional Responsibility warned that a corporation's lawyer who is sexually involved with a corporate constituent might, in the interest of continuing the sexual relationship, refrain from reporting the constituent's misconduct to higher authorities as might be required by Rule 1.13(b).

suggests, of course, is that, in some circumstances, a lawyer who is personally prohibited from having sex with an organizational constituent by Rule 1.8(j) would also have been prohibited from doing so by Rule 1.7. This would be a personal interest conflict, and at a minimum would require consent of an organizational constituent other than the lawyer's sexual partner. It might, however, even arise to a non-consentable conflict. Given the change to Rule 1.10 noted above, such a conflict would not be automatically imputed to others lawyers in the firm, but it would be imputed to them if the personal interest of the prohibited lawyer presents a significant risk of materially limiting the representation of the client by the remaining lawyers in the firm. While one could probably work such a plot line into a novel about corporate legal intrigue—*e.g.*, senior partner having illicit affair with CEO in circumstances in which CEO is engaged in misconduct that the lawyer might have to reveal to the board of directors by Rule 1.13(b)—the likelihood of such happenings in real life is sufficiently low that it should not be necessary to add sexual relationships to the firm's conflicts data base. More than enough said.

* * *

Profile of attorney professionalism. Lawyers and judges are often nervous about their use of social media, and rightfully so; cautionary tales abound of attorneys who have disclosed their clients' confidential information online, inadvertently created a risk of liability by offering legal advice without giving the matter due care, or engaged in improper electronic communications with prospective jurors or opposing parties. Nonetheless, these risks do not mean that lawyers should avoid communicating through social media. Lawyers and judges can benefit personally and professionally from maintaining a connection to the public, and social media makes that connection easier than ever before.

The following examples show that lawyers can use social media to offer information and humor and to reflect their personality while maintaining a high level of professionalism:

- Texas Supreme Court Justice Don Willett was featured in the New York Times for his prolific use of Twitter. *See* Jesse Wegman, *Some Judicial Opinions Require Only 140 Characters: Justice Don Willett of the Texas Supreme Court Lights Up Twitter*, N.Y. TIMES (Sept. 24, 2014). Justice Willett is careful to avoid commenting on matters that might come before his court, and also avoids controversial issues and partisan commentary, focusing instead on family, sports, and general current events. His posts often reflect his sense of humor ("sometimes corny and often funny," according to the *Times*). Before he makes a post, he reports that "[u]sually what goes through my mind before I hit the tweet button is, did I misspell or mis-grammatize anything, but also, is this worth polluting the interwebs with for posterity?" *Id.* Justice Willett finds social media to be a good way of keeping in touch with voters (judges in Texas must run for election), and has stated that he believes candidates who avoid social media are committing "political malpractice." *Id.* His Twitter handle is @JusticeWillett.

- Attorney Jessica Mederson, a partner at Hansen Reynolds Dickinson Crueger LLC in Wisconsin, also uses Twitter; in a recent article on social media, she commented that "I've met several other e-discovery lawyers on Twitter, as they retweet my posts and I retweet theirs. I've actually been at e-discovery conferences since I joined Twitter where I'm having conversations on Twitter with other conference attendees." Jessica C. Mederson, *5 Tips to Love and Live with Your Blog*, WISC. LAW., June 2014. In addition, Mederson writes for two separate blogs. The first, "e-Discovery Matters," at http://www.e-discoverymatters.com/, covers recent developments in electronic discovery. It provides a service to practicing lawyers by "analyz[ing] the court decisions and government actions/laws/regulations impacting e-discovery issues in U.S.-based litigation." Mederson has also teamed up with attorney Josh Gilliland to write a second blog, "The Legal Geeks," at http://thelegal geeks.com/blog/. Mederson and Gilliland offer a lighthearted take on the legal side of geekdom, covering "everything from Dune to Battlestar Galactica to the Rule Against Perpetuities." The blog makes occasional forays into legal ethics issues—in one post, Mederson analyzes the constitutional protections for some of the more amusing and outlandish lawyer ads found on YouTube. *Who You Gonna Call? 1-800-LawRocks*, at http://thelegalgeeks.com/blog/?p=7534. In another post, Gilliland asks "Can Daredevil Ethically Accept Iron Man's Gift of Sight?" *See* http://thelegalgeeks.com/blog/?p=7767. Gilliland analyzes that question under the California code and rules of professional conduct—but after studying this chapter, you should be able to analyze whether the answer would be the same under Model Rule of Professional Conduct 1.8.

SECTION 6

TERMINATION OF THE CLIENT-LAWYER RELATIONSHIP AND DUTIES TO FORMER CLIENTS

∎ ∎ ∎

Every client-lawyer relationship—both good and bad—will come to an end at some point in time. Typically this occurs when the lawyer or client terminates the representation or the lawyer completes the representation in a matter the lawyer is handling for the client. It is possible, of course, for a lawyer and a client to be in a client-lawyer relationship either before the lawyer begins to represent the client in a matter or after a representation in a matter has been completed or terminated either by the lawyer or the client. For present purposes, the triggering issue in the chapters in this part is whether a lawyer's client has become a former, rather than a current, client, because the client-lawyer relationship has come to an end. The end may come because the client fires the lawyer. The end may come because the lawyer fires the client. The end may come because the lawyer's job was done. The ending may be happy for both lawyer and client, for neither the lawyer nor the client, or for either the lawyer or the client, with the other being unhappy. The starting point, however, for the legal after-life of a client-lawyer relationship begins with its end. In Chapter 18 we introduce you to some of the issues that can arise in connection with termination of a lawyer's representation of a client. Then, in Chapter 19, we address the general duties owed by all lawyers and law firms to their former clients.

CHAPTER 18

TERMINATION OF THE
CLIENT-LAWYER RELATIONSHIP

■ ■ ■

Chapter hypothetical. Luther and Roseanne are law partners. Luther represents Carlene on a one-third contingent-fee basis in a personal injury action. Carlene is a bit of a pain. Carlene insists on talking to Luther at least three times a week, yet she frequently fails to assist Luther with information Luther needs from Carlene. Things came to a boiling point when, against Luther's strong advice, Carlene turned down a very reasonable settlement offer from the other side. Frustrated, Luther told Carlene he was quitting and filed a motion to withdraw as counsel, citing the details of Carlene's constant need for handholding, her failure to cooperate, and her rejection of the settlement offer as the basis. The court granted Luther's motion, and Carlene wound up representing herself at trial a few months later. Carlene lost and recovered nothing. Meanwhile, Roseanne has grown so tired of dealing with "irrational" clients that she has started to include a new provision in her contingent-fee agreements that requires a client to pay Roseanne at a rate of $200 per hour for all work performed if the client fires Roseanne without good cause. She recently attempted to enforce this provision after she was fired by her client, John. For several months, John had micromanaged Roseanne's work to the point that he insisted on reviewing, proofreading, and editing the pleadings that Roseanne drafted. Eventually, Roseanne refused to let John do so, while calling John "an ignorant hillbilly." John immediately fired Roseanne. Under Roseanne's agreement with John (and all her other clients), all disputes concerning fees are to be submitted to binding arbitration. As you read the material in the chapter, consider the following questions:

(A) Did Luther have grounds to withdraw from Carlene's representation?

(B) Luther sues Carlene, seeking to collect one-third of the settlement offer Carlene rejected. Alternatively, he seeks to recover for the reasonable value of the services he provided. Should he prevail? Would the answer be any different if Carlene had instead fired Luther because she lost faith in Luther after Luther advised Carlene to settle?

(C) Can Roseanne enforce her fee agreement against John?

* * *

A. TERMINATION BY CLIENT

**Please read ABA Model Rules of Professional Conduct,
Rule 1.16(a)(3) & (c) and Comments [4]–[6].**

* * *

1. GENERALLY

What do you think? Why, as Comment [4] provides, does a client have an absolute right to discharge a lawyer?

* * *

CAMPBELL V. BOZEMAN INVESTORS OF DULUTH

290 Mont. 374, 964 P.2d 41 (Mont., 1998)

NELSON, JUSTICE.

On December 3, 1992, Campbell was seriously injured when her vehicle collided with a van operated by Patrick Lund (Lund). The van was owned by Lund's employer, Bozeman Investors of Duluth d/b/a the Holiday Inn of Bozeman (Bozeman Investors). Bozeman Investors' insurer paid Campbell for the damage to her vehicle as well as $4,000 to $5,000 of her medical bills.

In January 1994, Bozeman Investors' insurer made an unsolicited offer to settle Campbell's claim for the sum of $22,000, less the amounts already paid for medical care and for the damage to Campbell's vehicle. Campbell, who had not yet consulted a physician to determine the extent of the injuries to her back, rejected the offer. On April 29, 1994, Campbell filed a personal injury action against Lund and Bozeman Investors.

[O]n December 8, 1994, Campbell entered into a contingent fee agreement with Hartelius and Morgan to render legal services in her suit against Bozeman Investors. The agreement provided that Campbell was to pay Hartelius and Morgan "33-1/3% OF ANY SETTLEMENT OBTAINED IN SAID CASE IF SAME IS SETTLED AT ANY TIME PRIOR TO INSTITUTING SUIT AND 40% OF ANY SETTLEMENT OBTAINED IN SAID CASE IF SAME IS SETTLED AT ANY TIME AFTER INSTITUTION OF SUIT."

. . .

On May 6, 1996, Campbell sent a letter to Hartelius and Morgan expressing dissatisfaction with their services and discharging them. Campbell later testified that she became dissatisfied with Hartelius and Morgan because they never wrote to Bozeman Investors' insurer requesting an advance payment for medical costs for surgery, did not request that a trial date be set, and did not adequately advise her about obtaining Social Security disability benefits. Hence, on June 6, 1996, Campbell filed a motion for substitution of counsel, requesting that Pohl be substituted as attorney of record in place of Hartelius and Morgan. The court granted her motion on June 25, 1996.

[The case eventually settled, and the amount of the settlement was kept confidential in accordance with the terms of the settlement.]

[Hartelius and Morgan sought payment of their fees from Campbell.] On March 5, 1997, the District Court entered its Findings of Fact and Conclusions of Law wherein the court determined that Hartelius was entitled to a fee of $6,600 and that Morgan was entitled to a fee of $2,200. The court entered judgment in accordance with these findings and conclusions on March 14, 1997.

Campbell appeals from the District Court's judgment regarding attorney fees and Hartelius and Morgan cross appeal.

Issue 1.

Whether the District Court erred in concluding that Hartelius and Morgan are entitled to attorney fees totaling $8800.

The District Court concluded that a client's right to discharge an attorney employed under a contingency fee contract is an implicit term of the contract and the client's discharge of the attorney, with or without cause, does not constitute a breach of that contract. The court further concluded that a client who discharges an attorney employed under a contingency fee contract for cause has no obligation to pay a fee to that attorney unless the attorney has substantially performed the services for which he was retained.

On that basis, the court determined that Campbell had not breached the contract by discharging Hartelius and Morgan. Moreover, the court determined that although Hartelius and Morgan were discharged for cause, they substantially performed the services for which they were retained prior to their discharge. Therefore, they were entitled to a fee limited to the reasonable value of their services. Thus, the court awarded $6600 to Hartelius and $2200 to Morgan.

First, we must determine whether, as Hartelius and Morgan contend, a client's discharge of his or her attorney is a breach of contract thus entitling the attorney to contract damages. We hold that it is not and does not.

In 1916, the New York Court of Appeals held that a contract under which an attorney is employed by a client has peculiar and distinctive features which differentiate it from ordinary contracts of employment, thus a client may, at any time for any reason or without any reason, discharge his or her attorney. Martin v. Camp (1916), 219 N.Y. 170, 114 N.E. 46, 47–48, modified 220 N.Y. 653, 115 N.E. 1044. Thus, the court reasoned that if the client has the right to terminate the relationship of attorney and client at any time without cause, the client cannot be compelled to pay damages for exercising a right which is an implied condition of the contract. *Martin*, 114 N.E. at 48. The court held that although the attorney may not recover damages for breach of contract, the attorney may recover the reasonable value of the services rendered. *Martin*, 114 N.E. at 48.

A majority of jurisdictions have since adopted the "client discharge rule" as set forth in *Martin*. (For a list of these jurisdictions, see Lester Brickman, *Setting the Fee when the Client Discharges a Contingent Fee Attorney* (Spring 1992), 41 Emory L.J. 367 n.37.) One such jurisdiction noted:

> The attorney-client relationship is one of special trust and confidence. The client must rely entirely on the good faith efforts of the attorney in representing his interests. This reliance requires that the client have complete confidence in the integrity and ability of the attorney and that absolute fairness and candor characterize all dealings between them. These considerations dictate that clients be given greater freedom to change legal representatives than might be tolerated in other employment relationships.

Rosenberg v. Levin (Fla.1982), 409 So.2d 1016, 1021. Another jurisdiction stated the following regarding the payment of damages for exercising the right to discharge an attorney:

> To allow an attorney to recover damages for services not actually rendered prior to termination of the attorney-client relationship would penalize the client in direct contravention of the client's absolute right to discharge his attorney.

> The right to discharge is obviously meaningless if the client is penalized by having to pay for services that have not been rendered. The client could conceivably be required to pay duplicate charges consisting of fees to the discharged attorney for services not rendered, in addition to those incurred by a newly appointed attorney for the same work.

Olsen and Brown v. City of Englewood (Colo.1995), 889 P.2d 673, 676–77 (citations omitted).

Finding considerable merit in the "client discharge rule" as expressed in *Martin*, *Rosenberg*, and *Olsen*, we follow those jurisdictions in holding that the discharge of an attorney by a client is not a breach of contract and does not give rise to contract damages. Therefore, we affirm the District Court on this issue.

We next must determine whether Hartelius and Morgan are entitled to a fee and on what basis that fee, if any, should be determined. The District Court concluded that Hartelius and Morgan were discharged for cause, however, they substantially performed the services for which they were retained and are thus entitled to a fee based on the reasonable value of the services rendered. Campbell alleges error in the court's determination arguing instead that this Court should formally adopt a rule that an attorney discharged for cause is not entitled to any fee. . . .

Instead, we agree with those jurisdictions that hold that regardless of whether an attorney was discharged with or without cause, that attorney is entitled to a quantum meruit recovery for the reasonable value of his services rendered to the time of discharge. Fracasse v. Brent (1972), 6 Cal.3d 784, 100 Cal.Rptr. 385, 494 P.2d 9, 14–15. We note one exception to this general rule, however-situations where the discharge occurs "on the courthouse steps," just prior to settlement and after much work by the attorney. In those cases some reviewing courts have, on appropriate facts, found that the entire fee was the reasonable value of the attorney's services. *Fracasse*, 100 Cal.Rptr. 385, 494 P.2d at 14. Here, however, Hartelius and Morgan were not discharged "on the courthouse steps," and, accordingly, we need not address this exception. Rather, the general quantum meruit rule applies.

Moreover, in the case *sub judice*, because we have determined that the general rule applies, it is not necessary for us to entertain a discussion of the reasons why Campbell discharged Hartelius and Morgan or whether those reasons constituted "cause." Rather, we review whether the District Court was correct in concluding that the reasonable value of the services rendered by Hartelius and Morgan was $6600 and $2200, respectively.

[The court held that the District Court did not abuse its discretion in awarding attorney fees to Hartelius in the amount of $6600 and to Morgan in the amount of $2200.]

Hartelius and Morgan contend that the District Court should have required Campbell to reveal the amount of the settlement. They argue that the court cannot effectively determine the amount of attorney fees owed until the settlement amount is known. We disagree. The amount of the settlement would only be necessary if the attorney fees were to be based on a percentage of that figure. Since we have already determined that Hartelius and Morgan are entitled only to the value of the services rendered, the amount of the settlement is immaterial.

Accordingly, we affirm the District Court's denial of Hartelius and Morgan's request to force Campbell to disclose the settlement amount.

* * *

Termination for cause vs. termination without cause. As *Campbell* hints at, the law among jurisdictions varies as to how much a lawyer working under a contingent-fee arrangement may recover when fired and whether the fact that the lawyer was fired "for cause" impacts the analysis. Should a lawyer recover anything if the lawyer was fired for good cause? Did Campbell have good cause to fire Hartelius and Morgan?

Limitations on a lawyer's right of recovery. Would Hartelius and Morgan have been able to recover the reasonable value of their services if Campbell had recovered nothing? The normal rule is that a lawyer's right to recover "accrues only upon the occurrence of the contingency." Plaza Shoe Store v. Hermel, Inc., 636 S.W.2d 53 (Mo. 1982). What if the reasonable value of the lawyer's services is determined to be more than what the client ended up recovering?

* * *

2. WRONGFUL DISCHARGE OF IN-HOUSE COUNSEL

Problem 18.1. Julia was employed by Brockman Industries as associate general counsel in its legal department. While working in this capacity, she reported to Brockman's General Counsel, Katherine. Eventually, Julia discovered that Katherine, who held herself out as a licensed attorney, did not possess a license to practice law. (Katherine had passed the bar exam, but had never passed the Multistate Professional Responsibility Examination.) Julia became concerned that Katherine was engaged in the unauthorized practice of law and discussed those concerns with Katherine. Katherine advised Julia to keep her mouth shut. Eventually, Julia decided that she was ethically obligated to report Katherine to the state's Board of Professional Responsibility. Upon learning that Julia had gone to the Board, Katherine fired Julia.

Julia has now sued Brockman on a theory of retaliatory discharge in violation of public policy. The relevant jurisdiction employs the "client discharge rule" described above and also employs the at-will employment rule, meaning that an employer is legally free to fire an employee for any reason. However, the jurisdiction has recognized an exception to the general at-will employment rule where an employee is fired for complying with an ethical or legal obligation and the firing offends public policy. Brockman argues that, given a lawyer's duty of confidentiality and the special relationship of trust between an in-house lawyer and her employer, the exception should not be available to an in-house lawyer who has been discharged. Should the court recognize this exception and permit Julia to bring her retaliatory discharge claim?

* * *

B. TERMINATION BY LAWYER

Please read ABA Model Rules of Professional Conduct, Rule 1.16 (a)–(c) and Comments [2]–[4], [7] & [8].

* * *

KRIEGSMAN V. KRIEGSMAN

150 N.J.Super. 474, 375 A.2d 1253 (App. Div. 1977)

MICHELS, J. A. D.

Appellants Messrs. Rose, Poley, Bromley and Landers (hereinafter "the Rose firm") appeal from an order of the Chancery Division denying their application to be relieved as attorneys for plaintiff Mary-Ann Kriegsman in this matrimonial action.

On December 22, 1975 plaintiff, who had been previously represented by other counsel, retained the Rose firm to represent her in a divorce action against her husband, defendant Bernard Kriegsman. The Rose firm requested and received consent to substitution of attorneys from plaintiff's former attorney. Plaintiff then paid an initial retainer of $1,000, plus $60 in court costs, with the understanding that she would be responsible for additional fees and expenses as litigation progressed. In March 1976 plaintiff paid the Rose firm another $1,000, plus $44 which was to be applied against costs.

During the 3½ months that the Rose firm represented plaintiff prior to its motion the firm had made numerous court appearances and had engaged in extensive office work in plaintiff's behalf. The unusual amount of work required was necessitated in part by the fact that defendant appeared pro se, was completely uncooperative and had refused to comply with some of the orders entered by the court. As of April 5, 1976 the Rose firm alleged that it had spent 110 hours on plaintiff's case, billed at $7,354.50, and had incurred disbursements of approximately $242. Since, by then, plaintiff was on welfare and since she apparently did not have sufficient funds to pay the additional fees incurred, the Rose firm contended that they were entitled to be relieved from further representation. Plaintiff opposed the application before the court, pointing out

> ... first of all, this case, I think, has accumulated a file this thick. I think at this point, for another attorney to step in, it would be very difficult to acquaint himself with every motion that has been brought up before this court. I feel that Mr. Koserowski (an associate in the Rose firm) has been with me, representing me, for four months, and when this case finally does go to trial, hopefully soon, he has all this knowledge at his

fingertips. Whereas another attorney would have to, I don't know how they can, wade through all of this, and really become acquainted with it. That's the first thing. Secondly, when I first went to this law firm, I spoke to Mr. Rose, and he knew exactly my circumstances. He knew that there were very few assets in the marriage. He knew that I would have to borrow money from relatives to pay the thousand dollar retainer fee that they asked for. They knew that my husband was going to represent himself, which would be a difficult situation. They also knew that he had done certain bizarre things, such as sending letters to people, and doing strange things; so, therefore, we might expect a difficult case from him. Yet, they consented to take my case. Of course, I don't think any attorney can guess, when he consents to represent somebody, what might occur. I imagine some cases go to trial immediately things get resolved, and my case is probably the other extreme, where everything possible has happened. I think it's unfortunate, and I think they've done a very fine job of representing me. I feel they should continue.

Judge Cariddi in the Chancery Division agreed with plaintiff and denied the application of the Rose firm, but set the case down for trial within the month. The Rose firm appealed. . . .

When a firm accepts a retainer to conduct a legal proceeding, it impliedly agrees to prosecute the matter to a conclusion. The firm is not at liberty to abandon the case without justifiable or reasonable cause, or the consent of its client. We are firmly convinced that the Rose firm did not have cause to abandon plaintiff's case, and that the trial judge properly exercised his discretion when he denied the firm's application and scheduled an early trial date. It was to plaintiff's and the firm's advantage that the matter be heard and disposed of as expeditiously as possible. With trial imminent, it would be extremely difficult for plaintiff to obtain other representation, and therefore she clearly would be prejudiced by the Rose firm's withdrawal.

Since the Rose firm undertook to represent plaintiff and demanded and was paid a retainer of $2,000, they should continue to represent plaintiff through the completion of trial. The firm should not be relieved at this stage of the litigation merely because plaintiff is unable to pay to them all of the fees they have demanded. We are not unmindful of the fact that the Rose firm has performed substantial legal services for plaintiff and clearly is entitled to reasonable compensation therefor. Nevertheless, an attorney has certain obligations and duties to a client once representation is undertaken. These obligations do not evaporate because the case becomes more complicated or the work more arduous or the retainer not as profitable as first contemplated or imagined. Attorneys must never lose sight of the fact that "the profession is a branch of the administration of justice and not a mere money-getting trade." Canons of Professional Ethics, No. 12. As Canon 44 of the Canons of Professional Ethics so appropriately states: "The lawyer should not throw up the unfinished task to the detriment of his client except for reasons of honor or self-respect." Adherence to these strictures in no way violates the constitutional rights of the members of the firm.

Affirmed.

* * *

WHITING V. LACARA

187 F.3d 317 (2d Cir. 1999)

PER CURIAM:

Garrett R. Lacara appeals from two orders of Judge Spatt denying Lacara's motions to withdraw as counsel for plaintiff-appellee Joseph M. Whiting. Although the record before Judge Spatt justified denial of the motions, amplification of Whiting's position at oral argument persuades us to reverse.

BACKGROUND

In July 1996, appellee, a former police officer, filed a civil rights action against Nassau County, the Incorporated Village of Old Brooksville, the Old Brooksville Police Department, other villages, and various individual defendants. The action was based on the termination of his employment as an officer. He sought $9,999,000 in damages.

Appellee's initial counsel was Jeffrey T. Schwartz. In October 1996, Robert P. Biancavilla replaced Schwartz. A jury was selected in October 1997 but was discharged when Biancavilla withdrew from the case with appellee's consent.

Whiting retained Lacara in December 1997. In June 1998, the district court partially granted defendants' summary judgment motion and dismissed plaintiff's due process claims. . . . The court scheduled the remaining claims, one free speech claim and two equal protection claims, for a jury trial on August 18, 1998. On July 20, 1998, the district court denied appellee's motion to amend his complaint to add a breach of contract claim and another due process claim. . . .

On August 6, 1998, Lacara moved to be relieved as counsel. In support, he offered an affidavit asserting that appellee "[had] failed to follow legal advice," that appellee "[wa]s not focused on his legal rights," and that appellee "demand[ed] publicity against legal advice." Lacara also asserted that appellee had failed to keep adequate contact with his office, was "not sufficiently thinking clearly to be of assistance at the time of trial," and would "be of little or no help during trial." Furthermore,

Lacara stated that appellee had "demand[ed] that [Lacara] argue collateral issues which would not be allowed in evidence," demanded that Lacara continue to argue a due process claim already dismissed by the court, and drafted a Rule 68 Offer without Lacara's consent and demanded that he serve it on defendants. Finally, Lacara asserted that on July 30, 1998, Whiting had entered his office and, without permission, had "commenced to riffle [Lacara's] 'in box.'" Lacara stated that he had to call 911 when Whiting had refused to leave the office. Lacara offered to provide further information to the court in camera. Whiting's responsive affidavit essentially denied Lacara's allegations. Whiting stated that he would not be opposed to an order relieving counsel upon the condition that Lacara's firm refund the legal fees paid by Whiting.

On August 13, Judge Spatt denied Lacara's motion to withdraw as counsel. Judge Spatt subsequently issued a written order giving the reasons for denying appellant's motion. . . .

On August 13, 1998, Lacara filed a notice of appeal and moved for an emergency stay of the district court's order and to be relieved as appellee's attorney. We granted Lacara's motion for an emergency stay pending appeal but denied his request for relief on the merits at that time. . . . At a status conference on September 23, 1998, the district court entertained another motion from Lacara to withdraw as counsel, which Judge Spatt again denied. Lacara filed a timely appeal, which was consolidated with the earlier appeal.

DISCUSSION

a) *Appellate Jurisdiction*

We first discuss whether we have jurisdiction over this appeal. The district court's order denying Lacara's motion to withdraw is neither a final judgment under 28 U.S.C. § 1291 nor an interlocutory order certified under 28 U.S.C. § 1292(b). Thus, we have jurisdiction, if at all, only under the collateral order doctrine, "a narrow exception to the general rule that interlocutory orders are not appealable as a matter of right." . . .

The collateral order doctrine "is limited to trial court orders affecting rights that will be irretrievably lost in the absence of an immediate appeal." . . . To fit within the collateral order exception, the interlocutory order must: "[i] conclusively determine the disputed question, [ii] resolve an important issue completely separate from the merits of the action, and [iii] be effectively unreviewable on appeal from a final judgment." . . .

The denial of Lacara's motion to withdraw as counsel satisfies each of the three requirements. An order denying counsel's motion to withdraw " 'conclusively determine(s) the disputed question,' because the only issue is whether . . . counsel will . . . continue his representation." . . . Moreover, whether Lacara must continue to serve as appellee's counsel is in the present circumstances an issue completely separate from the merits of the underlying action.

Finally, once a final judgment has been entered, the harm to Lacara will be complete, and no relief can be obtained on appeal. Unlike an order granting or denying a motion to disqualify an attorney, which primarily affects the interests of the underlying litigants, . . . an order denying counsel's motion to withdraw primarily affects the counsel forced to continue representing a client against his or her wishes. . . . Denial of a motion to withdraw is directly analogous to a denial of immunity or of a double jeopardy claim, which are reviewable under the collateral order doctrine on the ground that having to go through a trial is itself a loss of the right involved. . . . The injury to a counsel forced to represent a client against his will is similarly irreparable, and the district court's decision would be effectively unreviewable upon final judgment. We therefore have appellate jurisdiction.

b) *The Merits*

We review a district court's denial of a motion to withdraw only for abuse of discretion. . . . District courts are due considerable deference in decisions not to grant a motion for an attorney's withdrawal. . . . The trial judge is closest to the parties and the facts, and we are very reluctant to interfere with district judges' management of their very busy dockets.

Judge Spatt denied Lacara's motion pursuant to Rule 1.4 of the Civil Rules of the United States District Court for the Southern and Eastern Districts of New York, which provides that

> [a]n attorney who has appeared as attorney of record for a party may be relieved or displaced only by order of the court and may not withdraw from a case without leave of the court granted by order. Such an order may be granted only upon a showing by affidavit or otherwise of satisfactory reasons for withdrawal or displacement and the posture of the case, including its position, if any, on the calendar.

In addressing motions to withdraw as counsel, district courts have typically considered whether "the prosecution of the suit is [likely to be] disrupted by the withdrawal of counsel." . . .

Lacara does not claim that he faces mandatory withdrawal. Rather, he asserts three bases for "[p]ermissive withdrawal" under the Model Code: (i) Whiting "[i]nsists upon presenting a claim or defense that is not warranted under existing law and cannot be supported by good faith argument for an extension, modification, or reversal of existing law," Model Code DR 2–110(C)(1)(a); (ii) Whiting's "conduct [has] render[ed] it unreasonably difficult for [Lacara] to carry out employment effectively," DR 2–110(C)(1)(d); and (iii) Whiting has "[d]eliberately disregard[ed] an agreement or obligation to [Lacara] as to expenses or fees," DR 2–110(C)(1)(f). Although the Model Code "was drafted solely for its use in disciplinary proceedings and cannot by itself serve as a basis for granting a [m]otion to withdraw as counsel," we continue to believe that "the Model Code provides guidance for the court as to what constitutes 'good cause' to grant leave to withdraw as counsel." . . . However, a district court has wide latitude to deny a counsel's motion to withdraw, as here, on the eve of trial, where the Model Code merely permits withdrawal.

In the instant matter, we would be prepared to affirm if the papers alone were our only guide. Although Lacara has alleged a nonpayment of certain disputed fees, he has not done so with sufficient particularity to satisfy us that withdrawal was justified on the eve of trial. . . . Moreover, there is nothing in the district court record to suggest error in that court's finding that "Whiting has been very cooperative and desirous of assisting his attorney in this litigation." . . . To be sure, we are concerned by Lacara's allegation that appellee trespassed in his office and that appellant had to call 911 to get Whiting to leave. However, Whiting disputes Lacara's description of these events. Moreover, we strongly agree with the district court that, as the third attorney in this case, Lacara had ample notice that appellee was a difficult client. . . .

Nevertheless, we reverse the denial of appellant's motion for withdrawal under Model Code DR 2–110(C)(1)(a). Among Lacara's allegations are that Whiting insisted upon pressing claims already dismissed by the district court and calling witnesses Lacara deemed detrimental to his case. At oral argument, Whiting confirmed Lacara's contention that Whiting intends to dictate how his action is to be pursued. Whiting was asked by a member of the panel:

> Are you under the impression that if we affirm Judge Spatt's ruling, you will be able to tell Mr. Lacara to make the arguments you want made in this case? . . . [T]hat, if Mr. Lacara says, "That witness doesn't support your case," and you don't agree with that, are you under the impression that if we affirm Judge Spatt's ruling you'll be able to force him to call that witness?

> To which Whiting replied, "Yes I am."

Moreover, in his statements at oral argument, Whiting made it clear that he was as interested in using the litigation to make public his allegations of corruption within the Brookville police department as in advancing his specific legal claims. For example, Whiting thought it relevant to inform us at oral argument that police officers in the department were guilty of "illegal drug use, acceptance of gratuities, [and] ongoing extramarital affairs while they were on duty." Appellee stated that he wanted to call an officer to testify that the officer could not "bring up anything criminal about the lieutenant, the two lieutenants, or the chief, which could get them in trouble or make the department look bad." Finally, Whiting made clear that he disagreed with Lacara about the handling of his case partly because Whiting suspects that Lacara wants to cover up corruption. Appellee stated: "For some strange reason, Mr. Lacara states that he doesn't want to put certain witnesses on the stand. . . . The bottom line is he does not want to make waves and expose all of the corruption that's going on within this community."

Also, at oral argument, appellee continued to bring up the already-dismissed due process claims. He asserted: "They found me guilty of something which was investigated by their department on two separate occasions and closed as unfounded on two separate occasions." We thus have good reason to conclude that Whiting will insist that Lacara pursue the already dismissed claims at trial.

Finally, appellee indicated that he might sue Lacara if not satisfied that Lacara provided representation as Whiting dictated. After admitting that he did not consider Lacara to be the "right attorney" for him in this case, Whiting asserted that he deemed Lacara "ineffective." The following exchange also occurred:

Question from Panel:

If you think that Mr. Lacara is ineffective in representing you as you stand here now, doesn't Mr. Lacara face the prospect of a . . . malpractice suit, by you, against him, if he continues in the case?

Appellee's Reply:

Yes, I believe he absolutely does.

Question from Panel:

Then, isn't that all the more reason to relieve him? So that what you say is ineffective and is in effect a distortion of the attorney-client relationship, doesn't continue?

Appellee's Reply:

I believe I do have grounds to sue Mr. Lacara for misrepresentation. . . .

We believe that appellee's desire both to dictate legal strategies to his counsel and to sue counsel if those strategies are not followed places Lacara in so impossible a situation that he must be permitted to withdraw.

Model Code DR 2–110(C)(1)(a) limits the obligations of attorneys to follow their clients' dictates in how to conduct litigation. Attorneys have a duty to the court not to make "legal contentions . . . [un]warranted by existing law or by a nonfrivolous argument for the extension, modification, or reversal of existing law. . . ." . . . We have determined that "an attorney who continues to represent a client despite the inherent conflict of interest in his so doing [due to possible Rule 11 sanctions] risks an ethical violation." . . . In this case, appellee's belief that he can dictate to Lacara how to handle his case and sue him if Lacara declines to follow those dictates leaves Lacara in a position amounting to a functional conflict of interest. If required to continue to represent Whiting, Lacara will have to choose between exposure to a malpractice action or to potential Rule 11 or other sanctions. To be sure, such a malpractice action would have no merit. However, we have no doubt it would be actively pursued, and even frivolous malpractice claims can have substantial collateral consequences.

As previously noted, the interest of the district court in preventing counsel from withdrawing on the eve of trial is substantial. Moreover, we would normally be loath to allow an attorney to withdraw on the eve of trial when the attorney had as much notice as did Lacara that he was taking on a difficult client. However, the functional conflict of interest developed at oral argument causes us to conclude that the motion to withdraw should be granted.

We therefore reverse and order the district court to grant appellant's motion to withdraw as counsel. We note that Lacara agreed in this court to waive all outstanding fees and to turn over all pertinent files to Whiting.

* * *

Model Rules comparison. *Kriegsman* and *Whiting* were decided under rules of professional conduct that differ from the ABA's Model Rules. Which sections of Rule 1.16(b) would have applied in the two cases?

* * *

Problem 18.2. Refer back to the Chapter Hypothetical. Did Luther have grounds to withdraw from Carlene's representation?

Good cause as a prerequisite to compensation. A lawyer in a contingent fee agreement must have good cause to withdraw before being entitled to any compensation for work performed. *See, e.g.,* Bell & Marra, PLLC v. Sullivan, 6 P.3d 965, 970 (Mont. 2000). Does the fact that a court has permitted a lawyer to withdraw establish that the lawyer had the good cause to withdraw that is necessary to establish a right to compensation? According to one author, not necessarily: "[T]he vast majority of courts, and all of them that actually considered the issue, have held that cause sufficient to require or permit a lawyer to withdraw is insufficient to constitute just cause to withdraw but still be paid." David Hricik, *Dear Lawyer: If You Decide It's Not Economical to Represent Me, You Can Fire Me as Your Contingent Fee Client, But I*

Agree I Will Still Owe You a Fee, 64 MERCER L. REV. 363, 376 (2013). What should qualify as the cause sufficient to allow a lawyer who has withdrawn from a contingent fee agreement to be paid? Although no bright-line rule exists for determining "just cause," one court has said that just cause exists "where the client attempts to assert a fraudulent claim; fails to cooperate; refuses to pay for services; degrades or humiliates the attorney; or retains other counsel with whom the original attorney cannot work." *Bell & Marra*, 6 P.3d at 970.

Hybrid fee agreements and termination. In an attempt to protect themselves from client decisions that adversely affect their right to compensation, some lawyers modify their contingent fee agreements to give greater protection. "Generally, the provisions (a) either restrict the client's ability to terminate the lawyer, or expand the lawyer's right to withdraw from representing the client; (b) increase the compensation due if the client terminates the lawyer or the lawyer withdraws; or (c) a combination of those two approaches." Hricik, *supra*, at 364–65. In light of a client's absolute rights to terminate a relationship and to make certain decisions concerning the representation under Rule 1.2 (e.g., whether to settle), should a lawyer be subject to discipline for including such a provision in a fee agreement? Should courts enforce such agreements? *See* New York County Lawyers' Association Committee on Professional Ethics, Formal Opinion Number 736 (2006); Compton v. Kittleson, 171 P.3d 172, 174, 180 (Alaska 2007); Gilbert v. Evan, 822 So. 2d 42, 46 (La. Ct. App. 2002).

Problem 18.3. Refer back to the Chapter Hypothetical. Assume that Luther sues Carlene, seeking to collect one-third of the settlement offer Carlene rejected. Alternatively, he seeks to recover for the reasonable value of the services he provided. Should he prevail? Would the answer be any different if Carlene had instead fired Luther because she lost faith in Luther after Luther advised Carlene to settle?

* * *

C. RETURNING CLIENT PROPERTY AND RESOLVING FEE DISPUTES UPON TERMINATION OF THE RELATIONSHIP

Sometimes the termination of a client-lawyer relationship results in animosity. As the *Campbell* decision, *supra*, illustrates, sometimes it results in confusion as to how much, if anything, the client owes the lawyer for the lawyer's services. The following section examines the steps lawyers may take to obtain their fees and ways in which the parties may resolve their fee disputes.

* * *

1. IMPOSING ATTORNEYS' LIENS

Please read ABA Model Rules of Professional Conduct, Rule 1.16(d) and Comments [4]–[6] & [9]; Rule 1.8(i)(1) and Comment [16]; and Rule 1.15(d).

* * *

A Pennsylvania ethics opinion describes the two common types of attorney liens:

> A retaining lien permits a lawyer to retain money, papers or other property in the lawyer's possession to secure payment of costs and fees from the client. Charging liens are divided into two sub-categories: equitable charging liens and legal charging liens. An equitable charging lien gives a lawyer a right to be paid out of a fund in the control or possession of the court, which fund resulted from the skill and labor of the lawyer, and such payment may be applied only to a particular case. A legal charging lien applies to funds of a client in the lawyer's possession and may be applied to all outstanding debts of the client owed to the lawyer.

Pennsylvania Bar Ass'n Committee on Legal Ethics & Prof'l Resp. Formal Op. No. 94–35 (1994), *superseded* by Formal Op. No. 2006–300.

The use of charging liens is common in contingent fee arrangements. The use of retaining liens is more controversial. As described in the Pennsylvania decision, the general or retaining lien gives a lawyer the right "to retain possession of documents, money or other property of his client coming into his hands by virtue of the professional relationship, until he has been paid for his services; or until he voluntarily surrenders possession of the property, with or without payment."

An attorney's assertion of a retaining lien potentially deprives a client or former client of property. This creates a certain amount of tension with Model Rule 1.16(d), which advises that upon termination of representation, "a lawyer shall take steps to the extent reasonably practicable to protect a client's interests, such as . . . surrendering papers and property to which the client is entitled." To some extent, this begs the question as to which papers and property a client is entitled. State ethics opinions and rules of professional conduct take a variety of approaches. Below are some examples:

- Montana Rules 1.8(j) & 1.16(d): "a lawyer may not acquire or assert a retaining lien to secure payment due for the lawyer's services against any client property, papers or materials other than those related to the matter for which payment has not been made."

- D.C. Rule 1.8(i): "a lawyer shall not impose a lien upon any part of a client's files, except upon the lawyer's own work product, and then only to the extent that the work product has not been paid for. This work product exception shall not apply when the client has become unable to pay, or when withholding the lawyer's work product would present a significant risk to the client of irreparable harm."

- North Dakota Rule 1.19: a lawyer may not assert a retaining lien against a client's "files, papers, or property," which includes "[a]ll pleadings, motions, discovery, memoranda, and other litigation materials which have been executed and served or filed regardless of whether the client has paid the lawyer for drafting and serving and/or filing the document(s)."

* * *

Problem 18.4. Assume that in *Campbell, supra,* Ms. Campbell was experiencing financial difficulties at the time she fired Hartelius and Morgan since she was not working and had not received further payment for her medical bills from Bozeman Investors. Assume further that after they were fired by Campbell, Hartelius and Morgan refused to turn over her file to her new lawyer, Pohl, and asserted a retaining lien for their legal fees. As a result, Pohl did not have any of the pre-existing medical records, bills, pleadings, or other papers contained in the file when he entered into settlement negotiations with Bozeman Investors. Assess whether the conduct of Hartelius and Morgan have been permissible under the three approaches identified above.

* * *

2. RETURNING CLIENT FILES

Assume that Alice terminates her relationship with Lawyer Bob and hires Lawyer Carol to represent her. Alice does not owe Bob any legal fee. On Alice's behalf, Carol requests that Bob forward Alice's file to Carol so that she may begin work on Alice's matter. Again, Model Rule 1.16(d) provides that upon termination of the relationship, a lawyer should surrender the papers and property to which the client is entitled but provides limited guidance as to which parts of the file a client is entitled. Below are two very different state rules regarding what files a lawyer must return to a former client:

- Montana Rule 1.16(d): A lawyer is entitled to retain papers or materials personal to the lawyer or created or intended for internal use by the lawyer. (Examples include notes taken by the attorney during witness or client interviews, while conducting a fact investigation or in preparation for a deposition, and internal notes to other members of the firm.)

- Oregon State Bar Formal Op. No. 2005–125 (2005): "As a general proposition, and absent viable attorney liens, a lawyer is obligated to deliver a former client's entire file to the former client. By *entire file*, we mean papers and property that the client provided to the lawyer; litigation materials, including pleadings, memoranda, and discovery materials; all correspondence; all items that the lawyer has obtained from others, including expert opinions, medical or business records, and witness statements. The client file also includes the lawyer's notes or internal memoranda that may constitute "attorney work-product."

Which do you prefer?

To what extent can Lawyer Bob charge Alice for the costs associated with copying the file? The Oregon opinion above concludes that a lawyer cannot charge for copies "of original documents given by the client to the lawyer." A lawyer may charge for the copying costs of other material in the file in accordance with the fee agreement outlined in the retainer agreement. If, however, copying costs are not provided for in the agreement, the client is entitled to a copy of the file, free of charge. This would include the labor costs associated with copying the files. While this is a common approach to the issue of copying costs, some state rules permit copying costs to be borne by the former client. *See* Michigan State Bar Formal Op. R-19 (2000). Is Oregon's standard too onerous for attorneys, or does it best reflect the fiduciary nature of the attorney-client relationship?

* * *

3. ARBITRATING FEE DISPUTES

Lawyers have increasingly relied upon mandatory arbitration as a means of resolving fee disputes. ABA Formal Ethics Opinion 02–425 (2002) concluded that a lawyer may permissibly include in a retainer agreement a provision that requires the binding arbitration of disputes concerning fees and malpractice claims. However, to be effective, the client must be "fully apprised of the advantages and disadvantages of arbitration" and must give her informed consent to the inclusion of the arbitration provision in the retainer agreement. Many bar associations now have fee arbitration programs that lawyers and clients may utilize.

Despite the general acceptance of binding mandatory arbitration of fee disputes, a word of caution is in order. Some states take a dimmer view of mandatory arbitration as a means of resolving fee disputes. *See* Ohio Op. No. 96–9 (1996) ("An engagement letter between a lawyer and an individual client should not contain language requiring a client to prospectively agree to arbitrate fee disputes."). When dealing with unsophisticated clients, the lawyer needs to be particularly careful about explaining the advantages and disadvantages of arbitration. *See* Marino v. Tagaris, 480 N.E.2d 286 (Mass. 1985) (vacating arbitration award where client did not understand her rights as described in the material contained in bar-sponsored pamphlet explaining arbitration of fee agreements). Finally, arbitration agreements may be unenforceable on common law grounds (for example, the rules regarding unconscionability).

* * *

Problem 18.5. Refer back to the Chapter Hypothetical. Considering all of the information covered in this chapter, can Roseanne enforce her fee agreement against John?

* * *

Profile of attorney professionalism. Following a $24.4 million verdict in favor of his client LBDS Holding Company, LLC, Texas lawyer Sanford E. Warren and his co-counsel received a Rule 11 Motion for Sanctions. In the motion, Defendants asserted that LBDS had falsified evidence it had relied upon at trial and that its witnesses had testified falsely.

Attorney Warren immediately forwarded the motion to his client and set up a call with an LBDS principal—a person who also had been a fact witness in the case. That individual confirmed that the allegations in the Rule 11 motion were "essentially correct" and that a key contract offered as evidence at trial "was not authentic" because it contained forged schedules. He also admitted that LBDS employees had set up a fictitious domain name and sent emails from that fake domain that were introduced into evidence at trial.

Upon learning that he had offered false, material evidence at trial, Warren attempted to persuade his client to correct or withdraw the evidence as he was required to do under Texas Disciplinary Rules. *See* Texas Disciplinary Rule of Professional Conduct 3.03(b). When a client fails to act in that situation, the disciplinary rule requires that the attorney "take reasonable remedial measures, including disclosure of the true facts." *Id.*

Consistent with this authority, when LBDS failed to disclose its fraud to the court, Warren and his co-counsel informed the court. As part of this disclosure, the attorneys sought leave to withdraw as counsel to LBDS. They relied upon Texas Disciplinary Rule 1.15 (which is similar to Model Rule 1.16) to state grounds to withdraw as counsel. The LBDS attorneys explained that the client had used the law firm's services to perpetrate a fraud on the court, which is a basis to withdraw under Texas

Disciplinary Rule of Professional Conduct 1.15(b)(3). They also noted that the disciplinary rule requires a lawyer to withdraw if the continued representation will result in the violation of professional conduct rules. *See* Texas Disciplinary Rule of Professional Conduct 1.15(a)(1). They then explained that the continuing representation would violate the disciplinary rule prohibiting a lawyer from furnishing testimony adverse to the lawyer's client if the lawyers were compelled to testify in the present matter or a related criminal matter. They also noted that the conflict of interest rule would be violated because the attorneys' representation of LBDS would be adversely limited by their own interests and obligations to follow the disciplinary rules. On these bases, the attorneys sought leave to withdraw. *See* Notice to Court Pursuant to Texas Disciplinary Rule of Professional Conduct 3.03 and Unopposed Motion to Withdraw as Counsel for Plaintiff, LBDS Holding Company, LLC, v. ISOL Technology Inc. et al., No. 6:11–cv–00428–LED (E.D. Tex. filed May 21, 2014).

While it is difficult to disclose false testimony of a client and withdraw from a representation, Sanford Warren and his colleagues took the steps they determined necessary under Texas Disciplinary Rules.

CHAPTER 19

CONFLICTS OF INTEREST ARISING FROM PRIOR REPRESENTATION

■ ■ ■

Chapter Hypothetical. Attorney Taylor has requested an opinion based on the following fact situation: Taylor's practice is limited to representation of parents and children in special education matters. Taylor has two clients, both with children enrolled in special education programs. One client (Ms. Green) is also a special education teacher. Taylor helped Ms. Green obtain after-school tutoring for her child six months ago. Ms. Green is satisfied with the current academic support her child is receiving, and has not asked Taylor for further assistance since the tutoring was initiated.

The other client (Mr. Blue) has a child in Ms. Green's class in public school. Mr. Blue is not satisfied with his child's educational program, and he recently asked the school district to place his child in a private school to meet the child's special needs. The district denied the request, and Taylor's firm has filed for a special education hearing for the father. At the hearing, the board of education will likely call Ms. Green to testify about whether the needs of Mr. Blue's child can be met in the public school setting. In order to represent Mr. Blue at the hearing, Taylor expects to cross-examine the teacher, Ms. Green.

Taylor seeks your advice on several issues:

(A) What aspects of the situation give rise to conflicts of interest?

(B) Why does it matter whether Ms. Green should be considered former client rather than a current client, and how should Taylor determine which category Ms. Green fits into?

(C) If Taylor wants to seek Ms. Green's consent for the attorney to represent Mr. Blue, what information would need to be disclosed to Ms. Green in order to obtain her consent? What information would need to be disclosed to Mr. Blue?

(D) Assume hypothetically that Ms. Green should be considered to be a current client, and assume further that she declines to consent to Taylor's representation of Mr. Blue. Could

Taylor terminate her representation in order to take Mr. Blue's case?

* * *

A. GENERAL PRINCIPLES

Please read ABA Model Rules of Professional Conduct, Rule 1.9 and Comments.

Previously we have considered conflict of interest problems arising from the duties of loyalty and confidentiality a lawyer owes to a client during an ongoing attorney-client relationship ("concurrent conflicts"). Now that we have considered situations in which an attorney-client relationship has been terminated, we focus on "successive conflicts"—that is, the "after-life" of the representation. To what extent does the lawyer continue to owe a duty of loyalty or confidentiality to her now-former client, and how will these duties affect the lawyer's freedom to undertake the representation of new clients in a matter in which the interests of the new clients will be adverse to the interests of the former clients?

The first step in analyzing a potential conflict of interest problem must determining whether it involves a "concurrent conflict" under 1.7 or a "successive conflict" under 1.9. This analysis is important, because the rules are different: under 1.7, suing a party in one matter while the attorney is representing that same party in another matter is "direct adversity" even if the subjects of the litigation are completely different. Under 1.9, however, a lawyer may sue a former client—even without that client's consent—as long as the new litigation is not substantially related to the earlier representation. Thus, it is important to consider whether the representation of the original client has in fact terminated. A lawyer who wants to take on a lucrative new case against a client he or she has represented in the past will have an incentive to view the opposing party as a "former client" rather than a current client. Note, however, that the rules generally characterize the relationship from the point of view of the client, not the attorney. See Rule 1.3, Comment [4] (providing that when a lawyer has represented a client "over a substantial period in a variety of matters," the client may reasonably assume that "the lawyer will continue to serve on a continuing basis unless the lawyer gives notice of withdrawal," and putting the burden on the lawyer to clarify the end of that relationship, "preferably in writing," in order to avoid a situation where the client might "mistakenly suppose the lawyer is looking after the client's affairs when the lawyer has ceased to do so.").

If the attorney-client relationship with the first client has terminated, then Model Rule 1.9 governs the attorney's analysis of whether a duty to the former client may preclude accepting representation of the new client. Note another difference between Model

Rule 1.7 and 1.9: under 1.9, successive conflicts of interest are always waivable by the original client; there are no non-consentable conflicts under Rule 1.9. If the former client is willing to consent to the attorney's representation of the new client—even in a substantially related matter— then Rule 1.9 will not prohibit the attorney from doing so.

Finally, however, it is important to see that 1.7 may still regulate some aspects of the representation, even in cases involving successive conflicts. For example, an attorney's ongoing friendship with, or loyalty to, a former client may create a "material limitation" that interferes with the attorney's ability to diligently represent the new client's interests, especially where those interests might diverge with the former client's interests. In spite of the fact that the analysis involves a former client, this is actually a "concurrent conflict" governed by Rule 1.7 because it involves an ongoing limitation on the attorney's ability to effectively represent a current client.

* * *

B. CONFLICTS OF INTEREST BETWEEN CURRENT AND FORMER CLIENTS

1. MATERIAL ADVERSITY

Sometimes a lawyer will represent two or more clients whose interests appear to be aligned; often, they are co-clients suing a common defendant. It is not uncommon in such situations that one or more of the clients will terminate the lawyer's representation. In such cases, the lawyer may want to continue representing the other client or clients. The requirements of Model Rule 1.9 may preclude the lawyer from doing so, however, if the matters are related and the representation would be materially adverse to the now-former client. The next case gives an example of such a conflict.

McGRIFF V. CHRISTIE
477 Fed.Appx. 673 (11th Cir. 2012)

PER CURIAM.

Movants-Appellants George W. McGriff and Eric Emanuel Wyatt ("Counsel") appeal following the final order of the district court granting summary judgment in favor of Defendants-Appellees, in a discrimination suit brought by Plaintiff Russell Adkins, MD. Specifically, Counsel appeal from the district court's earlier order granting the Defendants' motion to disqualify Counsel from representing Dr. Adkins. . . . After thorough review, we affirm.

The relevant facts are these. On July 15, 2003, Dr. Adkins, a urologist, operated on patient Sharon Kornegay at Houston Medical Center ("HMC"). The next day, Ms. Kornegay bled profusely and returned to HMC. Staff called Dr. Adkins, who informed Ms. Kornegay that he was out of town but would have a doctor see her. During the next eleven hours, while Ms. Kornegay lay bleeding and in pain, nurses told her that Dr. Adkins was not responding to their pages and did not believe their descriptions of her condition. They also said they could not call another physician because Dr. Adkins had not asked anyone to cover his patients before he left town. That evening, urologist Dr. Daniel Deighton arrived and performed another surgery on Ms. Kornegay. He confirmed that Dr. Adkins had not asked him for coverage.

About two months later, Ms. Kornegay filed a complaint with HMC about the care she had received following an initial surgery Dr. Adkins had performed on her on June 23, 2003, and during her visit on July 16, 2003. Ms. Kornegay questioned whether Dr. Adkins had engaged in malpractice and described his unavailability, unprofessional conduct, and failure to arrange for a back-up physician.

In October 2003, Dr. Adkins's privileges at HMC were summarily suspended on grounds that his practice reflected a pattern of problems regarding: availability and timely response to emergency room call and consultation in-house; timely completion of medical records; compliance with protocol for pre-admission of surgical patients; and attendance of meetings. By way of example, the letter referenced Dr. Adkins's treatment of Sharon Kornegay. Dr. Adkins then called Ms. Kornegay, told her about the suspension and asked to see her complaints. Dr. Adkins advised that they were both victims of race discrimination at HMC, and that she should talk to his attorney. Within days, Dr. Adkins formally secured the legal representation of Counsel.

Counsel then visited the Kornegays. Ms. Kornegay told Counsel that she had contacted a few lawyers about a malpractice claim against Dr. Adkins and that she was uncomfortable talking to Counsel unless he agreed to represent her. Counsel said that Dr. Adkins had done nothing wrong in treating her and that two physicians had confirmed this. Counsel further said that HMC was targeting Dr. Adkins because of his race and that Ms. Kornegay likely also had a race-based claim against HMC. At this point, Counsel suggested that he represent Ms. Kornegay. The Kornegays asked whether Counsel's representation of both Ms. Kornegay and Dr. Adkins would create a conflict of interest, which Counsel denied, reiterating that Dr. Adkins had done nothing wrong. Ms. Kornegay finally agreed to Counsel's representation.

Thereafter, the Kornegays repeatedly expressed concerns to McGriff about whether he suffered from a conflict of interest and about his insistence that she had no malpractice claim against Dr. Adkins. Counsel brought in a nurse to convince Ms. Kornegay that hospital staff had not repeatedly called Dr. Adkins on July 16th, as she believed, and that Dr. Adkins was guilty of no wrongdoing. Counsel never requested a retainer from Ms. Kornegay, never conducted any investigation into the merits of any potential malpractice or abandonment claims, and never advised Ms. Kornegay that she may have potential claims against Dr. Adkins.

About six months after filing this suit, Counsel McGriff told Ms. Kornegay that attorney Dwight Johnson should represent her in her state-court fall claim against HMC, while McGriff would consider moving for her to intervene in Dr. Adkins's federal civil rights case. Ms. Kornegay agreed, and Counsel McGriff later admitted that at this time (late 2004), he was representing Ms. Kornegay "with Mr. Johnson."

Around this time, HMC sought to depose Ms. Kornegay, and Counsel requested that Ms. Kornegay sign a waiver of conflict. Ms. Kornegay, however, refused and specifically informed Counsel that the Kornegays did not consent to the use of any of their communications with Counsel in Dr. Adkins's federal litigation. In April 2005, attorney Melanie Webre notified Counsel that the Kornegays had retained new counsel to pursue any claims they had against Dr. Adkins and HMC.

In May 2005, Counsel moved to withdraw from the present case, identifying a conflict of interest that had been created by his joint representation of Dr. Adkins and Ms. Kornegay. In the motion, Counsel cited concerns about Georgia Rules of Professional Conduct 1.7 and 1.9, regarding conflicts of interests between current and former clients, and conceded that withdrawal "was necessary to avoid using confidential information of a former client." The district court granted the motion.

Dr. Adkins secured new representation, but four years later, Dr. Adkins's new counsel was unable to continue due to illness and also withdrew. Counsel then served an Entry of Appearance in this case. The Defendants moved to disqualify Counsel, claiming that the conflict still existed. The district court granted the motion to disqualify, and this timely appeal follows.

First, we are unpersuaded that the Defendants lacked standing to move for Counsel's disqualification. A party who is not a former client of opposing counsel nevertheless has standing to raise the issue of opposing counsel's conflict of interest if there is "a violation of the rules which is sufficiently severe to call in question the fair and efficient administration of justice." As the district court reasoned, it is clearly improper for a lawyer to simultaneously represent two clients when he is unable to maintain loyalty to both clients and may need to breach client confidentiality. Because this circumstance breeds prejudice and delay and undermines the credibility of our judicial system, we agree that the

Defendants identified a violation of the Georgia Rules of Professional Conduct severe enough to call into question the fair and efficient administration of justice. Counsel have offered nothing to dispute the seriousness of these allegations.

We are also unpersuaded that the fact that Ms. Kornegay might have given testimony favorable to Dr. Adkins resolved any conflict in their representation of both the Kornegays and Dr. Adkins. In fact, Counsel acknowledge that "Ms. Kornegay may have provided testimony that could be construed as unfavorable" to Dr. Adkins and/or Counsel. That statement alone recognizes that she may have had some complaints, and potentially, claims, against Dr. Adkins. Thus, on this record, we cannot find any error, much less clear error, in the district court's findings, nor in the evidence it relied upon to making those findings. . . .

[W]e find no merit to Counsel's claim that the district court erred in applying Rule 1.9(a) of the Georgia Rules of Professional Conduct, which provides:

> A lawyer who has formerly represented a client in a matter shall not thereafter represent another person in the same or a substantially related matter in which that person's interests are materially adverse to the interests of the former client unless the former client consents after consultation.

A violation of this rule depends on whether: (1) there was a previous attorney-client relationship and, if so, (2) that relationship involved a matter substantially related to the current proceeding. It is clear, as the district court found, that there was a "previous attorney-client relationship" between Counsel and Ms. Kornegay, and that Counsel's representation of Ms. Kornegay and Dr. Adkins is "not only logically and materially related, but the two involved exactly the same events, and both involved the present litigation." . . .

Counsel also claim that Ms. Kornegay had no reasonable expectation when she hired Counsel that her communications would not be shared with Dr. Adkins. Counsel rely on Ms. Kornegay's statement that, "I assumed that [McGriff's] reason for coming to me and inquiring was because later on down the road he intended to file a discrimination suit for Dr. Adkins. But when I agreed to give him private information surrounding me, at that point I felt like he was going to do the same for me too." Yet this is not evidence that she authorized Counsel to share all her confidences with Dr. Adkins, nor even that she understood that McGriff would bring a single lawsuit for both Ms. Kornegay and Dr. Adkins and that Dr. Adkins would be privy to every communication between McGriff and Ms. Kornegay. Indeed, McGriff could have secured a written waiver from Ms. Kornegay and a joint representation agreement with all parties, but did not. Further, when Ms. Kornegay terminated her representation with Counsel, she specifically refused to consent to the use of any of the Kornegays' communications with Counsel in Dr. Adkins's federal litigation.

Counsel further claim that they would not be taking a position "materially adverse" to Ms. Kornegay's interests by representing Dr. Adkins. However, Ms. Kornegay is adversely affected if information she previously disclosed to Counsel is used to undermine her trial testimony. The key issues in Dr. Adkins's federal case include whether he was available on July 16th, contrary to Ms. Kornegay's position that he told her that he was out of town, and whether he provided sufficient coverage for his patients in his absence (and indeed, Counsel admits that the facts surrounding this dispute—including why HMC did not immediately treat Ms. Kornegay that day—were "amongst the ultimate facts to be decided by the factfinder in this case"). What's more, the fact that some of Dr. Adkins's and Ms. Kornegay's interests are aligned does not make up for the fact that they are materially adverse in other ways.

Counsel also contend that any injury to Ms. Kornegay's confidentiality can be remedied by having another attorney cross-examine Ms. Kornegay at trial. But the district court did not find this approach practical, and we agree. Counsel's use of Ms. Kornegay's confidential information may also be used in strategy and argument. We therefore find no error in the district court's findings or conclusions about Rule 1.9. . . .

Accordingly, we affirm.

* * *

The "hot potato" rule. As the court discussed in *McGriff*, a conflict of interest that develops between two clients sometimes results in the lawyer being unable to represent either client. In other cases, however, the model rule would not necessarily have such an effect: because Model Rule 1.7 is broader than 1.9, a conflict that develops between two clients in unrelated cases could theoretically be solved by terminating representation of one client in favor of maintaining representation of the other. This creates a problematic incentive for lawyers to terminate their representation of clients when they are offered more lucrative opportunities to take cases adverse to their (now former) clients. In order to prevent this situation, courts apply a common law prohibition called the "hot potato" rule. Picker Int'l., Inc. v. Varian Assoc., Inc., 670 F. Supp. 1363, 1365 (N.D. Ohio 1987) ("A firm may not drop a client like a hot potato, especially if it is in order to keep happy a far more lucrative client."). Permitting a firm to solve a conflict by dropping the less lucrative conflict would not only raise loyalty concerns, but would also undermine public confidence in the legal profession. This "hot potato doctrine" is now well established. If a conflict arises between adverse parties and both do not consent to the conflict, the presumption is that the affected law firm must withdraw from representing *both* parties in the matters.

One notable exception to this general rule is when a conflict is "thrust upon" a firm through no fault of its own. An ethics opinion from the Association of the Bar of the City of New York defined "thrust-upon" conflicts as

> conflicts between two clients that (1) did not exist at the time either representation commenced, but arose only during the ongoing representation of both clients, where (2) the conflict was not reasonably foreseeable at the outset of the representation, (3) the conflict arose through no fault of the lawyer, and (4) the conflict is of a type that is capable of being waived . . . but one of the clients will not consent to the dual representation.

Committee on Professional Ethics of the New York City Bar Association, Formal Opinion 2005–05. While recognizing that law firms have a duty to consider potential conflicts at the outset of representation, the opinion concludes that a "flexible approach" that balances interests of the affected parties is appropriate in the case of "thrust upon" conflicts.

2. SUBSTANTIALLY RELATED

Please read ABA Model Rules of Professional Conduct, Rule 1.9 and Comment [3].

* * *

STATE EX REL. WAL-MART STORES, INC. V. KORTUM
559 N.W.2d 496 (Neb. 1997)

CONNOLLY, JUSTICE.

This is an original action for a peremptory writ of mandamus brought by relator, Wal-Mart Stores, Inc. (Wal-Mart). We are asked to determine whether a writ should issue disqualifying the law firm of Van Steenberg, Chaloupka, Mullin, Holyoke, Pahlke, Smith, Snyder, and Hofmeister, P.C. (Van Steenberg), from representing a party in an action against Wal-Mart because of the firm's prior representation of Wal-Mart in another case.

. . .

BACKGROUND

The factual statement of this case is taken largely from the findings of fact made by District Judge Donald E. Rowlands II, who was appointed as special master by this court for the taking of evidence and for recommending findings of fact and conclusions of law. Additional facts were taken from the pleadings, the proceedings before the district court on the original motion to disqualify counsel, and various exhibits.

On July 21, 1994, Debra J. Holden filed suit against the Scottsbluff Wal-Mart store through her counsel, Leonard W. Shefren of Omaha, Nebraska. In her petition, Holden asserts that Wal-Mart was negligent in failing to properly maintain and/or warn of a hole in the store's parking lot and that this negligence caused her personal injury when she fell into the hole on July 1, 1992. Subsequent to Wal-Mart's filing an answer, Shefren withdrew as attorney of record. On or about September 7, 1995, Tylor Petitt, an attorney with Van Steenberg, entered an appearance as Holden's counsel.

Van Steenberg had previously defended Wal-Mart, through its partner Steve Smith, in four tort cases in the district court for Scotts Bluff County: *Ramirez v. Wal-Mart Stores, Inc.*, docket 34217; *Sanderson v. Wal-Mart Stores, Inc.*, docket 34218; *Pottorff v. Wal-Mart Stores, Inc.*, docket 38913; and *Nebarez v. Wal-Mart Stores, Inc.*, docket 41412.

The *Ramirez* and *Sanderson* cases involved claims of false arrest and malicious prosecution and ended in 1987 with summary judgments in favor of Wal-Mart. The *Pottorff* case involved claims that Wal-Mart was negligent in failing to properly maintain and/or warn of a dangerous condition in the floor of the store and that this negligence caused personal injury when the customer slipped and fell in an area that had previously been wet-mopped. The *Pottorff* case concluded in June 1993, with a jury verdict in favor of the plaintiff, approximately 1 year after Holden was injured but 2 years before Petitt entered an appearance as Holden's counsel. The *Nebarez* case involved claims by a customer who was injured in an assault inside the store and concluded in August 1994, with summary judgment in favor of Wal-Mart.

Wal-Mart does not have an outside claims administration firm or insurance agency that handles claims made against it. Instead, Wal-Mart relies on its staff of in-house attorneys to administer all claims and to hire legal counsel. A Wal-Mart attorney, Michelle Johnson, retained Smith to defend Wal-Mart in the aforementioned cases. In preparation for its defenses in those cases, Smith had complete access to the Scottsbluff Wal-Mart store and to its managers and staff.

While assisting Smith in preparation for Wal-Mart's defenses, Johnson related to Smith Wal-Mart's general defense strategy, internal policies, and the conduct of similar lawsuits in other parts of the country. In addition, Kern Radtke, manager of the Scottsbluff store, gave Smith complete access to procedure manuals, lists, and sales information. After Smith concluded his representation of Wal-Mart in the *Nebarez* case, he was informed by Wal-Mart that neither he nor Van Steenberg would represent Wal-Mart in any further matters.

The district court entered an order denying Wal-Mart's motion to disqualify Van Steenberg from further representation of Holden in her tort action against Wal-Mart. Wal-Mart brought this original action seeking a peremptory writ of mandamus from this court compelling the district court to vacate its order.

The special master appointed by this court found that during the time Wal-Mart was represented by Smith, the policies, procedures, and practices of which he was informed did not include any confidential information, trade secrets, or anything that was not discoverable. However, the special master recommended that a peremptory writ of mandamus be issued directing the district court to disqualify Petitt and Van Steenberg from further representation of Holden in her action against Wal-Mart. The special master reasoned that "the nexus between [the Pottorff case and the instant case], both in type and time of occurrence, is too close to avoid the appearance of impropriety, whether in the subjective eyes of Wal-Mart employees, or of the legally recognized reasonable person."

ANALYSIS . . .

"Substantially Related" Test

Our first inquiry, and to a great extent the resolution of this action, involves a determination of what is meant by the phrase "substantially related subject matter." In State ex rel. Freezer Servs., Inc. v. Mullen, 235 Neb. 981, 987, 458 N.W.2d 245, 249–50 (1990), this court announced the rule that " '[a]n attorney, after receiving the confidence of a client, may not enter the service of others whose interests are adverse to such client, in the same subject-matter to which the confidence relates, or in matters so closely allied thereto as to be, in effect, a part thereof.' " In *State ex rel. FirsTier Bank v. Buckley*, 244 Neb. at 45, 503 N.W.2d at 844, this court expanded the rule announced in *State ex rel. Freezer Servs., Inc.*, by stating that

> an attorney must avoid the present representation of a cause against a client of a law firm . . . which he or she . . . formerly [represented], and which cause involves a subject matter which is the same as or substantially related to that handled by the former firm while the present attorney was associated with that firm.

. . . However, this general rule arose, and has only been applied, in the context where an attorney or attorneys ceased working for a law firm that represented a particular client and then began working for another law firm in a position adversarial to that client.

In the instant case, no attorneys switched law firms. Instead, Smith of Van Steenberg formerly defended Wal-Mart, and Petitt of Van Steenberg is now suing Wal-Mart. Nonetheless, this court has made it patently clear that "confidences and secrets possessed by an attorney are presumptively possessed by other members of the attorney's firm." As such, an attorney or law firm must avoid the present representation of a cause against a client that the attorney or law firm formerly represented, and which cause involves a subject matter which is the same as or substantially related to that formerly handled by the attorney or law firm.

In *State ex rel. FirsTier Bank v. Buckley*, 244 Neb. at 44, 503 N.W.2d at 843, we stated that "[i]n defining 'substantially related,' the court looked at whether counsel may have received confidential information from the former client that could be used against it in the subsequent representation." However, it is now necessary to further define what constitutes a "substantially related subject matter."

In fashioning a "substantially related subject matter" test, a court must balance several competing considerations, including the privacy of the attorney-client relationship, the prerogative of a party to choose counsel, and the hardships that disqualification imposes on parties and the entire judicial process. However, the preservation of client confidences is given greater weight in that balancing.

Mindful of these competing interests, we determine that the subject matters of two causes are "substantially related" if the similarity of the factual and legal issues creates a genuine threat that the affected attorney may have received confidential information in the first cause that could be used against the former client in the present cause.

Simply stated, if the court determines that the unique factual and legal issues presented in both cases are so similar that there exists a genuine threat that confidential information may have been revealed in the previous case that could be used against the former client in the instant case, then disqualification must ensue.

A nonexhaustive list of the factors a court may consider in making this determination includes: whether the liability issues presented are similar; whether any scientific issues presented are similar; whether the nature of the evidence is similar; whether the lawyer had interviewed a witness who was a key in both causes; the lawyer's knowledge of the former client's trial strategies, negotiation strategies, legal theories, business practices, and trade secrets; the lapse of time between causes; the duration and intimacy of the lawyer's relationship with the clients; the functions being performed by the lawyer; the likelihood that actual conflict will arise; and the likely prejudice to the client if conflict does arise.

Clearly, the "appearance of impropriety" and attempted screening procedures ... do not address whether two causes are "substantially related" and, thus, are not factors that may be considered in determining whether or not to disqualify an attorney or firm.

Whether Causes Are "Substantially Related"

... It is not disputed that Van Steenberg's interests are materially adverse to Wal-Mart's or that the information Smith acquired through his previous defenses of Wal-Mart is imputed to the entire Van Steenberg law firm. Thus, it is only left to be determined whether any of the previous cases in which Van Steenberg defended Wal-Mart are "substantially related" to the instant case against Wal-Mart.

Of the four cases in which Van Steenberg defended Wal-Mart, the case with factual and legal issues most closely related to the instant case is *Pottorff v. Wal-Mart Stores, Inc.*, Scotts Bluff County District Court, docket 38913. As such, we must determine whether the *Pottorff* case and the instant case are substantially related.

In the instant case, Holden asserts that Wal-Mart's negligence caused her to suffer a strained knee and sprained ankle when she fell into a hole located in the store's parking lot. Approximately 1 year after Holden was injured, but 2 years before Petitt entered an appearance as Holden's counsel, Van Steenberg concluded its defense of Wal-Mart in the Pottorff case. In the *Pottorff* case, the jury found that Wal-Mart's negligence caused Pottorff to suffer a bulging disk, an injured elbow, headaches, and leg pain when she slipped and fell in an area inside the store that had previously been wet-mopped.

Wal-Mart asserts that these cases are substantially related because in both cases a customer was injured in a fall on Wal-Mart's premises, the petitions alleged that Wal-Mart was negligent in failing to properly maintain its premises and in failing to warn of dangerous conditions, and Wal-Mart asserted contributory negligence and assumption of risk as defenses. Conversely, Van Steenberg, appearing amicus curiae, asserts that these cases are not substantially related because the *Pottorff* case involved a slip and fall on a slick floor, while the instant case involves a fall into a hole; the *Pottorff* case involved a floor, while the instant case involves a parking lot; and the accident in the *Pottorff* case happened inside the store, while the accident in the instant case happened outside the store.

Wal-Mart correctly asserts that the pleadings in these cases are similar. However, the mere fact that the pleadings are similar does not make the two cases substantially related. The differences in the factual and legal issues, where a plaintiff falls into a hole in a parking lot as opposed to where a plaintiff falls on a wet floor inside a store, are crucial and are not outweighed by the similarities.

We agree with the special master's findings that during the time Wal-Mart was represented by Smith, the policies, procedures, and practices Smith was told about did not include any trade secrets or anything that was not discoverable. Courts have recognized that defense strategies are confidential information that may be factored into the disqualification decision. . . . However, the defense strategies utilized in these types of relatively uncomplicated slip-and-fall actions are generally commonplace and routine. Wal-Mart did not assert that Van Steenberg became privy to any defense strategies that are unique, unexpected, unusual, or novel. Thus, we determine that an outside firm, with no prior association with Wal-Mart, would have the same or similar practical knowledge of how Wal-Mart would defend against this action and would have the same discovery opportunities.

Because Van Steenberg did not acquire any specialized knowledge of defense strategies or any other discovery advantages, we conclude that the similarity of the factual and legal issues does not create a genuine threat that Van Steenberg may have received confidential information from Wal-Mart that could be used against Wal-Mart in the instant case.

Because Wal-Mart failed to meet its burden of clearly showing that it has a legal right to the relief sought, we determine that the district court had no alternative but to deny Wal-Mart's motion to disqualify Van Steenberg. Since the district court did not have a clear legal duty to act at the time the writ was applied for, we decline to issue the requested writ.

* * *

Problem 19.1. Bob is suing Alice and her business, Alice's Auctions, Inc., for negligence and conversion. Bob had consigned a statue for auction to Alice's Auctions; however, due to a mistake, the high bidder was allowed to take the statue away after the auction without paying for it. Bob is now suing to recover the costs associated with retrieving the item. Ordinarily, individual shareholders of a corporation are not individually liable for the corporation's debts. In this case, however, Bob is attempting to "pierce the corporate veil" and hold Alice, the sole shareholder of Alice's Auctions, individually liable. Under the relevant law in the jurisdiction, if Bob is able to establish that Alice's Auctions "failed to follow corporate formalities, had nonfunctioning officers or directors, or failed to maintain corporate records," it would be appropriate for a court to pierce the corporate veil and allow Alice to be held individually liable. Alice has moved to disqualify Bob's attorneys, the law firm of Able, Baker, and Charlie LLC. In 1985, the firm helped Alice incorporate Alice's Auctions. Two years later, after conducting a "legal checkup" of the procedures being followed by Alice's Auctions, the firm sent Alice a letter reminding her of the need to maintain corporate records for the business to support its role as a separate entity and to help maintain a barrier against personal liability. The firm terminated representation of Alice after the legal checkup in 1987. Should the court grant Alice's motion to disqualify Able, Baker, and Charlie?

Problem 19.2. Lawyer represents Jane in an employment discrimination case against Waking Universe Corp. Lawyer had formerly served for 14 years as an in-house attorney for Waking Universe. During that time, he helped craft the corporation's employment policies, advised company officials and managers how to act pursuant to those policies and how to make hiring and firing decisions, and was involved in nearly 600 employment-related matters. Some of the officials and managers he advised will be witnesses in Jane's case, and some of them were also involved in some of the prior employment matters. Should Jane's lawyer be disqualified in the present matter?

Problem 19.3. Lawyer briefly represented Tobin in a drug trafficking prosecution, but was discharged by Tobin after only one meeting. During that meeting, Tobin described in general terms the events surrounding his arrest. All of the information disclosed also appeared in the police report accompanying Tobin's arrest. Now, six months later, Lawyer has been hired to represent Mick in a drug trafficking and felony murder prosecution. The prosecutor charges that Mick had been a longtime member of a drug trafficking ring of which Tobin was also a member. Tobin faces separate drug trafficking charges resulting from the same incident that led to Mick's arrest. Mick's anticipated defense involves placing some of the blame for the drug deal and its consequences on Tobin. The prosecution has now moved to disqualify Lawyer from representing Mick. Should the motion be granted?

* * *

C. MOBILE LAWYERS AND SCREENING

**Please read ABA Model Rule of Professional Conduct,
Rule 1.9(b) and Comments [4]–[7] & [9]; and Rule 1.10(b)
& (c) and Comments [5]–[7].**

* * *

In 2009, the ABA amended Model Rule 1.10 to allow for screening in the case of an imputed conflict when lawyers moved from one firm to another. At the time new Model Rule 1.10 was enacted, the majority of jurisdictions did not permit screening absent the consent of the affected former client, although a significant number did allow for at least some forms of nonconsensual limited screening.

Not all states have adopted the screening rule. Model Rule 1.10 is more permissive in terms of screening in some respects than existing rules in many jurisdictions. In some jurisdictions, screening is not permitted when the personally prohibited lawyer played a substantial role in the same or a substantially related matter. *See, e.g.*, Ariz. Rules of Prof'l Conduct R. 1.10(d). At the same time, Model Rule 1.10 is more restrictive than the screening rules in some jurisdictions. For example, a handful of jurisdictions do not require (as does Model Rule 1.10) that the affected client be given notice that the firm is employing screening procedures. Ill. Rules of Prof'l Conduct, Rule 1.10(e). A few provide that screening is permitted, but impose no express requirement (like that found in Model Rule 1.10) that the screening be "timely." Comment [4] lists three policy considerations that Model Rule 1.9(b) attempts to balance in the case of a lawyer making a lateral move. As you read the following materials, ask yourself whether the rule has succeeded in balancing these interests. Also, are there other policy interests that are implicated in the laterally-mobile lawyer situation and, if so, how should those be taken into account?

The following case addresses screening for a paralegal who has moved to a new firm. The case arises from a state that does not follow the Model Rule in allowing mobile attorneys to use screening as a means of avoiding imputation. Nonetheless, as you read the case you should analyze the arguments it makes in favor of allowing screening for a paralegal, and you should consider in what ways the issues might be similar or different for attorneys. You should also focus on the court's analysis of the procedures used for screening. In the states that do allow screening for mobile attorneys, compliance with these screening procedures is key to determining whether the firm can continue representation or whether the imputed conflict will lead to disqualification.

* * *

HODGE V. UFRA-SEXTON, LP
758 S.E.2d 314 (Ga. 2014)

HUNSTEIN, J.

We granted certiorari in this case to determine whether the Court of Appeals correctly held that a conflict of interest involving a nonlawyer can be remedied by implementing proper screening measures in order to avoid disqualification of the entire law firm. For the reasons set forth below, we hold that a nonlawyer's conflict of interest can be remedied by implementing proper screening measures so as to avoid disqualification of an entire law firm. In this particular case, we find that the screening measures implemented by the nonlawyer's new law firm were effective and appropriate to protect against the nonlawyer's disclosure of confidential information. However, we remand this case to the trial court for a hearing to determine whether the new law firm promptly disclosed the conflict.

On January 3, 2010, Monica Renee Williams was shot and killed at an apartment complex managed by Appellees UFRA-Sexton, LP and Signature Management Corporation (hereinafter "UFRA-Sexton"). Appellant Belinda Ann Hodge is the sister of Williams. Kristi Bussey had known Hodge for approximately ten years prior to Williams' death. Bussey assisted Hodge in obtaining her appointment as administratrix of Williams' estate and Hodge's appointment as the legal guardian for Williams' son.

Hodge retained attorney Craig Brookes of the law firm Hanks Brookes, LLC to pursue claims associated with the death of Williams. Bussey was a paralegal at Hanks Brookes and had worked there in that capacity since January 2007. Bussey was Hodge's primary contact with Hanks Brookes while she was employed at the firm. Bussey assisted with, and personally conducted, much of the investigation regarding Williams' death and the apartment complex where the death occurred. Bussey communicated regularly with Hodge about Hanks Brookes' investigation of the case, counsel's thoughts about the case, legal work being performed, and strategy for moving forward. Bussey participated in every face-to-face meeting Hodge had with Brookes while Bussey was employed with Hanks Brookes. Brookes spoke directly to Bussey about the status of her investigation, the results of his own investigation, his thoughts about the case, the strategies to be employed, and pertinent legal and factual considerations in the case.

Meanwhile, on March 29, 2010, UFRA-Sexton's insurer, Scottsdale Insurance Company, retained the firm of Insley & Race, LLC to represent UFRA-Sexton in the Williams matter. For the next six months, Insley & Race conducted a pre-suit investigation and evaluation of the incident, including numerous interviews, review of documents, and a detailed assessment.

In October 2010, Bussey left her position as a paralegal with Hanks Brookes and began working as a legal assistant at another law firm. In early 2011, Bussey applied for a paralegal position at Insley & Race. Brynda Rodriguez Insley personally called, and obtained a reference from, J.R. Hanks at Hanks Brookes. Hanks never disclosed any possible conflict with regard to Bussey or Hanks Brookes' work on the Williams case. Hanks was unaware that UFRA-Sexton was represented by Insley & Race in the Williams case.

Bussey began work as a paralegal at Insley & Race on March 15, 2011. At this time, neither Bussey nor Insley & Race was aware of any potential conflict regarding Bussey's work at Hanks Brookes, and Bussey did not know that Insley & Race was involved in a pre-suit investigation of Williams' death. Accordingly, Insley & Race did not employ any screening measures at that time.

On October 5, 2011, Bussey became aware of Insley & Race's involvement in the Williams case. Bussey immediately informed Insley & Race of her work with Hanks Brookes on the Williams case. Insley & Race immediately implemented screening measures, discussed more fully below, to protect against Bussey's disclosure of confidential information she had gained from working on the Williams case at Hanks Brookes.

Later that same evening, Insley sent an email to Brookes and other counsel for Hodge advising of the firm's representation of UFRA-Sexton and acknowledging the receipt of Hodge's demand letter. Insley did not mention any potential conflict involving Bussey.

On November 7, 2011, Hodge filed a complaint against UFRA-Sexton, and Insley & Race subsequently filed an answer on behalf of UFRA-Sexton. On December 6, 2011, counsel at Insley & Race disclosed Bussey's employment to Hodge's counsel. Hodge filed a motion to disqualify Insley & Race, requesting that Insley & Race voluntarily withdraw, and in the alternative, that the trial court issue an order disqualifying the firm from representing UFRA-Sexton in the Williams matter. UFRA-Sexton responded to Hodge's motion stating that Insley & Race was its counsel of choice and that it would not voluntarily withdraw.

The trial court denied Hodge's motion, finding that Insley & Race was UFRA-Sexton's counsel of choice, had developed specialized knowledge by working on the case for 18 months before learning of any potential conflict of interest, and had implemented appropriate and effective screening measures to protect against any disclosure of confidential information between Bussey and Insley & Race. Pursuant to Hodge's request, the trial court certified its order denying the motion to disqualify for immediate review. The Court of Appeals affirmed, finding that the trial court did not abuse its discretion in denying the motion to disqualify. We subsequently granted certiorari.

We review the trial court's ruling on a motion to disqualify for an abuse of discretion. We approach motions to disqualify with caution due to the consequences that could result if the motion is granted, such as the inevitable delay of the proceedings and the unique hardship on the client including the loss of time, money, choice of counsel, and specialized knowledge of the disqualified attorney. Additionally, we are mindful of counsel using motions to disqualify as a dilatory tactic. Accordingly, we view disqualification as an extraordinary remedy that should be granted sparingly.

It is well established that an attorney has a professional obligation to maintain client confidences and secrets. Ga. Rules of Prof'l Conduct, Rule 1.6(a). To protect this attorney-client relationship, the Georgia Rules of

Professional Conduct provide that a "lawyer who has formerly represented a client in a matter shall not thereafter represent another person in the same or a substantially related matter in which that person's interests are materially adverse to the interests of the former client unless the former client gives informed consent, confirmed in writing." Rule 1.9(a). "When a lawyer has been directly involved in a specific transaction, subsequent representation of other clients with materially adverse interests in that transaction clearly is prohibited." Id., Comment [2]. This Rule aims to protect former clients, avoid the appearance of any impropriety, and maintain public confidence in the integrity of our adversarial system.

Pursuant to Rule 1.10(a), " 'if one attorney in a firm has an actual conflict of interest, we impute that conflict to all the attorneys in the firm, subjecting the entire firm to disqualification.' " This Rule aims to give effect to the principle of loyalty to the client. Rule 1.10, Comment [6]. "Such situations can be considered from the premise that a firm of lawyers is essentially one lawyer for purposes of the rules governing loyalty to the client, or from the premise that each lawyer is vicariously bound by the obligation of loyalty owed by each lawyer with whom the lawyer is associated." Id.

Nonlawyers are also privy to confidential client information because it is often necessary for them to have access to this information to assist their attorney employers. However, our Rules do not regulate nonlawyers. Thus, the question presented here is how to protect the client's confidences, avoid impropriety, and maintain public confidence in the integrity of our adversarial system when nonlawyers change firms to work for opposing counsel.

There is a split of authority among the courts on this issue. The minority approach, which is what Hodge argues we should apply here, is to treat nonlawyers the same way we treat lawyers. Under this approach, when a nonlawyer moves to another firm to work for opposing counsel, the nonlawyer's conflict of interest is imputed to the rest of the firm, thereby disqualifying opposing counsel. UFRA-Sexton argues that we should adopt the majority approach and treat nonlawyers differently from lawyers. Under this approach, rather than automatic imputation and disqualification of the new firm, lawyers hiring the nonlawyer can implement screening measures to protect any client confidences that the nonlawyer gained from prior employment. After reviewing both approaches, we join today with "the majority of professional legal ethics commentators, ethics tribunals, and courts[, which] have concluded that nonlawyer screening is a permissible method to protect confidences held by nonlawyer employees who change employment."

We believe that screening measures are appropriate for nonlawyers, rather than imputed disqualification, for several reasons. First, nonlawyers generally have neither a financial interest in the outcome of a particular litigation nor a choice about which clients they serve, which reduces the appearance of impropriety. Second, nonlawyers have different training, responsibilities, and discovery and use of confidential information compared to lawyers. Third, as noted above, disqualification of the new firm would present a hardship to the new firm's client, such as delays, further expenses, and a loss of specialized knowledge.

Fourth, if imputation and disqualification were automatic, nonlawyers' employment mobility could be "unduly restricted." In recommending that screening measures be allowed for nonlawyers, the ABA Committee on Ethics and Professional Responsibility recognized that it was important for nonlawyers to "have as much mobility in employment opportunity as possible consistent with the protection of clients' interests." ABA Comm. on Ethics and Prof'l Responsibility, Informal Op. 88–1526, at 2. The ABA Committee noted that clients as well as the legal profession would be harmed by limiting nonlawyers' employment opportunities and requiring them to leave the careers for which they are trained. "A potential employer might well be reluctant to hire a particular nonlawyer if doing so would automatically disqualify the entire firm from ongoing litigation." Nonlawyers in sparsely populated towns or counties as well as nonlawyers previously employed by massive firms and involved in extensive litigation would be especially hard hit by the rule of imputed disqualification. "[A] lawyer may always practice his or her profession regardless of an affiliation to a law firm. Paralegals, legal secretaries, and other employees of attorneys do not have that option." If we were to impute the nonlawyers conflict of interest to the entire firm, "employers could protect themselves against unanticipated disqualification risks only by refusing to hire experienced people." Restatement (Third) of Law Governing Lawyers § 123, Comment (f) (2000).

Fifth, our Rules recognize that screening is effective at protecting a client's confidences. Our Rules explicitly allow screening with regard to lawyers who are former judges and arbitrators or former public officers and employees. Rules 1.11, 1.12. The purpose of screening measures in Rules 1.11 and 1.12 is "to assure the affected parties that confidential information known by the personally disqualified lawyer remains protected." Rule 1.0, Comment [8]. The use of a screen for nonlawyers has the same purpose.

Finally, while our Rules do not regulate nonlawyers, they do regulate attorneys' conduct with regard to supervising nonattorneys. Our Rules require that (1) a lawyer who has supervisory authority over a nonlawyer must make reasonable efforts to ensure that the nonlawyer's conduct is compatible with the professional obligations of a lawyer; (2) a lawyer may not order or ratify a nonlawyer's conduct if it would violate the Rules; and (3) those with managerial authority over a nonlawyer must make reasonable efforts to ensure that the firm itself has measures in place to give reasonable assurance that the nonlawyer's conduct is compatible with the professional obligations of the lawyer. Rule 5.3(a), (b), (c).6 These professional obligations include protecting a client's confidences. See Rule 1.6(a). Thus, our Rules require that attorneys be held accountable for their nonlawyer employees' conduct, particularly where there is a threat to attorney-client confidentiality and the integrity of our judicial process. We are not suggesting that lawyers always have a duty to an opposing party to maintain that party's confidences in the absence of a prior attorney-client relationship. However, we are mindful that the former employee's attorney has no effective means of protecting against the nonlawyer's disclosure of the client's confidences once the nonlawyer leaves the attorney's employment. Therefore, the responsibility for protecting the confidentiality of attorney-client communications must fall to the new lawyer or firm hiring the nonlawyer and the implementation of screening measures.

Accordingly, as a matter of first impression, we set forth the following guidance for disqualification of a law firm based on a nonlawyer's conflict of interest. Once the new firm knows of the nonlawyer's conflict of interest, the new firm must give prompt written notice to any affected adversarial party or their counsel, stating the conflict and the screening measures utilized. cf. Rule 1.11(a)(2) (regarding successive government and private employment, requiring that "written notice is duly given to the client and appropriate government entity"); Rule 1.12(c)(2) (regarding former judge or arbitrator, requiring that "written notice is promptly given to the appropriate tribunal"). The adversarial party may give written consent to the new firm's continued representation of its client with screening measures in place.

Absent written consent, the adversarial party may move to disqualify the new firm. The adversarial party must show that the nonlawyer actually worked on a same or substantially related matter involving the adversarial party while the nonlawyer was employed at the former firm. If the moving party can show this, it will be presumed that the nonlawyer learned confidential information about the matter. This prevents the nonlawyer from having to disclose the very information that should be protected.

Once this showing has been made, a rebuttable presumption arises that the nonlawyer has used or disclosed, or will use or disclose, the confidential information to the new firm. The new firm may rebut this by showing that it has properly taken effective screening measures to protect against the nonlawyer's disclosure of the former client's confidential information If the new firm can sufficiently rebut the presumption and show that it promptly gave written notice of the nonlawyer's conflict, then disqualification is not required.

The specific screening measures that the new firm must implement will vary based on the particular circumstances in each case. See Rule 1.0, Comment [9] ("screening measures that are appropriate for the particular matter will depend on the circumstances"). Courts must evaluate whether the new firm took sufficient measures to reduce the potential for the breach of confidences by the nonlawyer. Courts may also consider the amount of time that has elapsed since the nonlawyer's work on the case in question at the previous firm, the size of the new and previous firms, and the number of individuals presumed to have confidential information.

At a minimum,

> [a] lawyer should give [nonlawyers] appropriate instruction and supervision concerning the ethical aspects of their employment, particularly regarding the obligation not to disclose information relating to representation of the client, and should be responsible for their work product. The measures employed in supervising nonlawyers should take account of the fact that they do not have legal training and are not subject to professional discipline.

Rule 5.3, Comment [1]. A lawyer should "screen" the nonlawyer, which our Rules define as isolating the nonlawyer "from any participation in a matter through the timely imposition of procedures within a firm that are reasonably adequate under the circumstances to protect information that the isolated [non]lawyer is obligated to protect under these Rules or other law." Rule 1.0(p).

> The personally disqualified [nonlawyer] should acknowledge the obligation not to communicate with any of the other lawyers in the firm with respect to the matter [and] other lawyers in the firm who are working on the matter should be informed that the screening is in place and that they may not communicate with the personally disqualified [nonlawyer] with respect to the matter.

Rule 1.0, Comment [9]. It may also be appropriate for the firm to institute procedures to prevent the nonlawyer from having contact with, or access to, any firm files or other materials relating to the matter. Id. It may also be prudent for the firm to present periodic reminders of the screen to the nonlawyer and all other firm personnel. Id. "In order to be effective, screening measures must be implemented as soon as practical after a [nonlawyer,] lawyer[,] or law firm knows or reasonably should know that there is a need for screening." Id. at Comment [10].

On the other hand, the new firm will be disqualified where (1) the nonlawyer has already revealed the confidential information to lawyers or other personnel in the new firm; (2) screening would be ineffective; or (3) "the nonlawyer necessarily would be required to work [or has actually worked at the new firm] on the other side of the same or a substantially related matter on which the nonlawyer [previously] worked." If these situations occur, the new firm must withdraw from representing its client because the confidentiality of the former client has been destroyed and the appearance of impropriety will result.

2. Having found that screening is appropriate for nonlawyers, we must now evaluate the measures used by Insley & Race in this particular case. First, we begin by noting that Hodge has not waived the conflict of interest by giving written consent for Insley & Race to continue to represent UFRA-Sexton, and UFRA-Sexton has expressly requested that Insley & Race continue to represent it as their counsel of choice. Additionally, Bussey attests in her affidavit that she has neither discussed nor disclosed any confidential information that she obtained about the Williams matter during her employment with Hanks Brookes to any person at Insley & Race, and Bussey has not worked on the Williams case while at Insley & Race. Accordingly, automatic disqualification is not warranted.

Next, there is no dispute that Bussey worked on the Williams case while at Hanks Brookes, and therefore, it is presumed that Bussey learned confidential information about the Williams case. The burden now shifts to Insley & Race to rebut the presumption that Bussey used or disclosed, or will use or will disclose, confidential information about the Williams case to Insley & Race.

Bussey states in her affidavit that she was unaware of Insley & Race's involvement in the Williams case when she was hired on March 15, 2011, and Insley attests that the firm was unaware of any potential conflict in hiring Bussey. Bussey states that she did not learn of her new firm's involvement in the Williams case until October 5, 2011. Upon discovering that Insley & Race was counsel for UFRA-Sexton, Bussey immediately informed her co-workers, Insley, and the firm administrator. Insley immediately instructed Bussey not to be involved in the Williams case at Insley & Race in any way or to have any discussions with anyone about the case or her knowledge about it. Furthermore, Insley instructed Bussey that she would be restricted from any access to the electronic file and that Insley would make sure that appropriate screening measures were in place at Insley & Race. The firm administrator immediately implemented and confirmed electronic screening measures with Bussey, including taking steps to restrict Bussey's access to any information about the Williams case, implementing security measures to prevent Bussey from accessing any computerized information maintained by Insley &

Race regarding the Williams case, and testing the security measures he implemented to ensure their success. Since October 5, Bussey has been unable to access the case management system used by Insley & Race for the Williams matter, including any calendar events, contact information, documents, and billing information for the Williams case. Additionally, the physical file was removed from the general file room and securely placed in the office of an associate.

Bussey and Insley state in their affidavits that Bussey will continue to fully abide by the screening and restrictive measures implemented at Insley & Race; Bussey will not have access to the electronic or physical file in the Williams case; and Bussey will not discuss or disclose any confidential information about the Williams case to anyone at Insley & Race. Insley as well as the firm administrator attest that the screening and restrictive measures implemented on October 5, 2011, have and will remain in place throughout the duration of the case to prevent the disclosure of confidential information.

We find that in this particular case Insley & Race's screening measures were, and are, appropriate and effective to protect against Bussey's disclosure of confidential information she learned while working on the Williams case at Hanks Brookes. Insley & Race took sufficient screening measures to reduce the potential for the breach of confidences by Bussey, and therefore, Insley & Race has rebutted the presumption that Bussey used or disclosed, or will use or disclose, the confidential information.

Hodge contends that Insley & Race should be disqualified because the firm did not perform adequate conflict checks to detect whether Bussey had worked on the Williams case. Insley & Race responds that Hanks Brookes should have disclosed its involvement in the Williams case when Insley called Hanks to discuss hiring Bussey in March 2011. Although we agree that it would be prudent for a potential employer to conduct conflict checks before hiring a new nonlawyer, so as to implement appropriate screening measures and avoid the possibility of subsequent disqualification, in this case the potential conflict was missed, regardless of whether the blame rests with Insley & Race or Hanks Brookes. Importantly, Insley & Race implemented effective screening measures as soon as Bussey informed the firm of the conflict to ensure that Bussey would not disclose confidential information about the Williams case, and Bussey has not actually disclosed such confidential information.

Hodge also argues that Insley & Race did not timely disclose Bussey's conflict to Hanks Brookes on October 5, and instead waited until December 6 to do so. Hodge raised this argument before the trial court and the Court of Appeals, but neither court addressed this issue. Based on the guidelines we have established today, once Insley & Race knew of

Bussey's conflict of interest, Insley & Race was required to give prompt written notice to Hodge or her counsel, stating the conflict and the screening measures implemented at Insley & Race. Therefore, we remand this case to the Court of Appeals to remand to the trial court for a hearing to determine whether Insley & Race gave prompt written notice to Hodge or her counsel.

Judgment vacated and case remanded with direction.

* * *

Screening lawyers. *Hodge* dealt with a mobile paralegal. Under the Model Rule, a similar analysis would apply to mobile lawyers. Do you agree with the Model Rule position that screening should be allowed even for attorneys? Or do you agree with the court in *Hodge* that lawyers should be subject to a stricter rule?

Screening in transactional settings vs. litigation. Some jurisdictions permit screening in transactional representation, but not in the litigation setting. Tennessee's Rule 1.10(d) does not allow screening to be used to avoid imputed disqualification if "the lawyer's representation of the former client was in connection with an adjudicative proceeding that is directly adverse to the interests of a current client of the firm." Tenn. Rules of Prof'l Conduct R. 1.10(d). Is there a compelling reason to afford less protection in terms of confidentiality in transactional practice than is afforded in litigation?

Government lawyers. The *Hodge* case discussed Rule 1.11. As Comment [3] to Rule 1.11 points out, a conflict exists where the lawyer now represents a private client whose interests are aligned with those of the lawyer's former government agency client. In other words, adversity between the old client and the new client is not required for disqualification. Does this make sense? Whose interests are being protected by this provision?

Judges. Compare Model Rule 1.11 with 1.12. What is the underlying purpose of Rule 1.12? Is it to facilitate judge mobility (i.e., to ensure that judges are not unduly inhibited from moving back and forth from the bench to private practice)? If so, how does the rule effectuate this purpose? As amended by the ABA in 2002, Rule 1.12 also applies to mediators and other dispute resolution neutrals.

Rule 1.12(b) and law clerks. Rule 1.12(b) permits a law clerk for a judge to "negotiate for employment with a party or lawyer involved in a matter in which the clerk is participating personally and substantially, but only after the lawyer has notified the judge . . . " What purpose does notifying the judge serve here?

Duties of lawyers left behind when laterally mobile lawyers leave a firm and take clients with them. What happens when a lawyer who leaves her former firm takes one or more of the firm's clients with her when she moves to a new firm? These clients become former clients of the lawyers who remain at the firm that had previously represented them. Under what circumstances can the lawyers left behind represent clients with interests adverse to the clients who followed the lawyer who left the firm? Re-read Model Rule 1.10(b) and consider the following problem:

* * *

Problem 19.4. While Jill was a partner in the Biggs Law Firm, she was primarily responsible for the representation of Farley Corp. in its antitrust suit against Harrison Co. Jill supervised a team of several lawyers in this matter, including Cheyenne, who interviewed Farley Corp. company officials and reviewed confidential documents as part of the representation. Jill eventually left the Biggs Law Firm to start her own firm and brought several clients (including Farley Corp.) along with her as well as several lawyers from the Biggs firm. Cheyenne decided not to leave the Biggs firm. Pappas Industries has now approached the Biggs Law Firm about the possibility of the firm representing Pappas against Farley Corp. in a matter that is substantially related to the Farley Corp./Harrison Co. antitrust dispute. Can the Biggs firm represent Pappas in this matter?

* * *

Profile of attorney professionalism. Lawyers Ted Olson and David Boies were used to being adversaries. Olson, politically conservative and present at the 1982 meeting founding the Federalist Society, had worked in the Reagan administration and had later served as Solicitor General under George W. Bush. Boies, a self-described liberal, had argued in favor of greater regulation of business and had served as an outside consultant on the Clinton administration's antitrust lawsuit against Microsoft. The pair had famously opposed each other in litigating Bush v. Gore, 531 U.S. 98 (2000). In spite of their differences—and in spite of the fact that they opposed each other in court several more times—Boies and Olson grew to be friends.

In 2009, they decided to team up to represent a client with a cause they both believed in: marriage equality. The pair represented a California resident who was challenging Proposition 8, which restricted same-sex marriage rights. Boies and Olson won their case at trial, and the state of California elected not to appeal the ruling. Although other intervenors sought to appeal, Olson and Boies successfully argued on appeal that the inervenors lacked standing, and thus successfully defended their trial victory. Hollingsworth v. Perry, 133 S. Ct. 2652 (2013).

Olson and Boies describe their friendship, their litigation decisions, and their experience taking the case from trial, to appeal, and ultimately the Supreme Court, in DAVID BOIES AND THEODORE B. OLSON, REDEEMING THE DREAM: THE CASE FOR MARRIAGE EQUALITY (2014). In the book, they discuss how their prior legal work played into the decision to hire them, noting that Olson's success in *Bush v. Gore* raised concern, as some believed that the Bush victory paved the way for Proposition 8 and other restrictions on marriage rights. Nevertheless, that concern was overshadowed by both lawyers' strings of litigation success and by their obvious dedication to the case. Furthermore, they pointed out, "the irony of a former intimate of the Clinton White House teaming up with someone who had been an outspoken Clinton critic" was expected to spark media interest early on, bringing attention to the client's cause and, potentially, helping to "persuad[e] the public that the cause was just."

PART 4

REPRESENTING CLIENTS

■ ■ ■

In Part 3, we examined the legal relationship between the lawyer and the lawyer's client. Although many of the issues we discussed arose in connection with the lawyer's representation of the client in the client's dealings with others—either an opposing party in a lawsuit or a party to a business transaction—our focus was on the relative rights and responsibilities of the lawyer and client vis à vis each other. In this part of the book, we now shift our focus to the interaction of the lawyer, acting on behalf of the client, with third persons (including opposing parties), counsel and witnesses in lawsuits, judges and other governmental officials, and persons who are otherwise dealing with the lawyer or being affected by actions the lawyer is taking on behalf of the lawyer's client.

The central organizing theme for Part 4 is the assumption that the lawyer is obligated to diligently—some would say zealously—do whatever the lawyer reasonably believes will accomplish the client's objectives for the representation, as determined by the client, subject to the requirement that the lawyer comply with any rules of professional conduct or other law that afford protections to persons other than the lawyer's client. It is these rules and law that we will examine in Part 4. Because these issues are most commonly addressed in connection with the lawyer's representation of clients in judicial proceedings—either criminal prosecutions or civil lawsuits—we will start by examining the professional roles, rights, and responsibilities of lawyers who are representing clients in connection with the resolution of their disputes. Because there are many clients who need the help of a lawyer in matters that do not involve the resolution of a dispute with another person, but rather anticipate cooperation in a business transaction or business relationship with another, or want to effectuate the gratuitous transfer of property to another, we also include a chapter that focuses on the roles, rights, and responsibilities of lawyers who help their clients do deals, rather than win lawsuits or secure the favorable resolution of a dispute with another.

* * *

In the Chapters to follow, we examine the roles, responsibilities, and rights of lawyers who are helping a client—a person or an organization— secure a favorable resolution of a dispute with another person or organization. Here we have in mind litigators and lawsuits and all the activities in which litigators may engage in connection with the prosecution or defense of a lawsuit: factual investigation, filing claims and motions, discovery, settling cases, trying cases, appealing adverse judgments, and collecting judgments. We begin, however, with the following discussion of the adversary system of justice within which all of the above occurs and which ultimately provides the frame of reference for our thinking about the roles, responsibilities, and rights of lawyers who are representing clients in connection with prospective or pending lawsuits. As you consider the adversary system and the various matters addressed in this section, please keep in mind the variety of lawsuits— e.g., criminal and civil, with civil actions including class actions and shareholder derivative actions, and the different roles lawyers may play in such lawsuits—e.g., the criminal defense lawyer, the prosecutor or other government lawyer engaged in a law enforcement investigation or proceeding, a plaintiff's lawyer, or a defendant's lawyer in a civil action. Also bear in mind that many lawyers specialize in particular types of lawsuits and particular types of clients—e.g., a plaintiff's lawyer who only handles medical malpractice, or less commonly, legal malpractice. The question to keep in mind is how this variety affects the regulation of litigator conduct. Can one rule fit all? Is what is good for the goose—e.g., a rule governing the conduct of a criminal defense lawyer representing a person charged with a crime—good for the gander—e.g., a lawyer representing a plaintiff in a civil action?

* * *

CHARLES W. WOLFRAM, MODERN LEGAL ETHICS

563–568 (West 1986)

§ 10.1 CONCEPT OF THE ADVERSARY SYSTEM

Significance of the Adversary System

In discussions of the character of litigation and other representations by lawyers in the United States, the almost universally accepted term is the *adversary system*. It is often stated that one of the major problems of legal ethics is to determine the proper role for lawyers functioning within that system. A careful speaker would, however, be none too comfortable employing the phrase, because it suggests a kind of ordered arrangement of uniform practices and institutional features that simply does not exist. Lawyers and judges differ sharply over such vital matters as methodology and values. Moreover, the patterns of actual rules and customary litigational practices are themselves quite nonuniform, differing significantly from state to state, from nation to state, from city to town, within the different courts in the same community, and sometimes between one courtroom and another. One has only to spend a few hours observing the summary and uncontested proceedings in a Monday morning drunk court; the later morning observing the pomp, circumstance, and orderly discussion at the Supreme Court; and the afternoon observing a trial involving skillful commercial trial litigators to realize the profoundly different "systems" being employed. A preferable phrase would be "adversary conception," for it is really a generalized ideal to which lawyers and judges most often mean to refer.

A second, and perhaps more important, reservation concerns the extent to which the concept of the adverbial lawyer might be carried beyond the realm of litigation. The core context in which the adversary system is typically discussed is that of the criminal defense lawyer. From there, consideration often moves to civil representation as well, sometimes without noting the profoundly different setting. Once conclusions have been drawn about the proper role of a lawyer in those contexts, they are often generalized into the lawyer's proper function for a client in any other context, including representations that have nothing to do with criminal defense or even with litigation. . .

Features of the Adversary System

The adversary system, if it means to refer to the common features of litigation in American civil and criminal courts, seems generally to refer to the following features.

(1) The parties initiate and control the definition of the issues and the presentation of evidence. The initiating party in a criminal prosecution must be the state. In civil proceedings, the decision to sue is made by individuals or entities.

(2) The presentations of the parties' cases are representational. The interested parties do not participate directly, except possibly as witnesses, in their own proceeding. Almost invariably each litigant acts through a hired advocate. The judge deals primarily with the advocates in discussing proceedings in the case, and the system allows the advocates a large amount of discretion to act for and to bind their principals.

(3) The exploration of issues and presentation of evidence is party-centered and contentious from beginning to end. The procedure calls for reciprocating, but largely non-cooperative, statement and counterstatement, proof and counterproof.

(4) Judge and jury are both neutral and passive. They come to the proceeding without demonstrable bias for or against one of the parties. Although the judge rules on motions, objections, and the like, that is almost always in response to a request to act by one of the parties. Neither judge nor jury takes personal initiative in interjecting issues, acquiring or examining evidence, or staking out new directions that the unfolding drama should take.

(5) The proceedings are governed by procedural rules that attempt, for the most part in harmony with the above general features, to regularize the proceedings and make them efficient in terms of expenditures of public resources.

(6) Finally, law and procedures formulate remedial endings to the litigation that are largely either-or in nature (either the plaintiff wins or the defendant, but not both partially) and that must be based only on the issues and evidence that the parties have presented.

* * *

Objectives of the Adversarial System

There is no reason to think that the adversary system sprang fully intellectualized from the brows of a Solon. Many of the rules and practices of the adversarial system are important products of history or culture. The adversary system in the United States is culture-bound beyond an extent that most lawyers would prefer to admit. The same social system that supports professional prizefighting and football, but outlaws chicken fighting, can be seen mirrored in the set of contradictory rules that limit yet then allow aggression and competition in the legal arena. Yet it would be wrong to assume that the adversarial system has not been powerfully shaped by ideas about its proper working.

Several justifying claims for the adversary system are commonly asserted. Most of them can be subsumed under three general claims, which will be examined in turn. Truth, it is claimed, first, is best discovered through the adversarial system. Second, individual legal rights are better protected and vindicated through it. Third, litigants are more likely to be personally satisfied with the results of an adversarial trial. The justifications of the adversary system have not, of course, gone without challenge.

Truth. Most commentators agree that, either as a goal in itself or as an instrumental goal to achieve fair outcomes, the adversarial system should lead to truth. For example, for someone who is primarily interested in the protection of individual rights through the adversarial system, truth about occurrences is an essential ingredient in defining the circumstances so that a correct invocation of rights can be made.

Ascertaining truth is argued to be one of the chief justifications of the adversarial system. It is claimed that it is designed to lead to the truth more surely than competing models for litigation. The lawyers, committed to seeking a partisan victory in the trial by any legal means, are motivated to search diligently for facts and to test the evidence offered by the opposing party through cross-examination and counterevidence. Through the reciprocating process of proof and challenge to proof, the fact finder is best able to determine where the truth lies. The efficiency of the system is also enhanced because the parties, with their trained advocates, are able to reduce the issues to those that truly divide them instead of having the inquisitor canvass all possible issues and differences of fact.

The adversary process is often contrasted with an arbitral system, in which a single inquisitor is to decide a dispute between parties without advocacy from either side. The paradoxical position of the inquisitorial judge is that, as a matter of psychology, one searching for facts and for the limits and nuances of the law is much more likely driven to creative and tireless effort if one is committed to discovering support for a thesis. But once the judge forms and proceeds upon a thesis, the natural human instinct is to resist sloughing off that thesis, and such support as has been gathered for it, in order to investigate conflicting or variant theses.

The inquisitorial system in use in most of the countries of Europe other than Britain is sometimes posed as a model for comparison with the adversarial system. Indeed, some scholars have proposed that some of its features should replace the adversarial system. In the inquisitorial system the process of gathering and sifting facts is performed primarily by judges and not by parties. The judges, however, lack motivation, other than professional esprit, to take a sustained and dispassionate look at the case before forming relatively firm conclusions.

It is often objected that adversarial trials cannot be an effective search for truth because one or perhaps both advocates come to the proceedings prepared to obfuscate, conceal, and distort the truth—to the considerable extent permissible under the rules of perjury, false evidence, and contempt of court. "How the edifice of justice can be supported by the efforts of liars at the bar and ex-liars on the bench is one of the paradoxes of legal logic which the man in the street has never solved." Some have argued that the adversary system nonetheless discovers truth through the same process of discovery that is often employed, when the work is well done, in such fields as science and history. There proposed truth is subjected to the winnowing process of skeptical investigation by other researchers attempting to demonstrate the error of the thesis being tested. The important difference, however, is that scientific and historical investigators do not purposefully use manipulation and half-truths and do not generally argue against known fact as lawyers do. Lawyers are not necessarily attempting to persuade the fact finder to find the truth; they attempt to persuade the fact finder to find facts favoring their clients.

Rights Vindication. The belief that the adversary system is the system best suited to lead to the vindication of individual rights is founded on two different conceptions of rights. One is the substantive conception of rights as things to be possessed and enjoyed. Here the argument is that the adversarial system is the best way for individuals to secure such rights. A different conception is that the autonomy and privacy of individuals is not sufficiently respected by a state unless deprivations and obligations that are imposed by law are exacted only following a public process in which the person charged with a civil or criminal wrong is given many procedural and forensic advantages. The extreme illustration is the presumption of innocence and all that it procedurally brings with it in the idealized criminal trial.

Particularly when litigation is between individuals or nonpublic institutions, discussions of rights vindication associate the laissez-faire philosophy of economic competition with the adversarial concept of litigational competition. If the economic and litigational institutions share a common historical and theoretical base, then one would expect to find at bottom of each a conception of persons that includes as essential postulates possessive individualism in the substantive realm and a belief in a variety of procedures for regulation that share with Darwin a survival-of-the-fittest sort of resort to procedural governance. The difference between Darwin's world of natural science and the courtroom, however, is important. In the courtroom there are rules designed to assure, to an extent, that the competition is fair. In the adversary system justificatory arguments, belief in fairness constraints results in a strong emphasis upon the process and a corresponding belief in outcomes.

The concept of competitiveness consists of large strains of aggressiveness. For that reason, it is sometimes asserted that the present-day adversarial system "descends in part from trial by battle, in which the government official present at the trial simply refereed the contest." Such statements invoke historical metaphors rather than historical roots or causes. The adversarial system is clearly not a direct, lineal descendant of trial by battle in the sense of sympathetic modeling. The present methods of trial developed specifically as rationalized replacements of battle, test, and oath with their crude and superstitious invocations of divine judgment. It might nonetheless be true that battlelike characteristics that have survived in trials are atavistic emergences of the human qualities that the social arrangement of trials was meant to displace. A similar critique that also looks to the contentious nature of trials is that the adversary system displays a "sporting theory of justice." Others, however, have justified the adversarial system as a kind of acceptable social arrangement in which parties play a fair game with fair rules as a way of working out differences.

Litigant Satisfaction. The third justification for the adversary system is that it affords litigants more satisfaction than competing models of adjudication. That claim also has at least two principal assets—the intellectual and the emotional.

At the intellectual level, a litigant who has suffered a loss in adversarial litigation at least has the satisfaction of knowing that the result occurred at the end of a process in which the litigant played a major role. The litigant was not forced to sit by as mere observer while governmental officials, over whom the litigant had no hope of control, "lost" the litigant's claim. The participatory justification for the adversary system fits comfortably with related concepts such as citizen participation in governance through voting. But commentators who question the adversary system note that the claims of rights vindication are plausible on their own terms only if one has confidence that the system in fact works as described. The same is true, of course, for claims that the adversary system best finds the truth. But if, as often happens, the parties' lawyers are of significantly different ability or if one party is able to marshal more resources for a sustained fight, the results of litigation can often turn out to frustrate otherwise valid legal claims.

At the emotional level, the aggressiveness of the adversary system may serve for clients the valuable function of permitting them to resolve doubts and qualms about their own aggressive feelings toward an adversary, giving the litigant an occasion for playing out deeply conflicting social conflicts, such as those between order and freedom, or personal conflicts, such as anger and guilt. As a justification for the adversary system, the rationale must assume that the adversarial occasion for harmless aggressive displays replaces and deflects aggressions that would otherwise be acted out in socially harmful ways. It must also assume that the official permission to act aggressively does not dysfunctionally spawn more divisiveness and aggression than would otherwise exist. The literature of alternative dispute resolution argues, or assumes, that the adversarial system does indeed have the socially undesirable effect of creating conflict in society rather than diminishing it.

* * *

What do you think? Given our longstanding and deep commitment to the adversary system of justice, how do you explain the increased resort by lawyers to alternative dispute resolution and "collaborative lawyering?" Does this development call into question our love affair with the adversary system of justice?

* * *

We do not have answers for these questions about the extent to which it may be inappropriate to export ideas about an adversary system of justice that have their greatest force in the context of the defense of an accused in a criminal prosecution to other spheres of social life in which a lawyer may represent a client. For the moment, however, it is simply our goal to plant a seed of awareness that the rules you will be studying in the chapters to come are built upon various assumptions about the desirability of an adversarial system in which lawyers are expected to act as zealous partisans maximizing the power of their clients as the clients seek to prevail in their struggles against their opponents. Based on these assumptions, the rules seek to impose some limits on means lawyers can use as they act as partisan and zealous advocates or advisors on behalf of their clients.

SECTION 1

LITIGATION PRACTICE

■ ■ ■

This section includes four chapters that focus on the legal and disciplinary rules that are most relevant to a lawyer engaged in litigation practice. That said, many of the concepts discussed have application beyond the litigation setting. Chapter 20 deals with pre-trial practice, while Chapter 21 deals with special issues involved in trial practice. Chapter 22 focuses specifically on criminal law practice, an area where ethical rules often overlap with constitutional rules. While nearly every lawyer engaged in the practice of law can expect to interact with judges, litigators interact with judges on a regular basis. Therefore, Chapter 23 covers some of the relevant rules that apply to such interactions.

CHAPTER 20

PRE-TRIAL ADVOCACY

■ ■ ■

Chapter hypothetical. The Lilith Corporation's president, Linus Coverdale, asks you to represent the company in a lawsuit filed by Necco Corporation. Necco manufactures and sells lift trucks and parts through authorized dealers. For many years, Lilith was an authorized Necco dealer but was terminated as a dealer in January 2013.

Necco sued Lilith for violation of the Computer Fraud and Abuse Act, computer trespass, misappropriation of trade secrets, and tortious interference with contract and business relations. Necco alleges that after Lilith was terminated as a dealer in 2013, some of its employees gained unauthorized access to Necco's dealer website. According to Necco's complaint, the Lilith employees used a password obtained from Jane McLachlan, an employee of Hampstead Corporation. (Hampstead is an authorized Necco dealer). Necco asserts that Lilith's unauthorized access only ceased when Necco deactivated and replaced Hampstead's password in February 2014.

Lilith was served with the Necco lawsuit on June 1, 2014. Lilith's president contacted you the next day. He tells you that he was not aware of the issues alleged in the case until he received the complaint.

* * *

A. INFORMAL FACT INVESTIGATION

* * *

Please read ABA Model Rules of Professional Conduct, Rule 3.4(a), (b) & (f) and Comments [1], [2] & [4].

* * *

1. SEEKING INFORMATION FROM INDIVIDUALS REPRESENTED BY COUNSEL

Please read ABA Model Rules of Professional Conduct, Rule 4.2 and Comments [1]–[4] & [7]–[9]; and Rule 3.4(f).

* * *

Model Rule 4.2, the "no contact" rule, prevents an attorney from contacting a person represented by counsel absent counsel's consent. ABA Formal Ethics Opinion 95–396 explains that such rules prevent interference in the attorney-client relationship by opposing counsel and reduce the risk that a client will reveal information that will harm the client's interests.

The rule also applies to contact with certain constituents of an organizational client that is represented by counsel. Use Comment [7] to Rule 4.2 and Rule 3.4(f) to answer Problem 20.1.

* * *

Problem 20.1. Lilith Corporation's president Linus Coverdale tells you that Lilith employees who may have been involved in the unauthorized website access work in the company's Parts Group. They are Lora McDonald, Carlee Hixon, and Russell Marcus. Linus tells you that Dora Merigo was a member of the Parts Group until she was fired from Lilith in January 2014. She also may have been involved in accessing the Necco website. Finally, Linus notes that Jane McLachlan (the alleged source of the password) worked in the Lilith Parts Group for many years but left for Hampstead in 2012. Hampstead has not been named a party in the case and is not represented by counsel in the matter.

Consistent with Rule 4.2, which of these individuals may you interview at this time? Is Necco's counsel able to interview any of these individuals without violating Rule 4.2? Is it appropriate under the professional conduct rules for you to instruct any or all of these individuals that they should not talk to Necco's counsel if they receive a call or contact from her?

* * *

2. COMMUNICATING WITH UNREPRESENTED PERSONS AND CLARIFYING YOUR PARTISAN ROLE AND REFRAINING FROM RENDERING LEGAL ADVICE TO UNREPRESENTED PERSONS

Please read ABA Model Rules of Professional Conduct, Rule 4.3 and Comments [1] & [2].

* * *

Problem 20.2. You decide to contact Jane McLachlan, the alleged source of the password who now works at Hampstead (see the facts in Problem 20.1). You explain your role in the case as an attorney for Lilith. Jane admits that she was the source of the password for Lilith employees. She gave the password to Carlee Hixon and knew the Parts Group would use it to access the protected area of the Necco website. Jane asks you if you think Necco has a cause of action against her if Necco finds out that she was the source of the password. What do you tell her?

* * *

B. PREPARING PLEADINGS, MOTIONS AND OTHER PAPERS

As a general rule, a lawyer owes no duty to exercise reasonable care on behalf of a nonclient. However, a lawyer who files a frivolous claim or motion on behalf of a client could potentially face a number of tort theories of liability. At the same time, a lawyer who files a frivolous claim or motion might also face sanctions or professional discipline.

* * *

1. TORT LIABILITY STEMMING FROM THE FILING OF FRIVOLOUS CLAIMS AND MOTIONS

Malicious prosecution. One tort theory that might apply to the filing of a frivolous claim is malicious prosecution or wrongful initiation of civil proceedings. The party who has been forced to defend against a frivolous claim must prove (1) that the prior proceeding on the underlying matter terminated in the party's favor, (2) the absence of probable cause for those proceedings, and (3) "malice" on the part of the party who brought the underlying action. Friedman v. Dozroc, 312 N.W.2d 585 (Mich. 1981). The malice element is frequently defined to mean that the party had an improper purpose for bringing the action, i.e., "a purpose other than that of securing the proper adjudication of the claim in which the proceedings are based." Restatement (Second) of Torts § 674. The key conflict in many malicious prosecution cases is the issue of probable cause, which the Restatement (Second) of Torts defines in this manner:

One who takes an active part in the initiation, continuation or procurement of civil proceedings against another has probable cause for doing so if he reasonably believes in the existence of the facts upon which the claim is based, and either:

(a) correctly or reasonably believes that under those facts the claim may be valid under the applicable law, or

(b) believes to this effect in reliance upon the advice of counsel, sought in good faith and given after full disclosure of all relevant facts within his knowledge and information.

Restatement (Second) of Torts § 675.

* * *

Problem 20.3. (This problem is unrelated to the chapter hypothetical). Dr. Friedman successfully defended against a medical malpractice suit brought by Jeff, an attorney, on behalf of one of Dr. Friedman's former clients. The trial judge in the medical malpractice action entered judgment as a matter of law against Jeff's client. Now, Dr. Friedman has sued Jeff for malicious prosecution, claiming Jeff lacked probable cause to institute the malpractice action. Specifically, Dr. Friedman points to Jeff's ethical obligation of competence, which requires inquiry into the factual and legal elements of a case. *See* Model Rule 1.1, Comment [5]. Dr. Friedman alleges that if Jeff had conducted a reasonable investigation into the facts instead of relying solely on his client's version of events, he would have quickly realized that his client did not have a valid basis on which to pursue the malpractice claim. He also alleges that the medical malpractice claim amounts to a "nuisance suit," filed simply to force Dr. Friedman to settle rather than incur the cost and aggravation of defending himself. Assuming Jeff simply took his client's word for the facts Jeff ultimately alleged in the malpractice complaint, does Dr. Friedman have a valid malicious prosecution claim? *See* Friedman v. Dozroc, 312 N.W.2d 585 (Mich. 1981).

* * *

Abuse of process. The tort of abuse of process is a close cousin to the malicious prosecution or wrongful initiation tort. "The usual case of abuse of process is one of some form of extortion, using [a legal] process to put pressure upon [another] to compel him to pay a different debt or to take some other action or refrain from it." Restatement (Second) of Torts § 682 cmt. b.

Defamation. Where a lawyer makes false and defamatory statements about an individual, a defamation claim against the lawyer filing the complaint may be a possibility. However, the "litigator's privilege," which covers "communications preliminary to a proposed judicial proceeding, or in the institution of, or during the course and as a part of, a judicial proceeding" (provided the communication has some relation to the proceeding), should ordinarily protect the attorney who makes false and defamatory statements in a complaint or motion. Restatement (Second) of Torts § 586. In most jurisdictions, the privilege is absolute in nature. Thus, the fact the lawyer acted with knowledge that the statements were false is irrelevant. The privilege is absolute, the Restatement (Second) of Torts explains, so as not to deter lawyers from vigorously asserting their clients' rights. *See id.* § 586 cmt. a.

Tortious interference. Another possibility is a claim of tortious interference with contractual relations. For example, in Mantia v. Hanson, 79 P.3d 404, 406 (Or. Ct. App. 2003), the plaintiff sued one of its former employees on a tortious interference theory after the employee had filed allegedly frivolous claims against the plaintiff as part of an attempt to interfere with the plaintiff's business. In addition, the plaintiff sued the former employee's lawyers for asserting the allegedly frivolous claims on the employee's behalf. The court chose not to extend the litigator's privilege to interference claims. However, the court held that when an interference claim is based on the institution of legal proceedings, the plaintiff must establish that the lawyer employed "improper means" in interfering with the plaintiff's business relations with another. The court then defined the concept of "improper means" so that the definition tracked exactly the elements of a malicious prosecution or wrongful initiation claim. *Id.* at 414. Thus, a plaintiff in such cases faces the same difficult burden faced in a malicious prosecution or wrongful initiation claim. *See* Alex B. Long, *Attorney Liability for Tortious Interference: Interference with Contractual Relations or Interference with the Practice of Law*, 18 GEO. J. LEGAL ETHICS 471 (2005) (discussing the use of interference claims resulting from litigation tactics).

* * *

2. SANCTIONS FOR FILING FRIVOLOUS CLAIMS AND MOTIONS

* * *

Please read ABA Model Rules of Professional Conduct, Rule 3.1 and Comments; and Rule 3.2 and Comments.

Please read Federal Rules of Civil Procedure, Rule 11.

* * *

GARR V. U.S. HEALTHCARE, INC.
22 F.3d 1274 (3d Cir. 1994)

GREENBERG, CIRCUIT JUDGE.

I. INTRODUCTION

. . . This action arose in the aftermath of an article in the *Wall Street Journal* published on November 4, 1992, entitled "U.S. Healthcare Insiders Sold Stock Before Last Week's 17% Price Decline." The article recited that U.S. Healthcare, Inc. insiders, including Leonard Abramson, its chairman and president, had been heavy sellers of its stock before a 17% two-day drop in its price in the week before publication of the article. The article indicated the drop had been precipitated by disappointing earnings.

James R. Malone, Jr., a member of the Haverford, Pennsylvania, law firm of Greenfield & Chimicles, who read the article on the morning it was published, was interested in its contents because his firm specialized in securities litigation. Indeed, . . . Greenfield & Chimicles maintained a list of corporate stockholders available to become plaintiffs in securities litigation[1]. Robert K. Greenfield was on that list.[2] It is undisputed that after Malone read the article he examined a "representative sampling of stories relating to U.S. Healthcare," as well as a report on background information on the company. He also obtained considerable other information about U.S. Healthcare, including filings it had made with the Securities and Exchange Commission.

Malone does not contend that at the time that he was doing this research he had a client who had expressed any interest in the article to him. Rather, Malone was seeking to generate a lawsuit. Thus, in the pithy words of the district court, "[h]aving a case but no client," he called Greenfield, who lives in Florida, to discuss the U.S. Healthcare situation. Malone described the *Wall Street Journal* article to Greenfield and established that he owned stock in U.S. Healthcare. Malone asked Greenfield whether he would like Greenfield & Chimicles to file a suit on his behalf if the firm believed that there had been actionable wrongdoing, and Greenfield answered affirmatively. Within hours Malone determined that a certain class of U.S. Healthcare stockholders had "a legitimate and cognizable legal claim" stemming in part from the insiders' stock sales.

Events continued to unfold rapidly on November 4, 1992, for on that day Malone prepared and filed a class action complaint on behalf of Greenfield under section 10(b) of the Securities Exchange Act of 1934. . . . The gravamen of the complaint was that U.S. Healthcare and Abramson had issued false and misleading statements which were filed with the Securities and Exchange Commission and which caused Greenfield and the stockholder class to purchase U.S. Healthcare stock at artificially inflated prices. The complaint asserted controlling person liability against Abramson under section 20 of the Securities Exchange Act. . . . In the complaint, Malone recited that Greenfield fairly and adequately could represent the interest of the class of stockholders on whose behalf the action was being brought. Inasmuch as Malone mailed the complaint to Greenfield on November 4, 1992, Malone filed it before Greenfield received it. Obviously Malone did not think it important for Greenfield to see the complaint before it was filed even though Malone regards Greenfield as a distinguished retired corporate attorney.

On November 5, 1992, Malone on behalf of Allen Strunk filed a second class action against U.S. Healthcare and Abramson. The *Strunk* action repeated the allegations word for word from the Greenfield case

---

[1] This arrangement reverses the traditional regime which contemplates that the client start the steps towards formation of an attorney-client relationship by seeking legal representation.

[2] Robert K. Greenfield is not related to the Richard D. Greenfield of Greenfield & Chimicles.

except that the name of the plaintiff and the number of shares he owned were changed. Malone filed this action after Fred Taylor Isquith, an attorney in New York, contacted him and asked him to represent Strunk.

Malone and Strunk's New York lawyers were not the only attorneys interested in the U.S. Healthcare situation. On November 4, 1992, appellant Arnold Levin of the Philadelphia firm of Levin, Fishbein, Sedran & Berman, also read the *Wall Street Journal* article. Levin and his firm have what he characterized as "a long-standing professional relationship" with Greenfield & Chimicles, and Levin had a high regard for Greenfield & Chimicles' ethical standards and skill in handling federal securities law suits. On November 4, 1992, after Levin had read the article, Malone called him to discuss the merits of bringing a section 10(b) action against U.S. Healthcare and Abramson. Malone mentioned the *Wall Street Journal* article, and said he had done research into whether a section 10(b) action could be brought. Malone also told Levin that he had prepared such a complaint. Levin requested that Malone fax him a copy of the complaint, and Malone promptly did so. Levin then read the *Greenfield* complaint and reread the Wall Street Journal article and concluded, as he set forth in his affidavit, that "[b]ased upon my experience and understanding from the two documents," and in "reliance on the integrity of the pre-filing investigation of Greenfield & Chimicles," the section 10(b) action had merit.

There was even more interest in the U.S. Healthcare situation for on November 4, 1992, appellant Harris J. Sklar, a Philadelphia attorney in individual practice, also read the article. According to his affidavit, Sklar discussed the possibility of bringing an action against U.S. Healthcare with his client Scott Garr who was a U.S. Healthcare stockholder, and Garr authorized Sklar to bring the case on a class action basis. Sklar, however, saw the need to obtain co-counsel and consequently called Levin, as he had worked with him in the past. Levin then told Sklar of his dealings with Malone, and Levin and Sklar discussed the possibility of a suit. Sklar asked Levin to fax him a copy of the *Greenfield* complaint and Levin did so. Sklar then reviewed the complaint and, in his words as set forth in his affidavit, "[b]ased on my understanding of the securities laws and the facts as described in the *Wall Street Journal*," he determined that the complaint had merit. Sklar thus again spoke to Levin and indicated that Levin could file the class action on behalf of Scott Garr and Patricia Garr, his wife. On November 6, 1992, Levin and Sklar filed that complaint which replicated the *Greenfield* and *Strunk* complaints except that the names of the plaintiffs and the number of shares they owned were changed.

There was now an extraordinary development. On November 6, 1992, the same day that Levin and Sklar filed the *Garr* complaint, U.S. Healthcare and Abramson moved in the district court for the imposition of sanctions pursuant to Rule 11 in the *Greenfield, Strunk*, and *Garr* actions. This motion was a formidable document, as with attachments it exceeded 100 pages. At oral argument we asked U.S. Healthcare's attorney, Alan J. Davis, how it was possible that he filed this motion on the same day the Garr complaint was filed. He explained that he had anticipated that following the filing of the *Greenfield* complaint there would be additional complaints and accordingly his firm had a person waiting in the clerk's office to obtain copies of them when they were filed. . . .

In their brief, U.S. Healthcare and Abramson . . . asserted that Malone, Levin, and Sklar failed to conduct "even the most cursory factual and legal investigation" of the case and that if they had done so they would have determined that the complaints had no basis in fact or law. The brief indicated that the three complaints demonstrated the "all too familiar pattern of an instant class action lawsuit based on newspaper reports followed by a covey of cut and paste copycat complaints."

As if what we have described is not remarkable enough, there was yet an additional extraordinary development in the *Greenfield* case. On November 8, 1992, Robert K. Greenfield finally read the complaint, and at that time came to the realization that he had made a mistake in bringing the action because he knew of no basis for it and because his son had substantial business dealings with U.S. Healthcare. Thus, he directed Malone to withdraw the complaint. When U.S. Healthcare and Abramson learned of Robert K. Greenfield's position, they supplemented their motion for Rule 11 sanctions to assert that Malone had failed to make a reasonable inquiry into whether Greenfield fairly and adequately could protect the interests of the plaintiff class.

. . . [T]he court found that Malone could not be sanctioned under Rule 11 with respect to the accuracy of the information on which he had predicated the *Greenfield* complaint because his inquiry into the underlying facts "was reasonable under the circumstances." . . . However, the court found that Malone had violated Rule 11 with respect to the allegation in the complaint that Greenfield fairly and adequately could protect the interests of the class. . . . But it also found that it could not say that Malone had made an inadequate inquiry into Strunk's ability fairly and adequately to protect the class. Accordingly, as Malone's factual inquiry into the merits of the case against U.S. Healthcare and Abramson had been reasonable, the court did not impose sanctions in the *Strunk* action.

The district court next discussed whether sanctions should be imposed on Levin and Sklar. . . . The court rejected Levin's argument that he could rely on the integrity of the investigation by Greenfield & Chimicles, and it therefore ruled that Sklar could not rely on that investigation either. Ultimately the court held "that Levin and Sklar sought to act more quickly than fulfilling their duty would have allowed" and that "Levin['s] and Sklar's inquiry, or lack thereof, was unreasonable under the circumstances and a violation of Rule 11." . . .

The court provided for the following sanctions. It required that Malone, Levin, and Sklar pay all of U.S. Healthcare's and Abramson's reasonable costs and attorney's fees incurred to that time, that the *Greenfield* and *Garr* complaints be dismissed without prejudice, and that the matter be referred to the Disciplinary Board of the Supreme Court of Pennsylvania for an investigation into whether the conduct of Malone, Levin, and Sklar constituted a violation of the Pennsylvania Rules of Professional Conduct. . . . Of course, the court did not dismiss the *Strunk* action as there had been no Rule 11 violation in that case. Nevertheless, that case was dismissed without prejudice by stipulation on February 23, 1993. At oral argument, we were advised that none of the dismissed actions have been reinstated. . . . Malone paid his sanction and did not thereafter appeal, but Levin and Sklar obtained stays and have appealed.

II. DISCUSSION

[The court quotes Fed. R. Civ. P. 11.]

. . . It is clear that the signer has a "personal, nondelegable responsibility" to comply with the requirements of Rule 11 before signing the document.

A signer's obligation personally to comply with the requirements of Rule 11 clearly does not preclude the signer from any reliance on information from other persons. For example, no one could argue fairly that it would be unreasonable for an attorney to rely on witnesses to an accident before bringing a personal injury action. . . . [A] determination of whether there has been " 'a reasonable inquiry may depend on . . . whether [the signer] depended on forwarding counsel or another member of the bar.' " . . . [I]nasmuch as the standard under Rule 11 is "fact specific," the court must consider all the material circumstances in evaluating the signer's conduct. . . .

It is also important to observe that when the court examines the sufficiency of the inquiry into the facts and law, it must avoid drawing on the wisdom of hindsight and should test the signer's conduct by determining what was reasonable when the document was submitted. Thus, if under an objective standard, the signer made a reasonable inquiry both as to the fact and the law at the time a document was submitted, subsequent developments showing that the signer's position was incorrect will not subject the signer to Rule 11 sanctions for having submitted the document. On the other hand, a signer making an inadequate inquiry into the sufficiency of the facts and law underlying a document will not be saved from a Rule 11 sanction by the stroke of luck

that the document happened to be justified. As the court indicated in
Vista Mfg., Inc. v. Trac-4 Inc., 131 F.R.D. 134, 138 (N.D. Ind. 1990), "A
shot in the dark is a sanctionable event, even if it somehow hits the
mark." The court in *Vista* correctly stated the law, for if a lucky shot could
save the signer from sanctions, the purpose of Rule 11 "to deter baseless
filings" would be frustrated. Cooter & Gell v. Hartmarx Corp., 496 U.S.
384, 393 (1990).

There is also a temporal element in a determination of whether an
inquiry was reasonable. Thus, we have recognized that a factor in
ascertaining the reasonableness of the signer's inquiry is the amount of
time available to investigate the facts and law involved. Accordingly, if a
client comes into an attorney's office for an initial consultation concerning
a possible case one day before the statute of limitations will run, the
attorney might be justified in filing a complaint predicated on an inquiry
which would be inadequate if the attorney had more time for
investigation. On the other hand, an attorney with a great deal of time to
file a document might be expected to make a more comprehensive inquiry
than an attorney working under severe time constraints.

In reviewing a district court's Rule 11 determination, we use the
abuse of discretion standard. . . .

Application of the foregoing principles requires us to affirm. . . . As
Levin and Sklar explain in their brief: "Here, Levin acquired the
knowledge from one whom he knew to be competent securities law
counsel, Malone, coupled with the knowledge Levin obtained from the
Wall Street Journal, and his experienced understanding of the securities
laws. [sic] Levin passed this information on to Sklar so that he too could
make the same certification." Brief at 17.

We do not doubt that sometimes it is difficult to reconcile the tension
between the requirement that a signer personally discharge the Rule 11
obligations and the acknowledgment that a signer may rely on another
party's inquiry in some cases. But this appeal presents no difficulties.
Malone's declaration described the scope of his inquiry in great detail. He
obtained a representative sampling of stories regarding U.S. Healthcare
and a "disclo" report giving a great deal of financial information regarding
U.S. Healthcare, including five-year figures showing sales, net income,
earnings per share, and growth rate. He also considered financial ratios
and examined forms filed with the Securities and Exchange Commission
showing trading in U.S. Healthcare stock by insiders.[7] In fact, in the
district court's view, Malone's inquiry was inadequate only as to
Greenfield's status as the class representative.

---

[7] Malone obtained this information rapidly through the use of computer information
retrieval services.

On the other hand, Levin and Sklar relied only on the *Wall Street Journal* article, the *Greenfield* complaint, and Malone. They made no effort to examine the numerous materials Malone assembled, and they cannot justify their failure to have done so. They do not contend that Malone would not at their request have sent the materials to them. Alternatively, we see no reason why they could not have seen the materials by traveling the short distance from their offices in Philadelphia to Malone's office in Haverford, a Philadelphia suburb. We also point out that the documents on which Malone relied were all accessible to the public so that Levin and Sklar could have obtained them themselves.

Furthermore, there were no time constraints requiring Levin and Sklar to file the *Garr* complaint on an expedited basis. The *Wall Street Journal* article was published on November 4, 1992, and Levin and Sklar filed the *Garr* complaint two days later. Levin and Sklar do not contend that they were confronted with a statute of limitations problem compelling immediate action. . . .

We also point out that Levin and Sklar have advanced no other reason why the *Garr* complaint had to have been filed within two days of the publication of the article. They do not contend, for example, that the Garrs needed emergency relief, nor do they suggest that U.S. Healthcare or Abramson might have evaded process or concealed assets if the suit had not been filed so quickly. . . .

At bottom, there is no escape from the conclusion that Levin and Sklar abdicated their own responsibilities and relied excessively on Malone contrary to Rule 11. . . . We recognize that it could be argued that it would have been pointless for Levin and Sklar to make an inquiry into the merits of the case sufficient to satisfy Rule 11 as Malone already had done so. Yet Rule 11 requires that an attorney signing a pleading must make a reasonable inquiry personally. The advantage of duplicate personal inquiries is manifest: while one attorney might find a complaint well founded in fact and warranted by the law, another, even after examining the materials available to the first attorney, could come to a contrary conclusion. Overall, we conclude that the Rule 11 violation in this case is so clear that even on a plenary review, we would uphold the sanctions imposed on Levin and Sklar. Accordingly, under the deferential abuse of discretion standard, we certainly must affirm the district court's determination that sanctions were required.

    . . .

ROTH, CIRCUIT JUDGE, dissenting:

Although I share the majority's view that Levin and Sklar's conduct fell far short of the ideal, I do not share its belief that Rule 11 sanctions are appropriate in this situation. Instead, I believe that, when a court finds that an attorney has filed a meritorious complaint, the court should not go on to inquire whether the attorney conducted an adequate investigation prior to filing the complaint. I therefore respectfully dissent.

Except for changes in the named plaintiffs and the number of shares they owned, the complaint filed by Levin and Sklar on behalf of the Garrs was identical to the complaints filed by Malone on behalf of Greenfield and Strunk. As the majority notes, the district court did not dismiss the *Strunk* complaint, thereby implicitly finding that on its face it stated a valid claim. Presumably, had the district court not determined that Levin and Sklar violated Rule 11, it would not have dismissed the *Garr* complaint. Thus it is safe to assume that the district court believed that the *Garr* complaint on its face was meritorious.

In holding that the imposition of sanctions was appropriate in this case, the majority relies on the following statement in an opinion from a district court in another circuit: "A shot in the dark is a sanctionable event, even if it somehow hits the mark." Vista Mfg., Inc. v. Trac-4, Inc., 131 F.R.D. 134, 138 (N.D. Ind. 1990). Though this statement has the virtue of being colorful, . . .the majority's conclusion that the *Vista* rule is necessary to further the purposes of Rule 11 is the product of an incomplete analysis of both the policies animating Rule 11 and the impact of that rule on the effectiveness of Rule 11. . . .

. . . The Supreme Court has stated that

the central purpose of Rule 11 is to deter baseless filings in the District Court and thus, consistent with the Rule Enabling Act's grant of authority, streamline the administration and procedure of the federal courts. . . . Although the rule must be read in light of concerns that it will spawn satellite litigation and chill vigorous advocacy . . . any interpretation must give effect to the rule's central goal of deterrence.

Cooter & Gell v. Hartmarx Corp., 496 U.S. 384, 393 (1990). Similarly, the Advisory Committee indicated that the purpose of Rule 11 is "to discourage dilatory or abusive tactics and to help streamline the litigation process by lessening frivolous claims or defenses."

On the whole, the goals of deterring abuses of the system and streamlining litigation would be better served by the standard I advocate. Because the vast majority of "shots in the dark" will not hit their target, almost all of them will be subject to sanction. I find it difficult to believe that this slightly reduced probability of sanction will encourage lawyers to take blind shots. The deterrent function of Rule 11 to prevent baseless filings will not be undermined by not sanctioning when a complaint on its face does have merit. . . .

* * *

Filing time-barred claims. According to ABA Formal Ethics Opinion 94–387 (1994), an attorney does not violate professional conduct rules by filing a claim barred by the statute of limitations. The ABA committee reasoned that the running of the statute of limitations is an affirmative defense that must be raised or it is waived and that opposing counsel may fail to raise the defense.

Do you agree that an attorney can ethically file a claim that she knows to be barred by the statute of limitations? Consider Model Rules 3.1 and 3.3 as you think about your answer.

* * *

C. DISCOVERY

Please read ABA Model Rules of Professional Conduct, Rule 3.4.

Please read Federal Rules of Civil Procedure, Rules 26 & 37.

1. PRESERVATION AND SPOLIATION

Please read ABA Model Rules of Professional Conduct, Rule 3.4(a).

* * *

When a client reasonably anticipates litigation (whether as a plaintiff or a defendant), the client has an obligation to preserve information that may be relevant to the case. Culpable destruction of such material is referred to as spoliation and may be punished by a court. In your civil procedure class, you likely studied the legal authorities that govern the range of sanctions for spoliation. Possible penalties include additional discovery, monetary sanctions, adverse inference instructions, and even dismissal or a default judgment.

In the information age, it is more challenging than ever for attorneys to guide their clients in preserving evidence. Because electronic information is stored in so many formats and in so many locations, attorneys must be skilled at asking the right questions of the right people to identify, collect, and preserve a client's information. Further, it can be tempting for clients who do not understand the consequences and the likelihood of detection to delete embarrassing or harmful information. Attorneys must educate their clients of the hazards of spoliation.

When attorneys do not competently guide their clients in preserving evidence, both client and attorney may face sanctions and other adverse consequences in the underlying case. Sanctions for discovery violations are on the rise in the ediscovery era, and sanctions for spoliation top the list of most frequently imposed sanctions. *See* Dan H. Willoughby, Jr., et al, *Sanctions for E-Discovery Violations: By the Numbers*, 60 DUKE L. J. 789, 803 (2010). Additionally, an attorney responsible for spoliation may also be disciplined for violating the jurisdiction's version of Model Rule 3.4(a) which prohibits an attorney unlawfully obstructing access to evidence or unlawfully altering, destroying, or concealing evidence (or counseling or assisting in such misconduct).

The following case is one of the best-known preservation cases from the dawn of the modern ediscovery era. Though the case is over a decade old now, it is still instructive about the complexity of an attorney's obligations in guiding clients in preservation.

* * *

ZUBULAKE V. UBS WARBURG LLC ("ZUBULAKE V")
229 F.R.D. 422 (S.D.N.Y. 2004)

SCHEINDLIN, J.

Commenting on the importance of speaking clearly and listening closely, Phillip Roth memorably quipped, "The English language is a form of communication! . . . Words aren't only bombs and bullets—no, they're little gifts, containing meanings!" What is true in love is equally true at law: Lawyers and their clients need to communicate clearly and effectively with one another to ensure that litigation proceeds efficiently. When communication between counsel and client breaks down, conversation becomes "just crossfire," and there are usually casualties.

I. INTRODUCTION

This is the fifth written opinion in this case, a relatively routine employment discrimination dispute in which discovery has now lasted over two years. Laura Zubulake is once again moving to sanction UBS for its failure to produce relevant information and for its tardy production of such material. In order to decide whether sanctions are warranted, the following question must be answered: Did UBS fail to preserve and timely produce relevant information and, if so, did it act negligently, recklessly, or willfully?

This decision addresses counsel's obligation to ensure that relevant information is preserved by giving clear instructions to the client to preserve such information and, perhaps more importantly, a client's obligation to heed those instructions. Early on in this litigation, UBS's counsel—both in-house and outside—instructed UBS personnel to retain relevant electronic information. Notwithstanding these instructions, certain UBS employees deleted relevant e-mails. Other employees never produced relevant information to counsel. As a result, many discoverable e-mails were not produced to Zubulake until recently, even though they were responsive to a document request propounded on June 3, 2002. In addition, a number of e-mails responsive to that document request were deleted and have been lost altogether.

Counsel, in turn, failed to request retained information from one key employee and to give the litigation hold instructions to another. They also failed to adequately communicate with another employee about how she maintained her computer files. Counsel also failed to safeguard backup tapes that might have contained some of the deleted e-mails, and which would have mitigated the damage done by UBS's destruction of those e-mails.

The conduct of both counsel and client thus calls to mind the now-famous words of the prison captain in Cool Hand Luke: "What we've got here is a failure to communicate." Because of this failure by both UBS and its counsel, Zubulake has been prejudiced. As a result, sanctions are warranted.

II. FACTS

The allegations at the heart of this lawsuit and the history of the parties' discovery disputes have been well-documented in the Court's prior decisions. . . . In short, Zubulake is an equities trader specializing in Asian securities who is suing her former employer for gender discrimination, failure to promote, and retaliation under federal, state, and city law.

A. Background

Zubulake filed an initial charge of gender discrimination with the EEOC on August 16, 2001. Well before that, however—as early as April 2001—UBS employees were on notice of Zubulake's impending court action.[7] After she received a right-to-sue letter from the EEOC, Zubulake filed this lawsuit on February 15, 2002.

Fully aware of their common law duty to preserve relevant evidence, UBS's in-house attorneys gave oral instructions in August 2001—immediately after Zubulake filed her EEOC charge—instructing employees not to destroy or delete material potentially relevant to Zubulake's claims, and in fact to segregate such material into separate files for the lawyers' eventual review. This warning pertained to both electronic and hard-copy files, but did not specifically pertain to so-called "backup tapes," maintained by UBS's information technology personnel. In particular, UBS's in-house counsel, Robert L. Salzberg, "advised relevant UBS employees to preserve and turn over to counsel all files,

---

[7]   See Zubulake IV, 220 F.R.D. at 217 ("Thus, the relevant people at UBS anticipated litigation in April 2001. The duty to preserve attached at the time that litigation was reasonably anticipated.").

records or other written memoranda or documents concerning the allegations raised in the [EEOC] charge or any aspect of [Zubulake's] employment." Subsequently—but still in August 2001—UBS's outside counsel met with a number of the key players in the litigation and reiterated Mr. Salzberg's instructions, reminding them to preserve relevant documents, "including e-mails." Salzberg reduced these instructions to writing in e-mails dated February 22, 2002—immediately after Zubulake filed her complaint—and September 25, 2002. Finally, in August 2002, after Zubulake propounded a document request that specifically called for e-mails stored on backup tapes, UBS's outside counsel instructed UBS information technology personnel to stop recycling backup tapes. Every UBS employee mentioned in this Opinion (with the exception of Mike Davies) either personally spoke to UBS's outside counsel about the duty to preserve e-mails, or was a recipient of one of Salzberg's e-mails.

. . .

C. The Instant Dispute

The essence of the current dispute is that . . . Zubulake has now presented evidence that UBS personnel deleted relevant e-mails, some of which were subsequently recovered from backup tapes (or elsewhere) and thus produced to Zubulake long after her initial document requests, and some of which were lost altogether. Zubulake has also presented evidence that some UBS personnel did not produce responsive documents to counsel until recently, depriving Zubulake of the documents for almost two years.

. . .

Zubulake now moves for sanctions as a result of UBS's purported discovery failings. In particular, she asks . . . that an adverse inference instruction be given to the jury that eventually hears this case.

III. LEGAL STANDARD

Spoliation is "the destruction or significant alteration of evidence, or the failure to preserve property for another's use as evidence in pending or reasonably foreseeable litigation." "The determination of an appropriate sanction for spoliation, if any, is confined to the sound discretion of the trial judge, and is assessed on a case-by-case basis." The authority to sanction litigants for spoliation arises jointly under the Federal Rules of Civil Procedure and the court's inherent powers.

. . . A party seeking an adverse inference instruction (or other sanctions) based on the spoliation of evidence must establish the following three elements: (1) that the party having control over the evidence had an obligation to preserve it at the time it was destroyed; (2) that the records were destroyed with a "culpable state of mind" and (3)

495

that the destroyed evidence was "relevant" to the party's claim or defense such that a reasonable trier of fact could find that it would support that claim or defense.

In this circuit, a "culpable state of mind" for purposes of a spoliation inference includes ordinary negligence. When evidence is destroyed in bad faith (i.e., intentionally or willfully), that fact alone is sufficient to demonstrate relevance. By contrast, when the destruction is negligent, relevance must be proven by the party seeking the sanctions. In the context of a request for an adverse inference instruction, the concept of "relevance" encompasses not only the ordinary meaning of the term, but also that the destroyed evidence would have been favorable to the movant.... This is equally true in cases of gross negligence or recklessness; only in the case of willful spoliation does the degree of culpability give rise to a presumption of the relevance of the documents destroyed.

IV. DISCUSSION

In *Zubulake IV*, I held that UBS had a duty to preserve its employees' active files as early as April 2001, and certainly by August 2001, when Zubulake filed her EEOC charge. Zubulake has thus satisfied the first element of the adverse inference test. As noted, the central question implicated by this motion is whether UBS and its counsel took all necessary steps to guarantee that relevant data was both preserved and produced. If the answer is "no," then the next question is whether UBS acted willfully .... If UBS acted wilfully, this satisfies the mental culpability prong of the adverse inference test and also demonstrates that the deleted material was relevant. If UBS acted negligently or even recklessly, then Zubulake must show that the missing or late-produced information was relevant.

A. Counsel's Duty to Monitor Compliance

In *Zubulake IV*, I summarized a litigant's preservation obligations:

Once a party reasonably anticipates litigation, it must suspend its routine document retention/destruction policy and put in place a "litigation hold" to ensure the preservation of relevant documents. As a general rule, that litigation hold does not apply to inaccessible backup tapes (e.g., those typically maintained solely for the purpose of disaster recovery), which may continue to be recycled on the schedule set forth in the company's policy. On the other hand, if backup tapes are accessible (i.e., actively used for information retrieval), then such tapes would likely be subject to the litigation hold.

A party's discovery obligations do not end with the implementation of a "litigation hold"—to the contrary, that's only the beginning. Counsel must oversee compliance with the litigation hold, monitoring the party's efforts to retain and produce the relevant documents. Proper communication between a party and her lawyer will ensure (1) that all relevant information (or at least all sources of relevant information) is discovered, (2) that relevant information is retained on a continuing basis, and (3) that relevant non-privileged material is produced to the opposing party.

1. Counsel's Duty to Locate Relevant Information

Once a "litigation hold" is in place, a party and her counsel must make certain that all sources of potentially relevant information are identified and placed "on hold," to the extent required in *Zubulake IV*. To do this, counsel must become fully familiar with her client's document retention policies, as well as the client's data retention architecture. This will invariably involve speaking with information technology personnel, who can explain system-wide backup procedures and the actual (as opposed to theoretical) implementation of the firm's recycling policy. It will also involve communicating with the "key players" in the litigation, in order to understand how they stored information. In this case, for example, some UBS employees created separate computer files pertaining to Zubulake, while others printed out relevant e-mails and retained them in hard copy only. Unless counsel interviews each employee, it is impossible to determine whether all potential sources of information have been inspected. A brief conversation with counsel, for example, might have revealed that [UBS employee] Tong maintained "archive" copies of e-mails concerning Zubulake, and that "archive" meant a separate on-line computer file, not a backup tape. Had that conversation taken place, Zubulake might have had relevant e-mails from that file two years ago.

To the extent that it may not be feasible for counsel to speak with every key player, given the size of a company or the scope of the lawsuit, counsel must be more creative. It may be possible to run a system-wide keyword search; counsel could then preserve a copy of each "hit." Although this sounds burdensome, it need not be. Counsel does not have to review these documents, only see that they are retained. For example, counsel could create a broad list of search terms, run a search for a limited time frame, and then segregate responsive documents. When the opposing party propounds its document requests, the parties could negotiate a list of search terms to be used in identifying responsive documents, and counsel would only be obliged to review documents that came up as "hits" on the second, more restrictive search. The initial broad cut merely guarantees that relevant documents are not lost.

In short, it is not sufficient to notify all employees of a litigation hold and expect that the party will then retain and produce all relevant information. Counsel must take affirmative steps to monitor compliance so that all sources of discoverable information are identified and searched. This is not to say that counsel will necessarily succeed in locating all such sources, or that the later discovery of new sources is evidence of a lack of effort. But counsel and client must take some reasonable steps to see that sources of relevant information are located.

2. Counsel's Continuing Duty to Ensure Preservation

Once a party and her counsel have identified all of the sources of potentially relevant information, they are under a duty to retain that information . . . and to produce information responsive to the opposing party's requests. Rule 26 creates a "duty to supplement" those responses. Although the Rule 26 duty to supplement is nominally the party's, it really falls on counsel. As the Advisory Committee explains,

Although the party signs the answers, it is his lawyer who understands their significance and bears the responsibility to bring answers up to date. In a complex case all sorts of information reaches the party, who little understands its bearing on answers previously given to interrogatories. In practice, therefore, the lawyer under a continuing burden must periodically recheck all interrogatories and canvass all new information.

To ameliorate this burden, the Rules impose a continuing duty to supplement responses to discovery requests only when "a party[,] or more frequently his lawyer, obtains actual knowledge that a prior response is incorrect. This exception does not impose a duty to check the accuracy of prior responses, but it prevents knowing concealment by a party or attorney."

The continuing duty to supplement disclosures strongly suggests that parties also have a duty to make sure that discoverable information is not lost. Indeed, the notion of a "duty to preserve" connotes an ongoing obligation. Obviously, if information is lost or destroyed, it has not been preserved.

The tricky question is what that continuing duty entails. What must a lawyer do to make certain that relevant information—especially electronic information—is being retained? Is it sufficient if she periodically re-sends her initial "litigation hold" instructions? What if she communicates with the party's information technology personnel? Must she make occasional on-site inspections?

Above all, the requirement must be reasonable. A lawyer cannot be obliged to monitor her client like a parent watching a child. At some point, the client must bear responsibility for a failure to preserve. At the same time, counsel is more conscious of the contours of the preservation obligation; a party cannot reasonably be trusted to receive the "litigation hold" instruction once and to fully comply with it without the active supervision of counsel.

There are thus a number of steps that counsel should take to ensure compliance with the preservation obligation. While these precautions may not be enough (or may be too much) in some cases, they are designed to promote the continued preservation of potentially relevant information in the typical case.

First, counsel must issue a "litigation hold" at the outset of litigation or whenever litigation is reasonably anticipated. The litigation hold should be periodically re-issued so that new employees are aware of it, and so that it is fresh in the minds of all employees.

Second, counsel should communicate directly with the "key players" in the litigation, i.e., the people identified in a party's initial disclosure and any subsequent supplementation thereto. Because these "key players" are the "employees likely to have relevant information," it is particularly important that the preservation duty be communicated clearly to them. As with the litigation hold, the key players should be periodically reminded that the preservation duty is still in place.

Finally, counsel should instruct all employees to produce electronic copies of their relevant active files. Counsel must also make sure that all backup media which the party is required to retain is identified and stored in a safe place. In cases involving a small number of relevant backup tapes, counsel might be advised to take physical possession of backup tapes. In other cases, it might make sense for relevant backup tapes to be segregated and placed in storage. Regardless of what particular arrangement counsel chooses to employ, the point is to separate relevant backup tapes from others. One of the primary reasons that electronic data is lost is ineffective communication with information technology personnel. By taking possession of, or otherwise safeguarding, all potentially relevant backup tapes, counsel eliminates the possibility that such tapes will be inadvertently recycled. . . .

. . .

a. UBS's Discovery Failings

UBS's counsel—both in-house and outside—repeatedly advised UBS of its discovery obligations. In fact, counsel came very close to taking the precautions laid out above. First, outside counsel issued a litigation hold in August 2001. The hold order was circulated to many of the key players in this litigation, and reiterated in e-mails in February 2002, when suit was filed, and again in September 2002. Outside counsel made clear that the hold order applied to backup tapes in August 2002, as soon as backup tapes became an issue in this case. Second, outside counsel communicated directly with many of the key players in August 2001 and attempted to impress upon them their preservation obligations. Third, and finally, counsel instructed UBS employees to produce copies of their active computer files. . . .

b. Counsel's Failings

On the other hand, UBS's counsel are not entirely blameless. "While, of course, it is true that counsel need not supervise every step of the document production process and may rely on their clients in some respects," counsel is responsible for coordinating her client's discovery efforts. In this case, counsel failed to properly oversee UBS in a number of important ways, both in terms of its duty to locate relevant information and its duty to preserve and timely produce that information.

With respect to locating relevant information, counsel failed to adequately communicate with Tong about how she stored data. . . .

With respect to making sure that relevant data was retained, counsel failed in a number of important respects. First, neither in-house nor outside counsel communicated the litigation hold instructions to Mike Davies, a senior human resources employee who was intimately involved in Zubulake's termination. Second, even though the litigation hold instructions were communicated to [UBS employee] Kim, no one ever asked her to produce her files. And third, counsel failed to protect relevant backup tapes; had they done so, Zubulake might have been able to recover some of the e-mails that UBS employees deleted.

. . .

c. Summary

Counsel failed to communicate the litigation hold order to all key players. They also failed to ascertain each of the key players' document management habits. By the same token, UBS employees—for unknown reasons—ignored many of the instructions that counsel gave. This case represents a failure of communication, and that failure falls on counsel and client alike.

. . . .

I therefore conclude that UBS acted wilfully in destroying potentially relevant information. . . . Because UBS's spoliation was willful, the lost information is presumed to be relevant.

B. Remedy

. . . I recognize that a major consideration in choosing an appropriate sanction—along with punishing UBS and deterring future misconduct—is to restore Zubulake to the position that she would have been in had UBS faithfully discharged its discovery obligations. That being so, I find that the following sanctions are warranted.

First, the jury empaneled to hear this case will be given an adverse inference instruction with respect to e-mails deleted after August 2001. . . .

Second, . . . UBS is ordered to pay the costs of any depositions or re-depositions required by the late production.

Third, UBS is ordered to pay the costs of this motion.

Finally, I note that UBS's belated production has resulted in a self-executing sanction. Not only was Zubulake unable to question UBS's witnesses using the newly produced e-mails, but UBS was unable to prepare those witnesses with the aid of those e-mails. Some of UBS's witnesses, not having seen these e-mails, have already given deposition testimony that seems to contradict the newly discovered evidence. . . .

. . .

VI. POSTSCRIPT

The subject of the discovery of electronically stored information is rapidly evolving. When this case began more than two years ago, there was little guidance from the judiciary, bar associations or the academy as to the governing standards. Much has changed in that time. There have been a flood of recent opinions—including a number from appellate courts—and there are now several treatises on the subject. In addition, professional groups such as the American Bar Association and the Sedona Conference have provided very useful guidance on thorny issues relating to the discovery of electronically stored information. Many courts have adopted, or are considering adopting, local rules addressing the subject. Most recently, the Standing Committee on Rules and Procedures has approved for publication and public comment a proposal for revisions to the Federal Rules of Civil Procedure designed to address many of the issues raised by the discovery of electronically stored information.

Now that the key issues have been addressed and national standards are developing, parties and their counsel are fully on notice of their responsibility to preserve and produce electronically stored information. The tedious and difficult fact finding encompassed in this opinion and others like it is a great burden on a court's limited resources. The time and effort spent by counsel to litigate these issues has also been time-consuming and distracting. This Court, for one, is optimistic that with the guidance now provided it will not be necessary to spend this amount of time again. It is hoped that counsel will heed the guidance provided by these resources and will work to ensure that preservation, production and spoliation issues are limited, if not eliminated.

* * *

Problem 20.4. When Linus Coverdale asked you to represent Lilith in the Necco case, you knew that electronic information would play a major role in the litigation. Using *Zubulake V* as a guide, what steps do you plan to take to ensure that information relevant to the case is preserved? Who would you like to meet with at Lilith in order to identify, collect, and preserve discoverable information?

* * *

2. MANIPULATING EVIDENCE

Please read ABA Model Rules of Professional Conduct, Rule 3.4(a)–(c) & (f) and Comments [1]–[4].

* * *

The scope of Rule 3.4(a). Note that Model Rule 3.4(a) applies not just to altering or obstructing access to tangible documents and electronic evidence, but also to procuring the absence of a witness. In re Geisler, 614 N.E.2d 939 (Ind. 1993) (involving lawyer who helped witness avoid service). This includes making threats against witnesses. State ex rel. Bar Ass'n v. Cox, 48 P.3d 780 (Okla. 2002) (involving lawyer who threatened to "dig up dirt" about potential witness if he testified).

Retention of physical evidence to conduct an examination. Comment [2] notes that applicable law may allow a lawyer to take temporary possession of physical evidence of client crimes for the purpose of conducting a limited examination. Any tests conducted, however, must not alter or destroy material characteristics of the evidence. Section 119 of the Restatement (Third) of the Law Governing Lawyers repeats this idea, noting that as long as the examination is "for the lawful purpose of assisting in the trial of criminal cases, . . . criminal laws that generally prohibit possession of contraband or other evidence of crimes are inapplicable to the lawyer." Once the examination is complete, however, criminal law may require that a defense lawyer turn the evidence over to law enforcement.

* * *

3. FRIVOLOUS DISCOVERY REQUESTS AND OBJECTIONS AND DILATORY TACTICS

Please read ABA Model Rules of Professional Conduct, Rule 3.4(c) & (d).

* * *

Problem 20.5. After several months of litigation, you work with Lilith employees to prepare "Lilith's Objections and Answers to Necco's Interrogatories." You provide a draft of the document to president Linus Coverdale who is going to sign on behalf of the Lilith. You ask him to review the answers and let you know if he has any questions or suggested changes. You receive the following email from Linus:

Thanks for sending me the draft of "Lilith's Objections and Answers to Necco's Interrogatories." I see that you objected to producing information protected by the attorney-client privilege and there were a few spots where you objected that a word or phrase was ambiguous. But it looks like for the most part, you answered the questions.

I have to tell you, I wish we could make this a little more difficult for Necco. I have worked with other lawyers in the past who could come up with a full page of objections for each and every interrogatory. Is there any reason why we don't want to do that in this case? Let me know what you think about trying that approach.

Thanks,

Linus

You do not think there are legitimate objections that you have not already asserted. You know that many attorneys would throw in a handful of objections just to be difficult, but you think that tends to hurt your relationship with opposing counsel and the court. It has been your experience that if you only object when there is a solid basis for doing so, opposing counsel is more likely to accept your objection as legitimate. And if opposing counsel files a motion to compel, the court is more likely to side with you when you have not objected to every interrogatory (or request for production) on questionable grounds. Further, you believe that you have more success in discovery when you do not make things unnecessarily difficult for opposing counsel. Opposing attorneys are more likely to provide information to you without a fight when you are doing the same in return. In the end, you think your approach to discovery is much more cost effective, too.

In light of your views on these issues, draft a brief response to Linus's email. Explain why it is in the company's interest (and consistent with your legal and professional conduct obligations) for you to provide answers to interrogatories without asserting additional objections.

* * *

4. DISCLOSURE OF A CLIENT'S PERJURED TESTIMONY DURING A DEPOSITION

Please read ABA Model Rules of Professional Conduct, Rule 3.3(a)(3) and Comment [1].

* * *

State Bar of Michigan Standing Committee on Professional and Judicial Ethics Opinion Number RI-13

March 21, 1989

SYLLABUS

A lawyer who knows that a client has given false testimony in a deposition has a duty to rectify the consequences of the client's act.

A lawyer may not reveal client confidences or secrets based on a mere suspicion, rather than knowledge, of a client's false testimony.

Termination of the attorney-client relationship does not discharge the duty of a lawyer to rectify the consequences of a client's fraudulent act.

OPINION

A lawyer was discharged by the lawyer's clients, a financial institution and its Chief Executive Officer [CEO], the day following the CEO's deposition testimony which was not completed and had been adjourned to a later date. The financial institution and the CEO were defendants, and the lawyer is concerned that the CEO made two statements that could "possibly be considered perjured testimony." The lawyer is not absolutely certain the CEO testified falsely, although the lawyer has "more than a mere suspicion" that the CEO has done so.

The lawyer asks whether there is a duty to correct the deposition of the former client or to advise the tribunal of the former client's tactics.

If a client has presented false testimony at a deposition, the lawyer's duty is clear. Under MRPC 3.3(a)(4), the lawyer shall take reasonable remedial measures to correct the false testimony or rectify the consequence of the client's act. In this case, the lawyer is not certain the deposition testimony was false, and thus there is no duty to correct or rectify.

May a client relieve a lawyer of any duty to take "reasonable remedial measures" to ensure the client's truthful testimony by discharging the lawyer? Under MRPC 3.3(b), "the duties continue to the conclusion of the proceeding, and apply even if compliance requires disclosure of information otherwise protected by Rule 1.6." Discharge or withdrawal of the lawyer does not affect this duty.

Has the client, in effect, coerced the lawyer into being a party to fraud on the court if the testimony turns out to be false? MRPC 3.3 uses the language "knows to be false." The lawyer's "more than a mere suspicion" is not enough. See Hazard, The Law of Lawyering, Prentice-Hall, 1988 Supplement, pp. 354; CI-392. MRPC 3.3(c) gives a lawyer discretion in deciding whether to present evidence whose truthfulness is in serious doubt. But that remedy is not available to a lawyer who has been discharged.

Does a lawyer have an obligation to proceed further to make inquiry in some manner to determine whether the deposition was perjured? MRPC 1.6(c)(3) states:

(c) A lawyer may reveal:

. . . .

"(3) confidences and secrets to the extent reasonably necessary to rectify the consequences of a client's illegal or fraudulent act in the furtherance of which the lawyer's services have been used."

This Rule also requires knowledge of the illegal or fraudulent act. Similarly, MRPC 1.13 requires "knowledge."

In conclusion, since the deposition testimony is not known to be perjured, the lawyer may not reveal confidences and secrets to the tribunal or to the opposing party. There is no duty to investigate the truth of the testimony once the lawyer is discharged. The termination of the relationship does not affect a lawyer's duty to rectify the client's act if the lawyer had knowledge of perjury.

* * *

5. PROTECTING PRIVILEGE AND WORK PRODUCT AND ADDRESSING INADVERTENT DISCLOSURE

Please read ABA Model Rules of Professional Conduct, Rule 1.1; Rule 1.6(c); and Rule 4.4(b).

* * *

Recall that Chapter 15 discussed an attorney's obligation to protect privileged and work product protected information from disclosure in discovery. The chapter also considered the obligations of a recipient of an inadvertent disclosure. Review that material to complete the following problem.

* * *

Problem 20.6. You are reviewing "Necco's Objections and Responses to Lilith's First Requests for Production of Documents." As you begin to look at some of the documents, you come across a letter from Necco's litigation counsel addressed to Necco's general counsel. In the letter, Necco's attorney discusses how much the company should consider accepting to settle the Lilith litigation. With citation to authority, discuss the steps you will take next, including whether you will forward the letter to Lilith's President Linus Coverdale.

* * *

Profile of attorney professionalism. When Judge Shira Scheindlin wrote the fifth *Zubulake* opinion in 2004 (excerpted earlier in this chapter), the concept of electronic discovery was brand new; she had little precedent to guide her. Judge Scheindlin had become interested in the intersection of technology and litigation procedure in the late 1990s, while serving as a member of the Advisory Committee on Civil Rules. By the time she authored the opinion in *Zubulake*, Judge Scheindlin had already given substantial thought to how discovery procedures could work with emerging technologies and the storage of electronic data. When the *Zubulake* decision was released, Judge Scheindlin's opinion in the case instantly became the leading guide for lawyers and companies trying to figure out how to deal with electronically stored information. Some of Judge Scheindlin's analysis from *Zubulake* was later incorporated into the Federal Rules of Civil Procedure.

Judge Scheindlin has remained interested in electronic discovery, and, along with co-authors Daniel Capra and The Sedona Conference, has published a law school casebook: ELECTRONIC DISCOVERY AND DIGITAL EVIDENCE: CASES AND MATERIALS (West, 2d ed. 2012).

In a podcast interview with an e-discovery website, Judge Scheindlin explained that e-discovery is no longer merely a subset of all discovery; instead, with the proliferation of electronically stored documents and data, all discovery has become e-discovery. In the interview, Judge Scheindlin discussed the expense of discovery and the difficulties in litigating when one party has substantially greater financial resources than the other. She emphasized how the discovery rules interact with the lawyer's duties to the court and to the adversary, explaining that a party facing a burdensome discovery request has an obligation to handle it within the framework established by the rules of civil procedure:

> [T]hat's the key point. You can't use self-help. You either go for protection by coming to court or you comply. [You can't] just ignore it, put your head in the sand . . . and then say, "Well the reason I didn't do better is it was too expensive."

Podcast: Electronic Discovery and Law School Curriculums, ESI Bytes, March 18, 2009 *available at* http://esibytes.com/electronic-discovery-and-law-school-curriculums/.

CHAPTER 21

TRIAL AND APPELLATE ADVOCACY

■ ■ ■

Chapter hypothetical. You serve as a law clerk to U.S. District Court Judge Martha Moore. Judge Moore has a busy docket that includes the matters discussed in the problems in this chapter.

* * *

A. USING IRRELEVANT OR INADMISSIBLE INFORMATION

Please read ABA Model Rules of Professional Conduct, Rules 3.4(e) & 8.4(d).

A clear example of conduct that violates Model Rule 3.4(e) is alluding in trial to the fact that a party is covered by insurance, evidence which is inadmissible under the Federal Rules of Evidence. Falkowski v. Johnson, 148 F.R.D. 132 (D. Del. 1993). In most instances, this type of misconduct is dealt with through objections by opposing parties, contempt citations, and new trials. However, professional discipline remains a possibility.

* * *

Problem 21.1. Judge Moore recently presided over the criminal trial of Carrie Anderson for the alleged murder of her child. During opening statement, Anderson's attorney suggested to the jury that the child was not murdered but accidentally drowned in the family swimming pool. At trial, Anderson did not testify and no evidence was presented that the child drowned. Analyze whether Anderson's attorney violated Rule 3.4(e) through her opening statement.

* * *

B. INVOLVING YOURSELF IN A CASE OTHER THAN IN YOUR CAPACITY AS AN ADVOCATE OF YOUR CLIENT'S CAUSE

Please read ABA Model Rules of Professional Conduct, Rules 3.4(e) & 3.7.

Lawyers are also prohibited from improperly involving themselves in cases. So, for example, a lawyer may not interject her personal beliefs into arguments or vouch for the honesty of a witness. Perhaps the most common example of a lawyer blurring the line between advocate and witness is the case in which a lawyer acts as a witness at trial. A court's decision on the issue of whether a lawyer should be disqualified from serving as counsel at trial based on the fact that the lawyer is likely to be a necessary witness involves a balancing of competing interests. On one hand, there is the concern that disqualifying a lawyer may mean depriving a client of the client's choice of counsel and permitting the opposing side to use the disqualification rules as a tactical weapon. On the other hand, there are the concerns that "the attorney will not be a fully objective witness and . . . that the trier of fact will confuse the roles of advocate and witness and erroneously grant special weight to an attorney's arguments." McElroy v. Gaffney, 529 A.2d 889 (N.H. 1987).

* * *

Problem 21.2. For over three years, Judge Moore has presided over a multi-million dollar case involving multiple plaintiffs and defendants. One defendant in the case is Amalgamated Aluminum Associates (AAA). While AAA denies it, the other parties claim that a settlement agreement was reached and that AAA has now reneged on the deal. These parties have filed a motion to enforce the purported settlement agreement. Judge Moore has scheduled an evidentiary hearing on the motion.

Throughout the years of litigation, AAA has been represented by Rhett and Murray, two lawyers from the firm of Palsgraf & Pennoyer. The lawyers for the other parties are now seeking to disqualify Rhett, Murray, and the firm of Palsgraf & Pennoyer from (a) appearing as counsel at the evidentiary hearing on the motion, and (b) appearing as counsel in any future litigation involving the case if the motion is denied.

Judge Moore tells you that she will consider Model Rule 3.7 in determining her ruling on the disqualification motion. Analyze how she should rule on the issue.

* * *

C. COMMUNICATING WITH JURORS, THE JUDGE, AND COURT OFFICERS

Please read ABA Model Rules of Professional Conduct, Rule 3.5(a)–(c) and Comments [1]–[3].

The most obvious example of improper communication during the course of a proceeding is lawyer's communication with a judge outside the presence of opposing counsel. This is true regardless of whether the judge or the lawyer initiates the communication. Lawyers are also prohibited from communicating with jurors during a proceeding—however innocent the communication might seem. *See* Fla. Bar v. Peterson, 418 So. 2d 246 (Fla. 1982) (disciplining lawyer who allowed himself to be seated with jurors at lunch during a recess).

* * *

Problem 21.3. You are returning from a lunch break during the third week of a jury trial in Judge Moore's courtroom. You are following a group of people back into the courthouse. You see that one of the lawyers from the trial, Maureen Fischer, is holding the door for two of the jurors. As one of the jurors passes Maureen, the juror gives her a "thumbs up" sign. Maureen smiles and says, "Thanks." Should you tell Judge Moore about the exchange between attorney and juror? Do you think Maureen Fischer violated Rule 3.5?

* * *

D. DISRUPTIVE AND DISRESPECTFUL BEHAVIOR

Please read ABA Model Rules of Professional Conduct, Rule 3.5(d) and Comment [4].

Disruptive behavior in court is often addressed through a court's power to hold lawyers in contempt. But sometimes disruptive behavior in the courtroom has also resulted in professional discipline. Examples range from the dramatic to the childish. *See, e.g.,* Fla. Bar v. Martocci, 791 So. 2d 1074 (Fla. 2001) (imposing discipline on lawyer who, *inter alia,* made faces and stuck out his tongue during proceeding). The rule has also been applied to conduct occurring outside the courtroom that was designed to disrupt the tribunal. *See* People v. Maynard, 238 P.3d 672 (Colo. 2009) (disciplining lawyer who filed multiple motions seeking the judge's recusal as a tactic to delay the proceeding).

* * *

Problem 21.4. Judge Moore is presiding over a wrongful death jury trial. The decedent, a twenty-eight-year-old mother of two, lost her life when a semi-truck driver fell asleep at the wheel and slammed into her car. During closing argument, the plaintiff's lawyer, Mitch Murphy, broke down and cried. At one point, he stopped speaking so that he could wipe his eyes with a handkerchief as he braced himself by holding onto the rail in front of the jury box. Judge Moore called both attorneys to the bench and asked Murphy if he needed a short break to collect himself. He said he was fine, but when he continued the closing he started crying again.

Judge Moore believes the crying was an attempt by Murphy to disrupt the proceeding, to endear himself to the jury, and to influence the verdict. Advise Judge Moore about whether Murphy's crying amounts to professional misconduct under Model Rule 3.5(d) or any other professional conduct rule. Beyond referring Murphy to the bar for discipline, are there other steps Judge Moore can take to address what she perceives as misconduct in her courtroom?

* * *

E. DECEPTION AND TRICKERY

UNITED STATES V. THOREEN
653 F.2d 1332 (9th Cir. 1981)

EUGENE A. WRIGHT, CIRCUIT JUDGE:

I.   INTRODUCTION

The issue before us is whether an attorney may be found in criminal contempt for pursuing a course of aggressive advocacy while representing his client in a criminal proceeding such that, without the court's permission or knowledge, he substitutes someone for his client at counsel table with the intent to cause a misidentification, resulting in the misleading of the court, counsel, and witnesses; a delay while the government reopened its case to identify the defendant; and violation of a court order and custom.

We affirm the district court's finding of criminal contempt. . . .

II. FACTS

. . . .

In February 1980, [Attorney Thoreen] represented Sibbett, a commercial fisher, during Sibbett's non-jury trial before Judge Tanner for criminal contempt for three violations of a preliminary injunction against salmon fishing. In preparing for trial, Thoreen hoped that the government agent who had cited Sibbett could not identify him. He decided to test the witness's identification.

He placed next to him at counsel table Clark Mason, who resembled Sibbett and had Mason dressed in outdoor clothing denims, heavy shoes, a plaid shirt, and a jacket-vest. Sibbett wore a business suit, large round glasses, and sat behind the rail in a row normally reserved for the press. Thoreen neither asked the court's permission for, nor notified it or government counsel of, the substitution. On Thoreen's motion at the start of the trial, the court ordered all witnesses excluded from the courtroom. Mason remained at counsel table.

Throughout the trial, Thoreen made and allowed to go uncorrected numerous misrepresentations. He gestured to Mason as though he was his client and gave Mason a yellow legal pad on which to take notes. The two conferred. Thoreen did not correct the court when it expressly referred to Mason as the defendant and caused the record to show identification of Mason as Sibbett.

Because of the conduct, two government witnesses misidentified Mason as Sibbett. Following the government's case, Thoreen called Mason as a witness and disclosed the substitution. The court then called a recess. When the trial resumed, the government reopened and recalled the government agent who had cited Sibbett for two of the violations. He identified Sibbett, who was convicted of all three violations.

. . . .

Judge Tanner found Thoreen in criminal contempt for the substitution because it was imposed on the court and counsel without permission or prior knowledge; the claimed identification issue did not exist; it disrupted the trial; it deceived the court and frustrated its responsibility to administer justice; and it violated a court custom. He found Mason's presence in the courtroom after giving the order excluding witnesses another ground for contempt because Thoreen planned that Mason would testify when the misidentification occurred. Judge Tanner held also that Thoreen's conduct conflicted with DR 1–102(A)(4)[4], DR 7–102(A)(6)[5], and DR 7–106(C)(5)[6] of the Washington Code of Professional Responsibility.

Thoreen's principal defense is that his conduct was a good faith tactic in aid of cross-examination and falls within the protected realm of zealous advocacy. He argues that as defense counsel he has no obligation to ascertain or present the truth and may seek to confuse witnesses with misleading questions, gestures, or appearances. . . .

. . . .

---

[4] "(A) A lawyer shall not: (4) Engage in conduct involving dishonesty, fraud, deceit, or misrepresentation."

[5] "(A) In his representation of a client, a lawyer shall not: (6) Participate in the creation or preservation of evidence when he knows or it is obvious that the evidence is false."

[6] "(C) In appearing in his professional capacity before a tribunal, a lawyer shall not: (5) Fail to comply with known local customs of courtesy or practice of the bar or a particular tribunal without giving to opposing counsel timely notice of his intent not to comply."

1. Zealous Advocacy

. . . .

Vigorous advocacy by defense counsel may properly entail impeaching or confusing a witness, even if counsel thinks the witness is truthful, and refraining from presenting evidence even if he knows the truth. . . . When we review this conduct and find that the line between vigorous advocacy and actual obstruction is close, our doubts should be resolved in favor of the former.

The latitude allowed an attorney is not unlimited. He must represent his client within the bounds of the law. As an officer of the court, he must "preserve and promote the efficient operation of our system of justice."

Thoreen's view of appropriate cross-examination, which encompasses his substitution, crossed over the line from zealous advocacy to actual obstruction . . . . Moreover, this conduct harms rather than enhances an attorney's effectiveness as an advocate. It is fundamental that in relations with the court, defense counsel must be scrupulously candid and truthful in representations of any matter before the court. This is not only a basic ethical requirement, but it is essential if the lawyer is to be effective in the role of advocate, for if the lawyer's reputation for veracity is suspect, he or she will lack the confidence of the court when it is needed most to serve the client.

2. Criminal Contempt

18 U.S.C. § 401 (1976) provides

A court of the United States shall have power to punish by fine or imprisonment, at its discretion, such contempt of its authority, and none other as

(1) Misbehavior of any person in its presence or so near thereto as to obstruct the administration of justice; . . .

(3) Disobedience or resistance to its lawful writ, process, order, rule, decree, or command.

. . . .

Because Thoreen's conduct was in the court's presence, our inquiry turns to whether it constituted contumacious misbehavior that obstructed the administration of justice.

. . . .

Contumacious misbehavior by an attorney includes disobeying a court's rulings or instructions, and deceiving the court. Examples of contumacious deceptive behavior are misrepresenting oneself as a practicing attorney, Bowles v. United States, 50 F.2d 848, 851 (4th Cir.), *cert. denied*, 284 U.S. 648 (1931); an attorney's swearing to and filing of admittedly false affidavits and supplemental complaint, plus the pursuit of meritless litigation, Letts v. Icarian Development Co., S.A., No. 74 C 2252 (N.D. Ill., Sept. 15, 1980); and an attorney's presentation of false evidence, United States v. Ford, 9 F.2d 990, 991 (D. Mont. 1925).

Making misrepresentations to the court is also inappropriate and unprofessional behavior under ethical standards that guide attorneys' conduct. These guidelines, in effect in Washington and elsewhere, decree explicitly that an attorney's participation in the presentation or preservation of false evidence is unprofessional and subjects him to discipline.

Substituting a person for the defendant in a criminal case without a court's knowledge has been noted as an example of unethical behavior by the ABA Committee on Professional Ethics. *See* Informal Opinion No. 914, 2/24/66 (decided under the former ABA Code of Professional Responsibility).

Ethical standards establish the outermost limits of appropriate and sanctioned attorney conduct. While we acknowledge that a court's power to discipline or disbar an attorney " 'proceeds upon very different grounds' from those which support a court's power to punish for contempt," Cammer v. United States, 350 U.S. 399, 408 n.7 (1956), we consider and apply ethical benchmarks when determining whether an attorney's conduct is inappropriate to his role and thus constitutes contumacious misbehavior.

Counsel's conduct must cause an actual obstruction of justice before criminal contempt lies.

. . . .

Making misrepresentations to the fact finder is inherently obstructive because it frustrates the rational search for truth. It may also delay the proceedings. . . .

The record supports Judge Tanner's conclusion that Thoreen's substitution was misbehavior that obstructed justice. . . .

. . . .

To be held in criminal contempt, the contemnor must have the requisite intent. "[A]n attorney possesses the requisite intent only if he knows or reasonably should be aware in view of all the circumstances, especially the heat of the controversy, that he is exceeding the outermost limits of his proper role and hindering rather than facilitating the search for truth.". . . .

Thoreen admits he planned and intended the substitution, but defends by asserting that (1) it was a good faith effort to prove misidentification and attack the credibility of the government witnesses;

(2) he never intended to misrepresent any facts to the court or to obstruct justice; and (3) he believed the court knew Sibbett's identity from the pretrial hearing.

The record shows that Sibbett's identification was not an issue, contradicting the need to attack credibility. The testimony about Sibbett's violations was thorough, credible, and not in conflict. Thoreen's alleged belief that the court would remember Sibbett from a pretrial proceeding is unrealistic because that hearing took place several months earlier and Sibbett was but one of many persons cited for violating the salmon fishing injunction.

His alleged lack of intent to deceive the court or to obstruct justice is irrelevant. Section 401(1) does not require specific intent. It suffices that he should have been aware that his conduct exceeded reasonable limits and hindered the search for truth.

IV. CONCLUSION

Thoreen's error in judgment was unfortunate. The court's ire and this criminal contempt conviction could have been avoided easily and the admirable goal of representing his client zealously preserved if only he had given the court and opposing counsel prior notice and sought the court's consent.[7]

We AFFIRM the contempt conviction. . . .

* * *

F. CROSS-EXAMINING A WITNESS THE LAWYER KNOWS IS TELLING THE TRUTH AND USING A WITNESS'S TRUTHFUL BUT ERRONEOUS TESTIMONY FOR THE ADVANTAGE OF A CLIENT

Please read ABA Model Rules of Professional Conduct, Rule 3.3(a)(1); Rule 3.4(e); Rule 4.4(a); and Rule 8.4(c).

* * *

Criminal defense lawyer vs. prosecutor. ABA Standard Relating to the Defense Function 4–7.6(b) provides that a criminal defense lawyer's "belief or knowledge that the witness is telling the truth does not preclude cross-examination." The parallel standard for prosecutors repeats this idea, but also adds the following: "A prosecutor should not

---

[7]   While finding Thoreen's tactic misleading and obstructive of justice, we acknowledge that certain variations are acceptable. If identification is at issue, an attorney could test a witness's credibility by notifying the court and counsel that it is and by seeking the court's permission to (1) seat two or more persons at counsel table without identifying the defendant; *see* Duke v. State, 260 Ind. 638, 298 N.E.2d 453 (1973); (2) have no one at counsel table; (3) hold an in-court lineup.

use the power of cross-examination to discredit or undermine a witness if the prosecutor knows the witness is testifying truthfully." ABA Standard Relating to the Prosecution Function 3–5.7(b). Is there a good reason for the greater latitude given to criminal defense lawyers? Is it permissible to attempt to discredit a truthful witness in *civil* litigation, or would such conduct violate the rules listed above?

* * *

G. DISCRIMINATORY COMMENTS AND ACTIONS

Please read ABA Model Rules of Professional Conduct, Rule 8.4(d) and Comment [3].

Chapter 3 previously discussed Model Rule 8.4(d)'s prohibition on conduct prejudicial to the administration of justice. Comment [3] specifically notes that discriminatory words or conduct manifesting bias on the basis of race and other characteristics interferes with the proper administration of justice. The rule has been applied to improper statements at trial, *see* In re Thomsen, 837 N.E.2d 1011 (Ind. 2005) (disciplining lawyer who made repeated reference before the jury to the fact that the ex-wife (a white woman) of his client was living with "a black man" or "a black guy"), as well as discriminatory comments made to opposing counsel outside the courtroom, *see* Fla. Bar v. Martocci, 791 So. 2d 1074 (2001) (disciplining lawyer who engaged in "sexist, racial, and ethnic insults" during depositions).

* * *

H. TRIAL PUBLICITY

Please read ABA Model Rules of Professional Conduct, Rule 3.6 and Comments; and Rule 3.8(f) and Comments [5] & [6].

* * *

In Gentile v. State Bar of Nevada, 501 U.S. 1030 (1991), the Court held that a state can permissibly regulate an attorney's speech outside the courtroom that creates a "substantial likelihood of material prejudice" to a fair trial. The Court reasoned that this standard

> is designed to protect the integrity and fairness of a State's judicial system, and it imposes only narrow and necessary limitations on lawyers' speech. The limitations are aimed at two principal evils: (1) comments that are likely to influence the actual outcome of the trial, and (2) comments that are likely to prejudice the jury venire, even if an untainted panel can ultimately be found. Few, if any, interests under the

Constitution are more fundamental than the right to a fair trial by "impartial" jurors, and an outcome affected by extrajudicial statements would violate that fundamental right. . . .

Justice O'Connor, concurring, noted, "Lawyers are officers of the court and, as such, may legitimately be subject to ethical precepts that keep them from engaging in what otherwise might be constitutionally protected speech."

Application of the litigation privilege. Be careful what you say outside the court. Although lawyers enjoy a judicial privilege against civil liability for defamatory statements made in litigation, recent cases have held that a communication of the same statements to a reporter and post-trial comments to the media about a case are not protected by the privilege. *See* Bochetto v. Gibson, 860 A.2d 67 (Pa. Sup. Ct. 2004); Brown v. Gatti, 99 P.3d 299 (Or. Ct. App. 2004).

* * *

Problem 21.5. Following the arrest of Conner Anders, an alleged armed purse-snatcher, Anders' attorney held a press conference. He told the gathered media that Anders was wearing a leather jacket and boots at the time of arrest, but that "according to my police sources" the victim described the perpetrator as wearing a hooded sweatshirt and running shoes.

The prosecutor then issued a press release in which she stated,

> I want to address the suggestion that we have the wrong person in custody. Despite Anders' attorney's assertion to the contrary, the victim never described the perpetrator as wearing a hooded sweatshirt and running shoes. She said he was wearing a leather jacket and boots. This is exactly what Conner Anders was wearing when he was arrested less than two blocks away from the crime scene. The public can rest assured that we have the right guy.

Assume that both attorneys believe that they have truthfully communicated facts through the media. Nonetheless, did Anders' attorney violate Model Rule 3.6? Did the prosecutor violate Model Rules 3.6 or 3.8(f)?

* * *

I. REPRESENTING CLIENTS IN NON-ADJUDICATIVE PROCEEDINGS

Please read ABA Model Rules of Professional Conduct, Rule 3.9 and Comment.

J. TRUTHFULNESS AND CANDOR

1. REPRESENTATIONS TO THE TRIBUNAL

Please read ABA Model Rules of Professional Conduct, Rule 3.3(a)(1) & (d) and Comments [1]–[3] & [14]; and Rule 1.0(m).

* * *

Candor toward the tribunal vs. candor toward others. Note that under Model Rule 4.1(a), a lawyer is only prohibited from making a false statement of *material* fact or law to a third person. Under Model Rule 3.3(a)(1), *any* false statement of fact or law to a tribunal may subject the lawyer to discipline.

* * *

2. DISCLOSURE OF ADVERSE LEGAL AUTHORITY

Please read ABA Model Rules of Professional Conduct, Rule 3.3(a)(1) & (2) and Comment [4].

* * *

TYLER V. STATE
47 P.3d 1095 (Alaska Ct. App. 2001)

[Following the Alaska Court of Appeals' dismissal of an appeal brought on behalf of defendant Tyler, criminal defense attorney Eugene B. Cyrus was ordered by the court to show cause why sanctions should not be imposed against him for his behavior during the appeal. In addition to misstating facts in his appellate brief, Cyrus knowingly failed to cite a decision of the Alaska Supreme Court that was directly adverse to his contention on appeal on behalf of his client. The case involved a felony charge of driving while intoxicated. The issue on appeal was as follows: "If Tyler were allowed to withdraw his no contest pleas to the two prior DWI charges, but if the State then succeeded in re-convicting Tyler of these same charges, would those two DWI convictions still be 'prior convictions,' so that Tyler could properly be charged with felony DWI in the current case? Or would the re-convictions be 'new' convictions, so that

Tyler would technically be a 'first offender' for purposes of his current case (and thus guilty of only misdemeanor DWI)?"]

The State argued that if Tyler was convicted again of the two earlier charges (either following trial or after entering counseled pleas of no contest), Tyler would continue to be a third offender for purposes of his current offense, and therefore his current felony DWI conviction would remain valid. Mr. Cyrus argued the opposite. He contended that even if Tyler was re-convicted of the two previous DWIs, those convictions would be new—that is, they would no longer be "prior" to Tyler's current DWI offense. According to Mr. Cyrus's argument, even if the State re-convicted Tyler of the two earlier DWIs, Tyler would still be a "first offender" for purposes of his current offense, and thus his current offense would be a misdemeanor, not a felony.

When the parties submitted their pleadings on this issue, neither Mr. Cyrus nor the State's attorney alerted us to *McGhee v. State*, the Alaska Supreme Court decision that addresses this re-conviction issue in the context of an administrative revocation of a driver's license for a third-offense DWI. The State's attorney apparently did not find the *McGhee* case when he researched the State's motion to dismiss Tyler's appeal—for if the State's attorney had found *McGhee*, he doubtless would have cited it. But Mr. Cyrus plainly knew of the supreme court's decision in *McGhee*: he was the attorney who represented McGhee in the supreme court.

Alaska Professional Conduct, Rule 3.3(a)(3) declares that a lawyer shall not knowingly "fail to disclose . . . legal authority in the controlling jurisdiction" if the lawyer knows that this legal authority is "directly adverse to the position of the [lawyer's] client" and if this authority has "not [been] disclosed by opposing counsel." *McGhee* was decided by our supreme court, so it is "legal authority in the controlling jurisdiction." Mr. Cyrus knew about the *McGhee* decision, and he knew that the State's attorney had not brought *McGhee* to our attention. The remaining question is whether Mr. Cyrus knew that *McGhee* was "directly adverse" to his legal position-directly adverse to his contention that Tyler would have to be treated as a "first offender" even if he was re-convicted of the two prior DWIs.

Our decision in *Tyler v. State*—i.e., our dismissal of Tyler's appeal-is clearly premised on our conclusion that *McGhee* is, in fact, directly adverse to Mr. Cyrus's legal position. However, it would be unfair to judge Mr. Cyrus's ethical duties in hindsight. Obviously, Mr. Cyrus had not read our decision when he wrote his brief. The question is whether, at the time Mr. Cyrus wrote his brief, he knew that McGhee was directly adverse to his position.

(a) Mr. Cyrus's response to our order to show cause

In his response to our order to show cause, Mr. Cyrus asserts that he did not tell us about the *McGhee* decision because he believed that *McGhee* did not control the outcome of Tyler's case. Mr. Cyrus contends that "*McGhee* is unique because of its fact pattern" and, because of this, he did not believe (and still does not believe) that *McGhee* was "controlling authority" in Tyler's case. To back up his argument, Mr. Cyrus points out that at least one superior court judge shared his views concerning *McGhee*:

> [J]ust four months previous to my writing [Tyler's] brief . . . , a detached neutral judicial officer of the Anchorage Superior Court in a litigated case of mine, [the *Sjoblom* case], . . . ruled that *McGhee* was not controlling authority on a similar issue regarding the propriety of an attack on a prior conviction. . . . [I]f an attorney [knows of] a written judicial opinion verifying his belief that a case is not applicable, . . . it is not possible to [condemn the] attorney [for] intentionally withholding controlling authority. Simply [put], if attorneys could disagree as to [whether a case is] controlling authority, there should not be a violation [of Professional Conduct, Rule 3.3(a)(3)]."Response to Order to Show Cause" dated June 18, 2001 (File No. A-7779), pages 5–6 (emphasis in the original).

Mr. Cyrus did not tell the superior court about the *McGhee* decision, and the State's attorney did not find it. Superior Court Judge Dan A. Hensley discovered *McGhee* on his own, but he concluded that it was factually distinguishable.

To summarize: Mr. Cyrus offers two defenses to our order to show cause. First, he argues that even though we relied on *McGhee* when we dismissed Tyler's appeal, we were wrong to do so. Mr. Cyrus contends that because of *McGhee*'s procedural context (an attack on the ruling of an administrative agency), the case had little or no relevance to the proper decision of Tyler's criminal appeal. Second, Mr. Cyrus argues that even if this court was right when we concluded that *McGhee* was dispositive of Tyler's appeal, this conclusion was reasonably debatable. Based on Judge Hensley's analysis in *Sjoblom*, Mr. Cyrus points out that competent attorneys and judges might reasonably conclude that *McGhee* was factually distinguishable from Tyler's case—and that, therefore, *McGhee* did not control the outcome of Tyler's appeal. Mr. Cyrus argues that if reasonable attorneys could conclude that *McGhee* was not controlling authority in Tyler's appeal, he was under no obligation to cite the case in his brief.

Of the two defenses advanced by Mr. Cyrus, this second one is clearly the stronger. Judge Hensley's decision [in the *Sjoblom* case] shows that

Mr. Cyrus was not alone in thinking that *McGhee* should be limited to an administrative context and should not be viewed as controlling authority in criminal cases that raise the same re-conviction issue. And if reasonable attorneys and judges could disagree on the question of whether *McGhee* was controlling authority in Tyler's case, then regardless of whether this court correctly interpreted *McGhee* when we decided Tyler's appeal, it would be improper to fault Mr. Cyrus for taking another reasonable view of the matter.

We agree with Mr. Cyrus that, for present purposes, it does not matter whether our decision in *Tyler* was correct, or whether our decision in *Tyler* is arguably inconsistent with Judge Hensley's decision in *Sjoblom,* or whether Judge Hensley was right or wrong when he concluded that *McGhee* did not control Sjoblom's case. Instead, as Mr. Cyrus correctly points out, Judge Hensley's decision shows that reasonable judges might differ as to whether *McGhee* precludes the type of post-conviction claim presented by *Sjoblom* or the appellate claim made by Tyler the claim that if a defendant is convicted of felony DWI but later wins a plea withdrawal in one of the prior DWI cases, then even if the defendant is re-convicted of that prior offense, the superior court must set aside the felony DWI conviction. Thus, Mr. Cyrus might reasonably have concluded that the *McGhee* decision did not control the outcome of Tyler's appeal.

But Mr. Cyrus's defense to our order to show cause also hinges on his assertion that Professional Conduct, Rule 3.3(a)(3) only requires attorneys to reveal "controlling" court decisions and statutes. This is not correct.

(b) As used in Professional Conduct, Rule 3.3(a)(3), "directly adverse" is not synonymous with "controlling" or "dispositive"

Fortified by Judge Hensley's decision . . . , Mr. Cyrus argues that "if attorneys could [reasonably] disagree as to [whether *McGhee* was] controlling authority," then his failure to cite McGhee cannot constitute a violation of Professional Conduct Rule 3.3(a)(3). The problem with Mr. Cyrus's argument is that Rule 3.3(a)(3) does not speak of an attorney's failure to cite "controlling authority." Instead, it speaks of an attorney's failure to cite authority in the "controlling jurisdiction" if that authority is "directly adverse to the [lawyer's] position."

McGhee was decided by our state supreme court, so it clearly constitutes "authority in the controlling jurisdiction." The next question is whether *McGhee* was "directly adverse" to Mr. Cyrus's position in Tyler's appeal. The legislative history of Professional Conduct Rule 3.3(a)(3) and the commentaries on the rule show that "directly adverse" does not mean "controlling." It refers to a broader range of cases and statutes.

The meaning of "directly adverse" is explained in Formal Opinion No. 280 issued by the American Bar Association's Committee on Professional Ethics and Grievances. The Committee had been asked to clarify the "duty of a lawyer . . . to advise the court of decisions adverse to his client's contentions that are known to him and unknown to his adversary." The Committee wrote:

> We would not confine the [lawyer's duty] to "controlling authorities"—i.e., those decisive of the pending case—but, in accordance with the tests hereafter suggested, would apply it to a decision directly adverse to any proposition of law on which the lawyer expressly relies, which would reasonably be considered important by the judge sitting on the case. . . .
>
> . . . In a case involving a [settled question of law], there would seem to be no necessity whatever of citing even all the relevant decisions in the jurisdiction, much less those from other states or by inferior courts. [But w]here the question is a new or novel one, such as the constitutionality or construction of a statute, on which there is a dearth of authority, the lawyer's duty may be broader.

The Committee then defined the duty of disclosure:

> The test in every case should be: Is the decision which opposing counsel has overlooked one which the court should clearly consider in deciding the case? Would a reasonable judge properly feel that a lawyer who advanced, as the law, a proposition adverse to the undisclosed decision, was lacking in candor and fairness to him? Might the judge consider himself misled by an implied representation that the lawyer knew of no adverse authority?
>
> . . .

In March 1984, the American Bar Association's Committee on Ethics and Professional Responsibility issued Informal Opinion No. 84–1505, in which the Committee . . . concluded that the lawyer was obligated to disclose the decision, although the lawyer could "[o]f course . . . challenge the soundness of the other decision, attempt to distinguish it from the case at bar, or present other reasons why the court should not follow or even be influenced by it." . . .

Under the interpretation of Rule 3.3(a)(3) espoused in these ABA ethics opinions, a court decision can be "directly adverse" to a lawyer's position even though the lawyer reasonably believes that the decision is factually distinguishable from the current case or the lawyer reasonably believes that, for some other reason, the court will ultimately conclude that the decision does not control the current case.

(c)   Using this definition of "directly adverse," did Mr. Cyrus
know that McGhee was directly adverse to the position
he was advancing in Tyler's appeal?

Turning to the facts of Tyler's appeal, and using the test explained in the previous section, it is evident that the supreme court's decision in *McGhee* was "directly adverse" to the position that Mr. Cyrus was arguing in Tyler's appeal.

McGhee is the only Alaska Supreme Court decision (to our knowledge) that addresses the question raised in Tyler's appeal—the effect of a withdrawn plea and a re-conviction of DWI when a defendant faces harsher penalties if the defendant is found to be a repeat offender. The result reached in *McGhee* is the opposite of the result that Mr. Cyrus advocated in Tyler's appeal. And, although the matter was obviously debatable, one could reasonably interpret *McGhee* as being directly inconsistent with, or at least substantially undercutting, the argument that Mr. Cyrus was making in Tyler's case. Further, even if Mr. Cyrus thought that *McGhee* was distinguishable because of its procedural context, Tyler's appeal involved a novel issue on which there was a dearth of authority, and *McGhee* was the only Alaska decision that came close to addressing this issue.

Given these circumstances, *McGhee* was "directly adverse" to Mr. Cyrus's position for purposes of Professional Conduct Rule 3.3(a)(3). In the words of ABA Formal Ethics Opinion 280, *McGhee* is a decision "which would reasonably be considered important" by this court, a decision "which the court should clearly consider in deciding [Tyler's] case."

We recognize that advocacy invariably includes a process of separating wheat from chaff, of deciding which arguments and legal authorities are important to a case. Moreover, as we stated earlier, an attorney's ethical duties must not be judged in hindsight. When an attorney consciously decides not to cite a court decision or a statute, the attorney's choice should not—and does not—become a violation of Professional Conduct Rule 3.3(a)(3) simply because the court later concludes that the omitted decision or statute is directly adverse to the attorney's position. Rather, an attorney violates Rule 3.3(a)(3) only if the attorney knew that the omitted legal authority was directly adverse to the attorney's position.

. . .

We assume that reasonable attorneys and judges might conclude that *McGhee* did not dictate our decision in Tyler's case (because of its different procedural setting). Nevertheless, *McGhee* was directly adverse to Mr. Cyrus's position within the meaning of Professional Conduct Rule 3.3(a)(3). Mr. Cyrus was the attorney who litigated *McGhee*: he knew about the case, and he understood its relevance to Tyler's appeal. Even assuming that Mr. Cyrus had a good faith and reasonable belief that *McGhee* could be distinguished, he was obliged to bring *McGhee* to our attention once he realized that the State's attorney had failed to cite the case.

We readily acknowledge that appellate litigation is a contest, not a seminar. The lawyers who appear before us do so as adversaries and advocates. Our adversary system is based on the belief that the fairest results and the best rules of law are discovered through vigorous presentation of opposing viewpoints. But attorneys are officers of the court, and they owe a duty of candor to the court. . . .

In Great Britain, barristers are under "an unquestioned obligation" to cite all relevant law, both favorable and unfavorable. Professional Conduct Rule 3.3(a)(3) does not impose such a broad duty on Alaska attorneys. But although our state's duty of disclosure is narrower, enforcement of this duty remains important.

The process of deciding appeals involves the joint efforts of counsel and the court. As the Supreme Court of New Jersey has noted, "[i]t is only when each branch of the profession performs its function properly that justice can be administered to the satisfaction of both the litigants and society." Only then can an appellate court "[develop] a body of decisions . . . that will be a credit to the bar, the courts[,] and the state."

When a lawyer practicing before us fails to disclose a decision of the Alaska Supreme Court (or one of our own published decisions) that is directly adverse to the lawyer's position, the lawyer's conduct will, at the very best, merely result in an unneeded expenditure of judicial resources- the time spent by judges or law clerks in tracking down the adverse authority. At worst, we will not find the adverse authority and we will issue a decision that fails to take account of it, leading to confusion in the law and possibly unfair outcomes for the litigants involved. This potential damage is compounded by the fact that our decision, if published, will be binding in future cases

Professional Conduct Rule 3.3(a)(3) is based on the notion that "[t]he function of an appellate brief is to assist, not mislead, the court." We endorse the words of the Florida Court of Appeal in Forum v. Boca Burger, Inc., 788 So.2d 1055 (Fla. App.2001):

> Although we have an adversary system of justice, it is one founded on the rule of law. Simply because our system is adversarial does not make it unconcerned with outcomes. . . . We do not accept the notion that outcomes should depend on who is . . . [most] able to misdirect a judge.

Although we accept Mr. Cyrus's assertion that he honestly and reasonably believed that *McGhee* could be distinguished from Tyler's case, Mr. Cyrus does not contend that he was unaware of *McGhee*'s potential importance to the decision of Tyler's appeal. *McGhee* was the only Alaska appellate decision that discussed, or came close to discussing, the issue that Mr. Cyrus knew would determine the validity of Tyler's . . . plea. And the result in *McGhee* was the opposite of the result advocated by Mr. Cyrus in Tyler's case.

Mr. Cyrus knew that *McGhee* could reasonably be interpreted as rejecting or casting substantial doubt on his position. *McGhee* was therefore "directly adverse" authority for purposes of Professional Conduct Rule 3.3(a)(3), and Mr. Cyrus was obligated to bring *McGhee* to our attention when he realized that the State had not cited it. Mr. Cyrus failed in that duty. [The court imposed a fine upon Cyrus.]

* * *

Zealous advocacy? Doesn't it hurt your client's case to disclose adverse authority? The short answer is not necessarily, if done correctly. *See* Michael J. Higdon, *When the Case Gives You Lemons: Using Negative Authority in Persuasive Legal Writing,* 46 TENN. B.J. 14 (March 2010) (demonstrating that given the critical nature of the legal reader, including adverse case law in legal documents not only will help an attorney discharge her ethical obligation, but also will make the document more persuasive, and offering specific suggestions on incorporating negative authority in a manner that enhances the strength of the advocate's argument.)

* * *

Problem 21.6. Judge Moore has asked you to draft an order ruling on a motion for summary judgment. During your legal research, you find a case that is on point, that helps the moving party (and that is inconsistent with an argument made by the opposing party), and that was not cited by either party. Have both attorneys violated Model Rule 3.3?

* * *

3. PROTECTING THE TRIBUNAL AGAINST PERJURY AND OTHER OFFENSES AGAINST THE ADMINISTRATION OF JUSTICE

Please read ABA Model Rules of Professional Conduct, Rule 3.3(a)(3), (b) & (c) and Comments [9]–[15].

* * *

In Nix v. Whiteside, 475 U.S. 157 (1986), the U.S. Supreme Court held that a criminal defendant was not denied effective assistance of counsel when his appointed counsel threatened to withdraw because he believed his client intended to commit perjury at his trial. The Court held that the lawyer's performance fell within the "range of reasonable professional assistance," as measured by "[p]revailing norms of practice as reflected in American Bar Association Standards and the like. . . ." There, the defendant, Whiteside, was charged with murder. Whiteside told his lawyer, Robinson, that he stabbed the victim because he believed the victim was reaching for a gun, although he had not actually seen a gun. Shortly before trial, he changed his story, telling Robinson that he had seen the victim reaching for something "metallic." Whiteside also insisted on testifying at his trial. Robinson told him that

> we could not allow him to [testify falsely] because that would be perjury, and as officers of the court we would be suborning perjury if we allowed him to do it; . . . I advised him that if he did do that it would be my duty to advise the Court of what he was doing and that I felt he was committing perjury; also, that I probably would be allowed to attempt to impeach that particular testimony.

The Court noted that "Robinson also indicated he would seek to withdraw from the representation if Whiteside insisted on committing perjury." Whiteside did take the stand, but did not testify that he saw "something metallic." After he was convicted of murder, Whiteside alleged that Robinson had not provided effective assistance of counsel, due to his threats of disclosure and withdrawal if Whiteside testified to seeing "something metallic." The Court indicated its approval of Robinson's conduct:

> Although counsel must take all reasonable lawful means to attain the objectives of the client, counsel is precluded from taking steps or in any way assisting the client in presenting false evidence or otherwise violating the law. . . . Whether Robinson's conduct is seen as a successful attempt to dissuade his client from committing the crime of perjury, or whether seen as a "threat" to withdraw from representation and disclose the illegal scheme, Robinson's representation of Whiteside falls well within

accepted standards of professional conduct and the range of reasonable professional conduct. . . .

* * *

Knowledge of intent to commit perjury. Model Rule 3.3(a)(3) prohibits a lawyer from offering evidence the lawyer knows to be false. But how often does a lawyer "know" in advance that a witness will testify falsely? Model Rule 1.0(f) defines the term "knows" as denoting actual knowledge. In State v. McDowell, 681 N.W.2d 500, 514 (Wis. 2004), the Wisconsin Supreme Court stated that "[a]bsent the most extraordinary circumstances, such knowledge must be based on the client's expressed admission of intent to testify untruthfully." Other courts have not gone so far as to require actual knowledge under these circumstances. *See* State v. Hischke, 639 N.W.2d 6, 10 (Iowa 2002) (holding that rule applies when a lawyer has "good cause to believe the defendant's proposed testimony would be deliberately untruthful"); United States ex rel. Wilcox v. Johnson, 555 F.2d 115, 122 (3d Cir.1977) (stating lawyer must have "firm factual basis" that client will testify falsely before lawyer is permitted to raise concerns with trial judge). Given the competing policy concerns, what standard should apply?

So what do I do? The Court's discussion of Robinson's actions, coupled with a careful reading of Rule 3.3 and its Comments, yields a plausible sequence of responses to threatened or actual client perjury:

- If the client threatens to testify falsely, the lawyer must attempt to persuade the client not to do so.

- If the lawyer's attempt at persuasion is unsuccessful and the client still intends to commit perjury, the lawyer's strategy depends upon whether her client is a criminal defendant or a party to a civil action. If a criminal defendant, the client must be permitted to testify unless the lawyer "knows" that she will commit perjury. If a civil party, and if the lawyer "reasonably believes" that she will commit perjury, the client may be permitted to testify or may be kept off the stand, at the lawyer's discretion.

- If, despite the lawyer's best efforts, the lawyer "knows" that the client has testified falsely, the lawyer must "remonstrate" with the client and attempt to persuade her to rectify the false testimony. Model Rule 3.3, Comment [10].

- If the client refuses to rectify the false testimony, the lawyer must first seek to withdraw from the representation, and if withdrawal is refused, "must make such disclosure to the tribunal as is reasonably necessary to remedy the situation, even if doing so requires the lawyer to reveal information that otherwise would be protected by Rule 1.6." Model Rule 3.3, Comment [10].

Narrative testimony as an alternative. *Nix* illustrates one approach to dealing with anticipated client perjury. Some jurisdictions permit an alternative approach. For example, in Florida, when a lawyer knows that a client charged with a crime intends to testify falsely,

> the lawyer's first duty is to attempt to persuade the client to testify truthfully. If the client still insists on committing perjury, the lawyer must threaten to disclose the client's intent to commit perjury to the judge. If the threat of disclosure does not successfully persuade the client to testify truthfully, the lawyer must disclose the fact that the client intends to lie to the tribunal and . . . information sufficient to prevent the commission of the crime of perjury.

Amendment to the Rules Regulating The Florida Bar, 875 So.2d 448, 507–08 (Fla. 2004). If, at that point, the court does not permit the lawyer to withdraw, the lawyer must then allow the defendant to testify in a narrative fashion:

> [T]he defendant's attorney does not elicit the perjurious testimony by questioning nor argue the false testimony during closing argument. The attorney, of course, is not precluded from arguing sound, non-perjurious testimony or attacking the state's case. Under this procedure, a defendant is afforded his right to speak to the jury under oath and the constitutional right to assistance of counsel is preserved, but the defense attorney is protected from participating in the fraud. Under such a formula, the responsibility for committing or not committing fraud on the tribunal lies with the defendant, and not with his attorney, and the jury will decide whether the defendant's testimony is credible.

Sanborn v. State, 474 So. 2d 309, 313 (Fla.Dist. Ct. App. 1985).

* * *

Problem 21.7. In a bench trial pending before Judge Moore, the parties dispute whether a key document in the case is real or a forgery. The plaintiff testified that the document is authentic. You noticed, though, that her attorney relied entirely on other evidence (and never mentioned the controversial document) during closing argument. If the plaintiff's attorney believed that his client falsely testified about the document, has he addressed the issue in an acceptable way under Rule 3.3?

* * *

K. FRIVOLOUS APPEALS

* * *

Federal Rule of Appellate Procedure 38 provides that "[i]f a court of appeals determines that an appeal is frivolous, it may, after a separately filed motion or notice from the court and reasonable opportunity to respond, award just damages and single or double costs to the appellee."

According to the Seventh Circuit Court of Appeals, "An appeal is frivolous within the meaning of Rule 38, when it 'was prosecuted with no reasonable expectation of altering the district court's judgment and for purposes of delay or harassment or out of sheer obstinacy.'" Flexible Manufacturing Systems, Inc. v. Super Prods. Corp., 86 F.3d 96 (7th Cir. 1996).

In Nagle v. Alspach, 8 F.3d 141 (3d Cir. 1993), the trial court granted summary judgment to the defendant based upon four separate grounds. The defendant appealed on only two of those grounds. Thus, even had the appellate court reversed on those two grounds, the two unchallenged grounds would have supported the trial court's judgment. Because the appeal was "doomed to failure from the moment the plaintiff-appellants' brief was filed in this court," the Third Circuit held that the appeal was "frivolous" under Fed. R. App. P. 38. The Court explained:

> The purpose of Rule 38 damages is to compensate appellees who are forced to defend judgments awarded them in the trial court from appeals that are wholly without merit, and to "preserve the appellate court calendar for cases worthy of consideration." Another important purpose is to discourage litigants from unnecessarily wasting their opponents' time and resources.). Moreover, even though an appellee makes no request for Rule 38 damages, the court may raise the issue *sua sponte.*

> Damages under Rule 38 are appropriate when an appeal is "wholly without merit." [citations omitted]. Our inquiry is an objective one, focusing "on the merits of the appeal regardless of good or bad faith." . . .

> . . .

> We are well aware that injudicious awards of Rule 38 damages may have the potential to chill the zeal for pursuing novel questions and difficult appeals. . . .[S]ometimes a questionable appeal may be due to mere overzealousness or inexperience of counsel, and it is sometimes difficult to draw the line "between the tenuously arguable and the frivolous." Hence, we move with caution and will not label an appeal frivolous unless it lacks colorable support or is wholly without merit. Here, however,

there was no possibility of success, and it is patently unfair to allow appellees who have been damaged financially by a frivolous appeal to go uncompensated. We see no chilling effect whatsoever in requiring an attorney, once a proper decision to appeal has been made, to be professional and diligent in prosecuting it. Indeed, any other rule would prejudice the very clients whose interests the attorney is duty-bound to protect, and who properly rely on their attorneys to zealously advocate their causes.

We also believe it is appropriate to impose the burden for payment of these damages upon appellants' counsel rather than on the appellants. . . . [T]he burden for payment of Rule 38 damages may be imposed upon counsel for appellant when the frivolous appeal stems from counsel's professional error. Appellants' counsel has offered no reason to show that the fault for the frivolous appeal lies anywhere but with him. Moreover, it is inconceivable that appellants would request that their attorney not challenge alleged errors when the failure to do so would result in a certain loss. In [a previous case], we set the standard that

> attorneys have an affirmative obligation to research the law and to determine if a claim on appeal is utterly without merit and may be deemed frivolous. We conclude that if counsel ignore or fail in this obligation to their client, they do so at their peril and may become personally liable to satisfy a Rule 38 award. The test is whether, following a thorough analysis of the record and careful research of the law, a reasonable attorney would conclude that the appeal is frivolous.

Appellants' counsel should have known that unless all four conclusions reached by the district court in support of its summary judgment were challenged, the appeal he filed had no chance whatsoever of success. It is manifestly evident that the responsibility for paying these damages rests squarely upon counsel.

Id. at 145–46.

Compare the standards for attorney conduct under Fed. R. Civ. P. 11 and Fed. R. App. P. 38. Which rule provides more guidance for attorneys? Which rule is easier to comply with? We learned earlier that clients are generally in charge of the objectives of the representation, while lawyers are generally in charge of the means of achieving the client's objectives. How does that division of authority apply in the decision whether to file an appeal?

* * *

Profile of attorney professionalism. Violette Neatley Anderson, born in 1882, was the first African-American woman admitted to practice before the United States Supreme Court. Before becoming a lawyer, Anderson worked as a court reporter for fifteen years (from 1905 to 1920). Her time in the courtroom developed her interest in trial practice, and she attended law school at the University of Chicago while continuing to work as a court reporter. In 1920, Anderson graduated from law school, passed the Illinois bar exam, and immediately began litigating cases as a solo practitioner. Anderson took both civil and criminal cases, and her career quickly skyrocketed. In 1922, Anderson gained media attention for successfully defending a woman accused of murdering a male lodger; Anderson persuaded the jury that her client had acted in self-defense. A Chicago newspaper reported that it was "to the credit of Attorney Anderson that her client was acquitted after a three days' battle before judge and jury." THE BROAD AX, July 29, 1922. Soon after her success at the highly publicized trial, Anderson was offered a position as an assistant prosecutor for the City of Chicago. She accepted the job in December of 1922, becoming the city's first female prosecutor as well as its first African-American prosecutor. In 1926, after Anderson had been licensed and in good standing for five years, she was admitted to practice before the United States Supreme Court.

In addition to her legal work, Anderson also engaged in political advocacy and community service. She served as president of the Friendly Big Sisters League of Chicago, vice-president of the Cook County Bar Association, and national president of the Zeta Phi Beta Sorority. Anderson worked to secure passage of the Bankhead-Jones Act, which authorized low-interest loans to enable sharecroppers and tenant farmers to buy land for themselves. In addition to personally lobbying the congressional representatives from Illinois, she also used her position as sorority president to organize a nationwide lobbying effort by sorority members. Anderson lived to see the bill signed into law in the summer of 1937 by President Franklin D. Roosevelt, but was struck ill with cancer shortly thereafter. In December of 1937, at 55 years of age, Anderson passed away.

CHAPTER 22

CRIMINAL LAW PRACTICE

■■■

Chapter hypothetical. Cole was on trial for first-degree murder. At trial, the prosecution's key witness, Ann, testified that Cole had confessed to the murder. A few days later and while the trial was still ongoing, the assistant prosecutor handling the case, Ben, informed Cole's lawyer, Denise, that, before trial, Ann had cut a deal with the district attorney, Edward, under which pending charges against Ann for writing bad checks would be dropped in exchange for her testimony against Cole. Ben explained to Denise that he had only learned of this information that same day. He explained that the district attorney, Edward, was overseeing the prosecution of Ann but had failed to inform Ben of the deal. Outraged, Denise held a press conference in which she accused Edward's office of attempting to "railroad an innocent person" and of "gross misconduct, which calls into question the fairness of the entire criminal justice system." When asked at a separate press conference about whether the incident might impact the public's opinion as to Cole's guilt, Ben responded, "I doubt many members of the public would doubt Cole's guilt if they had seen the DNA test results that I have."

The incident involving Cole caused several local criminal defense lawyers to come forward with similar stories about the failure of Edward's office to disclose information relevant to their cases in a timely manner. This prompted the appellate lawyers for Francis, a convicted murderer on death row, to do some additional investigation into Francis' case. Eventually they learned that Gary, one of the assistant district attorneys in Edward's office, had spoken to Francis outside the presence of her court-appointed lawyer about her case. Francis had requested the meeting in order to discuss the possibility of a plea deal and voluntarily consented to the interview outside the presence of her lawyer. At trial, the prosecution introduced statements made by Francis during the interviews that it claimed cast doubt on her veracity. During their investigation, Francis' appellate lawyers also uncovered a bombshell: DNA evidence that was known to the assistant district attorney trying Francis' case but that was never disclosed to Francis' lawyer, which strongly pointed to another individual as being the actual murderer.

As you read the material in this chapter, consider the following issues:

(A) Is Gary subject to discipline under Model Rule 4.2? If so, should his violation result in a new trial?

(B) Has there been a violation of Cole's constitutional rights due to the failure to disclose the prosecution's deal with Ann? Is Ben subject to discipline under Model Rule 3.8(d)?

(C) If Francis wants to sue Edward or his office for the failure to disclose the exculpatory DNA evidence, is she likely to prevail?

(D) Is Denise subject to discipline for her statements to the press? Is Ben?

* * *

A. THE PROSECUTOR'S ROLE

**Please read ABA Model Rules of Professional Conduct,
Rule 3.8 and Comment [1].**

* * *

BERGER V. UNITED STATES
295 U.S. 78 (1935)

. . . .

[The prosecutor] is the representative not of an ordinary party to a controversy, but of a sovereignty whose obligation to govern impartially is as compelling as its obligation to govern at all; and whose interest, therefore, in a criminal prosecution is not that it shall win a case, but that justice shall be done. As such, he is in a peculiar and very definite sense the servant of the law, the twofold aim of which is that guilt shall not escape or innocence suffer. He may prosecute with earnestness and vigor—indeed he should do so. But, while he may strike hard blows, he is not at liberty to strike foul ones. It is as much his duty to refrain from improper methods calculated to produce a wrongful conviction as it is to use every legitimate means to bring about a just one.

. . . .

* * *

ROBERT H. JACKSON, *THE FEDERAL PROSECUTOR*
24 J. AM. JUD. SOC'Y 18 (1940)

It would probably be within the range of that exaggeration permitted in Washington to say that assembled in this room is one of the most powerful peace-time forces known to our country. The prosecutor has more control over life, liberty, and reputation than any other person in America. His discretion is tremendous. He can have citizens investigated and, if he is that kind of person, he can have this done to the tune of public statements and veiled or unveiled intimations. Or the prosecutor may choose a more subtle course and simply have a citizen's friends interviewed. The prosecutor can order arrests, present cases to the grand jury in secret session, and on the basis of his one-sided presentation of the facts, can cause the citizen to be indicted and held for trial. He may dismiss the case before trial, in which case the defense never has a chance to be heard. Or he may go on with a public trial. If he obtains a conviction, the prosecutor can still make recommendations as to sentence, as to whether the prisoner should get probation or a suspended sentence, and after he is put away, as to whether he is a fit subject for parole. While the prosecutor at his best is one of the most beneficent forces in our society, when he acts from malice or other base motives, he is one of the worst. . . .

Nothing better can come out of this meeting of law enforcement officers than a rededication to the spirit of fair play and decency that should animate the federal prosecutor. Your positions are of such independence and importance that while you are being diligent, strict, and vigorous in law enforcement you can also afford to be just. Although the government technically loses its case, it has really won if justice has been done. The lawyer in public office is justified in seeking to leave behind him a good record. But he must remember that his most alert and severe, but just, judges will be the members of his own profession, and that lawyers rest their good opinion of each other not merely on results accomplished but on the quality of the performance. Reputation has been called "the shadow cast by one's daily life." Any prosecutor who risks his day-to-day professional name for fair dealing to build up statistics of success has a perverted sense of practical values, as well as defects of character. Whether one seeks promotion to a judgeship, as many prosecutors rightly do, or whether he returns to private practice, he can have no better asset than to have his profession recognize that his attitude toward those who feel his power has been dispassionate, reasonable and just. . . .

The qualities of a good prosecutor are as elusive and as impossible to define as those which mark a gentleman. And those who need to be told would not understand it anyway. A sensitiveness to fair play and sportsmanship is perhaps the best protection against the abuse of power, and the citizen's safety lies in the prosecutor who tempers zeal with human kindness, who seeks truth and not victims, who serves the law and not factional purposes, and who approaches his task with humility.

* * *

B. PROMULGATION AND ENFORCEMENT OF STANDARDS OF CONDUCT FOR PROSECUTORS

The only Model Rule to speak directly and in detail to any special ethical obligations on the part of prosecutors is Rule 3.8. However, as the rest of this chapter discusses, many of the other disciplinary rules raise special issues in the case of prosecutors. For example, there are several disciplinary rules that prohibit a lawyer's use of deception. Yet, deception is a fundamental part of the work of undercover police investigators, who often work under the direction of a prosecutor. As we have seen in previous chapters, Model Rule 4.2 prohibits a lawyer, in the course of representation, from communicating about the subject of the representation with a person the lawyer knows to be represented by another lawyer in the matter, unless the lawyer has the consent of the other lawyer or is authorized to do so by law or a court order. It is, of course, the job of the police and prosecutors to investigate and prosecute crimes. Are police officials acting under the direction of a prosecutor "authorized" to interview criminal defendants who are represented by lawyers despite Rule 4.2's prohibition? The *State of Minnesota v. Clark* case below examines this and related issues pertaining to Rule 4.2.

In addition, there is the issue of whether state disciplinary rules may regulate the actions of *federal* prosecutors. In 1989, the Department of Justice, under the Bush Administration, asserted that the Supremacy Clause to the Constitution prohibited states from regulating the conduct of federal prosecutors to the extent a regulation "conflict[s] with the federal law or with the attorneys' federal responsibilities." Bruce A. Green, *Whose Rules of Conduct Should Govern Lawyers in Federal Court and How Should These Rules Be Created?*, 64 GEO. WASH. L. REV. 460, 474 (1996). Under the Clinton Administration, DOJ took a similar view, at least with respect to certain rules.

Congress eventually resolved the matter with the passage of the Citizens Protection Act. 28 U.S.C. § 530(b). The Citizens Protection Act dispensed with DOJ's claims and declared that "[a]n attorney for the Government shall be subject to State laws and rules, and local federal court rules, governing attorneys in each State where such attorney engages in that attorney's duties, to the same extent and in the same manner as other attorneys in that State."

To address some of the special ethical issues raised in the prosecutorial setting, the ABA has also produced its Standards of Criminal Justice Relating to the Prosecution Function [ABA Prosecution Function Standards]. Some jurisdictions have adopted these standards. In others, courts will sometimes look to them for guidance. This chapter occasionally references these standards.

* * *

C. STANDARDS OF CONDUCT FOR PROSECUTORS

1. INVESTIGATING AND SUPERVISING INVESTIGATION

Please re-read ABA Model Rules of Professional Conduct, Rules 4.1–4.4; and Rule 8.4.

Problem 22.1. District Attorney Edward is overseeing a sting operation involving the sale of stolen credit cards. Under Edward's supervision, police officers will pose as potential buyers. Would Edward be subject to discipline under Model Rule 8.4(c) based on the officers' deception?

* * *

As any regular viewer of the NBC television series *Law and Order* knows, "In the criminal justice system, the people are represented by two separate yet equally important groups: the police, who investigate crime, and the district attorneys, who prosecute the offenders." As the television show demonstrates, prosecutors and police do, in fact, have a close relationship. ABA Prosecution Function Standard 3–2.7 counsels that "[t]he prosecutor should provide legal advice to the police concerning the police functions and duties in criminal matters." Standard 3–2.7 also advises that prosecutors should even provide resources "to aid in training police in the performance of their function in accordance with the law."

However, despite the close relationship between prosecutors and police, prosecutors are constrained by ethical limitations that do not necessarily constrain police. ABA Prosecution Function Standard 3–3.1 recognizes the distinction between the police role and the prosecutor role: "A prosecutor ordinarily relies on police and other investigative agencies for investigation of alleged criminal acts, but the prosecutor has an affirmative responsibility to investigate suspected illegal activity when it is not adequately dealt with by other agencies." As you read the following materials, ask yourself how the ethical rules governing prosecutors are designed to differentiate them from "the police, who investigate crime."

* * *

a. Communicating with Represented Persons

Please read Model Rules of Professional Conduct, Rule 4.2 and Comment [5].

* * *

STATE OF MINNESOTA V. CLARK
738 N.W.2d 316 (Minn. 2007)

ANDERSON, PAUL H., JUSTICE.

Courtney Bernard Clark was convicted in Ramsey County for murdering Rodney Foster and attempting to murder Foster's girlfriend, B.B., while committing or attempting to commit aggravated robbery, kidnapping, and criminal sexual conduct. At Clark's trial, the state introduced over Clark's objection three recorded interviews between Clark and the police. In the first and second interviews, Clark denied involvement in the charged offenses. In the third interview, Clark admitted tying up Foster and B.B. and robbing Foster, and he stated that Foster died "by accident." ... On appeal, Clark argues that the district court erred on several grounds when it admitted the recorded interviews .... We affirm.

St. Paul Police Sergeant Steven Frazer, the primary investigator on Foster's case, testified regarding three interviews he conducted with Clark after Clark was arrested—two on July 26 and one on August 3. Frazer said that he conducted the interviews together with Minneapolis Police Officer Michael Doran, for whom Clark had worked as a paid informant. The state played for the jury an audiotape of the first interview and videotapes of the second and third interviews. [The first interview on July 26 took place before Clark's arraignment. Clark was not yet represented by counsel. At the start of the interview, Frazer and Doran obtained a signed *Miranda* waiver form from Clark. The second interview on July 26 took place after Clark had been arraigned and a lawyer from the public defender's office, Tom Handley, had been appointed to represent him. A police officer testified that the interview came about after Clark had requested to speak further to the police and that the public defender's office was "aware of the situation." The third interview was conducted on August 3 at the request of Clark. There was disputed testimony about how and when the public defender's office had been notified about the planned interview. The parties had difficulty establishing a time when Clark's lawyer could be present during police questioning, and assistant district attorney Charles Balck prevented the police from speaking with Clark outside the presence of his lawyer on several occasions prior to August 3. Shortly after 8:40 p.m. on August 3, however, Balck left a voicemail message at the public defender's office, indicating that Clark had requested to speak to the police and that "there would be contact with the police as a result of the defendant's contact." No one from the public defender's office was present when the third interview began shortly after 9 p.m.]

We now turn to Clark's claims regarding violations of his Sixth Amendment right to counsel and Minn. R. Prof. Conduct 4.2 with respect to the second July 26 interview and the August 3 interview (post-arraignment interviews). In his brief, Clark characterized these claims as related, if not overlapping. Specifically, he asserted that "part of" an accused person's right to counsel "is based on" Rule 4.2. But at oral argument, Clark conceded that a Sixth Amendment claim is analytically distinct from a Rule 4.2 claim and that each is governed by a different body of law. Having made this distinction, Clark focused his argument on the state's alleged violation of Rule 4.2. It is not clear whether Clark's comments at oral argument constituted an implicit withdrawal of his Sixth Amendment claim. Accordingly, we first address whether the state violated Clark's Sixth Amendment right to counsel, and second, whether the state violated Rule 4.2. . . .

Sixth Amendment Right to Counsel

The Sixth Amendment to the U.S. Constitution guarantees that "[i]n all criminal prosecutions, the accused shall enjoy the right to * * * have the assistance of counsel for his defence." U.S. Const. amend. VI. This right attaches as soon as the accused person is subject to adverse judicial proceedings, including arraignments. *See, e.g.,* United States v. Gouveia, 467 U.S. 180, 187–88 (1984). An accused person can waive his Sixth Amendment right to counsel, but the government bears the burden of proving that the person "understood that he had a right to have counsel present during an interrogation and that he intentionally relinquished or abandoned that known right." Giddings v. State, 290 N.W.2d 595, 597 (Minn.1980). In deciding whether the government has met its burden, courts consider the circumstances of each case, including the age, experience, and background of the defendant. *Giddings,* 290 N.W.2d at 597.

In this case, the district court concluded that the state met its burden of proving that Clark "voluntarily, knowingly, and intelligently abandoned or relinquished" his known right to counsel during his post-arraignment interviews. [The court held that the district court did not err when it concluded that the state did not violate Clark's Sixth Amendment right to counsel by conducting the post-arraignment interviews.]

Minnesota Rule of Professional Conduct 4.2

Minnesota Rule of Professional Conduct 4.2 provides:

> In representing a client, a lawyer shall not communicate about the subject of the representation with a person the lawyer knows to be represented by another lawyer in the matter, unless the lawyer has the consent of the other lawyer or is authorized to do so by law or a court order.

"[O]ur case law clearly establishes that [Rule] 4.2 applies to prosecutors involved in custodial interviews of a charged suspect." State v. Miller, 600 N.W.2d 457, 464 (Minn.1999). Moreover, police contact with a suspect may be attributed to a prosecutor when the prosecutor orders or ratifies the police contact, as apparently happened in this case. *Id.* The purpose of Rule 4.2 is to protect the represented individual "from the supposed imbalance of legal skill and acumen between the lawyer and the party litigant." *Id.* at 463 (quotation marks omitted).

In this case, the district court admitted Clark's statements from the post-arraignment interviews after finding that Clark's lawyer had notice of the interviews and an opportunity to be present. Clark essentially argues that the district court misconstrued what Rule 4.2 requires, and that the state violated the rule by failing to obtain his lawyer's consent before conducting the interviews. The state argues that the court properly construed and applied Rule 4.2, and further, that suppression of Clark's statements would be unwarranted even if the state did violate the rule. In light of these arguments, we first consider what steps the state must take when Rule 4.2 applies before interviewing a represented criminal defendant outside the presence of the defendant's lawyer. We then decide whether the state took those steps here, and if not, whether the state's violation of Rule 4.2 warrants suppression of Clark's statements.

Rule 4.2 Requirements

Precisely what Rule 4.2 requires of the state in the context of a criminal case is a question of law we review de novo. *See* Lennartson v. Anoka-Hennepin Indep. Sch. Dist. No. 11, 662 N.W.2d 125, 129 (Minn.2003). In *Miller*, we described the scope of Rule 4.2 as follows:

> [Rule] 4.2 protects the right of counsel to be present during any communication between the counsel's client and opposing counsel. The focus of [Rule] 4.2 is on the obligation of attorneys to respect the relationship of the adverse party and the party's attorney. * * * [T]he party cannot waive the application of [Rule 4.2]—only the party's attorney can approve the direct contact and only the party's attorney can waive the attorney's right to be present during a communication between the attorney's client and opposing counsel.

600 N.W.2d at 464 (citing United States v. Lopez, 4 F.3d 1455, 1462 (9th Cir.1993)). . . . Based on the passage above and the plain language of Rule 4.2, we agree with Clark that a lawyer representing a criminal defendant is owed more than notice and an opportunity to be present before the state interviews the defendant about the subject of the representation. We also agree that the operative word in Rule 4.2 is "consent."

The more difficult question is precisely what the defendant's lawyer must consent to before the state may permissibly communicate with the defendant. Our language in *Miller* could support an interpretation of Rule 4.2 requiring the state to obtain the lawyer's consent before communicating with the defendant outside the lawyer's presence. Under this interpretation, the state could interview a defendant who insists on speaking to the police over his lawyer's objection, as long as the lawyer is present during the interview. This interpretation denies the defense lawyer "veto power" over a defendant's decision to speak with the police, while arguably helping to achieve the Rule's purpose-protecting the defendant from being "taken advantage of." *See Miller*, 600 N.W.2d at 463 (quotation marks omitted).

An alternative interpretation of Rule 4.2 is that the state must obtain consent from the defendant's lawyer before engaging in any communication with the defendant, even when the defendant has requested contact with the police after being counseled against such contact and the defendant's lawyer is present. This interpretation is troubling in that it substantially infringes on a defendant's autonomy in favor of his lawyer's beliefs as to the defendant's best interests. *See* Carl A. Pierce, *Variations on a Basic Theme: Revisiting the ABA's Revision of Model Rule 4.2 (Part III)*, 70 TENN. L.REV. 643, 648 (2003) ("[T]he no-contact rule * * * is simply too paternalistic and does not accord sufficient respect for the client's autonomy or the client's freedom to speak without the prior consent of [his] lawyer."); John Leubsdorf, *Communicating with Another Lawyer's Client: The Lawyer's Veto and the Client's Interests*, 127 U. PA. L.REV. 683, 689 (1979) ("A legal system valuing informed personal choice should not assume that a client aided by his lawyer cannot make a sound decision whether to communicate with opposing counsel."). Such an infringement on personal autonomy is arguably unnecessary in the criminal law context, given the protections that the Constitution and case law provide to criminal defendants against government overreaching. As previously stated, these protections are entirely independent of Rule 4.2.

Notwithstanding the concerns set forth above, we conclude that when a government attorney is involved in a matter such that Minn. R. Prof. Conduct 4.2 applies, the state may not have any communication with a represented criminal defendant about the subject of the representation unless (1) the state first obtains the lawyer's consent; (2) the communication is "authorized by law" as discussed below; or (3) the state obtains a court order authorizing the communication. We reach our conclusion on the plain and unambiguous language of the rule as currently written.[10] Accordingly, to the extent that any of our past cases suggest that the state can meet the requirements of Rule 4.2 by providing the defendant's lawyer notice and an opportunity to be present, those cases are no longer good law.

Whether the State Violated Rule 4.2

With the foregoing principles in mind, we must now decide whether the state violated Rule 4.2 when officers Frazer and Doran conducted the post-arraignment interviews with Clark. There was no court order authorizing the interviews; accordingly, the state must establish either that Clark's lawyer consented to the interviews or that the interviews were authorized by law. The record contains no evidence that Clark's lawyer consented to the August 3 interview between Clark and the police. But the record is more ambiguous with respect to the second July 26 interview in light of testimony from Balck and Handley, as well as Clark's indication to Frazer and Doran that he had spoken to Handley and Handley was "pissed off." While this evidence could support an argument that Handley gave tacit consent for the interview, we conclude that tacit consent-even to the extent it existed here-is not sufficient to meet the requirements of Rule 4.2.

We also conclude that the post-arraignment interviews of Clark were not communications "authorized by law" for the purposes of Rule 4.2. The comments following Rule 4.2 provide examples of communications authorized by law, including

> communications by a lawyer on behalf of a client who is exercising a constitutional or other legal right to communicate with the government. Communications authorized by law may also include investigative activities of lawyers representing governmental entities, directly or through investigative agents, *prior to the commencement of criminal or civil enforcement proceedings.*

Minn. R. Prof. Conduct 4.2 cmt. 5 (emphasis added). There is no dispute in this case that the second July 26 interview and the August 3 interview took place after criminal proceedings were commenced against Clark. Further, we do not conclude that Clark was "exercising a constitutional or other legal right" when he communicated with the police during these

---

[10] We recognize that one undesirable consequence of our interpretation of Rule 4.2 may be that the police-in order to avoid a potential obstacle to admissibility of a statement under the Rule-will be less likely to obtain legal advice before proceeding to interview a represented defendant who has expressed the desire to speak with them. In light of this possible consequence and the other concerns we have articulated in this opinion, we invite a review by the appropriate committee(s) of Rule 4.2 as it relates to government lawyers' contact with represented criminal defendants.

interviews. Finally, we discern no other basis on which to conclude that the interviews in this case were authorized by law.

For all of the foregoing reasons, we conclude that the state violated Rule 4.2 by conducting the post-arraignment interviews with Clark.

Whether Suppression Is Warranted

Having concluded that the state violated Rule 4.2, we must determine whether the sanction that Clark seeks in this appeal-that is, suppression of the post-arraignment interview statements-is warranted. As a preliminary matter, we note that Rule 4.2 is a rule of professional conduct, not a constitutional or statutory provision. "The rules are designed to provide guidance to lawyers and to provide a structure for regulating conduct through disciplinary agencies." Minn. R. Prof. Conduct, Scope cmt. 20. Accordingly, a rule violation is "a basis for invoking the disciplinary process," id. cmt. 19, and "does not necessarily warrant any * * * nondisciplinary remedy," *Id.* cmt. 20.

Based on analogous principles underlying their own rules of professional conduct, "nearly every court that has ruled on [a no-contact rule violation in a criminal law context] has found that suppression of a [statement] is an inappropriate remedy for a lawyer's ethical violation." State v. McCarthy, 819 A.2d 335, 341 (Me.2003) (footnote omitted); *see, e.g.,* State v. Johnson, 318 N.W.2d 417, 437 (Iowa 1982) (concluding that suppression of a defendant's statements is not an appropriate remedy for the government's violation of the no-contact rule) . . . .

Unlike these jurisdictions, we have not adopted a per se rule placing suppression of defendant's statements outside the ambit of possible sanctions for a violation of Rule 4.2. Rather, we have taken a case-by-case approach to determining whether the state's conduct is so egregious as to compromise the fair administration of justice. *See* State v. Ford, 539 N.W.2d 214, 224–25 (Minn.1995). In cases where the state's conduct is sufficiently egregious, we may determine that suppression is warranted.

One such case is State v. Lefthand, 488 N.W.2d 799 (Minn.1992). We had not yet articulated the egregiousness standard when we decided *Lefthand*, a case that references Rule 4.2 indirectly in the broader context of constitutional protections against self-incrimination. *Id.* at 801 n.6. Nonetheless, we concluded that suppression of Lefthand's inculpatory statement was warranted regardless of his apparent waiver of constitutional protections given the circumstances under which the police obtained the statement. *Id.* at 801–02; *see also Ford*, 539 N.W.2d at 224 (noting that Lefthand was advised of and waived his constitutional rights). Specifically, the police interviewed Lefthand with permission from the prosecutor assigned to the case but without notification to the defendant's lawyer. *Lefthand*, 488 N.W.2d at 800. At the time of the interview, Lefthand, who had made his first court appearance in connection with two alleged homicides, was in custody pending a court-ordered Rule 20 mental competency examination. *Id.* We did not indicate in *Lefthand* how the interview came to occur, but we noted in a subsequent case that Lefthand initiated contact with the police. *Ford*, 539 N.W.2d at 224.

. . . .

[W]hen we consider all the evidence in the record, we do not perceive Balck's actions as evidencing the bad faith or blatant disregard of professional obligations that we have previously associated with the phrase "egregious conduct." . . . Balck tried to reach Clark's lawyer on August 2 and refused to allow a police interview to occur because Balck was unable to "get [a] message through." We see no basis to discount as unreliable Frazer's sworn testimony that after Balck made several unsuccessful attempts to reach Clark's lawyer on August 2, Balck told Frazer that "we're just going to have to wait until we get this thing ironed out" and "[i]t isn't going to happen today." Moreover, Frazer indicated that Balck expressed his intention that the state "take the high road" with respect to Clark's case. This intention is apparent in Balck's actions on July 27 and August 2, actions which indicate that he tried to meet Rule 4.2's requirements as he understood them.

. . . .

At a minimum, the record supports a conclusion that there was poor communication between both offices that may have led to frustration on both sides; this frustration may have led to Balck's lapse in judgment when he did not attempt to prevent the 9 p.m. interview on August 3. [W]e conclude that in light of all the testimony before the district court, Balck's failure to prevent the August 3 interview to proceed is more appropriately characterized as a lapse of professional judgment under frustrating circumstances [than a flagrant display of professional misconduct.]

. . . .

For all of the foregoing reasons, we conclude that the district court did not err when it denied Clark's motion to suppress the statements Clark made to the police during the post-arraignment interviews on July 26 and August 3.

* * *

Problem 22.2. Refer back to the Chapter Hypothetical. Is Gary subject to discipline under Model Rule 4.2? If so, should his violation result in a new trial?

Pre-arrest contact with represented persons. What about the situation in which a criminal suspect has not yet been arrested or arraigned, but has nonetheless hired a lawyer in connection with a criminal investigation? Can law enforcement agents, acting under the direction of a prosecutor, speak with the represented individual outside the presence of the individual's lawyer? Are such actions "authorized by law" under Rule 4.2?

Some states have attempted to provide clearer standards. For example, Utah's Rule 4.2(c) provides as follows:

A government lawyer engaged in a criminal or civil law enforcement matter, or a person acting under the lawyer's direction in the matter, may communicate with a person known to be represented by a lawyer if:

(c)(1) the communication is in the course of, and limited to, an investigation of a different matter unrelated to the representation or any ongoing, unlawful conduct; or

(c)(2) the communication is made to protect against an imminent risk of death or serious bodily harm or substantial property damage that the government lawyer reasonably believes may occur and the communication is limited to those matters necessary to protect against the imminent risk; or

(c)(3) the communication is made at the time of the arrest of the represented person and after that person is advised of the right to remain silent and the right to counsel and voluntarily and knowingly waives these rights; or

(c)(4) the communication is initiated by the represented person, directly or through an intermediary, if prior to the communication the represented person has given a written or recorded voluntary and informed waiver of counsel, including the right to have substitute counsel, for that communication.

Comment [11] explains:

Paragraph (c) of this Rule makes clear that this Rule does not prohibit all communications with represented persons by state or federal government lawyers (including law enforcement agents and cooperating witnesses acting at their direction) when the communications occur during the course of civil or criminal law enforcement. The exemptions for government lawyers contained in paragraph (c) of this Rule recognize the unique responsibilities of government lawyers to enforce public law. Nevertheless, where the lawyer is representing the government in any other role or litigation (such as a contract or tort claim, for example) the same rules apply to government lawyers as are applicable to lawyers for private parties.

* * *

b. Providing Exculpatory Evidence to the Defense

Please read Model Rules of Professional Conduct, Rule 3.8(d) and Comments [1] & [3].

BRADY V. MARYLAND
373 U.S. 83 (1963)

Opinion of the Court by MR. JUSTICE DOUGLAS, announced by MR. JUSTICE BRENNAN.

Petitioner and a companion, Boblit, were found guilty of murder in the first degree and were sentenced to death, their convictions being affirmed by the Court of Appeals of Maryland. Their trials were separate, petitioner being tried first. At his trial Brady took the stand and admitted his participation in the crime, but he claimed that Boblit did the actual killing. And, in his summation to the jury, Brady's counsel conceded that Brady was guilty of murder in the first degree, asking only that the jury return that verdict "without capital punishment." Prior to the trial petitioner's counsel had requested the prosecution to allow him to examine Boblit's extrajudicial statements. Several of those statements were shown to him; but one dated July 9, 1958, in which Boblit admitted the actual homicide, was withheld by the prosecution and did not come to petitioner's notice until after he had been tried, convicted, and sentenced, and after his conviction had been affirmed.

Petitioner moved the trial court for a new trial based on the newly discovered evidence that had been suppressed by the prosecution. Petitioner's appeal from a denial of that motion was dismissed by the Court of Appeals without prejudice to relief under the Maryland Post Conviction Procedure Act. The petition for post-conviction relief was dismissed by the trial court; and on appeal the Court of Appeals held that suppression of the evidence by the prosecution denied petitioner due process of law and remanded the case for a retrial of the question of punishment, not the question of guilt. The case is here on certiorari.

. . . .

We agree with the Court of Appeals that suppression of this confession was a violation of the Due Process Clause of the Fourteenth Amendment. The Court of Appeals relied in the main on two decisions from the Third Circuit Court of Appeals —United States ex rel. Almeida

v. Baldi, 195 F.2d 815, and United States ex rel. Thompson v. Dye, 221 F.2d 763—which, we agree, state the correct constitutional rule.

This ruling is an extension of Mooney v. Holohan, 294 U.S. 103, 112, where the Court ruled on what nondisclosure by a prosecutor violates due process:

> It is a requirement that cannot be deemed to be satisfied by mere notice and hearing if a state has contrived a conviction through the pretense of a trial which in truth is but used as a means of depriving a defendant of liberty through a deliberate deception of court and jury by the presentation of testimony known to be perjured. Such a contrivance by a state to procure the conviction and imprisonment of a defendant is as inconsistent with the rudimentary demands of justice as is the obtaining of a like result by intimidation.

In Pyle v. Kansas, 317 U.S. 213, 215–216 we phrased the rule in broader terms:

> Petitioner's papers are inexpertly drawn, but they do set forth allegations that his imprisonment resulted from perjured testimony, knowingly used by the State authorities to obtain his conviction, and from the deliberate suppression by those same authorities of evidence favorable to him. These allegations sufficiently charge a deprivation of rights guaranteed by the Federal Constitution, and, if proven, would entitle petitioner to release from his present custody. Mooney v. Holohan, 294 U.S. 103.

The Third Circuit in the *Baldi* case construed that statement in *Pyle v. Kansas* to mean that the "suppression of evidence favorable" to the accused was itself sufficient to amount to a denial of due process. 195 F.2d at 820. In Napue v. Illinois, 360 U.S. 264, 269, we extended the test formulated in *Mooney v. Holohan* when we said: "The same result obtains when the State, although not soliciting false evidence, allows it to go uncorrected when it appears." . . .

We now hold that the suppression by the prosecution of evidence favorable to an accused upon request violates due process where the evidence is material either to guilt or to punishment, irrespective of the good faith or bad faith of the prosecution.

The principle of *Mooney v. Holohan* is not punishment of society for misdeeds of a prosecutor but avoidance of an unfair trial to the accused. Society wins not only when the guilty are convicted but when criminal trials are fair; our system of the administration of justice suffers when any accused is treated unfairly. An inscription on the walls of the Department of Justice states the proposition candidly for the federal domain: "The United States wins its point whenever justice is done its citizens in the courts." A prosecution that withholds evidence on demand of an accused which, if made available, would tend to exculpate him or reduce the penalty helps shape a trial that bears heavily on the defendant. That casts the prosecutor in the role of an architect of a proceeding that does not comport with standards of justice, even though, as in the present case, his action is not "the result of guile," to use the words of the Court of Appeals.

* * *

Problem 22.3. Refer back to the Chapter Hypothetical. Has there been a violation of Cole's constitutional rights due to the failure to disclose the prosecution's deal with Ann? Is Ben subject to discipline under Model Rule 3.8(d)?

Extending *Brady* to law enforcement. Subsequent decisions have established that a prosecutor has a duty under *Brady* to disclose not only evidence that the prosecutor personally knows of, but also "any favorable evidence known to the others acting on the government's behalf in the case, including the police." Kyles v. Whitley, 514 U.S. 419, 437 (1995).

***Brady* vs. Model Rule 3.8(d).** *Brady* held "that the suppression by the prosecution of evidence favorable to an accused upon request violates due process where the evidence is material either to guilt or to punishment." Note the way in which Rule 3.8(d) departs from the *Brady* standard in this regard. Read Rule 3.8(d) carefully and note other ways in which the ethical rule differs from the constitutional rule.

Problem 22.4. Assistant district attorney Ben is scheduled to appear at a preliminary hearing in order to determine whether sufficient evidence exists in a domestic violence case to bring the case to trial. While examining the file, Ben finds a recent statement by the victim that incriminates the defendant but is somewhat inconsistent with her earlier statements in terms of the details of the incident. Objectively, there is still more than enough evidence to warrant a trial, despite the inconsistency. Ben decides not to disclose the statement to defense counsel until after the preliminary hearing, reasoning that the statement is not "material" under *Brady* since it would almost certainly have not altered the outcome of the preliminary hearing. Ben discloses the statement to defense counsel a few days after the preliminary hearing. Did Ben comply with his obligations under *Brady*? Under Rule 3.8(d)?

Remedies for *Brady* violations. Refer back to the Chapter Hypothetical in which Edward's office failed to turn over exculpatory DNA evidence concerning Francis. If Francis were to sue Edward or his office, would she be able to recover? As *Brady* itself illustrates, a prosecutor's failure to disclose exculpatory evidence material to guilt or to punishment may result in a conviction being overturned. In theory, a criminal defendant might also have a claim under 42 U.S.C. § 1983 for violation of his constitutional rights. However, a § 1983 plaintiff faces a number of fairly substantial obstacles to recovery. *See* Heck v. Humphrey, 512 U.S. 477 (1994) (holding that a § 1983 plaintiff may not recover unless the conviction or sentence has been overturned); Imbler v. Pachtman, 424 U.S. 409 (1976) (holding that prosecutors are entitled to absolute immunity for claims stemming from the performance of the advocacy function of the prosecutor); Villasana v. Wilhoit, 368 F.3d 976 (8th Cir. 2004) (concluding that the absolute immunity described in *Imbler* applies to claims based a trial prosecutor's *Brady* violation). The Supreme Court has also limited the ability of plaintiffs to recover from district attorneys who supervise the prosecutors who fail to turn over *Brady* material, as well as from the district attorney's office itself. *See* Van de Kamp v. Goldstein, 555 U.S. 335 (2009) (concluding that supervising prosecutor is absolutely immune from § 1983 liability based on improper supervision or training); Connick v. Thompson, 131 S.Ct. 1350 (2011) (holding that municipality could not be held liable based upon D.A. office's policy of not training prosecutors on their *Brady* obligations since the resulting failure to disclose exculpatory evidence was not so obviously a consequence of the failure as to amount to deliberate indifference on the part of the D.A.'s office).

* * *

2. SUBPOENAS TO LAWYERS

Please read Model Rules of Professional Conduct, Rule 3.8(e) and Comment [4].

* * *

The purpose of Model Rule 3.8(e). In light of the fact that lawyers owe their clients a duty of confidentiality that would generally prevent them from testifying about client communications, what is the concern with permitting a prosecutor to subpoena a criminal defense lawyer to provide grand jury testimony concerning a client?

* * *

D. FILING CRIMINAL CHARGES AND NEGOTIATING PLEAS

Please read ABA Model Rules of Professional Conduct, Rule 3.8(a) and Comment [1].

The disciplinary standard of "probable cause" contained in Model Rule 3.8(a) parallels the constitutional requirement that a prosecutor must have probable cause to believe that the accused committed the charged offense. Bordenkircher v. Hayes, 434 U.S. 357, 363 (1978). This standard does not require probable cause to believe that a conviction can be attained, just probable cause to believe the defendant, in fact, committed the crime. Given the relatively low threshold established by the probable cause standard, disciplinary action under Rule 3.8(a) is uncommon. *But see* Iowa Supreme Court Attorney Disciplinary Bd. v. Howe, 706 N.W.2d 360 (Iowa 2005) (suspending prosecutor from the practice of law for, *inter alia*, charging individuals with violation of obsolete traffic ordinance requiring drivers to have at least two cowl lamps [which were common on the Ford Model A in the 1920s] affixed to their vehicles). In contrast, the ABA Prosecution Function Standards also provide that a prosecutor should not bring criminal charges "in the absence of sufficient admissible evidence to support a conviction." Standard 3–3.9(a).

Selective prosecution. What about the case where a prosecutor engages in selective prosecution against an individual or group of individuals? The prosecutor in that case may have probable cause or sufficient admissible evidence to support a conviction, but the prosecutor only chooses to initiate proceedings against an individual or group, while ignoring violations committed by others. In Oylder v. Boles, 368 U.S. 448, 456 (1962), the Supreme Court rejected the argument that "the conscious exercise of some selectivity" is by itself a violation of the equal protection component of the Due Process Clause of the Constitution. However, when the decision is based on "an unjustifiable standard such as race, religion, or other arbitrary classification," there is a violation.

Prosecutors' liability resulting from initiation of charges. What remedy does a criminal defendant have against a prosecutor if the prosecutor lacked probable cause to bring charges against the defendant, or (worse still) the prosecutor framed the defendant? In theory, a tort claim of malicious prosecution might be one possibility. However, a public prosecutor enjoys absolute immunity in such cases, provided the prosecutor acts in his or her official capacity. Restatement (Second) of Torts § 656. Another possibility might be a constitutional tort claim under 42 U.S.C. § 1983. However, as alluded to above in conjunction with the *Brady* decision, prosecutors had long enjoyed absolute immunity in § 1983 actions for their actions occurring *during* trial. This includes knowingly presenting false evidence at trial. *See* Imbler v. Pachtman, 424 US 409 (1976). However, there is currently a circuit split on the question of whether prosecutors who *prepare* false evidence prior to trial are also entitled to immunity. *Compare* Michaels v. New Jersey, 222 F.3d 118 (3d Cir. 2000) (yes) *with* McGhee v. Pottawattamie Cnty., 547 F.3d 922 (8th Cir. 2008) (no). Why should prosecutors have immunity for actions occurring during trial?

* * *

E. TRIAL PUBLICITY

Please read ABA Rules of Professional Conduct, Rule 3.6; and Rule 3.8(f) and Comments [5] & [6].

As comment [1] to ABA Model Rule 3.6 notes, the rules regarding trial publicity attempt to balance several competing policy interests. Some lawyers believe that the duty of competent and diligent representation may require them to make public statements on behalf of their clients. In addition, the public has a legitimate interest in receiving information concerning the judicial process, particularly where the criminal law is concerned. On the other hand, there is an equally strong interest in preserving fairness in the trial process, again, particularly in the criminal context. Model Rule 3.6 applies to all lawyers, but Rule 3.6 and 3.8(f) note special concerns associated with trial publicity generated by a prosecutor.

* * *

Problem 22.5. Refer back to the Chapter Hypothetical. Is Denise subject to discipline for her statements to the press? Is Ben?

Problem 22.6. Below are three statements made by lawyers involved in the investigation or litigation of criminal matters. The first two are by a district attorney during press conferences. Has the district attorney violated Rules 3.6 and/or 3.8(f)? The third is by a defense lawyer. Does Rule 3.6 permit the defense lawyer to make the statement?

(1) At a press conference announcing that police were going to charge a suspect with murder, the district attorney stated the suspect had confessed to the murder and had "provided incredible details that only the murderer would have known."

(2) At another press conference announcing that a different individual, Mr. Lucas, had just been charged with a different murder, the district attorney announced that the police "had been able to determine definitively that indeed it was Mr. Lucas who had committed the crime."

(3) In response to the widespread publicity generated by the prosecutor's statement in number (2) above, Mr. Lucas' lawyer tells a reporter that he is confident that the results from a recent DNA test will exonerate his client.

The *Gentile* decision. In Gentile v. State Bar, 501 U.S. 1030 (1991), the United States Supreme Court held that, as a constitutional matter, a state need not demonstrate that extrajudicial statements by a lawyer during the pendency of a trial present a "clear and present danger" of prejudice to the trial before they may be restricted. Instead, given the heightened dangers associated with extrajudicial statements occurring during the pendency of a trial, states may constitutionally prohibit statements having a substantial likelihood of prejudicing the proceeding. ABA Model Rule 3.6 now reflects this standard.

Public condemnation. What concern underlies Model Rule 3.8(f)'s prohibition on statements by a prosecutor that heighten public condemnation of the accused?

* * *

F. NEWLY-DISCOVERED EVIDENCE

Please read ABA Rules of Professional Conduct, Rule 3.8(g) & (h).

What do you think? Why are prosecutors (but not other lawyers) subject to the special requirements of Model Rules 3.8(g) and (h)?

* * *

G. CONSTITUTIONALLY INEFFECTIVE ASSISTANCE OF COUNSEL

Allegations of lawyer incompetence may arise as convicted felons seek to have their convictions overturned because of their counsel's alleged ineffective assistance during their trial or sentencing. These claims are based on the Sixth Amendment right to counsel and the Supreme Court's holdings that the right to counsel is the right to the *effective* assistance of counsel. The issue can also arise under similar provisions of state constitutions.

The Supreme Court established the legal principles that govern claims of ineffective assistance of counsel in Strickland v. Washington, 466 U.S. 668 (1984). There are two components to such a claim. First a petitioner must show that defense counsel's performance was deficient. To establish deficient performance, a petitioner must demonstrate that counsel's representation "fell below an objective standard of reasonableness," as measured under prevailing professional norms. Next, the petitioner must show that the deficiency prejudiced the defense. To establish prejudice, a "defendant must show that there is a reasonable probability that, but for counsel's unprofessional errors, the result of the proceeding would have been different. A reasonable probability is a probability sufficient to undermine confidence in the outcome."

For example, in Wiggins v. Smith, 539 U.S. 510 (2003), the Court considered the petitioner's claim that his attorneys' failure to investigate his background and present mitigating evidence of his horrific life history dating back to childhood at his capital sentencing proceedings violated his

Sixth Amendment right to counsel. The trial court judge observed "that he could not remember a capital case in which counsel had not compiled a social history of the defendant, explaining, '[n]ot to do a social history, at least to see what you have got, to me is absolute error. I just—I would be flabbergasted if the Court of Appeals said anything else.' " Nonetheless, both the trial court and the Maryland Court of Appeals denied the petition for post-conviction relief, concluding that "when the decision not to investigate ... is a matter of trial tactics, there is no ineffective assistance of counsel." The Supreme Court disagreed:

> [S]tandard practice in Maryland in capital cases at the time of Wiggins' trial included the preparation of a social history report. ... Despite the fact that the Public Defender's office made funds available for the retention of a forensic social worker, counsel chose not to commission such a report. ... Counsel's conduct similarly fell short of the standards for capital defense work articulated by the American Bar Association (ABA)—standards to which we long have referred as "guides to determining what is reasonable." ... The ABA Guidelines provide that investigations into mitigating evidence "should comprise efforts to discover *all reasonably available* mitigating evidence and evidence to rebut any aggravating evidence that may be introduced by the prosecutor." ... Despite these well-defined norms, however, counsel abandoned their investigation of petitioner's background after having acquired only rudimentary knowledge of his history from a narrow set of sources.

In addition, the Court found that "[g]iven both the nature and the extent of the abuse petitioner suffered,"—which included physical torment, sexual molestation, and repeated rape during his childhood— there was "a reasonable probability that a competent attorney, aware of this history, would have introduced it at sentencing in an admissible form" and that the jury would have returned with a lesser sentence.

* * *

Profile of attorney professionalism. Norm Maleng served as Prosecutor for King County, Washington, for 28 years. In that capacity, he created Washington's first Special Assault Unit, which "became a national leader in developing innovative techniques to make the criminal-justice system more humane and less terrifying to vulnerable victims." Judge Robert S. Lasnik & David Boerner, *The Legacy of Norm Maleng*, 84 Wash. L. Rev. 3, 5 (2009).

According to a judge, "Although he was the lawyer for county government and its elected officials, Norm never lost sight of the fact that he and his deputies represented the people of King County. If elected officials violated that trust, they could not expect the King County Prosecutor to cover up or defend that dereliction of duty. Norm Maleng's client was always the people of his community." *Id.* at 7.

Maleng became a state and national leader in prosecutorial circles. But he is probably most famous for his actions with respect to the death penalty. As a prosecutor, Maleng sought the death penalty. However, "he never delegated these decisions, recognizing that the people had entrusted this responsibility to him personally. He approached each case knowing that his responsibility was to arrive at a just decision, sensitive to the victim, the community, and the defendant." *Id.* at 9–10.

Maleng oversaw the prosecution of the Green River Killer, a serial killer in Washington and California who pled guilty to the murders of 49 women. Maleng chose not to seek the death penalty in the case "in return for a plea of guilty and the killer's cooperation in recovering bodies and closing cases where families were unsure what had happened to their loved ones." *Id.* at 10. Reflecting upon Maleng's death years later, a judge made the following observation:

Dr. Martin Luther King, another of Norm's personal heroes, once observed:

> On some positions, cowardice asks the question, Is it expedient? And then expedience comes along and asks the question, Is it politic? Vanity asks the question, Is it popular? Conscience asks the question, Is it right? There comes a time when one must take the position that is neither safe nor politic nor popular, but he must do it because conscience tells him it is right.

His decision on the Green River case was not safe, politic, or popular. But once Norm determined that the decision was right, he had all he needed to go forward.

Norm was respected by all, and he was loved by many. Love is not an emotion one commonly associates with a prosecutor, but Norm's unique nature earned him this love. In Justice Jackson's words, he tempered zeal with kindness, sought truth and not victims, served the law and not factions. He exercised the power the people gave him with humility and wisdom. Norm's legacy lives in all of us he inspired.

Id.

CHAPTER 23

LAWYERS AND JUDGES

■ ■ ■

Chapter hypothetical. The Francois Federation of Teachers, which represents public school teachers in Francois, New Dakota, recently went on strike. The Francois School Board obtained a temporary injunction prohibiting continuance of the strike. Despite this, the teachers continued their strike, prompting the board to file a motion seeking to hold the union in contempt. Judge Reinhold was assigned the case and found the union in contempt. Prior to the contempt hearing, the union's lawyer, Claude, made a motion in court seeking Judge Reinhold's recusal on three grounds. First, Claude alleged recusal was required because, prior to being appointed to the bench three years ago, Reinhold had represented the School Board in another matter. Second, two months earlier (before Francois teachers went on strike), Judge Reinhold had given a speech to newly admitted lawyers in which he referenced a similar strike taking place in another state and opined that the teachers were behaving in a "lawless and uneducated" manner and that public employees should never strike. Third, Claude alleged recusal was required because a year earlier, Claude had been quoted in the local newspaper as saying that Judge Reinhold's elevation to the bench had been a "disaster for the working people in this State since everyone knows the judge is in the pocket of management and lacks any common sense." In addition, several months ago, Claude had filed an ethics complaint against Judge Reinhold that is still pending with the New Dakota Judicial Conduct Commission. The Francois Federation of Teachers has now appealed Judge Reinhold's contempt finding on the grounds that the judge erred in denying their motion for recusal.

* * *

A. CRITICIZING JUDGES

Please read ABA Model Rules of Professional Conduct, Rule 8.2(a) and Comments [1] & [3].

* * *

STANDING COMMITTEE ON DISCIPLINE V. YAGMAN
55 F.3d 1430 (9th Cir. 1995)

KOZINSKI, CIRCUIT JUDGE.

Never far from the center of controversy, outspoken civil rights lawyer Stephen Yagman was suspended from practice before the United States District Court for the Central District of California for impugning the integrity of the court and interfering with the random selection of judges by making disparaging remarks about a judge of that court. We confront several new issues in reviewing this suspension order.

I

The convoluted history of this case begins in 1991 when Yagman filed a lawsuit pro se against several insurance companies. The case was assigned to Judge Manuel Real, then Chief Judge of the Central District. Yagman promptly sought to disqualify Judge Real on grounds of bias.[1] The disqualification motion was randomly assigned to Judge William Keller, who denied it . . . and sanctioned Yagman for pursuing the matter in an "improper and frivolous manner."[2]

A few days after Judge Keller's sanctions order, Yagman was quoted as saying that Judge Keller "has a penchant for sanctioning Jewish lawyers: me, David Kenner and Hugh Manes. I find this to be evidence of anti-semitism." Susan Seager, *Judge Sanctions Yagman, Refers Case to State Bar*, L.A. DAILY J., June 6, 1991, at 1. The district court found that Yagman also told the *Daily Journal* reporter that Judge Keller was "drunk on the bench," although this accusation wasn't published in the article. . . .

Around this time, Yagman received a request from Prentice Hall, publisher of the much-fretted-about *Almanac of the Federal Judiciary*,[3]

---

[1] As the basis for this claim, Yagman cited an earlier case where Judge Real had granted a directed verdict against Yagman's clients and thereafter sanctioned Yagman personally in the amount of $250,000. . . .

[2] The sanctions order harshly reprimanded Yagman, stating that "neither monetary sanctions nor suspension appear to be effective in deterring Yagman's pestiferous conduct" . . . and recommended that he be "disciplined appropriately" by the California State Bar. On appeal, we affirmed as to disqualification but reversed as to sanctions. Yagman v. Republic Ins., 987 F.2d 622 (9th Cir. 1993).

[3] The *Almanac* is a loose-leaf service consisting of profiles of federal judges. Each profile covers the judge's educational and professional background, noteworthy rulings, and anecdotal items of interest. One section—which many judges pretend to ignore but in fact read

for comments in connection with a profile of Judge Keller. Yagman's response was less than complimentary.[4]

A few weeks later, Yagman placed an advertisement (on the stationary of his law firm) in the *L.A. Daily Journal*, asking lawyers who had been sanctioned by Judge Keller to contact Yagman's office.

Soon after these events, Yagman ran into Robert Steinberg, another attorney who practices in the Central District. According to Steinberg, Yagman told him that, by levelling public criticism at Judge Keller, Yagman hoped to get the judge to recuse himself in future cases. Believing that Yagman was committing misconduct, Steinberg described his conversation with Yagman in a letter to the Standing Committee on Discipline of the U.S. District Court for the Central District of California (the Standing Committee). . . .

A few weeks later, the Standing Committee received a letter from Judge Keller describing Yagman's anti-Semitism charge, his inflammatory statements to Prentice Hall and the newspaper advertisement placed by Yagman's law firm. Judge Keller stated that "Mr. Yagman's campaign of harassment and intimidation challenges the integrity of the judicial system. Moreover, there is clear evidence that Mr. Yagman's attacks upon me are motivated by his desire to create a basis for recusing me in any future proceeding." . . . Judge Keller suggested that "[t]he Standing Committee on Discipline should take action to protect the Court from further abuse." . . .

After investigating the charges in the two letters, the Standing Committee issued a Petition for Issuance of an Order to Show Cause why Yagman should not be suspended from practice or otherwise disciplined. . . . [T]he matter was then assigned to a panel of three Central District judges, which issued an Order to Show Cause and scheduled a hearing. Prior to the hearing, Yagman raised serious First Amendment objections to being disciplined for criticizing Judge Keller. . . .

     . . . .

---

assiduously—is styled "Lawyers' Evaluation." Perhaps because the comments are published anonymously, they sometimes contain criticism more pungent than judges are accustomed to. . . .

   [4] The portion of the letter relevant here reads as follows:

     . . . It is an understatement to characterize the Judge as "the worst judge in the central district." It would be fairer to say that he is ignorant, dishonest, ill-tempered, and a bully, and probably is one of the worst judges in the United States. If television cameras ever were permitted in his courtroom, the other federal judges in the Country would be so embarrassed by this buffoon that they would run for cover. One might believe that some of the reason for this sub-standard human is the recent acrimonious divorce through which he recently went: but talking to attorneys who knew him years ago indicates that, if anything, he has mellowed. One other comment: his girlfriend . . . , like the Judge, is a right-wing fanatic.

III

Local Rule 2.5.2 contains two separate prohibitions. First, it enjoins attorneys from engaging in any conduct that "degrades or impugns the integrity of the Court." Second, it provides that "[n]o attorney shall engage in any conduct which . . . interferes with the administration of justice." The district court concluded that Yagman violated both prongs of the rule. . . . Because different First Amendment standards apply to these two provisions, we discuss the propriety of the sanction under each of them separately.

A

1.   We begin with the portion of Local Rule 2.5.2 prohibiting any conduct that "impugns the integrity of the Court." As the district court recognized, this provision is overbroad because it purports to punish a great deal of constitutionally protected speech, including all true statements reflecting adversely on the reputation or character of federal judges. A substantially overbroad restriction on protected speech will be declared facially invalid unless it is "fairly subject to a limiting construction."

To save the "impugn the integrity" portion of Rule 2.5.2, the district court read into it an "objective" version of the malice standard enunciated in New York Times Co. v. Sullivan, 376 U.S. 254 (1964). Relying on United States Dist. Ct. v. Sandlin, 12 F.3d 861 (9th Cir. 1993), the court limited Rule 2.5.2 to prohibit only false statements made with either knowledge of their falsity or with reckless disregard as to their truth or falsity, judged from the standpoint of a "reasonable attorney." . . .

[In] *Sandlin* . . . we held that the purely subjective standard applicable in defamation cases is not suited to attorney disciplinary proceedings. . . . Instead, we held that such proceedings are governed by an objective standard, pursuant to which the court must determine "what the reasonable attorney, considered in light of all his professional functions, would do in the same or similar circumstances." . . . The inquiry focuses on whether the attorney had a reasonable factual basis for making the statements, considering their nature and the context in which they were made.[13]

. . . In *Sandlin*, we held that there are significant differences between the interests served by defamation law and those served by rules of professional ethics. Defamation actions seek to remedy an essentially

---

[13] This inquiry may take into account whether the attorney pursued readily available avenues of investigation. Sandlin, for example, wrongfully accused a district judge of ordering his court reporter to alter the transcript of court proceedings. Though the judge had agreed to let the reporter be deposed, Sandlin didn't wait to see what the deposition would disclose before making his accusation. Sandlin thus lacked a reasonable factual basis for his accusation because he failed to pursue readily available means of verifying his charge of criminal wrongdoing. . . .

private wrong by compensating individuals for harm caused to their reputation and standing in the community. Ethical rules that prohibit false statements impugning the integrity of judges, by contrast, are not designed to shield judges from unpleasant or offensive criticism, but to preserve public confidence in the fairness and impartiality of our system of justice. . . .

. . . *Sandlin* held that an objective malice standard strikes a constitutionally permissible balance between an attorney's right to criticize the judiciary and the public's interest in preserving confidence in the judicial system: Lawyers may freely voice criticisms supported by a reasonable factual basis even if they turn out to be mistaken.

Attorneys who make statements impugning the integrity of a judge are, however, entitled to other First Amendment protections applicable in the defamation context. To begin with, attorneys may be sanctioned for impugning the integrity of a judge or the court only if their statements are false; truth is an absolute defense. Moreover, the disciplinary body bears the burden of proving falsity.

It follows that statements impugning the integrity of a judge may not be punished unless they are capable of being proved true or false; statements of opinion are protected by the First Amendment unless they "imply a false assertion of fact." Even statements that at first blush appear to be factual are protected by the First Amendment if they cannot reasonably be interpreted as stating actual facts about their target. Thus, statements of "rhetorical hyperbole" aren't sanctionable, nor are statements that use language in a "loose, figurative sense."

With these principles in mind, we examine the statements for which Yagman was disciplined.

2.   We first consider Yagman's statement in the *Daily Journal* that Judge Keller "has a penchant for sanctioning Jewish lawyers: me, David Kenner and Hugh Manes. I find this to be evidence of anti-semitism." Though the district court viewed this entirely as an assertion of fact, . . . we conclude that the statement contains both an assertion of fact and an expression of opinion.

Yagman's claim that he, Kenner and Manes are all Jewish and were sanctioned by Judge Keller is clearly a factual assertion: The words have specific, well-defined meanings and describe objectively verifiable matters. . . . Thus, had the Standing Committee proved that Yagman, Kenner or Manes were not sanctioned by Judge Keller, or were not Jewish, this assertion might have formed the basis for discipline. The committee, however, didn't claim that Yagman's factual assertion was false, and the district court made no finding to that effect. We proceed, therefore, on the assumption that this portion of Yagman's statement is true.

The remaining portion of Yagman's *Daily Journal* statement is best characterized as opinion; it conveys Yagman's personal belief that Judge Keller is anti-Semitic. As such, it may be the basis for sanctions only if it could reasonably be understood as declaring or implying actual facts capable of being proved true or false. . . .

In applying this principle, we are guided by section 566 of the Restatement (Second) of Torts, which distinguishes between two kinds of opinion statements: those based on assumed or expressly stated facts, and those based on implied, undisclosed facts. . . .

. . . .

A statement of opinion based on fully disclosed facts can be punished only if the stated facts are themselves false and demeaning. The rationale behind this rule is straightforward: When the facts underlying a statement of opinion are disclosed, readers will understand they are getting the author's interpretation of the facts presented; they are therefore unlikely to construe the statement as insinuating the existence of additional, undisclosed facts. Moreover, "an opinion which is unfounded reveals its lack of merit when the opinion-holder discloses the factual basis for the idea"; readers are free to accept or reject the author's opinion based on their own independent evaluation of the facts. A statement of opinion of this sort doesn't "imply a false assertion of fact," . . . and is thus entitled to full constitutional protection.

. . . .

Yagman's *Daily Journal* remark is protected by the First Amendment as an expression of opinion based on stated facts. . . . Yagman disclosed the basis for his view that Judge Keller is anti-Semitic and has a penchant for sanctioning Jewish lawyers: that he, Kenner and Manes are all Jewish and had been sanctioned by Judge Keller. The statement did not imply the existence of additional, undisclosed facts; it was carefully phrased in terms of an inference drawn from the facts specified rather than a bald accusation of bias against Jews. Readers were "free to form another, perhaps contradictory opinion from the same facts," . . . as no doubt they did.

3.   The district court also disciplined Yagman for alleging that Judge Keller was "dishonest." This remark appears in the letter Yagman sent to Prentice Hall in connection with the profile of Judge Keller in the *Almanac of the Federal Judiciary*. The court concluded that this allegation was sanctionable because it "plainly impl[ies] past improprieties." . . . Had Yagman accused Judge Keller of taking bribes, we would agree with the district court. Statements that "could reasonably be understood as imputing specific criminal or other wrongful acts" are

not entitled to constitutional protection merely because they are phrased in the form of an opinion. . . .

When considered in context, however, Yagman's statement cannot reasonably be interpreted as accusing Judge Keller of criminal misconduct. The term "dishonest" was one in a string of colorful adjectives Yagman used to convey the low esteem in which he held Judge Keller. The other terms he used—"ignorant," "ill-tempered," "buffoon," "sub-standard human," "right-wing fanatic," "a bully," "one of the worst judges in the United States"—all speak to competence and temperament rather than corruption; together they convey nothing more substantive than Yagman's contempt for Judge Keller. Viewed in context . . . , the word "dishonest" cannot reasonably be construed as suggesting that Judge Keller had committed specific illegal acts. . . . Yagman's remarks are thus statements of rhetorical hyperbole, incapable of being proved true or false. *Cf.* In re Erdmann, 33 N.Y.2d 559, 347 N.Y.S.2d 441, 441, 301 N.E.2d 426, 427 (1973) (reversing sanction against attorney who criticized trial judges for not following the law, and appellate judges for being "the whores who became madams"); State Bar v. Semaan, 508 S.W.2d 429, 431–32 (Tex. Civ. App. 1974) (attorney's observation that judge was "a midget among giants" not sanctionable because it wasn't subject to being proved true or false).

Were we to find any substantive content in Yagman's use of the term "dishonest," we would, at most, construe it to mean "intellectually dishonest"—an accusation that Judge Keller's rulings were overly result-oriented. Intellectual dishonesty is a label lawyers frequently attach to decisions with which they disagree. An allegation that a judge is intellectually dishonest, however, cannot be proved true or false by reference to a "core of objective evidence." Because Yagman's allegation of "dishonesty" does not imply facts capable of objective verification, it is constitutionally immune from sanctions.

4. Finally, the district court found sanctionable Yagman's allegation that Judge Keller was "drunk on the bench." Yagman contends that, like many of the terms he used in his letter to Prentice Hall, this phrase should be viewed as mere "rhetorical hyperbole." The statement wasn't a part of the string of invective in the Prentice Hall letter, however; it was a remark Yagman allegedly made to a newspaper reporter. Yagman identifies nothing relating to the context in which this statement was made that tends to negate the literal meaning of the words he used. We therefore conclude that Yagman's "drunk on the bench" statement could reasonably be interpreted as suggesting that Judge Keller had actually, on at least one occasion, taken the bench while intoxicated. Unlike Yagman's remarks in his letter to Prentice Hall, this statement implies actual facts that are capable of objective verification. For this reason, the statement isn't protected under [prior cases].

For Yagman's "drunk on the bench" allegation to serve as the basis for sanctions, however, the Standing Committee had to prove that the statement was false. . . . This it failed to do; indeed, the committee introduced no evidence at all on the point. . . . By presuming falsity, the district court unconstitutionally relieved the Standing Committee of its duty to produce evidence on an element of its case. Without proof of falsity, Yagman's "drunk on the bench" allegation, like the statements discussed above, cannot support the imposition of sanctions for impugning the integrity of the court. . . .

B

As an alternative basis for sanctioning Yagman, the district court concluded that Yagman's statements violated Local Rule 2.5.2's prohibition against engaging in conduct that "interferes with the administration of justice." The court found that Yagman made the statements discussed above in an attempt to "judge-shop"—i.e., to cause Judge Keller to recuse himself in cases where Yagman appeared as counsel.

[The court observed that the Supreme Court had held in the context of pending litigation that, in order to justify a restriction on lawyer free speech, the government must merely establish that the speech poses a "substantial likelihood" of prejudicing the proceedings. Gentile v. State Bar of Nevada, 501 U.S. 1030, 1074–75 (1991). Where, however, no case is pending before a court, the Court had held that a state must satisfy the more demanding standard of showing that the restricted speech poses a "clear and present danger" to the administration of justice.]

The district court found that Yagman's statements interfered with the administration of justice because they were aimed at forcing Judge Keller to recuse himself in cases where Yagman appears as counsel. Judge-shopping doubtless disrupts the proper functioning of the judicial system and may be disciplined. But after conducting an independent examination of the record, . . . we conclude that the sanction imposed here cannot stand.

Yagman's criticism of Judge Keller was harsh and intemperate, and in no way to be condoned. It has long been established, however, that a party cannot force a judge to recuse himself by engaging in personal attacks on the judge: "Nor can that artifice prevail, which insinuates that the decision of this court will be the effect of personal resentment; for, if it could, every man could evade the punishment due to his offences, by first pouring a torrent of abuse upon his judges, and then asserting that they act from passion. . . ." Respublica v. Oswald, 1 U.S. (1 Dall.) 319, 326, 1 L. Ed. 155 (Pa. 1788). Modern courts continue to adhere to this view, and with good reason. . . .

Criticism from a party's attorney creates an even remoter danger that a judge will disqualify himself because the federal recusal statutes, in all but the most extreme circumstances, require a showing that the judge is (or appears to be) biased or prejudiced against a party, not counsel. . . .

Notwithstanding this well-settled rule, judges occasionally do remove themselves voluntarily from cases as a result of harsh criticism from attorneys. As the district court recognized, then, a lawyer's vociferous criticism of a judge could interfere with the random assignment of judges. But a mere possibility—or even the probability—of harm does not amount to a clear and present danger. . . .

. . . Public criticism of judges and the decisions they make is not unusual, . . . yet this seldom leads to judicial recusal. Federal judges are well aware that "[s]ervice as a public official means that one may not be viewed favorably by every member of the public," and that they've been granted "the extraordinary protections of life tenure to shield them from such pressures." Because Yagman's statements do not pose a clear and present danger to the proper functioning of the courts, we conclude that the district court erred in sanctioning Yagman for interfering with the administration of justice.

Conclusion

We can't improve on the words of Justice Black in *Bridges*, 314 U.S. at 270–71:

> The assumption that respect for the judiciary can be won by shielding judges from published criticism wrongly appraises the character of American public opinion. For it is a prized American privilege to speak one's mind, although not always with perfect good taste, on all public institutions. And an enforced silence, however limited, solely in the name of preserving the dignity of the bench, would probably engender resentment, suspicion, and contempt much more than it would enhance respect.

REVERSED.

* * *

Actual malice and the disciplinary process. The court in *Yagman* wrestled with the question of whether the standards articulated by the Supreme Court in cases dealing with the applicability of the First Amendment to state law defamation claims are applicable to the lawyer disciplinary process. In New York Times Co. v. Sullivan, 376 U.S. 254 (1964), the Supreme Court held that the free speech clause of the First Amendment prohibits a public official from recovering damages in a defamation action relating to his public conduct unless he proves that the defamatory statement was made with "actual malice," i.e., knowledge that the statement was false or that it was made with reckless disregard as to its truth or falsity. Other constitutional rules (such as the rules mentioned in *Yagman* concerning burdens of proof and when statements of opinion or statements involving rhetorical hyperbole are actionable) soon developed and were incorporated into disciplinary decisions involving criticism of judges. But it is *Sullivan*'s "actual malice" standard that has proven most troublesome in the disciplinary context.

Model Rule 8.2(a) addresses a lawyer's criticism of a judge and utilizes *Sullivan*'s language regarding knowledge of falsity or reckless disregard as to falsity. But what does that phrase mean? In *Sullivan* and subsequent cases, the Supreme Court clarified that one acts with "reckless disregard" when one entertains serious doubts as to a statement's truth. This is a subjective standard. The speaker must actually entertain such doubts, regardless of whether a reasonable person under the same circumstances would have entertained such doubts. Some courts have interpreted their jurisdictions' versions of Rule 8.2(a) in this manner. In re Green, 11 P.3d 1078 (Colo. 2000); Restatement (Third) of the Law Governing Lawyers § 114 (2000); *see* State ex rel. Okla. Bar Ass'n v. Porter, 766 P.2d 958, 969 (Okla. 1988) (stating that government officials must be subjected to the stringent requirements of *New York Times Co. v. Sullivan* and its progeny). The majority of courts—for reasons similar to those expressed in *Yagman*—have utilized the *Yagman* approach and adopted an objective formulation of *Sullivan*'s "actual malice" standard for use in the disciplinary process. *See, e.g.*, In re Cobb, 838 N.E.2d 1197 (Mass. 2005); Florida Bar v. Ray, 797 So.2d 556 (Fla. 2001). The comments to Rule 8.2 shed no light on the proper interpretation of the language.

* * *

Problem 23.1. Refer back to the Chapter Hypothetical. Is Claude subject to discipline for his statements in the newspaper concerning Judge Reinhold?

* * *

Civility. Although the case hinged on the truth or falsity of the statements in question, *Yagman* involved a local rule of the court prohibiting conduct that "impugns the dignity of the Court." Some states have similar rules of professional conduct. *See* Grievance Adm'r v. Fieger, 719 N.W.2d 123 (Mich. 2006) (upholding discipline under a rule prohibiting undignified or discourteous conduct toward a tribunal where an attorney made crude comments about members of the Michigan Court of Appeals while appearing on a radio show).

Lawyer bias as grounds for recusal. In *Yagman*, the court noted "the federal recusal statutes, in all but the most extreme circumstances, require a showing that the judge is (or appears to be) biased or prejudiced against a party, not counsel." Indeed, 28 U.S.C. § 455, the recusal statute governing federal judges, does not list a judge's bias against a party's lawyer as a basis for recusal. Part B below explores the issue of judicial recusal in detail. However, it is worth mentioning that Rule 2.11(A)(1) of the ABA's Code of Judicial Conduct (CJC), which has been adopted in whole or in part by many states, does list bias concerning a party's lawyer as grounds for recusal.

* * *

B. REGULATING THE INTERACTION BETWEEN LAWYERS AND JUDGES

1. INTERACTING WITH JUDGES IN CONNECTION WITH JUDICIAL PROCEEDINGS

a. Ex parte Communication

Please re-read ABA Model Rules of Professional Conduct, Rules 3.5(a) & (b).

Please read ABA Model Code of Judicial Conduct, Rule 2.9

* * *

Problem 23.2. Judge Reinhold ruled in favor of lawyer Ronnie's motion for attorney's fees in a matter in the presence of Ronnie and opposing counsel, Neil. Reinhold instructed Ronnie to draft an order for the judge's signature awarding the fees. After receiving the draft, Reinhold telephoned Ronnie outside of Neil's presence and instructed Ronnie to rewrite an awkwardly-phrased sentence. Has Reinhold engaged in an improper ex parte communication?

* * *

b. Judicial Monitoring of Lawyer Conduct

i. *Reporting Lawyer Misconduct to Disciplinary Authorities*

Please read ABA Model Code of Judicial Conduct, Canon 2, Rules 2.14–2.16.

* * *

What do you think? The Model Code of Judicial Conduct did not require judges to report lawyer misconduct until 1990. One author notes that "the conventional wisdom suggests that this is still a duty that is largely ignored." Arthur F. Greenbaum, *Judicial Reporting of Lawyer Misconduct*, 77 UMKC L. REV. 537, 539–40 (2009). For example, in one year, the Utah Office of Professional Conduct reported that only 0.5 percent of all disciplinary referrals came from judges. *Id.* at 540 n.9. Assuming the conventional wisdom is accurate, why don't judges report lawyer misconduct?

* * *

ii. Holding Lawyers in Contempt

**Hawaii Revised Statutes § 710–1077,
Criminal Contempt of Court**

(1) A person commits the offense of criminal contempt of court if:

> (a) The person recklessly engages in disorderly or contemptuous behavior, committed during the sitting of a court in its immediate view and presence, and directly tending to interrupt its proceedings or impair the respect due to its authority;

> (b) The person creates a breach of peace or a disturbance with intent to interrupt a court's proceedings;

> (c) As an attorney, clerk, or other officer of the court, the person knowingly fails to perform or violates a duty of the person's office, or knowingly disobeys a lawful directive or order of a court;

> (d) The person knowingly publishes a false report of a court's proceedings;

> . . . .

(2) Except as provided in subsections (3) and (7), criminal contempt of court is a misdemeanor.

(3) The court may treat the commission of an offense under subsection (1) as a petty misdemeanor, in which case:

> (a) If the offense was committed in the immediate view and presence of the court, or under such circumstances that the court has knowledge of all of the facts constituting the offense, the court may order summary conviction and disposition; and

> (b) If the offense was not committed in the immediate view and presence of the court, nor under such circumstances that the court has knowledge of all of the facts constituting the offense, the court shall order the defendant to appear before it to answer a charge of criminal contempt of court; the trial, if any, upon the

charge shall be by the court without a jury; and proof of guilt beyond a reasonable doubt shall be required for conviction.

. . . .

(5) Whenever any person is convicted of criminal contempt of court or sentenced therefor, the particular circumstances of the offense shall be fully set forth in the judgment and in the order or warrant of commitment. In any proceeding for review of the judgment, sentence, or commitment, no presumption of law shall be made in support of the jurisdiction to render the judgment, pronounce the sentence, or order the commitment. A judgment, sentence, or commitment under subsection (3)(a) shall not be subject to review by appeal, but shall subject to review in an appropriate proceeding for an extraordinary writ or in a special proceeding for review.

All other judgments, sentences, or commitments for criminal contempt of court shall be subject to review by appeal, in a proceeding for an appropriate extraordinary writ, or in a special proceeding for review.

* * *

c. Lawyer Monitoring of Judicial Conduct

i. *Motions for Recusal*

Please re-read ABA Model Rules of Professional Conduct, Rule 3.1.

Please read ABA Model Code of Judicial Conduct, Canon 2, Rule 2.11.

* * *

CHENEY v. U.S. DIST. COURT FOR DIST. OF COLUMBIA
541 U.S. 913 (2004)

Memorandum of JUSTICE SCALIA.

[The Sierra Club made a motion seeking Justice Scalia's recusal in a pending case in which the group sought records relating to the participation of energy industry officials in a federal energy task force headed up by Vice President Dick Cheney. The suit named Vice President Cheney and other members of the Bush Administration as defendants.]

I

The decision whether a judge's impartiality can " 'reasonably be questioned' " is to be made in light of the facts as they existed, and not as they were surmised or reported. *See* Microsoft Corp. v. United States, 530

U.S. 1301, 1302, 121 S.Ct. 25, 147 L.Ed.2d 1048 (2000) (REHNQUIST, C.J., respecting recusal). The facts here were as follows:

For five years or so, I have been going to Louisiana during the Court's long December-January recess, to the duck-hunting camp of a friend whom I met through two hunting companions from Baton Rouge, one a dentist and the other a worker in the field of handicapped rehabilitation. The last three years, I have been accompanied on this trip by a son-in-law who lives near me. Our friend and host, Wallace Carline, has never, as far as I know, had business before this Court. He is not, as some reports have described him, an "energy industry executive" in the sense that summons up boardrooms of ExxonMobil or Con Edison. He runs his own company that provides services and equipment rental to oil rigs in the Gulf of Mexico.

During my December 2002 visit, I learned that Mr. Carline was an admirer of Vice President Cheney. Knowing that the Vice President, with whom I am well acquainted (from our years serving together in the Ford administration), is an enthusiastic duck hunter, I asked whether Mr. Carline would like to invite him to our next year's hunt. The answer was yes; I conveyed the invitation (with my own warm recommendation) in the spring of 2003 and received an acceptance (subject, of course, to any superseding demands on the Vice President's time) in the summer. The Vice President said that if he did go, I would be welcome to fly down to Louisiana with him. (Because of national security requirements, of course, he must fly in a Government plane.) That invitation was later extended—if space was available—to my son-in-law and to a son who was joining the hunt for the first time; they accepted. The trip was set long before the Court granted certiorari in the present case, and indeed before the petition for certiorari had even been filed.

We departed from Andrews Air Force Base at about 10 a.m. on Monday, January 5, flying in a Gulfstream jet owned by the Government. We landed in Patterson, Louisiana, and went by car to a dock where Mr. Carline met us, to take us on the 20-minute boat trip to his hunting camp. We arrived at about 2 p.m., the 5 of us joining about 8 other hunters, making about 13 hunters in all; also present during our time there were about 3 members of Mr. Carline's staff, and, of course, the Vice President's staff and security detail. It was not an intimate setting. The group hunted that afternoon and Tuesday and Wednesday mornings; it fished (in two boats) Tuesday afternoon. All meals were in common. Sleeping was in rooms of two or three, except for the Vice President, who had his own quarters. Hunting was in two-or three-man blinds. As it turned out, I never hunted in the same blind with the Vice President. Nor was I alone with him at any time during the trip, except, perhaps, for instances so brief and unintentional that I would not recall them—walking to or from a boat, perhaps, or going to or from dinner. Of course we said not a word about the present case. The Vice President left the camp Wednesday afternoon, about two days after our arrival. I stayed on to hunt (with my son and son-in-law) until late Friday morning, when the three of us returned to Washington on a commercial flight from New Orleans.

II

Let me respond, at the outset, to Sierra Club's suggestion that I should "resolve any doubts in favor of recusal." Motion to Recuse 8. That might be sound advice if I were sitting on a Court of Appeals. There, my place would be taken by another judge, and the case would proceed normally. On the Supreme Court, however, the consequence is different: The Court proceeds with eight Justices, raising the possibility that, by reason of a tie vote, it will find itself unable to resolve the significant legal issue presented by the case. Thus, as Justices stated in their 1993 Statement of Recusal Policy: "We do not think it would serve the public interest to go beyond the requirements of the statute, and to recuse ourselves, out of an excess of caution, whenever a relative is a partner in the firm before us or acted as a lawyer at an earlier stage. Even one unnecessary recusal impairs the functioning of the Court." (Available in Clerk of Court's case file.) Moreover, granting the motion is (insofar as the outcome of the particular case is concerned) effectively the same as casting a vote against the petitioner. The petitioner needs five votes to overturn the judgment below, and it makes no difference whether the needed fifth vote is missing because it has been cast for the other side, or because it has not been cast at all.

Even so, recusal is the course I must take-and will take-when, on the basis of established principles and practices, I have said or done something which requires that course. I have recused for such a reason this very Term. *See* Elk Grove Unified School Dist. v. Newdow, 540 U.S. 945, 124 S.Ct. 384, 157 L.Ed.2d 274 (cert.granted, Oct. 14, 2003). I believe, however, that established principles and practices do not require (and thus do not permit) recusal in the present case.

A

My recusal is required if, by reason of the actions described above, my "impartiality might reasonably be questioned." 28 U.S.C. § 455(a). Why would that result follow from my being in a sizable group of persons, in a hunting camp with the Vice President, where I never hunted with him in the same blind or had other opportunity for private conversation? The only possibility is that it would suggest I am a friend of his. But while friendship is a ground for recusal of a Justice where the personal fortune or the personal freedom of the friend is at issue, it has traditionally not been a ground for recusal where official action is at issue, no matter how important the official action was to the ambitions or the reputation of the Government officer.

A rule that required Members of this Court to remove themselves from cases in which the official actions of friends were at issue would be utterly disabling. Many Justices have reached this Court precisely because they were friends of the incumbent President or other senior officials-and from the earliest days down to modern times Justices have had close personal relationships with the President and other officers of the Executive. [Justice Scalia listed numerous examples.]

It is said, however, that this case is different because the federal officer (Vice President Cheney) is actually a named party. That is by no means a rarity. At the beginning of the current Term, there were before the Court (excluding habeas actions) no fewer than 83 cases in which high-level federal Executive officers were named in their official capacity—more than 1 in every 10 federal civil cases then pending. That an officer is named has traditionally made no difference to the proposition that friendship is not considered to affect impartiality in official-action suits. Regardless of whom they name, such suits, when the officer is the plaintiff, seek relief not for him personally but for the Government; and, when the officer is the defendant, seek relief not against him personally, but against the Government. That is why federal law provides for automatic substitution of the new officer when the originally named officer has been replaced. See Fed. Rule Civ. Proc. 25(d)(1); Fed. Rule App. Proc. 43(c)(2); this Court's Rule 35.3. . . .

Richard Cheney's name appears in this suit only because he was the head of a Government committee that allegedly did not comply with the Federal Advisory Committee Act (FACA), 5 U.S.C.App. § 2, p. 1, and because he may, by reason of his office, have custody of some or all of the Government documents that the plaintiffs seek. . . .

The recusal motion, however, asserts the following:

> Critical to the issue of Justice Scalia's recusal is understanding that this is not a run-of-the-mill legal dispute about an administrative decision. . . . Because his own conduct is central to this case, the Vice President's "reputation and his integrity are on the line." (Chicago Tribune.) Motion to Recuse 9.

I think not. Certainly as far as the legal issues immediately presented to me are concerned, this is "a run-of-the-mill legal dispute about an administrative decision." I am asked to determine what powers the District Court possessed under FACA, and whether the Court of Appeals should have asserted mandamus or appellate jurisdiction over the District Court. Nothing this Court says on those subjects will have any bearing upon the reputation and integrity of Richard Cheney. Moreover, even if this Court affirms the decision below and allows discovery to proceed in the District Court, the issue that would ultimately present itself still would have no bearing upon the reputation and integrity of Richard Cheney. That issue would be, quite simply, whether some private individuals were de facto members of the National Energy Policy Development Group (NEPDG). It matters not whether they were caused to be so by Cheney or someone else, or whether Cheney was even aware of their de facto status; if they were de facto members, then (according to D.C. Circuit law) the records and minutes of NEPDG must be made public.

. . . .

To be sure, there could be political consequences from disclosure of the fact (if it be so) that the Vice President favored business interests, and especially a sector of business with which he was formerly connected. But political consequences are not my concern, and the possibility of them does not convert an official suit into a private one. That possibility exists to a greater or lesser degree in virtually all suits involving agency action. To expect judges to take account of political consequences-and to assess the high or low degree of them-is to ask judges to do precisely what they should not do. It seems to me quite wrong (and quite impossible) to make recusal depend upon what degree of political damage a particular case can be expected to inflict.

In sum, I see nothing about this case which takes it out of the category of normal official-action litigation, where my friendship, or the appearance of my friendship, with one of the named officers does not require recusal.

B

[Justice Scalia also rejected the argument that he should recuse himself because he had received "a gift" by being allowed to fly on the Vice President's plane.]

. . . .

V

Since I do not believe my impartiality can reasonably be questioned, I do not think it would be proper for me to recuse. That alone is conclusive; but another consideration moves me in the same direction: Recusal would in my judgment harm the Court. If I were to withdraw from this case, it would be because some of the press has argued that the Vice President would suffer political damage if he should lose this appeal, and if, on remand, discovery should establish that energy industry representatives were de facto members of NEPDG-and because some of the press has elevated that possible political damage to the status of an impending stain on the reputation and integrity of the Vice President. But since political damage often comes from the Government's losing official-action suits; and since political damage can readily be characterized as a stain on reputation and integrity; recusing in the face of such charges would give elements of the press a veto over participation of any Justices who had social contacts with, or were even known to be friends of, a named official. That is intolerable.

My recusal would also encourage so-called investigative journalists to suggest improprieties, and demand recusals, for other inappropriate (and increasingly silly) reasons. The Los Angeles Times has already suggested that it was improper for me to sit on a case argued by a law school dean whose school I had visited *several weeks before-visited not at his invitation, but at his predecessor's. See* New Trip Trouble for Scalia, Feb. 28, 2004, p. B22. The same paper has asserted that it was improper for me to speak at a dinner honoring Cardinal Bevilacqua given by the Urban Family Council of Philadelphia because (according to the *Times*'s false report) that organization was engaged in litigation seeking to prevent same-sex civil unions, and I had before me a case presenting the question (whether same-sex civil unions were lawful?-no) whether homosexual sodomy could constitutionally be criminalized. *See* Lawrence v. Texas, 539 U.S. 558, 123 S.Ct. 2472, 156 L.Ed.2d 508 (2003). While the political branches can perhaps survive the constant baseless allegations of impropriety that have become the staple of Washington reportage, this Court cannot. The people must have confidence in the integrity of the Justices, and that cannot exist in a system that assumes them to be corruptible by the slightest friendship or favor, and in an atmosphere where the press will be eager to find foot-faults. . . .

. . . .

There are, I am sure, those who believe that my friendship with persons in the current administration might cause me to favor the Government in cases brought against it. That is not the issue here. Nor is the issue whether personal friendship with the Vice President might cause me to favor the Government in cases in which he is named. None of those suspicions regarding my impartiality (erroneous suspicions, I hasten to protest) bears upon recusal here. The question, simply put, is whether someone who thought I could decide this case impartially despite my friendship with the Vice President would reasonably believe that I cannot decide it impartially because I went hunting with that friend and accepted an invitation to fly there with him on a Government plane. If it is reasonable to think that a Supreme Court Justice can be bought so cheap, the Nation is in deeper trouble than I had imagined.

As the newspaper editorials appended to the motion make clear, I have received a good deal of embarrassing criticism and adverse publicity in connection with the matters at issue here-even to the point of becoming (as the motion cruelly but accurately states) "fodder for late-night comedians." Motion to Recuse 6. If I could have done so in good conscience, I would have been pleased to demonstrate my integrity, and immediately silence the criticism, by getting off the case. Since I believe there is no basis for recusal, I cannot. The motion is Denied.

* * *

Problem 23.3. Refer back to the Chapter Hypothetical. Is Judge Reinhold's recusal required on any of the asserted grounds?

* * *

Party bias as grounds for recusal. 28 U.S.C. § 455 governs the recusal of federal judges (including Supreme Court justices). Like Rule 2.11(A)(1) of the ABA's CJC, § 455 requires recusal in a proceeding in which the judge's impartiality might reasonably be questioned, including where the judge has a personal bias or prejudice concerning a party.

The fox guarding the henhouse? Although 28 U.S.C. § 455 applies to Supreme Court justices, there is a rather gaping hole in the law. As Professor Caprice L. Roberts has observed, the decision as to whether to recuse is left to the individual Justice and there is no review mechanism in place. "In other words, when any one Justice weighs the perilous issue of whether recusal is proper, there is no review mechanism, no opinion or public reasoning required, no legal accountability, and no mechanism to handle replacement when recusal occurs." Caprice L. Roberts, *The Fox Guarding the Henhouse?: Recusal and the Procedural Void in the Court of Last Resort*, 57 RUTGERS L. REV. 107, 109 (2004) (quotations omitted). Indeed, at one point in the *Cheney* decision, Justice Scalia states that "[s]ince I don't believe my impartiality can reasonably be questioned, I do not think it would be proper for me to recuse. That alone is conclusive." Really? Should the belief of the justice in question as to the appropriateness of recusal be conclusive?

* * *

Problem 23.4. In which of the following circumstances is recusal most likely to be required?

(A) The judge formerly practiced law with one of the lawyers representing a party in a case pending before the judge.

(B) The judge's son is a partner in the law firm that is representing a party in a case pending before the judge.

(C) The judge's former law clerk is one of the lawyers representing a party in a case pending before the judge.

(D) The plaintiff in a discrimination case claim he was discriminated against because of his religion. The judge shares the same religion as the plaintiff.

* * *

Bias and waiver of disqualification. Rule 2.11(c) of the Code of Judicial Conduct explains the procedure through which the lawyers for the parties may waive a judge's disqualification. The judge is supposed to disclose the basis for his or her disqualification on the record and give the parties and their lawyers the opportunity (outside the presence of the judge) to decide whether to waive the disqualification. The one basis for disqualification that the parties cannot waive, however, is bias concerning a party or lawyer or personal knowledge of facts in dispute in the proceeding under Rule 2.11(A).

* * *

Problem 23.5. Judge Reinhold is currently considering two recusal motions. In the first, a borrower being sued by a bank has moved to disqualify Reinhold on the grounds that the bank holds the mortgage on Reinhold's home. In the second, a cell phone company is suing another cell phone company in a multi-billion dollar lawsuit for patent infringement concerning the second company's major product. The first company has moved to disqualify Reinhold on the grounds that his wife owns stock in the second company valued at $70,000. Reinhold was stunned to learn of his wife's investment, which she had kept hidden from him. Is the judge's disqualification required under ABA CJC Rule 2.11(A) in either case? Is he otherwise subject to discipline under Rule 2.11(B)?

* * *

ii. Reporting Judicial Misconduct

Please re-read ABA Model Rules of Professional Conduct, Rule 8.3(b).

Please read ABA Model Code of Judicial Conduct, Canon 2, Rule 2.11.

* * *

Problem 23.6. Lawyer Ronnie and his opposing counsel, Neil, have both noticed some erratic behavior from Judge Reinhold during trial. On one occasion, the judge fell asleep during trial. On another, the judge's speech was slurred. There are rumors around the courthouse that the judge is sometimes drunk on the bench, and Ronnie could swear he caught a whiff of alcohol coming from the judge when he passed the judge in the courthouse hallway. Both lawyers are concerned about Reinhold's behavior but fear retribution if they report their concerns. Are Ronnie and Neil obligated to report the judge's conduct to the state's judicial conduct organization?

* * *

2. AVOIDING COMPLICITY IN JUDICIAL MISCONDUCT

Please read ABA Model Rules of Professional Conduct, Rule 8.4(f).

What do you think? In several reported cases, lawyers have been charged with violations of Model Rule 8.4(f) for engaging in conduct that conferred an improper benefit upon a judge. *See* In re Corboy, N.E.2d 694 (Ill. 1998) (involving lawyers who made improper gifts or loans to a judge). Should the rule be limited to these kinds of situations, or should it apply more broadly to situations in which a lawyer "assists" a judge in conduct that is in violation of the rules of judicial conduct but in no way benefits the judge? *See* In re Wilder, 764 N.E.2d 617 (Ind. 2002) (imposing discipline upon a lawyer who obtained a temporary restraining order for his client following an impermissible ex parte meeting with the judge presiding in the case).

* * *

Profile of attorney professionalism. Penny White is the Director of the Center for Advocacy and Dispute Resolution and the Elvin E. Overton Distinguished Professor of Law at the University of Tennessee College of Law. Before beginning her teaching career, White practiced law as a solo practitioner and successfully argued a case in the United States Supreme Court in 1988. Later, White served as the first female Circuit Judge in the First Judicial District in Tennessee. She went on to serve as a judge at every level of the state court system and became only the second woman to serve on the Tennessee Court of Criminal Appeals and the Tennessee Supreme Court.

In 1996, the Tennessee Supreme Court voted, in a death penalty case, to affirm the conviction of a criminal defendant on the crime of rape and murder but vacated the death penalty and remanded for resentencing. White joined the majority decision. Later that year, White was the only member of the court standing for election as part of Tennessee's retention system for judges. She was targeted by a variety of groups who pointed to the prior majority decision as evidence that White was "soft on crime." She lost the retention election in a campaign that proponents of judicial independence still point to as an example of the dangers associated with judicial elections.

White went on to become a law professor who focuses on teaching through experiential learning. Her scholarship focuses on criminal law, judicial ethics, and judicial selection. Rather than distance herself from the bench and bar following her retention defeat, White routinely teaches continuing legal education courses for judges on matters of evidence and judicial ethics.

SECTION 2

TRANSACTIONAL PRACTICE AND THE REPRESENTATION OF ORGANIZATIONAL CLIENTS

■ ■ ■

In many ways, the ethical and fiduciary duties a lawyer owes to an organizational client are no different than the duties owed to an individual client. A lawyer must act competently and diligently in pursuing the client's objectives, the lawyer must maintain client confidences, and the lawyer must act loyally. But the nature of representing an organizational client poses some special challenges in those regards. How, for example, does a lawyer determine what an organization's objectives really are when individuals within that organization have conflicting views on the subject or at least have conflicting views as to how to pursue those objectives? At the same time, while lawyers engaged in transactional practice face many of the same issues as litigators, some of those issues—such as the ethics of negotiation—may be more acute for the transactional lawyer. Therefore, this section focuses on some of the special issues involved in transactional practice and the representation of organizational clients. Chapter 24 addresses special issues facing the transactional lawyer, whereas Chapter 25 addresses some of the special issues involved in representing organizational clients.

Problem 24.4. For many years, you have been outside counsel to the Taylor Corporation. You frequently advise the company and represent it in contract negotiations with suppliers. Other lawyers in your firm represent the corporation in employment, intellectual property, and business litigation matters. The company's CEO asks if you would consider serving on the corporation's board of directors. What are the possible adverse consequences of taking a seat on the board?

Problem 24.5. Assume that you represented both Stacy and John in forming a Limited Liability Company (LLC). Eighteen months after they hired you, Stacy is unhappy with the LLC Agreement; she thinks that you drafted the document in a way that gives John a disproportionate amount of power in the management of the business. With citation to specific provisions of the Restatement (Third) of the Law Governing Lawyers, describe the causes of action Stacy could assert against you in a lawsuit.

* * *

B. REPRESENTING CLIENTS IN NON-LITIGATION MATTERS

In litigation, a lawyer is presented with a factual scenario that occurred in the past: a contract may have been breached, an employee may have been discriminated against, a tort may have been committed. It is litigation counsel's job to zealously advocate on the client's behalf, making the most persuasive arguments under the law and facts that the subject conduct should (in the case of plaintiff's counsel) or should not (in the case of defense counsel) result in liability. Assuming that litigation counsel was not involved in the underlying conduct, there is no chance that counsel will be found liable for the conduct that is the subject of the litigation.

An attorney's role is somewhat different in non-litigation matters. In a transactional practice, an attorney typically is addressing a client's future conduct. Rather than making the best of facts that have occurred in the past (as litigation counsel must do), the transactional attorney has the opportunity—and the obligation—to competently advise the client about how to comply with legal obligations and avoid liability. The client needs this information in order to decide how to proceed. But this may mean giving the client advice that he or she does not want.

In these representations, the transactional lawyer faces a risk that is not an issue for litigation counsel. Because the lawyer may be a participant in the client's conduct, it is possible for the lawyer to face criminal and civil liability for the lawyer's actions. *See* Restatement (Third) of the Law Governing Lawyers § 8, 56, 57 (2000). In the transactional setting, fraud is a typical basis of liability for both lawyer and client in civil litigation and criminal prosecutions.

As a fiduciary, the lawyer must act competently, diligently, and loyally in the interest of the client. *See* Restatement (Third) of the Law Governing Lawyers §§ 16, 52(1) (2000). Professional conduct rules provide some (but not a great deal of) guidance to attorneys concerning meeting these duties to clients in non-litigation settings. *See, e.g.,* Model Rule 1.1, 2.1. Other rules remind lawyers that they cannot participate in client crime and fraud. *See, e.g.,* Model Rules 1.2(d), 1.4(a)(5), 4.1(b), 1.16(a). Following these rules should result in both lawyer and client avoiding serious forms of misconduct and liability.

The following four Parts address these legal and professional conduct issues in transactional lawyering. Part 1 addresses the legal and ethical issues surrounding advising clients. Then, Part 2 considers professional conduct rules that govern attorney conduct in negotiations and other interactions with third parties. Thereafter, Part 3 discusses tools the lawyer may use to avoid participating in client misconduct when the client insists upon a course of conduct the lawyer has advised against. Finally, Part 4 looks at the consequences lawyers may suffer when they become participants in client misconduct.

* * *

1. ADVISING CLIENTS

**Please read ABA Model Rules of Professional Conduct,
Rule 2.1 and Comments;
Rule 1.2(d) and Comments [9]–[13]; and Rule 1.4(a)(5).**

**Please read Restatement (Third) of the Law Governing
Lawyers §§ 16, 52(1) & 94.**

* * *

Clients—even sophisticated business clients—often see the law in black and white terms. They understand the law as a line that they cannot cross. They want their lawyers to tell them if a proposed course of conduct is "legal" or "illegal."

Most legal issues that clients face are not so simple. While a client's planned conduct may not be "illegal" it may certainly lead to substantial liability and should be avoided. This is the advice that competent lawyers must provide to clients. Clients cannot make an informed decision about how to proceed if lawyers only provide technical advice about black and white violations of the law.

Instead, lawyers must explain how a prosecutor may view an issue and why a client's plan may lead to a criminal prosecution. A lawyer must explain that silence may amount to fraud if a client has a duty to share information and is concealing information in an attempt to mislead another party. Lawyers must help clients understand the breadth of the law and the consequences of viewing it in a narrow or technical way.

Model Rule 2.1 provides some guidance in this regard. The rule encourages lawyers to "exercise independent professional judgment" and "render candid advice." Comment [1] notes that lawyers may have to tell the client things that the client does not want to hear. Highlighting the relationship between unethical conduct and legal liability, Comment 2 provides, "[M]oral and ethical considerations impinge upon most legal questions and may decisively influence how the law will be applied."

Other rules remind lawyers that they need to make a judgment call and not participate in conduct that may amount to a crime or fraud. Rule 1.2(d) prohibits counseling a client to engage in or assisting a client in conduct the lawyer knows is criminal or fraudulent. Rule 1.4(a)(5) requires the lawyer to explain to the client that the lawyer cannot provide such assistance. Rules that will be discussed later in this chapter (Rules 4.1, 1.6(b), and 1.16) provide additional guidance for lawyers who believe they are being asked to participate in (or have already participated in) criminal or fraudulent conduct. Lawyers read such rules narrowly at their own and their client's peril. Neither lawyer nor client should be inclined to play fast and loose with the possibility of engaging in criminal and fraudulent conduct.

* * *

Problem 24.6. You represent a small family-owned corporation, The Good Egg, Inc. Father and son owners Jim Dale Coster and Jim Dan Coster are engaged in the day-to-day operations of the company. Recently, Jim Dan mentioned to you that changes in egg safety rules have made it more difficult than ever to get eggs approved for shipment by USDA egg inspectors. Jim Dan explained, "The risk of salmonella is actually quite low. But after other foodborne illness outbreaks in the US in recent years, the feds are watching us more closely than ever. It's killing us." You asked, "Is there anything I can do to help?" Jim Dan responded, "I think Dad has it covered for now. He's found an inspector who doesn't mind making an extra buck once in a while. I guess it's just the new cost of doing business."

You understood Jim Dan's comment to mean that Jim Dale is bribing a USDA egg inspector to allow shipments of bad eggs. You know that the company and the Costers will face criminal penalties if their eggs cause a salmonella outbreak under the circumstances. Beyond that, plaintiffs will line up to sue if a salmonella outbreak is traced to The Good Egg.

How would you advise The Good Egg in these circumstances? Should you ask additional questions to determine if bribes are being paid or defer to Jim Dan's assessment that this is the "new cost of doing business?"

Problem 24.7. Your client, the Peanut Company of America (PCA), has asked you for advice about a planned tax position PCA is considering. PCA has made some recent expenditures that it wants to deduct as expenses. After researching the issue, you conclude that if the Internal Revenue Service (IRS) challenges this deduction, PCA's position is unlikely to prevail. Indeed, you are unable to find any substantial authority in support of PCA's position. That concerns you because you know that the Internal Revenue Code imposes a penalty on a taxpayer for substantial understatement of tax liability that can be avoided if the taxpayer had substantial authority for the position taken. Nonetheless, you believe that PCA's position is actually warranted under a literal reading of the relevant position of the Code, even if it is unlikely to withstand IRS review. Can you advise PCA that it can take the deduction? If so, what will you say when you provide this advice?

* * *

2. HONESTY IN NEGOTIATIONS AND OTHER INTERACTIONS WITH THIRD PARTIES

Please read ABA Model Rules of Professional Conduct, Rule 4.1 and Comments.

* * *

Because a lawyer is an agent of the client, a client faces liability for fraudulent misrepresentations that a lawyer makes on the client's behalf. Further, the lawyer faces personal liability for his or her fraudulent misrepresentations even if they were made in the context of representing a client.

If a lawyer abides by Rule 4.1, the lawyer can avoid this liability for client and self. The rule prohibits the lawyer making a false statement to a third party or failing to disclose a material fact when disclosure is necessary to avoid assisting in a crime or fraud unless disclosure is prohibited by Rule 1.6. (As you will see in Part 3, the exceptions to Rule 1.6 allow disclosure to prevent a client from committing a crime or fraud under these circumstances).

As you read the following case, note all of the parties that Wright sued and the basis for Wright's claims against them. If Pennamped had followed Rule 4.1, would this case have been avoided?

WRIGHT V. PENNAMPED

657 N.E.2d 1223 (Ind. App. 1995)

SHARPNACK, CHIEF JUDGE.

Donald H. Wright appeals the trial court's order of summary judgment in favor of the defendant-appellees, Bruce M. Pennamped and his law firm, Lowe Gray Steele & Hoffman ("the Appellees"). Wright is seeking damages arising from the Appellees' alleged deceptive and fraudulent conduct during a commercial loan transaction. Wright raises four issues for our review, which we consolidate and restate as whether the trial court erred in granting summary judgment. We affirm in part and reverse in part.

[Wright was a self-employed general contractor and real estate developer who was looking to refinance the apartment complex he owned, the Diplomat Apartments, in the amount of $500,000.00. On May 29, 1991, Ray Krebs, the vice president of mortgage banking at SCI Financial Corporation ("SCI"), submitted a proposal of financing to Wright. Wright accepted the proposal on June 3, 1991. The proposal contained a prepayment provision that Wright did not understand, but he anticipated that he would have his attorney, Richard L. Brown, explain any provisions he did not understand when Brown received the proposed loan documents prior to closing. After signing the proposal, Wright provided Brown's name, address, and telephone number to Krebs. Krebs then relayed this information to Pennamped. Pennamped, a partner in the law firm of Lowe Gray Steele & Hoffman, became involved in the loan transaction on July 2, 1991, when he had a luncheon meeting with Krebs. SCI retained Pennamped and the firm to represent its interests and to prepare the necessary loan documents. Pennamped drafted the loan documents on July 31, 1991, and forwarded copies marked "DRAFT DATED 7–31–91" to Krebs and Brown. The draft contained a prepayment provision.

On Friday, August 2, 1991, Brown reviewed the draft documents and discussed them with Wright. Brown and Wright discussed the prepayment provision as well as additional terms in the draft documents. Wright did not indicate to Brown that the prepayment provision in the draft note was any different than the one in the proposal for financing. Based on their discussion, both Wright and Brown accepted and approved the form and substance of the draft documents. In the meantime, Don Wilson, Senior Vice President of the funding bank, Kentland Bank, reviewed the draft and requested of Krebs that changes be made to the prepayment penalty provision. On August 5th, Pennamped and Wright's attorney, Brown, discussed the loan agreement. Pennamped never mentioned any changes to the document. Pennamped asked Brown if he had any problems with the proposed loan documents, and Brown responded that he did not. Brown informed Pennamped he had two cases set for the following morning and he would be unable to attend the closing set for 9:00 a.m. the next day. Pennamped completed the changes to the loan documents that Wilson had requested on the afternoon of August 5, 1991. No one informed Brown or Wright about the changes, although Pennamped told Krebs that he should speak to Wright and explain the changes. Krebs said he would do so, but never did. Pennamped never made any further inquiry regarding the matter.

Because Brown was in court, Wright attended the closing alone. No one ever informed him about the changes to the agreement. Wright executed the documents. Wright learned of the new prepayment provision when he attempted to payoff the loan. Under the terms of the original agreement, Wright's prepayment penalty would have been $4,931.49. Under the terms as modified the prepayment penalty was $97,504.38.]

[O]n July 18, 1993, Wright filed a complaint for damages against Kentland Bank, Krebs, SCI, Pennamped, and Lowe Gray Steele & Hoffman. Wright sought recovery from the defendants based on fraud, constructive fraud and breach of fiduciary relationship, obtaining money and property by false pretenses, deception, criminal mischief, conversion and theft, and forgery. Wright subsequently amended his complaint to include a count based on breach of implied contract.

On September 8, 1993, the Appellees filed their motion for summary judgment. On December 1, 1993, Wright filed his opposition to the motion for summary judgment. Following a hearing on December 21, 1993, the trial court took the motion under advisement. On March 4, 1994, the trial court issued its order granting the Appellees' motion for summary judgment. The trial court found that an essential element of each of Wright's non-contractual theories is the intent to deceive and that Wright failed to come forward with any evidence supporting an inference of fraud. The court held that the Appellees had no contractual duty to Wright and therefore, Wright's breach of implied contract claim must fail. The trial held there was no just cause for delay and ordered the entry of final judgment in favor of the Appellees. Wright appeals this judgment.

. . .

II. Actual Fraud

The elements of actual fraud are: (1) the fraud feasor must have made at least one representation of past or existing fact; (2) which was false; (3) which the fraud feasor knew to be false or made with reckless disregard as to its truth or falsity; (4) upon which the plaintiff reasonably relied; (5) and which harmed the plaintiff. Scott, 571 N.E.2d at 319. An intent to deceive, or "scienter," is an element of actual fraud, whether classified as a knowing or reckless misrepresentation or as an additional element to a knowing or reckless misrepresentation. . . . Fraud may be proven by circumstantial evidence, provided there are facts from which the existence of all of the elements can be reasonably inferred. . . .

[The court agreed with Wright that there was sufficient evidence of actual fraud to survive summary judgment.]

We conclude, therefore, that the trial court erred in granting summary judgment on Wright's claim for actual fraud.

III. Constructive Fraud

The elements of constructive fraud include:

" '1. a duty owing by the party to be charged to the complaining party due to their relationship,

2. violation of that duty by the making of deceptive material misrepresentations of past or existing facts or remaining silent when a duty to speak exists,

3. reliance thereon by the complaining party,

4. injury to the complaining party as a proximate result thereof, and

5. the gaining of an advantage by the party to be charged at the expense of the complaining party.' "

. . . Contrary to the trial court's ruling in the present case, intent to deceive is not an element of constructive fraud. . . . Instead, the law infers fraud from the relationship of the parties and the surrounding circumstances. The Appellees contend that the trial court nonetheless properly entered summary judgment in their favor on Wright's claim for constructive fraud because there is an absence of the type of relationship which may form a basis of a claim for constructive fraud. Furthermore, Appellees contend this relationship did not give rise to a legal duty to disclose. . . .

As we have observed previously, however, "Defendants are mistaken in arguing that constructive fraud can *only* exist where there is a confidential or fiduciary relationship. In Indiana, the term constructive fraud encompasses several related theories. All of these theories are premised on the understanding that there are situations which might not amount to actual fraud, but which are so likely to result in injustice that the law will find a fraud despite the absence of fraudulent intent. Defendants are correct in asserting that a constructive fraud may be found where one party takes unconscionable advantage of his dominant position in a confidential or fiduciary relationship. This is not, however, the exclusive basis for the theory of constructive fraud. In Indiana constructive fraud also includes what other jurisdictions have termed 'legal fraud' or 'fraud in law.' *This species of constructive fraud recognizes that certain conduct should be prohibited because it is inherently likely to create an injustice. . . ."* Scott, 571 N.E.2d at 323–24 (emphasis added). Thus, we find the Appellees' reliance upon Hardy and Comfax to be of no avail. . . .

Considering the facts in the light most favorable to Wright and contrary to the Appellees' contentions on appeal, this case is amenable to the application of the doctrine of constructive fraud. The facts as alleged by Wright suggest a situation that is so likely to result in injustice that the law will find a fraud despite the absence of fraudulent intent. See Scott, 571 N.E.2d at 323–24. The material alteration of loan documents after the review and approval of those documents by opposing counsel and the presentation of the revised documents for execution with no indication that changes have been made is the sort of conduct which "should be prohibited because it is inherently likely to create an injustice. . . ." Id. at 324.

In the alternative, Appellees contend this relationship did not give rise to a legal duty. Appellees claim that Pennamped did not owe Wright a duty to disclose the changes made to the loan documents. Furthermore, Appellees argue that even if Pennamped did have a duty, Pennamped satisfied this duty by delegating the performance to Krebs. We disagree.

A party to a contract has a duty to the other party to disclose changes. Peoples Trust & Savings Bank v. Humphrey (1983), Ind.App., 451 N.E.2d 1104, 1112. The Appellees argue that although Pennamped altered the contract, he did not owe a duty to Wright because Pennamped was not a party to the contract.

Contrary to Appellees' contention, as discussed previously, we find that Pennamped had a duty to disclose. As the drafting attorney, Pennamped assumed a duty to inform Wright of any changes to the loan documents prior to their execution. . . . In opposing the motion for summary judgment, Wright submitted the affidavit of Richard L. Johnson, the senior partner in the law firm of Johnson Smith Densborn Wright & Heath. The significance of this affidavit was to establish the customs and practices of financing transactions. Johnson commenced the practice of law in 1972 and has concentrated his practice in the areas of banking law, real estate law, and commercial law. After setting forth his qualifications and extensive experience as lender's counsel and in drafting or preparing documents to be used in lending transactions, Johnson's affidavit states:

"Based upon my experience as lender's counsel, I believe the following to be the customs and practices in the industry in relation to real estate and/or commercial financing transactions:

(a) At any time changes or revisions are made to draft or proposed loan documents by the attorney charged with the responsibility of drafting such documents—no matter how trivial or seemingly insignificant such changes or revisions may be—it is expected and understood by all other attorneys involved in the transaction that the drafting attorney will take whatever steps are necessary and/or appropriate to fully disclose and identify all such document changes and revisions to other attorneys involved in the transaction.

(b) Typically, when any changes or revisions are made to proposed or draft loan documents, the drafting attorney will circulate, in writing, a 'red-lined' copy or some other written materials which will highlight and/or more particularly identify and/or describe the changes and revisions that have been or are contemplated to be made.

(c) At the very least, the drafting attorney is responsible to verbally disclose to all other attorneys involved in the transaction—prior to execution of final documents—any and all changes and revisions that the drafting attorney has made to previously-distributed draft documents.

(d) Any changes or revisions to the substance or form of documents which have been previously circulated to the participating attorneys should be fully disclosed to such other attorneys.

(e) The closing of the transaction should not occur until final revisions to the loan documents have been fully disclosed to and approved by all parties and their respective counsel."

Based on this relationship, Wright could expect that Pennamped would inform him of any changes in the loan documents. Therefore, Pennamped had a duty to disclose material information to Wright concerning the loan documents.

Furthermore, Appellees' argument is in contradiction with Rule 4.1(b) of the Rules of Professional Conduct which states, "[i]n the course of representing a client a lawyer shall not knowingly ... (b) fail to disclose that which is required by law to be revealed." Ind. Professional Conduct, Rule 4.1(b). As previously stated, the drafting attorney assumes a duty to disclose any changes in the documents prior to execution to the other parties. See id.

Courts hold attorneys to a separate and more demanding standard than the attorneys' clients. Fire Insurance Exchange, 643 N.E.2d at 312. Pennamped may have assisted his client, Krebs, in the commission of constructive fraud by failing to disclose to Wright that Pennamped changed the loan documents. Since Pennamped knew the documents were altered, he had a duty to disclose.

Lastly, we address whether Pennamped delegated his duty to Krebs. Pennamped may have created an agency relationship where he was the principal and Krebs was his agent within this narrow scope of disclosing changes to Wright. Therefore, Pennamped may have discharged his duty by delegating it to Krebs. However, this raises a question of whether Pennamped actually instructed Krebs to inform Wright of the changes. The existence of an agency is a question of fact, therefore this issue should be decided by a trier of fact and not decided upon summary judgment. Bryan Mfg. Co. v. Harris (1984), Ind.App. 459 N.E.2d 1199, 1204.

We conclude, therefore, that the trial court erred in granting summary judgment on Wright's claim for constructive fraud.

To sum up, while we affirm the trial court's entry of summary judgment for the defendant on the theory of quasi-contract, we reverse summary judgment on the theories of actual and constructive fraud. The case is remanded to the trial court for further proceedings consistent with this opinion.

* * *

Problem 24.8. Mick Stirts hired you to represent him in negotiations with Cost-Mart Big Box Stores. Cost-Mart is interested in purchasing a lot that Mick owns and has been unable to sell for ten years. (Mick told you that the site was once home to a gas station, and that is why he has had trouble selling the lot). Cost-Mart is in the process of purchasing several adjoining lots where it will build a Cost-Mart Wholesale Club, which will include a gas station on the lot currently owned by Mick. You successfully negotiated a "conditional agreement" in which Cost-Mart agreed to pay Mick $50,000 for the lot, conditioned on its purchase of the adjoining lots within 90 days. Mick was thrilled with the price. The last offer he had received for the land was for $7,000—and that was three years ago.

This morning, Mick tells you that he needs you to take care of one last detail. He says that he "technically co-owns the lot with a former business partner" named Ginny Sampson. Mick would like you to offer Ginny $5,000 for her interest in the land. He feels certain she will take the offer. Legally, you know that Mick owes his co-owner and business partner a duty to disclose the $50,000 conditional agreement with Cost-Mart. You tell him this. But Mick insists, "You need to keep the deal quiet. At this point, it is conditional and even that wouldn't have happened without me. Why should I share that with Ginny? Just work out a deal with her for $5,000."

Under applicable professional conduct rules, can you negotiate the $5,000 deal with Ginny without revealing the conditional agreement?

What are the possible legal consequences for you personally if you handle the negotiations with Ginny as Mick has suggested? What are the possible legal consequences for Mick?

* * *

3. TOOLS LAWYERS CAN USE TO AVOID LIABILITY FOR PARTICIPATING IN CLIENT MISCONDUCT

Please read ABA Model Rules of Professional Conduct, Rule 1.6(b)(2) & (3) and Comments [7] & [8]; Rule 4.1(b) and Comment [3]; and Rule 1.16(a) & (b) and Comments [2] & [7].

* * *

Even though clients may choose to engage in misconduct against the lawyer's advice, the lawyer cannot participate in that misconduct. Professional conduct rules require a lawyer to withdraw if the representation "will result in violation of the rules of professional conduct or other law." Model Rule 1.16(a)(1). Even if the lawyer is not certain that conduct will violate law or professional conduct rules, a lawyer is nonetheless permitted to withdraw if the lawyer "reasonably believes" the client is using the lawyer's services to perpetrate a crime or fraud. Model Rule 1.16(b)(2).

Other rules allow a lawyer who has been engaged in a client's fraudulent misconduct to make a disclosure to prevent or mitigate damages to a third party. Model Rule 1.6(b)(2) permits disclosure to prevent a client from committing a crime or fraud likely to cause substantial injury to a third party, while Model Rule 1.6(b)(3) allows disclosure to "prevent, mitigate, or rectify" financial injury caused by a client's crime or fraud. In both cases, it is necessary that the client used the lawyer's services to commit the crime or fraud. Similarly, Model Rule 4.1(b) requires a lawyer to disclose a fact when doing so is necessary to avoid assisting a client in a crime or fraud unless prohibited by Model Rule 1.6. In light of today's Model Rule 1.6 exceptions (particularly the exceptions highlighted in this paragraph), the duty to disclose under Model Rule 4.1(b) is broad.

These rules effectively give the lawyer an avenue to protect him or herself from liability for fraud. But they may also lead clients to change course. Explaining what the lawyer plans to do under the authority of professional conduct rules may cause a client to re-think a plan that would have resulted in liability for the client.

Finally, lawyers should note that organizational clients do not have the same autonomy as clients that are natural persons when it comes to questions of engaging in misconduct. Chapter 25 addresses the organizational client's lawyer to take additional steps to protect the client from constituent misconduct.

* * *

Problem 24.9. Refer to the facts in Problem 24.8. Assume for purposes of this problem that you told Mick that you would not negotiate the purchase of Ginny's interest in the property without revealing the Cost-Mart conditional agreement to her. Mick responded, "That's fine. I'll negotiate the deal myself. I will just need your help drafting the contract. Leave the purchase amount blank and I'll fill it in after I work out the price with her." Under applicable professional conduct rules, what steps are you permitted or required to take at this point? What would you do?

* * *

4.   LAWYER CRIMINAL AND CIVIL LIABILITY FOR PARTICIPATING IN CLIENT MISCONDUCT

Please Read Restatement (Third) of the Law Governing Lawyers §§ 8, 56, 57 & 95.

* * *

This chapter has noted that a lawyer may face civil or criminal liability for conduct undertaken on a client's behalf. In limited circumstances, defenses and exceptions to liability apply because of the lawyer's role. *See* Restatement (Third) of the Law Governing Lawyers § 8 (explaining that the "traditional and appropriate activities" of the lawyer representing a client should be considered in determining the propriety of a lawyer's conduct under the criminal law); § 57 (defining limited exceptions and defenses to civil liability for conduct undertaken on a client's behalf). Otherwise, a lawyer can expect to face liability to the same extent and on the same basis as a non-lawyer. *See* Restatement (Third) of the Law Governing Lawyers § 8 (except as noted, a lawyer is "guilty of a [criminal] offense for an act committed in the course of representing a client to the same extent and on the same basis as would a non-lawyer acting similarly."); § 56 (unless an exception or defense applies, "a lawyer is subject to liability . . . when a non-lawyer would be in similar circumstances); § 95 (a lawyer counseling or assisting a client in conduct that violates the rights of a third person is subject to liability unless an exception or defense applies).

The following case concerns lawyer Joseph Collins' criminal conviction for participating in a corporate client's fraudulent scheme. During the years of fraud described in the case, attorney Collins was a partner in the global law firm Mayer Brown. When the fraud was revealed, client Refco, Inc. had no choice but to file for bankruptcy. Several company executives were tried and convicted for the roles they played in the fraudulent scheme.

* * *

UNITED STATES V. COLLINS

No. 13–2902, 581 Fed. Appx. 59 (2d Cir. Oct. 22, 2014)

Present DENNIS JACOBS, GUIDO CALABRESI and CHRISTOPHER F. DRONEY, CIRCUIT JUDGES.

SUMMARY ORDER

UPON DUE CONSIDERATION, IT IS HEREBY ORDERED, ADJUDGED AND DECREED that the judgment of the district court be AFFIRMED.

Joseph Collins appeals from a judgment of the United States District Court for the Southern District of New York (Preska, Ch. J.), sentencing Collins principally to one year and one day imprisonment after a jury convicted him of conspiracy, securities fraud, false filings with the Securities and Exchange Commission, and wire fraud. We assume the parties' familiarity with the underlying facts, the procedural history, and the issues presented for review.

Collins was outside counsel for Refco, Inc., from as early as 1997 until revelations of accounting fraud in 2005 forced the corporation into bankruptcy. The government eventually charged Collins with supporting Refco executives' scheme to conceal large amounts of intercompany debt. The scheme was based on a series of artfully timed loans, euphemistically called "short-term financings," which bounced the debt back and forth between a Refco subsidiary and Refco's parent company immediately before and after audits. The short-term financings kept the growing intercompany debt hidden from auditors, banks, customers, and regulators throughout a 2004 leveraged buyout of Refco and throughout a 2005 initial public offering.

Collins prepared documents for many of the individual transactions that, in aggregate, effected the short-term financings. However, Collins claimed in his defense that he did not know of the fraud scheme motivating these transactions. The government's showing that Collins was aware (or consciously avoided awareness) of the fraud included: Collins' work in drafting a Proceeds Participation Agreement ("PPA") in 2002, which revealed Refco's desperate capital shortage and buried the intercompany debt in a side letter; Collins' failure to disclose the PPA in the 2004 leveraged buyout, when the terms of the PPA might have raised the buyers' suspicions; Collins' ready willingness to opine in 2002 that Refco's $700 million in intercompany debt was enforceable and collectable; and conversations with another attorney in 2004, negotiating a sale of Refco stock, in which Collins was explicitly confronted about the existence of $1.1 billion of debt.

In 2013, after a five-week trial, a jury convicted Collins of seven counts related to the fraud. Collins now appeals his conviction, challenging the district court's exclusion of opinion testimony and the delivery of a jury instruction on conscious avoidance. Neither decision represents prejudicial error.

1. The district court excluded the opinion testimony of two lawyers. This Court "review[s] a district court's evidentiary rulings for manifest error." Raskin v. Wyatt Co., 125 F.3d 55, 65–66 (2d Cir.1997). Opinion testimony is inadmissible if it is not "helpful to . . . determining a fact in issue." Fed.R.Evid. 701(b); see id. R. 702(a). An opinion is unhelpful and therefore may not be received in evidence if, for example, the testimony would merely recapitulate aspects of the evidence that the jury can already perceive on its own, see Cameron v. City of New York, 598 F.3d 50, 62 (2d Cir.2010); the testimony "would merely tell the jury what result to reach," United States v. Rea, 958 F.2d 1206, 1215 (2d Cir.1992) (quoting Fed.R.Evid. 704 Advisory Committee Note); or an expert's testimony would deal with matters within "the ken of the average juror," United States v. Castillo, 924 F.2d 1227, 1232 (2d Cir.1991).

Collins' counsel sought to elicit opinions from one lay witness and one expert regarding the materiality of the PPA during the 2004 leveraged buyout. According to Collins' proffer, both witnesses would have testified that the PPA would have appeared immaterial to the leveraged buyout in the eyes of a lawyer unaware of Refco's fraud. The expert, a mergers and acquisitions lawyer, would also have testified generally about the work of transactional lawyers. The district court rejected both proffers on the grounds that the testimony would not be helpful to the jury, that the opinions depicting the PPA as immaterial would be conclusory, that Collins could alternatively establish immateriality through cross-examination of government witnesses, that a "war of experts" should be avoided, and that the materiality vel non of the PPA was within the competence of a jury unassisted by opinion testimony. As it transpired, fact witnesses proved sufficient for Collins' counsel to present the defense view of the PPA's materiality, including testimony that rights under the PPA were "extinguished" before the leveraged buyout closed. The district court's evidentiary rulings were valid exercises of its discretion.

2. The district court delivered a conscious avoidance charge over Collins' objection. When the parties in a trial dispute the element of knowledge, a conscious avoidance charge is appropriate if "the evidence

would permit a rational juror to conclude beyond a reasonable doubt that the defendant was aware of a high probability of the fact in dispute and consciously avoided confirming that fact." United States v. Cuti, 720 F.3d 453, 463 (2d Cir.2013) (quotation marks omitted). This test is satisfied "where[ ] a defendant's involvement in the criminal offense may have been so overwhelmingly suspicious that the defendant's failure to question the suspicious circumstances establishes the defendant's purposeful contrivance to avoid guilty knowledge." United States v. Svoboda, 347 F.3d 471, 480 (2d Cir.2003) (internal quotation marks and alteration omitted); see United States v. Goffer, 721 F.3d 113, 127–28 (2d Cir.2013). The evidence supporting that overwhelming suspiciousness is often the same evidence used to demonstrate actual knowledge. See Svoboda, 347 F.3d at 480.

Collins argues on appeal that the government introduced insufficient evidence to support a conscious avoidance charge.[1] This argument is untenable in view of the government's evidence that Collins provided a 2002 legal opinion regarding $700 million in intercompany debt, at a time when Refco's public filings reported only $179 million in intercompany debt. Further undercutting Collins' argument is the trial evidence that another lawyer told him in 2004 that Refco's CEO had revealed the existence of a $1.1 billion debt while negotiating the price of an equity sale. This evidence was sufficient to support the district court's conscious avoidance charge.

For the foregoing reasons, and finding no merit in Collins' other arguments, we hereby AFFIRM the judgment of the district court.

* * *

Problem 24.10. Consider the first time when Refco executives asked Joseph Collins to prepare the documentation for the short-term financings that were part of the fraudulent scheme. Of course, company executives did not say, "This is part of a fraudulent scheme." Instead, they described the need to document a short-term loan that had no purpose other than to remove debt from the company's books for a short period of time. With citation to authorities referenced throughout this chapter, describe the steps Collins should have taken to gather information, advise his client, and withdraw from the representation if necessary.

* * *

---

[1] Collins further argues that the district court's instruction misstated the legal standard for conscious avoidance, but he concedes that controlling precedent of this Court supports the district court's instruction. See Goffer, 721 F.3d at 128. Given that precedent, we see no fault in the content of the conscious avoidance instruction.

Profile of attorney professionalism. Tamar Frankel, a professor at Boston University School of Law, focuses her teaching and writing on issues of fiduciary law, corporate governance, mutual funds, securitization, and financial system regulation. Her book titles include *Trust and Honesty, America's Business Culture at a Crossroad* (2006), *Fiduciary Law* (2010), and *The Ponzi Scheme Puzzle* (2012). Professor Frankel wants to help lawyers and the public at large understand that "[l]aw is not the enemy of business. It the enemy of crooked business." Tina Spee, *Conversations with Tamar Frankel*, http://www.tamarfrankel. com/conversations-with-tamar-frankel.html.

Professor Frankel's work in the area of fiduciary duty law has been recognized by the Institute for the Fiduciary Standard's establishment of the "Frankel Fiduciary Prize" to honor individuals who advance fiduciary principles.

Since beginning her legal career in 1948, Tamar Frankel has practiced law in both her native Israel and in the U.S. Her experiences have ranged from being an attorney in the legal department of the Israeli Department of Justice to designing the corporate structure of the Internet Corporation for Names and Numbers ("ICANN"). She has been a visiting scholar at the Securities and Exchange Commission and has lectured at schools including Oxford University, Tokyo University, and Harvard Law School.

Professor Frankel has been a trailblazer for women teaching corporate law. She began her law-teaching career at Boston University School of Law in 1967. She was one of only twelve women teaching corporations law at a U.S. law school prior to 1980 who went on to become tenured, full professors. Margaret V. Sachs, *Women in Corporate Law Teaching: A Tale of Two Generations*, 65 MD. L. REV. 666, 666–67 (2006). In discussing her approach to teaching, Professor Frankel has said it is important "not to get stuck in your own generation." She combats that by "listen[ing] to the new generation" and "[trying] to understand a very different world." Tina Spee, *Conversations with Tamar Frankel*, http:// www.tamarfrankel.com/conversations-with-tamar-frankel.html.

CHAPTER 25

REPRESENTING ORGANIZATIONAL CLIENTS

■ ■ ■

Chapter hypothetical. The attorneys in this chapter's problems represent Trucker's Fuel Stop, Inc. ("TFS"). TFS is the country's second largest truck stop chain, with locations in forty-eight states.

TFS is a privately held company. Members of the Hanson family own approximately 70% of the company's stock. All Hanson family members who own company stock are also members of the board, with one exception: family matriarch Patty Hanson owns company stock but is no longer involved in the business. TFS employees own the remaining 30% of company shares. Company stock is not available for purchase by the general public.

* * *

When a client is an organization, such as a partnership, limited liability company, corporation, or governmental body, a lawyer owes the client all of the same legal and ethical duties discussed in other chapters of this book. In this chapter, though, we look at the unique challenges of representing a client that cannot speak for itself. The organizational client must speak through its agents (referred to as "constituents" in the Model Rules). While this may seem like a minor matter, it significantly complicates the lawyer's job in a number of ways.

First, what should the lawyer do when the agents of the company are engaged in conduct that may result in substantial liability to the organization—such as criminal penalties or civil liability for fraud or breach of fiduciary duty? Certainly a competent lawyer has a duty to advise any client (whether an individual or organization) about the risks of engaging in such misconduct and the lawyer cannot participate in such misconduct. Does the attorney for an organizational client have any additional duties to protect the organization from liability?

Second, when the client is an organization, which communications between employees and attorneys are privileged? To whom within the organization can the lawyer disclose confidential information without risking attorney-client privilege? During internal investigations, what should the company's lawyer explain to employees about privilege, client identity, and the prospect of privilege waiver?

Third, lawyers must be especially mindful of conflicts of interest when they represent organizational clients. In the course of representing these clients, when can the lawyer also represent agents of the organization? When can the attorney represent the organization in matters adverse to agents of the organization, and when should the attorney refuse to do so? In what circumstances can the company lawyer represent management in a derivative suit brought by shareholders?

All of these questions turn on the issue of loyalty: what does it mean to be loyal to a client that is an entity and not a person? Loyalty to an entity can be confusing, because the organization's lawyer necessarily deals with people who speak on the organization's behalf. *See* Model Rule 1.13(a) and Comment [1] (organizations act through their authorized constituents). Understandably, the lawyer may sometimes think of these people as the client even though they are not or may feel loyalty to these individuals more than to the actual client. This chapter is aimed at providing you a framework for addressing these issues in practice.

* * *

A. PROTECTING ORGANIZATIONAL CLIENTS FROM CONSTITUENT MISCONDUCT

Please read ABA Model Rules of Professional Conduct, Rule 1.13(a)–(e) and Comments [1]–[9].

Please read Standards of Professional Conduct for Attorneys Appearing and Practicing Before the Commission in the Representation of an Issuer, 17 C.F.R. § 205.

* * *

In 2002, Congress passed the Sarbanes-Oxley Act in response to accounting fraud in publicly traded companies, including Enron and WorldCom. The fraudulent conduct by the companies' own executives ultimately destroyed these companies and caused company stockholders to lose their investments. The Sarbanes-Oxley Act was aimed at protecting companies—and their investors—from future fraud. Among its numerous provisions, § 307 of the Act addresses the role that lawyers should play in preventing corporate fraud. That section required the Securities and Exchange Commission (SEC) to adopt attorney conduct rules that would guide attorneys in reporting violations of law to higher authorities in the company so that the company could appropriately address the misconduct.

In response to this directive, in 2003, the SEC adopted "Standards of Professional Conduct for Attorneys Appearing and Practicing Before the Commission in the Representation of an Issuer," codified at 17 C.F.R. Part 205. These rules provide detailed direction to attorneys for publicly traded companies concerning their obligation to report violations of law "up-the-ladder" within the corporation. Another provision of the SEC rule gives an attorney permission to disclose confidential client information to the SEC if doing so will protect the company or its investors from substantial injury. The latter type of rule is sometimes described as a "loyal disclosure" rule because it permits disclosure of client confidences out of loyalty to the organizational client. In short, the disclosure is allowed for the purpose of protecting the client from the negative consequences of agent misconduct.

In 2002, the ABA formed the Task Force on Corporate Responsibility to consider rule amendments to address the same issues of corporate fraud. In 2003, the ABA strengthened its up-the-ladder reporting rule (Model Rule 1.13(b)) and adopted a loyal disclosure rule (Model Rule 1.13(c)) similar to those that had just been adopted by the SEC. Numerous states followed the ABA's lead and incorporated such provisions into their professional conduct rules. The ABA and SEC rules will be discussed in greater detail in the following sections.

At the outset, it may be helpful to briefly consider how these rules fit within the legal and ethical framework discussed in Chapter 24. Recall that attorneys have an ethical and legal obligation to competently advise their clients about the legal consequences of proposed conduct. Nonetheless, a client that is a natural person can choose to engage in conduct that is contrary to the attorney's advice. If the conduct could result in liability for the lawyer, he or she should withdraw (Model Rule 1.16(a), (b)), and may be permitted (Model Rule 1.6(b)) or required (Model Rule 4.1(b)) to disclose confidential information to avoid assisting in client misconduct. But the attorney need not protect the client from itself.

Organizational clients are different though. Such clients act through agents who may be engaged in conduct that: (1) is in the agent's personal interest but harms the organization, or (2) that is part of a misguided plan that will ultimately result in liability for the organization. The Model Rules recognize an organization's agents usually speak for it, but that the lawyer should stop listening when the lawyer determines the agents are engaged in such misconduct. *See* Model Rule 1.13(b) and Comment [3]. The up-the-ladder reporting and loyal disclosure rules are intended to prompt lawyers to take further steps to protect an organizational client from agents who may harm it through misconduct. This is consistent with a lawyer's fiduciary duty of loyalty to the client: the lawyer must put the interests of the client before the interests of any third party, including an agent.

1.   UP-THE-LADDER REPORTING

Please read ABA Model Rules of Professional Conduct, Rule 1.13(b) and Comments [1] & [3]–[5].

Please read Standards of Professional Conduct for Attorneys Appearing and Practicing Before the Commission in the Representation of an Issuer, 17 C.F.R. § 205.

The ABA's up-the-ladder reporting rule applies to all organizational clients, not just companies with registered securities. Though the text is slightly more complex than this summary, Model Rule 1.13(b) essentially provides that the organization's attorney should alert higher authorities in the organization (including the organization's highest authority) when a constituent of the organization is engaged in: (1) a violation of a legal obligation to the organization; or (2) a violation of law that if imputed to the organization would result in substantial injury to the organization.

The SEC's up-the-ladder reporting rule requires attorneys appearing and practicing before the SEC in the representation of an issuer (a company with registered securities) to report "evidence of a material violation" to higher authorities of the corporation. A "material violation" is defined as a "material violation of an applicable United States federal or state securities law, a material breach of fiduciary duty arising under United States federal or state law, or a similar material violation of any United States federal or state law." 17 C.F.R. § 205.2(i).

Section 205.3(b) requires that an attorney report to the corporation's chief legal officer (or both the chief legal officer and the chief executive officer). 17 C.F.R. § 205.3(b)(1). The attorney then must determine if he or she has received an "appropriate response," defined as a response that causes the attorney to believe: (1) there is no material violation; (2) the company has adopted appropriate remedial measures; or (3) the company has retained an attorney to review the material violation and either (i) has implemented that attorney's remedial recommendations; or (ii) has been advised that the attorney may assert a "colorable defense" on behalf of the company. 17 C.F.R. § 205.2(b).

If the attorney reasonably believes that he or she has not received an "appropriate response," then the attorney must report the evidence to the audit committee, or a committee of directors who are not employees of the company (if there is no audit committee), or to the full board of directors (if there is no committee of directors not employed by the company). 17 C.F.R. § 205.3(b)(3). As an alternative to reporting up-the-ladder under § 205.3(b), the attorney may instead report evidence of a material violation to the corporation's qualified legal compliance committee. 17 C.F.R. § 205.3(c).

* * *

Problem 25.1. Doug Michaels, an attorney in TFS's general counsel's office, works primarily on negotiating and drafting TFS contracts. For the past year, Doug has worked with TFS Vice President Hank Silvers on all new rebate contracts with TFS customers. These contracts provide customers a rebate based on numerous factors, including the volume of fuel purchased each quarter. The rebate contracts are an important part of TFS's business model because the rebates encourage customers to purchase all of their fuel from TFS.

Hank and Doug were recently negotiating a rebate contract between TFS and Missouri Trucklines. As the negotiations were drawing to a close, Doug had a troubling conversation with TFS customer billing supervisor Charlene Mills. Doug called Charlene to ask her to estimate the rebate Missouri Trucklines could expect given certain assumptions about their quarterly purchases. He asked Charlene to run the numbers by applying the rebate formula contained in most of TFS's rebate contracts. Doug wanted the information so he could provide Missouri Trucklines with an estimate of the rebates they should expect if they signed the contract.

Charlene responded, "Do you want to know how the rebate formula actually works or how it is supposed to work?"

"Isn't that the same thing?" Doug asked.

Charlene then explained that for the past two years, at the direction of Hank Silvers, the customer billing department has been adjusting rebate numbers by applying a secondary formula. She then described why the secondary formula is unlikely to be detected by customers. With a laugh she noted, "No one has caught on yet." Charlene concluded by telling Doug that the secondary formula has saved the company approximately $12.5 million over the past two years.

As a fiduciary, what legal obligation does Doug owe TFS as he addresses the rebate issue? Analyze whether Doug has an up-the-ladder reporting obligation in light of the information provided by Charlene. (Note on applicable professional conduct rules: The state where Doug practices has adopted a professional conduct rule identical to Model Rule 1.13(b). You should assume that SEC attorney conduct rules do not apply to Doug because TFS is not an "issuer.").

* * *

2. LOYAL DISCLOSURE

Please read ABA Model Rules of Professional Conduct, Rule 1.13(c) & (d) and Comments [6]–[8].

Please read Standards of Professional Conduct for Attorneys Appearing and Practicing Before the Commission in the Representation of an Issuer, 17 C.F.R. § 205.

Loyal disclosure is only permitted under Model Rule 1.13(c) when up-the-ladder reporting fails, i.e., when the highest authority capable of acting either insists upon or fails to timely and appropriately address "an action or a refusal to act that is clearly a violation of law." Then, the attorney may disclose confidential information if the attorney "reasonably believes" the conduct (that is clearly a violation of law) "is reasonably certain to result in substantial injury to the organization," but such disclosure is allowed "only if and to the extent the lawyer reasonably believes necessary to prevent substantial injury to the organization." The rule does not define who can (or cannot) be the recipient of such disclosure. *Id.* The ABA rule does not permit disclosure by an attorney investigating the alleged violation of law or defending the organization or any of its constituents against a claim arising out of an alleged violation of law. Model Rule 1.13(d).

The SEC's loyal disclosure rule allows an attorney to disclose confidential client information to the SEC "to the extent the attorney reasonably believes necessary" to prevent the client's commission of a "material violation" that is "likely to cause substantial injury" to the issuer client. 17 C.F.R. § 205.3(d)(2)(i).[1] The rule also allows disclosure to the extent the attorney reasonably believes necessary "to rectify the consequences of a material violation" (when the attorney's services were used in furtherance of the violation) that "caused or may cause substantial injury" to the financial interest or property of the issuer client. 17 C.F.R. § 205.3(d)(2)(iii). Though not explicitly stated in the text of the SEC rule, it is implicit that disclosure outside the corporation can occur only after "reporting up" efforts have failed—the rule only permits disclosure "to the extent" necessary.

It can be hard for attorneys to envision that it might be in the client's interest to disclose information that the client is involved in illegal conduct. Attorneys may even rationalize that if the conduct is unlikely to be discovered and is actually profitable to the company, it would not be in the company's interest to disclose it. These loyal disclosure rules

---

[1] Another provision of the rule—section 205.3(d)(2)(ii)—is not a loyal disclosure provision because it is not aimed at protecting the company but rather its purpose is to allow disclosure to prevent an issuer from committing or suborning perjury or perpetrating a fraud on the SEC. This provision is more akin to Model Rule 3.3 than to Model Rule 1.13(c).

recognize, though, that it is not in the company's long-term interest to be engaged in misconduct for which the company could suffer substantial financial harm. Prior professional conduct rules gave attorneys no mechanism to encourage legal compliance in the case of financial fraud: an attorney's only option was to withdraw from the representation under the prior Model Rule 1.13(b). Under loyal disclosure rules, though, the attorney can explain that he or she has the power to protect the organization through disclosure if management chooses to do nothing. Even if loyal disclosure itself is rare, perhaps the possibility of it will discourage financial fraud.

* * *

Problem 25.2. Assume that Doug discussed the rebate issue (discussed in Problem 24.1) with Frank Silvers, then with TFS general counsel Jane Harmon, and ultimately with the TFS board of directors. Everyone Doug has met with insists that the rebate plan is profitable and unlikely to be detected, so there is no reason to change what the company is doing.

Doug is now considering whether he has a legal and professional conduct obligation of "loyal disclosure." (Note on applicable professional conduct rules: The state where Doug practices has adopted a professional conduct rule identical to Model Rule 1.13(c). Recall that SEC rules do not apply because TFS is not an "issuer.").

Which factors weigh in favor of loyal disclosure? Against loyal disclosure? If Doug determines that loyal disclosure is appropriate, to whom should Doug disclose the information?

* * *

B. ORGANIZATIONAL CLIENTS AND ATTORNEY-CLIENT PRIVILEGE

Please read ABA Model Rules of Professional Conduct, Rule 1.13(f) and Comments [2], [10] & [11].

Please read Restatement (Third) of the Law Governing Lawyers §§ 73 & 74.

1. COMMON ORGANIZATIONAL CLIENT ATTORNEY-CLIENT PRIVILEGE ISSUES

Whether a client is an organization or an individual, the same attorney-client privilege applies. For a communication to be privileged, it must be made in confidence, between attorney and client, for the purpose of seeking or giving legal advice. Restatement (Third) of the Law Governing Lawyers § 73.

But even though the privilege is the same, the nature of the organizational entity can complicate the privilege analysis. One issue is who can speak on behalf of the corporation to create a privileged communication. As discussed in Chapter 15, courts follow different approaches to determine which of a corporation's agents can have privileged conversations with counsel. In federal court, *Upjohn v. United States* guides the corporate privilege analysis. States are not bound by *Upjohn*, so some take a different approach to determining which agents' communications with counsel are protected by privilege. *See, e.g.,* Consolidation Coal Co. v. Bucyrus-Erie Co., 432 N.E.2d 250, 257–58 (Ill. 1982) (adopting a modified control group test). *See also* Restatement (Third) of the Law Governing Lawyers § 73(2) and comment d. Because of the differences in approach, research is necessary in each case to determine the contours of the privilege.

Whether legal advice was the purpose of a communication between company and lawyer is another hurdle in analyzing organizational attorney-client privilege. In-house attorneys for organizations often wear two hats, sometimes addressing business concerns and other times advising about legal matters. If the communication is not for the purpose of seeking or giving legal advice, it will not be protected by privilege. In *Higgins v. Eichler*, the court determined that numerous documents evidencing communications with in-house counsel, Glenn Madere, were not privileged. In several instances, the court explained the documents did not reflect that Madere (who was also a corporate officer) was acting "in his capacity as counsel" or that he was "giving, sharing, or receiving legal advice." 1998 WL 181825, *1–4 (E.D. Pa. 1998). *See also In re* Kellogg Brown & Root, Inc., 756 F.3d 754 (D.C. Cir. 2014) (holding that "[i]n the context of an organization's internal investigation, if *one of the significant purposes* of the internal investigation was to obtain or provide legal advice, the privilege will apply.") (emphasis added).

A related problem is that constituents of the organization may forward documents to counsel or copy counsel on email under the mistaken belief that an attorney's involvement creates a privileged communication. *See, e.g.,* Simon v. G.D. Searle & Co., 816 F.2d 397 (8th Cir. 1987) (noting that business documents sent to the company's attorneys "do not become privileged automatically."); *In re* Vioxx Products Liability Litigation, 501 F.Supp.2d 789, 800–01 (E.D. La. 2007) (explaining that despite extensive regulation of its industry, a corporation cannot assume that everything sent to the legal department will be protected by the attorney-client privilege). It is important for the organization's personnel to understand that they must be seeking legal advice in order for the privilege to attach.

An organization's attorney-client privilege can also be put at risk through a lack of confidentiality. Even though an organization may have many employees, not every employee needs to know the content of communications with counsel. Because confidentiality is a necessary component of privilege, organizational clients can jeopardize the privilege by forwarding privileged communications beyond those persons within the company who need to know. *See, e.g.,* In re Grand Jury Subpoenas, 561 F.Supp.1247, 1258–59 (E.D.N.Y. 1982) (finding documents not privileged because they were forwarded to a constituent of the company who did not need to know the information); Restatement (Third) of the Law Governing Lawyers § 73(4). The lawyer's professional conduct obligation in regard to confidentiality is similar. Comment [2] to the organizational client professional conduct rule (Model Rule 1.13) notes that lawyers cannot disclose confidential client information to agents of the organization except when authorized to carry out the representation.

* * *

Problem 25.3. TFS has been sued by Fanny's Pie Factory for breach of contract. Maureen Albright, an attorney at the firm Spinner, Ahern & Albright, was hired by TFS to represent TFS in the case. In discovery, Fanny's Pie Factory has requested that TFS produce all communications by TFS employees during a defined time period that "refer or relate to the TFS contract with Fanny's Pie Factory and/or Fanny's Pie Factory product quality." Analyze whether Maureen will be successful in asserting that the following documents are privileged.

Assume that state law (and not federal law) is applicable and that the state follows the *Upjohn* approach regarding which agents of the company may have privileged communications with counsel. You may also rely upon cases cited in this part of the text and the Restatement as you answer the following questions:

(A) An email from TFS accounts payable supervisor Bif Allington to in-house attorney Doug Michaels. Bif noted that he recalls that Doug negotiated the TFS contract with Fanny's. Bif asked Doug for advice about whether, under the terms of the contract, TFS should refuse to pay Fanny's for approximately $500 worth of product that was past its sell-by date when it was received by TFS. Bif suggested that alternatively he can pay the full invoiced amount and seek a refund from Fanny's.

(B) An email from TFS employee Kitty Blair to TFS employees Herb Strobel, Annika Overhoffer, and Benton Tucker. All of these employees manage various TFS truck stops. Kitty stated, "I just wonder if other people have had problems with the Fanny's pies lately. We keep receiving pies that are already expired, meaning they arrive after their 'sell-by-this-date' sticker." She included a "cc" of the email to Regional Vice President Harley Crandall. Harley then forwarded the email to in-house attorney Doug Michaels with a note, "What should we do about this?"

(C) A memo from Doug Michaels to TFS Regional Managers. Doug asked for the managers' opinion regarding whether the Fanny's Pies contract should be renegotiated when it expires or if there is another supplier that the company would like to consider. Also in the memo, Doug noted reports of product inconsistency as a reason to think about a new supplier.

2. ORGANIZATIONAL ATTORNEY-CLIENT PRIVILEGE AND INTERNAL INVESTIGATIONS

Another privilege issue unique to organizational clients arises when attorneys receive information from company agents in an investigation. This information may reveal a possible basis for criminal or civil liability of the agent, the organization, or both. Even though attorneys want to encourage company employees to be candid in these discussions, the promise of privilege could be confusing. While it is true the conversations may be protected by privilege, the privilege belongs to the organization and not to the individual providing information. The organization may later wish to waive privilege, even though it is against the interests of the individual who disclosed the information.

Professional conduct rules and case law address what a company's lawyer should communicate to company employees in this situation. Model Rule 1.13(f) provides that a lawyer should explain the client's identity—that it is the organization and not the individual—in dealings with company agents if the agent's interests are adverse to the organization. Comments 10 and 11 elaborate that in a situation of adversity between organizational client and constituent, the lawyer should explain whom the lawyer represents and the impact on attorney-client privilege.

Alerting a client's employees of such issues at the outset of an internal investigation is often referred to as providing an "*Upjohn* warning" or "corporate *Miranda* warning." This warning should include notice to the employee of the following: (1) the lawyer represents the organization and not the individual; (2) the privilege belongs to the organization and not the individual; (3) the organization may later choose to waive the privilege; (4) the individual should keep the conversation confidential; and (5) the individual may wish to consult his or her own attorney. To avoid any uncertainty about the content of these warnings to employees, lawyers are encouraged to put them in writing.

Without this warning, the client's agent might reasonably believe he or she has an attorney-client relationship with the lawyer. This misapprehension could harm the corporate client who might be prohibited from disclosing the information from the agent's interview even though it is in the corporate client's interest to do so. Further, such a misapprehension could result in the lawyer violating fiduciary duties to the agent/client, as well as professional conduct obligations, prohibiting conflicts of interest (the dual representation of parties with adverse interests) and disclosure of client confidences (if the lawyer disclosed information at the corporate client's direction but against the wishes of the agent/client). The following case considers the sufficiency of counsel's *Upjohn* warning to constituents of AOL Time Warner.

IN RE GRAND JURY SUBPOENA: UNDER SEAL
415 F.3d 333 (4th Cir. 2005).

WILSON, DISTRICT JUDGE.

This is an appeal by three former employees of AOL Time Warner ("AOL") from the decision of the district court denying their motions to quash a grand jury subpoena for documents related to an internal investigation by AOL. Appellants in the district court [asserted] that the subpoenaed documents were protected by the attorney-client privilege. Because the district court concluded that the privilege was AOL's alone and because AOL had expressly waived its privilege, the court denied the appellants' motion. We affirm.

I.

In March of 2001, AOL began an internal investigation into its relationship with PurchasePro, Inc. AOL retained the law firm of Wilmer, Cutler & Pickering ("Wilmer Cutler") to assist in the investigation. Over the next several months, AOL's general counsel and counsel from Wilmer Cutler (collectively referred to herein as "AOL's attorneys" or the "investigating attorneys") interviewed appellants, AOL employees Kent Wakeford, John Doe 1, and John Doe 2.[1]

The investigating attorneys interviewed Wakeford, a manager in the company's Business Affairs division, on six occasions. At their third interview, and the first one in which Wilmer Cutler attorneys were present, Randall Boe, AOL's General Counsel, informed Wakeford, "We represent the company. These conversations are privileged, but the privilege belongs to the company and the company decides whether to waive it. If there is a conflict, the attorney-client privilege belongs to the company." Memoranda from that meeting also indicate that the attorneys explained to Wakeford that they represented AOL but that they "could" represent him as well, "as long as no conflict appear[ed]." The attorneys interviewed Wakeford again three days later and, at the beginning of the interview, reiterated that they represented AOL, that the privilege belonged to AOL, and that Wakeford could retain personal counsel at company expense.

---

[1]   Because the grand jury has indicted Wakeford, we refer to him by name.

The investigating attorneys interviewed John Doe 1 three times. Before the first interview, Boe told him, "We represent the company. These conversations are privileged, but the privilege belongs to the company and the company decides whether to waive it. You are free to consult with your own lawyer at any time." Memoranda from that interview indicate that the attorneys also told him, "We can represent [you] until such time as there appears to be a conflict of interest, [but] . . . the attorney-client privilege belongs to AOL and AOL can decide whether to keep it or waive it." At the end of the interview, John Doe 1 asked if he needed personal counsel. A Wilmer Cutler attorney responded that he did not recommend it, but that he would tell the company not to be concerned if Doe retained counsel.

AOL's attorneys interviewed John Doe 2 twice and followed essentially the same protocol they had followed with the other appellants. They noted, "We represent AOL, and can represent [you] too if there is not a conflict." In addition, the attorneys told him that, "the attorney-client privilege is AOL's and AOL can choose to waive it."

In November, 2001, the Securities and Exchange Commission ("SEC") began to investigate AOL's relationship with PurchasePro. In December 2001, AOL and Wakeford, through counsel, entered into an oral "common interest agreement," which they memorialized in writing in January 2002. The attorneys acknowledged that, "representation of [their] respective clients raise[d] issues of common interest to [their] respective clients and that the sharing of certain documents, information, . . . and communications with clients" would be mutually beneficial. As a result, the attorneys agreed to share access to information relating to their representation of Wakeford and AOL, noting that "the oral or written disclosure of Common Interest Materials . . . [would] not diminish in any way the confidentiality of such Materials and [would] not constitute a waiver of any applicable privilege."

Wakeford testified before the SEC on February 14, 2002, represented by his personal counsel. Laura Jehl, AOL's general counsel, and F. Whitten Peters of Williams & Connolly, whom AOL had retained in November 2001 in connection with the PurchasePro investigation, were also present, and both stated that they represented Wakeford "for purposes of [the] deposition." During the deposition, the SEC investigators questioned Wakeford about his discussions with AOL's attorneys. When Wakeford's attorney asserted the attorney-client privilege, the SEC investigators followed up with several questions to determine whether the privilege was applicable to the investigating attorneys' March-June 2001 interviews with Wakeford. Wakeford told them he believed, at the time of the interviews, that the investigating attorneys represented him and the company.

John Doe 1 testified before the SEC on February 27, 2002, represented by personal counsel. No representatives of AOL were present. When SEC investigators questioned Doe about the March-June 2001 internal investigation, his counsel asserted that the information was protected and directed Doe not to answer any questions about the internal investigation "in respect to the company's privilege." He stated that Doe's response could be considered a waiver of the privilege and that, "if the AOL lawyers were [present], they could make a judgment, with respect to the company's privilege, about whether or not the answer would constitute a waiver."

On February 26, 2004, a grand jury in the Eastern District of Virginia issued a subpoena commanding AOL to provide "written memoranda and other written records reflecting interviews conducted by attorneys for [AOL]" of the appellants between March 15 and June 30, 2001. While AOL agreed to waive the attorney-client privilege and produce the subpoenaed documents, counsel for the appellants moved to quash the subpoena on the grounds that each appellant had an individual attorney-client relationship with the investigating attorneys, that his interviews were individually privileged, and that he had not waived the privilege. Wakeford also claimed that the information he disclosed to the investigating attorneys was privileged under the common interest doctrine.

The district court denied John Doe 1's and John Doe 2's motions because it found they failed to prove they were clients of the investigating attorneys who interviewed them. The court based its conclusion on its findings that: (1) the investigating attorneys told them that they represented the company; (2) the investigating attorneys told them, "we *can* represent you," which is distinct from "we *do* represent you"; (3) they could not show that the investigating attorneys agreed to represent them; and (4) the investigating attorneys told them that the attorney-client privilege belonged to the company and the company could choose to waive it.

The court initially granted Wakeford's motion to quash because it found that his communications with the investigating attorneys were privileged under the common interest agreement between counsel for Wakeford and counsel for AOL. Following a motion for reconsideration, the court reversed its earlier ruling and held that the subpoenaed documents relating to Wakeford's interviews were not privileged because it found that Wakeford's common interest agreement with AOL postdated the March-June 2001 interviews. In addition, the court held that Wakeford failed to prove that he was a client of the investigating attorneys at the time the interviews took place. The court based its conclusion on its findings that: (1) none of the investigating attorneys understood that Wakeford was seeking personal legal advice; (2) the investigating attorneys did not provide any personal legal advice to him; and (3) the investigating attorneys believed they represented AOL and not Wakeford. This appeal followed.

II.

Appellants argue that because they believed that the investigating attorneys who conducted the interviews were representing them personally, their communications are privileged. However, we agree with the district court that essential touchstones for the formation of an attorney-client relationship between the investigating attorneys and the appellants were missing at the time of the interviews. There is no evidence of an objectively reasonable, mutual understanding that the appellants were seeking legal advice from the investigating attorneys or that the investigating attorneys were rendering personal legal advice. Nor, in light of the investigating attorneys' disclosure that they represented AOL and that the privilege and the right to waive it were AOL's alone, do we find investigating counsel's hypothetical pronouncement that they *could* represent appellants sufficient to establish the reasonable understanding that they *were* representing appellants. Accordingly, we find no fault with the district court's opinion that no individual attorney-client privilege attached to the appellants' communications with AOL's attorneys.[2]

We apply a two-fold standard of review in this case. We give deference to the district court's determination of the underlying facts, and review those findings for clear error. In re Grand Jury Subpoena v. Under Seal, 341 F.3d 331, 334 (4th Cir.2003); *see also In re Allen et al.,* 106 F.3d 582, 601 (4th Cir.1997) (noting the two-fold standard of review). A finding of fact is clearly erroneous, despite the presence of evidence to support it, when the reviewing court, after carefully examining all the evidence, is "left with the definite and firm conviction that a mistake has been committed." Anderson v. City of Bessemer City, 470 U.S. 564, 573, 105 S.Ct. 1504, 84 L.Ed.2d 518 (1985). We review the application of legal principles *de novo. In re Grand Jury Subpoena,* 341 F.3d at 334.

"The attorney-client privilege is the oldest of the privileges for confidential communications known to the common law." Upjohn v. United States, 449 U.S. 383, 389, 101 S.Ct. 677, 66 L.Ed.2d 584 (1981). "[W]hen the privilege applies, it affords confidential communications between lawyer and client complete protection from disclosure." Hawkins v. Stables, 148 F.3d 379, 383 (4th Cir.1998). Because its application

---

[2] The grand jury's return of an indictment against Wakeford does not moot his appeal because the government continues to seek records from the March-June 2001 interviews for trial as to Wakeford and through a second grand jury as to others. Given this high probability of reoccurrence, our opinion is in no way advisory. *See In re Grand Jury Proceedings,* 33 F.3d 342, 347 (4th Cir.1994) (applying the "capable of repetition, yet evading review" exception to the mootness doctrine in the context of expired grand jury).

interferes with "the truth seeking mission of the legal process," United States v. Tedder, 801 F.2d 1437, 1441 (4th Cir.1986), however, we must narrowly construe the privilege, and recognize it "only to the very limited extent that ... excluding relevant evidence has a public good transcending the normally predominant principle of utilizing all rational means for ascertaining the truth." Trammel v. United States, 445 U.S. 40, 50, 100 S.Ct. 906, 63 L.Ed.2d 186 (1980). Accordingly, the privilege applies only to "[c]onfidential disclosures by a client to an attorney made in order to obtain legal assistance." Fisher v. United States, 425 U.S. 391, 403, 96 S.Ct. 1569, 48 L.Ed.2d 39 (1976).[3] "The burden is on the proponent of the attorney-client privilege to demonstrate its applicability." *Jones,* 696 F.2d at 1072.

The person seeking to invoke the attorney-client privilege must prove that he is a client or that he affirmatively sought to become a client. "The professional relationship ... hinges upon the client's belief that he is consulting a lawyer in that capacity and his manifested intention to seek professional legal advice." United States v. Evans, 113 F.3d 1457, 1465 (7th Cir.1997). An individual's subjective belief that he is represented is not alone sufficient to create an attorney-client relationship. *See* United States v. Keplinger, 776 F.2d 678, 701 (7th Cir.1985)("We think no individual attorney-client relationship can be inferred without some finding that the potential client's subjective belief is minimally reasonable"); *see also,* In re Grand Jury Subpoena Duces Tecum, 112 F.3d 910, 923 (8th Cir.1997) ("[W]e know of no authority ... holding that a client's beliefs, subjective or objective, about the law of privilege can transform an otherwise unprivileged conversation into a privileged one."). Rather, the putative client must show that his subjective belief that an attorney-client relationship existed was reasonable under the circumstances.[4]

---

[3] This circuit has adopted the classic test to determine whether the attorney-client privilege applies to certain communications or documents. The privilege applies only if (1) the asserted holder of the privilege is or sought to become a client; (2) the person to whom the communication was made (a) is a member of the bar of a court, or his subordinate and (b) in connection with this communication is acting as a lawyer; (3) the communication relates to a fact of which the attorney was informed (a) by his client (b) without the presence of strangers (c) for the purpose of securing primarily either (i) an opinion on law or (ii) legal services or (iii) assistance in some legal proceeding, and not (d) for the purpose of committing a crime or tort; and (4) the privilege has been (a) claimed and (b) not waived by the client. United States v. Jones, 696 F.2d 1069, 1072 (4th Cir.1982).

[4] This court addressed the question of whether a corporate employee could personally assert the attorney-client privilege for communications with corporate counsel conducting an internal investigation in United States v. Aramony, 88 F.3d 1369 (4th Cir.1996). In *Aramony,* this court affirmed the finding of the district court that Aramony was not the client of internal investigation counsel. The court noted that Aramony did not seek legal advice; Aramony could not have reasonably believed that the information he disclosed would be kept confidential; and internal investigation counsel told Aramony that they were retained to represent the company. *Id.* at 1390–92.

With these precepts in mind, we conclude that appellants could not have reasonably believed that the investigating attorneys represented them personally during the time frame covered by the subpoena. First, there is no evidence that the investigating attorneys told the appellants that they represented them, nor is there evidence that the appellants asked the investigating attorneys to represent them. To the contrary, there is evidence that the investigating attorneys relayed to Wakeford the company's offer to retain personal counsel for him at the company's expense, and that they told John Doe 1 that he was free to retain personal counsel. Second, there is no evidence that the appellants ever sought personal legal advice from the investigating attorneys, nor is there any evidence that the investigating attorneys rendered personal legal advice. Third, when the appellants spoke with the investigating attorneys, they were fully apprised that the information they were giving could be disclosed at the company's discretion. Under these circumstances, appellants could not have reasonably believed that the investigating attorneys represented them personally.[5] Therefore, the district court's finding that appellants had no attorney-client relationship with the investigating attorneys is not clearly erroneous.[6]

The appellants argue that the phrase "we *can* represent you as long as no conflict appears," manifested an agreement by the investigating attorneys to represent them. They claim that, "it is hard to imagine a more straightforward assurance of an attorney-client relationship than 'we can represent you.' " We disagree. As the district court noted, "we *can* represent you" is distinct from "we *do* represent you." If there was any evidence that the investigating attorneys had said, "we *do* represent you," then the outcome of this appeal might be different. Furthermore, the statement actually made, "we *can* represent you," must be interpreted within the context of the entire warning. The investigating attorneys' statements to the appellants, read in their entirety, demonstrate that the attorneys' loyalty was to the company. That loyalty was never implicitly or explicitly divided. In addition to noting at the outset that they had been retained to represent AOL, the investigating attorneys warned the appellants that the content of their communications during the interview "belonged" to AOL. This protocol put the appellants on notice that, while their communications with the attorneys were considered confidential,

---

[5] The district court made no finding as to whether the appellants, in fact, believed that the investigating attorneys represented them personally.

[6] Appellants maintain the district court improperly relied on In re Bevill, Bresler, & Schulman Asset Mgmt. Corp., 805 F.2d 120, 123 (3d Cir.1986), in determining that appellants did not have an attorney-client relationship with the investigating attorneys. They contend that *Bevill* creates a litmus test this circuit has not adopted for determining whether there is an attorney-client relationship between corporate employees and corporate counsel. It is unnecessary to decide whether we find *Bevill* fully consistent with our views on this matter because based on the circumstances we have identified, it would not have been objectively reasonable for appellants to believe that the investigating attorneys represented them personally.

the company could choose to reveal the content of those communications at any time, without the appellants' consent.

We note, however, that our opinion should not be read as an implicit acceptance of the watered-down "*Upjohn* warnings" the investigating attorneys gave the appellants. It is a potential legal and ethical mine field. Had the investigating attorneys, in fact, entered into an attorney-client relationship with appellants, as their statements to the appellants professed they could, they would not have been free to waive the appellants' privilege when a conflict arose. It should have seemed obvious that they could not have jettisoned one client in favor of another. Rather, they would have had to withdraw from all representation and to maintain all confidences. Indeed, the court would be hard pressed to identify how investigating counsel could robustly investigate and report to management or the board of directors of a publicly-traded corporation with the necessary candor if counsel were constrained by ethical obligations to individual employees. However, because we agree with the district court that the appellants never entered into an attorney-client relationship with the investigating attorneys, they averted these troubling issues.

III.

[The court determined there was no evidence that Wakeford and AOL shared a common interest before December 2001 and found no error in the district court's conclusion that Wakeford had no joint defense privilege before that time].

IV.

After review of the district court's factual findings and legal conclusions, we find no clear error. . . . The district court therefore properly denied the appellants' motions.

AFFIRMED

* * *

Problem 25.4. Doug Michaels approached the TFS board a second time with his concerns about rebate fraud. This time, the board agreed that the company should hire a law firm to conduct an investigation to determine if TFS is engaged in illegal conduct. The company hired Loretta Sawyer from the firm Sawyer & Bernstein to conduct the investigation and prepare a report on her findings.

Loretta worked with in-house attorney Doug to create a list of individuals who are knowledgeable about the rebate issue. She has decided to interview TFS Vice President Hank Silvers first. Draft an *Upjohn* warning that Loretta can present to Hank at the start of his interview. If you complete additional research to prepare your *Upjohn* warning, please make a note the source or sources that you find most useful.

* * *

C. ORGANIZATIONAL CLIENTS, CONSTITUENTS, AND CONFLICTS OF INTEREST

Please read ABA Model Rules of Professional Conduct, Rule 1.13(g) and Comments [12]–[14].

* * *

Professional conduct rules acknowledge that, subject to the conflict of interest rules, an attorney may simultaneously represent an organizational client and its officers, employees, directors, and other constituents. Model Rule 1.13(g). Accordingly, there is no conflict if: (1) organization and constituent are not directly adverse, (2) there is not a significant risk that the representation of the organization would materially limit the representation of the constituent and vice versa, and (3) there is not a significant risk that the representation of either will be materially limited by lawyer's responsibility to another (current client, former client, or third party) or the lawyer's own personal interest. Model Rule 1.7(a). Even if there is a conflict or potential conflict in representing the organization and individual, the lawyer may still proceed with the representation if the lawyer believes he or she can competently and diligently represent both, they will not assert claims against one another, and both provide informed consent. Model Rule 1.7(b). Apply these rules as you consider the proposed simultaneous representation in Problem 25.5.

Another possible conflict can arise when a lawyer is asked to represent the company in a matter adverse to one of the company's agents—perhaps even an agent the lawyer has worked with closely in the past on matters for the company. The lawyer should consider several factors when determining whether there is a conflict of interest in accepting the representation. Obviously, if the agent is a current client of the lawyer or the lawyer's firm—even in a completely unrelated matter— the representation is prohibited. Model Rule 1.7(a)(1). Also, if the lawyer's personal relationship with the agent will limit the lawyer's ability to represent the organization, the lawyer should refuse to accept the case. Model Rule 1.7(a)(2).

Further, if the agent is a former client of the lawyer or the lawyer's firm, the representation also is problematic if the new matter for the organization is substantially related to the former representation of the agent. Model Rule 1.9(a). This is the issue that was raised in Problem 24.3 in the Transactional Practice chapter.

Finally, another possible conflict scenario arises with a derivative suit. A derivative suit is a lawsuit filed by a shareholder (or other owner) on behalf of the company. *See, e.g.,* Fed. R. Civ. P. 23.1 (explaining procedural requirements for a derivative suit in federal court). Company managers may seek representation in the matter from the lawyers who currently represent the company in other matters or that have represented the company in the past. Even though the derivative lawsuit is brought in the name of the company, the Model Rules recognize that it is not necessarily a conflict for counsel to represent management. Comments [13] and [14] to Model Rule 1.13 address this issue. Refer to these comments, as well as Model Rule 1.7, when you answer Problem 25.6.

* * *

Problem 25.5. Last month, the IRS and FBI raided the corporate offices of TFS; their search warrant allowed them to collect evidence of the rebate fraud scheme. It now appears imminent that the U.S. Attorney will pursue criminal charges (mail fraud, wire fraud, and perhaps others) against TFS and Hank Silvers. TFS has retained attorney Maggie Haynes to represent TFS during the criminal investigation and in any future criminal prosecution. TFS's board has asked Maggie to consider also representing Hank Silvers. The board's thinking is that the company's interests are aligned with Frank's: both deny that fraudulent conduct occurred and both want to avoid a conviction. Analyze the appropriateness of Maggie representing both TFS and Hank Silvers.

Problem 25.6. TFS's employee shareholders (who own approximately 30% of company stock) have filed a derivative suit on behalf of the company against the current board. The lawsuit alleges that the board intentionally and affirmatively encouraged the rebate fraud, in breach of the board's fiduciary duties of care and loyalty to TFS. The board has reached out to Loretta Sawyer from the law firm Sawyer & Bernstein to represent the board in the matter. (Recall that Loretta is the attorney who conducted the internal investigation on behalf of the company in Problem 24.4). Should Loretta represent the board in this case?

* * *

Profile of attorney professionalism. Roger Balla was employed as in-house counsel of Gambro, Inc., a distributor of kidney dialysis equipment. In July 1985, he learned that Gambro's German affiliate planned to ship to Gambro kidney dialyzers that did not comply with regulations of the U.S. Food and Drug Administration ("FDA"). Specifically, the German affiliate advised Gambro:

For acute patients risk is that acute uremic situation will not be improved in spite of the treatment. . . . The chronic patient may note the effect as a slow progression of the uremic situation and depending on the interval between medical check-ups the medical risk may not be overlooked.

Roger Balla informed Gambro's president that the dialyzers must be rejected because of their failure to meet FDA requirements. Initially, the president followed Mr. Balla's advice and notified the German affiliate that the dialyzers would not be accepted. Later, though, the president alerted the German affiliate that Gambro would accept and re-sell the dialyzers.

When Roger Balla learned of this decision, he again approached Gambro's president with his concern that the company was engaging in illegal conduct. This time, Mr. Balla said he would do "whatever is necessary" to stop the sale of the dialyzers. Shortly thereafter, Gambro's president fired attorney Balla.

As an Illinois-licensed attorney, Balla consulted Illinois professional conduct rules and concluded that he was required to disclose information about the dialyzers. At the time, Illinois's Rule 1.6(b) provided, "A lawyer shall reveal information about a client to the extent it appears necessary to prevent the client from committing an act that would result in death or serious bodily injury." Following the rule's mandate, attorney Balla disclosed information about the non-compliant dialyzers to the FDA. Relying on this information, the FDA seized the shipment of dialyzers.

Chapter 6 of this text includes a note about Roger Balla's litigation against Gambro. The Illinois Supreme Court refused to allow him to pursue a cause of action for retaliatory discharge against his employer. The facts in this profile are contained in the court's decision. Balla v. Gambro, 584 N.E.2d 104 (Ill. 1991).

Beyond its significance as a retaliatory discharge case, Roger Balla's case provides important insight about the challenges faced by corporate counsel. Attorney Balla took concerns of illegal conduct up-the-ladder of the corporation in an effort to protect both the company and future users of the non-compliant dialyzers. When his advice was ignored, he persisted in voicing his concerns and lost his job as a result. Ultimately, Balla took additional steps to prevent the sale of the dialyzers because he was required to do so under applicable professional conduct rules. While some attorneys may have deferred to the president, Balla took the more difficult path required of an attorney.

PART 5

LOOKING FORWARD TO FUTURE OPPORTUNITIES AND TO LOOKING BACKWARD AT YOUR CAREER AS A LAWYER

■ ■ ■

Now that you have completed law school, have been admitted to the bar of a state, have acquired clients, and have represented them ethically, you can begin thinking about roles and opportunities that typically arise only after a lawyer has earned a stellar reputation in the practice of law. We have already touched on some of the roles a lawyer can play: prosecutor, in-house counsel, etc. In this section, we consider two additional roles that may be available to you as a competent and ethical practitioner: judge and leader within your law office as well as the broader community. We also touch on the topic of law-related businesses, as many lawyers use their legal training and experience as background for providing services that are related to law, though not necessarily constituting the "practice of law." Finally, as you read the final chapter, we ask that envision yourself ten, twenty, or even fifty years down the road from your law school graduation and at the end of your legal career. Where will you be?

CHAPTER 26

BECOMING AND SERVING AS A JUDGE

■ ■ ■

Chapter hypothetical. Ione is a lawyer who is running for local judicial office in New Dakota against the incumbent, Judge Lloyd. On the eve of the election, Ione ran a television ad that contained the following lines: "For too long, Judge Lloyd has been giving the benefit of the doubt to criminal defendants in his courtroom. Isn't it time we had a judge who trusts law enforcement officers to do their job and give *them* the benefit of the doubt? Vote for Ione." Ione's ad was funded by Adam, a former litigant in Judge Lloyd's courtroom who is still bitter at what he views as his mistreatment at Lloyd's hands. Ione learned of Adam's dislike of Lloyd and personally asked him to fund her ad. Adam also produced and paid for a series of anti-Lloyd ads through an independent political organization not affiliated with Ione's campaign. Lloyd lost the race and promptly filed disciplinary charges against Ione. He also went out the next night and got arrested for driving under the influence. The case against him is still pending. As luck would have it, shortly after assuming office, Ione was assigned a civil case involving Adam's son, Mike, in which Mike was accused of fraud. The plaintiff's lawyer moved to disqualify Ione, but Ione refused to recuse herself. As you read the material in this chapter, consider the following issues:

(A) Is Ione subject to discipline for the statements in her advertisement?

(B) Is Ione subject to discipline for her communications with Adam soliciting his support?

(C) Does Ione's failure to recuse amount to a violation of the plaintiff's due process rights?

(D) Is Lloyd subject to discipline for his DUI arrest?

* * *

A. INTRODUCTION

Being a judge is potentially a pretty good gig. Your work can be intellectually stimulating, your decisions may have a dramatic impact on the lives of those who appear before you, and the jokes you tell at bar association meetings and among lawyers are funnier than when you were a practicing lawyer. The pay—although a bone of contention for many judges—is not too bad. In 2013, the salary for federal district judges was $174,000 and the salary for federal appellate judges was over $184,000. Being a judge also carries with it at least some job security. The term of office for many state judges extends over a period of several years. Federal judges have life tenure during good behavior. Perhaps it is no surprise that many lawyers aspire to the bench. Even if you have no judicial aspirations, you will probably have to deal with judges on occasion during your career. Moreover, you will be impacted by the judicial selection process at the state and federal level, at least in a professional capacity. Therefore, it is important that lawyers understand the process by which judges are selected, the potential conflicts that may arise as a result of a judge's words and actions during the selection process, and the restrictions judges face on their judicial and extrajudicial actions.

1. JUDICIAL SELECTION—ELECTION, APPOINTMENT, OR OTHER METHOD

Judicial selection methods vary widely. Federal judges are appointed by the President with the advice and consent of the Senate. Article III of the federal Constitution provides that federal judges "shall hold their Offices during good Behaviour." In contrast, judicial elections are common at the state level. According to one estimate, 87% of state judges are selected or retained on the basis of popular election. Judith L. Maute, *Selecting Justice in State Courts: The Ballot Box or the Backroom?*, 41 S. TEX. L. REV. 1197, 1203 (2000).

Historically, this was not the case. "Eight of the original thirteen states placed the control over judicial selection in the hands of the legislature. In the remaining states, the governor held the power of appointment alone or shared it jointly with his council. None entrusted the electorate with the task." Alex B. Long, *An Historical Perspective on Judicial Selection Methods in Virginia and West Virginia*, 18 J.L. & POL. 691, 712 (2002).

Beginning with Mississippi's decision in 1832 to adopt a system of popular election of judges, a strong trend toward popular election quickly developed. Historians have debated the causes of this trend, with many focusing on the rise of Jacksonian democracy and the attendant fear that the selection of judges was the product of backroom swaps among political elites. Regardless of the causes, popular election soon became common. Between 1846 and 1860, nineteen of the twenty-one constitutional conventions held among the states approved constitutions that allowed citizens to elect their judges. Every state that entered the Union between 1846 and 1912 provided for judicial elections. *Id.* at 719–20.

Gradually, more states began to experiment with a third form of judicial selection: merit selection. Merit selection combines elements of appointive and elective systems while (proponents argue) reducing some of the harmful effects of both. Under a merit selection plan (sometimes also called the "Missouri Plan" for the state from which it originated), judges are typically appointed by the governor, who chooses from a list of applicants screened and prepared by a merit selection commission. After the initial appointment, the judge must then stand for a retention election on annual basis. Voters simply vote "yes" or "no" on the question of whether the judge should be retained in office. Thus, in theory, judges and judicial candidates are spared some of the problems associated with running in a contested election while still being subject to the will of the voters.

Today, the majority of states employ either partisan or non-partisan elections to select some or all of their appellate and/or general jurisdiction trial court judges. Only a handful retain a system of pure gubernatorial or legislative appointment. The rest rely upon some sort of merit selection. Brian T. Fitzpatrick, *The Constitutionality of Federal Jurisdiction-Stripping Legislation and the History of State Judicial Selection and Tenure*, 98 VA. L. REV. 839, 860–61 (2012).

* * *

2. JUDICIAL INDEPENDENCE AND JUDICIAL ACCOUNTABILITY

A system of judicial appointment with life (or at least long) tenure during good behavior is said to be essential to preserving a judge's decisional independence. Proponents argue that an appointive system helps shield the decision making process of judges from the influences of the political process. If judges were forced to stand for reelection, their decisions might be influenced by the fear of voter disapproval. *See* Penny J. White, *Using Judicial Performance Evaluations to Supplement Inappropriate Voter Cues and Enhance Judicial Legitimacy*, 74 MO. L. REV. 635 (2009). Proponents of popular election counter that voter accountability is actually desirable in light of the fact that judicial decisions often have dramatic policy ramifications. Moreover, election proponents argue that an appointive system merely substitutes one form of politics for another. As you read the rules and decisions that follow, ask yourself which value—judicial independence or judicial accountability—the legal profession should prize more highly?

* * *

3. SEEKING SELECTION AS A JUDGE

**Please read ABA Model Code of Judicial Conduct,
Canon 4, Rule 4.1A(1)–(7) & (B); and Rule 4.2B(4) & C.**

* * *

What is the point of the prohibitions contained in Rules 4.1A(1)–(7)? Why, for example, is a candidate for judicial office (whether elected or appointed) prohibited from publicly endorsing or opposing a presidential candidate or candidate for the state legislature? The *Republican Party of Minnesota v. White* case that follows addresses this general idea.

* * *

B. POLITICAL AND CAMPAIGN ACTIVITIES OF JUDICIAL CANDIDATES IN PUBLIC ELECTIONS

The popular election of judges raises special concerns. As the rules above demonstrate, the ethical rules governing judges impose limitations on campaign speech. However, as the first case below also illustrates, these limitations on speech are subject to the First Amendment. As the second case illustrates, the federal Constitution may itself impose some limitations on judicial campaign speech, or at least a judge's ability to hear a case after getting elected.

* * *

1. LIMITATIONS ON CAMPAIGN ACTIVITIES AND FREE SPEECH CONCERNS

REPUBLICAN PARTY OF MINNESOTA V. WHITE
536 U.S. 765 (2002)

SCALIA, J., delivered the opinion of the Court.

The question presented in this case is whether the First Amendment permits the Minnesota Supreme Court to prohibit candidates for judicial election in that State from announcing their views on disputed legal and political issues.

I

... Since 1974, [Minnesota State Judicial Elections] have been subject to a legal restriction which states that a "candidate for a judicial office, including an incumbent judge," shall not "announce his or her views on disputed legal or political issues." This prohibition, promulgated by the Minnesota Supreme Court and based on Canon 7(B) of the 1972 American Bar Association (ABA) Model Code of Judicial Conduct, is known as the "announce clause." Incumbent judges who violate it are subject to discipline, including removal, censure, civil penalties, and suspension without pay. Lawyers who run for judicial office also must comply with the announce clause. . . . Those who violate it are subject to, *inter alia*, disbarment, suspension, and probation.

[Gregory Wersal has twice been a candidate for associate justice of the Minnesota Supreme Court. During his 1996 campaign, his campaign literature included criticism of Minnesota Supreme Court decisions on issues such as crime, welfare, and abortion. A complaint against Wersal was filed. The complaint was dismissed due to doubts as to whether the clause could constitutionally be enforced. Wersal subsequently withdrew from the election, fearing that further complaints would negatively affect his ability to practice law. In 1998, Wersal again sought the same office. Wersal alleged that he was forced to refrain from announcing his views on disputed issues during the 1998 campaign, to the point where he declined response to questions put to him by the press and public, out of concern that he might run afoul of the announce clause. He filed suit, seeking a declaration that the announce clause violates the First Amendment. The Eighth Circuit held that the announce clause did not violate the First Amendment.]

II

Before considering the constitutionality of the announce clause, we must be clear about its meaning. Its text says that a candidate for judicial office shall not "announce his or her views on disputed legal or political issues." Minn. Code of Judicial Conduct, Canon 5(A)(3)(d)(I) (2002).

We know that "announcing . . . views" on an issue covers much more than *promising* to decide an issue a particular way. The prohibition extends to the candidate's mere statement of his current position, even if he does not bind himself to maintain that position after election. All the parties agree this is the case, because the Minnesota Code contains a so-called "pledges or promises" clause, which *separately* prohibits judicial candidates from making "pledges or promises of conduct in office other than the faithful and impartial performance of the duties of the office," *ibid.*—a prohibition that is not challenged here and on which we express no view.

There are, however, some limitations that the Minnesota Supreme Court has placed upon the scope of the announce clause that are not (to put it politely) immediately apparent from its text. . . . The Judicial Board issued an opinion stating that judicial candidates may criticize past decisions . . . . The Eighth Circuit relied on the Judicial Board's opinion in upholding the announce clause, 247 F.3d at 882, and the Minnesota Supreme Court recently embraced the Eighth Circuit's interpretation, *In re Code of Judicial Conduct*, 639 N.W.2d 55 (2002).

There are yet further limitations upon the apparent plain meaning of the announce clause: In light of the constitutional concerns, the District Court construed the clause to reach only disputed issues that are likely to come before the candidate if he is elected judge. 63 F. Supp. 2d at 986. The Eighth Circuit accepted this limiting interpretation by the District Court, and in addition construed the clause to allow general discussions of case law and judicial philosophy. 247 F.3d at 881–882. The Supreme Court of Minnesota adopted these interpretations as well when it ordered enforcement of the announce clause in accordance with the Eighth Circuit's opinion. *In re Code of Judicial Conduct, supra.*

It seems to us, however, that—like the text of the announce clause itself—these limitations upon the text of the announce clause are not all that they appear to be. First, respondents acknowledged at oral argument that statements critical of past judicial decisions are *not* permissible if the candidate also states that he is against *stare decisis.* Thus, candidates must choose between stating their views critical of past decisions and stating their views in opposition to *stare decisis.* Or, to look at it more concretely, they may state their view that prior decisions were erroneous only if they do not assert that they, if elected, have any power to eliminate erroneous decisions. Second, limiting the scope of the clause to issues likely to come before a court is not much of a limitation at all. One would hardly expect the "disputed legal or political issues" raised in the course of a state judicial election to include such matters as whether the Federal Government should end the embargo of Cuba. Quite obviously, they will be those legal or political disputes that are the proper (or by past decisions have been made the improper) business of the state courts. And within that relevant category, "there is almost no legal or political issue that is unlikely to come before a judge of an American court, state or federal, of general jurisdiction." *Buckley* v. *Illinois Judicial Inquiry Bd.,* 997 F.2d 224, 229 (CA7 1993). Third, construing the clause to allow "general" discussions of case law and judicial philosophy turns out to be of little help in an election campaign. At oral argument, respondents gave, as an example of this exception, that a candidate is free to assert that he is a " 'strict constructionist.' " But that, like most other philosophical generalities, has little meaningful content for the electorate unless it is exemplified by application to a particular issue of construction likely to come before a court—for example, whether a particular statute runs afoul of any provision of the Constitution. Respondents conceded that the announce clause would prohibit the candidate from exemplifying his philosophy in this fashion. Without such application to real-life issues, all candidates can claim to be "strict constructionists" with equal (and unhelpful) plausibility.

In any event, it is clear that the announce clause prohibits a judicial candidate from stating his views on any specific nonfanciful legal question within the province of the court for which he is running, except in the context of discussing past decisions—and in the latter context as well, if he expresses the view that he is not bound by *stare decisis.*

Respondents contend that this still leaves plenty of topics for discussion on the campaign trail. These include a candidate's "character," "education," "work habits," and "how [he] would handle administrative duties if elected." Brief for Respondents 35–36. Indeed, the Judicial Board has printed a list of preapproved questions which judicial candidates are allowed to answer. These include how the candidate feels about cameras in the courtroom, how he would go about reducing the caseload, how the costs of judicial administration can be reduced, and how he proposes to ensure that minorities and women are treated more fairly by the court system. Whether this list of preapproved subjects, and other topics not prohibited by the announce clause, adequately fulfill the First Amendment's guarantee of freedom of speech is the question to which we now turn.

III

As the Court of Appeals recognized, the announce clause both prohibits speech on the basis of its content and burdens a category of speech that is "at the core of our First Amendment freedoms"—speech about the qualifications of candidates for public office. 247 F.3d at 861, 863. The Court of Appeals concluded that the proper test to be applied to determine the constitutionality of such a restriction is what our cases have called strict scrutiny, *id.,* 247 F.3d at 864; the parties do not dispute that this is correct. Under the strict-scrutiny test, respondents have the burden to prove that the announce clause is (1) narrowly tailored, to serve (2) a compelling state interest. *E.g., Eu* v. *San Francisco County Democratic Central Comm.,* 489 U.S. 214, 222, 103 L. Ed. 2d 271, 109 S. Ct. 1013 (1989). In order for respondents to show that the announce clause is narrowly tailored, they must demonstrate that it does not "unnecessarily circumscribe protected expression." *Brown* v. *Hartlage,* 456 U.S. 45, 54, 71 L. Ed. 2d 732, 102 S. Ct. 1523 (1982).

The Court of Appeals concluded that respondents had established two interests as sufficiently compelling to justify the announce clause: preserving the impartiality of the state judiciary and preserving the appearance of the impartiality of the state judiciary. 247 F.3d at 867. Respondents reassert these two interests before us, arguing that the first is compelling because it protects the due process rights of litigants, and that the second is compelling because it preserves public confidence in the judiciary. Respondents are rather vague, however, about what they mean by "impartiality." Indeed, although the term is used throughout the Eighth Circuit's opinion, the briefs, the Minnesota Code of Judicial Conduct, and the ABA Codes of Judicial Conduct, none of these sources bothers to define it. Clarity on this point is essential before we can decide whether impartiality is indeed a compelling state interest, and, if so, whether the announce clause is narrowly tailored to achieve it.

A

One meaning of "impartiality" in the judicial context—and of course its root meaning—is the lack of bias for or against either *party* to the proceeding. Impartiality in this sense assures equal application of the law. That is, it guarantees a party that the judge who hears his case will apply the law to him in the same way he applies it to any other party. This is the traditional sense in which the term is used. *See* Webster's New International Dictionary 1247 (2d ed. 1950) (defining "impartial" as "not partial; esp., not favoring one more than another; treating all alike; unbiased; equitable; fair; just"). It is also the sense in which it is used in the cases cited by respondents and *amici* for the proposition that an impartial judge is essential to due process. *Tumey* v. *Ohio,* 273 U.S. 510, 523, 531–534, 71 L. Ed. 749, 47 S. Ct. 437, 5 Ohio L. Abs. 839, 25 Ohio L. Rep. 236 (1927) (judge violated due process by sitting in a case in which it would be in his financial interest to find against one of the parties) . . .

We think it plain that the announce clause is not narrowly tailored to serve impartiality (or the appearance of impartiality) in this sense. Indeed, the clause is barely tailored to serve that interest *at all,* inasmuch as it does not restrict speech for or against particular *parties,* but rather speech for or against particular *issues.* To be sure, when a case arises that turns on a legal issue on which the judge (as a candidate) had taken a particular stand, the party taking the opposite stand is likely to lose. But not because of any bias against that party, or favoritism toward the other party. *Any* party taking that position is just as likely to lose. The judge is applying the law (as he sees it) evenhandedly.

B

It is perhaps possible to use the term "impartiality" in the judicial context (though this is certainly not a common usage) to mean lack of preconception in favor of or against a particular *legal view.* This sort of impartiality would be concerned, not with guaranteeing litigants equal application of the law, but rather with guaranteeing them an equal chance to persuade the court on the legal points in their case. Impartiality in this sense may well be an interest served by the announce clause, but it is not a *compelling* state interest, as strict scrutiny requires. A judge's lack of predisposition regarding the relevant legal issues in a case has never been thought a necessary component of equal justice, and with good reason. For one thing, it is virtually impossible to find a judge who does not have preconceptions about the law. As then-Justice Rehnquist observed of our own Court: "Since most Justices come to this bench no earlier than their middle years, it would be unusual if they had not by that time formulated at least some tentative notions that would influence them in their interpretation of the sweeping clauses of the Constitution and their interaction with one another. It would be not merely unusual, but extraordinary, if they had not at least given opinions as to constitutional issues in their previous legal careers." *Laird* v. *Tatum*, 409 U.S. 824, 835, 34 L. Ed. 2d 50, 93 S. Ct. 7 (1972) (memorandum opinion). Indeed, even if it were possible to select judges who did not have preconceived views on legal issues, it would hardly be desirable to do so. "Proof that a Justice's mind at the time he joined the Court was a complete *tabula rasa* in the area of constitutional adjudication would be evidence of lack of qualification, not lack of bias." *Ibid.* The Minnesota Constitution positively forbids the selection to courts of general jurisdiction of judges who are impartial in the sense of having no views on the law. Minn. Const., Art. VI, § 5 ("Judges of the supreme court, the court of appeals and the district court shall be learned in the law."). And since avoiding judicial preconceptions on legal issues is neither possible nor desirable, pretending otherwise by attempting to preserve the "appearance" of that type of impartiality can hardly be a compelling state interest either.

C

A third possible meaning of "impartiality" (again not a common one) might be described as openmindedness. This quality in a judge demands, not that he have no preconceptions on legal issues, but that he be willing to consider views that oppose his preconceptions, and remain open to persuasion, when the issues arise in a pending case. This sort of impartiality seeks to guarantee each litigant, not an *equal* chance to win the legal points in the case, but at least *some* chance of doing so. It may well be that impartiality in this sense, and the appearance of it, are desirable in the judiciary, but we need not pursue that inquiry, since we do not believe the Minnesota Supreme Court adopted the announce clause for that purpose.

Respondents argue that the announce clause serves the interest in open-mindedness, or at least in the appearance of openmindedness, because it relieves a judge from pressure to rule a certain way in order to maintain consistency with statements the judge has previously made. The problem is, however, that statements in election campaigns are such an infinitesimal portion of the public commitments to legal positions that judges (or judges-to-be) undertake, that this object of the prohibition is implausible. Before they arrive on the bench (whether by election or otherwise) judges have often committed themselves on legal issues that they must later rule upon. More common still is a judge's confronting a legal issue on which he has expressed an opinion while on the bench. Most frequently, of course, that prior expression will have occurred in ruling on an earlier case. But judges often state their views on disputed legal issues outside the context of adjudication-in classes that they conduct, and in books and speeches. Like the ABA Codes of Judicial Conduct, the Minnesota Code not only permits but encourages this. See Minn.Code of Judicial Conduct, Canon 4(B) (2002) ("A judge may write, lecture, teach, speak and participate in other extra-judicial activities concerning the law . . . "); Minn.Code of Judicial Conduct, Canon 4(B), Comment. (2002) ("To the extent that time permits, a judge is encouraged to do so . . . "). That is quite incompatible with the notion that the need for open-mindedness (or for the appearance of open-mindedness) lies behind the prohibition at issue here.

The short of the matter is this: In Minnesota, a candidate for judicial office may not say "I think it is constitutional for the legislature to prohibit same-sex marriages." He may say the very same thing, however, up until the very day before he declares himself a candidate, and may say it repeatedly (until litigation is pending) after he is elected. As a means of pursuing the objective of open-mindedness that respondents now articulate, the announce clause is so woefully underinclusive as to render belief in that purpose a challenge to the credulous. . . .

. . . .

IV

. . . .

There is an obvious tension between the article of Minnesota's popularly approved Constitution which provides that judges shall be elected, and the Minnesota Supreme Court's announce clause which places most subjects of interest to the voters off limits. (The candidate-speech restrictions of all the other States that have them are also the product of judicial fiat.) The disparity is perhaps unsurprising, since the ABA, which originated the announce clause, has long been an opponent of judicial elections. . . . That opposition may be well taken (it certainly had the support of the Founders of the Federal Government), but the First Amendment does not permit it to achieve its goal by leaving the principle of elections in place while preventing candidates from discussing what the elections are about. . . .

The Minnesota Supreme Court's canon of judicial conduct prohibiting candidates for judicial election from announcing their views on disputed legal and political issues violates the First Amendment. Accordingly, we reverse the grant of summary judgment to respondents and remand the case for proceedings consistent with this opinion.

It is so ordered.

[Concurring opinion of JUSTICE KENNEDY and dissenting opinions of JUSTICE STEVENS and JUSTICE GINSBURG, with whom JUSTICE STEVENS, JUSTICE SOUTER, and JUSTICE BREYER join, omitted.]

JUSTICE O'CONNOR, concurring

I join the opinion of the Court but write separately to express my concerns about judicial elections generally. Respondents claim that "[t]he Announce Clause is necessary ... to protect the State's compelling governmental interes[t] in an actual and perceived ... impartial judiciary." Brief for Respondents 8. I am concerned that, even aside from what judicial candidates may say while campaigning, the very practice of electing judges undermines this interest.

We of course want judges to be impartial, in the sense of being free from any personal stake in the outcome of the cases to which they are assigned. But if judges are subject to regular elections they are likely to feel that they have at least some personal stake in the outcome of every publicized case. Elected judges cannot help being aware that if the public is not satisfied with the outcome of a particular case, it could hurt their reelection prospects. *See* Eule, *Crocodiles in the Bathtub: State Courts, Voter Initiatives and the Threat of Electoral Reprisal*, 65 U. COLO. L.REV. 733, 739 (1994) (quoting former California Supreme Court Justice Otto Kaus' statement that ignoring the political consequences of visible decisions is " 'like ignoring a crocodile in your bathtub' "); Bright & Keenan, *Judges and the Politics of Death: Deciding Between the Bill of Rights and the Next Election in Capital Cases*, 75 B.U.L.REV. 759, 793–794 (1995) (citing statistics indicating that judges who face elections are far more likely to override jury sentences of life without parole and impose the death penalty than are judges who do not run for election). Even if judges were able to suppress their awareness of the potential electoral consequences of their decisions and refrain from acting on it, the public's confidence in the judiciary could be undermined simply by the possibility that judges would be unable to do so.

Moreover, contested elections generally entail campaigning. And campaigning for a judicial post today can require substantial funds. Unless the pool of judicial candidates is limited to those wealthy enough to independently fund their campaigns, a limitation unrelated to judicial skill, the cost of campaigning requires judicial candidates to engage in fundraising. Yet relying on campaign donations may leave judges feeling indebted to certain parties or interest groups. . . . Even if judges were able to refrain from favoring donors, the mere possibility that judges' decisions may be motivated by the desire to repay campaign contributors is likely to undermine the public's confidence in the judiciary. . . .

. . . .

Minnesota has chosen to select its judges through contested popular elections instead of through an appointment system or a combined appointment and retention election system along the lines of the Missouri Plan. In doing so the State has voluntarily taken on the risks to judicial bias described above. As a result, the State's claim that it needs to significantly restrict judges' speech in order to protect judicial impartiality is particularly troubling. If the State has a problem with judicial impartiality, it is largely one the State brought upon itself by continuing the practice of popularly electing judges.

* * *

Restrictions on campaign speech. The "announce clause" at issue in *White* originally appeared in the 1972 version of the ABA's Model Code of Judicial Conduct (CJC). By 1990, the ABA had dropped the "announce" language from the CJC, but some jurisdictions (like Minnesota) continued to use it. Regarding the issue in *White*, Rule 4.1(A)(13) now prohibits judges and candidates for elected judicial office from making "pledges, promises, or commitments that are inconsistent with the impartial performance of the adjudicative duties of judicial office" in connection with "cases, controversies, or issues that are likely to come before the court." Similarly, Rule 4.1(A)(12) prohibits judicial candidates from making statements that might affect the outcome or otherwise impair the fairness of pending or impending cases. Judicial campaigns have become increasingly contentious in recent years. Rule 4.1(A)(11) addresses the problem of candidates making false charges during a campaign and adopts the "actual malice" standard articulated by the Supreme Court in New York Times Co. v. Sullivan, 376 U.S. 254 (1964).

* * *

Problem 26.1. Refer back to the Chapter Hypothetical. Assuming New Dakota's Code of Judicial Conduct is identical to the ABA's CJC, is Ione subject to discipline for the statements in her advertisement?

Problem 26.2. Would Rule 4.1(A)(13) survive a First Amendment challenge under the standard articulated in *White*?

Appearing to commit oneself. CJC Rule 2.11(A)(5) also addresses situations in which a candidate or judge makes public statements that do not necessarily pledge or promise a particular result but that may *appear* to commit the candidate or judge to rule a certain way. Rather than prohibiting such statements, Rule 2.11(A)(5) requires the speaker to recuse himself or herself in the matter in question. The CJC was rewritten following *White* to include this provision.

Problem 26.3. Refer back to the Chapter Hypothetical. If Judge Ione is found not to have violated Rule 4.1 through her statements in the advertisements, is she nonetheless required under Rule 2.11(A)(5) to disqualify herself in cases that come before her that involve law enforcement?

Problem 26.4. Refer back to the Chapter Hypothetical and Rules 4.1(A)(7) & (8) and Rule 4.2(B)(5). Is Ione subject to discipline for her communications with Adam soliciting his support? Based on your reading of *White* and its application of strict scrutiny, could these rules withstand a constitutional challenge on First Amendment grounds? Are any of the other prohibitions in Rule 4.1(A) subject to constitutional challenge?

* * *

2. CAMPAIGN ACTIVITIES AND DUE PROCESS CONCERNS

CAPERTON V. A.T. MASSEY COAL CO., INC.
556 U.S. 868 (2009)

JUSTICE KENNEDY delivered the opinion of the Court.

In this case the Supreme Court of Appeals of West Virginia reversed a trial court judgment, which had entered a jury verdict of $50 million. Five justices heard the case, and the vote to reverse was 3 to 2. The question presented is whether the Due Process Clause of the Fourteenth Amendment was violated when one of the justices in the majority denied a recusal motion. The basis for the motion was that the justice had received campaign contributions in an extraordinary amount from, and through the efforts of, the board chairman and principal officer of the corporation found liable for the damages.

Under our precedents there are objective standards that require recusal when "the probability of actual bias on the part of the judge or decisionmaker is too high to be constitutionally tolerable." *Withrow v. Larkin*, 421 U.S. 35, 47, 95 S.Ct. 1456, 43 L.Ed.2d 712 (1975). Applying those precedents, we find that, in all the circumstances of this case, due process requires recusal.

I

In August 2002 a West Virginia jury returned a verdict that found respondents A.T. Massey Coal Co. and its affiliates (hereinafter Massey) liable for fraudulent misrepresentation, concealment, and tortious interference with existing contractual relations. The jury awarded petitioners Hugh Caperton, Harman Development Corp., Harman Mining Corp., and Sovereign Coal Sales (hereinafter Caperton) the sum of $50 million in compensatory and punitive damages.

In June 2004 the state trial court denied Massey's post-trial motions challenging the verdict and the damages award, finding that Massey "intentionally acted in utter disregard of [Caperton's] rights and ultimately destroyed [Caperton's] businesses because, after conducting cost-benefit analyses, [Massey] concluded it was in its financial interest to do so." In March 2005 the trial court denied Massey's motion for judgment as a matter of law.

Don Blankenship is Massey's chairman, chief executive officer, and president. After the verdict but before the appeal, West Virginia held its 2004 judicial elections. Knowing the Supreme Court of Appeals of West Virginia would consider the appeal in the case, Blankenship decided to support an attorney who sought to replace Justice McGraw. Justice McGraw was a candidate for reelection to that court. The attorney who sought to replace him was Brent Benjamin.

In addition to contributing the $1,000 statutory maximum to Benjamin's campaign committee, Blankenship donated almost $2.5 million to "And For The Sake Of The Kids," a political organization formed under 26 U.S.C. § 527. The § 527 organization opposed McGraw and supported Benjamin. Blankenship's donations accounted for more than two-thirds of the total funds it raised. This was not all Blankenship spent, in addition, just over $500,000 on independent expenditures-for direct mailings and letters soliciting donations as well as television and newspaper advertisements—" 'to support . . . Brent Benjamin.' "

To provide some perspective, Blankenship's $3 million in contributions were more than the total amount spent by all other Benjamin supporters and three times the amount spent by Benjamin's own committee. Caperton contends that Blankenship spent $1 million more than the total amount spent by the campaign committees of both candidates combined.

Benjamin won. He received 382,036 votes (53.3%), and McGraw received 334,301 votes (46.7%).

In October 2005, before Massey filed its petition for appeal in West Virginia's highest court, Caperton moved to disqualify now-Justice Benjamin under the Due Process Clause and the West Virginia Code of Judicial Conduct, based on the conflict caused by Blankenship's campaign involvement. Justice Benjamin denied the motion in April 2006. He indicated that he "carefully considered the bases and accompanying exhibits proffered by the movants." But he found "no objective information . . . to show that this Justice has a bias for or against any litigant, that this Justice has prejudged the matters which comprise this litigation, or that this Justice will be anything but fair and impartial." In December 2006 Massey filed its petition for appeal to challenge the adverse jury verdict. The West Virginia Supreme Court of Appeals granted review.

In November 2007 that court reversed the $50 million verdict against Massey [in a 3–2 decision]. . . .

Caperton sought rehearing, and the parties moved for disqualification of three of the five justices who decided the appeal. Photos had surfaced of Justice Maynard vacationing with Blankenship in the French Riviera while the case was pending. Justice Maynard granted Caperton's recusal motion. On the other side Justice Starcher granted Massey's recusal motion, apparently based on his public criticism of Blankenship's role in the 2004 elections. In his recusal memorandum Justice Starcher urged Justice Benjamin to recuse himself as well. He noted that "Blankenship's bestowal of his personal wealth, political tactics, and 'friendship' have created a cancer in the affairs of this Court." Justice Benjamin declined Justice Starcher's suggestion and denied Caperton's recusal motion.

The court granted rehearing. . . . Caperton moved a third time for disqualification, arguing that Justice Benjamin had failed to apply the correct standard under West Virginia law-i.e., whether "a reasonable and prudent person, knowing these objective facts, would harbor doubts about Justice Benjamin's ability to be fair and impartial." . . . Justice Benjamin again refused to withdraw. . . .

In April 2008 a divided court again reversed the jury verdict, and again it was a 3-to-2 decision. . . .

Four months later—a month after the petition for writ of certiorari was filed in this Court—Justice Benjamin filed a concurring opinion. He defended the merits of the majority opinion as well as his decision not to recuse. He rejected Caperton's challenge to his participation in the case under both the Due Process Clause and West Virginia law. Justice Benjamin reiterated that he had no " 'direct, personal, substantial, pecuniary interest' in this case.' " ___ W.Va., at ___, 679 S.E.2d, at ___, 2008 WL 918444; App. 677a (quoting *Lavoie, supra,* at 822, 106 S.Ct. 1580). Adopting "a standard merely of 'appearances,' " he concluded, "seems little more than an invitation to subject West Virginia's justice system to the vagaries of the day-a framework in which predictability and stability yield to supposition, innuendo, half-truths, and partisan manipulations." ___ W.Va., at ___, 679 S.E.2d, at ___, 2008 WL 918444; App. 692a.

We granted certiorari.

II

It is axiomatic that "[a] fair trial in a fair tribunal is a basic requirement of due process." *Murchison, supra,* at 136, 75 S.Ct. 623. As the Court has recognized, however, "most matters relating to judicial disqualification [do] not rise to a constitutional level." *FTC v. Cement Institute,* 333 U.S. 683, 702, 68 S.Ct. 793, 92 L.Ed. 1010 (1948). The early and leading case on the subject is *Tumey v. Ohio,* 273 U.S. 510, 47 S.Ct. 437, 71 L.Ed. 749 (1927). There, the Court stated that "matters of kinship, personal bias, state policy, remoteness of interest, would seem generally to be matters merely of legislative discretion." *Id.*, at 523, 47 S.Ct. 437.

The *Tumey* Court concluded that the Due Process Clause incorporated the common-law rule that a judge must recuse himself when he has "a direct, personal, substantial, pecuniary interest" in a case. *Ibid.* This rule reflects the maxim that "[n]o man is allowed to be a judge in his own cause; because his interest would certainly bias his judgment, and, not improbably, corrupt his integrity." The Federalist No. 10, p. 59 (J. Cooke ed.1961) (J. Madison); *see* Frank, *Disqualification of Judges*, 56 YALE L.J. 605, 611–612 (1947) (same). Under this rule, "disqualification for bias or prejudice was not permitted"; those matters were left to statutes and judicial codes. Lavoie, *supra*, at 820, 106 S.Ct. 1580; *see also* Part IV, *infra* (discussing judicial codes). Personal bias or prejudice "alone would not be sufficient basis for imposing a constitutional requirement under the Due Process Clause." *Lavoie, supra*, at 820, 106 S.Ct. 1580.

As new problems have emerged that were not discussed at common law, however, the Court has identified additional instances which, as an objective matter, require recusal. These are circumstances "in which experience teaches that the probability of actual bias on the part of the judge or decisionmaker is too high to be constitutionally tolerable." *Withrow*, 421 U.S., at 47, 95 S.Ct. 1456. To place the present case in proper context, two instances where the Court has required recusal merit further discussion.

[Summarizing these decisions, the Court observed, "The inquiry is an objective one. The Court asks not whether the judge is actually, subjectively biased, but whether the average judge in his position is 'likely' to be neutral, or whether there is an unconstitutional 'potential for bias.' "]

III

Based on the principles described in these cases we turn to the issue before us. This problem arises in the context of judicial elections, a framework not presented in the precedents we have reviewed and discussed.

[In considering the recusal motions, Justice Blankenship inquired whether he was actually biased in Massey's favor.] Justice Benjamin conducted a probing search into his actual motives and inclinations; and he found none to be improper. We do not question his subjective findings of impartiality and propriety. Nor do we determine whether there was actual bias.

The difficulties of inquiring into actual bias, and the fact that the inquiry is often a private one, simply underscore the need for objective rules. Otherwise there may be no adequate protection against a judge who simply misreads or misapprehends the real motives at work in deciding the case. The judge's own inquiry into actual bias, then, is not one that the law can easily superintend or review, though actual bias, if disclosed, no doubt would be grounds for appropriate relief. In lieu of exclusive reliance on that personal inquiry, or on appellate review of the judge's determination respecting actual bias, the Due Process Clause has been implemented by objective standards that do not require proof of actual bias. *See Tumey*, 273 U.S. at 532, 47 S.Ct. 437; *Mayberry*, 400 U.S. at 465–466, 91 S.Ct. 499; *Lavoie*, 475 U. S., at 825, 106 S.Ct. 1580. In defining these standards the Court has asked whether, "under a realistic appraisal of psychological tendencies and human weakness," the interest "poses such a risk of actual bias or prejudgment that the practice must be forbidden if the guarantee of due process is to be adequately implemented." *Withrow*, 421 U.S. at 47, 95 S.Ct. 1456.

We turn to the influence at issue in this case. Not every campaign contribution by a litigant or attorney creates a probability of bias that requires a judge's recusal, but this is an exceptional case. . . . We conclude that there is a serious risk of actual bias—based on objective and reasonable perceptions—when a person with a personal stake in a particular case had a significant and disproportionate influence in placing the judge on the case by raising funds or directing the judge's election campaign when the case was pending or imminent. The inquiry centers on the contribution's relative size in comparison to the total amount of money contributed to the campaign, the total amount spent in the election, and the apparent effect such contribution had on the outcome of the election.

Applying this principle, we conclude that Blankenship's campaign efforts had a significant and disproportionate influence in placing Justice Benjamin on the case. Blankenship contributed some $3 million to unseat the incumbent and replace him with Benjamin. His contributions eclipsed the total amount spent by all other Benjamin supporters and exceeded by 300% the amount spent by Benjamin's campaign committee. Caperton claims Blankenship spent $1 million more than the total amount spent by the campaign committees of both candidates combined.

. . . .

. . . Due process requires an objective inquiry into whether the contributor's influence on the election under all the circumstances "would offer a possible temptation to the average . . . judge to . . . lead him not to hold the balance nice, clear and true." *Tumey, supra*, at 532, 47 S.Ct. 437. In an election decided by fewer than 50,000 votes (382,036 to 334,301), *see* ___ W.Va., at ___, 679 S.E.2d, at ___, 2008 WL 918444. Blankenship's campaign contributions-in comparison to the total amount contributed to the campaign, as well as the total amount spent in the election-had a significant and disproportionate influence on the electoral outcome. And the risk that Blankenship's influence engendered actual bias is sufficiently substantial that it "must be forbidden if the guarantee of due process is to be adequately implemented." *Withrow, supra,* at 47, 95 S.Ct. 1456.

The temporal relationship between the campaign contributions, the justice's election, and the pendency of the case is also critical. It was reasonably foreseeable, when the campaign contributions were made, that the pending case would be before the newly elected justice. The $50 million adverse jury verdict had been entered before the election, and the Supreme Court of Appeals was the next step once the state trial court dealt with post-trial motions. So it became at once apparent that, absent recusal, Justice Benjamin would review a judgment that cost his biggest donor's company $50 million. Although there is no allegation of a quid pro quo agreement, the fact remains that Blankenship's extraordinary contributions were made at a time when he had a vested stake in the outcome. Just as no man is allowed to be a judge in his own cause, similar fears of bias can arise when-without the consent of the other parties-a man chooses the judge in his own cause. And applying this principle to the judicial election process, there was here a serious, objective risk of actual bias that required Justice Benjamin's recusal.

. . . On these extreme facts the probability of actual bias rises to an unconstitutional level.

IV

Our decision today addresses an extraordinary situation where the Constitution requires recusal. Massey and its amici predict that various adverse consequences will follow from recognizing a constitutional violation here-ranging from a flood of recusal motions to unnecessary interference with judicial elections. We disagree. The facts now before us are extreme by any measure. The parties point to no other instance involving judicial campaign contributions that presents a potential for bias comparable to the circumstances in this case.

. . . .

One must also take into account the judicial reforms the States have implemented to eliminate even the appearance of partiality. Almost every State—West Virginia included—has adopted the American Bar Association's objective standard: "A judge shall avoid impropriety and the appearance of impropriety." ABA Annotated Model Code of Judicial Conduct, Canon 2 (2004). . . . The ABA Model Code's test for appearance of impropriety is "whether the conduct would create in reasonable minds a perception that the judge's ability to carry out judicial responsibilities with integrity, impartiality and competence is impaired." Canon 2A,

Commentary; *see also* W. Va.Code of Judicial Conduct, Canon 2A, and Commentary (2009) (same).

The West Virginia Code of Judicial Conduct also requires a judge to "disqualify himself or herself in a proceeding in which the judge's impartiality might reasonably be questioned." Canon 3E(1); *see also* 28 U.S.C. § 455(a) ("Any justice, judge, or magistrate judge of the United States shall disqualify himself in any proceeding in which his impartiality might reasonably be questioned."). Under Canon 3E(1), " '[t]he question of disqualification focuses on whether an objective assessment of the judge's conduct produces a reasonable question about impartiality, not on the judge's subjective perception of the ability to act fairly.' " *State ex rel. Brown v. Dietrick*, 191 W.Va. 169, 174, n. 9, 444 S.E.2d 47, 52, n. 9 (1994); *see also Liteky v. United States*, 510 U.S. 540, 558, 114 S.Ct. 1147, 127 L.Ed.2d 474 (1994) (KENNEDY, J., concurring in judgment) ("[U]nder [28 U.S.C.] § 455(a), a judge should be disqualified only if it appears that he or she harbors an aversion, hostility or disposition of a kind that a fair-minded person could not set aside when judging the dispute."). Indeed, some States require recusal based on campaign contributions similar to those in this case. *See, e.g.,* Ala.Code §§ 12–24–1, 12–24–2 (2006); Miss.Code of Judicial Conduct, Canon 3E(2) (2008).

These codes of conduct serve to maintain the integrity of the judiciary and the rule of law. The Conference of the Chief Justices has underscored that the codes are "[t]he principal safeguard against judicial campaign abuses" that threaten to imperil "public confidence in the fairness and integrity of the nation's elected judges." Brief for Conference of Chief Justices as Amicus Curiae 4, 11. This is a vital state interest:

> "Courts, in our system, elaborate principles of law in the course of resolving disputes. The power and the prerogative of a court to perform this function rest, in the end, upon the respect accorded to its judgments. The citizen's respect for judgments depends in turn upon the issuing court's absolute probity. Judicial integrity is, in consequence, a state interest of the highest order." *Republican Party of Minn. v. White*, 536 U.S. 765, 793, 122 S.Ct. 2528, 153 L.Ed.2d 694 (2002) (KENNEDY, J., concurring).

It is for this reason that States may choose to "adopt recusal standards more rigorous than due process requires." *Id.*, at 794, 122 S.Ct. 2528. . . .

"The Due Process Clause demarks only the outer boundaries of judicial disqualifications. Congress and the states, of course, remain free to impose more rigorous standards for judicial disqualification than those we find mandated here today." *Lavoie, supra,* at 828, 106 S.Ct. 1580. Because the codes of judicial conduct provide more protection than due process requires, most disputes over disqualification will be resolved without resort to the Constitution. Application of the constitutional standard implicated in this case will thus be confined to rare instances.

The judgment of the Supreme Court of Appeals of West Virginia is reversed, and the case is remanded for further proceedings not inconsistent with this opinion.

* * *

Problem 26.5. Refer back to the Chapter Hypothetical. Does Ione's failure to recuse amount to a violation of the plaintiff's due process rights?

What do you think? Justice Kennedy downplayed concerns that the *Caperton* decision would lead to a dramatic increase in recusal motions. Are you convinced? In his dissent (which has been omitted), Chief Justice Roberts criticized the majority for providing "no guidance to judges and litigants about when recusal will be constitutionally required" and predicted an increase in the number of recusal motions filed. He then proceeded to list 40 "fundamental questions" left unanswered by the majority's "probability of bias" standard. These included, "How much money is too much money? What level of contribution or expenditure gives rise to a 'probability of bias'?"; "How long does the probability of bias last? Does the probability of bias diminish over time as the election recedes? Does it matter whether the judge plans to run for reelection?"; and "What if the candidate draws 'disproportionate' support from a particular racial, religious, ethnic, or other group, and the case involves an issue of particular importance to that group?" 129 S.Ct. at 2269–72 (Roberts, C.J., dissenting). Are Chief Justice Roberts' concerns valid? *See* Penny J. White, *Relinquished Responsibilities*, 123 HARV. L. REV. 120 (2009).

Other ways of dealing with campaign contributions. In the majority opinion, Justice Kennedy references various provisions pertaining to recusal in the ABA's Model Code of Judicial Conduct. Rule 2.11(A)(4) provides that recusal is required where a judge learns that a party, a party's lawyer, or the law firm of a party's lawyer has recently made aggregate contributions exceeding $___ (with the dollar amount to be supplied by the adopting jurisdiction). To date, only a few jurisdictions have adopted this approach. In Alabama, lawyers appearing before a judge are required to disclose campaign contributions made by the lawyers or the parties they represent. If the contributions made by the opposing side exceed a designated amount ($4,000 in the case of appellate judges and $2,000 in the case of circuit judges), a party may "file a written notice *requiring* recusal of the justice or judge." Ala. Code. § 12–24–2(c) (emphasis added). Is this a better way to handle these kinds of issues?

Citizens United. In January 2010, the Supreme Court decided in Citizens United v. Federal Election Commission, 558 U.S. 310 (2010), that a federal law that prohibited corporations from using their own funds to make independent expenditures for campaign speech that advocates the election or defeat of a candidate for office amounted to a violation of the First Amendment. What impact might that decision have on judicial elections? How will *Citizens United* and *Caperton* interact?

What do you think? Having now read these two decisions, what are your thoughts about judicial elections? Do the benefits outweigh the problems? Is either merit selection or the federal model of executive appointment a better approach?

* * *

C. ACTIVITIES OF CANDIDATES FOR APPOINTIVE JUDICIAL OFFICE

Please read ABA Model Code of Judicial Conduct, Canon 4, Rule 4.3; re-read Rule 4.1(A)(13); and re-read Rule 2.11(A)(5).

* * *

Confirmation hearings. In theory, Senate confirmation hearings provide an opportunity for Senators to question judicial nominees and learn more about a nominee's qualifications and judicial philosophy. In light of the prohibitions contained in Rules 2.11(A)(5) and Rule 4.1(A)(13), is there much of anything a nominee can say in response to questioning that would shed light on her judicial philosophy?

* * *

D. STANDARDS OF CONDUCT FOR JUDGES

Canon 1 of the ABA Model Code of Judicial Conduct articulates a broad standard of conduct for judges. Not only must judges comply with the law under Rule 1.1, they must, at *all times*, act in a manner that promotes public confidence in the independence, integrity, and impartiality of the judiciary. *See* In re Removal of a Chief Judge, 592 So. 2d 1025 (Fla. 1992) (removing a judge from office after the judge made racially insensitive remarks during a newspaper interview because his comments "eroded public confidence in the judiciary and cast doubt on his impartiality"). Moreover, Rule 1.2 requires that they avoid even the *appearance* of impropriety. In addition, Rule 1.3 prohibits judges from abusing the prestige of judicial office to advance their own interests or the interests of others, and it also prohibits them from allowing others to do so. One could be excused for thinking that these sweeping rules might cover all forms of judicial misconduct. However, the Model Code articulates a host of other, more specific rules governing the conduct of judges on and off the bench.

* * *

Problem 26.6. Refer back to the Chapter Hypothetical. Is Lloyd subject to discipline for his DUI arrest?

* * *

1. ASSURING THE QUALITY OF JUSTICE

The Model Code includes numerous rules addressing a judge's responsibilities with respect to assuring the quality of justice. Judges must be competent and diligent under Rule 2.5, and they must perform their duties without bias or prejudice under Rule 2.3. They must require order and decorum in the courtroom and must be "patient, dignified, and courteous" to individuals in the courtroom under Rule 2.8. *See* Spruance v. Commission On Judicial Qualifications, 532 P.2d 1209 (Cal. 1975) (disciplining a judge who, *inter alia*, made a "raspberry" during defendant's testimony and gave "the finger" to a party in court). With limited exceptions, a judge may not engage in ex parte communications outside the presence of the parties or their lawyers concerning a pending matter under Rule 2.9(A). While *Republican Party of Minnesota v. White* dealt with constitutional issues related to a judge's campaign speech, Rule 2.10 imposes a stricter standard on judges concerning their public statements regarding pending or impending cases. A judge may not make any public statement that might reasonably be expected to affect the outcome or impair the fairness of a pending or impending manner and is also prohibited from making "pledges, promises, or commitments" that are inconsistent with the impartial performance of the judge's duties in connection with matters that are likely to come before the court.

* * *

2. PERSONAL AND EXTRAJUDICIAL ACTIVITIES

a. Restrictions on Civic Engagement

**Please read ABA Model Code of Judicial Conduct,
Canon 3, Rules 3.1–3.4.**

* * *

Problem 26.7. In which of the following instances would Judge Ione be subject to professional discipline?

(A) The judge voluntarily testifies before a legislature about the need to increase judicial salaries.

(B) The judge suggests to a former law clerk that the judge testify as a character witness at the criminal trial of the former clerk and then voluntarily testifies.

(C) The judge voluntarily testifies before a legislature about the need to revise criminal sentencing guidelines.

(D) The judge accepts an appointment by the governor to chair a special committee on improving access to justice.

* * *

b. Restrictions on Freedom of Association

Please read ABA Model Code of Judicial Conduct, Canon 3, Rule 3.6; and Rule 3.7.

* * *

Membership in organizations that practice "invidious" discrimination. Prior to her confirmation hearing, Supreme Court Justice Sonia Sotomayor was a member of the Belizean Grove, "an all-female networking club ... founded as a counterpart to the all-male Bohemian Grove, a legendary club of elite politicians, businessmen and other leaders who meet every year at a retreat in California." http://blogs. wsj.com/law/2009/06/16/will-senators-make-hay-out-of-sotos-all-female-networking-club/ after questions were raised about her membership in the group, Sotomayor resigned her membership. Was she required to do so?

* * *

c. Restrictions on Professional Engagements and Extrajudicial Remunerative Activities

Please read ABA Model Code of Judicial Conduct, Canon 3, Rules 3.8–3.12; Rule 3.14; and Rule 3.15.

* * *

Problem 26.8. In which of the following situations would Judge Ione be subject to professional discipline?

(A) After giving a lecture at a law school, the judge's travel expenses are paid for by the law school.

(B) After giving a lecture at a law school, the judge accepts a gift from the law school of a baseball cap and coffee mug.

(C) The judge, without receiving compensation, acts as a lawyer for her mother in a breach of contract claim in small claims court in a different jurisdiction than the one in which the judge sits.

(D) On weekends, the judge participates in running a family-owned bait and tackle store at the lake.

* * *

d. Restrictions on Accepting Gifts and Loans

**Please read ABA Model Code of Judicial Conduct,
Canon 3, Rule 3.13; and Rule 3.15.**

* * *

Restrictions on accepting gifts and loans. As we saw in Chapter 25, a judge's acceptance of a loan or gift may require the judge's recusal. Even where recusal is not required, a judge may still be required to publicly report the receipt of a gift or loan under Rule 3.13. Putting these questions aside, what qualifies as "ordinary social hospitality" for purposes of Rule 3.13(B)(3)? How about tickets to a professional baseball game? Would the judge have to report this gift pursuant to Rule 3.15? What if the tickets came from a law firm that regularly appears before the judge? *See* In re Luzzo, 756 So.2d 76 (Fla. 2000). Edward Bennett Williams, the former owner of the Washington Redskins, reportedly gave tickets to Redskins games to several members of the Supreme Court, despite the fact that Williams, a lawyer, also appeared as a lawyer before the Court. Richard H. Underwood, *What Gets Judges in Trouble?*, 23 J. NAT'L ASS'N ADMIN. L. JUDGES 101, 122 (2003). Was it proper for the justices in question to accept the tickets? If the same thing were to happen today, could a judge accept the tickets if he reported the receipt pursuant to Rule 3.15? Would a lawyer in Williams' position be subject to discipline?

* * *

Profile of attorney professionalism. Judge Robert R. Merhige, Jr. was appointed to the federal bench in Richmond, Virginia in 1967. Merhige was in private practice as a trial lawyer for over twenty years when he was appointed. Said one longtime Richmond lawyer, "I remember being very enthusiastic about him going on the bench because everybody felt he was pretty much the best lawyer in town." Bill Lohmann, *A Judge's Legacy*, RICH. L., Summer 2005, at 15–17, http://law magazine.richmond.edu/archives/Sum05/pdfs/Features/Merhige_Sum05. pdf.

Merhige was known as a stickler for courtroom decorum and once expelled his own father from court for falling asleep on the front row. *Id.*

Only 5% of his decisions were reversed on appeal. Over the course of his career, he oversaw numerous high-profile cases, including the bankruptcy reorganization of A.H. Robins, the manufacturer of the Dalkon Shield. He also ordered the University of Virginia to admit women in 1970.

But Merhige was perhaps most famous for having ordered the desegregation of dozens of Virginia school systems. His decisions in this area provoked considerable public scorn. "He was widely considered the most hated man in Richmond in the early 1970s, and required 24-hour protection by U.S. marshals. Segregationists threatened his family, spat in his face and shot his dog to death after tying its legs. Protesters held weekly parades outside his home. A guest cottage on his property, where his mother-in-law lived, was burned to the ground." Patricia Sullivan, *Federal Judge Robert R. Merhige Dies*, WASH. POST, Feb. 20, 2005, http://www.washingtonpost.com/politics/federal-judge-robert-r-merhige-dies/2012/05/31/gJQAdkJ4FV_story.html. Said one local lawyer, "He was doing, in my mind, exactly what the law required him to do." Lohmann, *supra*, at 16, http://lawmagazine.richmond.edu/archives/Sum05/pdfs/Features/Merhige_Sum05.pdf.

Merhige retired from the bench in 1998. Looking back on the desegregation cases, he observed, "If I had gotten off (the bench), the kooks would have said they won ... I wouldn't give them the satisfaction." *Id.*

CHAPTER 27

SERVING AS A LEADER IN A LAW FIRM, THE LEGAL PROFESSION, AND THE COMMUNITY

■ ■ ■

Chapter Hypothetical. The law firm of Avett & Connell consists of seven partners, ten associates, and one retired partner whom the firm lists as being "of counsel." The firm also occasionally contracts with temporary lawyers to assist with document review on specific matters. The firm's partners have made Ian the firm's managing partner and have delegated all of the authority with respect to the promulgation of internal firm policies to Ian. Simone is a contract lawyer currently working on a matter handled by James, a semi-retired partner in the firm who now holds an of-counsel position. Simone is concerned that she does not have adequate time to conduct the document review she was hired to do. Unless the firm contracts with another temporary lawyer to help her out, Simone is afraid she will have to start cutting corners and the quality of her work will suffer. James assigned the matter to Simone after he agreed to assume a leadership role in the state bar that required him to do extensive traveling. As a result, James hasn't checked in on the case in several weeks and is unaware of Simone's troubles. To compound matters, Simone believes she may have a previously-undiscovered conflict of interest in the matter. She just discovered the problem two days ago, and when she tried to ask Ian, the managing partner, about the issue, Ian told her to talk to James about it "since it's his case." However, James hasn't responded to any of Simone's emails or voicemails.

(A) Is James subject to discipline for his supervision of Simone?

(B) Is Ian subject to discipline for his supervision of Simone? Are any of the other partners? The firm itself?

(C) Must the firm advise the client that it is employing a temporary lawyer to assist on the client's matter?

(D) Assume that Simone really does have a conflict of interest. Is her conflict imputed to the firm since she is not an employee of the firm?

* * *

Chapter 6 examined the rules that apply to the relationship of supervising and subordinate attorneys. While most recent law graduates will end up taking orders from others at their first job and thus being "subordinate lawyers," if you practice long enough, you may one day be one of those giving the orders. Anyone thinking of opening up their own shop upon graduation and assuming the role of manager would be well advised to take a course on law office management. But even if being a solo or small-firm practitioner is not in your plans, it's important to understand the responsibilities of those whom the Model Rules call "partners, managers, and supervisory lawyers" since you will be dealing with them on a regular basis. In a traditional law firm, these lawyers may owe fiduciary duties to the firm. But even with respect to other kinds of law offices, those with managerial authority have special obligations under the Model Rules, including a duty of supervision of other lawyers and non-lawyers. This chapter also briefly explores some of the business decisions that firm managers make on behalf of the firm. This includes an examination of the special rules regarding engaging in what the Model Rules call "law-related services" and buying and selling a law practice or practice area, including the special ethical obligations facing lawyers who are considering retirement. But in a larger sense, this chapter is about lawyers as leaders. While the primary focus is on lawyers as leaders of the offices in which they work, by the time a lawyer has reached this stage of her career, she may have assumed a leadership more generally within the community. Therefore, the chapter closes with an examination of the concept of lawyers as leaders in the community.

* * *

A. RESPONSIBILITIES OF PARTNERS, MANAGERS, AND SUPERVISORY LAWYERS

**Please read ABA Model Rules of Professional Conduct,
Rule 5.1 and Comments [1]–[5]; and Rule 5.2 and
Comments [1] & [2].**

* * *

Although the Model Rules use the terms "firm" or "law firm," the Terminology section makes clear that those terms cover not just traditional law firms but other types of law offices as well, including "a legal service organization or the legal department of a corporation or other organization." Model Rule 1.0(c). Within a traditional law firm, the management of the firm is, of course, traditionally left to the partners. However, partners are not necessarily all created equal. In recent years, many firms have created a distinction between equity partners (or profit-sharing partners) and non-equity partners (or income partners), who are paid a salary from the firm's profits instead of sharing in the firm's profits. Non-equity partners frequently do not participate in the governance of the firm. Robert W. Hillman, *Law, Culture, and the Lore of Partnership: Of Entrepreneurs, Accountability, and the Evolving Status of Partners*, 40 WAKE FOREST L. REV. 793, 821 (2005). Many firms delegate the management of the firm's business to an individual or group of individuals, who may have few, if any, other duties within the firm. Elizabeth Chambliss, *The Nirvana Fallacy in Law Firm Regulation Debates*, 33 FORDHAM URB. L.J. 119, 127 (2005).

Law firm associates are, of course, employees of the firm. But again, as a practical matter, there may be important distinctions among associates. Associates on the cusp of partnership may have supervisory authority over other associates in a given matter. A third category of law firm lawyers is the lawyer who is "of counsel." This term can potentially apply to a variety of lawyers, including a lawyer who practices in association with a firm but on a part-time basis, a retired partner, or a firm lawyer who occupies a position in between that of partner and associate with no expectation of one day becoming partner. But, as ABA Formal Ethics Opinion 90–357 (1990) explains, the "core characteristic" of an "of counsel" relationship with a firm is a " 'close, regular, personal relationship'; but a relationship which is neither that of a partner . . . with the shared liability and/or managerial responsibility implied by that term; nor [that of an] 'associate,' which is to say a junior non-partner lawyer, regularly employed by the firm."

* * *

1. RESPONSIBILITIES WITH RESPECT TO SUBORDINATE ATTORNEYS

Rule 5.1(a) and "ethical infrastructures." As we saw in an earlier chapter, Model Rules 5.1 and 5.2 envision a situation in which law firm partners and those with comparable authority will establish "ethical infrastructures" that will, among other things, help subordinate lawyers resolve any ethical dilemmas they may come across. Ted Schneyer, *Professional Discipline for Law Firms?*, 77 CORNELL L. REV. 1, 10 (1991). According to Professor Schneyer, "a law firm's organization, policies, and operating procedures . . . may have at least as much to do with causing and avoiding unjustified harm as do the individual values and practice skills of [the firm's] lawyers." *Id.* Thus, Comment [2] to Model Rule 5.1 provides that a lawyer with managerial authority over the professional work of a firm must make "reasonable efforts to establish internal policies and procedures designed to provide reasonable assurance that all lawyers in the firm will conform to the Rules of Professional Conduct."

Comment [3] lists a number of examples of the types of internal policies and procedures that a firm might utilize to help ensure that its lawyers are practicing in an ethical manner. One study found that the most common policies and procedures used in law firms were informal in nature. For example, relatively few of the 156 respondents reported having a formal mentor system in place for associates (33%) or formal training for associates (23%). When asked what an associate should do if the associate had a question about his or her ethical responsibilities in a matter or those of another firm lawyer, the majority of respondents (54%) said that the associate should refer the matter to the firm's managing partner or practice group leader. Would you feel comfortable doing that if you were a new associate? When asked how associates learn of these types of policies and procedures, the majority of respondents (61%) said that the policies were not in written form but were instead passed along by word of mouth. Alex B. Long, *Is Your Firm Focused on Providing a Culture of Ethical Practice and Behavior?*, 45 TENN. B.J. 14 (Dec. 2009). Other studies have produced similar findings. Susan Saab Fortney, *Soul for Sale: An Empirical Study of Associate Satisfaction, Law Firm Culture, and the Effects of Billable Hour Requirements*, 69 UMKC L. REV. 239 (2000) (finding that 54% of associates surveyed reported that their firms did not have procedures in place for dealing with the ethical concerns of firm attorneys and that 24% did not know if their firms had any procedures in place).

Is this what Rule 5.1(a) contemplates? How much instruction, guidance, or hand-holding do new lawyers need?

Recall also from Chapter 6 that Rule 5.3 imposes a similar duty with respect to the supervision of non-lawyer employees.

The use of ethics counsel. Many larger firms have a designated ethics expert or in-house ethics counsel. In some firms, the designation is informal in nature ("Sandy's the ethics expert"), whereas in others the position is a full-time one. For obvious reasons, there are fewer designated ethics experts in smaller firms.

Individual liability vs. firm liability. All of the duties set forth in the Model Rules are duties imposed upon individual lawyers. Even the vicarious responsibility of the supervisory lawyer under Model Rule 5.1(c) is imposed on the individual supervisory lawyer. There is no possibility under the Model Rules of imposing professional discipline upon a law firm as an entity. Might it be useful to impose some professional responsibilities on a law firm or legal department considered as an entity distinct from the individual lawyers who act on its behalf? In New York, for example, the Rule 5.1 duties are imposed on the firm itself. N.Y. Lawyer's Code of Prof'l Responsibility DR 1–104(A).

* * *

Problem 27.1. Refer back to the Chapter Hypothetical. Is James subject to discipline for his supervision of Simone? Is Ian subject to discipline for his supervision of Simone? Are any of the other partners? The firm itself?

* * *

2. RESPONSIBILITIES WITH RESPECT TO CONTRACT LAWYERS

STATE BAR OF MICHIGAN
STANDING COMMITTEE ON PROFESSIONAL
AND JUDICIAL ETHICS
Opinion Number RI-310

A "Professional Employer Organization" (PEO), also known as an Employee Leasing Company (ELC), seeks to "rent" out lawyers for temporary employment with a law firm. The ELC administers all payroll and benefit services for the law firm, pays the wages of the worker, and has the right to reassign, discipline, and terminate the leased employees. The ELC is in effect, a separate entity from the law firm, which seeks to utilize leased services of an attorney.

. . . This opinion addresses only the abstract question as to whether a lawfully "leased" attorney can be utilized in an appropriate situation.

The possibility of unethical activity has lead [sic.] some states to determine that such arrangements are unethical. It has been said that the lack of economic independence of the leased attorney impairs the ability of the attorney to exercise independent judgment on behalf of clients. North Carolina Ethics Op 365 (1985). This has not been found to be a direct sharing of fees in another state. New Jersey Ethics Op 90–23 (1991).

Absent a more definitive rule on the subject, an opinion prohibiting the conduct in absolute terms would be inappropriate. The ability to enter into such an arrangement has been specifically approved, although there has always been stated caveats. ABA Op 88–356 (1988), sets forth the commonly referred to limitations stating:

> "In order to satisfy the requirements of the Model Rules and predecessor Model Code when a lawyer is engaged temporarily to work for clients of a law firm (including a corporate legal department), the lawyer and the firm must exercise care, in accordance with the guidelines in this opinion, to avoid conflicts of interest, to maintain confidentiality of information relating to the representation of clients, to disclose to clients the arrangement between the lawyer and the firm in some

circumstances, and to comply with other applicable provisions of the Rules and Code. The use of a lawyer placement agency to obtain temporary lawyer services where the agency's fee is a proportion of the lawyers compensation does not violate the Model Rules or predecessor Model Code as long as the professional independence of the lawyer is maintained without interference by the agency, the total fee paid by the client to the law firm is reasonable, and the arrangement is otherwise in accord with the guidelines in this opinion."

Compliance with the Michigan Rules of Professional Conduct (MRPC) provides equal limitations on the practical use of such an arrangement. A non-exhaustive sampling of some ethical considerations follows:

MRPC 5.1(a) and (b) states:

"(a) A partner in a law firm shall make reasonable efforts to ensure that the firm has in effect measures giving reasonable assurance that all lawyers in the firm conform to the Rules of Professional Conduct.

"(b) A lawyer having direct supervisory authority over another lawyer shall make reasonable efforts to ensure that the other lawyer conforms to the Rules of Professional Conduct."

Any arrangement, which impaired the ability of the firm to exercise such reasonable efforts, would be unethical. The arrangement cannot be considered to absolve the employing firm of the duty to see to it that the leased attorney, and the firm itself follows ethical practices.

The individual lawyer that is leased to the firm is likewise bound by the rules without regard to the nature of the lawyer's supervision. [See MRPC 5.2(a).]

The nature of temporary employment may increase the likelihood that a leased attorney will be confronted with conflicts of interest. However, the temporary or dual nature of the employment does not lessen the stringent requirements to avoid conflicts of interest. The temporarily employed lawyer must comply with MRPC 1.7, 1.8, 1.9 and 1.10. The leased attorney must be considered to be "associated" with the leasing firm, as well as any prior leasing firms, for purposes of MRPC 1.9 and 1.10. The supervising firm and the individual lawyer shall have a duty to see to it that a reasonable procedure is designed to determine if the leased attorney shall have a duty to see to it that a reasonable procedure is designed to determine if the leased attorney has been associated with firms that have represented clients with adverse interests. The requirements of rules pertaining to resolutions of any conflicts would then have to be met.

. . . .

MRPC 1.4(b) states:

"(b) A lawyer shall explain a matter to the extent reasonably
necessary to permit the client to make informed decisions
regarding the representation."

. . . .

The firm and the lawyer must affirmatively advise the client of the
temporary nature of the relationship at the point that this information is
necessary to make an informed decision as to the firm's representation.
This is true even if there has been no expressed or implied suggestion
that the leased attorney is a member of the employing firm. No
exhaustive statement can be made as to what situation requires
disclosure, but certain situations can illustrate the factors involved.

The lawyer that interviews the client, and actually agrees to the
firm's representation is clearly of importance in the attorney-client
relationship. A client would reasonably infer that the attorney that
outwardly represents the firm is also a member of the firm. Disclosure of
the leased nature of the employment would therefore be required.

In addition, when decisions of the leased employee involve the
ongoing direction of a file or legal matter, then the nature of the
relationship would be necessary to allow the client to make an informed
decision. However, if the acts of the leased attorney are subject to
approval by firm attorneys, and the independent actions are closely
supervised, no disclosure would be required. For example, a brief
submitted as drafted and signed by a leased attorney in a significant
aspect of the case would require disclosure. However, a brief reviewed
and approved by a firm attorney is subject to the firm's own independent
judgment. The fact that the leased attorney had written a prior "draft," or
engaged in research used by a firm attorney would likely not be sufficient
to require disclosure.

A client has a right to know if any significant discretion or judgment
resides in an attorney that is not a member of the firm that the client has
chosen to retain. The client has legitimate expectations that the firm
retained is making the decisions of importance to his or her legal matter.
Failure to disclose would defeat these reasonable expectations.

. . . .

The arrangement to lease an attorney must be consistent with the
requirements set forth herein and any other ethical considerations that a
specific factual scenario may present. However, if the arrangement
complies with other legal requirements unrelated to ethical
considerations, and is also consistent with the Michigan Rules of

Professional Conduct, it is not per se unethical. The duty to see to it that the arrangement is in fact consistent with ethical considerations resides with the firm leasing the attorney, as well as any leased attorney.

* * *

Problem 27.2. Refer back to the Chapter Hypothetical. Must the firm advise the client that it is employing a temporary lawyer to assist on the client's matter?

Problem 27.3. Refer back to the Chapter Hypothetical. Assume that Simone really does have a conflict of interest. Is her conflict imputed to the firm since she is not an employee of the firm?

* * *

3. OUTSOURCING LEGAL WORK

The practice of law is also a business, and like many businesses, law offices sometimes "outsource" work to lawyers in other countries. According to the ABA, "in each of the last three years, the legal outsourcing industry has grown by 60 percent . . . In India alone, its estimated $80 million industry expects to grow to $4 billion by 2015." *ABA Says "Yes" to Legal Outsourcing*, YOUR ABA (Sep. 2008), available at www.abanet.org/media/youraba/200809/article09.html. ABA Formal Opinion 08–451 (2008) examined some of the potential ethical concerns raised in such cases. The opinion noted some of the potential benefits of outsourcing, including the potential reduction in costs for legal services to a client. However, the opinion is also clear that the supervisory obligations imposed by Rule 5.1(b) can apply to the outsourcing situation. Indeed, given the differences in legal education and training in other countries and the practical difficulties raised by trying to supervise the work of someone a thousand miles and several time zones away, the opinion explains that "it will be more important than ever for the outsourcing lawyer to scrutinize the work done by foreign lawyers." The opinion advised that "[a]t a minimum," a law firm outsourcing legal services should consider conducting reference checks on the lawyer in question. Also, the outsourcing lawyer "should consider investigating the security of the provider's premises, computer network, and perhaps even its recycling and refuse disposal procedures."

* * *

B. PROVIDING LAW-RELATED SERVICES

**Please read ABA Model Rules of Professional Conduct,
Rule 5.4 and Comments; and Rule 5.7 and Comments.**

* * *

Innovative law firms are always seeking ways to better serve clients while expanding their market share. One way some firms have accomplished these goals is through the offering of law-related services. Model Rule 5.7 defines law-related services (also sometimes known as "ancillary services") as "services that might reasonably be performed in conjunction with and in substance are related to the provision of legal services, and that are not prohibited as unauthorized practice of law when provided by a nonlawyer." A comment provides numerous examples. Professor Ted Schneyer has explained the rise of these types of services:

> In the 1980s, law firms, most notably in Washington, D.C., began to experiment with arrangements for providing their clients with the law-related services of professionals such as accountants, economists, lobbyists and environmental engineers. Some firms hired these nonlawyers directly, while others placed them in subsidiary consulting firms that provided services to the affiliated law firm's clients and other customers. Law firms often considered the subsidiary form attractive because ethics rules barred lawyers from having nonlawyer-partners in their firms, but top-notch experts often preferred to participate in these ventures as principals.

Ted Schneyer, *"Professionalism" as Pathology: The ABA's Latest Policy Debate on Nonlawyer Ownership of Law Practice Entities*, 40 FORDHAM URB. L.J. 75, 110 n. 126 (2012). Eventually, the ABA amended the Model Rules to address these types of arrangements. Although permitted under the rules, offering law-related services may raise a number of potential ethical concerns.

* * *

NORTH CAROLINA STATE BAR
RECEIVING FEE OR COMMISSION FOR FINANCIAL
SERVICES AND PRODUCTS PROVIDED
TO LEGAL CLIENTS
2010 Formal Ethics Opinion 13

Inquiry:

Lawyer would like to establish an ancillary business that provides financial services to clients and non-clients. Services would include assistance in the selection, purchase, and disposition of securities, life insurance, and annuities. Lawyer would be compensated through consulting fees, investment advisory fees, and commissions. The ancillary services would be provided by an entity separate and distinct from the lawyer's legal practice.

May Lawyer offer financial services to his legal clients and receive a fee or commission based on the provision of the financial services and the sale of financial products?

Opinion:

Yes. The ethical responsibilities for a lawyer who provides law-related services are set out in Rule 5.7. When law-related services are provided under circumstances that are not distinct from the provision of legal services, the law firm will be subject to all of the Rules of Professional Conduct with respect to the provision of the law-related services. If the law-related services are provided by a separate entity, the law firm will still be subject to the Rules of Professional Conduct unless the law firm takes "reasonable measures" to ensure that a person obtaining the law-related services knows that the services are not legal services and that the protections of the lawyer-client relationship do not exist. See Rule 5.7(a)(2).

Even when a lawyer provides law-related services through a separate entity, and takes the necessary measures to ensure that the consumer of the law-related services knows that the services are not legal services, the lawyer is still bound by the Rules of Professional Conduct as to the referral of his legal clients to the ancillary business. Comment [6] to Rule 5.7 provides that when a client-lawyer relationship exists with a person who is referred by a lawyer to an ancillary business controlled by the lawyer, the lawyer must comply with Rule 1.8(a) pertaining to business transactions with clients. See also Rule 1.8, cmt. [1]. Pursuant to Rule 1.8(a) a lawyer may only enter into a business transaction with a client if: (1) the transaction and terms are fair and reasonable to the client and are fully disclosed and transmitted in writing in a manner that can be reasonably understood by the client; (2) the client is advised in writing of the desirability of seeking and is given a reasonable opportunity to seek the advice of independent legal counsel on the transaction; and (3) the client gives informed consent, in writing signed by the client, to the essential terms of the transaction and the lawyer's role in the transaction. Accordingly, a lawyer must make these disclosures and secure the requisite consent before providing financial services and products to a client.

. . . .

Although the previous prohibition on receiving fees or commissions for ancillary business transactions related to legal representation has been eliminated, when dealing with his legal clients, Lawyer has an ethical duty to avoid conflicts created by his own personal interests. *See* Rule 1.7(a)(2). Rule 1.7(b) provides that a lawyer shall not represent a client with respect to a matter if the lawyer's professional judgment on behalf of the client may be materially limited by the lawyer's own personal interest. Comment [10] to Rule 1.7 specifically states that a lawyer may not allow related business interests to affect representation, "for example, by referring clients to an enterprise in which the lawyer has an undisclosed financial interest." The lawyer's self-interest in promoting his financial services company must not distort his independent professional judgment in the provision of legal services to the client, including referring a client to the lawyer's own ancillary business. Rule 1.7; Rule 2.1.

Although a conflict of interest exists in providing financial products to legal clients, the potential problems and risks can be avoided in most transactions if the lawyer makes the disclosures required by Rules 1.8(a) and 1.7(b), and obtains the client's informed written consent. Rule 1.7(b) allows a lawyer to represent a client despite a conflicting personal interest if the lawyer reasonably believes his representation of the client will not be affected and the client gives written consent after disclosure of the existence and nature of the possible conflict and the possible adverse consequences of the representation. Prior to entering into a business transaction with a client, Rule 1.8(a) requires the lawyer to fully disclose the terms of the transaction to the client, including the lawyer's role in the transaction, in a manner that can be reasonably understood by the client. In such circumstances, a client should have sufficient information from which to decide whether to enter into an ancillary business transaction with the client's lawyer. Each transaction should be evaluated in accordance with its individual circumstances.

. . . .

Assuming that the financial services are provided under circumstances that are distinct from the provision of legal services, and Lawyer ensures that the consumer of the financial services knows that the services are not legal services, Lawyer may offer his financial services to his legal clients and receive payment for the services so long as he complies with the requirements set out in 1.8 and 1.7.

Lawyer must first determine that his professional judgment on behalf of the client will not be adversely affected by his personal interest in making a profit. If Lawyer cannot reasonably make such a determination, then the lawyer should not refer the client to his financial services company. See Rule 1.7(b)(1). Lawyer then must make an independent professional determination that the financial products and services offered by his company would best serve his client's interests. Prior to recommending his financial services and products to the client,

Lawyer must make full disclosure of his personal interest in the financial services company, as required by Rule 1.7(b) and Rule 1.8(a) so that the client can make a fully informed choice.

* * *

Problem 27.4. Assume that the lawyer from the above ethics opinion goes ahead and sets up his law-related business. He has recently been talking to one of his legal clients about the possibility of offering his services in the selection of securities. What sort of information should the lawyer include in a written disclosure to the client concerning the proposed transaction?

* * *

Non-lawyer ownership of law firms. While the ABA amended the rules to specifically address the provision of law-related services by lawyers, it has been unwilling to amend the rule to permit non-lawyer ownership of law firms. Model Rule 5.4 explicitly prohibits lawyers from sharing legal fees with non-lawyers and forming partnerships involving the practice of law with non-lawyers. In contrast, the U.K. Legal Services Act of 2007 permits non-lawyers to manage, invest in, and own businesses that provide legal services. The goal of the Act is to encourage greater competition and efficiency.

Reread Rule 5.4. Why are non-lawyers not permitted to own or manage law firms? Do the justifications make sense in today's legal environment? For a discussion of the general issue, see Renee Newman Knake, *Democratizing the Delivery of Legal Services*, 73 OHIO ST. L.J. 1, 9 (2012).

* * *

C. SALE OF A LAW PRACTICE OR AN AREA OF PRACTICE

**Please read ABA Model Rules of Professional Conduct,
Rule 1.17 and Comments; Rule 5.4(a)(2);
and Rule 5.6 and Comment [3].**

* * *

Problem 27.5. Helen is a local solo practitioner who has a lucrative estate planning practice with numerous wealthy clients. She also handles a few adoption matters a year. Helen has been a practicing lawyer for over forty years and is now considering selling her law practice and retiring. She hasn't completely ruled out practicing law on a part-time basis, but she knows that she no longer wants to do estate-planning work and may instead handle the occasional adoption matter. Ian, the managing partner at Avett & Connell, learns of Helen's plans at a local bar meeting. As it so happens, the partners at Avett & Connell have been thinking about expanding the firm's practice to include estate planning. Ian's first preference would be to purchase some of Helen's more lucrative open client matters, but he is willing to consider purchasing Helen's entire estate planning practice. The firm has no interest in Helen's adoption practice. Are either of these arrangements permissible under the Model Rules?

Client confidences. Presumably, Ian will want to know more about Helen's clients and their ongoing matters before he makes an offer on behalf of Avett & Connell. Will Helen be violating her duty of confidentiality under Model Rule 1.6 if she provides Ian with this information? ABA Model Rule 1.17—more specifically Comment [7]— attempts to provide guidance for lawyers and protections for clients concerning disclosure of information relating to the representation of clients in connection with the sale and purchase of a law practice. Does the comment provide adequate guidance? The relevant section of the Ohio Rules of Professional Conduct, for example, provides:

> The selling lawyer and prospective purchasing lawyer may engage in general discussions regarding the possible sale of a law practice. Before the selling lawyer may provide the prospective lawyer with information relative to client representation or confidential information contained in client files, the selling lawyer shall require the prospective purchasing lawyer to execute a confidentiality agreement. The confidentiality agreement shall bind the prospective purchasing lawyer to preserve information relating to the representation of the client of the selling lawyer, consistent with Rule 1.6 as if those clients were the clients of the prospective purchasing lawyer.

Comment [7] adds that "[a]fter the confidentiality agreement has been signed and before the prospective purchaser reviews client-specific information, a conflict check should be completed to assure that the prospective purchaser does not review client-specific information concerning a client whom the prospective purchaser cannot represent because of a conflict of interest." Is this helpful? Why not require client consent, unless the selling lawyer is unable to communicate with the client or, as the case may be, former client?

Planning for the inevitable. As lawyers near retirement, they need to consider how any unresolved client matters will be taken care of upon retirement. Even younger lawyers for whom the thoughts of retirement and death are not in the front of their minds need to plan for the unfortunate possibility of an untimely death. This is particularly true in the case of solo practitioners. ABA Formal Ethics Opinion 92–369 (1992) considered what steps lawyers should take to ensure that their clients' matters will not be neglected in the event of their death. According to the opinion, a lawyer's duties of competence and diligent representation require that a solo practitioner have a plan in place to protect their clients upon the death of the lawyer. "Such a plan should at a minimum include the designation of another lawyer who would have the authority to look over the sole practitioner's files and make determinations as to which files needed immediate attention, and provide for notification to the sole practitioner's clients of their lawyer's death."

* * *

D. SERVING AS A LEADER IN THE LEGAL PROFESSION AND IN THE COMMUNITY

In addition to serving as leaders within law firms, lawyers may serve as leaders in other capacities. When Thomas Jefferson designed the first law school curriculum at the College of William & Mary in 1780, he did so with the idea that newly-trained lawyers would help preserve America's constitutional republican government and so would need to be "virtuous leaders who would place the public interest above their own private interest . . . [and be] well positioned to provide direction and leadership to the new nation." Davison M. Douglas, *The Jeffersonian Vision of Legal Education*, 51 J. LEGAL EDUC. 185, 185 (2001). In order to receive their degrees, aspiring lawyers were required to study math, philosophy, logic, literature, rhetoric, natural law, law of nations, geography, and ancient and modern languages. *Id.* at 205. These requirements were all intended to train aspiring lawyers "to assume positions of leadership in the secular world." *Id.* at 196.

As Professor Deborah L. Rhode has observed, lawyers serve as leaders in a variety of capacities:

> The legal profession has supplied a majority of American presidents, and in recent decades, almost half of Congress, and ten percent of S&P 500 companies' CEOs. Lawyers occupy leadership roles as governors, state legislators, judges, prosecutors, general counsel, law firm managing partners, and heads of government and nonprofit organizations.

Deborah L. Rhode, *Lawyers and Leadership*, 20 PROFESSIONAL LAWYER, No. 3, at 1 (2010). Rhode notes that lawyers serve as leaders in other capacities as well: "Even recent law school graduates and other members of the bar who do not land at the top of the pecking order frequently play leadership roles in teams, committees, campaigns, and other group efforts." *Id.*

Another way in which lawyers serve as leaders is with respect to professional organizations. Local and state bar associations offer a variety of programs designed to improve the legal profession and the quality of justice. Most state and local bars have committees devoted to improving access to justice, relations between judges and practicing lawyers, professional development for young lawyers, continuing legal education, judicial selection, and increasing diversity within the legal profession.

A group of researchers on the subject of effective leadership identified four components of enduring success:

> happiness (feelings of pleasure and contentment); achievement (accomplishments that compare favorably against similar goals others have strived for); significance (the sense that you've made a positive impact on people you care about); and legacy (a way to establish your values or accomplishments so as to help others find future success).

Laura Nash & Howard Stevenson, *Success That Lasts*, HARV. BUS. REV., Feb. 2004, at 104. As Professor Rhode notes, "The challenge for leaders is setting priorities that strike a balance among all four goals." Deborah L. Rhode, *What Lawyers Lack: Leadership*, 9 U. ST. THOMAS L.J. 471, 495 (2011).

* * *

Profile of attorney professionalism. One example of a lawyer who used his legal training to serve as a leader within his community is Mahatma Gandhi. Before returning to India to help lead India's independence movement, Gandhi was a lawyer in South Africa for nearly twenty years. As described by Professor Charles DiSalvo in his book *M.K.Gandhi, Attorney at Law: The Man Before the Mahatma* (2013), Gandhi developed a successful commercial law practice by representing Indian merchants in South Africa. Upon arriving in South Africa, he found that European colonists were seeking to deny Indians their civil and economic liberties. Having becoming a respected figure in South Africa's Indian community, Gandhi's merchant clients turned to him for assistance. In this capacity, "Gandhi acted as the community's political organizer, not as the community's lawyer." Charles R. DiSalvo, *Attorney Gandhi's Questions*, W. VA. LAWYER (Jan-Mar. 2014), at 37. In his time outside of his practice, Gandhi helped organize citizens and sought to bring the denial of Indian civil rights to the attention of government officials.

DiSalvo describes the second phase of Gandhi's legal career:

> When the attacks on Indian rights nevertheless continued, Gandhi altered the shape of his practice and his life. In this second phase, Gandhi began to devote some of his professional

work and time to defending his community. When the colonial
government, for example, attempted to drive Indians out of
businesses by denying them the necessary operating licenses,
Gandhi and a colleague went to court to fight this effort. . . .
Gandhi performed this work while continuing to operate, and
indeed expand, his commercial law practice. Alongside his
community work, he continued his business practice. The two
aspects of his practice operated parallel with, but separate from,
each other.

Id.

Eventually, when the attacks on Indian civil liberties continued,
many Indians engaged in civil disobedience. "When his Indian
compatriots resisted the law and found themselves prosecuted in criminal
court by the government, it was Gandhi who was at their side. In this
portion of his life, Gandhi dedicated his entire practice to defense work.
The needs of his clients and his community commanded his complete
professional attention and entirely defined his practice." *Id.*

CHAPTER 28

REFLECTIONS ON A REWARDING CAREER AS A LAWYER

■ ■ ■

Chapter hypothetical. After many years of practicing law, you are ready to retire and enjoy the good life. As you start to look back on your life as a lawyer, how do you hope you will be remembered?

* * *

This book has been organized around the concept of the professional life of a lawyer. A lawyer cannot know at the beginning of his or her career what the future holds. For example, Richard Baumgartner was a lawyer who graduated from law school in 1978. Over the years, he became a respected criminal lawyer and eventually became judge of the state felony trial court in his city. Baumgartner presided over a number of high-profile criminal cases and gained the respect of the lawyers who appeared before him. He was described as "brilliant." He was also progressive; in 2000 he founded the local Drug Court, which was designed "to provide nonviolent offenders with substance-abuse treatment and job training." The program became a model for other programs in the state. In short, Baumgartner appeared well on his way to leaving behind a lasting legacy as a lawyer and judge. But by 2012, his judicial career was over. He had become an alcoholic and developed an addiction to painkillers. He was arrested and pleaded guilty to purchasing drugs. Many of the convictions in cases Baumgartner presided over were overturned due to the fact that he was impaired during the time. *See* Jamie Satterfield, *Court of Secrecy*, KNOXVILLE NEWS SENTINEL, Feb. 12, 2012.

Baumgartner's story serves as a cautionary tale for aspiring lawyers. Yet, this book has also included numerous examples of lawyers whose careers serve as models for future lawyers. More examples follow in this chapter. What is it that accounts for the different paths that some lawyers' professional lives take?

* * *

THE LAWYERS KNOW TOO MUCH
CARL SANDBURG (1878–1967)

The lawyers, Bob, know too much.
They are chums of the books of old John Marshall.
They know it all, what a dead hand wrote,
A stiff dead hand and its knuckles crumbling,
The bones of the fingers a thin white ash.
The lawyers know
a dead man's thoughts too well.

In the heels of the higgling lawyers, Bob,
Too many slippery ifs and buts and howevers,
Too much hereinbefore provided whereas,
Too many doors to go in and out of.

When the lawyers are through
What is there left, Bob?
Can a mouse nibble at it
And find enough to fasten a tooth in?

Why is there always a secret singing
When a lawyer cashes in?
Why does a hearse horse snicker
Hauling a lawyer away?

The work of a bricklayer goes to the blue.
The knack of a mason outlasts a moon.
The hands of a plasterer hold a room together.
The land of a farmer wishes him back again.
Singers of songs and dreamers of plays
Build a house no wind blows over.
The lawyers—tell me why a hearse horse snickers
hauling a lawyer's bones.

* * *

What do you think? Professionals are not usually subject to criticism for knowing too much. According to the poem, in what sense do lawyers "know too much"? Summarize in your own words the critique of lawyers that the poem presents. If a new lawyer asked you for advice about how to avoid having the hearse horse snicker as he hauls the lawyer's bones away, what would you say?

* * *

Ripples in a pond. Many lawyers have had a positive influence on the legal profession. The impact one lawyer can have is often like a ripple in a pond, creating ever-widening circles of inspiration. One such lawyer was Thurgood Marshall.

Thurgood Marshall was the first African-American to serve on the United States Supreme Court. Born in 1908 in Baltimore, Maryland, he was educated in the segregated public schools of his hometown. He received his undergraduate degree from Lincoln University in Pennsylvania and then obtained his law degree in 1933 from Howard University School of Law in Washington, D.C., where he graduated first in his class.

Marshall began his career in solo practice but quickly began his affiliation with the NAACP. In 1940 he became the founder and Executive Director of the NAACP Legal Defense and Education Fund. Continuing the work begun by his mentor, Howard Law School Dean Charles Hamilton Houston, he filed lawsuits across the country challenging racial segregation. His most famous victory came in 1954, in *Brown vs. Board of Education*, which he argued before the U.S. Supreme Court.

In 1961 President John F. Kennedy appointed Marshall to the United States Court of Appeals for the Second Circuit, and in 1965 President Lyndon B. Johnson appointed him to serve as the U.S. Solicitor General. As the first African-American to serve in that role, he represented the United States before the Supreme Court in many civil rights cases. In fact, he argued frequently before the Court, making 32 arguments in all and winning 29 of those cases.

In 1967 President Lyndon Johnson appointed him to the U.S. Supreme Court, where he became a staunch advocate of civil rights. He consistently opposed the death penalty, and he was a strong supporter of trial by jury. Dissenting in *Apodaca v. Oregon,* in which the Supreme Court held that a criminal defendant could be convicted of a felony by a less-than-unanimous verdict, he stated:

> Each time this Court has approved a change in the familiar characteristics of the jury, we have reaffirmed the principle that its fundamental characteristic is its capacity to render a commonsense, laymen's judgment, as a representative body drawn from the community. To fence out a dissenting juror fences out a voice from the community, and undermines the principle on which our whole notion of the jury now rests. [The other dissenting Justices] have pointed to the danger, under a less-than-unanimous rule, of excluding from the process members of minority groups, whose participation we have elsewhere recognized as a constitutional requirement. It should be emphasized, however, that the fencing-out problem goes beyond the problem of identifiable minority groups. The juror whose dissenting voice is unheard may be a spokesman, not for any minority viewpoint, but simply for himself—and that, in my view, is enough. The doubts of a single juror are in my view

evidence that the government has failed to carry its burden of proving guilt beyond a reasonable doubt. I dissent.

Apodaca v. Oregon, 404 U.S. 356, 402–03 (1972).

Thurgood Marshall influenced generations of lawyers. One of his law clerks was now-Justice Elena Kagan. Another one of his protégés became the first African-American woman appointed to the federal bench.

Constance Baker Motley was born in 1921 in New Haven, Connecticut. She grew up to become one of the nation's leading civil rights advocates, a United States District Judge, and a recipient of the Presidential Citizens Medal.

Motley was a first-generation American, her parents having emigrated from the West Indies. During her childhood, her New Haven neighborhood was diverse, made up largely of families of recent immigrants—Polish, Italian, Jewish, and Irish. After attending college for a time at Fisk University in Nashville, she earned her bachelor's degree at New York University. She earned her J.D. from Columbia University Law School, where she met Thurgood Marshall, who hired her as a law clerk for the NAACP's Legal Defense and Education Fund (LDEF).

After graduating from law school, she worked with Marshall at the LDEF, where she participated in many of the landmark cases of the civil rights era, including *Brown v. Board of Education*. Recalling that decision, she said, "I thought we had talked ourselves out of our jobs. But instead of seeing the end in sight, we see newer horizons all the time." Allan Morrison, *Top Woman Civil Rights Lawyer*, EBONY, Jan. 1963, at 58. She also became the first African-American woman to argue a case before the United States Supreme Court when she argued the case of James Meredith, who had been denied admission to the University of Mississippi. In Southern courtrooms she endured the hostility of white citizens and judges to defend freedom riders and Dr. Martin Luther King, Jr.

In 1966 President Lyndon B. Johnson appointed her to the United States District Court for the Southern District of New York, making her the first African-American woman to serve as a federal judge. Her appointment was supported by both New York Senators, Robert F. Kennedy, a Democrat, and Jacob K. Javits, a Republican. She continued to serve until her death in 2005. Upon her death, the United States Senate passed a resolution honoring her for her "lifelong commitment to the advancement of civil rights and social justice." S. Res. 272, 151 Cong. Rec. 22642 (2005).

Civil rights lawyer and law professor Lani Guinier, at 12 years old, watched the television image of James Meredith being escorted into the University of Mississippi by Constance Baker Motley. She was struck by Motley's "erect and imposing figure," her "proud image." Guinier saw that

Motley "did not flinch even as the crowd yelled epithets." Although Motley was guarded by U.S. Marshals, Guinier thought, "she could . . . have been alone. . . . She was that determined. I thought: I can do that. I can be a civil rights lawyer." LANI GUINIER, LIFT EVERY VOICE: TURNING A CIVIL RIGHTS SETBACK INTO A NEW VISION OF SOCIAL JUSTICE 68 (1998).

* * *

What do you think? Constance Baker Motley was inspired by the example of Thurgood Marshall. Who inspired you to choose a legal career? Who are the inspiring lawyers of today? Does the prevalence of lawyer jokes and the generally cynical attitude about lawyers indicate that there is a paucity of inspiring lawyers? What are the characteristics of an inspiring lawyer?

What do you think? Both Marshall and Motley were acutely aware of the obstacles faced by African-Americans entering the legal profession. Do the barriers they describe still exist for African-Americans or members of other racial or ethnic minorities? If so, what should the legal profession do to erase these obstacles?

What do you think? Both Marshall and Motley believed in the law as an instrument of social change, and both pursued legal careers, in part at least, because of their commitment to certain social ideals. Can the law change society? What social changes comparable to racial integration should the law help to bring about in the future? Have you been motivated to study law because of your commitment to certain social ideals? If so, how would you describe your commitment?

* * *

Most lawyers never achieve the fame of a Thurgood Marshall or a Constance Baker Motley. But they too are remembered. Consider, for example, John C. Dods, longtime partner at Kansas City's Shook, Hardy and Bacon. He died in 2008, at age 74, shortly after the article below was published, and was memorialized in the obituary that follows.

DEBBIE CALTON, CELEBRATING 50 YEARS AT SHB: JOHN C. DODS
SHB CityLink, Feb. 7, 2008

The "Chief," as he was known to any young lad who had ever been a boy scout, was H. Roe Bartle, later the mayor of Kansas City and for whom the K.C. Chiefs were named. An early encounter with the Chief changed the direction of John C. Dods's education and ultimately contributed to Dods's 50-year career at SHB [Shook, Hardy & Bacon L.L.P.].

In the spring of his senior high school year, Dods was summoned by Bartle. "Everyone knew that when the Chief summoned, you responded. I appeared as commanded in Bartle's office, not knowing why," Dods said.

Bartle told Dods, that he should attend Missouri Valley College, a small church-related college in Marshall, Missouri. Bartle always spoke in a booming, stentorian voice and told Dods he would have " . . . a grand and glorious future at Valley." Dods thought he had been commanded from on-high. He knew little about the small college where Bartle was interim president, but after talking to the Chief, Dods abandoned his plans to attend K.U. and spent the next two years at Valley.

Marshall, Missouri, plays an important role in the history of Shook, Hardy & Bacon. Unknown to Dods at the time, the firm began in Marshall, where founder Frank Payne Sebree first opened an office and where both Edgar Shook and Charlie Bacon had practiced. It was through Bacon, who was then on the Board of Trustees of the college, that Dods later gained an interview with the firm, where he was hired as an associate in 1958.

Now, 50 years later, Dods is still with the firm and still has a connection to Marshall and Valley, where he serves on the board of trustees of the college.

John grew up in a middle-class neighborhood in the old northeast part of Kansas City where he attended the same public schools as had his mom and dad, and he lived within walking distance of both paternal and maternal grandparents. "A kid couldn't get in too much trouble in the neighborhood," Dods says, "because everyone knew all the kids and would rat out on us for any prank or mischievous activity."

Dods was president of the student council in high school and often was called upon to make speeches to the P.T.A. and other groups, through which he developed an interest in public speaking and debate and the strong speaking voice now often heard on public radio, as well as in the courtroom.

No one in his family had any connection with the legal profession (he was the first member of his family to graduate from college) and he went through all the usual sophomoric phases of deciding on a career choice which ranged from wanting to be a college professor of philosophy, a youth social worker, a clergyman, and ultimately a lawyer. After two years at Valley, Dods decided to aim for law school and transferred to the University of Kansas, from which he received his undergraduate degree and where he attended the first year of law school.

At K.U. Dods was president of a Scholarship Hall. At the time, immediately after the U.S. Supreme Court decision in *Brown v. Board of Education,* Dods led efforts to have the resident hall become the first racially integrated housing facility at the university. "Rooming with the first African-American to integrate a facility at K.U. made me acutely aware of the racial prejudice that permeated society. It was an experience that reshaped my life."

Dods transferred to the University of Kansas City School of Law (now U.M.K.C.) and graduated in 1957. After a brief period of active duty in the Army, Dods contacted Charlie Bacon, who introduced him to David R. Hardy, who offered him a job in February 1958. "Hardy told me he wasn't sure the firm—which then had 14 lawyers—could afford to hire two lawyers in one year," Dods says. The going rate in Kansas City was $350.00 a month but Hardy said the firm would only pay new associates $300, because a young lawyer would get more and better experience at the firm than elsewhere.

"My car payment and my rent totaled almost exactly what I got paid, after taxes, but I jumped at the chance to work for the firm," Dods relates, "and it was the best decision I ever made. But I did eat a lot of pasta and other cheap meals until I got my first raise, a whopping $50 a month!"

Dods tells great stories of his early days with the firm and how he got to work with Hardy, Bacon, Ed Shook, Sam Sebree, Jim Ottman, Lane Bauer, Dave Clark, and the other great trial lawyers. His interest in the long history of the firm has earned him the unofficial title of "firm historian" and he remains a reservoir of tales and anecdotes about the firm's early days and its growth. He frequently makes presentations to new associates and staff members on the history of the firm, weaving in tales of the firm's big cases and the great lawyers who have practiced with the firm.

Dods has spent his career as a trial lawyer handling everything from personal injury defense work to antitrust, intellectual property, and myriad business litigation matters. He served a number of years as chair of the business litigation division of the firm. Before the time of the firm having a managing partner, he was the "administrative partner" and served on the firm executive committee.

Long active in the local bar, Dods is a past-president of the Kansas City Metropolitan Bar Association and currently a member of the association's board, as current chair of the Past Presidents group.

Dods has been president of the K.C. International Visitors Council through which he has met with foreign visitors from around the world. (Ask him to recount how these experiences led him and his wife to have visited the inner most spaces of the Vatican, including waiving from the top of St. Peter's to the crowd in the square below.)

He has served as President of Legal Aid of Western Missouri; as President of the Law Foundation of U.M.K.C; and as chair of the Citizens Advisory Board of public radio station KCUR.

Plaques and numerous other awards adorn the walls and shelves of his office ("Dust catchers," Dods call them). In 2006 he was presented the Presidents Award by the Missouri Bar Association for his years of leadership as chair of the Advisory Committee of the Missouri Supreme Court. Later this month he will be presented with the Purcell award by the bar, recognizing "an exceptional degree of competency, integrity and civility in both professional and civic activities."

Even after what he calls "over 15,000 days of happily coming to work at SHB," Dods still gets a sparkle in his eye and a broad smile when asked about his career. "SHB has long been committed to legal excellence, community involvement, and that special collegiality that we call the 'Spirit' of SHB. What better place to spend 50 years working in a challenging profession with such a great group of people. I hope the Good Lord (and the managing partner, a more immediate concern) lets me continue."

AARON BAILEY, KANSAS CITY LEGAL 'GIANT' JOHN C. DODS III DIES

Daily Record and the Kansas City Daily News-Press (June 4, 2008)
Reprinted courtesy of Missouri Lawyers Media

After a half century of working in the Kansas City legal arena, prominent attorney John C. Dods III died Monday. He was 74.

Dods had practiced at Shook, Hardy & Bacon since 1958, specializing in business and commercial litigation. Dods, who became a partner at Shook in 1963, is a former chair of the firm's litigation division and business litigation section and was a prolific civic contributor through the years.

"John lived his whole career with the thought that the practice of law was a profession, and everyone engaging in it should be treated with dignity and respect," Shook Chairman John Murphy said. "Those weren't just words to him—that was his whole life."

Dods was diagnosed with lung cancer last February and hospitalized last week due to the illness.

Dods was one of The Daily Record's Legal Leaders in 2004, its inaugural year. At the time, Dods described why he felt compelled to civic duty during his career.

"My thesis is that lawyers by reason of their training, their interests and their experiences owe something back to their community," he said.

Dods was busy when he wasn't in the courtroom. Among other endeavors, he served as chair for the Missouri Supreme Court's Advisory Committee for more than a decade.

"He was a giant of a person, in every way," said Jennifer Gille Bacon, of Shughart Thomson & Kilroy, who took over the committee when Dods stepped down in March. "He was big person, with a big personality and a wonderful temperament. He was admired, if not adored, by the people he worked with."

Dods was a lifelong friend of Bacon's husband, Charles "Bud" Bacon, who said his passing "leaves a huge hole in the community and a lot of people's lives."

Bacon's father was the named partner at Shook. He said he remembers Dods leaving an impression even when he was just a youngster, sharpening pencils in his dad's office when Dods was a new associate.

"There's a lot that has been lost in the practice of law in this day and age in terms of cordiality and civility," said Bacon, general counsel for the Federal Reserve in Kansas City. "John never lost sight of the need for that, and he did whatever he could to engender that in younger attorneys."

Missouri Supreme Court Chief Justice Laura Denvir Stith said Dods was her mentor during her time at Shook and that she was honored to present him with a certificate of appreciation from the court several months ago for his work for the bench and bar.

"He took a special joy in the practice of law and in helping others, a joy that could not help but inspire those around him to do likewise," Stith said in an e-mailed statement. "John's unique combination of professionalism, intellect, good humor and common sense will be sorely missed."

Larry Ward, the long-time chair of Shughart who stepped down earlier this year to focus on litigating cases, met Dods in 1960 when he worked as a law clerk for Shook. Ward said Dods was "a consummate professional and gentleman" who showed several generations of attorneys how to be a professional in and out of the courtroom.

"There probably aren't any attorneys in this city who didn't personally know him, or at least knew him by his name and fame," Ward said. "He was an example for every lawyer at any age."

Dods had plenty of opportunities to showcase his professionalism, representing clients in front of the U.S. Supreme Court and a number of federal courts among other local courtrooms.

Dods served as president of Legal Aid of Western Missouri, the Kansas City Metropolitan Bar Association and the Law Foundation of the University of Missouri-Kansas City. He was active with UMKC's School of Law, where he graduated with a juris doctorate in 1957.

Dods had reaped many awards during his career, including lifetime achievement awards from the KCMBA last year and UMKC's Law Foundation in 1997.

Murphy said memorial services are pending. Dods, who was born in Kansas City and lived in the Northland, was the 15th lawyer to join Shook when he was hired on Feb. 10, 1958. The firm now has more than 500 attorneys.

"In today's day and age, for someone to practice law at one firm for 50 years is amazing," Murphy said. "I don't know if this city will ever see that again."

In an interview with The Daily Record marking that anniversary earlier this year, Dods said the key to being a successful attorney is simple: "Devote everything to your client. And do good."

* * *

Finally, consider the following appreciation by a well-known professor of legal ethics, motivated by the simple obituary of a young lawyer.

STEVEN LUBET, A LIFE WELL LIVED
13 GEO. J. LEG. ETHICS 575 (2000)[1]

I learned everything I know about Felicia Presser by reading her obituary. . . . I distribute the obituary every year to the students in my Legal Ethics class, because it is the best lesson I can give them about . . . well, about themselves.

Though I seldom pay attention to newspaper obituaries, on September 5, 1998, one particular notice caught my eye as I paged forward to the op-ed section. The headline was "Felicia Presser, Juvenile Defense Lawyer," and it was accompanied by a photograph of a very young woman. I forced myself to read it, knowing that it had to be a tragic story.

Felicia Nekritz Presser graduated from law school in the Spring of 1996, taking a job with the juvenile section of the Ohio Public Defender's office. In December of that year she married Jay Presser. She was diagnosed with breast cancer just a few weeks later, and in less than a year she had passed away. Simply writing those facts still takes my

---

[1]   Reprinted with permission of the publisher, Georgetown Journal of Legal Ethics © 2000.

breath away. When I read them to my students, virtually everyone gasps in horror and then the entire class falls silent.

The first lesson is that life is fleeting and fragile. No one can ever be completely safe from that one devastating test result or accident that can cut short all of your hopes and aspirations. No matter how secure and successful your life may seem, it can all end suddenly and without warning.

And in those awful situations when the good die young, family and friends are left to search for meaning and solace. That is the second lesson. Here is what Felicia Presser's loved ones said about her:

"She believed absolutely in rehabilitation as opposed to incarceration of criminals," said her husband. "She believed in the inherent goodness of all people, and it was that basic belief that drove her."

"It was her heart that just drove everything and drove everybody to her," said her mother.

Others added that she was passionate about defending the underdog. She worked on death penalty cases and she volunteered legal assistance to the homeless. The main thing that stood out was that "she really cared about [her] clients."

That is the third lesson. Faced with an almost unimaginable loss, Felicia Presser's loved ones were able to find some measure of comfort in the fact that she had devoted her life to helping others. In what must have been the most sorrowful of times, they consoled each other by remembering the way that Felicia had lived, the good works she had done, the commitment that she valued.

As I explain each semester to my students, no one will ever look back upon the loss of wife or daughter and say, "What we remember most is that she billed 2200 hours every year." No one tempers the grief of a son's death by recalling that he always drove a new BMW, or that he wore a Rolex and went skiing in Aspen every year.

My point is not to embarrass my students about their materiality or to call them acquisitive. I have no standing to do that, considering my own comfortable life style. Anyhow, they would be justified in tuning me out if I ever tried to preach them out of their supposedly covetous ways. Rather, I hope to show the tremendous fulfillment, and ultimately the depth of meaning, that can come from using one's legal training to help others. It is not too hokey (or at least not *way* too hokey) to realize that when a career ends, as it does for everyone, the greatest satisfaction comes to those who have given the most. And this is true for legal careers that span the decades that we all hope for, or only a few short years.

There is astonishing pressure on contemporary law students to aspire to professional success in the most conventional terms: big firms, long hours, high salaries. None of those are bad in and of themselves, but conventional success can become self-defeating if it is allowed to crowd out the motivation to do good. Every attorney in every job can find some time for some sort of pro bono work, and it is that work that will stand out in the thoughts and memories of those who really care.

I commend to all of [us]—lawyers, law students, and law teachers—Felicia Presser's example of a life well lived.

* * *

What do you think? Looking forward to your career as a lawyer, what do you think might be said about your life by a eulogist? About your career as a lawyer? What do you hope will be said about you? Having imagined your eulogy, what do you plan to do to increase the likelihood that you will be remembered as you would like to be remembered?

* * *

In this final chapter, the authors of this text share profiles of the lawyers who have been professional role models, mentors, and friends to us.

Judy Cornett's profile of the lawyers of the University of Tennessee Legal Clinic Community Office. I never wanted to be a lawyer. Growing up, I didn't know any lawyers personally, and Perry Mason did not inspire me. Then, after getting my B.A. from the University of Tennessee, I went to work as a paralegal at the U.T. Legal Clinic Community Office. Working with the lawyers there made me want to be a lawyer too. Never before had I realized that law is a helping profession. These legal aid lawyers—men and women, some experienced, some fresh out of law school—toiled in the vineyards of public benefits, housing, consumer rights, and domestic relations. They went to work every day in an antique building with a temperamental elevator, dim lighting, and cramped offices. They represented clients who had little money and less hope. They listened to the client's story. They treated each client with dignity and compassion and reached for the referral list of community service agencies as often as they reached for the digest and the code. Sometimes these lawyers grew frustrated with how little they could do to help the client, but they always mobilized their legal knowledge and skills to help the client understand the legal system, to battle within the legal system, and sometimes to triumph. With no expectation of gain or glory, these lawyers changed the course of many lives, including mine.

Alex Long's profile of David Morrison. David Morrison is a lawyer with the law firm of Steptoe & Johnson in West Virginia. Years ago, he represented the employer on appeal in a discrimination case. The case boiled down to a question of the company's reasons for discharging the employee. According to the employee, he had been discriminated against on the basis of disability. According to the company, the employee had been fired due to his failure to abide by safety rules. Morrison's oral argument before the West Virginia Supreme Court of Appeals was going well when he was asked a crucial question by one of the justices: "Mr. Morrison, [your opposing counsel] says this company, with its long record of safety violations by employees, has never fired anyone for safety reasons. Is that true, Mr. Morrison?" The lawyer on the other side, Charles DiSalvo, describes Morrison's response:

> The lawyer could do what hundreds had done before him: choose an expedient answer that would serve the needs of the case, regardless of its truthfulness. The lawyer could lie, or the lawyer could obfuscate, or the lawyer could dodge.

> Without a moment's hesitation came the answer:

> "Yes, your honor, that is true."

> On that day in 1990, David Morrison's case was lost, but the system of justice was honored and a lawyer's reputation for integrity was built.

David took his responsibilities as a mentor seriously and once passed along the following piece of advice to me: someday, you'll be tempted to withhold a document or to be dishonest when answering a question posed by opposing counsel or a court. You have to remember that the case is not your case but your client's, and lying to help your client isn't worth the cost. Once you lose your integrity, you can never get it back.

Carl Pierce's profile of Baby Boomer lawyers. Please consider an "unsung" profile of professionalism of the "baby boomers" who entered the legal profession during the 1970s and are now "senior lawyers." This includes the many baby-boomer law students who faithfully prepared for and attended class, asked questions before, during and after class, and actually came for an exam review to learn what they had missed and how to improve their performance. They went on to graduate and pass the bar, and then embark on 40–45 year careers as lawyers in a local practice of law in a small firm, a legal aid office or as a solo practitioner, or as a district attorney or a public defender. Throughout their careers they represented their clients competently, diligently, conscientiously, and loyally. They cared for and respected those they represented as well as the legal system within which they worked. As lawyers they juggled many, often tedious tasks and worked long hours to get done on time all that needed to be done. They also strove to find or make time for their families and to give back to their chosen profession and the communities in which they lived. And they did this all without any fanfare.

These lawyers have provided us with a career-long profile of professionalism that includes but transcends compliance with the rules of professional conduct. It is their attitude toward their work and the values they embrace that are at the heart of their professionalism. It has been my privilege to both teach and thereafter observe the careers of many such lawyers throughout the 43 years since I was admitted to the bar.

Cassandra Robertson's profile of Tom Phillips. My role model is the former Chief Justice of Texas, Tom Phillips, who hired me as a law clerk. Chief Justice Phillips combines a strong work ethic with a constant sense of humor and kindness. He taught me a lot about legal writing in a very short time. It wasn't uncommon for his clerks to go through ten or more drafts of any written work we turned in to him. He would give us extensive feedback on each draft, making it stronger each time until he was satisfied with the final result. One of his goals was to ensure that his judicial opinions were written clearly enough that people did not need a legal education to understand them. He wanted the state's opinions to be accessible to everyone. After nearly twenty-five years of service as Chief Justice, Phillips stepped down from the Court and returned to private practice, as a partner in the appellate section of Baker Botts. However, he remains active in working for the public interest, and has been an especially strong voice advocating that states move away from partisan judicial elections and toward more neutral selection systems.

Paula Schaefer's profile of Ann Covington. When I was a senior in high school in the late 1980's, Ann Covington was appointed to the Missouri Supreme Court. She was the first woman to serve as a judge on the court. As a young woman thinking about law school, her appointment was important to me. It signified the opportunities that were possible for me as a woman in the legal profession. I was still in awe of her - and the historical significance of her presence on the court—when I started working for her in 1996. More than any other experience, clerking for Judge Covington had a lasting, positive impact on my development as a lawyer. She was a brilliant lawyer and judge, who encouraged her clerks to disagree with her because she thought it made her opinions better. She was a skilled writer and editor who worked tirelessly to develop these skills in her clerks. She had a strong work ethic, and simultaneously always put her children first. Everyone in her chambers knew that no matter how busy she was, she wanted to be interrupted if her daughter or son called. Through the years, she has been my most trusted and frequent advisor. And even when I did not ask for her advice, I often asked myself what she would do in a situation, whether I was teaching, writing, or struggling to balance work and motherhood.

INDEX

References are to Pages